# Footprint Cuzco & the Inca heartland



***Ben Box & Steve Frankham***

4th edition

*The Qoyllur Rit'i (Star of the Snow) ceremony draws pilgrims of Inca heritage to the glacial source of the Río Tinguimayo, an Amazon tributary. Some stay the night to sense the Earth "coming alive" under the seven-starred Pleiades, signalling the time to sow. At daybreak devotees bring down ice from Apu Colquepunku, the god-mountain, melt it and thicken the holy water with barley to make* api, *a rejuvenating beverage.*

Amazonia, *Loren McIntyre*

**1 Cuzco, Plaza de Armas**
The Incas' Place of Tears, page 61.

**2 Cuzco, Qoricancha**
Hidden in a Catholic church is the Incas' Temple of the Sun, page 69.

**3 Sacsayhuaman**
Striking zigzag walls and massive masonry define this Inca ceremonial centre, page 75.

**4 Pisac**
Don't miss the market in Pisac, with great Inca ruins above, page 126.

**5 Moray**
Huge depressions become crop laboratories beneath snow-capped peaks, page 136.

**6 Salineras**
White and brown salt pans tumble down a hillside, page 136.

**7 Ollantaytambo**
Another magnificent Inca fortress and temple, with a genuine Inca town below, page 138.

**8 Machu Picchu**
Where else? The focus of most people's visit to Peru and one of the world's finest archaeological ruins page 151.

**9 Salkantay**
Hike around this mountain on two alternative treks to Machu Picchu, page 165.

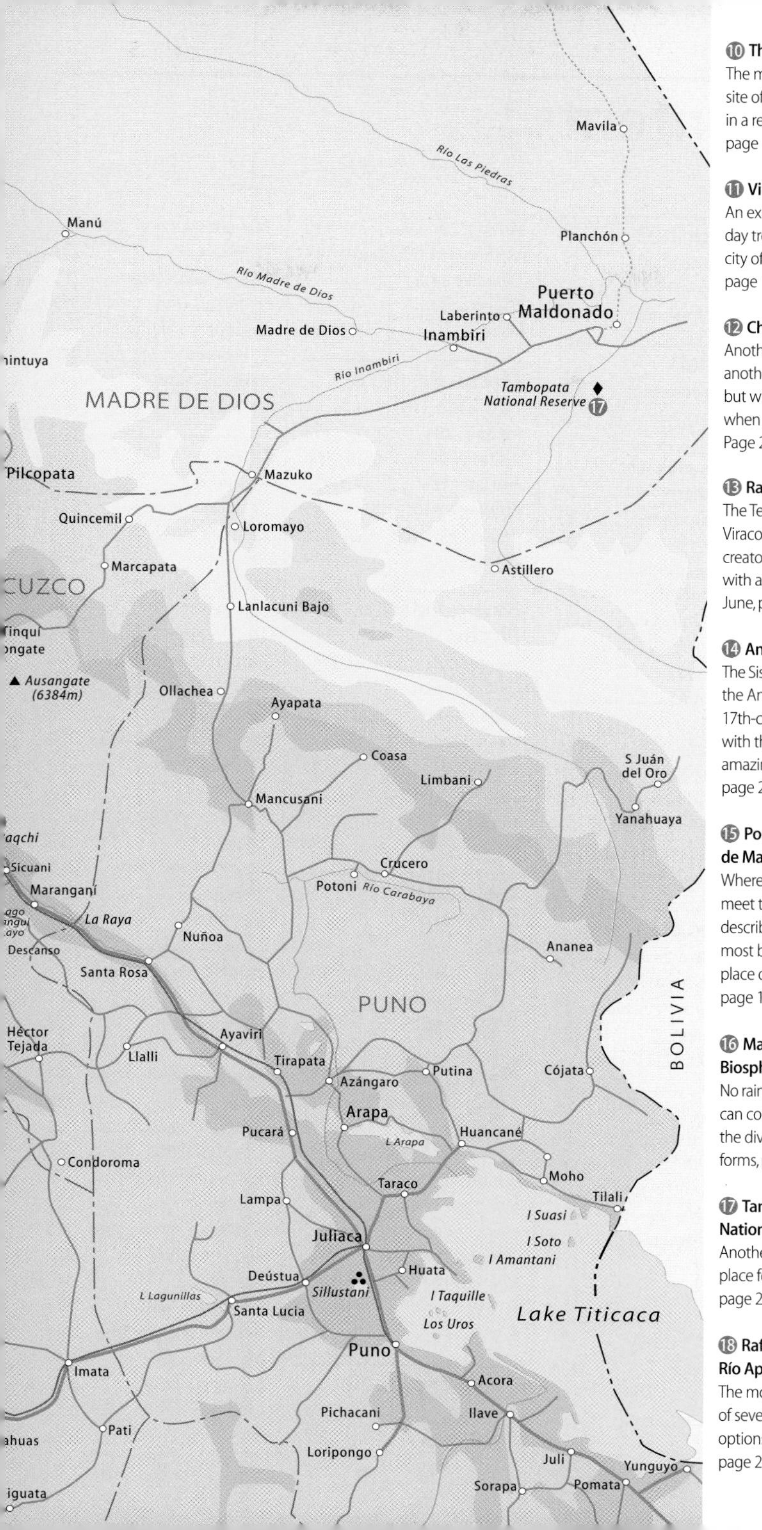


**10 The White Rock**
The most sacred site of the Incas, in a remote area, page 185.

**11 Vilcabamba**
An exhausting five-day trek to the last city of the Incas, page 186.

**12 Choquequirao**
Another lost city, another hard walk – but what a reward when you get there! Page 218.

**13 Raqchi**
The Temple of Viracocha, the creator of all things, with a festival on 24 June, page 212.

**14 Andahuaylillas**
The Sistine Chapel of the Andes: a simple 17th-century church with the most amazing frescoes, page 205.

**15 Pongo de Mainique**
Where the Andes meet the Amazon; described as the most beautiful place on earth, page 184.

**16 Manu Biosphere Reserve**
No rainforest reserve can compare for the diversity of life forms, page 231.

**17 Tambopata National Reserve**
Another great place for wildlife, page 240.

**18 Rafting on the Río Apurímac**
The most exacting of several rafting options in the area, page 21.

# Contents

**Mountain spirits**
*Tilled fields, long shadows and tiny houses are dwarfed by the flanks of the Sacred Valley, which rise to the peaks where, the Incas believed, the gods resided.*

1
2
4
5
7
8
10
11

1 *A precipitous path zigzags down into the Apurímac canyon.* ▸▸ *See page 217.*

2 *Alpaca yarn is dyed and dried before being made into luxurious shawls and sweaters for the tourist market.* ▸▸ *See page 34.*

3 *Calle Hatun Rumiyoc has some of Cuzco's best Inca stonework.* ▸▸ *See page 69.*

4 *High on the pampa above Urubamba, Chinchero's colourful Sunday market draws locals and tourists alike.* ▸▸ *See page 135.*

5 *Machu Picchu, voted one of the Seven Wonders of the World, continues to draw crowds of tourists, trekkers and pilgrims to its remarkably preserved buildings and awesome setting.* ▸▸ *See page 151.*

6 *The Fiesta of Virgen del Carmen is celebrated by masked dancers re-enacting a centuries-old story.* ▸▸ *See page 201.*

7 *The squirrel monkey is one of the more visible inhabitants of the marvellous rainforest in Tambopata National Reserve.* ▸▸ *See page 240.*

8 *The Manu Biosphere Reserve is one of the most biologically diverse places on the planet. Rivers are the principal means of access through the pristine tropical wilderness.* ▸▸ *See page 231.*

9 *The Inca site of Choquequirao is a true 'lost city', hidden in the Vilcabamba mountains west of Cuzco. It can only be reached on an exhilarating two-day trek.* ▸▸ *See page 218.*

10 *At the Salineras, thousands of terraced pre-Columbian saltpans cascade down the hillside and are still in production today.* ▸▸ *See page 136.*

11 *Llamas, traditional costume and Inca stonework are all part of the daily scene in Cuzco.* ▸▸ *See page 55.*

12 *Next door to the cathedral on Lima's Plaza de Armas is the archbishop's palace with one of the finest balconies for which the colonial city is renowned.* ▸▸ *See page 258.*

**Mountains and markets**

*The Inca ruins of Pisac occupy a commanding position above the Urubamba valley, while the town below has a fascinating Sunday market for local produce.*

# A foot in the door

Can you imagine a city laid out in the shape of a puma; a stone to tie the sun to; a city of fleas? Are you willing to meet the Earth Changer, Our Lord of the Earthquakes and Mother Earth? If so, prepare to follow the pilgrimage to Cuzco, the place that every Inca endeavoured to visit once in a lifetime. Navel of the world, Spanish colonial showpiece, gringo capital of South America, Cuzco is all these things and more.

Cuzco's position, high up in the Andes, kept it largely isolated until the beginning of the 20th century when the railway arrived. As a result, although it has grown into a city of almost 300,000 inhabitants, its centre still has the feel of a colonial town. But don't be lulled into thinking that a holiday here is going to be a stroll back in time. Cuzco is alive with the traditions of the Incas' descendants and the legacy of 300 years of Spanish rule – most visible in its long list of festivals – but the latest trends of 21st-century adventure tourism, hotel fashion, nightlife and internet culture also give the city a vibrancy that's hard to match.

The quintessential South American tourist site, Machu Picchu, is a mere train ride away from Cuzco – or a four-day hike along the Inca Trail. In recent years, the Trail has become a victim of its own success, eroded by countless pairs of boots, but the development of alternative, equally challenging Inca routes has widened the perspectives that you can get on this historic landscape. Also within easy reach of Cuzco are Andean markets selling essentials to the locals and handicrafts to the tourist, hot springs, charming places to stay and thrilling hikes that traverse 4000-m passes to reach lost cities. What's more, you have access to those features that make Peru one of the eight 'mega-diverse' countries on earth. Below snow-covered peaks, roads and trails drop into river canyons or descend the eastern slopes of the Andes to the vast lowlands of the Amazon.

## Culture clash

For all their elegance, the Spanish churches and opulent mansions of Cuzco have not fared as well as the matchless stonemasonry of the Inca foundations on which they were imposed. The best example of this uneasy marriage is the Qoricancha/Santo Domingo complex, the site of the Inca's Temple of the Sun.

## Mountains worship

From the huge zigzag walls of the ceremonial centre of Sacsayhuaman to the Inca suspension bridge of Qeswachaca, there are sites of historical interest in every direction. Just an hour from Cuzco is the market town of Pisac and its superb fortress. Follow the Río Urubamba west, beneath sacred mountains, to Ollantaytambo, which has a well-preserved Inca town and an unfinished temple, whose pre-Columbian stonework is among the finest in the country. All along the valley, with its fields of cereals and steep agricultural terracing, stand the *apus*, the imposing snow-capped peaks worshipped by the Incas.

## Lost cities of the Incas

Machu Picchu, the only major Inca retreat to escape Spanish looting, is Peru's most-visited archaeological site and, as such, with its accompanying comfortable train and the well-worn Inca Trail, has transcended the epithet 'lost' to become a universal symbol. In neighbouring valleys and on the hills are other Inca cities that are still being cleared of vegetation and retain a sense of mystery. These are the way-stations or the goals of exhilarating treks, which scale high passes, stride in the lee of glaciers and pass through isolated communities.

## Wilderness beckons

Cuzco is a city you can walk out of. In little more than 10 minutes you leave the crowds and enter the solitude of the *cordillera*. You can escape for an hour or two, or follow in the footsteps of Incas, *conquistadores* and *campesinos* for days at a time. The Ausangate Circuit, around the region's highest peak, is probably the most popular trek after the Inca Trail. Cuzco also has huge potential for other adventures. Mountain bikers can climb as many hills as their legs can take or plummet down 1500 m in two hours. Rafting ranges from gentle half-day trips to heart-stopping whitewater runs, and, if you prefer to fly, you can take to the air on a paraglider or in a balloon.

## Rainforest sanctuaries

In Peru's southern jungle are the Manu Biosphere Reserve and the Tambopata National Reserve, both brilliant places to see wildlife and both accessible from Cuzco. Manu is one of the largest protected areas of rainforest in the world, starting high in the Andes and going down through elfin, cloud and montane forest to the vast lowland jungle of the Amazon.

# Essentials

## Footprint features

# Planning your trip

To see Cuzco and the surrounding area properly you'll need between 10 and 14 days. This would allow you to explore the city, enjoy its nightlife, visit the towns and villages of the Urubamba Valley – including Pisac, Ollantaytambo, Urubamba and Chinchero – and, of course, hike one of the Inca trails, many of which lead to Machu Picchu (about four days). Added to that, you'll need at least four or five days for a jungle trip to Manu or Tambopata, plus a few more for mountain biking and whitewater rafting. Three or four weeks, therefore, would allow you to enjoy the region to its full, but the one problem with Cuzco is that it is all too easy to find a colonial café with a balcony, toss the guidebook aside and sit back in the blazing sun to watch the world go by.



## Where to go

Your first port of call should be Cuzco's **Plaza de Armas**, heart of the city since Inca times, and it is here that you will get an immediate feel for the city. Two grand churches and a series of arcades surround this great colonial space, which is filled with eating places, tourist businesses and people on the move. Behind the facade, you will gaze amazed at the gold altars of churches such as **La Compañía**, those even these will fade into insignificance on entering the complex of the **Temple of the Sun**. Here the Spanish *conquistadores* found so much gold it took them three months to melt it down. It takes only a little imagination to picture the solar garden as it once was: filled with life-sized replicas of men, women and children, insects, plants and flowers – all made from gold. The 700 gold and silver plates that once covered the temple walls here may have gone, but their disappearance has revealed the stunning craftsmanship of the Inca stonemasons whose blocks fit together so perfectly it is impossible to slide even a razorblade into the joints – and that after two major earthquakes.

Out of the city you have to travel only a few hours to discover the wonderful **Sacred Valley**. Take a one-day bus trip if you are on a tight schedule, otherwise see the spectacular Inca ruins, busy indigenous markets and beautiful scenery under your own steam and at your own pace. Some choose to take the bus, others to go off-road on a mountain bike. If you have the stomach for it, sign up for a condor's-eye view and paraglide it in tandem with a professional.

For many, Cuzco means one thing: **Machu Picchu**, one of only three places in the Americas that has been declared a World Heritage Site for both its natural beauty *and* its history (the other two are Palenque in Mexico and Tikal in Guatemala). Its global fame was assured in 2007 when it was voted one of the New Seven Wonders of the World.

The ancient **Inca Trail** is one of the world's classic trekking routes. After four days of climbing through dizzying 4000-m-plus mountain passes, the weary hiker emerges at the Sun Gate to look down at last on one of the most awe-inspiring sights in the world. And its wonder is not confined to the young and fit. The site is accessible by luxury train followed by a bus ride up a switchback road.

It has however been realized that the Inca Trail was not built for thousands of hiking boots and camping sites, and the authorities have been forced to reduce degradation by limiting the number of trekkers through strict controls and high prices. Fortunately, there are many other equally challenging trails which lead to Machu Picchu, or other remarkable Inca sites: to **Choquequirao** over the **Vilcabamba** mountain range; to the last Inca stronghold at **Espíritu Pampa**; or around – and up! – ice-capped

## How big is your footprint?

- Where possible choose a destination, tour operator or hotel with a proven ethical and environmental commitment – if in doubt ask.
- Spend money on locally produced (rather than imported) goods and services and use common sense when bargaining – your few dollars saved may be a week's salary to others.
- Use water and electricity carefully – travellers may receive preferential supply while the needs of local communities are overlooked.
- Learn about local etiquette and culture – consider local norms and behaviour and dress appropriately for local cultures and situations.
- Protect wildlife and other natural resources – don't buy souvenirs or goods made from wildlife unless they are clearly sustainably produced and are not protected under CITES legislation (CITES controls trade in endangered species). If you are concerned about the application of the principles of ecotourism, in Peru as elsewhere, you need to make an informed choice by finding out in advance how establishments such as jungle lodges cope with waste and effluent disposal, whether they create the equivalent of 'monkey islands' by obtaining animals in the wild and putting them in the lodge's property.
- Always ask before taking photographs or videos of people.
- Consider staying in local accommodation rather than foreign-owned hotels – the economic benefits for host communities are far greater – and there are far greater opportunities to learn about local culture.
- The heartbreaking sight of children begging for money, shining shoes and selling sweets and postcards often at midnight in Cuzco town centre leaves many visitors guilt-ridden if they refuse, or doubtful they have really helped if they do give money. The best advice is to give children food (fruit or a sandwich rather than sweets), or something to keep them warm such as a pair of gloves or a scarf.
- Otherwise make a donation to a local charitable organization such as **Los Niños** (see page 74), which is actively helping reverse the plight of hundreds of similar children.

**Ausangate,** the mountain that dominates Cuzco's eastern skyline. The passes here are over 5000 m. Thrill-seekers can combine a jungle experience with rafting the turbulent waters of the **Apurímac,** the true source of the Amazon. There cannot be many places in the world where you can cast off amid snow-capped mountain scenery and take a trip that later leaves you bumping through caiman-infested jungle. The rivers around Cuzco are between a gentle Grade II to a heady Grade V.

No trip of more than two weeks would be complete without discovering the beauty of the jungle in the **Manu Biosphere Reserve,** one of the largest conservation areas on earth, or the **Tambopata National Reserve**. Over 10% of all the species of birds in the world can be found at Manu. Your trip will take you through cloudforest on the eastern slopes of the Andes, past the upper tropical zone where blue-headed and military macaws can be found, to the untouched forests of the western Amazon.

### Packing for Peru

Everybody has their own preferences, but listed here are the most often mentioned. These include: an inflatable travel pillow for neck support; hiking boots; waterproof clothing; wax earplugs (vital for noisy hotels); rubber sandals (to wear in showers to avoid athlete's foot); a sheet sleeping bag to avoid sleeping on filthy sheets in cheap hotels; a clothes line; a water bottle; a universal bath – and basin – plug of the flanged type that will fit any wastepipe; Swiss Army knife (do not carry it in your hand luggage on flights); an alarm clock for those early morning departures; candles and/or a torch/flashlight; an adaptor, or the necessary equipment for recharging cameras, laptops, etc; padlocks (for doors of the cheapest hotels, tent zips, and backpacks as a deterrent to thieves); a small first aid kit; and a sun hat.

A list of useful medicines and health-related items is given in the Health section, see page 38. To these might be added some lip salve, with sun protection, and pre-moistened wipes (such as Wet Ones). Always carry toilet paper, which is especially important on long bus trips. Contact lens solution is readily available in pharmacies.



## When to go

There is no time of year when you will have Cuzco and Machu Picchu to yourself. Having said that, Peru's high season is from June to September and, at that time, Cuzco is bursting at the seams. This also happens to be the time of year which enjoys the most stable weather for hiking the Inca Trail or trekking and climbing elsewhere. The days are generally clear and sunny, but nights can be very cold at high altitude. The highlands can be visited at other times of the year, though during the wettest months from November to April some roads become impassable and hiking trails can be very muddy. April and May, at the tail end of the highland rainy season, is a beautiful time to see the Peruvian Andes, but the rain may linger, so be prepared.

On the coast, the summer months are from December to April. If you arrive in Lima between May and October you will find the area covered with what's known locally as *la garúa*, a thick blanket of cloud and mist. As your plane heads towards Cuzco in the *garúa* season, you will soon be into clear skies and the mountains below can be seen rising like a new coastline out of the sea of fog.

The best time to visit the jungle is during the dry season, from April to October. During the wet season, November to April, it is oppressively hot (40°C and above) and while it only rains for a few hours at a time, which is not enough to spoil your trip, it is enough to make some roads virtually impassable.

## Activities and tours

This is one of the very best parts of the world for a number of adventure sports, including trekking and climbing, whitewater rafting and mountain biking. Facilities for adventure tourism tend to develop in correlation with general tourist services so always make sure the infrastructure and equipment is adequate before signing up for a potential dangerous activity. Also check the experience and qualifications of operators and guides. Peru also offers probably the greatest wildlife viewing opportunities on the planet and it is unmatched anywhere for the sheer scale of its ancient ruins.

## Birdwatching

Peru is the number one country in the world for birds. Its varied geography and topography have endowed Peru with the greatest biodiversity and variety of birds on earth. About 20% of all the bird species in the world and 45% of all neotropical birds occur in Peru. More new species have been described in Peru in the last 30 years than any other country in the world: on average 2 new species a year. This is why Peru is the best South American destination for birds, on a continent that is itself dubbed 'the bird continent' by professional ornithologists.

A birding trip to Peru is possible during any month of the year, as birds breed all year round. There is, however, a definite peak in breeding activity – and consequently birdsong – just before the rains come in Oct, and this makes it rather easier to locate many birds between Sep and Christmas.

Rainwear is recommended for the mountains, especially during the rainy season between Dec and Apr. But in the tropical lowlands an umbrella is the way to go. Lightweight hiking boots are probably the best general footwear, but wellingtons (rubber boots) are preferred by many neotropical birders for the lowland rainforests.

Apart from the usual binoculars, a telescope is helpful in many areas, whilst a tape recorder and shotgun microphone can be very useful for calling out skulking forest birds, although experience in using this type of equipment is recommended, particularly to limit disturbance to the birds.

A great 3-week combination is about 16 days in Manu, then 2-3 days in the highlands at Abra Málaga. You can extend this by including one or more of the other highly recommended spots outside the scope of this guidebook.

### The birds

If your experience of neotropical birding is limited, the potential number of species which may be seen on a 3- or 4-week trip can be daunting. A 4-week trip can produce over 750 species, and some of the identifications can be tricky! You may want to take an experienced bird guide with you who can introduce you to, for example, the mysteries of foliage-gleaner and woodcreeper identification, or you may want to 'do it yourself' and identify the birds on your own.

Machu Picchu may be a nightmare for lovers of peace and solitude, but the surrounding bamboo stands provide excellent opportunities for seeing the Inca wren. A walk along the railway track near Puente Ruinas station can produce species which are difficult to see elsewhere. This is *the* place in Peru to see white-capped dipper and torrent duck.

The most accessible *polylepsis* woodlands in the Andes is only 2 hrs' drive from Ollantaytambo, whilst the humid temperate forest of Abra Málaga is only 45 mins further on. In the *polylepsis* some very rare birds can easily be seen, including royal cinclodes and white-browed tit-spinetail (the latter being one of the 10 most endangered birds on earth). The humid temperate forest is laden with moss and bromeliads, and mixed species flocks of multi-coloured tanagers and other birds are common.

See also Wildlife and vegetation, page 312.

**★ Head for ...**

**Abra Málaga**, page 183
**Machu Picchu**, page 151
**Manu Biosphere Reserve**, page 231
**Tambopata National Reserve**, page 240

## Climbing and trekking

While Peru has some of the best climbing in the world, Cuzco is not developed for the sport. Peru has some outstanding trekking circuits around the *nevados*, its snowcapped mountains. Among the best known is the Ausangate circuit. The other type of trekking for which Peru is justifiably renowned is walking among ruins, the prime example being the Inca Trail. Other exciting walks of this type in a region rich in archaeological heritage are being developed and you are encouraged to try them, if for no other reason than to protect the fragile Inca Trail.

Most walking is on clear trails well trodden by *campesinos* who populate most parts of the Peruvian Andes. If you camp on their land, ask permission first and, of course, do not leave any litter. Tents, sleeping bags, mats and stoves can easily be hired in Cuzco but check carefully for quality.

### Trekking and climbing conditions

May to Sep is the dry season in the Cordillera. Oct, Nov and Apr can be fine, particularly for trekking. Most bad weather comes from the east and temperatures plummet around twilight. The optimum months for extreme ice climbing are from late May to mid Jul. In early May there is a risk of avalanche from sheered *neve* ice layers. It is best to climb early in the day as the snow becomes slushy later on. After Jul successive hot sunny days will have melted some of the main support (compacted ice) particularly on north-facing slopes. On the other hand, high altitude rock climbs are less troubled by ice after Jul. On south-facing slopes, the ice and snow never consolidates quite as well.

### Maps

The following are the IGN 1:100,000 topographical sheets which apply to the treks. All sheets can be obtained through **South American Explorers** in Cuzco, see page 58. All names of mountains and other features given in the trek descriptions have been checked by the authors, even if they differ from those given on IGN or other sources.

Ausangate: Ocongate sheet (ref: 28-T). Choquequirao to Machu Picchu: Machupicchu sheet (ref: 27-Q). Salkantay to Santa Teresa: Machupicchu sheet (ref: 27-Q). Salkantay to Machu Picchu: Machupicchu sheet plus Urubamba sheet (27-Q and 27-R). Espíritu Pampa: Machupicchu sheet plus sheets to the west and northwest (27-Q, 27-P and 26-P). Ancascocha Trek: Urubamba sheet (27-R).

### ★ Head for ...

**Choquequirao**, page 218
**Cordillera Vilcabamba** for Salkantay (6271 m) peak, page 165, and **Cordillera Vilcanota**, for Ausangate (6398 m) peak, page 206.
**Inca Trail**, page 160
**Vilcabamba traverse trek**, page 185

## Cultural tourism

This covers more esoteric pursuits such as archaeology and mystical tourism. Several of the tour operators listed on page 47 offer customized packages for special interest groups. Local operators offering these more specialized tours are listed in the travelling text under the relevant location. Cultural tourism is a rapidly growing niche market.

Details of specialized shamanic healing and mystical tourism are listed under Cuzco Cultural tours, page 116.

### ★ Head for ...

**Cuzco**, page 55

### Contact

**PromPerú**, www.peru.info/perueng.asp, has 5 interesting community-based tourism projects around the country. Click on 'What do you want to do?' on the home page and then choose Experiential tourism from the drop-down menu. In the Cuzco area, the project involves activities in villages in the Sacred Valley and Raqchi.

## Kayaking

Peru offers outstanding whitewater kayaking for all standards of paddlers from novice to expert. Many first descents remain unattempted due to logistical difficulties, though they are slowly being ticked off by a dedicated crew of local and internationally renowned kayakers. For the holiday paddler, you are probably best joining up with a raft company who will gladly carry all your gear (plus any non-paddling companions) and provide you with superb food while you enjoy the river from an unladen kayak. There is a surprising selection of latest-model kayaks available in Peru for hire for US$10-20 a day.

For complete novices, some companies offer 2- to 3-day kayak courses on the Urubamba and Apurímac that can be booked locally. For expedition paddlers, bringing your own canoe is the best option though it is getting increasingly expensive to fly around Peru with your boats. A knowledge of Spanish is indispensable.

## Mountain biking

With its amazing diversity of trails, tracks and rough roads, Peru is surely one of the last great mountain bike destinations yet to be fully discovered. Whether you're into a 2-day downhill blast from the Andes to the Amazon jungle or an extended off-road journey, Peru has some of the world's best biking opportunities. The problem is finding the routes as trail maps are virtually nonexistent and the few main roads are often congested with traffic and far from fun to travel along. A few specialist agencies run by dedicated mountain bikers are now exploring the intricate web of paths, single tracks and dirt roads that criss-crosses the Andes, putting together exciting routes to suit everyone from the weekend warrior to the long-distance touring cyclist, the extreme downhiller to the casual day tripper.

If you are considering a dedicated cycling holiday, then it is best to bring your bike from home. It's pretty easy, just get a bike box from your local shop, deflate the tyres, take the pedals off and turn the handlebars. It is worth checking first that your airline is happy to take your bike: some are, some will want to charge. Make sure your bike is in good condition before you depart as spares and repairs are hard to come by, especially if your bike is very complicated (eg: XT V-brake blocks are virtually impossible to find and rear suspension/disc brakes parts are totally unavailable). A tip from a Peruvian mountain bike guide: take plenty of inner tubes, brake blocks, chain lube and a quick release seat. Leave all panniers at home and rely on the support vehicle whenever you get tired as there will be plenty more riding later.

If you are hiring a bike, be it for one day or longer, the basic rule is that you get what you pay for. For as little as US$5-10 a day you can get a cheap imitation of a mountain bike that will be fine on a paved road, but will almost certainly not stand up to the rigours of off- roading. For US$20-25 you should be able to find something half-decent with front shocks, V-brakes, helmet and gloves. Bear in mind high-quality, well-maintained bikes are rare in Peru so you should check any hire bike thoroughly before riding it.

### Choosing the right tour

When signing up for a mountain bike trip, remember that you are in the Andes so if you are worried about your fitness and the altitude, make sure you get a predominantly downhill route. Check there is a support vehicle available throughout the entire trip, not just dropping you off and meeting you at the end. Check the guide is carrying a first aid kit, at the very least a puncture repair kit (preferably a comprehensive tool kit) and is knowledgeable about bike mechanics. Bikes regularly go wrong, punctures are frequent and people do fall off, so it is essential that your company provides minimum cover.

On longer trips ask for detailed trip dossiers, describing the ups and downs and total distances of the routes, check how much is dirt road (suitable for anyone of reasonable fitness) and how much is single track (often requiring considerable experience and fitness). Also, find out what support will be provided in the way of experienced bike guides (they should have an official certificate of qualification), trained bike mechanics on hand, radio communications, spare bikes, cooking, dining and toilet facilities, etc.

### ★ Head for ...

All ideally require a guide as it's very easy to get lost in the Andes.

**Abra Málaga**, page 183. From 4200 m, an 80-km descent to the jungle or a radical Inca trail back to Ollantaytambo, both great rides.

**Chinchero–Moray–Maras–Las Salineras–Urubamba**, page 137. One of the finest day trips in Peru. Largely downhill on a mixture of dirt road and single track, this trip takes you to the interesting circular ruins of Moray and into the spectacular salt pans below Maras on an awesome mule track (watch out for mules!). Maras Moray Biking appears on the Urubamba Sheet (27-R); however, road information on this sheet is not accurate and to find the best off-road sections we recommend hiring a guide.

**Cuzco ruins** Cheat by taking a taxi to Puka Pukara and then enjoy a tarmac descent (if unguided) via Tambo Machay (page 82), Qenqo (page 76) and Sacsayhuaman (page 75) – don't forget your combined entrance ticket; see box, page 59. Or, with a guide, explore some of Cuzco's less-visited ruins, following the mass of old Inca tracks accessible only to those in the know.

**Cuzco–Puerto Maldonado** Possibly the greatest Trans-Andean challenge on a bike: 550 km of hard work up to 4700 m and down to 230 m on one of the roughest roads there is (with the odd full-on single track thrown in for good measure). Be prepared to get wet as there are a lot of river crossings, sometimes up to waist deep. Either a 9-day epic, or cheat on the hills and enjoy some of the biggest downhills out (3-4 days).

**Huchuy Cuzco**, page 128. For biking experts only, this unbelievable trip is best described as 'trekking with your bike'. Various routes, again hard to find, are followed by what must be one of the hairiest single tracks in the world, along the top of and down into the Sacred Valley of the Incas.

**Lares Valley**, page 130. This offers some incredible down and uphill options on 2- or 3-day circuits including a relaxing soak in the beautiful Lares hot springs. Lares Biking appears on the IGN Urubamba and Calca Sheets (27-R and 27-S); however, the trip stays fairly close to the road so IGN is perhaps not essential.

**Pisac–Tres Cruces–Manu** From Pisac to Manu is a 250-km, beautiful dirt road ride offering big climbs and an even bigger (2-day) descent. A side trip to Tres Cruces to see the sunrise is a must if time permits. Remember that the road to Manu only operates downhill every other day, so be sure to check you've got it right or else beware irate truck drivers not giving way on a very narrow road!

## Parapenting and hang-gliding

*Vuelo libre* is just taking off in Peru. The season in the sierra is May-Oct, with the best months being Aug and Sep. Some flights in Peru have exceeded 6500 m.

### ★ Head for ...

**Cerro Sacro** (3797 m), Pampa de Chincheros, 45 km from Cuzco, with 550 m clearance at take-off. aunch site for cross-country flights over the Sacred Valley, Sacsayhuaman and Cuzco.

**Mirador de Urubamba**, 38 km from Cuzco, at 3650 m, with 800 m clearance and views over Pisac. Particularly good for parapenting.

**Sacred Valley**, page 123, excellent launch sites, thermals and reasonable landing sites.

## Rafting

Peru is rapidly becoming one of the world's premier destinations for whitewater rafting. Several of its rivers are rated in the world's top 10 and a rafting trip is now high on any adventurer's list of activities while travelling in Peru. It is not just the adrenaline rush of big rapids that attracts, it is the whole experience of accessing areas beyond the reach of motor vehicles, whether tackling sheer-sided, mile-deep canyons, travelling silently through pristine rainforest, or canoeing across the stark Altiplano, high in the Andes.

Before you leap in the first raft that floats by, a word of warning and a bit of advice will help you ensure that your rafting trip of a lifetime really is as safe, as environmentally friendly and as fun as you want it to be.

The very remoteness and amazing locations that make Peruvian whitewater rivers so attractive mean that dealing with an emergency (should it occur) can be difficult, if impossible. As the sport of rafting has increased in popularity over the last few years, so too have the number of accidents (including fatalities), yet the rafting industry remains virtually unchecked. How then, do you ensure your safety on what are some of the best whitewater runs anywhere in South America if not the whole world?

If you are keen on rafting and are looking to join a rafting expedition of some length, then it is worth signing up in advance before you set foot in Peru. Some long expeditions have only a few scheduled departures a year and the companies that offer them only accept bookings well in advance as the trips are logistically extremely difficult to organize. For the popular day trips and expeditions on the Apurímac there are regular departures (the latter in the dry season only, see below). If you can spare a few days to wait for a departure then it's fine to book in Cuzco. It also gives you the chance to talk to the company who will be operating your tour and to meet the guides. There are day trip departures all year and frequent multi-day departures in the high season. Note that the difficulty of the sections changes between the dry and rainy seasons. Some become extremely difficult or impossible in the rainy season. The dry season is Apr/May to Sep (but can be as late as Nov), the rainy season Dec-Mar.

New legislation demands that Class 4+ guides hold the internationally recognized qualification of Swift Water Rescue Technician and hold a current first aid certificate. All rafting equipment will be checked regularly to ensure it meets basic safety standards, eg life jackets that actually float, etc. At present there are a number of guides with the relevant qualifications, but you will only find them at companies who operate the longer, multi-day trips. Moreover, equipment standards in some of the companies are woefully low and it may prove difficult to enforce the new rules, but at least it will be a step in the right direction.

At present (and probably in the foreseeable future), as with many of Peru's adventure options, it simply boils down to you get what you pay for. Rafting is an inherently dangerous sport and doing it in Peru with the wrong operator can seriously endanger your life. If price is all that matters bear in mind the following comments: the cheaper the price, the less you get, be it with safety cover, experience of guides, quality of equipment, quantity of food, emergency back-up and environmental awareness.

You will often be required to show proof that your **travel insurance** will cover you for whitewater rafting (occasionally you may be asked to sign an insurance disclaimer). If you are unsure about it, and are planning to go rafting, it is worth checking with your insurance company before you leave, as some policies have an additional charge. Very few policies cover Grade V rafting so read the small print.

When signing up you should ask about the experience of the **guides** or, if possible, meet them. At present there is no exam or qualification required to become a river guide, but certain things are essential. Firstly, find out their command of English (or whatever language; there are a few German-speaking guides available), essential if you are going to understand commands. Find out about their experience. How many times have they done this particular stretch of river? Many Peruvian guides have worked overseas. The more international experience a guide has, the more aware they will be of international safety practices. All guides should have some experience in rescue techniques. All guides must have knowledge of first aid. Ask when they last took a course and what level they are at.

Good **equipment** is essential for your safe enjoyment of your trip. If possible ask to see some of the gear provided. Essentials include self-bailing rafts for all but the calmest of rivers. Check how old your raft is and where it was made. Satellite phones are an indispensable piece of safety equipment on long trips in remote areas: does the company use them (they are not yet standard on the Apurímac)? Paddles should be of plastic and metal construction. Wooden paddles can snap, but a few companies use locally made ones which can be excellent, but expensive (in either case, losing a paddle should be of less importance to the company than the safety of the rafter). Helmets should always be provided and fit correctly (home-made fibreglass copies are inadequate). Life jackets must be of a lifeguard-recognized quality and be replaced regularly as they have a tendency to lose their flotation; locally made jackets don't float as well. Does your company provide wetsuits (some of the rivers are surprisingly cold), or, at the very least, quality splash jackets, as the wind can cause you to chill rapidly? On the longer trips, dry bags are provided – what state are these in? How old are they? Do they leak? There is nothing worse than a soggy sleeping bag at the end of a day's rafting. Are tents provided? And, most importantly for the jungle, do the zips on the mosquito net work and is it rain proof? Does the company provide mosquito netting dining tents? Tables? Chairs? These apparent excesses are a bonus when camping for some time at the bottom of a sandfly-infested canyon!

Ask to see the **first aid kit** and find out what is in there and, most importantly, do they know how to use it? When was it last checked? Or updated?

Ask about **food**. Good, wholesome food is relatively cheap in Peru and can make all the difference on a long trip. Once again, you pay for what you get. Ask if there's a vegetarian option. On the food preparation, simple precautions will help you stay healthy. Are all vegetables soaked in iodine before serving? Do the cooks wash their hands and is there soap available for the clients? Are the plates, pots and cutlery washed in iodine or simply swilled in the river? (Stop and think how many villages upstream use that river as their main sewage outlet.)

On the Apurímac, the operator should provide a chemical **toilet** and remove all toilet paper and other rubbish. In the past, certain beaches have been subject to a completely uncaring attitude over toilet paper and human excrement. At the very least your company should provide a lighter for burning the paper and a trowel to dig a hole; always bury it deep and watch out when burning the paper so as not to start a fire. It is normal practice for guides to check the campsite on arrival and then again before leaving to ensure it is clean. If your company does not, make it your responsibility to encourage other members of the group to keep the campsites clean of **rubbish**. When cooking, bottled gas is used; neither driftwood nor cut trees should be burnt.

Above all it is your **safety** on the river that is important. Some companies are now offering safety kayaks as standard, as well as safety catarafts on certain rivers. This is open to misuse. Sometimes safety kayakers have little or no experience of what they are required to do and are just along for the ride; sometimes they are asked to shoot video (rendering the safety cover useless). A safety cataraft is useless if weighed down with equipment. All companies should carry at the very least a wrap kit, consisting of static ropes, carabiners, slings and pulleys should a raft get stuck. But check if the guides know how to use it?

If this has not put you off, you are now equipped to go out there and find the company that offers what you are looking for at a price you think is reasonable. Bear in mind a basic day's rafting in the USA can cost between US$75-120. In Peru you might get the same for just US$25, but ask yourself what you are getting for so little. As it is, rafts and equipment cost more in Peru.

### ★ Head for ...

**The Abyss** Below Puente Cunyac is a section of rarely run whitewater. This extreme expedition involves days of carrying rafts around treacherous rapids; few have attempted it.

**Choquequirao**, page 218. Another rarely run section, this 10-day adventure involves a walk in with mules, a chance to visit the amazing ruins of Choquequirao and raft huge rapids in an imposing sheer-sided canyon all the way to the jungle basin.

**Chuquicahuana** (Rainy season, Grade IV to V+, dry season, Grade II to IV.) In the rainy season, this is a technically demanding day trip for genuine adrenaline junkies. In the dry season this section makes a good alternative from the now terribly polluted sections further downstream (Huambutío–Pisac, Ollantaytambo–Chilca, see above) and provides several hours of fun, with 3 km of rapids (technical) with much cleaner water and all in a very pretty canyon. Strict safety procedures are needed all year round.

**Cusipata**, page 211. (Rainy season, Grade III to IV, dry season Grade II to III.) Often used as a warm-up section in high water before attempting Chuquicahuana. This section has fun rapids and a beautiful mini-canyon, which, in low water, is ideal for inflatable canoes (duckies). Again the water purity is much better than the lower sections.

**Cuzco region**, page 55. This is probably the rafting capital of Peru, with more whitewater runs on offer than anywhere else in the country.

**Huambutío–Pisac**, page 200. (All year availability, Grade II.) A scenic half-day float with a few rapids to get the adrenaline flowing, right through the heart of the Sacred Valley of the Incas. Fits in perfectly with a day trip to Pisac market. A sedate introduction to rafting for all ages.

**Huarán Canyon**, page 130. (All year, Grade III+ to V+ depending on season.) A short section of fun whitewater that is occasionally rafted and used as the site of the Peruvian National Whitewater Championships for kayaking and rafting. Definitely not for beginners in the rainy season.

**Kiteni–Pongo Mainique** (the bit made famous by Michael Palin). An interesting jungle gorge, but logistically hard to reach and technically pretty average except in the rainy season.

**Ollantaytambo–Chilca** (all year availability, Grade III to IV+ depending on season). A fun half-day introduction to the exciting sport of whitewater rafting with a few challenging rapids and some beautiful scenery near the Inca 'fortress' of Ollantaytambo. This trip also fits in perfectly with the start of the Inca Trail. Try to go early in the morning as a strong wind picks up in the late morning.

**Pinipampa** (all year grade I to II). A fun and beautiful section, rarely paddled but relatively clean; no major rapids but a fun canoeing or ducky trip for beginners. Get out at the Huambutío start point, before the Huatanay disgorges Cuzco's raw sewage into the Urubamba.

**Puente Hualpachaca–Puente Cunyac** (May-Nov, Grade IV to V). 3-4 days of nonstop whitewater adventure through an awesome gorge just 5 hours' drive from Cuzco. Probably the most popular multi-day trip, this is one to book with the experts as there have been fatalities on this stretch.

**Río Apurímac**, page 217. Technically the true source of the Amazon, the Apurímac cuts a 2000-m-deep gorge through incredible desert scenery and offers some of the finest whitewater rafting on the planet.

**Santa María–Quillabamba** (dry season, Grade III to IV). A rarely rafted 2-day high jungle trip. A long way to go for some fairly good whitewater but mediocre jungle.

**Tambopata**, page 240. (Jun-Oct, Grade III-IV.) Wilderness, wildlife and whitewater, the Tambopata is the ultimate jungle adventure for those looking to get away from the standard organized jungle package. Starting with a drive from the shores of Lake Titicaca to the end of the road, the Tambopata travels through the very heart of the Tambopata National Reserve. 4 days of fun whitewater followed by 2 days of gentle meandering through virgin tropical rainforest where silent rafts make perfect wildlife watching platforms. The final stage is a visit to the world's largest macaw clay lick and a short flight out from Puerto Maldonado.

**Urubamba**, page 134. Perhaps the most popular day run Peru, but sadly one heavily affected in parts by pollution both from Cuzco (the Río Huatanay joins the Urubamba by Huambutio and is one of the main sewage outlets of Cuzco) and from the towns of the Sacred Valley, who regularly dump their waste directly into the river. A recent clean-up campaign organized by various rafting companies removed 16 tons of rubbish, predominantly plastic bags and bottles, but it just touched the surface of the problem. See also box, page 129.

# Getting there

## Air

Unless you are flying from Bolivia, it is not possible to take an international flight direct to Cuzco; you have to fly via Lima. While it may be possible to make a connection to get you to Cuzco the same day you land in Peru, as often as not you will have to spend some time in the capital before flying up to the highlands. Many organized tours build in a day or so in Lima as a matter of course. This allows you to get your bearings after your flight and see a bit of the city.

**Airport information** Lima's Jorge Chávez Airport will be your point of entry into Peru, see page 254.

**Airport departure tax** International airport departure tax: US$30; domestic airport departure tax US$4.50. The international tax is never included in the price of your ticket; it may be paid in dollars or soles. The national tax is payable at all airports in Peru. Tickets purchased in Peru will also have the 19% state tax, but this will be included in the price of the ticket.

**From Europe** There are direct flights to Lima only from Amsterdam (**KLM** via Bonaire) and Madrid (**Iberia** and **Lan**). From London or other European cities, connections must be made in Madrid, Caracas, or Brazilian or US gateways.

**From North America** Miami is the main gateway to Peru, together with Atlanta, Dallas, Houston, Los Angeles and New York. Airlines, not all direct, include **American Airlines, Continental, Delta, Lan, Copa** and **Aero Mexico**. Daily connections can be made from almost all major North American cities. **Air Canada** flies direct from Toronto, but from Vancouver you will have to make a connection at one of the above gateways.

**From Australia, New Zealand or South Africa** There are no obvious connecting flights from either Australia or New Zealand to Lima. One option would be to go to Buenos Aires from Sydney or Auckland (flights twice a week with **Aerolíneas Argentinas**) and fly on from there (several flights daily). Alternatively, fly to Los Angeles and travel down from there. From Johannesburg, make connections in Buenos Aires or São Paulo.

**From Latin America** There are regular flights (daily in many cases) to Peru from most South American countries. The **Lan** group has the most routes to Lima within the continent. The **Taca** group also has quite extensive coverage, including to Central America and Mexico.

**From Asia** From Hong Kong, Seoul and Singapore, connections have to be made in Los Angeles. Make connections in Los Angeles or Miami if flying from Tokyo.

**Baggage allowance** There is always a weight limit for your baggage, but there is no standard baggage allowance to Peru. If you fly via the USA you are allowed two pieces of luggage up to 32 kg per case. The American airlines are usually a bit more expensive but if you are travelling with a 40-kg bag of climbing gear, it may be worth looking into. On flights from Europe there is a weight allowance of 20 or 23 kg, although some carriers out of Europe use the two-piece system, but may not apply it in both directions. The two-piece system is gaining wider acceptance, but it is always best to check in advance. At busy times of the year it can be very difficult and expensive to bring items such as bikes and surfboards along. Many airlines will let you pay a penalty for overweight baggage – often this is US$5 per kg – but this usually depends on how full the flight is. Check first before you assume you can bring extra luggage. The weight limit for internal flights is often 20 kg or less per person.

**Prices and discounts** Most airlines offer discounted fares on scheduled flights through agencies who specialize in this type of fare. The very busy seasons are from 7 December to 15 January and from 10 July to 10 September. If you intend travelling during those times, book as far ahead as possible. From February to May and from September to November special offers may be available. Examples of fares on scheduled airlines are: from the UK a return with flexible dates will cost about US$1270, but travelling over the Christmas/New Year period can see prices rise to over US$1655. The picture is the same from the USA: a low season return costs as little as US$230 from Miami, but high season is US$315. From Los Angeles low season is US$455, high season US$600. From Sydney, Australia, a low season return is US$2765, whereas a Christmas/New Year return will cost US$4620.

*If you will be returning home at a busy time (eg Christmas or Easter), a booking is advisable on any type of open return ticket.*

## Discount flight agents

### In the UK and Ireland

**STA Travel**, T0870-163 0026, www.statravel.co.uk. They have 65 other branches in the UK, including many university campuses. Specialists in low-cost student/youth flights and tours, also good for student IDs and insurance.
**Trailfinders**, 194 Kensington High St, London, W8 7RG, T020-7938 3939, www.trailfinders.com. 18 branches throughout the UK. Also has a branch in Dublin and 5 travel centres in Australia.

### In North America

**Air Brokers International**, 685 Market St, Suite 400, San Francisco, CA 94105, T1-800-883 3273, www.airbrokers.com. Consolidator and specialist on RTW and Circle Pacific tickets.
**Discount Airfares Worldwide On-Line**, www.etn.nl/discount.htm. A hub of consolidator and discount agent links.
**STA Travel**, T1-800-781 4040, www.statravel.com. Branches all over the US and Canada.
**Travel CUTS**, in all major Canadian cities and on college campuses, T1-866-246 9762, www.travelcuts.com. Specialist in student discount fares, ID and other travel services. Also in California, USA.
**Travelocity**, www.travelocity.com. Online consolidator.

### In Australia and New Zealand

**Flight Centre**, T133 133, www.flight centre.com.au. Offices throughout Australia and other countries.
**STA Travel**, T1300-733035, www.statravel.com.au; 208 Swanston St, Melbourne, Victoria 3000, T03-9639 0599, and branches throughout Australia.
In NZ: 0508-782872, www.statravel.co.nz; 130 Cuba St, PO Box 6604, Wellington, T04-385 0561, cuba@statravel.co.nz. STA branches can also be found in major towns and university campuses.
**Travel.com.au**, 80 Clarence St, Sydney, NSW, T1300 130 481, www.travel.com.au.

**Note** Using the internet for booking flights, hotels and other services directly is increasingly popular and you can get some good deals this way. But don't forget that a travel agent can find the best flights to suit your itinerary, as well as providing advice on documents, insurance, safety, routes, lodging and times of year to travel. A reputable agent will also be bonded to give you some protection if things go wrong.

## Road

There are bus services from neighbouring countries to Peru. If coming from Bolivia, there are direct buses to Cuzco and Puno from La Paz. On rare occasions, customs officials at international borders may ask for a forward ticket out of the country. This means you'll have to buy the cheapest bus ticket out of Peru before they let you in. Note that these tickets are not transferable or refundable.

# Getting around

## Air

Low promotional tariffs are renewed monthly; often it is best to wait to purchase internal flights until your arrival. There are no deals for round-trip tickets and prices can rise within four days of the flight.

Lima to Cuzco is the main tourist axis in Peru and there are plenty of flights between the two cities. Most flights are in the morning, giving people in organized groups and independent travellers an early start. If you're on a tight schedule, then by far the best option is to fly from Lima to **Cuzco** (55 minutes, daily services), and then from Cuzco to **Puerto Maldonado**, if you're

*Sit on right side of the aircraft for the best view of the mountains when flying from Cuzco to Lima; it is worth checking in early to get these seats.*

## Domestic airlines

**Aero Cóndor**, Juan de Arona 781, San Isidro, Lima, T01-614 6000, www.aerocondor.com.pe. Flights from Lima to Andahuaylas, Arequipa, Ayacucho, Cajamarca, Cuzco, Ica, Iquitos, Juliaca, Nazca, Piura, Puerto Maldonado, Pucallpa, Tacna, Talara, Trujillo, Tumbes.
**Lan Perú**, Av José Pardo 513, Miraflores, Lima, T01-213 8200, www.lan.com. Flights from Lima to Arequipa, Chiclayo, Cuzco, Iquitos, Juliaca, Piura, Puerto Maldonado and Trujillo.
**LC Busre**, Los Tulipanes 218, Urb San Eugenio, Lima 14, T01-619 1300, www.lcbusre.com.pe. Flights from Lima to Andahuaylas, Ayacucho, Cajamarca, Huancayo, Huánuco and Huaraz.
**Star Perú**, Av José Pardo 485, Miraflores, Lima, T01-705-9000, www.starperu.com. Flights from Lima to Arequipa, Chiclayo, Cuzco, Iquitos, Juliaca, Pucallpa, Tarapoto and Trujillo.
**Taca Perú**, Av Pardo 811, Miraflores, Lima, T01-511 8222 or 01-800-1TACA (8222), www.grupotaca.com. Flights between Lima and Cuzco.



planning a trip to Tambopata (30 minutes, also daily services). Flights to **Boca Manu** for Manu are normally arranged through a tour operator (also 30 minutes). » *For details of Cuzco airport, see page 58.*

**Airlines and tickets** The main national airlines serving the most travelled routes (of which Cuzco is the prime example) are **Star Perú** and **Aero Cóndor. Lan** flies to many major cities and **Grupo Taca** (the Central American airline) also offers service on the Lima–Cuzco route. (**Lan** and **Taca** are generally reckoned to have the better service.) All these airlines generally cost the same, between US$65 and US$125 one-way anywhere in the country from Lima. Shorter flights may cost a bit less. The closer you get to departure date, the higher the fare. It is not unusual for the prices to go up at holiday times (Easter, May Day, Inti Raymi, 28-29 July, Christmas and New Year), and for elections. During these times, in school holidays (May, July, October and December to March) and the northern hemisphere summer, seats can be hard to come by, so book early. Internal flight prices are given in US dollars but can be paid in soles and the price should include the 19% sales tax. Tickets are not interchangeable between companies but sometimes exceptions will be made in the case of cancellations. Do check with companies for special offers.

**Advice and information** On the Cuzco–Lima route there is a high possibility of cancelled flights during the wet season; tourists are sometimes stranded for several days. It is possible for planes to leave early if the weather is bad. Always give yourself an extra day between national and international flights to allow for any schedule changes. Flights are often overbooked so it is very important to reconfirm your tickets at least 24 hours in advance of your flight and, in the high season, make sure you arrive at the airport two hours before departure to avoid problems. By law, the clerk can start to sell reserved seats to stand-by travellers 30 minutes before the flight. To save time and hassle, travel with carry-on luggage only (48cm x 24cm x 37cm). This will guarantee that your luggage arrives at the airport when you do.

## Road

Peru is no different from other Latin American countries in that travelling by road at night or in bad weather should be treated with great care. It is also true that there are many more unpaved than paved roads, so overland travel is not really an option if you only have a few weeks' holiday. Getting around the country overland can be a difficult task and this is to be expected in a country whose geography is dominated by the Andes, one of the world's major mountain ranges. Great steps have been taken to improve major roads and enlarge the paved network linking the Pacific coast with the Highlands. It is worth taking some time to plan a journey in advance, checking which roads are finished, which have roadworks and which will be affected by the weather. The highland and jungle wet season, from mid-October to late March, can seriously hamper travel. It is important to allow extra time if planning to go overland at this time.

In the Cuzco area a number of roads in the Sacred Valley are paved but, in the main, mountain roads are of dirt, some good, some very bad. Each year they are affected by heavy rain and mud slides, especially those on the eastern slopes of the mountains. Repairs can be delayed because of a shortage of funds. This makes for slow travel and frequent breakdowns. Note that some of these roads can be dangerous or impassable in the rainy season. Check beforehand with locals (not with bus companies, who only want to sell tickets) as accidents are common at these times.

**Bus** There are several bus lines that run between Lima and the towns en route to Cuzco. Many companies have regular (local) services and direct executive (*ejecutivo*) services; the difference between the two is often great and tickets for *ejecutivo* service buses can cost up to double those of the local service buses. (Note that different companies use different titles for their executive or top class service – eg **Imperial, Ideal, Royal**).

*Try to arrive during the day, when it is safer and easier to find accommodation.*

With the better companies or *ejecutivo* service you will get a receipt for your luggage, it will be locked under the bus and you shouldn't have to worry about it at stops because the storage is not usually opened. For mountain routes, take a fleece and sleeping bag as the temperature at night can drop quite low. Night buses along the coast and into main highland areas are generally fine but once you get off the beaten track, the quality of buses and roads deteriorates and you may want to stick to the day buses.

If your bus breaks down and you have to get on another bus, you will probably have to pay for the ticket, but keep your old ticket as some bus companies will give refunds. The back seats tend to be the most bumpy and the exhaust pipe is almost always on the left-hand side of the bus.

**Note** Prices of tickets are raised 60-100% during Semana Santa (Easter), Fiestas Patrias (Independence Day – 28 and 29 July), Navidad (Christmas) and special local events. Prices will usually go up a few days before the holiday and possibly remain higher a few days after. Tickets also sell out during these times so if travelling then, buy your ticket as soon as you know what day you want to travel.

**Car hire** The airport in Lima is the best and most cost-effective place to arrange car hire (see page 255). The minimum age for renting a car is 25. If renting a car, your home driving licence will be accepted for up to six months. Car hire companies are given in the text. They do tend to be very expensive, reflecting the high costs and accident rates. Hotels and tourist agencies will tell you where to find cheaper rates, but you will need to check that you have such basics as spare wheel, tool kit and functioning lights, etc.

Check exactly what the hirer's insurance policy covers. In many cases it will only protect you against minor bumps and scrapes, not major accidents, nor 'natural' damage (eg flooding). Ask if extra cover is available. Also find out, if using a credit card, whether the card automatically includes insurance. Beware of being billed for scratches which were on the vehicle before you hired it.

**Touring y Automóvil Club del Perú** ⓘ *Av Trinidad Morán 698, Lince, T01-211 9977, www.touringperu.com.pe*, offers help to tourists and particularly to members of the leading motoring associations. The Club publishes touring guides to northern, central and southern Peru.

**Combis, colectivos and trucks** Combis operate between most small towns in the Andes on one- to three-hour journeys. This makes it possible, in many cases, just to turn up and travel within an hour or two. On rougher roads, combis are minibuses, while on better roads there are also slightly more expensive and much faster car colectivos. Both operate in the Sacred Valley area. Colectivos are shared taxis that usually charge twice the bus fare and leave only when full. Most firms have offices. If you book one day in advance, they will pick you up at your hotel or in the main plaza. Trucks are not always much cheaper than buses. They charge 75% of the bus fare, but are wholly unpredictable. They are not recommended for long trips and comfort depends on the load.

**Cycling** Unless you are planning a journey almost exclusively on paved roads, a mountain bike is strongly recommended. The good-quality ones are incredibly tough and rugged, with low gear ratios for difficult terrain, wide tyres with plenty of tread for good road-holding, cantilever brakes, and a low centre of gravity for improved stability. A chrome-alloy frame is a desirable choice over aluminium as it can be welded if necessary. Once an aluminium frame breaks, it's broke.

**South American Explorers** (see page 46) have valuable cycling information that is continuously updated. The Expedition Advisory Centre, administered by the **Royal Geographical Society** ⓘ *1 Kensington Gore, London SW7 2AR*, has a useful monograph entitled *Bicycle Expeditions*, by Paul Vickers. It can be downloaded from the RGS's website, www.rgs.org. A useful website is **Cyclo Accueil Cyclo** (**CAC**), www.cci.asso.fr/cac/cac.htm, an organization of long-haul tourers who open their homes for free to passing cyclists.

**Hitchhiking** Hitchhiking is not easy, owing to the lack of private vehicles, and requires a lot of patience. It can also be a risky way of getting from A to B but, with common sense, it can be an acceptable way of travelling for free (or very little money) and a way to meet a range of interesting people. For obvious reasons, a lone female should not hitch by herself. Besides, you are more likely to get a lift if you are with a partner, be they male or female. The best combination is a male and female together. Three or more and you'll be in for a long wait. Your appearance is also important. Remember that you are asking considerable trust of someone.

**Note** Drivers usually ask for money but they don't always expect to get it. In mountain and jungle areas you usually have to pay drivers of lorries, vans and even private cars; ask the driver first how much they are going to charge, and then doublecheck with the locals.

**Motorcycling** The motorcycle should be off-road capable. A road bike can go most places an off-road bike can go at the cost of greater effort. Most hotels will allow you to bring the bike inside (see accommodation listings in the travelling text for details). Look for hotels that have a courtyard or more secure parking and never leave luggage on the bike overnight or whilst unattended.

**Taxis** Taxi prices are fixed and cost around US$0.75-1.20 in the urban areas. In Lima prices range from US$1.50-3, but fares are not fixed. Some drivers work for companies that do have standard fares. Ask locals what the price should be and always set the price beforehand. Taxis at airports are often a bit more expensive, but ask locals what the price should be as taxi drivers may try to charge you three times the correct price. Many taxi drivers work for commission from hotels and will try to convince you to go to that hotel. Feel free to choose your own hotel and go there. If you walk away from the Arrivals gate a bit, the fares should go down to a price that is reasonable.

### Train

Peru's national rail service was privatized in 1999. The lines in the Cuzco area are all run by **PerúRail SA** ⓘ *T084-238722, www.perurail.com*. Service has improved, but prices have also risen substantially. **PerúRail's** services are Cuzco-Machu Picchu (see box, page 154) and Cuzco-Juliaca-Puno.

## Sleeping

Cuzco is full of excellent-value hotels throughout the price ranges and finding a room to suit your budget should not present any problems. The exception to this is during Christmas and Easter, Carnival in June and Independence celebrations at the end of July, when all hotels seem to be crowded. It's advisable to book in advance at these times and during school holidays and local festivals (see page 33).

Accommodation, as with everything else, is more expensive in Lima, where good budget hotels are fewer and therefore tend to be busy. Remote jungle towns such as Puerto Maldonado also tend to be more expensive than the norm. And if you want a room with air conditioning expect to pay around 30% extra.

By law all places that offer accommodation now have a plaque outside bearing the letters **H (Hotel)**, **Hs (Hostal)**, **HR (Hotel Residencial)** or **P (Pensión)** according to type. A hotel has 51 rooms or more, a *hostal* 50 or fewer, but the categories do not describe quality or facilities. Generally speaking, though, a *pensión* or *hospedaje* will be cheaper than a hotel or *hostal*. Most mid-range hotels have their own restaurants serving lunch and dinner, as well as breakfast. Few budget places have this facility, though many now serve breakfast. Many hotels have safe parking for motor cycles. Most places are friendly, irrespective of the price, particularly smaller *pensiones* and *hospedajes*, which are often family run and will treat you as another member of the family. Cheaper places don't always supply soap, towels and toilet paper. In colder (higher) regions they may not supply enough blankets, so take your own or a sleeping bag.

### Youth hostels

The office of the **Youth Hostel Association of Peru** (Asociación Peruana de Albergues Turísticos Juveniles) ⓘ *Av Casimiro Ulloa 328, Miraflores, Lima, T01-446-5488, www.limahostell.com.pe/aphi/*, has information about youth hostels all around the world. For information about International Student Identity Cards (ISIC) and lists of discounts available to cardholders contact **Intej**, see page 45.

### Camping

This presents no problems in Peru. There can, however, be problems with robbery when camping close to a small village. Avoid such a location, or ask permission to camp in a backyard or *chacra* (farmland). Most Peruvians are used to campers. Be casual about it, do not unpack all your gear, leave it inside your tent (especially at night) and never leave a tent unattended.

## A bed for the night

**LL** (**over US$200**),
**L** (**US$151-200**), **AL** (**US$101-150**) and **A** (**US$66-100**) Hotels in these categories are usually only found in Cuzco, Lima and the main tourist centres. They should offer pool, sauna, gym, jacuzzi, all business facilities (including email), several restaurants, bars and often a casino. Most will provide a safe box in each room.

**B** (**US$46-65**) and **C** (**US$31-45**) The better-value hotels in these categories provide more than the standard facilities and a fair degree of comfort. Most will include breakfast and many offer 'extras' such as cable TV, minibar, and tea and coffee making facilities. They may also provide tourist information and their own transport. Service is generally better and most accept credit cards. At the top end of the range, some may have a swimming pool, sauna and jacuzzi.

**D** (**US$21-30**) and
**E** (**US$12-20**) These categories range from very comfortable to functional, but there are some real bargains. At these prices you should expect your own bathroom, hot water, towel, soap, toilet paper, TV, restaurant, communal sitting area and a reasonably sized, comfortable room with air conditioning (in tropical regions).

**F** (**US$6-11**) Usually in this range you can expect some degree of comfort and cleanliness, a private bathroom with hot water and perhaps continental breakfast thrown in. Again, the best value hotels will be listed in the travelling text. Many of those catering for foreign tourists in the more popular regions offer excellent value for money and many have their own restaurant and offer services such as cooking and laundry facilities, safe deposit box, money exchange and luggage store.

**G** (**under US$6**) A room in this price range varies from the functional, with a bed, window, table and chair, even your own bathroom, to not much more than a bed to sleep in and space to put your bags. Although there aren't many recommendable places in this range in Peru, those that operate for tourists tend to offer shared facilities, but include hot water and use of a kitchen.

Prices given in the accommodation listings are for two people sharing a double room with bathroom (shower and toilet) in the high season. Where possible, prices are also given per person, as some hotels charge almost as much for a single room.

Camping gas in little blue bottles is available. Those with stoves designed for lead-free gasoline should use *ron de quemar*, available from hardware shops (*ferreterías*). White gas is called *bencina*, also available from hardware stores. If you use a stove system that uses canisters make sure you dispose of the empty canisters properly. Keep in mind that you are responsible for the trash that your group, guide or mule driver may drop and it is up to you to say something and pick it up.

## Advice and suggestions

If travelling alone, it's usually cheaper to share with others in a room with three or four beds. If breakfast is included in the price, it will almost invariably mean continental breakfast. During the low season, when many places may be half empty, it's often possible to bargain the room rate down. Reception areas in hotels may be misleading, so it is a good idea to see the room before booking. Many hoteliers try to offload their least desirable rooms first. If you're shown a dark box without any furniture, ask if there's another room with a window or a desk for writing letters. The difference is often surprising.

When booking a hotel from an airport or station by phone, always talk to the hotel yourself; do not let anyone do it for you (except an accredited hotel booking service). You will be told the hotel of your choice is full and be directed to a more expensive one.

### Bathrooms and toilets

The electric showers used in many hotels (basic up to mid-range) are a health and safety nightmare. Avoid touching any part of the shower while it is producing hot water and always get out before you switch it off.

Except in the most upmarket hotels and restaurants, most Peruvian toilets are barely adequate at best. The further you go from the main population and tourist centres, the poorer the facilities, so you may require a strong stomach and the ability to hold your breath for a long time. Almost without exception used toilet paper or feminine hygiene products should not be flushed down the pan, but placed in the receptacle provided. This applies even in quite expensive hotels. Failing to observe this custom will block the pan or drain, which can be a considerable health risk.

## Eating and drinking

### Peruvian cuisine

Not surprisingly for a country with such a diversity of geography and climates, Peru boasts the continent's most extensive and varied menu. In fact, Peru is rivalled in Latin America only by Mexico in the variety of its cuisine. One of the least expected pleasures of a trip to Peru is the wonderful food on offer, and those who are willing to forego the normal traveller's fare of pizza and fried chicken are in for a tasty treat.

The best coastal dishes are those with **seafood** bases, with the most popular being the jewel in the culinary crown, *ceviche*. This delicious dish of raw white fish marinated in lemon juice, onion and hot peppers can be found in neighbouring countries, but Peruvian is best. Traditionally, *ceviche* is served with corn on the cob, *cancha* (toasted corn), yucca and sweet potatoes. Another mouth-watering fish dish is *escabeche*, fish with onions, hot green pepper, red peppers, prawns (*langostinos*), cumin, hard-boiled eggs, olives, and sprinkled with cheese. For fish on its own, don't miss the excellent *corvina*, or white sea bass. You should also try *chupe de camarones*, which is a shrimp stew made with varying and somewhat surprising ingredients. Other fish dishes include *parihuela*, a popular bouillabaisse with *yuyo de mar*, a tangy seaweed, and *aguadito*, a thick rice and fish soup said to have rejuvenating powers.

The staples of highland cooking, **corn** and **potatoes**, date back to Inca times and beyond and are found in a remarkable variety of shapes, sizes and colours. Two good potato dishes are *causa* and *carapulca*. *Causa* is made with yellow potatoes, lemons, pepper, hard-boiled eggs, olives, lettuce, sweet cooked corn, sweet potato, fresh cheese, and served with onion sauce. Another potato dish is *papa a la huancaína*, which is topped with a spicy sauce made with milk and cheese. The most commonly eaten corn dishes are *choclo con queso*, corn on the cob with cheese, and *tamales*, boiled corn dumplings filled with meat and wrapped in a banana leaf.

**Meat** dishes are many and varied. *Ollucos con charqui* is a kind of potato with dried meat, *sancochado* is meat and all kinds of vegetables stewed together and seasoned with ground garlic and *lomo a la huancaína* is beef with egg and cheese sauce. A dish almost guaranteed to appear on every restaurant menu is *lomo saltado*, a kind of stir-fried beef with onions, vinegar, ginger, chilli, tomatoes and fried potatoes,

## A limp excuse

Did you know there is a potato that has the opposite effect of Viagra? It's a tuber named *año* and Cuzqueña women have been known to use it to take revenge on cheating husbands. If a man is unfaithful, his wife will boil his trousers in a vat containing the potato – enough to stop him rising to any occasion!

Stories like these are part of the fun of discovering Cuzco's markets. Wandering round one is a great experience, packed with new sights, smells and the bright colours of unknown fruit and veg. At San Jerónimo you'll find *huacatay* (a mint grown at high altitude and used in the preparation of guinea pig), bulls' testicles (boiled, sliced and used in salads), huge sacks of dirt-cheap garlic, massive 20-25 kg pumpkins, *pepiño* (which has a creamy-coloured skin and is very refreshing), as well as strawberries from the coast, basil, coriander, green chilli peppers and spinach.

There is *caihua*, from the cucumber family, which grows only in sub-tropical valleys and which can be stuffed or chopped for stir-fry or salad. Then there is a dried black potato which smells of bad feet when it is cooked, but is favoured by locals nevertheless; they grind it up and add it to food.

Then there are potatoes frozen overnight as hard as rocks to bring out their flavour; these are mixed with salt and eaten with cheese. These, together with olives, oranges and tomatoes piled high in large mounds, are weighed out by indigenous women who proudly show off their region of origin by the different hats they wear.

Most Westerners will shrink from ever sampling these foodstuffs – especially when a lamb's head, complete with lipless, grinning teeth bobs to the surface of *caldo de cabeza*, the favourite soup here. (Locals pay a premium for this if it includes brain and tongue.) However, the sight of so much variety, of bright yellow bananas balanced chest-high, of brown guinea pigs scurrying around cages and of heady herbs sold by the sackful, is one worth seeking out. Just don't try the tuber named *año*!

served with rice. *Rocoto relleno* is spicy bell pepper stuffed with beef and vegetables, *palta rellena* is avocado filled with chicken or Russian salad, *estofado de carne* is a stew which often contains wine and *carne en adobo* is a cut and seasoned steak. Others include *fritos*, fried pork, usually eaten in the morning, *chicharrones*, deep fried chunks of pork ribs and chicken, and *lechón*, suckling pig. And not forgetting that popular childhood pet, *cuy* (guinea pig), which is considered a real delicacy.

Very filling and good value are the many **soups** on offer, such as *yacu-chupe*, a green soup which has a base of potato, with cheese, garlic, coriander leaves, parsley, peppers, eggs, onions, and mint, and *sopa a la criolla* containing thin noodles, beef heart, bits of egg and vegetables and pleasantly spiced. And not to be outdone in the fish department, *trucha* (trout) is delicious, particularly from Lake Titicaca.

The main ingredient in much **jungle cuisine** is fish, especially the succulent, dolphin-sized *paiche*, which comes with the delicious *palmito*, or palm-hearts, and the ever-present yucca and fried bananas. Other popular dishes include *sopa de motelo* (turtle soup), *sajino* (roast wild boar) and *lagarto* (caiman). *Juanes* are a jungle version of *tamales*, stuffed with chicken and rice.

The Peruvian sweet tooth is evident in the huge number of **desserts** and confections from which to choose. These include: *cocada al horno* – coconut, with yolk of egg, sesame seed, wine and butter; *picarones* – frittered cassava flour and eggs fried

## Eating out

| | | |
|---|---|---|
| ¥¥¥ | **Expensive** over US$12 | Prices for individual restaurant meals given in the text refer to a two-course meal for one person, without tips or drinks, or, where stated, the price of a main course only. |
| ¥¥ | **Mid-range** US$6-11 | |
| ¥ | **Cheap** under US$6 | |

in fat and served with honey; *mazamorra morada* – purple maize, sweet potato starch, lemons, various dried fruits, sticks of ground cinnamon and cloves and perfumed pepper; *manjar blanco* – milk, sugar and eggs; *maná* – an almond paste with eggs, vanilla and milk; *alfajores* – shortbread biscuit with *manjar blanco*, pineapple, peanuts, etc; *pastelillos* – yuccas with sweet potato, sugar and anise fried in fat and powdered with sugar and served hot; and *zango de pasas*, made with maize, syrup, raisins and sugar. *Turrón*, the Lima nougat, is worth trying. *Tejas* are pieces of fruit or nut enveloped in *manjar blanco* and covered in chocolate or icing sugar – delicious.

The various Peruvian **fruits** are wonderful. They include bananas, citrus fruits, pineapples, dates, avocados (*paltas*), eggfruit (*lúcuma*), custard apples (*chirimoyas*) which can be as big as your head, quince, paw paw, mango, guava, the passion fruit (*maracuyá*) and the soursop (*guanábana*). These should be tried as juices or ice cream – an unforgettable experience. » *For a food and drink glossary, see page 336.*

### Eating out

Lunch is the main meal, and apart from the most exclusive places, most restaurants have one or two set lunch menus, called *menú ejecutivo* or *menú económico*. The set menu has the advantage of being ready and is served almost immediately and it is usually cheap. The *menú ejecutivo* costs US$2 or more for a three-course meal with a soft drink and it offers greater choice and more interesting dishes than the *menú económico*, which costs US$1-2. Don't leave it too late, though, as most Peruvians eat lunch around 1230-1300. There are many Chinese restaurants (*chifas*) which serve good food at reasonable prices. For economically minded people the *comedores populares* found in the markets of most cities offer a standard three-course meal for as little as US$1.

For those who wish to eschew such good value, the menu is called *la carta*. An *à la carte* lunch or dinner costs US$5-8, but can go up to an expensive US$30 in a first-class Cuzco restaurant, with drinks and wine included (US$80 in Lima). Middle- and high-class restaurants may add 10% service, but do add the 19% sales tax to the bill (which foreigners do have to pay). This is not shown on the price list or menu, so check in advance. Less fancy restaurants charge only the tax, while cheap, local restaurants charge no taxes. Dinner in restaurants is normally about 1900 onwards, but choice may be more limited than lunchtime.

The situation for vegetarians is improving, but slowly. In Cuzco you should have no problem finding a vegetarian restaurant (or a restaurant that has vegetarian options), and the same applies to Lima. Elsewhere, choice is limited and you may find that, as a non-meat eater, you are not understood. Vegetarians and people with allergies should be able to list (in Spanish) all the foods they cannot eat. By saying *No como carne* (I don't eat meat), people may assume that you eat chicken and eggs. If you do eat eggs, make sure they are cooked thoroughly. Restaurant staff will often bend over backwards to get you exactly what you want but you need to request it.

## Drink

Peru's most famous drink is *pisco*, a grape brandy, used in the wonderful pisco sour, a deceptively potent cocktail which also includes egg whites and lime juice. The most renowned brands come from the Ica Valley. Other favourites are *chilcano*, a longer refreshing drink made with *guinda*, a local cherry brandy, and *algarrobina*, a sweet cocktail made with the syrup from the bark of the carob tree, egg whites, evaporated milk, *pisco* and cinnamon.

Some Peruvian wines are good, others are acidic and poor. The best are the Ica wines Tacama and Ocucaje, and both come in red, white and rosé, sweet and dry varieties. They cost around US$5 a bottle, or more. Tacama blancs de blancs and brut champagne have been recommended, also Gran Tinto Reserva Especial. Viña Santo Tomás, from Chincha, is cheap, but Casapalca is not for the discerning palate.

Peruvian beer is good but became pretty much the same the country over after many individual brewers were swallowed up by the multinational Backus and Johnson (itself a subsidiary of the multinational brewer SABMiller). This happened to the *Cuzqueña*, *Arequipeña*, *Pilsen Callao* and *Trujillo* brands. Other beers include *Cristal* from Lima but available nationwide, which is pretty good, and SABMiller's new product, *Barena*. Those who fancy a change from the ubiquitous pilsner type beers should look out for the sweetish *maltina* brown ale. A good dark beer is Trujillo Malta.

*Chicha de jora* is a strong but refreshing maize beer, usually home-made and not easy to come by, and *chicha morada* is a soft drink made with purple maize. Coffee in Peru is usually execrable. It is brought to the table in a small jug accompanied by a mug of hot water to which you add the coffee essence. If you want coffee with milk, a mug of milk is brought. Those who crave a decent cup of coffee will find recommended places listed in the café section of each town. There are many different kinds of herb tea: the commonest are *manzanilla* (camomile), *mate de coca* (often served in the highlands to stave off the discomforts of altitude sickness) and *hierbaluisa* (lemon grass).



# Entertainment

## Lima

The chances are you won't have much time in Lima and will want to move on to Cuzco as soon as possible. But if you do have a free night before flying you should check out the nightlife in Barranco, a pleasant, bohemian, seaside suburb of the capital. It's only a short taxi ride from Miraflores and at weekends is positively throbbing with young *limeños* out for a good time. It's also a great place for a romantic early evening drink while you watch the sun slip into the Pacific Ocean. There are lots of trendy bars and nightclubs in Miraflores, too. ⏩ *For listings, see Bars and clubs, page 274, and Entertainment, page 275.*

## Cuzco → *Look out for the vast range of flyers, which give you free entry plus a complimentary drink.*

One of Cuzco's main attractions – apart from Inca ruins, colonial architecture, great trekking, wonderful scenery and wild adventure sports – is its nightlife. There is a staggering selection of bars to suit all tastes and dispositions, all crammed into a few streets on and around the main Plaza de Armas. You can large it up in the frenzied atmosphere of the **Cross Keys**, get blissed out in the laid-back **Los Perros**, or go all Oirish in **Paddy Flaherty's**. The choice, as they say, is yours. After the bars close the nightclubs kick into action. The old favourites such as **Mama Africa** and **Ukuku's** have been joined by a rash of new pretenders, some with decent sound systems and DJs spinning the latest happening tunes. But it's not all techno and thumping drum 'n' bass. There are also places where you can wiggle your hips to the sensuous sounds of salsa and merengue. If all that brings you out in a cold sweat, there are *peñas* offering relatively sedate folklore shows. A side effect of all the competition to entertain you is that establishments may come and go, or reinvent themselves as something new. The main places tend to stay constant, but this season's favourite may have moved on next year, or vanished altogether. Be warned that Cuzco's nightlife is so prolific you may be so off your face every night that you won't even have the energy to do the Inca Trail. More seriously, though, take it easy on the booze when you first arrive. Having altitude sickness and a hangover is no joke. Also be aware of the potential dangers of trying to score drugs in nightclubs (see page 37). ⏩ *For listings, see Bars and clubs, page 96, and Entertainment, page 98.*



# Festivals and events

## Festivals

Every bit as important as knowing where to go and what the weather will be like, is Peru's festival calendar. At any given time of the year there'll be a festival somewhere in the country, at which time even the sleepiest little town or village is transformed into a raucous mixture of drinking, dancing and water throwing (or worse). Not all festivals end up as choreographed drunken riots, however. Some are solemn and ornate holy processions. All draw people from miles around; it helps a great deal to know about these festivals and when they take place.

Two of the major festival dates are **Carnaval**, which is held over the weekend before **Ash Wednesday**, and **Semana Santa** (Holy Week), which ends on **Easter Sunday**. Carnaval is celebrated in most of the Andean regions and Semana Santa throughout most of Peru. Accommodation and transport is heavily booked at these times and prices rise accordingly.

Another important festival is **Fiesta de la Cruz**, held on the first of May in much of the central and southern highlands and on the coast. In Cuzco, the entire month of June is one huge fiesta, culminating in **Inti Raymi**, on 24 June, one of Peru's prime tourist attractions. Accommodation can be very hard to find at this time in Cuzco.

The two main festivals in Lima are **Santa Rosa de Lima**, on 30 August, and **Señor de los Milagros,** held on several dates throughout October. Another national festival is **Todos los Santos** (All Saints) on 1 November, and on 8 December is **Festividad de la Inmaculada Concepción**. For more dates, check the websites of **PromPerú** and **South American Explorers** (see page 46). Also check out www.whatsonwhen.com.

## National holidays

Apart from the festivals listed above, the main holidays are: 1 January, New Year; 6 January, Bajada de Reyes; 1 May (Labour Day); 28-29 July, the Fiestas Patrias (Independence); 8 October, Battle of Angamos; 24-25 December, Christmas.

Most businesses such as banks, airline offices and tourist agencies close for the official holidays while supermarkets and street markets may be open. This depends a lot on where you are so ask around before the holiday. Sometimes holidays that fall during mid-week will be moved to the following Monday. Find out what the local customs and events are. Often there are parades, processions, special types of food or certain traditions (like yellow underwear at New Year) that characterize the event. The high season for foreign tourism in Peru is June to September while national tourism peaks on certain holidays, Navidad, Semana Santa and Fiestas Patrias. Prices rise and accommodation and bus tickets are harder to come by. If you know when you will be travelling buy your ticket in advance.

# Shopping

Almost everyone who visits Cuzco will end up buying a souvenir from the vast array of arts and crafts (*artesanía*) on offer. The best, and cheapest, place to shop for souvenirs, and almost anything else, is in the street markets which can be found everywhere.

## Bargaining

Sooner or later almost everyone has to bargain in Peru. Only the rich and famous can afford to pay the prices quoted by taxi drivers, receptionists and self-proclaimed guides. The great majority of Peruvians are honest and extremely hard working, but their country is poor and often in turmoil, the future is uncertain and the overwhelming majority of people live below the poverty line. Foreigners are seen as rich, even if they are backpackers or students. In order to bring prices down, it is extremely helpful to speak at least some Spanish and/or to convince locals that you live, work or study in Peru and therefore know the real price.

You can negotiate the price of a tour booked through a travel agency, but not an aeroplane, bus or train ticket. In fact, you will probably get a better price directly from the airline ticket office.

Bargaining is expected when you are shopping for artwork, handicrafts, souvenirs, or even food in the market. Remember, though, that most handicrafts, including alpaca and woollen goods, are made by hand. Ask yourself if it is worth taking advantage of the piteous state of the people you are buying from. Keep in mind, these people are making a living and the 50 centavos you save by bargaining may buy the seller two loaves of bread. You want the *fair* price not the lowest one, so bargain only when you feel you are being ripped off. Remember that some Peruvians are so desperate that they will have to sell you their goods at *any* price, in order to survive. Please, don't take advantage of it.

## What to buy

Good buys are: silver and gold handicrafts; hand-spun and hand-woven textiles; manufactured textiles in traditional designs; llama and alpaca wool products such as ponchos, rugs, hats, blankets, slippers, coats and sweaters; *arpilleras* (appliqué pictures of Peruvian life), which are made with great skill and originality by women in the shanty towns; and fine leather products which are mostly hand-made. Another good buy is clothing made from high quality Pima cotton, which is grown in Peru.

The *mate burilado*, or engraved gourd, found in every tourist shop, is cheap and one of the most genuine expressions of folk art in Peru. Alpaca clothing, such as sweaters, hats and gloves, is cheaper in the sierra, the best value being found in Puno. Nevertheless, Cuzco is one of the main weaving centres and a good place to shop for textiles, as well as excellent woodcarvings (see the Shopping section on page 101). **Note** Genuine alpaca is odourless wet or dry, wet llama 'stinks'. ⏩ *For a more detailed look at Peruvian arts and crafts, see page 303.*

Pre-paid Kodak slide film cannot be developed in Peru and is also very hard to find. Kodachrome is almost impossible to buy. Some travellers (but not all) have advised against mailing exposed films home. Either take them with you, or have them developed, but not printed, once you have checked the laboratory's quality. Note that postal authorities may use less-sensitive equipment for X-ray screening than the airports do. Developing black and white film is a problem. Often it is shoddily machine-processed and the negatives are ruined. Ask the store if you can see an example of their laboratory's work and if they hand-develop. Exposed film can be protected in humid areas by putting it in a balloon and tying a knot. Similarly, keeping your camera in a plastic bag may reduce the effects of humidity. In major tourist centres, such as Cuzco, there is no shortage of shops selling cards for digital cameras, but they are expensive. Many places will transfer digital photos to CD.

# Essentials A-Z

## Accident & emergency

Contact the relevant emergency service and your embassy (see pages 119 and 280). Make sure you obtain police/medical reports in order to file insurance claims.

**Emergency services**
Police T01-475 2995
Ambulance (Lima) T01-225 4040
Fire T116
Tourist police, Jr Moore 268, Magdalena at 28th block of Av Brasil, Lima, T01-460 1060.

## Children

Travel with children can bring you into closer contact with local families and, generally, presents no special problems – in fact the path is often smoother for family groups. Officials tend to be more amenable where children are concerned and they are pleased if your child knows a little Spanish. South American Explorers in Cuzco and Lima (see pages 58 and 257) can provide lots of useful information on travelling with children.

Getting from A to B usually involves a lot of time waiting for buses, trains and planes. You should take reading material with you. When travelling by road in the Sacred Valley, be prepared for cramped *colectivo* travel. On all long-distance buses you pay a fare for each seat and there are no half fares if the children occupy a seat each. For shorter trips it is cheaper, if less comfortable, to seat small children on your knee. On sightseeing tours you should *always* bargain for a family rate – often children can go free.

Food can be a problem if the children are not adaptable. A small immersion heater and jug for making hot drinks is invaluable, but remember that electric current varies. In restaurants, you can normally buy children's helpings, or divide one full-size helping between 2 children.

In all hotels, try to negotiate family rates. If charges are per person, always insist that 2 children will occupy 1 bed only, therefore counting as 1 tariff. You can almost always get a reduced rate at cheaper hotels. For details of health issues, see page 38.

See also box, page 36, and the useful website www.babygoes2.com.

## Customs & duty free

**Duty-free allowance** When travelling into Peru you can bring 20 packs of cigarettes (400 cigarettes), 50 cigars or 500 g of tobacco, 3 litres of alcohol and new articles for personal use or gifts valued at up to US$300. There are certain items that cannot be brought in duty free: these include computers (but laptops are OK). The value-added tax for items that are not considered duty free but are still intended for personal use is generally 20%. Personal items necessary for adventure sports such as climbing, kayaking and fishing are duty free. Most of the customs rules aren't a worry for the average traveller, but anything that looks like it's being brought in for resale could give you trouble.

**Export ban** It is illegal to take items of archaeological interest out of Peru. This means that any pre-Columbian pottery or Inca artefacts cannot leave the country. If you are buying extremely good replicas make sure the pieces have the artist's name on them or that they have a tag which shows that they are not originals. No matter how simple it seems, it is not worth your time to try and take anything illegal out of the country – this includes drugs. The security personnel and customs officials are experts at their job. Understand that this is a foolhardy idea and save yourself the horror of 10 years in jail.

## Disabled travellers

As with most underdeveloped countries, facilities for the disabled traveller are sadly lacking. Wheelchair ramps are a rare luxury and getting a wheelchair into a bathroom or toilet is well-nigh impossible, except in some of the more upmarket hotels. The entrance to many cheap hotels is up a narrow flight of stairs. Pavements are often in a poor state of repair (even able-bodied people need to look out for uncovered manholes and other unexpected traps).

## A child's survival guide to Peru

I went to Peru for three months and loved it. We lived in a place in Urubamba called K'uychi Rumi, which was brilliant because it shared a big garden with the other houses and we visited Cuzco a lot.

The ruins are interesting to visit but you don't want to spend your whole time trudging up and down them. There is plenty else to do.

I really liked the horse riding. To start, try riding from Sacsayhuaman to the X-Zone (I love that name!) and around to Qenqo. This was my first horse-riding trip ever, so if you haven't been before, don't worry. It was quite flat and even my seven-year-old brother Owen managed on his own horse. My other brother Leo, who's four, rode with Dad.

The next ride wasn't flat at all. We went up a very steep hill in the Sacred Valley, from Lamay to a ruin called Huchuy Cuzco. It was amazing. We went up a steep windy path between two hills and when I was on the path, I looked up and couldn't believe that I was going to do that – but we did.

After these trips you are fully prepared for camping in the High Andes. We went up to, wait for it, 4200 m and it was cool in every sense, including temperature. The two nights in a tent were the coldest I have ever been in my life – but don't let me put you off because it was great fun and it warmed up during the day.

River-rafting on the Urubamba was fab. The first bit was gentle, but the second part near Ollantaytambo got rough, including a Grade III bit, which had a 2-m waterfall that we went over.

After all that exercise you might need some food. The place to go in Cuzco is Jack's Café, which has toasted sandwiches, big breakfasts, chips and milkshakes. For a more fancy dessert, try the Dolce Vita ice cream place in Santa Catalina Ancha. My favourite flavour was *naranja* (orange)-split, and there are a lot of unusual flavours like *lúcuma* (egg-fruit) and *maracuya*.

In Urubamba, Los Geranios is recommended, as is anywhere which does fried chicken, which luckily is very popular around Cuzco.

By Daisy Thomson (aged 9)

Visually and hearing-impaired travellers are similarly poorly catered for, as a rule, but experienced guides can often provide tours with individual attention. Disabled Peruvians obviously have to cope with these problems and mainly rely on the help of others to get on and off public transport and generally move around.

The Ministerio de la Mujer y Desarrollo Social (Ministry for Women and Social Development) incorporates a National Council for the Integration of Disabled People (CONADIS, www.conadisperu.gob.pe, in Spanish only). CONADIS, together with PromPerú, SATH (see below) and Kéroul of Québec, has been involved in a project called Peru: Towards an Accessible Tourism; the first report on 'Accessibility in Peru for Tourists with Disabilities' was published in 2001. The report identifies many challenges in a selected number of major tourist sites. For instance, archaeological sites such as Machu Picchu, being a World Heritage Site, may not be altered for accessibility. Specially trained personnel, however, can provide assistance to those with disabilities in these cases.

Some travel companies are beginning to specialize in exciting holidays, tailor made for individuals depending on their level of disability. The Global Access Disabled Travel Network Site, www.globalaccessnews.com, is dedicated to providing information for 'disabled adventurers' and includes a number of reviews and tips from members of the public. Another informative site, with lots of advice on how to travel with specific disabilities, plus listings and links, belongs to the Society for Accessible Travel and

Hospitality (SATH), www.sath.org. You might want to read *Nothing Ventured*, edited by Alison Walsh (Harper Collins), which gives personal accounts of worldwide journeys by disabled travellers, plus advice and listings. One company in Cuzco which offers tours for disabled people is **Apumayo**, see Cuzco Activities and tours, page 111.

## Drugs

Soft and hard drugs are part of the scene in Cuzco and are easy to score but be aware that anyone found carrying even the smallest amount is automatically assumed to be a drug trafficker. The use or purchase of drugs is punishable by up to 15 years' imprisonment and the number of foreigners in Peruvian prisons on drug charges is still increasing. If arrested on any charge the wait for trial in prison can take up to a year and is particularly unpleasant. Be wary of anyone approaching you in a club and asking where they can score – the chances are they'll be plain-clothes police. If you are asked by the narcotics police to go to the toilets and have your bags searched, insist on taking a witness.

## Electricity

220 volts, 60 cycles (Arequipa 50 cycles). Most 4- and 5-star hotels have 110 volts AC. Plugs are either American flat-pin or twin flat and round pin combined.

## Embassies and consulates

**Australia**, 40 Brisbane Ave, Barton, ACT 2600, Canberra, T02-6273 7351, www.embaperu.org.au.
**Austria**, Gottfried Keller-Gasse 2/1-2, 1030 Vienna, T713 4377, embajada @embaperuaustria.at.
**Belgium** (consulate), rue de Praetere 2, 1000 Brussels, T32-2-641 8760, www.consulado-peru.be.
**Bolivia** (consulate), Av 6 de Agosto 2455 Of 402, Sopocachi, La Paz, T591-2-244 0631, www.conperlapaz.org.
**Canada**, 130 Albert St, Suite 1901, Ottawa, Ontario K1M 1W5, T1-613-238 1777, www.embassyofperu.ca.
**France**, 50 Ave Kleber, 75116 Paris, T33-1-5370 4200, www.amb-perou.fr/.
**Germany**, Mohrenstrasse 42, 10117 Berlin, T49-30-229 1455, www.embaperu.de.
**Israel**, 60 Medinat Hayehudin St, Herzliya Pituach, T972-9-9957 8835, emperu@012.net.il.
**Italy**, Via Siacci 2B, 2nd floor, 00197 Roma, T39-06-8069 1510, www.ambasciataperu.it.
**Japan** (consulate), COI Gotanda Bldg.6F, Higashi Gotanda, 1-13-12 Shinagawa-Ku, Tokio To 141-0022, T81-3-5793 4444, www.consuladodelperuentokio.org.
**Netherlands** (consulate), Amsteldijk 166-7E, 1079 LH, Amsterdam, T31-20-622 8580, www.consuladoperuamsterdam.com.
**New Zealand**, Level 8, 40 Mercer St, Cigna House, Wellington, T64-4-499 8087, www.embassyofperu.org.nz.
**South Africa**, Brooklyn Gardens, 235 Veale and Middel Sts, block B, 1st floor, Nieuw Muckleneuk, 0181 Pretoria, T27-12- 346 8744, emperu6@telkomsa.net.
**Spain**, C Príncipe de Vergara 36, 5to Derecha, 28001 Madrid, T34-91-431 4242, www.embajadaperu.es.
**Sweden**, Brunnsgatan 21 B, 111 38 Stockholm, T46-8-440 8740, www.peruembassy.se.
**Switzerland**, Thunstrasse No 36, CH-3005 Berne, T41-31-351 8555, www.embajadaperu.ch.
**UK**, 52 Sloane St, London, SW1X 9SP, T020-7235 1917, www.peruembassy-uk.com.
**USA**, 1700 Massachusetts Av NW, Washington DC 20036, T1-202-833 9860, www.peruvianembassy.us.

## Gay and lesbian travellers

**Movimiento Homosexual de Lima**, C Mariscal Miller 828, Jesús María, T01-332 2934, www.mhol.org.pe, has great information about the gay community in Lima. Online resources for gay travellers in Peru are http://lima.queercity.info/index.html (a good site, in English, with lots of links and information), www.deambiente.com/web and www.gayperu.com (both in Spanish). A tour operator in Peru is **Gayperu Travel**, Larco 101, of 309, T01-447 3366, www.gayperu.com/travel. In Cuzco the scene is not very active (perhaps the best place to enquire is the **Café Macondo**). This does not imply, however, that there is hostility towards gay and lesbian travellers. As a major tourist centre which welcomes a huge variety of visitors, Cuzco is probably more open than anywhere else in Peru.

## Health

Cuzco stands at 3310 m, so you'll need time to acclimatize to the high altitude. If flying from Lima, don't underestimate the shock to your system of going from sea level to over 3000 m in 1 hr – see also acute mountain sickness below. If you're arriving in Cuzco by air, it makes a lot of sense to get down to the Urubamba Valley, at 2800 m, 510 m lower than Cuzco itself, and make the most of your first couple of days. At this relatively low altitude you will experience no headaches and you can eat and sleep comfortably. There are doctors who speak English (and other foreign languages) in Cuzco and Lima who have particular experience in dealing with locally occurring diseases, but don't expect good facilities away from the major centres.

### Before you go

Ideally, you should see your GP/practice nurse or travel clinic at least 6 weeks before your departure for general advice on travel risks, malaria and vaccinations (see page 51). Your local pharmacist can also be a good source of readily accessible advice. Make sure you have travel insurance, get a dental check (especially if you are going to be away for more than a month), know your own blood group and, if you suffer a long-term condition such as diabetes or epilepsy, make sure someone knows or that you have a Medic Alert bracelet/necklace with this information on it.

### A-Z of health risks

**Acute mountain sickness** can strike from about 3000 m upwards and in general is more likely to affect those who ascend rapidly (for example by plane) and those who over-exert themselves. Acute mountain sickness takes a few hours or days to come on and presents with headache, lassitude, dizziness, loss of appetite, nausea and vomiting. Insomnia is common and often associated with a suffocating feeling when lying down in bed. You may notice that your breathing tends to wax and wane at night and your face is puffy in the mornings – this is all part of the syndrome. If the symptoms are mild, the treatment is rest and painkillers (preferably not aspirin-based) for the headaches. Should the symptoms be severe and prolonged it is best to descend to a lower altitude immediately and re-ascend, if necessary, slowly and in stages. The symptoms disappear very quickly – even after a few hundred metres of descent. The best way of preventing acute mountain sickness is a relatively slow ascent. When trekking to high altitude, some time spent walking at medium altitude, getting fit and acclimatizing is beneficial. When flying to places over 3000 m a few hours' rest and the avoidance of alcohol, cigarettes and heavy food will go a long way towards preventing acute mountain sickness. Remember to walk slowly.

If you are unlucky (or careless) enough to get a **bite or sting** from a venomous snake, spider, scorpion or sea creature, try to identify the culprit, without putting yourself in further danger (do not try to catch a live snake). Snake bites in particular are very frightening, but in fact rarely poisonous – even venomous snakes bite without injecting venom. Victims should be taken to a hospital or a doctor without delay. Snake bite antivenom is not usually carried by travellers as in inexperienced hands it can be dangerous. Reassure and comfort the victim frequently. Immobilize the limb with a bandage or a splint and get the patient to lie still. Do not slash the bite area and try to suck out the poison because this sort of heroism does more harm than good. If you know how to use a tourniquet in these circumstances, you will not need this advice. If you are not experienced, do not apply a tourniquet. Certain tropical fish inject venom into bathers' feet when trodden on, which can be exceptionally painful. Wear plastic shoes if such creatures are reported. The pain can be relieved by immersing the foot in hot water (as hot as you can bear) for as long as the pain persists.

**Dengue fever** is a viral disease spread by mosquitoes that tend to bite during the day. The symptoms are fever and often intense joint pains, also some people develop a rash. Symptoms last about a week but it can take a few weeks to recover fully. Dengue can be difficult to distinguish from malaria as both diseases tend to occur in the same countries. There are no effective vaccines or antiviral drugs though, fortunately, travellers rarely develop the more severe forms of the disease (these can prove fatal). Rest, plenty of fluids and paracetamol (not aspirin) is the recommended treatment.

**Diarrhoea** can refer to either loose stools or an increased frequency of bowel movement, both of which can be a nuisance. Symptoms should be relatively short-lived but if they persist beyond 2 weeks specialist medical attention should be sought. Also seek medical help if there is blood in the stools and/or fever. Adults can use an antidiarrhoeal medication such as Loperamide to control the symptoms, but only for up to 24 hrs. In addition keep well hydrated by drinking plenty of fluids and eat bland foods. Oral rehydration sachets taken after each loose stool are a useful way to keep well hydrated. These should always be used when treating children and the elderly. Bacterial traveller's diarrhoea is the most common form. Ciproxin (Ciprofloxacin) is a useful antibiotic and can be obtained by private prescription in the UK. You need to take one 500 mg tablet when the diarrhoea starts. If there are no signs of improvement after 24 hrs the diarrhoea is likely to be viral and not bacterial. If it is due to other organisms such as those causing giardia or amoebic dysentery, different antibiotics will be required.

The standard advice to prevent problems is to be careful with water and ice for drinking. Ask yourself where the water came from. If you have any doubts then boil it or filter and treat it. There are many filter/treatment devices now available on the market. Food can also transmit disease. Be wary of salads (what were they washed in? who handled them?), reheated foods or food that has been left out in the sun having been cooked earlier in the day. There is a simple adage that says wash it, peel it, boil it or forget it. Also be wary of unpasteurized dairy products as these can transmit a range of diseases.

**Hepatitis** means inflammation of the liver. Viral causes of the disease can be acquired anywhere in the world. The most obvious symptom is a yellowing of your skin or the whites of your eyes. However, prior to this all that you may notice is itching and tiredness. Pre-travel hepatitis A vaccine is the best bet. Hepatitis B (for which there is a vaccine) is spread through blood and unprotected sexual intercourse: both of these can be avoided.

**Malaria** can cause death within 24 hrs. It can start as something just resembling an attack of flu. You may feel tired, lethargic, headachy, feverish; or more seriously, develop fits, followed by coma and then death. Be suspicious of vague symptoms, which may actually be malaria. If you have a temperature, go to a doctor as soon as you can and ask for a malaria test. On your return home if you suffer any of these symptoms, get tested as soon as possible, even if any previous test proved negative, it could save your life.

Treatment is with drugs and may be oral or into a vein depending on the seriousness of the infection. Remember ABCD: Awareness (of whether the disease is present in the area you are travelling in), Bite avoidance, Chemoprophylaxis, Diagnosis. To prevent mosquito bites wear clothes that cover arms and legs, use effective insect repellents in areas with known risks of insect-spread disease and use a mosquito net treated with an insecticide. Repellents containing 30-50% DEET (Di-ethyltoluamide) are recommended when visiting malaria-endemic areas, lemon eucalyptus (Mosiguard) is a reasonable alternative. The key advice is to guard against contracting malaria by taking the correct anti-malarials (see above) and finishing the recommended course.

Remember that it is risky to buy medicinal tablets and in particular antimalarials in some developing countries because they may be sub-standard or counterfeit. If you are a popular target for insect bites or develop lumps quite soon after being bitten use antihistamine tablets and apply a cream such as hydrocortisone.

Remember that **rabies** is endemic throughout certain parts of the world so be aware of the dangers of the bite from any animal. Rabies vaccination before travel can be considered, but if bitten always seek urgent medical attention whether or not previously vaccinated, after cleaning the wound and treating with an iodine base disinfectant or alcohol.

Take heed of advice on **sun protection**. Overexposure can lead to sunburn and, in the longer term, skin cancers and premature skin ageing. The best advice is simply to avoid exposure to the sun by covering exposed skin, wearing a hat and staying out of the sun if possible, particularly between late morning and early afternoon. Apply a high factor sunscreen (greater than SPF15) to the skin and also make sure it screens against UVB. A further danger in hot climates is heat exhaustion or more seriously heat stroke. This can be avoided by good hydration, which means drinking water past the point of simply quenching thirst. Also, when first exposed to tropical heat, take time to acclimatize by avoiding strenuous activity in the middle of the day. If you cannot avoid heavy exercise in the tropics it is also a good idea to increase salt intake.

There are a number of ways of purifying **water**. Dirty water should first be strained through a filter bag and then boiled or treated. Bring water to a rolling boil for a few minutes. There are sterilizing methods that can be used and products generally contain chlorine (eg Puritabs) or iodine (eg Pota Aqua) compounds. There are a number of water sterilizers now on the market available in personal and expedition size. Make sure you take the spare parts or spare chemicals with you and do not believe everything the manufacturers say.

There are a range of **other insect-borne diseases** that are quite rare in travellers, but worth finding out about if going to particular destinations. Examples are sleeping sickness, river blindness and leishmaniasis. Fresh water can also be a source of diseases such as bilharzia and leptospirosis and it is worth investigating if these are a danger before bathing in lakes and streams.

**Unprotected sex** always carries a risk and extra care is required when visiting some parts of the world.

### Further information

**Fit for Travel**, www.fitfortravel.scot.nhs.uk. This site from Scotland provides a quick A-Z of vaccine and travel health advice requirements for each country.
**Foreign and Commonwealth Office** (FCO) (UK), www.fco.gov.uk.
**National Travel Health Network and Centre** (NaTHNaC), www.nathnac.org.
**Nomad Travel Store & Medical Centre**, 3-4 Wellington Terr, Turnpike Lane, London N8 0PX, T020-8889 7014, www.nomadtravel.co.uk. Travel health clinic and traveller's shop. Other stores in Victoria and Russell Square, London, as well as Bristol, Manchester and Southampton.
**World Health Organisation**, www.who.int.

## Insurance

Take out travel insurance before you set off and read the small print carefully. Check that the policy covers all your planned activities and those you may end up doing. Check whether the medical cover includes ambulance and helicopter rescue or emergency flights back home. Also check the payment protocol. You may have to cough up first (literally) before the insurance company reimburses you. It is always best to dig out all the receipts for expensive personal effects like jewellery or cameras. Take photos of these items and note down all serial numbers.

You are advised to shop around for the best insurance policy. Your travel agent can advise on the best deals available. **STA Travel** and other reputable student travel organizations offer good-value policies, including the International Student Insurance Service (ISIS) for young travellers from North America. In the UK, companies worth trying are **Direct Line Insurance**, T0845-246 8704, http://uk.directline.com, and the **Flexicover Group**, T0870-990 9292, www.flexicover.net.

Older travellers should note that some companies will not cover people over 65 or may charge higher premiums. The best policies for older travellers (UK) are offered by **Age Concern**, T0845-601 2234, www.ageconcern.org.uk, and **Saga**, T0800-056 5464, www.saga.co.uk.

## Internet

You can find internet access everywhere. Cuzco and Lima have internet cafés on almost every corner; many of them have net2phone. Internet cafés in smaller places are listed in the travelling text. Internet cafés are incredibly cheap to use, normally about US$0.50 per hour. When cyber cafés first open in the morning is often a good time as they are less busy then. Access is generally quick. Internet access is more expensive in hotel business centres and in more remote places.

## Language

The official language is Spanish. Quechua, the Andean language that predates the Incas, has been given some official status and there is much pride in its use. It is spoken by millions of people in the sierra who have little or no knowledge of Spanish. Another important indigenous language is Aymara, used in the area around Lake Titicaca. For more on the Quechua and Aymara languages, see page 300.

The jungle is home to a plethora of languages but Spanish is spoken in all but the remotest areas. English is not spoken widely, except by those employed in the tourism industry (eg hotel, tour agency and airline staff).

See page 330 for basic Spanish words and phrases and page 335 for pronunciation.

## Media

There are several national daily **newspapers**. The most informative are *El Comercio* and *La República*, www.larepublica.com.pe. *El Comercio*, www.elcomercioperu.com.pe, is good for international news and has a near monopoly on classified ads. It also has a good weekly tourism section. *La República* takes a more liberal-left approach. Also with an online edition is *Expreso*, www.expreso.com.pe. *Gestión*, www.gestion.com.pe, a business daily. Very popular are the sensationalist papers, written in raunchy slang and featuring acres of bare female flesh. For daily news (in Spanish only), see www.terra.com.pe and www.peru.com.

The most widely read **magazine** is the weekly news magazine *Caretas*, www.caretas.com.pe, which presents a considered angle on current affairs and is often critical of government policy. The bi-monthly *Rumbos* (in English, Spanish and German), www.rumbosdelperu.com, is a good all rounder.

**Radio** is far more important in imparting news to Peruvians than newspapers, partly due to the fact that limited plane routes make it difficult to get papers to much of the population on the same day. There are countless local and community radio stations which cover even the most far-flung places. The most popular stations are *Radioprogramas del Perú*, www.rpp.com.pe, which features round-the-clock news, and *Cadena Peruana de Noticias*, www.cpnradio.com.pe.

A shortwave (world band) radio offers a practical means to brush up on the language, keep abreast of current events, sample popular culture and absorb some of the varied regional music. International broadcasters such as the BBC World Service, the Voice of America, Boston-based Monitor Radio International (operated by Christian Science Monitor) and the Quito-based evangelical station, HCJB, keep the traveller informed in both English and Spanish. Detailed advice on radio models and wavelengths can be found in the annual publication, Passport to World Band Radio (International Broadcasting Services Ltd, USA). Details of local stations are listed in *World Radio TV Handbook* (WRTH Publications Ltd). Both of these, free wavelength guides and selected radio sets are available from the BBC World Service Bookshop, Bush House Arcade, Bush House, Strand, London WC2B 4PH, UK, T020-7557 2576.

Many hotels have **TV** in the rooms; the more expensive the hotel, the more cable channels there will be on the set. There will almost certainly be US channels, often the BBC, Italian and occasionally German channels. You can find movies, sports, music, nature/discovery and news (CNN in both English and Spanish). Local channels include América Televisión, www.americatv.com.pe, Cable Mágico, www.cablemagico.com.pe, Frecuencia Latina, www.frecuencialatina.com.pe, and 24 Horas, www.24horas.com.pe.

## Money

### Currency

The *nuevo sol* (new sol, S/.) is the official currency of Peru. It is divided in 100 *céntimos* (cents) with coins valued at S/.5, S/.2, S/.1 and 50, 20, 10 and 5 *céntimo* pieces, although the latter is being phased out as it is virtually worthless. Notes in circulation are S/.200, S/.100, S/.50, S/.20 and S/.10. Try to break down notes whenever you can as there is a country-wide shortage of change (or so it seems). It is difficult to get change in shops and museums and sometimes impossible from street vendors or cab drivers.



**Exchange rates** (Jan 2008)
US$1 = S/. 2.91
UK£1 = S/. 5.70
€1 = S/.4.32

Prices of airline tickets, tour agency services, non-backpacker hotels and hostels, among others, are almost always quoted in dollars. You can pay in soles or dollars but it is generally easiest to pay dollars when the price is in dollars, and in soles when the price is in soles. This will save you from losing on exchange rates. In Cuzco and Lima dollars are frequently accepted. Euros are also accepted for exchange into soles at many places, but cannot be used for direct purchases. Dollars are more commonly used.

Almost no one, certainly not banks, will accept dollar bills that are ripped, taped, stapled or torn. Do not accept torn dollars from anyone; simply tell them you would like another bill. Also ask your bank at home to give you only nice, crisp, clean dollars and keep your dollars neat in your money belt or wallet so they don't accidentally tear. Forgeries of dollars and soles are not uncommon. Always check the sol notes you have received, even at the bank. Money changers, especially at borders, mix fake notes with genuine banknotes when giving wads of soles for other currencies. Hold the notes up to the light to check the watermark. The line down the side of the notes in which the amount of the money is written should appear green, blue and pink at different angles; fake notes are only pink and have no hologram properties. There should be tiny pieces of thread in the paper (not glued on). Check to see that the faces are clear. The paper should not feel smooth like a photocopy but rougher and fibrous. Try not to accept brand new notes, especially if changing on the street, slightly used notes are less likely to be forgeries. There are posters in many restaurants, stores and banks explaining exactly what to look for in forged sol notes. In parts of the country, forged one- and five-sol coins are in circulation. Fakes are slightly off-colour; the surface copper can be scratched off and they tend to bear a recent date.

### Credit cards

Visa (by far the most widely accepted card in Peru), Plus, MasterCard, Maestro, American Express, Link and Diners Club are all valid. There is often a commission of between 8% and 12% for all credit card transactions. It may be cheaper to use your credit card to get money (dollars or soles) out of an ATM rather than to pay for your purchases with a card, although this depends on the interest rate for cash advances on your credit cards; ask your bank or card provider about this. Another option is to put extra money on your credit cards and use them as a bank card. Most banks are affiliated with the Visa/Plus system; those that you will find in Cuzco and Lima, and most towns, are **BCP** and **BBVA Continental**. **Interbank** ATMs accept Visa, Plus, Mastercard, Maestro, Cirrus and American Express. **Scotiabank** ATMs accept Visa, Plus, Mastercard, Maestro and Cirrus. There are also Red Unicard ATMs which accept Visa, Plus, Mastercard, Maestro and Cirrus.

Note that not every branch of each bank offers the same ATM services (even branches within the same city). In contrast with widespread ATM use, businesses displaying credit card symbols may not accept foreign cards. Credit cards are not commonly accepted in smaller towns so go prepared with cash. Make sure you carry the phone numbers that you need in order to report your card lost or stolen. In addition, some travellers have reported problems with their credit cards being 'frozen' by their bank as soon as a charge from a foreign country occurs. To avoid this problem, notify your bank that you will be incurring charges in Peru.

## Stop press

From the start of 2008, travellers can expect prices to rise in the areas of Peru covered in this edition, in part because of the relevant instability of the US dollar against other currencies, in part because of the removal of tax-free status from the southeast Amazon region. Many tour operators were considering a price increase of some 30% in 2008, regardless of any of the above factors. Without concrete figures to quote or advance knowledge of currency market changes, it would be unwise to publish speculative prices here, but readers should budget for rising costs.

### Credit card assistance

**American Express**, Travex SA, Av Santa Cruz 621, Miraflores, Lima, T01-690 0900, info@travex.com.pe.
**Diners Club**, Canaval y Moreyra 535, San Isidro, T01-221 2050.
**Mastercard**, Porta 111, 6th floor, Miraflores, T01-311 6000, T0800-307 7309.
**Visa Travel Assistance**, T108 and ask the operator for a collect call (*por cobrar*) to T410-902 8022 (English), T581-0120/9754 (Spanish), or T420-937 8091.

### Money exchange and TCs

US dollars and euros are the only currencies which should be brought into Peru from abroad (take some small notes) as other currencies carry high commission fees. There are no restrictions on foreign exchange. Banks are the most discreet places to change TCs cheques into soles. Some charge commission of 1-3%, some don't, and practice seems to vary from branch to branch, month to month. The services of the BCP have been repeatedly recommended; **Interbank** is also good. Changing money at a bank always gives a lower rate than with *cambistas* (street changers) or *casas de cambio* (exchange houses). Always count your money in the presence of the cashier. Street changers give the best rates for changing small amounts of dollars or euros in cash, avoiding paperwork and queuing, but you should take care: check your soles before handing over your money, check their calculators, etc, and don't change money in crowded areas. In Cuzco many of the *cambistas* congregate around the top of Av Sol. Think about taking a taxi after changing, to avoid being followed. Also, many street changers congregate near an office where the exchange 'wholesaler' operates; these will probably be offering better rates than elsewhere on the street. Soles can be exchanged into dollars at the banks and exchange houses at Lima airport.

American Express will sell TCs to cardholders only, but will not exchange cheques into cash. Amex will hold mail for cardholders at the Lima branch only. They are also very efficient at replacing stolen cheques, though a police report is needed. Most of the main banks accept American Express TCs and **BCP**, **Interbank** and **BSCH** accept Visa TCs. Travellers have reported great difficulty in cashing TCs in the jungle and other remote areas. Always sign TCs in blue or black ink or ballpen.

### Money transfer

To transfer money from one bank to another you must first find out which Peruvian bank works with your bank at home. You will then have to go to that bank and ask them what the process is to make a transfer. Depending on the bank, transfers can be completed immediately or will take up to five working days. Another option is to use **Western Union** (www.westernunion.com) which has widespread representation. **Moneygram** (www.moneygram.com) also has offices throughout the capital and the provinces; it exchanges most currencies and TCs.

### Cost of living and travelling

Living costs in the provinces are 20-50% below those in Lima and Cuzco. For a lot of low-income Peruvians, many items are simply beyond their reach.

The approximate budget for travelling is US$30-40 per person a day for living comfortably, or US$15-20 a day for low-budget travel, not including tours and entry tickets. Your budget will be higher when you add on flights (US$150-250 Lima-Cuzco return) and tours such as Machu Picchu (US$150-200) and the Inca Trail (US$450). Accommodation rates range from US$5 per person for the most basic *alojamiento*, but in Cuzco such places tend to be away from the centre, to US$15-30 for mid-range places, to over US$90 for top-of-the-range hotels in Cuzco (more in Lima; see also page 28). For meal prices, see box, page 31.

For 2008 prices, see also box, page 43.

## Post

Parcels and mail can be sent from any post office but Correo Central on the Plaza de Armas in Lima is the best place. The office is open Mon-Fri 0800-1800. Stamps, envelopes and cloth sacks (to send bigger parcels in) can all be bought there. It costs US$1 to mail a letter up to 20 g anywhere in the Americas, US$1.50 to Europe and US$1.70 to Australia. You can also mail letters 'expreso' for about US$0.55 extra to the Americas, US$0.90 to the rest of the world, and they will arrive a little more quickly. Don't put tape on envelopes or packages; wait until you get to the post office and use the glue they have. It is very expensive to mail large packages out of Peru so it is best not to plan to send things home from here. For emergency or important documents, **DHL** and **Federal Express** are also options in Lima.

For the post office in Cuzco, see page 122.

To receive mail, letters can be sent to Poste Restante/General Delivery (*lista de correos*), your embassy or, for cardholders, American Express offices. Members of **South American Explorers** (see page 46) can have post and packages sent to them at either of the Peruvian offices. Remember that there is no W in Spanish; look under V, or ask. For the minimal risk of misunderstanding, use title, initial and surname only. If having items sent to you by courier (eg DHL), do not use Poste Restante, but an address such as a hotel: a signature is required on receipt. Try not to have articles sent by post to Peru – taxes can be 200% of the value.

The name of the postal system is **Serpost**.

## Safety

More police patrol the streets, trains and stations in Cuzco than in the past, which has led to an improvement in security, but you still need to be vigilant. Look after your belongings, leaving valuables in safe keeping with hotel management, not in hotel rooms. Places in which to take care are: when changing money on the streets; in the railway and bus stations; the bus from the airport; the Santa Ana market; the San Cristóbal area and at out-of-the-way ruins. Also take special care during Inti Raymi. Avoid walking around alone at night on narrow streets, between the stations and the centre, or in the market areas. Stolen cameras often turn up in the local market and can be bought back cheaply. If you can prove that the camera is yours, contact the police.

On no account walk back to your hotel after dark from a bar, nightclub or restaurant; strangle muggings and rape are on the increase. For your own safety pay the US$1 taxi fare, but not just any taxi. Ask the club's doorman to get a taxi for you.

The tourist police in Lima are excellent and you should report any incidents to them (see page 281). Dealings with the tourist police in Cuzco have produced mixed reviews; you should double check that all reports written by the police in Cuzco actually state your complaint. There have been some mix-ups, and insurance companies seldom honour claims for 'lost' baggage. In the event of a vehicle accident in which anyone is injured, all drivers involved are automatically detained until blame has been established, and this does not usually take less than 2 weeks.

Check with **South American Explorers** (see page 46) for the latest travel updates.

It is wise to seek advice on security from your own consulate rather than from travel agencies. Before you travel, contact: **British Foreign and Commonwealth Office,** Travel Advice Team, T0845-850 2829, www.fco.gov.uk/travel; **US State Department's Bureau of Consular Affairs,** Overseas Citizens Services, T1-888-407 4747 (from overseas: T202-501 4444), http://travel.state.gov/, or the

Australian Department of Foreign Affairs, T02-6261 3305, www.smartraveller.gov.au.

### Advice and suggestions

Be especially careful arriving at or leaving from bus stations. These are obvious places to catch people (tourists or not) with a lot of important belongings. Do not set your bag down without putting your foot on it, even just to double check your tickets or look at your watch; it will grow legs and walk away. Take taxis to stations, when carrying luggage before 0800 and after dark (look on it as an insurance policy). Avoid staying in hotels too near to bus companies as drivers who stay overnight are sometimes in league with thieves. Also avoid restaurants near bus terminals; if you have all your luggage with you it is hard to keep an eye on all your gear when eating. Try to find a travel companion if alone, as this will reduce the strain of watching your belongings all the time.

Keep all documents secure and hide your main cash supply in different places or under your clothes. Keep cameras in bags, take spare spectacles (eyeglasses) and don't wear wristwatches (even cheap ones have been ripped off arms!) or jewellery. If you wear a shoulder-bag in a market, carry it in front of you. Backpacks are vulnerable to slashers: a good idea is to cover the pack with a plastic sack, which will also keep out rain and dust. It's best to use a pack which is lockable at its base. Make photocopies, or take digital photos of important documents and give them to your family, embassy and travelling companion, this will speed up replacement if documents are lost or stolen and will still allow you to have some ID while getting replacements. Alternatively, before you leave home, send yourself an email containing all your important details and addresses which you can access in an emergency. If someone tries to extract a bribe from you, insist on a receipt.

Ignore mustard smearers and paint or shampoo sprayers, and don't bend over to pick up money or other items in the street. These are all ruses intended to distract your attention and make you easy for an accomplice to steal from. Ruses involving 'plain-clothes policemen' are infrequent, but it is worth knowing that the real police only have the right to see your passport (not your money, tickets or hotel room). Before handing anything over, ask why they need to see it and make sure you understand the reason. Insist on seeing identification and know that you have the right to write it all down. Do not get in a cab with any police officer, real or not; tell them you will walk to the nearest police station. Do not hand over your identification freely and insist on going to the police station first. A related scam is for a 'tourist' to gain your confidence, then accomplices create a reason to check your documents.

We have received reports of nightclubs denying entrance to people on the basis of skin colour and assumed economic status. This has happened in Lima and in Cuzco. It is not possible to verify if this is the establishments' policy or merely that of certain doormen.

## Student travellers

If you are in full-time education you will be entitled to an International Student Identity Card, which is distributed by student travel offices and travel agencies in 77 countries. The ISIC gives you special prices on all forms of transport (air, sea, rail, etc), and access to a variety of other concessions and services. If you need to find the location of your nearest ISIC office contact the **ISIC Association**, Keizersgracht 174-176, 1016 DW Amsterdam, The Netherlands, T+31 (0)20-421 2800, www.istc.org.

Students can obtain very few reductions in Peru with an international student's card, except in and around Cuzco. To be any use in Peru, it must bear the owner's photo. An ISIC card can be obtained in Lima from **Intej**, Av San Martín 240, Barranco, T01-247 3230, www.intej.org. They can also extend student cards. In Cuzco student cards can be obtained from Portal de Panes 123, of 107 (CC Los Ruiseñores), T084-256367.

## Telephone

**Country code** +51
**IDD prefix** 00

All Peruvian phone numbers are made up of 6 digits except Lima, which has 7, plus the area code. All area codes are given with each number in the text. If calling Peru from abroad, dial the international access code (eg 00 from the UK), followed by Peru's country code (51), and then dial in the area code and number.

The main service provider is **Telefónica**, www.telefonica.com.pe (or **Telser** in Cuzco) which has offices in all large- and medium-sized towns. In some cases, the Telefónica office is administrative and phones are provided on the street outside.

Local, national and international calls can be made from public phone boxes with prepaid phone cards, or, less commonly, coins. To use phone cards, remove the card from its plastic covering (which should not be broken) and, on the back, scratch off the dark grey strip to reveal the card's number. You have to dial this number when told to do so by the operator. Cards for Telefónica services, of which there are several, can be bought at Telefónica offices or the many private phone offices (could be just a counter with a phone on the street). Also on sale in larger towns are cards for a number of other carriers for long-distance calls. Their rates are very competitive and there are usually seasonal offers to take advantage of. Each carrier has a prefix code which you must dial, as well as the card's secret code. Not every phone takes cards; Telefónica, for instance, has its own phones for its 147 service (national and international). The SuperPlus 147 card for one long-distance call is very good value at S/.20 (US$5.70) for 48 mins. So shop around for the best deal for the type of call you want to make, select a card which will give you the number of minutes you require and get dialling. Calls without cards from public phones cost US$1 per min to North America, US$1.40 to Europe and US$1.50 to Australia and New Zealand. Collect calls are possible to almost anywhere by ringing the international operator (108). You can also reach a variety of countries' operators direct if you wish to charge a call to your home calling card. By ringing 108 you can obtain all the 0-800 numbers for the international direct options and they speak English. Your home telephone company can give you the number to call as well. You can also receive calls at many Telefónica offices, the cost is usually around US$1 for 10 mins. Net Phones are popular, especially in Lima. Costs and service varies but can be as cheap as US$5 per hr to the USA. Calls to everywhere else are usually at least 50% more. For the Telefónica office in Cuzco, see page 122.

There are two main **mobile phone** networks in Peru, **Telefónica Movistar** and **Claro**, www.claro.com.pe. Mobile phones in Peru operate at 1900 mhz. If you need a mobile phone, your best bet is to buy one locally. Phones which take prepaid cards are easy to buy; special offers start as low as US$45. All mobile phone numbers are prefixed by 9.

## Time

Peru is 5 hrs behind GMT.

## Tipping

In most of the better restaurants a 10% service charge is included in the bill, but you can give an extra 5% as a tip if the service is good. The most basic restaurants do not include a tip in the bill, and tips are not expected. Taxi drivers are not tipped – bargain the price down, then pay extra for good service if you get it. Tip cloakroom attendants and hairdressers (very high class only), US$0.50-1; railway or airport porters, US$0.50; car wash boys, US$0.30; car 'watch' boys, US$0.20. If going on a trek or tour it is customary to tip the guide, as well as the cook and porters.

## Tourist information

Outside Peru, tourist information can be obtained from Peruvian embassies and consulates, see page 37. Also contact **South American Explorers**, 126 Indian Creek Rd, Ithaca, NY, 14850, T607-277 0488, www.saexplorers.org. SAE is the best place to get the most up-to-date information regarding everything from travel advisories to volunteer opportunities. Annual membership is currently US$50 per person and US$80 per couple, with a discount for researchers, archaeologists and scientists in exchange for information and/or presentations. If you're looking to study

Spanish in Peru, hoping to travel down the Amazon or in search of a quality Inca Trail tour company, SAE has the information you'll need to make it happen. Members can take advantage of many discounts arranged by SAE with many hotels, tour companies, etc. SAE has a superlative office in Lima (see page 257) and an office in Cuzco (see page 58). For tourist organizations within Peru, see below. For newspapers, radio and TV websites, see page 41.

In overall charge of tourism in Peru is the **Ministerio de Comercio Exterior y Turismo** Edificio Mincetur, C Uno 050, Urb Córpac, San Isidro, Lima, T01-513 6100, www.mincetur.gob.pe (for useful links go to Enlaces de interés). The promotion of tourism and information is handled from the same office by **PromPerú**, T01-224 3131, www.peru.info, which produces promotional material and runs an information and assistance service for visitors and **i perú**, T01-574 8000 (24 hrs), iperulima@promperu.gob.pe, which has offices in Lima, Cuzco and elsewhere.

## Tour operators

For Lima- and Cuzco-based operators, see Activities and tours, pages 104 and page 276.

### UK and Ireland

**Amazing Peru**, 9 Alma Rd, Manchester M19 2FG, T0808-234 6805 (freephone), www.amazingperu.com. UK managed with offices in Cuzco (C Yepez Miranda C-6, Magisterio, Cuzco) and Lima (C Ramon Ribeyro 264, Urb San Antonio, Miraflores).
**Andean Trails**, The Clockhouse, Bonnington Mill Business Centre, 72 Newhaven Rd, Edinburgh, EH6 5QG, T0131-467 7086, www.andeantrails.co.uk. For trekking, mountain biking and other adventure tours.
**Andes**, 37a St Andrews St, Castle Douglas, Kirkcudbrightshire, Scotland, DG7 1EN, T01556-503929, www.andes.org.uk. Climbing and trekking trips in Peru (and many other destinations in Latin America).
**Audley Latin America**, New Mill, New Mill Lane, Witney, Oxfordshire, OX29 9SX, T01993-838600 , www.audleytravel.com.

**Austral Tours**, 20 Upper Tachbrook St, London SW1V 1SH, T020-7233 5384, www.latinamerica.co.uk.

**Condor Journeys & Adventures**, 2 Ferry Bank, Colintraive, Argyll PA22 3AR, T01700-841318, www.condor journeys-adventures.com. Eco and adventure tourism with specially designed tours.

**Dragoman**, Camp Green, Debenham, Stowmarket, Suffolk IP14 6LA, T01728-861133, www.dragoman.co.uk. Overland camping and/or hotel journeys throughout South and Central America.

**Exodus Travels**, Grange Mills, 9 Weir Rd, London SW12 0NE, T020-8675 5550, www.exodus.co.uk. Experienced in adventure travel, including cultural tours and trekking and biking holidays.

**Explore Worldwide**, Nelson House, 55 Victoria Road, Farnborough, Hampshire GU14 7PA, T0870-333 4001, www.exploreworldwide.com. Highly respected operator, with 2- to 5-week tours in more than 90 countries including Peru.

**Guerba Adventure and Discovery Holidays**, Wessex House, 40 Station Rd, Westbury, Wiltshire BA13 3JN, T01373-826611, www.guerba.com. Specializes in adventure holidays, from trekking safaris to wilderness camping.

**Journey Latin America**, 12-13 Heathfield Terrace, Chiswick, London, W4 4JE, T020-8747 8315, and 12 St Ann's Sq, 2nd floor, Manchester, M2 7HW, T0161-832 1441, www.journeylatinamerica.co.uk. The world's leading tailor-made specialist for Latin America, running escorted tours throughout the region. They also offer a wide range of flight options.

**KE Adventure Travel**, 32 Lake Rd, Keswick, Cumbria, CA12 5DQ, T017687-73966, www.keadventure.com. Adventure tour specialist. 3-week cycling trips around Cuzco.

**Kumuka Expeditions**, 40 Earls Court Rd, London W8 6EJ, T020-7937 8855, www.kumuka.com. Overland tour operator.

**Last Frontiers**, Fleet Marston Farm, Aylesbury, Buckinghamshire HP18 0QT, T01296-653000, www.lastfrontiers.co.uk. South American specialist. Tailor-made itineraries as well as discounted air fares and air passes.

**Llama Travel**, Oxford House, 49A Oxford Rd, London, N4 3EY, T020-7263 3000, www.llama travel.com. Tours throughout Peru.

**Naturetrek**, Cheriton Mill, Cheriton, Alresford, Hampshire, SO24 0NG, T01962-733051, www.naturetrek.co.uk. Wildlife tours throughout the continent.

**New Worlds Ltd**, Holly Cottage, Holt Road, Cromer, Norfolk NR27 9JN, T01263-510105, www.newworlds.co.uk. Peru specialists offering tailor-made itineraries.

**Oasis Overland Ltd**, The Marsh, Henstridge, Somerset, BA8 0TF, T01963-363400, www.oasisoverland.co.uk. Trips across Peru, including the Inca Trail, Lake Titicaca and the Amazon jungle.

**Select Latin America** (incorporating **Galapagos Adventure Tours**), 79 Maltings Pl, 169 Tower Bridge Rd, London, SE1 3LJ, T020-7407 1478, www.selectlatinamerica.co.uk. Offers quality tailor-made holidays and small group tours.

**South American Experience**, Welby House, 96 Wilton Road, Victoria, London SW1V 1DW,

T0845-277 3366, www.southamerican experience.co.uk. Tailor-made trips and flights.

**Steppes Latin America**, 51 Castle St, Cirencester, Glos, GL7 1QD, T01285-885333, www.steppestravel.co.uk.

**Sunvil Latin America**, Sunvil House, Upper Sq, Old Isleworth, Middlesex, TW7 7BJ, T020-8568 4499, www.sunvil.co.uk. Small groups or individual tours.

**Tribes Travel**, 12 The Business Centre, Earl Soham, Woodbridge, Suffolk, IP13 7SA, T01728-685971, www.tribes.co.uk. Tour company with an associated charity that aims to relieve poverty in indigenous communities.

**Trips Worldwide**, 14 Frederick Place, Clifton, Bristol, BS8 1AS, T0117-311 4400, www.tripsworldwide.co.uk.

**Veloso Tours**, 34 Warple Way, London W3 0RG, T020-8762 0616, www.veloso.com.

### North America

**Discover Peru Tours**, 5775 Blue Lagoon Drive, Suite 190, Miami, FL 33126, T1-305-266 5827.

**eXito**, T1-800-655 4053 (USA), T1-800-670 2605 (Canada), www.exitotravel.com.

**4starSouthAmerica**, USA and Canada, T1-800-747 4540, Europe and New Zealand T00 (800)-747 45400, Australia T0011 (800)-747 45400, www.southamerica.travel. Online tour operator. For flights, visit the website.

**GAP Adventures**, 19 Charlotte St, Toronto, Ontario, M5V 2H5, T1-800-708 7761 (in North America), 0870-999 0144 (in UK), T+1-416-260 0999 (outside North America or UK), www.gapadventures.com.

**Ladatco Tours**, 2200 S Dixie Highway, Suite 704, Coconut Grove, FL 33133, T1-800-327 6162, www.ladatco.com. Based in Miami, runs themed explorer tours based around the Incas, mysticism, etc.

**Lost World Adventures**, T800-999 0558, T1-404-373 5820, www.lostworldadventures.com.
**Myths and Mountains**, 976 Tree Court, Incline Village, Nevada 89451, T1-800-670 6984, www.mythsandmountains.com.
**Pedal Peru**, PO Box 1921, Fraser, CO 80442, T1-800-708 8604, www.pedalperu.com. Multi-sport adventures.
**Peru for Less**, 919 East 49 1/2 Street, Austin, TX 78751, T1-877-269 0309 (toll free), www.peruforless.com. Guided and customized tours to Peru and other South American destinations. Office in Lima.
**Peru Mountain Bike**, in USA T1-866 865 BIKE, in UK T0871-871 6759, in Peru T01-447 2057. Organizes mountain bike trips in conjunction with Peruvian companies in Cuzco and other parts of Peru.
**Puchka Peru**, www.puchkaperu.com. Textiles, folk art and market tours.
**South American Journeys**, 9921 Cabanas Avenue, Tujunga, CA 91042, T1-800-884 7474, www.southamericaexp.com. Small group tours off the beaten track with Peruvian guides. Ecological projects.
**Tambo Tours**, 4405 Spring Cypress Rd Suite 210, Spring, TX, 77388, T1-888-2-GO-PERU (246-7378), T1-281-528 9448, www.2GOPERU.com. Long-established adventure and tour specialist with 20 years' experience in Peru, with offices in Peru and the USA. Customized trips for families, individuals and groups to the Amazon and archaeological sites.
**Wildland Adventures**, 3516 NE 155 St, Seattle, WA 98155-7412, T1-206-365 0686, www.wildland.com. Cultural and natural history tours to the Andes and the Amazon.

### Continental Europe

**Nouveaux Mondes**, Rte Suisse 7, CH-1295 Mies, Switzerland, T+41(0)22-950 9660, info@nouveauxmondes.com.
**South American Tours**, Stephanstrasse 13, D-60313, Frankfurt am Main, Germany, T+49 (0)69-405 8970, www.southamericantours.de. Peru office at Av Bolognesi 381, Miraflores, Lima, T01-446 3398, info@satperu.com.pe.

### Bolivia

#### Lake Titicaca

**Transturin**, Av Arce 2678, PO Box 5311, La Paz, T02-242 2222, www.travelbolivia.com. Runs catamarans on Lake Titicaca.

### Australia

**Adventure World**, Level 20, 141 Walker St, North Sydney, NSW 2060, T02-8913 0755; level 9, 40 St Georges Terrace, Perth, WA 6000, T08-9226 4525, www.adventureworld.com.au. Tour operator running a range of escorted group tours, locally escorted tours and packages to Peru and to other Latin American countries.
**Kumuka Expeditions** Level 4, 46-48 York St, Sydney, NSW 2000, T02-9279 0491, www.kumuka.com.
**Tucan Travel**, 217 Alison Road, Randwick, NSW 2031, T02-9326 6633, ozsales@tucantravel.com. In Cuzco: C Triunfo 356, T084-241123, cuzco@tucantravel.com.

## Useful resources

**Apotur** (**Asociación Peruana de Operadores de Turismo**), San Fernando 287, Lima 18, T01-446 4076, www.apoturperu.org.
**Aptae** (**Asociación Peruana de Turismo de Aventura y Ecoturismo**), Bolognesi 125, of 703, Miraflores, Lima 18, T01-447-8476, www.aptae.org.
**Indecopi**, T01-224 7777 in Lima, T0800-44040 in the rest of Peru (not available from payphones), www.indecopi.gob.pe. The government-run consumer protection and tourist complaint bureau. Friendly, professional and helpful.

### Websites

#### Cuzco and Machu Picchu

**www.aboutcusco.com** Information in English and Spanish.
**www.cuscoonline.com** In Spanish, English, French, German, Italian and Portuguese.
**www.cuscoperu.com** In English, Spanish, French and German.
**www.cusco.net** Useful.
**www.ex.ac.uk/~RDavies/inca/** A site by Ron Davies on the Inca Trail, with

descriptions of the hike, the sites along it and many links to other sites of interest.
**www.machu-picchu.info** Introductory information on Machu Picchu.
**www.machupicchu.perucultural.org.pe/** An overview in Spanish and English of the site, its history and related topics.
**http://whc.unesco.org/en/list/274/** The UNESCO World Heritage List entry for Machu Picchu.

**Peru**
**www.andeantravelweb.com/peru** Andean Travel Web, for adventure travel, with advice and more (Spanish and English).
**www.conam.gob.pe** The National Environmental Commission's site, in Spanish.
**www.geocities.com/perutraveller/** In English for independent travellers.
**www.perucultural.org.pe** An excellent site for information on cultural activities, museums and textiles (Spanish).
**www.perurail.com** The website of **Peru Rail** (trains in the Cuzco/Puno area).
**www.rree.gob.pe** Ministry of Foreign Relations' site, which contains addresses of all Peruvian embassies and consulates.
**www.terra.com.pe** Go to 'Turismo' for tourist information (in Spanish).
**www.traficoperu.com** Online travel agent with information in Spanish and English.
**http://travel.peru.com/travel/english/** Peru.com's travel page (Spanish version is at http://travel.peru.com/travel/spanish/).
**www.yachay.com.pe** **Red Científica Peruana**, click on 'Turismo' for travel.
www.livinginperu.com Informative guide in English for people living in Peru.

## Vaccinations

No vaccinations are compulsory for entry into Peru but the following vaccinations are commonly recommended for the region: polio, tetanus, typhoid, yellow fever (if you are travelling around South America it is best to get this vaccine since you will need it for the northern areas and some jungle areas; tours to Manu and Tambopata state that a yellow fever certificate is compulsory for entering the area), rabies (recommended if going to jungle and/or remote areas) and hepatitis A. Vaccination against cholera is not necessary. The final decision, however, should be based on your consultation with your GP or travel clinic.

## Visas and permits

No visa is necessary for citizens of member states of the European Union, many other West European countries, North or South (but not Central) America and the Caribbean, or for citizens of Andorra, Costa Rica, Iceland, Israel, Japan, Liechteinstein, Norway, Russia, Switzerland, Australia, New Zealand and South Africa. All other travellers should consult the Peru Embassy or consulate in their home country for details of up-to-date visa requirements. See also www.rree.gob.pe.

**Tourist cards** are obtained on flights arriving in Peru or at international border crossings. The tourist card, called TAM (Tarjeta Andina de Migración), allows you to stay in Peru for up to a maximum of 90 days. The form is in duplicate; you give up the original on arrival and keep the copy to give to officials on your departure. A new tourist card is issued on each re-entry to Peru and extensions to existing tourist cards can be obtained by taking the card and your passport to an immigration office. (For details of this process, see Renewals and extensions, below). If your tourist card is lost or stolen, apply to get a new one at **Inmigraciones**, Av España 734 y Av Huaraz, Breña, Lima, T01-330 4111, www.digemin.gob.pe, Mon-Fri 0800-1300. It shouldn't cost anything to replace your tourist card here.

**Tourist visas** for citizens of countries that are not listed above cost about US$38 or equivalent, for which you require a valid passport, a departure ticket from Peru, two colour passport photos, one application form and proof of your economic solvency.

All foreigners should be able to produce on demand some recognizable means of **ID**, preferably a **passport**. You must present your passport when reserving tickets for internal, as well as international, travel. An alternative is to photocopy the important pages of your passport, including the immigration stamp, and have it legalized by a *notario público*, which costs US$1.50. This way you can avoid showing your passport. Remember that it is your responsibility to ensure that your passport is stamped in and out when you arrive in the country or cross borders. The absence of entry and exit stamps can cause serious difficulties: seek out the proper migration offices if the stamping process is not carried out as you cross. You should always carry your passport in a safe place about your person or, if you're in one place for a few days, deposit it in the hotel safe. If staying in Peru for several weeks, it is worthwhile registering at your consulate. Then, if your passport is stolen, replacing it is simpler and faster.

Travellers arriving by air are not asked for an onward flight ticket at Lima airport, but it is quite possible that you will not be allowed to board a plane in your home country without showing an onward ticket.

If you want to stay in Peru for more than 90 days, you can make an **extension** to your tourist card or visa at the immigration office in Lima. The process is called *Prórroga de Permanencia*. Three extensions are permitted, up to a total of 90 extra days; you are not allowed to buy more than 30 days at a time. Peruvian law states that a tourist can remain in the country for a maximum of 6 months (180 days), after which time you must leave. Crossing the border out of Peru and returning immediately is acceptable. You will then receive another 90 day tourist card and the process begins again.

To obtain an extension at the address above in Lima, the process is: go to the 3rd floor and enter the long narrow hall with many 'teller' windows. Obtain form F-07 (free – it can be downloaded at www.digemin.gob.pe/formularios.asp). You will have to pay S/.25 (US$7.80) for the paperwork. Present your passport and TAM tourist card. The official will give you a receipt for US$20 (the cost of a 1-month extension) which you will pay at the *Banco de la Nación* on the same floor. Fill out the form and return to the 3rd floor. Give the official the paid receipt, the completed form, your passport and tourist card. Next, you will wait 2 mins for your passport to be stamped and signed.

To summarize: you are given 90 days upon entering the country. You can buy 90 more days (US$20 for each 30 day extension) for a total of 6 months (180 days). Once your 6 months is completed, you must leave Peru (no exceptions). This simply means crossing into a bordering country for the day (depending on where you cross, you can come back immediately) and returning with a fresh 90 days stamped in your passport. See www.digemin.gob.pe/informa/inmigra.htm.

If you exceed your 90 days, you will pay a US$1-per-day charge. If you know that your excess time will only be a day or two, it is better to pay this than buy a 30-day extension for US$20.

Visitors who are going to receive money from Peruvian sources must have a **business visa**: requirements are a valid passport, 2 colour passport photos, return ticket and a letter from an employer or Chamber of Commerce stating the nature of business, length of stay and guarantee that any Peruvian taxes will be paid. The visa costs £21.60, or equivalent. On arrival business visitors must register with the Dirección General de Contribuciones for tax purposes.

To obtain a 1-year **student visa** you must have: proof of adequate funds, affiliation to a Peruvian body, a letter of recommendation from your own and a Peruvian Consul, a letter of moral and economic guarantee from a Peruvian citizen and 4 photographs (frontal and profile). You must also have a health check certificate which takes 4 weeks to get and costs US$10. If applying within Peru, you will have to leave the country and collect your student visa from Peruvian immigration in La Paz, Arica or Guayaquil (US$20).

## Weights and measures

Peru uses the metric system.

## Women travellers

Generally women travellers should find visiting Peru an enjoyable experience. However, machismo is alive and well here and you should be prepared for this and try not to overreact. When you set out, err on the side of caution until your instincts have adjusted to the customs of a new culture. It is easier for men to take the friendliness of locals at face value; women may be subject to much unwanted attention. To help minimize this, do not wear suggestive clothing and do not flirt. By wearing a wedding ring, carrying a photograph of your 'husband' and 'children', and saying that your husband is close at hand, you may dissuade an aspiring suitor. If politeness fails, do not feel bad about showing offence and departing. When accepting a social invitation, make sure that someone knows the address and the time you left. Ask if you can bring a friend (even if you do not intend to do so).

If, as a single woman, you can befriend a local woman, you will learn much more about the country you are visiting as well as finding out how best to deal with the barrage of suggestive comments, whistles and hisses that will invariably come your way. Travelling with another *gringa* may not exempt you from this attention, but at least should give you moral support.

Unless actively avoiding foreigners like yourself, don't go too far from the beaten track. There is a very definite 'gringo trail' which you can join, or follow, if seeking company. This can be helpful when looking for safe accommodation, especially if arriving after dark (which is best avoided). Remember that for a single woman a taxi at night can be as dangerous as wandering around on her own. A good rule is always to act with confidence, as though you know where you are going, even if you do not. Someone who looks lost is more likely to attract unwanted attention.

## Working in Peru

There are many opportunities for volunteer work in Peru; **South American Explorers** (see page 46) has an extensive database. Some options in Cuzco are given in the box, page 74. The **Amauta Spanish School**, Suecia 480, Cuzco, T084-241422, www.amautaspanish.com, also offers volunteering opportunities.

There is some overlap between volunteering and gap year or career break tourism as many people who make this type of trip do some form of work. There is an increasing amount of help for students on a gap year and, in the UK at least, a well-planned and productive gap year can be an advantage when it comes to university and job application. The career-break market is growing fast and there is help online to guide you. Some organizations help from planning to finding something to do; others are quite specific in the type of project or country in which they operate.

See www.gapyear.com, www.gap.org.uk and www.yearoutgroup.org. For career breaks, see www.thecareerbreaksite.com, www.gapsforgrumpies.com, www.gapyearforgrownups.co.uk or www.goldengapyears.com. For a range of options, try www.gvi.co.uk (Global Vision International), or www.i-to-i.com. More specific (but not limited to South America) are www.rainforestconcern.org (Rainforest Concern), with environmental projects in Peru, www.handsupholidays.com, with projects in Peru, www.madventurer.com, www.questoverseas.com (Quest Overseas, which also organizes expeditions) and www.thepodsite.co.uk (Personal Overseas Development), with projects in Peru, and www.teaching-abroad.co.uk, for more than teaching.

An excellent place to start for low and zero-cost volunteer programmes in South America is Steve McElhinney's website, www.volunteersouthamerica.net. You can also investigate the publications of Vacation Work, www.vacationwork.co.uk.

# Cuzco

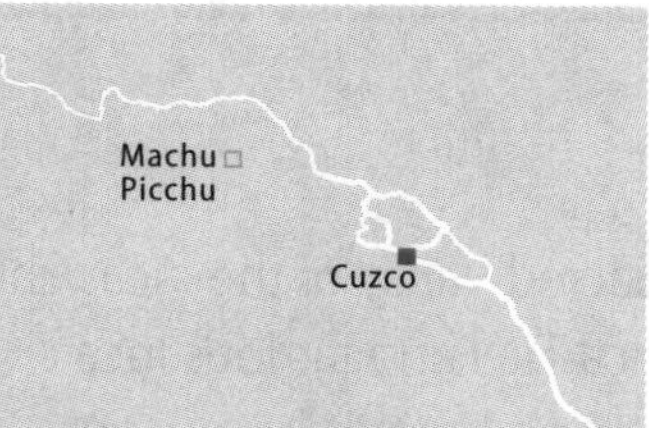




## Footprint features

# Introduction

Cuzco stands at the head of the Sacred Valley of the Incas and is the jumping-off point for the Inca Trail and famous Inca city of Machu Picchu. Not surprising, then, that this is the prime destination for the vast majority of Peru's visitors. In fact, the ancient Inca capital is now the 'gringo' capital of the entire continent. And it's easy to see why. There are Inca ruins aplenty, as well as fabulous colonial architecture, stunning scenery, great trekking, river rafting and mountain biking, beautiful textiles and other traditional handicrafts – all within easy reach of the nearest cappuccino or comfy hotel room.

The history books describe the Incas' mythical beginnings, their rapid rise to power, their achievements and their equally rapid defeat by the Spaniards, who converted the pulse of the Inca Empire into a jewel of their own. Yet Cuzco today is not some dead monument. Its history breathes through the stones and the Quechua people bring the city to life with a combination of prehispanic and Christian beliefs.

## Don't miss ...

1 **Church of San Blas** The carved pulpit is remarkable and you can buy traditional crafts in the surrounding streets, page 68.

2 **Santa Catalina** The museum of Cusqueño painting explains how European themes were adapted by local artists, page 68.

3 **Colonial palaces** Even if you are not staying there, visit one of the hotels that have been converted from colonial palaces; the Novotel, Libertador and Monasterio are the best examples, pages 82 and 83.

4 **Museo de Arte Precolombino** A fine new museum exhibiting Peru's pre-Columbian art in a world context, page 67.

5 **Shopping** The choice is endless, from piles of weavings to the most singular modern designs. Don't forget San Jerónimo market for weird and wonderful fruit and veg, pages 101 and 104.

6 **Sacsayhuaman** Take a car, horse, or go on foot, to Sacsayhuaman, Qenqo, Puka Pukara and Tambo Machay, the Inca sites outside the city on the way to Pisac, pages 75 and 81.

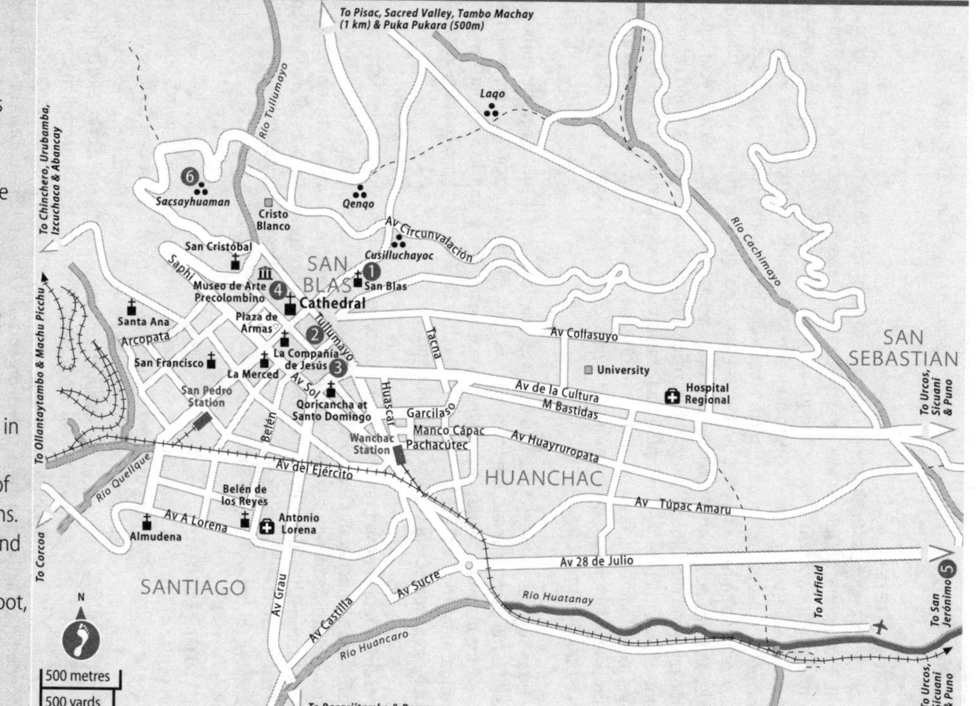

# Ins and outs → *Phone code 084. Colour map 2, B3. Population 275,000. Altitude 3310 m.*

## Getting there

**By air** Most travellers arriving from Lima will do so by air. No flights arrive in Cuzco at night. The airport is at Quispiquilla, near the bus terminal, southeast of the centre. Airport information, T084-222611/601. A taxi to and from the airport costs US$2 (US$4.50 by radio taxi). Colectivos charge US$0.30 from outside the airport car park to the centre. You can book a hotel at the airport through a travel agency, but this is not really necessary. Many representatives of hotels and travel agencies operate at the airport, offering transport to the hotel with which they are associated. Take your time to choose your hotel, at the price you can afford. There is a post office, phone booths, restaurant and cafeteria at the airport. There is also an **i perú** tourist information desk, which is helpful. Do not forget to reconfirm your flight before the day of your flight, nor to pay the airport tax at the appropriate desk before departure. ➤➤ *For flight information, see Getting there, page 21, and Getting around, page 23.*

**By bus** Services between Lima and Cuzco are improving as the road gets better but it is still a full-day's journey. The main route is Lima–Nazca–Abancay–Cuzco, which is paved for its entire length. All long-distance buses arrive and leave from the bus terminal near the Pachacútec statue in Ttio district. Transport to your hotel is not a problem as representatives are often on hand.

**By train** There are two train stations in Cuzco. To Juliaca and Puno, trains leave from the **Estación Wanchac** ⓘ *C Pachacútec, T084-238722, ext 318/319/320*. The office here offers direct information and ticket sales for all **PerúRail** services. When arriving in Cuzco, a tourist bus meets the train to take visitors to hotels whose touts offer rooms on the train. Machu Picchu trains leave from **Estación San Pedro** ⓘ *opposite the Santa Ana market.* ➤➤ *For further details, see Transport page 117.*

## Getting around

The centre of Cuzco is small and is easily explored on foot. Bear in mind, however, that at this altitude walking up some of the city's steep cobbled streets may leave you out of breath, so you'll need to take your time. It is even possible to walk up to Sacsayhuaman, but a better idea is to take a combi (minivan) to Tambo Machay and walk back downhill to town via Qenqo and Sacsayhuaman. Combis are the main form of public transportation in the city; they are well organized, cheap and safe. Taxis in Cuzco are also cheap and recommended when arriving by air, train or bus, and at night. ➤➤ *For further details, see Transport page 117.*

*! Motorists beware: many streets end in flights of steps not marked as such.*

If you wish to explore this area on your own, road map (*Hoja de ruta*) No 10 is an excellent guide. You can get it from the **Touring y Automóvil Club del Perú**, see page 118. They have other maps. There are, however, very few good maps of Cuzco available.

## Tourist information

The official **tourist office** ⓘ *Portal Mantas 117-A, next to La Merced church, T084-263176, 0800-2000*, is supplemented by tourist information desks run by **i perú** ⓘ *at the airport, T084-237364, daily 0600-1600; also at Av del Sol 103, of 102, Galerías Turísticas, T084-252974, iperucusco@promperu.gob.pe, daily 0830-1930*. The **Dircetur** office is at ⓘ *Av de la Cultura 734, 3rd floor, T084-223701, Mon-Fri 0800-1300*. It has a good map of the city centre. See box opposite for the offices of OFEC and INC for Machu Picchu.

**South American Explorers** ⓘ *Choquechaca 188, No 4, T084-245484, cuscoclub@saexplorers.org, Mon-Fri 0930-1700, Sat 0930-1300; also in Lima (see page 257)*, is an

## Visitors' tickets

A combined entry ticket to most of the main sites of historical and cultural interest in and around the city, called **Boleto Turístico General** (BTG), costs US$21 (S/.70) and is valid for 10 days. The price may rise in 2008. It permits entrance to: Santa Catalina convent and art museum, Museo de Sitio Qoricancha (but not Qoricancha itself), Museo Histórico Regional (Casa Garcilaso), Museo Palacio Municipal de Arte Contemporáneo, Museo de Arte Popular, Centro Qosqo de Arte Nativo, Monumento Pachacútec; the archaeological sites of Sacsayhuaman, Qenqo, Puka Pukara, Tambo Machay, Pisac, Ollantaytambo, Chinchero, Tipón and Piquillacta. A BTG costing US$12 (S/.40) permits entry to either the churches and museums in the city, or Sacsayhuaman, Tambo Machay, Puka Pukara and Qenqo, or Tipón, Piquillacta, Chinchero, Ollantaytambo and Pisac; these three options are valid for one day. It is payable in soles only.

The BTG can be bought at the office of **OFEC** (Casa Garcilaso), Plaza Regocijo, esquina Calle Garcilaso, T084-226919, Monday-Saturday 0800-1600, Sunday 0800-1200; at Avenida Sol 103, T084-227037, Monday-Friday 0800-1800, Saturday 0830-1230, or at any of the sites included in the ticket. There is a 50% discount for students with a green ISIC card, which is only available at the OFEC office (Casa Garcilaso) upon presentation of the student card. Take your ISIC card when visiting the sites, as some may ask to see it.

Entrance tickets for the Santo Domingo/Qoricancha, the Inka Museum (El Palacio del Almirante), and La Merced are sold separately while the Cathedral, the churches of El Triunfo, La Sagrada Familia, La Compañía and San Blas and the Museo de Arte Religioso del Arzobispado are included on a new religious buildings ticket, S/.36 (18 with ISIC card), US$10, valid for 10 days.

All sites and museums are very crowded on Sunday and many churches are closed to visitors. 'Official' visiting times are unreliable. Photography is not allowed in churches and museums. On the back of the BTG is a map of the centre of Cuzco with the main sites of interest clearly marked. It also includes a map of the tourist routes from Cuzco to the Sacred Valley, following the Río Urubamba towards Machu Picchu, as well as the southeastern area of Cuzco on the road to Puno.

Machu Picchu ruins and Inca Trail entrance tickets are sold at the **Instituto Nacional de Cultura (INC)**, San Bernardo s/n entre Mantas y Almagro, T084-236061, Monday-Friday 0900-1300, 1600-1800, Saturday 0900-1100.



excellent resource and haven for the traveller. The Cuzco club is only a couple of minutes' walk from the Plaza de Armas. They provide great information on the Cuzco area, along with an extensive English language library, expedition reports, maps, a laptop dedicated to www.leaplocal.org (for finding local guides and services who have no other means of publicising themselves) and, of course, free coffee and hot chocolate for members. They will also refill water bottles in an attempt to minimize plastic waste in Cuzco and they have a recycling centre. There are weekly presentations by local experts covering many aspects of Peruvian culture, and film nights showcasing Latin American movie classics.

**Perú Verde** ⓘ *Ricaldo Palma J-1, Santa Mónica, To84-226392, www.peruverde.org*, provides information and free video shows about Manu National Park and Tambopata National Reserve. The staff are friendly and also have information on programmes and research in the jungle area of Madre de Dios, as well as distributing the beautiful but expensive book on the Manu National Park by Kim MacQuarrie and André Bartschi.

**Tourist police** ⓘ *C Saphi 510, To84-249665/221961, or Ovalo de Pachacútec, To84-249654*, will type out a *denuncia* (a report for insurance purposes), which is available from the **Banco de la Nación**. Always go to the police when robbed, even though it will take a bit of time.

**Tourist Protection Bureau (Indecopi)** ⓘ *Av Manco Inca 209, Wanchac, To84-252987, mmarroquin@indecopi.gob.pe, or To800-44040*, protects the consumer rights of all tourists and helps with any problems or complaints. It can be useful in dealing with tour agencies, hotels or restaurants. ▸▸ *For Sleeping, Eating and other listings, see pages 82-122.*



# Background

The ancient Inca capital is said to have been founded around AD 1100. According to the central Inca creation myth, the Sun sent his son, Manco Cápac and the Moon sent her daughter, Mama Ocllo, to spread culture and enlightenment throughout the dark, barbaric lands. The Sun pitied the people of this savage region because they could not cultivate the land, clothe themselves, make houses, nor had they any religion. Manco and Mama Ocllo emerged from the icy depths of Lake Titicaca and began their journey in search of the place where they would found their kingdom. They were ordered to head north from the lake until a golden staff they carried could be plunged into the ground for its entire length. The soil of the altiplano was so thin that they had to travel as far as the valley of Cuzco where, on the mountain of Huanacauri, the staff fully disappeared and the soil was found to be suitably fertile. This was the sign they were looking for. They named this place Cuzco, meaning 'navel of the earth' according to popular legend (there is no linguistic basis for this). The local inhabitants, on seeing Manco Cápac and Mama Ocllo with their fine clothes and jewellery (including the adornments in their long, pierced ears, which became a symbol of the Incas) immediately worshipped them and followed their instructions, the men being taught by Manco Cápac, the women by Mama Ocllo. See also boxes on page 285 and page 141.

Thus the significance of Cuzco and the sacred Urubamba Valley was established for many centuries to come. As Peter Frost states in his *Exploring Cusco*: "Cusco was more than just a capital city to the Incas and the millions of subjects in their realm. It was a Holy City, a place of pilgrimage with as much importance to the Quechuas as Mecca has to the Moslems. Every ranking citizen of the empire tried to visit Cusco once in his lifetime; to have done so increased his stature wherever he might travel."

Today, the city's beauty cannot be overstated. It is a fascinating mix of Inca and colonial Spanish architecture: colonial churches, monasteries and convents and pre-Columbian ruins are interspersed with hotels, bars and restaurants that have sprung up to cater for the tourists who flock here for the atmosphere. Almost every central street has remains of Inca walls, arches and doorways. Many streets are lined with perfect Inca stonework, now serving as the foundations for more modern dwellings. This stonework is tapered upwards (battered); every wall has a perfect line of inclination towards the centre, from bottom to top. The curved stonework of the Temple of the Sun, for example, is probably unequalled in the world.

Cuzco has developed into a major commercial centre of 275,000 inhabitants, most of whom are Quechua. The city council has designated the Quechua, Qosqo, as the official spelling. Despite its growth, however, the city is still laid out much as it was in Inca times. The Incas conceived their capital in the shape of a puma and this can be seen from above, with the Río Tullumayo forming the spine, Sacsayhuaman the head and the main city centre the body. The best place for an overall view of the Cuzco Valley is from the puma's head – the top of the hill of Sacsayhuaman.



# Sights

Not even the most ardent tourist would be able to visit all the sights in Cuzco city. For those with limited time, or for those who want a whistle-stop tour, a list of must-sees would comprise the combination of Inca and colonial architecture at Qoricancha; the huge Inca ceremonial centre of Sacsayhuaman; the paintings of the Last Supper and the 1650 earthquake in the cathedral; the main altar of La Compañía de Jesús; the pulpit of San Blas; the high choir at San Francisco; the monstrance at La Merced; and the view from San Cristóbal. If you have the energy, take a taxi up to the White Christ and watch the sunset as you look out upon one of the most fascinating cities in the world. And if you only visit one museum, make it the Museo Inka, which has the most comprehensive collection.

Unless your Spanish is up to scratch a good guide can really improve your visit, as most of the sights do not have any information or signs in English. Either arrange this before you set out or hire one of those hanging around the sight entrances. The latter is much easier to do in the low season; good guides are often booked up with tour agencies at busy times of year. A tip is expected at the end of the tour; this gives you the chance to reward a good guide and get rid of a bad one!

## Plaza de Armas

The heart of the city in Inca days was *Huacaypata* (the place of tears) and *Cusipata* (the place of happiness), divided by a channel of the Río Saphi. Today, Huacaypata is the Plaza de Armas and Cusipata is Plaza Regocijo. This was the great civic square of the Incas, flanked by their palaces, and was a place of solemn parades and great assemblies. Each territory conquered by the Incas had some of its soil taken to Cuzco to be mingled symbolically with the soil of the Huacaypata, as a token of its incorporation into the empire.

As well as the many great ceremonies, the plaza has also seen its share of executions, among them the last Inca Túpac Amaru, the rebel *conquistador* Diego de Almagro the Younger, and the 18th-century indigenous leader Túpac Amaru II.

Around the present-day Plaza de Armas are colonial arcades and four churches. In the mid-1990s the mayor insisted that all the native trees be pulled down as they interrupted views of the surrounding buildings. The trees were replaced with the flowerbeds you see today. You may be forgiven for thinking the graceful, imposing church on the southeast side of the plaza is the cathedral. However, this is **La Compañía de Jesús**. When the Jesuits started building, the other Catholics asked the Pope to intervene, complaining it was too ornate and overshadowed the presence of the cathedral. The Pope failed to act in time and La Compañía de Jesús was completed in all its splendour.

### Cathedral

ⓘ *Daily 0500-1000 for worshippers only; Quechua Mass is held 0500-0600. Visiting hours Mon-Wed, Fri and Sat 1000-1130 and 1400-1730; Thu and Sun 1400-1730 only.*
The early 17th-century baroque cathedral (on the northeast side of the square) forms part of a three-church complex: the cathedral itself, Iglesia Jesús y María (1733) on the

# Cuzco centre

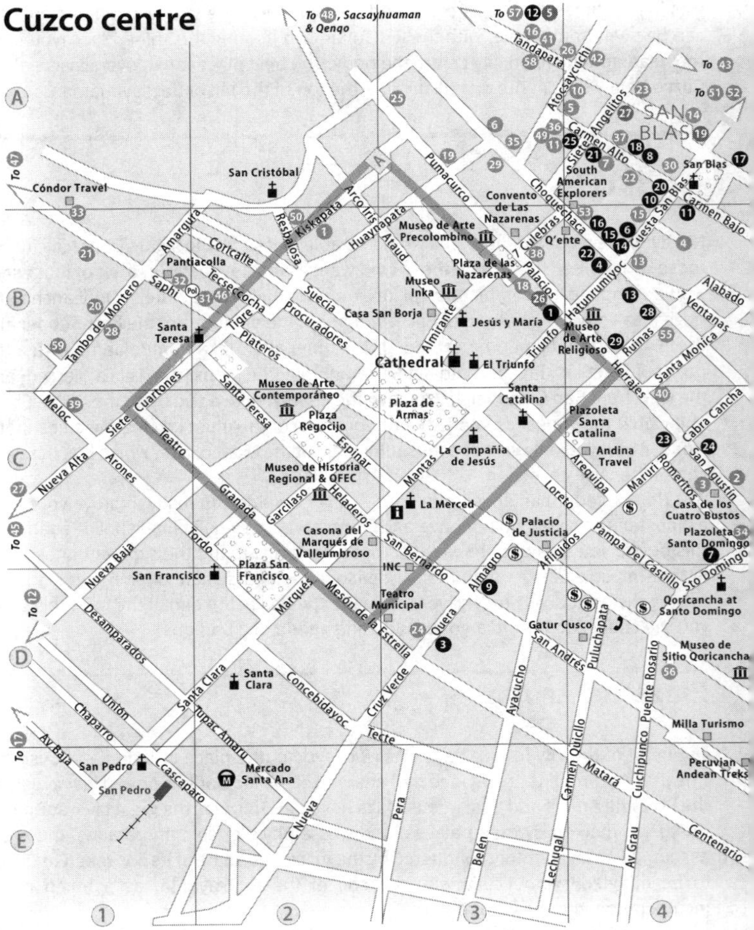

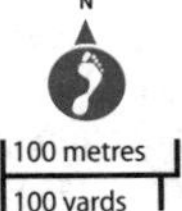


**Sleeping**

- Albergue Casa Campesina **3** *C4*
- Albergue Municipal **1** *B2*
- Andes de San Blas **7** *A4*
- Blue House **43** *A4*
- Cahuide **47** *A1*
- Casa Andina Koricancha **2** *C4*
- Casa Andina Private Collection Cusco **8** *C5*
- Casa Elena **53** *B4*
- Casa San Blas & Tika Bistro Gourmet **4** *B4*
- Casona Les Pleiades **14** *A4*
- Cusco Plaza 2 **32** *B1*
- El Arcano **5** *A4*
- El Arqueólogo **19** *A3*
- El Balcón Colonial **6** *A3*
- El Grial **36** *A3*
- El Monasterio **38** *B3*
- Estrellita **9** *C5*
- Hospedaje El Artesano de San Blas **51** *A5*
- Hospedaje Familiar Inti Quilla **10** *A4*
- Hospedaje Inka **52** *A5*
- Hospedaje Jhuno **11** *A3*
- Hospedaje Turístico San Blas **13** *B4*
- Hostal Amaru **15** *B4*
- Hostal Andenes de Saphy **33** *B1*
- Hostal Casa de Campo **16** *A3*
- Hostal Cusco Plaza **18** *B3*
- Hostal El Balcón **20** *B1*
- Hostal Familiar **21** *B1*
- Hostal Familiar Carmen Alto **22** *A4*
- Hostal Familiar Mirador del Inka **23** *A4*
- Hostal Killipata **59** *B1*
- Hostal Kuntur Wasi **57** *A3*
- Hostal Loki **45** *C1*
- Hostal Luzerna **17** *D1*
- Hostal Machu Picchu **24** *D3*
- Hostal María Esther **25** *A3*
- Hostal Osiris **49** *A3*
- Hostal Pakcha Real **26** *A4*
- Hostal Qorichaska **27** *C1*
- Hostal Rickch'airy **28** *B1*
- Hostal Rumi Punku **29** *A3*
- Hostal Sambleño **30** *A4*
- Hostal San Isidro Labrador **31** *B2*
- Hostal Tikawasi **58** *A3*
- Incatambo Hacienda **48** *A2*
- Libertador **34** *C4*
- Los Apus Hostal y Mirador **35** *A3*
- Maison de la Jeunesse **56** *D4*
- Marani **37** *A4*
- Niños **39** *C1*
- Niños 2 **12** *D1*
- Novotel **40** *C4*
- Pensión Alemana **41** *A3*
- Piccola Locanda & L'Osteria **50** *B2*
- Posada del Sol **42** *A4*
- Residencial Torre Dorada **44** *E6*
- Ruinas **55** *B4*
- Suecia II **46** *B2*

**Eating**

- A Mi Manera **1** *B3*
- Baco **28** *B4*
- Café Cultural Ritual **15** *B4*

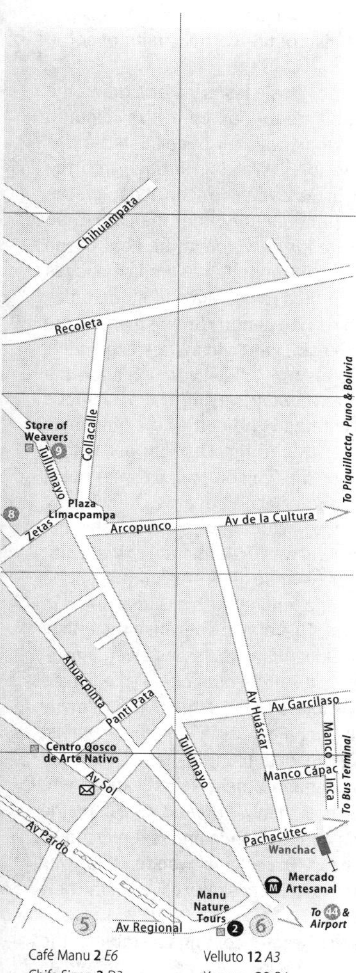


Café Manu **2** *E6*
Chifa Sipan **3** *D3*
Chocolate **16** *B4*
El Encuentro **13** *B4*
Granja Heidi **6** *B4*
Gypsy Pub **18** *A4*
Hatunrumiyoc **4** *B4*
Inka...fe **22** *B4*
Inkanato **7** *C4*
Jack's Café **14** *B4*
Juanito's Sandwich Café **21** *A4*
La Bodega **8** *A4*
Los Toldos **9** *D3*
Macondo **10** *A4*
Moni **24** *C4*
Mundo Hemp **25** *A4*
Muse **17** *A4*
Pachapapa **11** *B4*
Panadería El Buen Pastor **20** *A4*
Parrilla Andina **23** *C4*
Velluto **12** *A3*
Yanapay **29** *B4*

**Bars & clubs**
Bar 7 **5** *A3*
Km 0 (Arte y Tapas) **19** *A4*
Mandela's **26** *B3*
Siete Angelitos **27** *A4*

left as you look at it and El Triunfo (1533) on the right. There are two entrances; the cathedral doors are used during Mass but the tourist entrance is on the left-hand side through Iglesia Jesús y María.

Two interesting legends surround the western tower of the cathedral. According to the first, a captured Inca prince is bricked up in the tower. His only means of escape is for the tower to fall, at which point he will reclaim his people and land. Believers' hopes were raised when the tower was severely damaged in the 1950 earthquake, but it failed to fall before restoration started, incarcerating the prince until this very day.

The same tower holds the largest bell in the city, weighing 5980 kg. After two failed attempts at casting the bell, María Angola, an Afro-Peruvian woman, is said to have thrown a quantity of gold into the smelting pot on the third, successful attempt. The bell was then named after her. During the 1950 earthquake *María Angola* was damaged, so now her hoarse voice is only heard on special occasions.

The cathedral itself was built on the site of the Palace of Inca Wiracocha (*Kiswarcancha*). Stones from Sacsayhuaman were used in its construction after the architect, Juan Miguel de Veramendi, ordered the destruction of the Inca fortress. Although Spanish designers and architects supervised its construction, it took nearly 100 years of Quechuan blood, sweat and tears to build. The ground plan is in the shape of a Latin cross with the transept leading into the two side-churches.

Built on the site of *Suntur Huasi* (The Roundhouse), **El Triunfo** was the first Christian church in Cuzco. The name ('the Triumph') came from the Spanish victory over an indigenous rebellion in 1536. It was here that the Spaniards congregated, hiding from Manco Inca who had besieged the city, almost taking it from the invaders. The Spaniards claim to have witnessed two miracles here in their hour of need. First, they were visited by the Virgin of the Descent, who helped put out the flames devouring the thatched roofs, then came the equestrian saint, James the Greater, who helped kill many indigenous people. The two divinities are said to have led to the Spanish victory; not only was it the triumph of the Spaniards over the Incas, but also of the Catholic faith over the indigenous religion.

The gleaming, renovated gilded main altar of the **Iglesia Jesús y María** draws the eyes to the end of the church. However, take the time to look up at the colourful murals which have been partially restored. The two gaudy, mirror-encrusted altars towards the front of the church are also hard to miss. Walking through into the cathedral's transept, the oldest surviving painting in Cuzco can be seen. It depicts the 1650 earthquake. It also shows how, within only one century, the Spaniards had already divided the main plaza in two. *El Señor de los Temblores* (the Lord of the Earthquakes) can be seen being paraded around the Plaza de Armas while fire rages through the colonial buildings with their typical red-tiled roofs. Much of modern-day Cuzco was built after this event. The choir stalls, by a 17th-century Spanish priest, are a magnificent example of colonial baroque art (80 saints and virgins are exquisitely represented), as is the elaborate pulpit. On the left is the solid-silver high altar; the original *retablo* behind it is a masterpiece of native woodcarving by the famous Quechuan **Juan Tomás Tuyro Túpaq**. At the far right-hand end of the cathedral is an interesting local painting of the Last Supper. But this is the Last Supper with a difference, for Jesus is about to tuck into a plate of *cuy* (guinea pig), washed down with a glass of *chicha*. In the sacristy there is a good selection of artwork including portraits of all the bishops and archbishops of Cuzco, including Vicente de Valverde, the Dominican friar who accompanied Pizarro and who was instrumental in the death of Atahualpa. He was bishop of Cuzco until 1541, the year he died. The painting of the crucified Christ is strange because his body is rather effeminate. This is also noted in other paintings of Christ from the Cuzqueño school. This may be because the artists used female models, or could be simply how the Quechuan artists perceived him.



Many of the cathedral's treasures are hidden in a safe behind one of the carved doors. Much venerated is the crucifix of *El Señor de los Temblores*, the object of many pilgrimages and viewed all over Peru as a guardian against earthquakes. You may be forgiven for thinking he has a Quechuan complexion but this is actually due to many years' exposure to candle smoke! This is the most richly adorned Christ in the cathedral with his gold crown and his hands and feet pierced by solid gold, jewel-encrusted nails. The original wooden altar was destroyed by fire and dedicated locals are slowly covering the new plaster one with silver.

*Túpac Amaru was imprisoned next door, in San Ignacio chapel (now a craft market), before being executed in the plaza. His head was planted on a stick and placed on a hill by the main pass into the city.*

The chapel of **St James the Greater** contains a statue of the saint on horseback. The painting depicts him killing the local indigenous people as he appeared in the miracle.

Entering **El Triunfo** there is a stark contrast between the dark, heavy atmosphere of the cathedral and the light, simple structure of this serene church. The fine granite altar is a welcome relief from the usual gilding. Here the statue of the *Virgin of the Descent* resides and, above her, is a wooden cross known as the *Cross of Conquest*, said to be the first Christian cross on Inca land brought from Spain by Vicente de Valverde.

Going down into the **catacomb** (closed on Sundays), originally used to keep the bodies of important people, you will find a coffer containing half the ashes of the Cuzqueño chronicler Inca Garcilaso de la Vega, born of a Spanish father and Inca princess mother. The ashes were only sent back from Spain in 1978. The paintings of the parables, which used to hang on the central columns, have been moved to the Museo de Arte Religioso.

## La Compañía de Jesús

On the southeast side of the plaza is the beautiful church of La Compañía de Jesús, built in the late 17th century on the site of the *Amarucancha* (Palace of the Serpents),

## Around Plaza de Armas

### Plateros detail

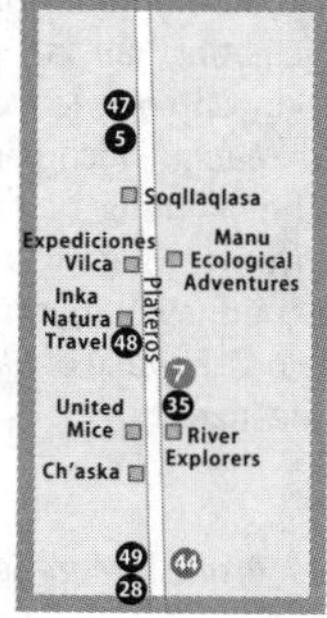


**Sleeping**

Casa Andina Catedral **15** *C3*
Casa Andina Plaza **20** *C2*
Del Prado Inn **5** *B3*
El Procurador del Cusco **1** *A2*
Emperador Plaza **2** *C3*
Hostal Carlos V **4** *A2*
Hostal Corihuasi **6** *A3*
Hostal Imperial Palace **8** *A2*
Hostal Plaza de Armas **10** *C2*
Hostal Q'Awarina **11** *A2*
Hostal Qosqo **12** *C2*
Hostal Resbalosa **13** *A3*
Hostal Royal Frankenstein **14** *B1*
Hostal Turístico Plateros **7** *Plateros detail*
La Casona Inkaterra **9** *B3*
Marqueses **3** *B1*
Munay Wasi **17** *A3*
Pensión Loreto **18** *C2*
Picoaga **19** *A1*
Royal Inka I **21** *B1*
Royal Inka II **22** *A1*
Sonesta Posadas del Inca **16** *B2*
The Point **23** *C1*
Tumi I **24** *A1*

**Eating**

Al Grano **1** *C3*
Amaru **49** *Plateros detail*
Ayllu **3** *B3*
Café Halliy **5** *Plateros detail*
Cicciolina **21** *C3*
Dolce Vita **10** *C3*
El Encuentro **34** *C3*
El Fogón **47** *Plateros detail*
El Molino **48** *Plateros detail*
El Patio **12** *B3*
El Truco & Taberna del Truco **13** *B1*
Fallen Angel **9** *B3*
Greens Organic **2** *C3*
Incanto **2** *C3*
Inka Grill **16** *B2*
Kapaj Ñan **26** *A2*
Kachivache **4** *B1*
Kintaro **17** *B1*
Kusikuy **18** *B3*
La Bondiet **29** *C1*
La Retama **19** *B2*
La Tertulia **20** *B2*
Los Candiles **49** *Plateros detail*
Maikhana **6** *C2*
MAP Café **32** *B3*
Paccha **15** *B2*
Pachacútec Grill & Bar **23** *B2*
Paloma Imbil **25** *A2*
Pizzería Marengo **27** *B2*
Pucará **28** *Plateros detail*
Real McCoy **35** *Plateros detail*
Trotamundos **30** *B2*
Tunupa **31** *B2*
Tupananchis **52** *C1*
Varayoc **14** *B2*
Víctor Victoria **33** *A2*
Witches Garden **7** *C2*
Yaku Mama **51** *A2*

**Bars & clubs**

Big Blue Martini **53** *A2*
Cross Keys Pub **58** *B2*
El Garabato Video Music Club **41** *B2*
Extreme **46** *B3*
Indigo **43** *A2*
Kamikaze **36** *B2*
Los Perros **37** *A2*
Mama Africa **55** *B2*
Mythology **8** *B3*
Norton Rat's Tavern **39** *C2*
Paddy Flaherty's **40** *C3*
Rosie O'Grady's **42** *C3*
Ukuku's **44** *Plateros detail*

 residence of the Inca Huayna Cápac. First it was given to Pizarro after the Spanish conquest, then it was bought by a family who eventually donated it to the Jesuits after their arrival in 1571. The church was destroyed in the earthquake of 1650. The present-day building took 17 years to construct and was inaugurated in 1668. When the Jesuits were expelled from Peru most of the valuables were taken to Spain. The altarpiece is a dazzling work of art. Resplendent in its gold leaf, it stands 21 m high and 12 m wide. It is carved in the baroque style, but the indigenous artists felt that this was too simple to please the gods and added their own intricacies in an attempt to reach perfection. Gold leaf abounds in the many *retablos* and on the carved pulpit. The painting on the left-hand side of the door as you enter is historically interesting. It depicts the marriage of Beatriz Qoya, niece of Túpac Amaru, to Martín García de Loyola, the nephew of one of Túpac's captors. Thus, de Loyola joins the line of succession for the Inca king's inheritance. The cloister is also noteworthy, though it has been closed for restoration for many years.



## North and northeast of the Plaza de Armas

### Museo Inka

ⓘ *Calle Ataud, T084-237380, Mon-Sat 0800-1730, US$3.*

The **Palacio del Almirante**, just north of the Plaza de Armas, is one of Cuzco's most impressive colonial houses. Note the pillar on the balcony over the door, showing a bearded man from inside and a naked woman from the outside. During the high season local Quechuan weavers can be seen working in the courtyard. The weavings are for sale, expensive but of very good quality. The palace houses the interesting Museo Inka, run by the Universidad San Antonio Abad, which exhibits the development of culture in the region from pre-Inca times to the present day. The museum has a good combination of textiles, ceramics, metalwork, jewellery, architecture, technology, photographs and 3-D displays. It has an excellent collection of miniature turquoise figures and other objects made as offerings to the gods. The display of skulls, deliberately deformed by trepanning, is fascinating, as is the full-size tomb complete with mummies stuck in urns! The section on coca leaves gives a good insight into the sacred Inca leaf. Old photographs of Machu Picchu are good to see after a visit, for 'then and now' comparisons. The painting of the garrotting of Inca Atahualpa, watched over by Vicente de Valverde, is gory but informative. There are no explanations in English so a guide is a good investment.

Opposite, in a small square on Cuesta del Almirante, is the colonial house of **San Borja**, which was a Jesuit school for the children of upper-class mestizos.

### Museo de Arte Religioso

ⓘ *Hatun Rumiyoc y Herrajes, 2 blocks northeast of Plaza de Armas, Mon-Sat, 0830-1130, 1500-1730.*

The **Palacio Arzobispal** was built on the site of the palace occupied in 1400 by the Inca Roca and was formerly the home of the Marqueses de Buena Vista. It contains the Museo de Arte Religioso which has a fine collection of colonial paintings, furniture and mirrors. The Spanish tiles are said to be over 100 years old and each carved wooden door has a different design. The collection includes the paintings of a 17th-century Corpus Christi procession by the indigenous master Diego Quispe Tito, which used to hang in the church of Santa Ana. They now hang in the two rooms at the back of the second smaller courtyard.

The first picture on the right-hand side in the first room is an example of a travelling picture. The canvas can be rolled up inside the cylindrical wooden box which becomes part of the picture when it is hanging. The stained-glass windows in the chapel were made in Italy. The one on the left-hand side depicts the Lord of the

66 99 The masks on the walls represent the Spaniards when they arrived in Cuzco – the eyes are red with greed and the skin yellow from all the gold they took ...

Earthquakes. The priest's vestments belonged to Vicente de Valverde; the black was used for funerals, white for weddings and red for ceremonial masses. There are many paintings of the Virgin of the Milk, in which the Virgin Mary is breastfeeding Jesus, a sight not seen in Western religious paintings. The throne in the old dining room is 300 years old and was taken up to Sacsayhuaman for the Pope to sit on when he visited in 1986. Visitors can also see a bed that Simón Bolívar slept in.

## Museo de Arte Precolombino

ⓘ *Plaza de las Nazarenas, daily 0900-2200, US$6, US$3 with student card.*

In the Casa Cabrera, on the northwest side of the plaza, this beautiful two-floor museum, set around a spacious courtyard, opened in June 2003. It is dedicated to the work of the great artists of pre-Colombian Peru. Within the expertly lit and well-organized galleries are many superb examples of pottery, metalwork (largely in gold and silver) and woodcarvings from the Moche, Chimú, Paracas, Nazca and Inca empires. There are some vividly rendered animistic designs, giving an insight into the way Peru's ancient peoples viewed their world and the creatures that inhabited it. All the exhibits carry extensive explanations in English and Spanish, and there are some illuminating quotes regarding the influence of pre-Colombian art in Europe and beyond, for example in the work of Pablo Picasso and his contemporaries. The museum, which is highly recommended, has a restaurant/café (see Eating, page 91) and stores such as a branch of the **Center for Traditional Textiles of Cusco**. One of two such stores in town (see page 101), you can often see local villagers weaving the pieces that are on sale using techniques that haven't changed in centuries.

## Convento de las Nazarenas

The Convento de las Nazarenas, on Plaza de las Nazarenas, is now an annexe of **El Monasterio** hotel. You can see the Inca-colonial doorway with a mermaid motif, but ask permission to view the lovely 18th-century frescos inside. **El Monasterio** itself is well worth a visit; ask at reception if you can have a wander around (see page 82). Built in 1595 on the site of an Inca palace, it was originally the **Seminary of San Antonio Abad** (a Peruvian National Historical Landmark). One of its most remarkable features is the baroque chapel, constructed after the 1650 earthquake. Look at the altar: to the right is a painting that slides to one side allowing access to a stairway, down which the statues of saints on high can be liberated for use in the Corpus Christi procession of June. Attempts have been made to restore the paintings outside in the cloister but, as can be seen in an alcove, the paint keeps peeling away and much is painted white. If you are not disturbing mealtimes, check out the dining room. This is where the monks used to sing. The masks on the walls represent the Spaniards when they arrived in Cuzco – the eyes are red with greed and the skin yellow from all the gold they took. Moving back to the second cloister, turn left at the restored painting in the alcove to see a small courtyard which used to be a farm; guests claim to have seen ghosts here. One last curiosity is *Samson's Martyrdom*, an

> ❢ *Only male visitors can see the place where monks were imprisoned for transgressions; today it's the men's toilet! In an inscription one monk tells how he was locked up for a day for ringing a bell 10 minutes late.*

 18th-century painting in the mestizo style, next to room 422. Look at the tray on the floor – those are Samson's eyes. Gruesome!

### San Blas

The San Blas district, called Tococache in Inca times, has been put on the tourist map by the large number of shops and galleries which sell local carvings, ceramics and paintings (see page 101). The **church of San Blas** ⓘ *Carmen Bajo, daily 1800-1130, 1400-1730, closed Thu mornings*, is a small and simple rectangular adobe building whose walls were reinforced with stone after the 1650 and 1950 earthquakes. It comes as some surprise to learn that it houses one of the most famous pieces of woodcarving found in the Americas, a beautiful mestizo pulpit carved from a single cedar trunk. Images of eight heretics are carved at the base of the pulpit; see if you can spot Henry VIII and Queen Elizabeth I of England among them. Above are carved the four Evangelists and, crowning the pulpit, supported by five archangels, is the statue of Saint Paul of Tarsus, although some believe it to be Jesus Christ. The skull is supposed to be that of the sculptor. There are many stories surrounding the artist. Some say he was an indigenous leper who dedicated his life to the carving after he was cleansed of the disease. The church was built and used by indigenous inhabitants and the Cuzco baroque altarpiece was designed to compete with any in the city.

> ❢ *There are many hostales and eating places on the steep, narrow streets, of San Blas, which are good for a daytime wander, but take care after dark.*



## East and southeast of the Plaza de Armas

### Santa Catalina

ⓘ *Arequipa at Santa Catalina Angosta, Sat-Thu 0900-1200, 1300-1700, Fri 0900-1200, 1300-1600. There are guided tours by English-speaking students; a tip is expected. Church open daily 0700-0800.*

The church, convent and museum are magnificent. Santa Catalina was the founder of the female part of the Dominican Order, which also founded the beautiful convent of the same name in Arequipa. The Cuzco convent is ironically built upon the foundations of the *Acllahuasi* (House of the Chosen Women), the most important Inca building overlooking the main plaza. The Quechuan women were chosen for their nobility, virtue and beauty to be prepared for ceremonial and domestic duties – some were chosen to bear the Inca king's children. No man was allowed to set eyes on the Chosen Women and if he had any relationship with one, he, his family and livestock would all be killed.

> ❢ *The most fascinating article in this museum is the trunk which unfolds to reveal a religious tableau used by travelling preachers to take the word of the Lord to remote villages.*

Today the convent is a closed order where the nuns have no contact with the outside world. There is a room at the back of the church where the nuns can participate in Sunday Mass. It is separated from the church by a heavy metal grill so although they cannot be seen their voices can still be heard. In this room there is the only signed painting in the museum. The artist was, of course, Spanish, as local artists were either forbidden or unable to sign their work. The church has an ornate, gilded altarpiece and a beautifully carved pulpit. The altarpieces are all carved by different craftsmen.

The museum has a wonderful collection of Cuzqueño school paintings spanning the decades of Spanish rule; a good guide can point out how the style changes from the heavy European influence to the more indigenous style. One obvious difference can be seen in the paintings of the Lord of the Earthquakes in the corridor. Early paintings show Christ wearing a white loincloth typical of European art, but in others he is seen wearing a very light, almost transparent skirt. The beautifully coloured murals in the Scriptures

## Heart of stone

Just wandering around the streets of Cuzco gives you a sense of the incredible craftsmanship of the Inca stonemasons. Some of the best examples can be seen in the **Callejón Loreto**, running southeast past La Compañía de Jesús from the main plaza. The walls of the Acllahuasi (House of the Chosen Women) are on one side, and of the Amarucancha on the other. There are also Inca remains in **Calle San Agustín**, to the east of the plaza. The famous **Stone of 12 Angles** is in **Calle Hatun Rumiyoc**, halfway along its second block, on the right-hand side going away from the plaza. The finest stonework is in the celebrated curved wall beneath the west end of **Santo Domingo**. This was rebuilt after the 1950 earthquake, when a niche that once contained a shrine was found at the inner top of the wall. Excavations revealed Inca baths below here, and more Inca retaining walls. Another superb stretch of late-Inca stonework is in **Calle Ahuacpinta**, outside Qoricancha, to the east or left as you enter. True Inca stonework is wider at the base than at the top and features ever-smaller stones as the walls rise. Doorways and niches are trapezoidal. The Incas clearly learnt that the combination of these four techniques helped their structures to withstand earthquakes. This explains why, during the two huge earthquakes in 1650 and 1950, Inca walls stayed standing while colonial buildings tumbled down. The walls of Hotel Libertador, near Santo Domingo, show an Inca stonemason following a Spanish architect – the walls are vertical and the doorways square. However, the stones are still beautifully cut and pieced together.



Room show the difference between the devoted lives of the religious order in the upper section and the frivolity of the courtier's life. The floral designs covering the lower section and the archways are the indigenous artists' way of paying tribute to *Pachamama*, Mother Earth. This can also be seen in the upstairs room, which has many paintings of the Virgin. The dresses are triangular, in the shape of mountains, which were seen as gods by the indigenous people. Another addition can be seen in the painting of the Virgin of Bethlehem. The baby Jesus is held at an awkward angle because he has been swaddled tightly from neck to feet in the manner of indigenous babies. The gold patterns are applied to these paintings by the use of a stamp. This is carried out by a separate artist once the painting has dried. Many of the works of art, bureaux and ornaments were given to the Order by the families of the joining novices.

Also worth a visit is the palace called **Casa de los Cuatro Bustos**, whose colonial doorway is at San Agustín 400. This palace is now the **Hotel Libertador**. The general public can enter the hotel from Plazoleta Santo Domingo, opposite the Temple of the Sun/Qoricancha.

### Qoricancha at Santo Domingo

ⓘ *Mon-Sat 0800-1700, Sun 1400-1600 (except holidays), US$2 (not on the BTG Visitor Ticket); the guides outside charge around US$2-3.*

This is one of the most fascinating sights in Cuzco. Behind the walls of the Catholic church are remains of what was once the centre of the vast Inca society. The Golden Palace and Temple of the Sun was a complex filled with such fabulous treasures of gold and silver it took the Spanish three months to melt it all down. You will be able to see what was the Solar Garden – where life-sized gold sculptures of men, women, children, animals, insects and flowers were placed in homage to the Sun God – and

## The festival of Inti Raymi

The sun was the principal object of Inca worship and at their winter solstice, in June, the Incas honoured the solar deity with a great celebration known as Inti Raymi, the sun festival. The Spanish suppressed the Inca religion, and the last royal Inti Raymi was celebrated in 1535.

However, in 1944 a group of Cuzco intellectuals, inspired by the contemporary 'indigenist' movement, revived the old ceremony in the form of a pageant, putting it together from chronicles and historical documents. The event caught the public imagination, and it has been celebrated every year since then on 24 June, now a Cuzco public holiday. Hundreds of local men and women play the parts of Inca priests, nobles, chosen women, soldiers (played by the local army garrison), runners, and the like. The coveted part of the Inca emperor Pachacuti is won by audition, and the event is organized by the municipal authorities.

It begins around 1000 at the Qoricancha – the former sun temple of Cuzco – and winds its way up the main avenue into the Plaza de Armas, accompanied by songs, ringing declarations and the occasional drink of chicha. At the main plaza, Cuzco's presiding mayor is whisked back to Inca times, to receive Pachacuti's blessing and a stern lecture on good government. Climbing through Plaza Nazarenas and up Pumacurcu, at about 1400 the procession reaches the ruins of Sacsayhuaman, where tens of thousands of people are gathered on the ancient stones.

Before Pachacuti arrives, the Sinchi (Pachacuti's chief general) ushers in contingents from the four Suyus (regions) of the Inca empire. Much of the ceremony is based around alternating action between these four groups of players. A Chaski (messenger) enters to announce the imminent arrival of the Inca and his Coya (queen). Men sweep the ground before him and women scatter flowers. The Inka takes the stage alone, and has a dialogue with the sun. Then he receives reports from the governors of the four Suyus. This is followed by a drink of the sacred chicha, the re-lighting of the sacred fire of the empire, the sacrifice (faked) of a llama, and the reading of auguries in its entrails. Finally the ritual eating of sankhu (corn paste mixed with the victim's blood) ends the ceremonies. The Inca gives a last message to his assembled children and departs. The music and dancing continues until nightfall.

marvel at near-complete temples with the best Inca stonework in Cuzco. On the walls were more than 700 gold sheets weighing about 2 kg each. The *conquistadores* sent these back intact to prove to the King of Spain how rich their discovery was.

The first Inca, Manco Cápac, is said to have built the temple when he left Lake Titicaca and founded Cuzco with Mama Ocllo. However, it was the ninth Inca, Pachacútec, who transformed it. When the Spaniards arrived, the complex was awarded to Juan Pizarro, the younger brother of Francisco. He in turn willed it to the Dominicans who ripped much of it down to build their church.

**The temple complex** Walk first into the courtyard then turn around to face the door you just passed through. Behind and to the left of the paintings (representing the life of Santo Domingo Guzmán) is Santo Domingo. This was where the Temple of the Sun stood, a massive structure 80 m wide, 20 m deep and 7 m in height. Only the curved wall of the western end still exists and will be seen (complete with a large crack from the 1950 earthquake) when you later walk left through to the lookout over the Solar Garden. The Temple of the Sun was completely covered with gold plates and there would have been a large solar disc in the shape of a round face with rays and flames. One story, with no historic basis to it, is that *conquistador* Mancio Sierra de Leguizamo was given this in the division of spoils but he lost it one night playing dice. Whether a *conquistador* lost it, or the Incas spirited it away, the solar disc has not been found.

Still in the baroque cloister, close by and facing the way you came in, turn left and cross to the remains of the **Temple of the Moon**, identifiable by a series of niches. The Moon, or Mamakilla, was the Sun's wife. The walls were covered in silver plates and the dark horizontal stripe in the niches shows where they were attached. Have a look at the stonework. This is a fantastic example of polished joints so perfectly made it is impossible to slip even a playing card in between. In fact, all the walls of the temples around this courtyard are fine examples of Inca stonemasonry.

Further round the courtyard, anticlockwise, is a double door-jamb doorway. Beyond this is the so-called **Temple of Venus and the Stars**. Stars were special deities used to predict weather, wealth and crops. There's a window around which, on the inside, holes can be seen where the Spaniards prised out precious stones. The roofs of all these temples would have been thatched, but on the ceiling here was a beautiful representation of the Milky Way. The 25 niches would have held idols and offerings to the cult of the stars and the walls around them were plated in silver (notice again the dark stripes). In the **Temple of Lightning** on the other side of the courtyard is a stone. Stand on this and you will appreciate how good the Incas were as stonemasons: all three windows are in perfect alignment. The Lightning was the Sun's servant while the Rainbow, subject of the next and last temple, was also important because it came from the Sun. A rainbow was painted onto the gold plates which coated the walls.

The gold thread used in the vestments of Catholic priests (on display in the sacristy which you pass on your way to the Solar Garden) pales into insignificance when you consider the vast quantities of gold housed in this most special of Inca temple complexes. Yet, to the Incas, gold and silver had little monetary value, and were prized only for their religious significance. As you gaze over the grass lawn to the Avenida Sol, this may help you believe that there truly was once a garden here filled with flowers, insects, animals and people, all fashioned in gold and silver. What a sight that must have been!

## Museo de Sitio Qoricancha

ⓘ *Mon-Sat 0900-1200, 1300-1700, Sun 0800-1400. Entrance by the BTG Visitor Ticket, or US$2. The staff will give a guided tour in Spanish, but please give a tip.*
The former Museo Arqueológico is now housed in an underground site on Avenida Sol, in the gardens below Santo Domingo. It contains a limited collection of pre-Columbian artefacts, a few Spanish paintings of imitation Inca royalty dating from the 18th century, photos of the excavation of Qoricancha, and some miniature offerings to the gods. It's a good idea to visit Santo Domingo before the museum, in order to understand better the scant information given.

## Other sights southeast of the centre

Between the centre and the airport on Alameda Pachacútec, the continuation of Avenida Sol, 20 minutes' walk from the Plaza de Armas, there is a statue of the **Inca Pachacútec** placed on top of a **Lookout Tower** ⓘ *1000-2000, free*, from which there are excellent views of Cuzco. Inside are small galleries and a coffee shop.

Avenida La Cultura, which runs southeast out of the city and eventually becomes the road to Sicuani and Lake Titicaca, passes through **Urbanización Magisterio**, one of the favoured areas to live in the city. Many foreigners, including overseas students, stay here. This is the other, modern side of Cuzco, with up-to-date services and just a US$1 taxi ride to the centre. Over the five blocks you'll find restaurants, including fast-food places with games for kids, every type of shop, internet cabins and long-distance phone services, laundries, safe long-term car parking, hairdressers, drugstores, pharmacies and video and DVD rental.

## South and southwest of the Plaza de Armas

### La Merced

ⓘ *Márques, monastery and museum Mon-Sat 1430-1700, church 0830-1200, 1530-1730, US$1.*

La Merced was originally built in 1534 by the religious order of Mercedarians (founded in 1223 by the French Saint Peter Nolasco), whose main aim was to redeem the natives. The church was razed in the 1650 earthquake and rebuilt by indigenous stonemasons in the late 17th century. The high altar is neoclassical with six gilded columns. There are a further 12 altars. Inside the church are buried Gonzalo Pizarro, half-brother of Francisco, and the two Almagros, father and son. Their tombs were discovered in 1946.

Attached is a very fine monastery. The first cloister is the most beautiful with its two floors, archways and pillars. The pictures on the first floor depict the saints of the order, but those on the second floor have been removed for restoration. The small museum can also be found here. This houses the order's valuables including the priceless monstrance (a vessel used to hold the consecrated host). It is 1.2 m high, weighs over 22 kg and is decorated with thousands of precious stones. Note the two huge pearls used for the body of a mermaid. There are many other precious religious objects including a small Christ carved in ivory, crowns and incense burners. The painting of the Holy Family is ascribed to Rubens. The superb choir stalls, reached from the upper floor of the cloister, can only be seen by male visitors and, then, only if you can persuade a Mercedarian friar to show them to you.



### Around Plaza Regocijo

**Museo de Historia Regional** ⓘ *Casa Garcilaso, C Garcilaso y Heladeros, daily 0730-1700; entrance with BTG tourist ticket (see box, page 59); a guide is recommended and is usually available at the ticket office; many of them speak English*, tries to show the evolution of the Cuzqueño school of painting. It also contains Inca agricultural implements, a mummy from Nazca complete with 1-m-long hair, colonial furniture and paintings, a small photographic exhibition of the 1950 earthquake and mementos of more recent times. Upstairs there is an exhibition room which holds temporary exhibits from photography to recently excavated finds. The museum is disjointed and even the Spanish explanations are minimal.

If you are walking up Garcilaso, the **Hotel Marqueses**, on the right, has one of the most unusual colonial courtyards. Attractive brick arches single this out from other patios in Cuzco as do the sculpted faces of the previous noble owners which stare out from above them. This house has been restored and converted from the old Hostal Los Marqueses into a hotel (see Sleeping, below).

**Museo de Arte Contemporáneo** ⓘ *Casa de Gobierno, Plaza Regocijo; free with BTG tourist ticket*, is only worth popping into if you are in the area and it is raining as it holds very few pieces.

### Around Plaza San Francisco

**San Francisco church** ⓘ *Plaza San Francisco, 3 blocks southwest of the Plaza de Armas, daily 0600-0800, 1800-2000*, is an austere church reflecting many indigenous influences, but it has a wonderful monastery, cloister and choir. The monastery is under reconstruction, so if you wish to visit, approach the door to the left

### Getting in a flap

Some love it, some hate it – but travel a couple of kilometres down the Avenida de la Cultura (the route to Paucartambo) and you won't miss it. Standing on a column six storeys high in the middle of the road is a massive condor, the Inca god called upon to protect the kingdom from the *conquistadores*. This modern-day marvel (or monstrosity, depending on your point of view) was built from the aluminium of a plane donated by the army. The artist (who died young) also created the monument of Pachacútec, the greatest Inca ruler of all, which visitors see on arrival at Cuzco airport. The condor's construction (which stands in sight of the poor barrios of San Sebastián) cost US$1.5 million and three people's lives in two accidents. The day of its inauguration, the massive bird caused a flap among the dignitaries below as an earth tremor started up and the wings began to move up and down! The beak is said to be gold, a sorry sight to the poor below who have no way of preying upon its treasure – the tower can be scaled only by locked stairs within.



of the church, shake it and, if the administrator appears, ask if he will show you around. Agree on a price before you enter. If he starts asking for money to take photographs and then a further tip at the end because of his good service ask him for a *boleta de venta* for the money you paid up front.

The cloister is the oldest in the city, built in the Renaissance style, but with diverse influences. The ground floor has several crypts containing human bones. Some of the bones have been used to write out phrases to remind the visitor of his or her mortality! The fabulous high choir contains 92 detailed carvings of martyrs and saints. The rotating lectern inlaid with ivory skulls (the Franciscan monks' symbol) was used to hold large books. Over the years the wooden ledge has been worn away by the continuous turning of pages.

On one of the stairways the largest painting in South America (12 m high, 9 m wide) can be seen. It records the 12 branches of the Franciscan Order – 683 people are present. Make sure you look up at the colourful, painted ceiling, restored after the 1950 earthquake.

## Around Mercado Santa Ana

Heading towards Santa Ana market and San Pedro station from Plaza San Francisco, you pass Santa Clara arch and the nuns' church of **Santa Clara** ⓘ *daily 0600-0700*. It is singular in South America for its decoration, which covers the whole of the interior. Its altars are set with thousands of mirrors.

**San Pedro** ⓘ *in front of the Santa Ana market, Mon-Sat 1000-1200, 1400-1700*, built in 1688, has two towers made from stones brought from an Inca ruin. The most interesting aspect of this church is the walk to it through the Santa Clara arch early in the morning. If you have only seen the Plaza de Armas and surrounding area a walk here will show you another side of Cuzco life. The street stallholders will be setting up and the Santa Ana market is worth a visit.

## Southern outskirts

The church of **Belén de los Reyes** ⓘ *Mon, Tue, Wed, Thu and Sat 1000-1200, 1500-1700*, was built by an indigenous architect in the 17th century. It has a striking main altar with silver embellishments at the centre and gold-washed *retablos* at the sides.

## Good Samaritans

"Shoeshine? Shoeshine?" Everyone who visits Cuzco will experience the sad sight of children as young as five struggling to shine shoes, sell sweets or postcards. Grubby, crouched in the gutter on a homemade box, knees poking through what's left of their jeans, these urchins have been banned from the Plaza de Armas, but persevere to survive by pestering every tourist in sight in the streets nearby. Their plight is extraordinary. Often the offspring of alcoholic parents, many of them sleep huddled together in shacks you wouldn't allow a pig to inhabit.

But equally amazing are the stories of a pair of Dutch backpackers who have set out to change the children's lives forever, and of two other foreigners who are working to help Cuzco's downtrodden and who need your help. Titus Bovenberg and his girlfriend, Jolanda, came as tourists to Cuzco in 1996. Twelve years later, they are still here, with a family of 12 adopted boys and a programme by the name of **Los Niños** that feeds and helps educate and clothe a further 250.

The 250 are the worst cases sent from three local schools. Many arrive with TB, bronchitis, pneumonia and numerous skin diseases. Some have been fainting through malnutrition; all are too small for their age. Doctors and dentists first attend to the children, then Los Niños give the youngsters healthy food, ensure they clean their teeth and shower 10 or 15 of them every day at their centre.

This is all funded by two excellent tourist hostels named **Niños Hotel**, its offshoot, **Niños 2**, and a set of apartments (see page 85). Staying here is a way of directly helping the street children (no volunteers are taken). Titus says: "We want to give these children not only food but hope that they can escape this; we must teach them they are human beings."

Meanwhile, in San Blas, another Dutch couple are battling for the underdogs through the **Hope Foundation**. In a dozen years Walter Meekes and his wife Tineke have built 20 schools in poor mountain villages and barrios around Cuzco. They have a programme to teach teachers and, in town, there is a 30-bed burns unit at the hospital that would have been just a dream were it not for their efforts. Again, work is funded by an excellent hostel called **Marani** (see page 89), where Walter will gladly tell you about his work. He does need volunteers.

In Urubamba, a British woman, Suzy Butler, is spearheading Cuzco's third amazing project, **Kiya Survivors**. At the Rainbow Centre street children and children with special needs are being given basic education, therapy and access to theatre and sports. There is no other provision for these children or their families locally. Kiya Survivors has also opened a children's home called Mama Cocha. Suzy says: "One of the kids is 16 and has Downs syndrome. She had been out of her family house only once in all her life. Within two days of coming to us she was like a new person, smiling and wanting to write."

Volunteers can work for one, two, three, four or six months and are asked to pay £750-1500, depending on the length of stay. All volunteers attend a training programme in the UK before starting.

To help **Los Niños** or the **Hope Foundation** simply book a room at their hostels. For details of **Kiya Survivors**, visit their website, www.kiyasurvivors.org, or write to Suite 41, 41-43 Portland Road, Hove, East Sussex, BN32DQ, UK, T+44 (0)1273-721092.

## West and northwest of the Plaza de Armas

Above Cuzco, on the road up to Sacsayhuaman, is **San Cristóbal**, built to his patron saint by Cristóbal Paullu Inca. The church's atrium has been restored and there is access to the Sacsayhuaman Archaeological Park. North of San Cristóbal, you can see the 11 doorway-sized niches of the great Inca wall of the **Palacio de Colcampata**, which was the residence of Manco Inca before he rebelled against the Spanish and fled to Vilcabamba. Above San Cristóbal church, to the left, is a private colonial mansion, **Quinta Colcampata**, once the home of the infamous explorer and murderer, Lope de Aguirre. It has also been home to many other important personages including Simón Bolívar and Hiram Bingham during the years of his excavation of Machu Picchu in 1915-1916. It has been restored but is not open to the public.

**Cristo Blanco**, arms outstretched and brilliantly illuminated at night, stands over the town and is clearly visible if you look north from the Plaza de Armas. He was given to the city as a mark of gratitude by Palestinian refugees in 1944. A quick glance in the local telephone directory reveals there is still a large Arab population in Cuzco.



## Sacsayhuaman and around

### Sacsayhuaman

ⓘ *30 mins' walk from the town centre; walk up Pumacurco from Plaza de las Nazarenas. Daily 0700-1730 (go earlier if you wish and definitely try to get there before midday when the tour groups arrive). Don't forget to take your BTG tourist ticket (see box, page 59) to gain entry to Sacsayhuaman and many of the other sites within walking/biking/riding distance of Cuzco. There are lights to illuminate the site at night.*

There are some magnificent Inca walls in the ruined ceremonial centre of Sacsayhuaman, on a hill in the northern outskirts. The Inca stonework is hugely impressive and the massive rocks, weighing up to 130 tons, are fitted together with absolute precision. Three walls run parallel for over 360 m and there are 21 bastions.

Sacsayhuaman was thought for centuries to be a fortress, but the layout and architecture suggest a great sanctuary and temple to the Sun, rising opposite the place previously believed to be the Inca's throne – which was probably an altar – carved out of the solid rock. Broad steps lead to the altar from either side. Zigzags in the boulders around the 'throne' are apparently '*chicha* grooves', channels down which maize beer flowed during festivals. Up the hill is an ancient quarry, the Rodadero, now used by children as a rock slide. Near it are many seats cut perfectly into the smooth rock.

The hieratic rather than the military hypothesis was supported by the discovery in 1982 of the graves of priests; it is unlikely that priests would have been buried in a fortress. The precise functions of the site, however, will probably continue to be a matter of dispute as very few clues remain, due to its steady destruction. The site survived the first years of the conquest. Pizarro's troops had entered Cuzco unopposed in 1533 and lived safely at Sacsayhuaman, until the rebellion of Manco Inca, in 1536, caught them off guard. The bitter struggle which ensued became the decisive military action of the conquest, for Manco's failure to hold Sacsayhuaman cost him the war and the empire. The destruction of the hilltop site began after the defeat of Manco's rebellion. The outer walls still stand, but the complex of towers and buildings was razed to the ground. From then until the 1930s Sacsayhuaman served as a kind of unofficial quarry of pre-cut stone for the inhabitants of Cuzco. As the site's tourism value has increased in recent years, so care and restoration have been given greater priority also.

> ❢ *Although robberies and other forms of aggression are rare in the countryside around Cuzco it's not unknown. It is always best to hike with a trusted guide or in a small group.*

## Sacsayhuaman to Tambo Machay

From Sacsayhuaman, the route leads east by northeast, part of the way along the modern paved highway, until reaching the turn-off for Qenqo, about 2 km away. First pass **Qenqo Chico**, then **Qenqo Grande** (see also page 81) and then following the exit road out of Qenqo – just before it joins the main paved highway running to the northeast, another smaller road feeds into it from the right. Follow this road which will soon curve left before reaching a large group of houses (Villa San Blas), about 200 m away, on the other side of a gully.

In the immediate vicinity of **Villa San Blas**, the paved road circles around a *huaca* (shrine) in the form of a small rock outcropping with finely cut and polished niches and little platforms. From that point, an older dirt track heads off in a northerly direction. Continue along this track for about 50 m, enough to steer comfortably clear of the houses, the children and the dogs, and then leave this secondary road altogether, striking off to the right, at right angles to it, and begin hiking east, skirting around fields and depressions (the remains of reservoirs), following any of several footpaths, but always maintaining a fairly straight course.

About 400 m away, there is a gentle descent into a shallow creek bed. After crossing it and walking on for almost 100 m, you will find some Inca stone walls. This marks the beginning of a semi-subterranean archaeological site similar to Qenqo. Because it does not protrude significantly above the level of the surrounding terrain, it is not easy to distinguish from many other rocky outcrops scattered throughout the area. It is, however, a conglomeration of large boulders with walkways and interconnecting galleries between them. The rocks are extensively sculpted with the usual array of niches and platforms and a great profusion of carvings, many of which represent monkeys and snakes, as well as what is thought to have been a large sculpted stone representing a toad. There are also remains of a liturgical fountain and a very battered, partially defaced, but still clearly perceptible stone sculpture of a large feline, possibly a puma, perhaps a jaguar (a plausible explanation given the presence of other examples of jungle fauna – the monkeys and snakes). This was once a *huaca* of great importance. The name given to this site is **Cusilluchayoc** ('place of the monkeys', from *kusillo*, monkey in Quechua). In Spanish it is sometimes called Templo de los Monos. The original Inca name is unknown.

Also unknown is the reason why so many of these *huacas* are partially or almost totally buried. Archaeological research has revealed as much as 3 m of niches, pedestals, carvings and masonry below present ground level. Throughout the Sacsayhuaman Archaeological Park all the lower sections of the various *huacas* uncovered over the last 25 years are much lighter in colour, in many cases almost white, in marked contrast to the weathered grey patina of the parts exposed for hundreds of years. The lower levels retain the original luminosity of the polished limestone, traces of what must have been a dazzling landscape. Did the Incas themselves attempt to conceal their religious shrines from the *conquistadores*? Or was it the fanatic persecution of heathen idolatry undertaken by the Christians during and after the conquest, which entombed the native places of worship? Alternatively, the consistency of the landfill and the uniformity of the depth throughout the area could suggest a natural or geological cause. Landslides brought about by earthquake or flooding are possibilities. Although records from the last 500 years detail devastating earthquakes in the Cuzco region, as well as floods and similar natural disasters, there are no specific references to great displacements of earth having obliterated this area.

> *Most of these hiking routes can also be done on horseback and perhaps as many can be ridden on a mountain bike. Horse and mountain bike rentals are readily available.*

After walking through Cusilluchayoc, you reach a well-defined, straight dirt track, flanked by sections of adobe walls with cacti and agave growing on them. This is a section of the ancient **Inca road** from Cuzco to Pisac, still used by highland folk descending from the hills to Cuzco. Turn left on this road and head northeast (away

## Dog eared advice

The further you go into the countryside, the more likely you are to run into large bands of working farm dogs, some of which are sometimes inclined to defend their patch. As with most animals, the best solution is to keep calm, face the dogs and make an organized retreat. Pick up a stick or a couple of stones just in case. Usually the dogs' owner will turn up and all will end *tranquilo*. Whatever you do, panicking and running is the most likely to end in a nasty bite. It's not common, but it sometimes happens.

from Cuzco) for about 300 m, towards a very prominent rock outcrop rising some 40 m above the surrounding fields. This is yet another important Inca *huaca*, currently known as **Laqo** (although the original Inca name is unknown). The INC is excavating the site, revealing the Inca complex. *Laqo* has more than one meaning in Quechua: it can be interpreted as 'confusing, misleading, enigmatic', but it is also the name of an algae found along Andean streams and marshes. And such a stream runs just below the site and so the place name would seem to derive from that. Still, it is also an enigmatic place. The name more commonly used by the local inhabitants is **Salonniyuc**, a hybrid Spanish-Quechua word roughly meaning 'place of the *salón* (hall or room)'. Another name is Salapunku or Salonpunku, with the same Spanish noun plus the Quechua *punku* (door, doorway). It is always Laqo on maps.

Laqo is a formation of grey, porous limestone, some 50 m high. A split, large enough to walk through, cuts into the rock. There are two large caves with remains of zoomorphic sculptures similar to those in Cusilluchayoc. Carved in the rock are niches and an altar upon which sunlight and moonlight fall at certain times of the



## Walks around Sacsayhuaman

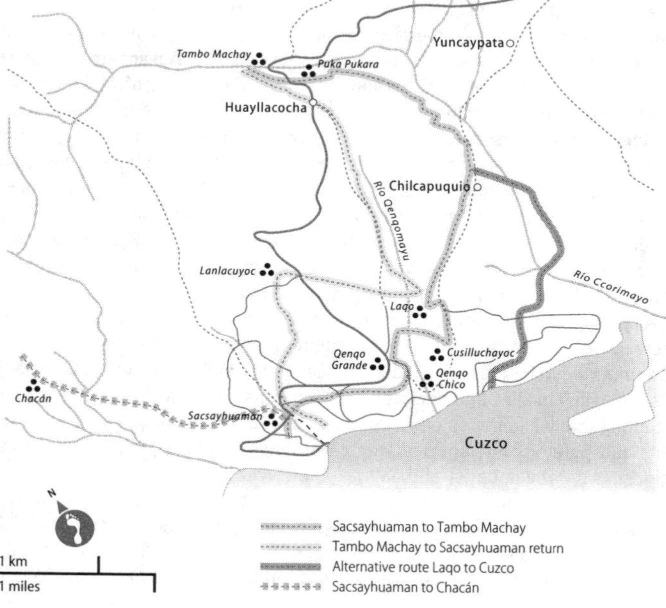

## Ceques – the cosmic dial

To understand the basis on which many Inca roads were laid out, one needs to know a little about the *ceque* system. This involves a complex series of lines and associated *huacas* (shrines) that radiated out from Cuzco and had astronomical, calendric and sacred connotations. The centre point of this giant dial is generally taken to be the Qoricancha, although some say a pillar and the tower of the Suntur Huasi on the Huacaypata (the Plaza de Armas) were the sighting points. Forty-one lines emanated from the hub, some hundreds of kilometres long. The lines were not necessarily marked on the ground, but ran dead straight towards the horizon. Four were the intercardinal roads to the four quarters of Tahuantinsuyo, others aimed at the equinox and solstice points, others to the points where different stars and constellations rise. On or near these rays, about 328 *huacas* (shrines) and survey points were distributed. The lines served various purposes: they were used for tracking the movements of sun and stars; they helped predict the best time for planting crops; they were instrumental in irrigation (about a third pointed to springs and other water sources). Certain *ceques* and their *huacas* were under the jurisdiction of particular *panacas* (clans). As well as delineating *panaca* property, the lines helped to define the organization of land, water and work and the rituals and ceremonies which began and closed work cycles.



year, filtered through the fissure above (hence another name for the place, Templo de la Luna – Temple of the Moon). The external surfaces also have carvings, sculptures, niches, stairways and the remains of a sundial, similar to the *intihuatanas* at Machu Picchu and Pisac.

Laqo has always been an observatory. Standing at the summit it is easy to appreciate why: it is the best single vantage point from which to view not only the Cuzco countryside, but also to see through the fabric of Andean time. To the southeast, about 100 km away as the crow flies, rises the great snowy peak of **Ausangate**, 'the one that pulls – or herds – the others', 6384 m above sea level, revered *apu* of the eastern Andes and grandfather of mountains. Some 70 km closer, in the same direction, loom the dark, jagged crags of **Pachatusan** 'pillar – or fulcrum – of the earth', at 4950 m, one of the children of Ausangate. And only 10 km away, aligned with father and grandfather, the young and green **Pikol**, one of the local *apus*, 4200 m high. Every mountain, every hill, is an *apu*, each possessing its individual identity and name. The *apus* are masculine and they all belong to a hierarchical order. At the same time, each *apu* is both offspring and consort of Mother Earth, *Pachamama*, source of all life, the indivisible and fundamental feminine element in nature.

Almost all the limestone outcrops scattered throughout the countryside are in effect *huacas*, all intricately carved and sculpted. There are also groves of eucalyptus trees, imported to Peru from Australia (via California) in the mid-19th century; adobe walls belonging to kilns and brickworks from colonial times; ancient irrigation canals contouring many kilometres of mountain slopes; fields of native amaranth, maize, beans and potatoes interspersed with other fields sown with cereals of European origin, such as wheat, barley and oats.

At the northern end of Laqo, there is a dirt road, about 10 m wide, running east to west. Beyond it lies a flat open field about 50 m long, which culminates on the side of a steep ravine with a shallow stream descending from the north. This runs through the many carved limestone outcrops, turns slightly to the southeast and flows on in the direction of Cuzco. The same Inca road followed from Cusilluchayoc to Laqo descends into this ravine, crosses the stream and continues its northeasterly course, gradually climbing and skirting around the southeastern flanks of the mountains, crossing into a small valley and then into a larger one, eventually reaching the village of **Chilcapuquio**, about 2 km from Laqo. The cliffs and rocky canyon walls along this section display many overhangs and cave-like openings, some at ground level and others many metres higher. These are the remains of burials dating back to Inca times. It is not uncommon to find remains of ceremonial offerings, such as bouquets of flowers, candles, coca leaves and tobacco, tributes by the people of today to the eternal spirits of the mountains.

Beyond Chilcapuquio, the main trail swerves to the right and gradually begins heading eastward, climbing about 100 m towards **Yuncaypata**, another, larger, community. Before the main trail reaches and crosses another stream, called the Ccorimayo on maps, it is best to strike away from it, following any of several smaller trails which will be found on the left heading north. These paths follow the course of the Ccorimayo, always on the left side of its ravine, gradually pulling away from it and climbing above it. About 2 km to the north of the point where one has struck off the main trail, and 200 m higher, poised atop a prominent rock buttress, lies the site of **Puka Pukara** and, a further kilometre beyond it, crossing the modern paved road from Cuzco to Pisac, are the ruins of **Tambo Machay** (see page 82) and the finishing point of this hike.

## The return from Tambo Machay

You can return from Tambo Machay to Cuzco by simply following the main paved road. There is also (time permitting) an interesting off-road alternative. Begin by following the main paved road going back to Cuzco, retracing your steps past Puka Pukara. The road soon reaches the vicinity of the modern community of **Huayllacocha**. On the left side of the road, a small ravine can be seen, descending southward. This is the **Qenqomayu**, the zigzagging river, the same which eventually flows 50 m past the northern end of Laqo and which the trail from there to Chilcapuquio and Puka Pukara earlier crosses. Several footpaths, along either the left or right slopes of the gully, descend for about 3 km to reach the vicinity of Laqo.

About 500 m after starting the descent there is a notable feature on the right bank of the canyon: the western canyon walls become vertical cliffs, extensively pockmarked with open holes, most of them many metres above ground level. They are graves (all looted) dating back to Inca times and representing one of the largest cemeteries in the department of Cuzco. A similar one can be seen opposite the northern side of the ruins of Pisac. Facing the vertical necropolis in the Qenqomayu gully is an Inca wall, of fine masonry, running for about 100 m. Its function is not known but it may indicate a shrine buried in the hill behind it, or some kind of canalization of the Qenqomayu, channelling its course toward Cuzco.

You approach Laqo but, to avoid visiting the site again, gradually climb above and away from the Qenqomayu in a southwesterly direction, eventually to descend and meet the dirt road which runs from east to west in front of the northern end of Laqo. Once on this road, head west for about 1 km, until rejoining the main paved highway from Pisac to Cuzco, now heading south toward Cuzco. Cross the highway, turn left, and less than 50 m south there is a turn-off to the right (west). Directly above lies another limestone promontory, the site of another enigmatic *huaca*. The outer surface displays many carvings, though none as fine as the ones in Laqo or Cusilluchayoc. The inner part of the *huaca* is a labyrinth of passageways and narrow caves. The official name of this site is **Lanlacuyoc**, which roughly translates as 'that which has an evil (or mischievous) spirit'. Its more popular name is **Zona X**, no doubt bestowed upon it 25 years ago during Cuzco's hippy period (the Kathmandu of the West, as it was called), when this particular archaeological site acquired a keen degree of interest. At the weekend, you may find these caves occupied by romantic couples and, occasionally, by a few young lads with a bit of alcohol in hand.

Leaving the recent and ancient past behind, follow the paved road for about 3 km, past the ruins of a colonial kiln, an Inca quarry, countless clumps of intricately carved limestone and occasional parked cars with romantic couples in pursuit of the timeless ritual. Soon after the first few turns, Sacsayhuaman comes into view. Any options for getting off the road, as long as they are on the left and head down towards Sacsayhuaman, are good.

## Variations on the route

Both of these hiking routes can be undertaken in reverse. It is also possible to hike northward from Laqo, after coming there from Cusilluchayoc, following the course of the Qenqomayu upward for about 3 km eventually reaching Huayllacocha on the main paved Cuzco to Pisac highway, a few hundred metres before Puka Pukara. This avoids the longer roundabout way from Laqo to Chilcapuquio. The routes can be modified and combined according to time limitations and weather conditions. Likewise, it is possible to take motor transport to the furthest point, in this case Tambo Machay, and from there begin walking back in the direction of Sacsayhuaman and Cuzco.



## An alternative route Laqo to Cuzco

After walking 1 km beyond Laqo, head northeast along the Inca road from Cusilluchayoc (which goes to Pisac) and follow it uphill to the right of the hill. The trail crosses from a narrow valley to a wider valley. After a grove of eucalyptus you will see well-preserved Inca terraces, to the right of which is **Inkiltambo**. Here is a vast area of carved niches, which housed the mummies of the ancestors of the Inca community that looked after the *huaca*.

From Inkiltambo you go down the *quebrada* (ravine) of **Choquequirau**, taking the trail on the right side of the stream. You pass colonial kilns and then take a trail that goes up the right side of the valley, leading to a superb view of the **Huatanay Valley** and **San Jerónimo** (see page 196). The outskirts of Cuzco are reached through a gap in the ridge. A dirt track crosses the hillside towards Cuzco to meet the paved road, which you follow to the right for about 100 m until you find the path again on the opposite side. This leads to **Titicaca** (or Tetekaka) *huaca*, which now has a cross and chapel. The shrine stands on the *ceque* (see page 78) of the winter solstice and Peter Frost (in his *Exploring Cusco*) associates this fact with the alignment of the *huaca* with the legendary birthplace of the sun in Lake Titicaca. Above the shrine, the path splits; take the upper fork and continue to the *huaca* called **Mesa Redonda**, so called for its flat, table-like rock. Beyond, you go downhill into the city.

## Sacsayhuaman to Chacán

You can reach the paved perimeter road around the north side of Sacsayhuaman from the centre of Cuzco on foot. From the Plaza de Armas walk up Calle Suecia (straight up from the Portal de Carnes), or up Cuesta del Almirante to Plaza Nazarenas (turn left onto Calle Pumacurco), or via Calle Saphi and any of the pedestrian streets to the right of this street (eg Resbalosa or Amargura staircase). All of these will lead you to a small ticket booth just a few metres above San Cristóbal church. Leave the paved road at the booth to climb a wide set of stone steps on the left of a small stream. This leads up the steep but obvious valley between the Cristo Blanco statue and the ruins' walls that are visible even from the town centre. Head north and up to the Sacsayhuaman archaeological site. The simplest way to find the Chacan Trail from the often-busy car park is to enter the site at the grassy flat esplanade. Ascending above the furthest wall from the city you'll find a gently sloping but clear trail, taking you up above the main body of the ruins and still further away from the city. As you walk away from Cuzco you'll pass a small ampitheatre-like structure on your left. A few minutes further on, just to your right is an oval rock several metres across and almost as tall. Its form has several carved steps cut into it, as do some other rocks in the area. Just above this point you hit the small paved road that cuts a wide arc above Sacsayhuaman. At this point it's significantly below its highest, but on the far side of the road is an obvious trail, that winds steeply up the hill in front of you.

A blue **INC** signboard reads: "Saqsaywaman – Patrimonio Cultural De La Nación", and "Sitio Arqueológico Hatun Chinkana". Below this there's a much smaller but clear sign pointing to the lefthand trail and Chacán. It reads: "Qhapaq Nan-Chakan-Nustha Pakana". Follow this trail uphill, heading generally northwards with the large river valley on your left and hill to your right. This now brings you to an irrigation channel made of concrete. Do not miss this channel, as it leads directly to **Chacán**. Follow the channel upstream for 2 km, where it meets the Tica Tica Valley. Here a natural bridge (Chacán means 'bridge place') carries the channel across the gorge while the stream runs 25 to 30 m below. Above this exceptional barrier stands a large carved rock built between stone walls. This is another of Cuzco's sacred *huacas*. If you cross the bridge and go down to your right towards the edge of the cliff, you will reach a lookout point at the front of a cave, which has Inca carvings. Below you can see the Río Tica Tica emerging from another cave, which runs beneath Chacán.

One kilometre upstream from Chacán are the ruins of **Ñustapacana**. The surroundings of this site are full of fine terraces, stone walls and another *huaca*.

*It is safest to visit the ruins in a group, especially if you wish to see them under a full moon. Take as few belongings as possible and hide your camera in a bag.*

Back at Chacán, walk west on the high trail above the river. Look for a eucalyptus plantation (or its remains, if it has been cut down) on the opposite side of the river. Walk down to the river at this point and cross over. Along this path you will see rocks carved in the shape of pyramids and other Andean religious motifs. Most prominent is a rock, some 2.5 m in height, whose central symbol has been defaced. This is **Quispe Wara** (Crystal Loincloth). Associated with this shrine are high-quality Inca walls and aqueducts, which can be seen on the return to Cuzco. Stay on the left bank of the river at Quispe Wara and climb straight uphill until you reach a narrow road. A leisurely 2-km descent passes, as a point of reference, the **Inca Tambo Hotel** on your left. After this, turn left for 100 m to get back to the paved road at the bend just below Sacsayhuaman.

With good navigational skills and plenty of time, it's also possible to hike directly cross country, between Zona X (Lanlacuyoc) and Chacán. This covers some beautiful rural valleys and Andean scenes a million miles from the tourist hustle and bustle of Cuzco: young boys guarding small herds of cattle; hardy Quechua folk ploughing the fields and taking mules and llamas to market in Cuzco's more rugged corners.

## Other sites near Cuzco

Along the road from Sacsayhuaman to Pisac, past a radio station, at 3600 m, is the temple and amphitheatre of **Qenqo**. These are not exactly ruins, but are some of the finest examples of Inca stone carving *in situ*, especially inside the large hollowed-out stone that houses an altar. The rock is criss-crossed by zigzag channels that give the place its name and which served to course *chicha*, or perhaps sacrificial blood, for purposes of divination. The open space that many refer to as the 'plaza' or 'amphitheatre' was used for ceremonies. The 19 trapezoidal niches, which are partially destroyed, held idols and mummies.

The Inca fortress of **Puka Pukara** (Red Fort) was actually more likely to have been a *tambo*, a kind of post-house where travellers were lodged and goods and animals housed temporarily. It is worth seeing for the views alone.

A few hundred metres up the road is the spring shrine of **Tambo Machay**, still in excellent condition. There are many opinions as to what this place was used for. Some say it was a resting place for the Incas and others that it was used by Inca Yupanqui as a hunting place – the surrounding lands, even today, hide many wild animals including deer and foxes. As this Inca was a living god, Son of the Sun, his palace would also have been a sacred place. There are three ceremonial water fountains built on different levels. As water was considered a powerful deity, it is possible that the site was the centre of a water cult. Water still flows by a hidden channel out of the masonry wall, straight into a little rock pool traditionally known as the Inca's bath.

Taking a guide to the sites mentioned above is a good idea and you should visit in the morning for the best photographs. Carry your multi-site ticket as there are roving ticket inspectors. You can visit the sites on foot; it's a pleasant walk through the countryside requiring half a day or more, though remember to take water and sun protection, and watch out for dogs. An alternative is to take the Pisac bus up to Tambo Machay (which costs US$0.35) and walk back. Another excellent way to see the ruins is on horseback, arranged at travel agencies. An organized tour (with guide) will go to all the sites for US$6 per person, not including entrance fees. A taxi will charge US$15-20 for three to four people. Some of these ruins are included in the many city tours available. » *For further details, see Activities and tours, page 104.*



## Sleeping

Prices given are for double rooms with bathroom in the high season of Jun-Sep. Tourists should not pay tax (IVA), but service may be extra to the bill. When there are fewer tourists hotels may drop their prices by as much as half. Always ask for discounts; the prices shown at reception are usually negotiable. Also, hotel prices, especially in the middle to upper categories, are often lower when booked through tour agencies, or on the internet. You should book more expensive hotels well in advance through a good travel agency, particularly for the week or so around **Inti Raymi**, when prices are much higher. Always reconfirm an advance reservation, in all price categories, particularly when you know that you will be arriving late in the city.

Be wary of unlicensed hotel agents for mid-priced hotels, they are often misleading about details; their local nickname is *jalagringos* (gringo pullers), or *piratas* (pirates). Taxis and tourist minibuses meet arriving trains and take you to the hotel of your choice for US$0.50, but be insistent.

It is cold at night in Cuzco and many hotels do not have heating. It is worth asking for an *estufa*, a heater, which some places will provide for an extra charge. When staying in the big, popular hotels, allow yourself plenty of time to check out if you have a plane or train to catch; front desks can be very busy. All the hotels listed below offer free luggage storage unless otherwise stated. Assume hotels have 24-hr hot water in pre-heated tanks (gas now being the most popular system) unless otherwise stated. Cuzco's low-power electric showers, frequently used in cheaper hotels, often do a poor job of heating the very cold water and their safety is sometimes questionable. Turning down the water pressure sometimes heats up the water to a reasonable level in electric showers.

### Plaza de Armas and around

*p61, maps p62 and p65*

**LL El Monasterio**, C Palacios 136, Plazoleta Nazarenas, T084-241777, www.monasterio.orient-express.com. This 5-star beautifully restored Seminary of San Antonio Abad is central and quite simply the best hotel in town for historical interest; it is worth a visit even if you cannot afford the price tag (see page 67). Soft Gregorian

*For an explanation of the sleeping and eating price codes used in this guide, see inside front cover. Other relevant information is found on pages 27-32.*

chants follow you as you wander through the baroque chapel, tranquil courtyards and charming cloisters, admiring the excellent collection of religious paintings. There are 106 spacious rooms with all facilities, including cable TV, as well as 20 suites, including 2 royal suites at US$1240 and 3 presidential suites at US$1025. Some rooms even offer an oxygen-enriched atmosphere to help clients acclimatize, for an additional fee of US$30. Staff, who all speak English, are very helpful and attentive. The price includes a great buffet breakfast (US$19 to non-residents) which will fill you up for the rest of the day. The restaurant, where the monks used to sing, serves lunch and dinner à la carte. The chapel is used as a conference centre and there is email for guests, open 0930-1300, 1730-2130. Recommended.

**LL La Casona Inkaterra**, Plazoleta Las Nazarenas 113, T084-245314, www.inkaterra.com. A new (2007), private, colonial-style boutique hotel in a converted 16th-century mansion, built on the site of Manco Cápac's palace. 11 exclusive suites, all facilities, concierge service with activities and excursions (prices US$500-1000).

**LL Libertador Palacio del Inka**, Casa de los Cuatro Bustos, Plazoleta Santo Domingo 259 (see page 69), T084-231961, www.libertador.com.pe. This splendid 5-star, award-winning hotel is built on Inca ruins (the walls can be seen in the restaurant and bar) and is set around courtyards. It has 254 well-appointed rooms; the attention to detail is so great there are even Nazca Lines drawn in the sand of the ashtrays! Enjoy Andean music and dance during dinner in the excellent **Inti Raymi** restaurant. Recommended.

**LL Novotel**, San Agustín 239, T084-581030, reservations@novotel.cusco.com.pe. 4-star, cheaper in modern section; price includes buffet breakfast. This is probably the best hotel converted from a colonial house in Cuzco. It was originally built as a home for *conquistador* Miguel Sánchez Ponce who accompanied Pizarro in the taking of Cajamarca. It was remodelled after the 1650 earthquake by General Pardo de Figueroa who built the lovely stone archways and commissioned paintings of the saints of his devotion on the grand stairway. Today the beautiful courtyard, roofed in glass, has sofas, coffee tables and pot plants around the central stone fountain. The modern 5-storey rear extension has 83 excellent, spacious, airy and bright rooms. All have sofas, cable TV, central heating and bathtubs. Those above the 2nd floor have views over Cuzco's red-tiled rooftops. The 16 in the colonial section are not much different but have high, beamed ceilings and huge, 2-m-wide beds. There are 2 restaurants and a French chef.

**L-AL Picoaga**, Santa Teresa 344 (2 blocks from the Plaza de Armas), T084-252330, www.picoagahotel.com. Price includes buffet breakfast. Originally the home of the Marqués de Picoaga, this beautiful colonial building has large original bedrooms set around a shady courtyard, and a modern section, with a/c, at the back. All have cable TV, minibar and safe. There are conference facilities, a tourist information office and the staff are very pleasant. Pricey but recommended.

**AL Casa Andina Private Collection Cusco**, Plazoleta de Limacpampa Chico 473, T084-232610, www.casa-andina.com. In a 16th-century mansion with 3 courtyards, this hotel is one of the recommended Casa Andina chain's upmarket establishments, with even higher standards of services and comfort than those listed above. It has all the main facilities, plus a gourmet restaurant serving local cuisine and a bar with an extensive *pisco* collection.

**AL Ruinas**, Ruinas 472, T084-260644, www.hotelruinas.com. A comfortable hotel conveniently located close to the Plaza de Armas (and **Rosie O' Grady's Irish Bar**). Good facilities (TV, minibar, etc) and comfortable beds, however it's possibly a little expensive given the competition in Cuzco. Helpful staff, price includes buffet breakfast.

**AL Sonesta Posadas del Inca**, Portal Espinar 108, T084-227061, www.sonesta.com. One block from the main square. Includes buffet breakfast, warmly decorated rooms with heating and cable TV, safe, some rooms on 3rd floor with view of Plaza, very helpful, English spoken, restaurant with Andean food, excellent service.

**AL-A Del Prado Inn**, Suecia 310, T084-224442, www.delpradoinn.com. A very smart hotel just off the plaza. 24-hr room service available and closed-circuit TV in the public areas for additional security. Suites with jacuzzi cost US$120-145.

A **Casa Andina Plaza**, Portal Espinar 142, T084-231733, www.casa-andina.com. 1½ blocks from the Plaza de Armas, this hotel has 40 rooms with cable TV, private bathroom, safe deposit box, heating, duvets on the beds and all the facilities common to this bright, cheerful chain.

Equally recommendable are the **Casa Andina Koricancha**, San Agustín 371, T084-252633, and the **Casas Andina Catedral**, Santa Catalina Angosta 149, T084-233661, and the AL **Casa Andina San Blas**, Chihuampata 278, San Blas, T084-263694, all of which are in the same vein (but the last 3 do not have an ATM).

A **Cusco Plaza 2**, Saphi 486, T084-263000, www.cuscoplazahotels.com. Under the same management as the **Hostal Cusco Plaza** (see below). The 24, nicely decorated rooms are set around 3 charming covered patios. Price includes American breakfast, and all rooms have cable TV and heating.

A **El Arqueólogo**, Pumacurco 408, T084-232522, www.hotelarqueologo.com. Price includes buffet breakfast. Services include oxygen, a library and hot drinks. A colonial building on Inca foundations, with rustic but stylish decor. Lovely sunny garden with comfy chairs and a small restaurant that serves interesting Peruvian food and fondue. French and English spoken. Also has a bed-and-breakfast *hostal* at Carmen Alto 294, T084-232760, C-D. **Vida Tours**, Ladrillo 425, T084-227750, www.vidatours.com. Traditional and adventure tourism.

A **Royal Inka I**, Plaza Regocijo 299, T084-231067, royalin@speedy.com.pe. Price includes buffet breakfast. The 29 bedrooms, with cable TV and heating, are set in a colonial house around an enclosed shady central patio. Those at the front have balconies overlooking the plaza. The building is decorated with heavy colonial furnishings and has a tranquil atmosphere. There is a bar and the restaurant has a set menu. Recommended.

A **Royal Inka II**, close by, on Santa Teresa, same phone and website as above. More modern and expensive but the price includes buffet breakfast, saunas and jacuzzi. Massages are an extra US$25. The old colonial facade hides a modern building, the rooms of which open out onto a huge atrium dominated by an incongruous, 3-storey-high mural. All rooms have cable TV and heating and are identical, except for No 218 and 3 others which are much larger for the same price. These hotels run a free bus for guests to Pisac at 1000 daily, returning at 1800.

A-B **Hostal Cusco Plaza**, Plaza Nazarenas 181 (opposite **El Monasterio**), T084-246161. Price includes continental breakfast. Situated on a lovely small plaza in the town centre, there are 33 clean rooms all with cable TV. Room 303 has the best view.

A-B **Incatambo Hacienda Hotel**, at Km 2, close to Sacsayhuaman, above the town, T084-221918 (Lima T01-224 0263). Price includes buffet breakfast and transport from the airport. Built on the site of Pizarro's original house, this 23-bedroom rustic-style hacienda is very peaceful, but this may not be enough to lure you out of town. The patio is a pleasant suntrap, but the garden is rough and, despite its height above the city, the views are not spectacular. Rooms have heaters and Peruvian-only TV. Horse riding can be arranged in the 60 ha of hotel grounds or around the nearby ruins.

A-C **Marqueses**, Garcilaso 256, T084-264249, marqueses@sastravelperu.com. Recently restored in Spanish colonial style, with 16th- and 17th-century-style religious paintings and 2 lovely courtyards. Rooms have heavy curtains and some are a little dark; luxury rooms have bath. Prices include buffet breakfast and discounts are available for guests booked on **SAS Travel** tours (see page 109).

B **Cahuide**, Saphi 845, T084-222771, www.hotelcahuide-cusco.com. Price (negotiate for a discount, especially for longer stays) includes American breakfast. Cable TV and heating in all rooms. This is a modern 45-room hotel with 1970s furniture and comfortable beds. Helpful staff.

B **Emperador Plaza**, Santa Catalina Ancha 377, T084-227412, emperador@terra.com.pe. Price includes buffet breakfast. A modern, light, airy hotel with friendly and helpful English-speaking staff. They will even order food for you from the Irish pub over the road! Rooms have cable TV, gas-heated showers and electric radiators. Winner of several hotel awards within its class.

**B Hostal Andenes de Saphy**, Saphi 848, T084-227561, www.andenesdesaphi.com. Very friendly little hotel with an artistic and cosmopolitan atmosphere. Each room is decorated in a different style, so have a good look around before choosing. The 4-bed family room is very nice. Price includes continental breakfast and all rooms have heaters. Lovely entertainment/games room and a small but pleasant garden.

**B Hostal Carlos V**, Tecseccocha 490, T084-223091, www.carlosvcusco.com. Price includes continental breakfast; heating is extra, TV costs more too. Take time to explore the 30 rooms and you should be able to find one with character and reasonable decor in the refurbished 1st-floor section. However, many bathrooms are shabby. With regard to prices, the owners are definitely open to negotiation. Worth a look.

**B Hostal El Balcón**, Tambo de Montero 222, T084-236738, balcon1@terra.com.pe. Price includes breakfast and you can pay with Visa, Amex, Diners and Visa Electron. This lovingly restored 1630 colonial house has 16 large rooms set around a beautiful, well-maintained garden. Ask for a TV if you want one – there is no extra charge. As well as a restaurant there is a kitchen for guests to use, and a laundry service. Homely atmosphere. Recommended.

**B Hostal Plaza de Armas**, Plaza de Armas, corner of Mantas, T084-231709, hostal_plaza @terra.com.pe. Price includes breakfast, from 0500. This is a clean, modern hotel with 28 rooms, each with cable TV, mineral water and heaters. However, in spite of its excellent position, only the lacklustre restaurant has views over the plaza.

**B Hostal Rumi Punku**, Choquechaca 339, T084-221102, www.rumipunku.com. A genuine Inca doorway leads to a sunny, tranquil courtyard. 30 large, comfortable, clean rooms, with private bathroom and 24-hr hot water (**C** low season). Helpful staff. Safe deposit box and luggage storage available. Highly recommended.

**B-C Hostal Corihuasi**, C Suecia 561, T084-232233, www.corihuasi.com. Price (Visa or Amex accepted) includes continental breakfast and airport pick-up. A tough climb up from the northernmost corner of the Plaza de Armas, this tranquil guesthouse is popular with tour groups. It is friendly and has some good views (the best is from room No 1) as well as cable TV in each room, solar heating. Recommended.

**B-C Hostal Qosqo**, Portal Mantas 115, near the Plaza de Armas, T084-252513, www.hostalqosqo.com. Bargain hard for a discount. Price includes continental breakfast, a heater and cable TV. The state of decor and quality of mattress varies from room to room but most stay here for its proximity to the plaza. Clean, friendly and helpful.

**C Hostal San Isidro Labrador**, Saphi 440, T084-226241, labrador@qnet.com.pe. Very pleasant 3-star hotel with elegant but simple decor. Colonial arches lead to a breakfast area (continental breakfast included in the price) and 2 lovely patios. The location is good, there's plenty of hot water and heating and telephone in all rooms. Recommended.

**C Niños**, C Meloc 442, T084-231424, www.ninoshotel.com. Spotless, beautiful rooms (cheaper without private bathroom) funding a fantastic charity established by Dutch couple, Titus and Jolande Bovenberg, who have converted this 17th-century colonial house into a stylish, comfortable place, typified by painted-wood floors and fresh lilies everywhere. All bedrooms lead onto a well-renovated courtyard. Those downstairs are named after the 12 street children Titus and Jolande have adopted and care for at the back of the hotel, while upstairs rooms bear the names of various benefactors. Price does not include the excellent breakfast (fruit salad, home-made wholemeal bread, locally produced jam, tea or coffee, fruit juice, etc). Services include the cafeteria and laundry. Dutch, English, German and French spoken. Also has the **Niños 2**, on C Fierro, a little further from the centre. **Niños 2** follows the same model as the first hotel, with 20 nicely decorated, clean and airy rooms, surrounding a central courtyard, and **AL-C Niños Hacienda** in the village of Huasao, with bungalows, rooms, pool, horse riding. Contact the main hotel for reservations and information. See also page 74 for further details of the Los Niños project.

**C Pensión Loreto**, Pasaje Loreto 115, Plaza de Armas (it shares the same entrance as **Norton Rat Tavern**), T084-226352, loreto@hloreto.com. Price includes continental breakfast and a heater which you will need, as the original Inca walls make the rooms cold. The best feature of this *hostal* is its location, although the rooms are spacious and they will serve you breakfast in bed if you are finding it too cold to get up. They have a laundry service and will help organize any travel services including guides and taxis. They also offer a free airport pick-up service. A bit pricey but where else can you fall out of a pub into bed?

**C-D Piccola Locanda**, Resbalosa 520, T084-252551, www.piccolalocanda.com. A steep walk up the hill behind the Plaza de Armas brings you to this friendly and colourful Peruvian/Italian-run B&B. If you've just arrived in Cuzco and the altitude is taking its toll, ask a taxi driver to drop you at San Cristóbal church and then stroll down to the hotel. The rooftop terrace has 360° views, excellent **L'Osteria** restaurant, TV/DVD room, pleasant courtyard and communal sofa area. Each of the small but cosy rooms has its own individual style, but not all have bathrooms. The *hostal*, restaurant and small **Perú Etico** tour company help to finance two children's projects, one in the village of Huaro, helping children with various physical and mental handicaps, and the other in Urubamba providing a home and learning centre for children facing parental abuse. Volunteers are sometimes required to aid these projects. Recommended.

**D Casa Elena**, Choquechaca 162, T084-241202, www.geocities.com/casa_elena. French/Peruvian hostel, very comfortable and friendly, breakfast included. Highly recommended.

**D Hostal Imperial Palace**, Tecseccocha 490-B, T084-223324, celazo1@hotmail.com. Cheaper without bathroom, price includes continental breakfast and some of the rooms have heaters. Hot water supply is patchy, with some rooms having a 24-hr supply, while others only have hot water in the early morning and evening. Rooms are large and have comfortable beds. There is a café, bar and restaurant. Very friendly.

**D Hostal Loki**, Cuesta Santa Ana 601, T084-243705, info@lokihostel.com. From **G** per person. Huge, ultra funky new hostel in a restored viceroy's residence on the super-steep Cuesta Santa Ana. Dorms and rooms are set around a beautiful courtyard, and the view from the bar alone, a condor's eye perspective of Cuzco, makes the climb well worth the effort. The beds have comfortable duvets, there's plenty of hot water, free internet access and lots of chill-out areas. A great place to meet other travellers.

**D Hostal María Esther**, Pumacurco 516, T084-224382. Price includes continental breakfast, but heating is extra. This very friendly, helpful place has a lovely garden in which to relax and a variety of rooms, including a lounge with sofas. Also car parking. Recommended.

**D Hostal Q'Awarina**, at the top of Suecia 575, T084-228130, www.qawarinahostal.com. Price includes continental breakfast, heating is extra, as is a TV in your room. No laundry service. Rooms are OK, ask for those with a view – they cost the same. There is a lovely living room with views across the city and the breakfast area upstairs is even better. Group rates available, good value. Recommended.

**D-E Hostal Turístico Plateros**, Plateros 348, T084-236878, plateroshostal@hotmail.com. Price includes continental breakfast. Clean, good-value *hostal* in a great location. There is a pleasant communal area with cable TV. The best rooms overlook the street.

**D-E Maison de la Jeunesse** (affiliated to Hostelling International), Av Sol, Cuadra 5, Pasaje Grace, Edificio San Jorge (down a small side street opposite Qoricancha), T084-235617, hostellingcusco@hotmail.com or maisondelajeunesse@hotmail.com. Very friendly hostel with a selection of dormitories and private rooms. TV and video room, hammocks strung on a sheltered balcony, cooking facilities and very hot water add to its appeal. Price includes breakfast.

**E El Balcón Colonial**, Choquechaca 350, T084-238129, balconcolonial@hotmail.com. Continental breakfast is available at extra cost. Use of the kitchen costs US$1 per day; laundry service. There is accommodation for 11 people in 6 rooms of this family house. Rooms are basic with foam mattresses but the hospitality of the owners, Liris and Yuli, is exceptional. Hot water most of the time. Free airport pick-up.

**E Hostal Familiar**, Saphi 661, T084-239353. Luggage deposit costs US$2.85 a day for a big pack. For over 25 years the owners have run this popular 32-bedroom *hostal* in a pleasing colonial house around a central courtyard, with benches, 3 blocks from the central plaza. Most beds are comfy and there is hot water all day. Recommended.

E **Hostal Killipata**, Killichapata 238, just off Tambo de Montero, T084-236668, www.geocities.com/killipata. G per person in shared rooms. Very clean, family-run lodging with good showers, hot water and fully equipped kitchen – it even has a pizza oven if culinary inspiration grabs you! Recommended.

E **Hostal Qorichaska**, Nueva Alta 458, T084-228974, www.qorichaskaperu.com. Cheaper with shared bath. Price includes continental breakfast, use of the well-equipped kitchen, internet and safe. Laundry service extra. Rooms in this colonial house are clean and sunny although watch out for the odd sagging mattress in the new section. Ask for the older rooms which are bigger and have traditional balconies overlooking the paved courtyard. Friendly and recommended.

E **Hostal Resbalosa**, Resbalosa 494, T084-224839. Breakfast is extra; laundry service. For superb views of the Plaza de Armas from a sun-drenched terrace look no further. The best rooms are those with a view (they cost extra). Others may be pokey and suffer from foam mattresses. The electric showers are reportedly cool, but most guests love this place. Owner Georgina is very hospitable. There is a safe in reception.

E **Hostal Rickch'airy**, Tambo de Montero 219, T084-236606. G without bathroom. This popular backpackers' haunt has views from the garden where travellers swap tales while waiting for their tents to dry. Owner Leo has tourist information and will collect guests from the station. Mixed reports of late.

E **Hostal Royal Frankenstein**, San Juan de Dios 260, 2 blocks from the Plaza de Armas, T084-236999, ludwig_roth@hotmail.com. One thing is for sure, you will never forget this place. Greeted by a grinning skull whose eye sockets light up as you enter, things just become more peculiar. Passing through the fully equipped kitchen (small charge to use), you can sit next to a (caged) tarantula while watching cable TV in the living room or gaze at Franken Fish. Rooms, fortunately, follow this theme in name only, thus you can stay in Mary Shelley or the Laboratorio. Nearly all 10 have excellent mattresses but few have outside windows. Downstairs, with one exception, they also run straight off the living room, which has an open fire. However, Ludwig, the mildly eccentric German owner, has 2 excellent *matrimoniales*/family rooms on the open-air top floor, which come with heaters. There is also a safe and laundry facilities. Recommended.

E-F **El Procurador del Cusco**, Coricalle 440, Prolongación Procuradores, at the end of Procuradores. T084-243559. G per person without bathroom. Price includes use of the basic kitchen (no fridge) and laundry area. The rooms are basic too and the beds somewhat hard, but upstairs is better. There is a place to relax and gaze over the city and the staff are very friendly and helpful. This is good value for money. Recommended.

E-F **Hostal Machu Picchu**, Quera 282, T084-231111. Cheaper without bathroom. There is a public phone, a safe but no TVs; laundry service. This very clean colonial house is a central, pleasant place to stay if you can afford the better rooms. Those with a bathroom are of a high standard but those *sin baño* are dark inside. Floors are stylishly tiled and there are plenty of places to relax in the flower-filled garden and escape the busy road outside.

E **Suecia II**, Tecseccocha 465, T084-239757 (it is wise to book ahead). G without bathroom, breakfast extra. You'll find Suecia II opposite **Los Perros Bar** close to Gringo Alley. Rooms are set around a glass-covered colonial courtyard and are consequently warm. Beds have foam mattresses but they are thick and guests can sit at tables on verandas overlooking the patio. Drawbacks: no seats on the toilets, water not always hot nor bathrooms clean, can be noisy and the luggage store is closed at night, but it's otherwise OK.

F **Albergue Casa Campesina**, Av Tullumayo 274, T084-233466, ccamp@apu.cbc.org.pe. Price includes breakfast, shared bathrooms only. A lovely place, set up to support the work of the **Casa Campesina** organization (www.cbc.org.pe/casacamp/), which is linked to local *campesina* communities. On the same site is the **Store of the Weavers** (see Shopping, page 102). The money that people pay for accommodation goes to this good cause. 23% discount for **SAE** members.

F **Albergue Municipal**, Kiskapata 240, near San Cristóbal, T084-252506, albergue@municusco.gob.pe. There are private rooms with double beds as well as dormitories in this very clean, helpful 56-bed youth hostel. Good communal area with cable TV and video. No rooms have bath. It has the added bonus of great views as well as a cafeteria and place to wash clothes (laundry service extra). Showers are electric and, unusually for a youth hostel, there is no kitchen.

F **Estrellita**, Av Tullumayo 445, parte Alta, T084-234134. Price includes breakfast and tea and coffee all day. There is a TV, video and old stereo system in the tiny communal sitting area and a very basic kitchen. 11 rooms are multiples with shared bathrooms and there are 2 with private bathrooms. It is basic but the wooden floors, good mattresses and clean decor make this excellent value. When you arrive ring the bell several times and wait; you will be given your own keys when you register. Cars and bikes can be parked safely. Recommended.

F **Hostal Luzerna**, Av Baja 205, near San Pedro train station (take a taxi at night), T084-232762. Price includes breakfast. A nice family runs this *hostal* which has hot water, good beds and is clean. It is safe to leave luggage. Recommended.

F **Munay Wasi**, Huaynapata 253, not far from Plaza de Armas, T084-223661. The price includes free hot drinks and laundry facilities. Bargain for a bed in this quiet, run-down colonial house. The 7 bedrooms are basic and very clean and most mattresses are sprung. The 2 front rooms have views of the Plaza de Armas. The owner is friendly and helpful.

F **The Point**, Mesón de la Estrella 172, T084-252266, www.thepointhostels.com. Price is per person in dormitory, also has doubles (**E**), includes breakfast, free internet, good beds, hot showers, clean, pleasant atmosphere.

F **Tumi 1**, Siete Cuartones 245, 2 blocks from Plaza de Armas, T084-244413. Price includes use of the kitchen and laundry area. There is a free book exchange but laundry service is extra. This lovely colonial house has 16 bedrooms (none with bath) around a sunny, paved courtyard. All are clean, traditional and huge with bare wooden floors and walls in need of a lick of paint. The toilets all lack a toilet seat and you have to pay for more than 1 shower (some are electric) a day. However, this is a very friendly, popular place and good value, especially if you bargain for longer stays.

## North and northeast of the Plaza de Armas *p66, map p62*

### San Blas *p68, map p62*

L-A **Casa San Blas**, Tocuyeros 566, just off Cuesta San Blas, T/F084-237900, www.casasanblas.com. An international standard boutique hotel boasting bright, airy rooms decorated with traditional textiles. Breakfast is served at the excellent **Tika Bistro** downstairs, wireless internet is included and upstairs a pleasant balcony gives you a more avian perspective of the city. Very attentive service, as you'd expect for a hotel in this price range. Suites upstairs are spacious and boast kitchen facilities – the largest even has a jacuzzi. The same owners have opened a hotel near Calca in the Sacred Valley and plan to open another near Sacsayhuaman, see www.pebhl.com.

A **Hotel y Mirador Los Apus**, Atocsaycuchi 515 y Choquechaca, T084-264243, www.losapushotel.com. Price includes buffet breakfast and airport pick-up; laundry costs US$1 per kg. Character and mod cons combine in this Swiss-owned hotel. It is all varnished wood, very clean and smart with beamed bedrooms fitted with cable TV and real radiators! Tall travellers will love the 2.3 m-long beds. Breakfast lookout on the top floor. Disabled facilities.

B **Hostal Casa de Campo**, Tandapata 296-B (at the end of the street), T084-244404, info@hotelcasadecampo.com. Price (10% discount for SAE members and *Footprint Handbook* owners) includes continental breakfast and free airport/rail/bus transfer with reservations. Guests get a work-out thrown in for free in the shape of many steep steps up to the multi-level hotel! Consequently the 46 bedrooms have fabulous views over Cuzco. There is a safe deposit box, laundry service, meals on request and a sun terrace. Dutch and English are spoken; take a taxi there after dark.

B **Hostal Tikawasi**, Tandapata 491, T084-231609, tikawasi@hotmail.com. Price includes breakfast and all rooms are heated. A family-run *hostal* with a lovely garden overlooking the city. Very stylish, softly lit rooms with lots of glass; great views come as standard. Comfortable beds and spotless bathrooms make this a good choice.

**B-C Casona Les Pleiades**, Tandapata 116, T084-506430, www.casona-pleiades.com. Small San Blas guesthouse in renovated colonial house, cosy and warm, generous hosts, hot water, cable TV, wireless connection, roof terrace, video lounge and book exchange, café, free airport pick-up with reservation, lots of information.

**C El Grial**, Carmen Alto 112, on the corner with Atocsaycuchi, T/F 084-223012, www.hotelelgrial.com. This handsome colonial building is shared with the South American Spanish School (www.spanish schoolscourses.com), and discounts are offered for students of the school. The comfortable whitewashed rooms have high ceilings and skylights. There's a large covered communal area and a TV and video room, plus free internet connection.

**C Hostal Amaru**, Cuesta San Blas 541, T084-225933, www.cusco.net/amaru (**E** without bathroom). Price includes breakfast and airport/train/bus pick-up. Services include oxygen, kitchen for use in the evenings only, laundry and free book exchange. Rooms around a pretty colonial courtyard, good beds, pleasant, relaxing, some Inca walls. Rooms in the first courtyard are best. Recommended. Also has **C Hostal Amaru II** at Chihuampata 642, San Blas, www.amaruhostal.com, and **E Hostería de Anita**, with bath, safe, quiet, good American breakfast.

**C Hospedaje Turístico San Blas**, Cuesta San Blas 526, T084-225781, www.sanblashostal.com. The price includes continental breakfast, free airport pick-up and there is cable TV in the comfortable, covered courtyard. The bedrooms are well decorated and the place is reasonable value for a mid-range *hostal* – rooms downstairs have no windows/outside views. Good views from the rooftop terrace.

**C Marani**, Carmen Alto 194, T084-249462, www.hostalmarani.com. Breakfasts available. Services include beginnings of a book exchange and information on Andean life and culture. Walter Meekes and his wife, Tineke, opened this spotless *hostal* in 2000. The rooms, set around a courtyard, are large with beamed ceilings and heaps of character. There is a breakfast room to the same standards. Some of the rooms are decorated with gifts of gratitude from communities the couple have helped through their association, the **Hope Foundation** (www.stichtinghope.or, see page 74). In 10 years the Dutch couple have built 20 schools in poor mountain villages and *barrios*, established a programme to teach teachers and set up a 30-bed burns unit in Cuzco general hospital. A great cause and highly recommended.

**C Pensión Alemana**, Tandapata 260, T084-226861. Price includes American breakfast; laundry is US$1.10 per kg. Car parking available. This Swiss-owned *pension* has clean, modern European decor with a comfy lounge area in which to watch cable TV or listen to music. There is a lovely garden with patio furniture. Recommended.

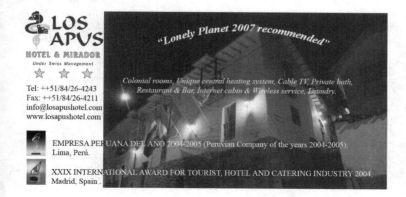

**D Posada del Sol**, Atocsaycuchi 296, T084-246394. Includes American breakfast, heater and airport pick-up. Cheerfully decorated with rustic charm, the hotel also has fantastic showers and a sun terrace with great views of Cuzco. Guests may use the kitchen and laundry costs only US$0.50/kg. Food is available. The *hostal* is up some steps and cannot be reached by taxi. Recommended.

**D-E El Arcano**, Carmen Alto 288, T084-232703. Breakfast and laundry are available, cheaper rooms with shared bath. On the one side there is a lovely little communal area with comfortable seating, covered by a colourful glass roof, and on the other there is a small breakfast area with cable TV and a book exchange. The owners are very friendly. Highly recommended.

**D-F Hostal Kuntur Wasi**, Tandapata 352-A, T084-227570. Cheapest without bathroom, services include a safe, use of the kitchen (for small charge) and laundry (also extra). There are great views from the terrace where you can breakfast. Owned by a very helpful, welcoming family. The showers are gas heated. A very pleasant place to stay.

**E Hostal Osiris**, Atocsaycuchi 616, T084-234572, www.hostalosiris.com. Belgian/Peruvian owned, all rooms with shared bath, hot water, kitchen, dining room, laundry, internet, trekking equipment for rent, yoga lessons, basic but warm, relaxed, clean and friendly.

**E Hostal Pakcha Real**, Tandapata 300, T084-237484, pakcharealhostal@hotmail.com. Price includes breakfast, the use of the kitchen and free airport/train/bus pick-up; heaters are an extra US$1.50. This is a family-run *hostal* where you can expect all the comforts of home including a large lounge with a fireplace and cable TV. There is a laundry service and they own the shop next door. The rooms are spotless although sparsely decorated and the front 2 rooms have great views. Taxis can drop you at the door. A friendly, relaxed place.

**E-F Andes de San Blas**, Carmen Alto 227, T084-242346, www.andesdesanblas@hotmail.com. Very friendly, family run hostel in an excellent location midway along Carmen Alto, between the **Splendid** laundry and **Juanitos Sandwich Café**. Great views of Cuzco, Sacsayhuaman and Cristo Blanco from the small rooftop terrace and some rooms. A basic breakfast is served, there's a living room with sofas and a TV for guests upstairs and internet access downstairs. The family can arrange budget tours, although you shouldn't feel under pressure to sign up. Rooms are clean and pleasant with basic decoration and comfortable beds. The only minor downside would be the slightly smelly drains in the bathrooms. Generally good.

**E-F Hospedaje Jhuno**, Carmen Alto 281, T084-233579. Breakfast is not included but guests can use the tiny kitchenette. A small, basic family-run *hospedaje* with 8 clean, well-decorated rooms and a family lounge with stereo. Very friendly.

**E-F Hostal Familiar Mirador del Inka**, Tandapata 160, off Plaza San Blas, T084-261384, miradordelinka@latinmail.com. Sprawling hostel set around large concrete courtyards. Not a lot of charm, but cheap (even more so without bath), prices include breakfast.

**E-F Hostal Sambleño**, Carmen Alto 114, T084-262979. A lovely jumble of staircases overlooks a central courtyard in this San Blas cheapie which has some rooms of varying quality. Breakfast is available and there is a laundry service. Beds are comfortable but the showers are electric. Recommended.

**F Hostal Familiar Carmen Alto**, Carmen Alto 197, first on the right down steps (no sign), T084-504658, carmencitadelperu@hotmail.com. If there's no answer when ringing the bell, go to the shop next door, it's run by the same family. Basic rooms with great character (in one case, constructed around a huge tree). Tranquil, family-run, use of kitchen and washing machine. Carmen makes an excellent breakfast for US$2. All rooms with shared bath, electric showers.

**G Hospedaje El Artesano de San Blas**, Suytucato 790, T084-263968, manosandinas@yahoo.com. Many clean, bright and airy rooms. As with the **Hospedaje Inka** (see below), you need to walk up from San Blas.

**G Hospedaje Familiar Inti Quilla**, Atocsaycuchi 281, T084-252659. Breakfast is not included and there are no facilities for either providing or making food. There are 6 colourfully decorated bedrooms around a pleasant little courtyard. It is situated on a quiet pedestrian street which means taxis cannot drop you off at the door. Friendly and good value.

**G Hospedaje Inka**, Suytucato 848, T084-231995. Taxis leave you at Plaza San Blas; walk steeply uphill for 5-10 mins, or phone the *hostal*. Price (per person) includes bath and breakfast. There are wonderful views, the rooms are spacious and owner Américo is very helpful, with lots of information.

G **The Blue House**, Kiskapata 291 (confusingly there are 2 Kiskapatas – this one runs parallel to and above Tandapata), T084-242407. Price per person. Snug little *hostal*, excellent value, with reductions for longer stays. Breakfast is included, DVD room, shared kitchen and great views with a small park in front.

### Elsewhere

A **Residencial Torre Dorada**, C los Cipreses N – 5, Residencial Huancaro, T084-241698, www.torredorada.com.pe. In a tranquil suburb to the west of the airport, this sparklingly clean modern hotel makes up in service for anything it might lose in location. Good-size rooms with very comfortable beds, heating and plenty of hot water in the well-appointed en suite bathrooms. Buffet breakfast is included, as is free transportation to and from the airport/bus/train station, and daily to the historical centre of Cuzco. Internet access is also available. This is an excellent option for people looking to stay in a quieter part of town. Highly recommended.



## Eating

### Plaza de Armas *p61, maps p62 and p65*

TTT **Cicciolina**, Triunfo 393, 2nd floor, T084-239510, cicciolinacuzco@yahoo.com. Sophisticated restaurant focusing largely on Italian/Mediterranean cuisine. Antipasti, salads and bruschettas are all excellent. Main dishes range from hand-made pasta, through excellent steaks to Moroccan lamb tagine. The impressive wine list draws from around the globe but the emphasis is on Latin American produce. Good atmosphere and great for a treat.

TTT **El Truco**, Plaza Regocijo 261. Excellent local and international dishes, frequently used by tour groups, buffet lunch served 1200-1500, nightly folk music at 2045; next door is **Taberna del Truco**, which is open 0900-0100.

TTT **Incanto**, Santa Catalina Angosta 135, T084-254753. Under same ownership as **Inka Grill** and with the same standards, serves pastas, grilled meats, pizzas, desserts, extensive wine list. Daily 1100-2400. There is also a Peruvian delicatessen on the premises. Upstairs is **Greens Organic** (see page 92).

TTT **Inka Grill**, Portal de Panes 115, T084-262992, 1000-2400 (Sun 1200-2400), www.inkagrillcusco.com. According to many the best food in town is served here. They specialize in *novo andino* cuisine (using native ingredients and 'rescued' recipes) and innovative dishes, also home-made pastas, wide vegetarian selection, live music, excellent coffee and home-made pastries to go. A good place to spoil yourself. Recommended.

TTT **La Retama**, Portal de Panes 123, 2nd floor, T084-226372. Excellent *novo andino* food and service. There is also a balcony, an enthusiastic music and dance group and art exhibitions.

TTT **Pachacútec Grill and Bar**, Portal de Panes 105. International cuisine including seafood and Italian specialities, also features folk music shows nightly.

TTT **Tunupa**, Portal Confiturías 233, 2nd floor (same entrance as **Cross Keys**). One of the finest restaurants on the plaza, its large dining room (accommodates 120-140) is often used by tour groups. Also has the longest (glassed-in) balcony but this is narrow and best for couples only. Food is international, traditional and *novo andino*. The wine list, as everywhere in Cuzco, is limited. Also an excellent buffet for US$15 including a *pisco sour* and a hot drink. In the evenings there is an excellent group playing 16th- and 17th-century-style Cuzqueña music of their own composition accompanied by dancers. Recommended.

TTT **Tupananchis**, Portal Mantas 180, T084-976 4494, tupananchis_rest_cusco@hotmail.com. Tasty, beautifully presented *novo andino* and fusion cuisine in a smart, sophisticated atmosphere – think Soho with alpaca steak. The café next door doesn't quite maintain the high standard of the restaurant, but generally **Tupananchis** is highly recommended

🍴🍴 **Al Grano**, Santa Catalina Ancha 398, T084-228032, 1000-2100, closed on Sun. Lunchtime menu US$3 is a good option if you are fed up with other menus. Evening serves 5 authentic Asian dishes for US$6, menu changes daily. Not a typical English curry but good and without doubt some of the best coffee in town, vegetarian choices. Also on the menu are breakfasts, including the 'full English' variety, dubbed the 'mother of all breakfasts', and jacket potatoes for those not smitten on all things hot and spicy! Recommended.

🍴🍴 **A Mi Manera**, (Culturas Peru), Triunfo 393, T084-222219, www.amimaneraperu.com. Remodelled in 2006, imaginative *novo andino* cuisine with open kitchen. Great hospitality and atmosphere.

🍴🍴 **El Patio**, Portal de Carnes 236, Plaza de Armas, left of the cathedral. Closed 1530-1830. In a colonial courtyard, this has a short menu (perfect for the indecisive!) with great pasta, Mediterranean dishes and salads as well as a good-value lunch. Good for a quick meal; get there early as the sun disappears around 1300-1330. Recommended.

🍴🍴 **Greens Organic**, Santa Catalina Angosta 135 p 2, T084-243379. Above **Incanto**, just off the Plaza. Entirely organic ingredients, plenty of superb vegetarian options; carnivores will find themselves in the minority, but there are always a couple of meaty possibilities. Recommended.

🍴🍴 **Kintaro**, Heladeros 149. 1200-2200, closed Sun. Excellent home-made food, set menu (1200-1500) particularly good value at US$3, Japanese run. Low-fat food is said to be good for high altitude. Slow service.

🍴🍴 **Kusikuy**, Suecia 339, T084-292870. Mon-Sat 0800-2300. Some say this serves the best *cuy* (guinea pig, US$10.90) in town and the owners say if you give them an hour's warning they will produce their absolute best. Many other typical Cuzco dishes on the menu. Set lunch is unbeatable value at only US$2. Good service, highly recommended.

🍴🍴 **Maikhana**, Av El Sol 106 (2nd floor), T084-252044, www.maikhana.net. Just off the Plaza, in a new mini-mall. Cuzco's only authentic Indian restaurant. Good filling curries, Indian breads and lassis. Chillies can be seriously hot, even for Thai and Indian food fans. Good for a change. Also has coffee house and sports bar.

🍴🍴 **Pizzería Marengo**, Plaza Regocijo 169, T084-264151. Excellent pizzas for US$7-8 per person. Ask for a table in the back room next to the cosy clay oven and watch your food being prepared. Also does deliveries.

🍴🍴 **Varayoc**, Espaderos 142, T084-232404. Open daily 0800-2400. Swiss-owned restaurant including Peruvian ingredients (try bircher muesli for breakfast; cheese fondue US$10-13 – the only place in Cuzco that serves it). Also has a variety of pastas, good desserts, 'tea time' beverage and pastry for US$2.80 accompanied by Andean harp music. It has a pleasant, literary atmosphere, established over 22 years and owner, Oscar, has a fine reputation.

🍴🍴 **Witches Garden**, Loreto 125, T084-244077, www.witchesgarden.net. New location for this warmly decorated little restaurant, serving good *novo andino* and international cuisine. The furry purple sofas are a highlight. There is a TV and video, with a selection of movies available for patrons.

🍴🍴-🍴 **Yanapay**, Ruinas 415, p 2, T255134. A good café serving breakfast, lunch and dinner. It is run by a charity which supports children's homes; head office at Av Alta 466, T084-245779, www.aldeayanapay.org. They welcome volunteers.

🍴 **El Encuentro**, Santa Catalina Ancha 384, T084-247977, and Choquechaca 136, T084-225496. One of the best-value eateries, 3 courses of good vegan food and a drink for US$1.35, very busy at lunchtime, more so at Santa Catalina than Choquechaca.

🍴 **Paccha**, Portal de Panes 167. Good for breakfast, it also has a bookstore, posters for sale, English and French spoken.

🍴 **Víctor Victoria**, Tecsecocha 466, T084-252854 (not to be confused with similar-sounding name at old address on Tigre). Israeli and local dishes, highly recommended for breakfast, good value.

### Cafés, delis, panaderías and heladerías

**Ayllu**, Portal de Carnes 208, to the left of the cathedral, is probably one of the oldest cafés in Cuzco and a great place to go. Fantastic breakfasts (try the special fruit salad), sandwiches, coffee and classical music as well as wonderful apple pastries. Very much a local venue – menu refreshingly all-Spanish. Service superb, handled by blue-jacketed waiters permanently on the run.

**Dolce Vita**, Santa Catalina Ancha 366. 1000-2100. Delicious Italian ice cream.

**La Bondiet**, corner of Av Márques and Heladeros. Clean, simple and inexpensive café with a huge selection of sweet and savoury pastries and decent sandwiches. Good juices and the coffee's OK.

**Trotamundos**, Portal Comercio 177, 2nd floor. Mon-Sat 0800-2400. This is one of the most pleasant cafés in the plaza, if a bit pricey. There is a balcony overlooking the plaza and a warm atmosphere especially at night with its open fire. Good coffees and cakes, safe salads, *brochetas*, sandwiches and pancakes as well as 4 computers with Wi-Fi internet access.

### Procuradores (Gringo Alley) *map p65*

Procuradores, or Gringo Alley as the locals call it, is good for a value feed and takes the hungry backpacker from Mexico to Italy to Spain and Turkey with its menus. Still a very popular spot, free drinks are offered as an incentive to get you inside amid cut-throat inter-restaurant competition. As Cuzco's restaurant scene has expanded and grown in sophistication (not forgetting price!) Gringo Alley has gradually faded, being somewhat outclassed. Some restaurants have closed, being taken over by travel agencies and shops, but – with the exception of the odd floppy pizza – most are still worth some experimentation.

🍴🍴 **Kapaj Ñan**, Procuradores 398, kapajnan@hotmail.com. Attentive service, an interesting mix of Peruvian, Asian and Italian cuisine. This one's a rustic, cosy little hole-in-the-wall and different from the Gringo Alley standard.

🍴 **Paloma Imbil**, Procuradores 362. Serves doner kebabs. The *rollo mixto* comes in delicious home-baked bread. For vegetarians and fans of Middle Eastern food the *rollo de falafel y queso* is a tasty option.

### Cafés, delis, panaderías and heladerías

**La Tertulia**, Procuradores 50, 2nd floor. The breakfast buffet, served 0630-1300, includes muesli, bread, yoghurt, eggs, juice and coffee, eat as much as you like for US$3, superb value, vegetarian buffet daily 1800-2200. Set dinner and salad bar for US$3.50, also fondue and gourmet meals, book exchange, newspapers, classical music, open till 2300.

**Yaku Mama**, Procuradores 397. Good for breakfast, unlimited fruit juice and coffee, good value but make sure you've got time – service can be painfully slow.

### Plateros *detail map p65*

Parallel with Gringo Alley but further south-west, Plateros also has good-value food.

🍴🍴 **Pucará**, Plateros 309. Mon-Sat 1230-2200. Peruvian and international food, Japanese owner does an excellent *ají de gallina* (garlic chicken) and cream of potato soup, pleasant atmosphere. Recommended.

🍴🍴 **The Real McCoy**, Plateros 326, 2nd floor, T084-261111, therealmccoycafelounge@yahoo.com. A fabulous retreat for homesick Brits and Aussies. The equal-best greasy-spoon breakfast in town (the other being **Jack's Café**), there's a good-value breakfast buffet (US$2), PG Tips and Heinz baked beans round up the early-morning highlights. On offer for dinner are some English classics: roast beef with Yorkshire pudding, etc. Finish it all off with banoffee pie or apple crumble with custard and cream – perfect!

🍴 **El Fogón**, Plateros 365. Huge local *menú del día* for US$2 – no messing around, just good solid food at reasonable prices. Very popular with locals and increasingly so with travellers.

🍴 **El Molino**, Plateros 339. Snug little place that serves excellent pizza.

🍴 **Los Candiles**, Plateros 323. Good set lunch for US$2.50.



### Cafés, delis, panaderías and heladerías

**Amaru**, Plateros 325, 2nd floor, T084-246976. Limitless coffee, tea, eggs, bread and juices served, even on non-buffet breakfasts. Colonial balcony catches the sun early in the morning. Excellent value and recommended.

**Café Halliy**, Plateros 363. Popular meeting place, especially for breakfast, good for comments on guides, has good snacks and *copa Halliy* (fruit, muesli, yoghurt, honey and chocolate cake, also vegetarian menu).

## North and northeast of the Plaza de Armas *p66, maps p62 and p65*

🍴🍴🍴 **El Monasterio**, Palacios 136, T084-241777. Even if you are not staying here, it is worth visiting for its food as well as its architecture. The dining room is where the monks used to sing. Main courses will set you back around US$15. Breakfasts are huge (perhaps 'epic' would be a better word) and cost US$19.

🍴🍴🍴 **Fallen Angel**, Plazoleta Nazarenas 320, T084-258184, www.fallenangelincusco.com. Mon-Sat 1100 till whenever (bar closes at midnight, kitchen at 2300), Tue and Sun opens at 1500. Like nowhere else. This is the second venture of Cuzco native Andrés Zúñiga (the other being **Macondo**, see page 95). The menu features steaks and some innovative pasta dishes. The cocktails are excellent. Live DJ at night. Regular parties/fashion shows are always events to remember. Free Wi-Fi internet. Always phone to reserve.

🍴🍴🍴 **MAP Café**, Plaza de las Nazarenas 231, a glass structure in the **Museo de Arte Precolombino**, T084-242476, www.map-cafe.com. Operates as a café 1000-1830; from 1830-2200, serves excellent Peruvian-Andean and international cuisine, with an innovative children's menu. It has a very good list of wines and *piscos*.

🍴🍴 **Baco**, Ruinas 465, T242808. Wine bar and bistro-style restaurant, same owner as **Cicciolina** (see page 91). Specializes in BBQ and grilled meats, also veggie dishes, pizzas and good wines. Unpretentious and comfy, groups welcome.

🍴🍴 **L'Osteria della Locanda**, Quiskapata 215, T084-252551, riserve@osteriadella locanda.com. In the same group as **Piccola Locanda** and an Italian/Peruvian-run tour company. Closed Sun, open Mon-Sat, evenings only; book in advance if possible. Excellent hand-made Italian food, fresh pasta, pizza and lasagna created as you wait with imported olive oil and parmesan. US$0.50 per table goes towards 2 family-run children's projects in the area.

🍴 **Café Cultural Ritual**, Choquechaca 140. Good value and tasty vegetarian *menú*, including some decent Indian dishes, for US$2.20.

### Cafés, delis, panaderías and heladerías

**Chocolate**, Choquechaca 162, T975 2172 (mob). Good for coffee and cakes but the real highlights are the fresh gourmet chocolates – these come up to European standards. Great for an indulgence or as a gift to chocoholic friends.

## San Blas *p68, map p62*

🍴🍴🍴 **Tika Bistro Gourmet**, Tocuyeros 566, 084-237900, www.tikabistro.com. This snug and beautifully decorated little eatery, tucked in under the **Casa San Blas**, really does offer an eating experience on par with London or Paris. Dishes range from filling and beautifully presented stuffed meats with spicy risottos, through to oriental plates of spicy beef wantons and spring rolls of various flavours, served with a variety of mouthwatering sauces. The wine list, largely

Latin American, is excellent, as is the service.

**Jack's Café**, Choquechaca y San Blas, T084-806960. Excellent and varied menu with very generous portions, all in a light and relaxed atmosphere. The American-style pancakes are multi-storey masterpieces and the freshly ground local coffee really gets you started in the morning. Excellent Thai curry, salads and the tortillas. Opens at 0630, making this a good bet for pre-tour breakfast; *El Gordo* is a contender for the best English breakfast in town. Lunchtime can be very busy.

**La Bodega**, 146 Carmen Alto. Snug Dutch- and Peruvian-owned café/restaurant of just 7 tables. Sip creamy hot chocolate by candlelight in the afternoons and read one of the English magazines. *House of the Rising Sun* sums up choice in music. The chicken curry is very good. Dishes come with side trip to salad bar. They also serve a decent American breakfast for US$2.50, and the US$1.50 lunch menu is a bargain. Highly recommended.

**Macondo**, Cuesta San Blas 571, T084-229415. Bit pricier than others in this range but fantastic. Walking into Macondo is like walking into an artistic creation. Owner Andrés has dreamed up a casual, cosy, arty and comfortable restaurant with sofas of iron bedsteads covered in dozens of cushions, mixed with chairs, tables and candles. Walls are decorated with local art, which changes every fortnight. Andrés' mum cooks in the kitchen of this colonial house that belonged to his grandmother. Popular, gay-friendly and a steep 3-block walk from the central plaza, Macondo has dishes of local ingredients with an artistic twist – eg vinaigrette of passion fruit with Amazonian salad. It is also renowned for its tasty *alpaca mignon à la Parisienne* and its desserts – the Marquis au Chocolate is great. Daiquiris are delicious. Happy hour 1500-1800. The tree house upstairs is great if you are 5 ft tall, otherwise take a seat fast! Visa attracts 10% surcharge. Recommended.

**Mundo Hemp**, Qanchipata 596, www.mundohemp.com. Focaccia bread, interesting savoury pancakes, quiche and good fresh juices. Good atmosphere with a beautiful sunny courtyard, lots of cushions inside, a colourful place and great for chilling, but the food's overpriced for what you get. Also has a shop with a range of hemp products on offer.

**Pachapapa**, Plazoleta San Blas 120, opposite church of San Blas, T084-241318. A beautiful patio restaurant in a wonderful old colonial house. Very good Cuzqueño dishes, including *pachamanca* (previous reservation required). At night diners can sit in their own private colonial dining room. Recommended.

**Granja Heidi**, Cuesta San Blas 525, T084-238383. US$5 gets you a 3- or 4-course *menú del día* in a clean and relaxed environment. There are usually vegetarian options on offer.

**Gypsy Pub**, Carmen Alto 162-C. Comfortable bar/restaurant a little further down the street from La Bodega. Good *menú del día* for US$2 and the chicken is some of the best in Cuzco. Unpretentious, a great place to talk to your mates.

**Hatunrumiyoc**, on the corner of Hatunrumiyoc and Choquechaca. Good location on the 2nd floor with a nice balcony. Decent set menu at lunchtime, often including lasagne and sometimes trout. Served with a drink and soup this will set you back around US$2.50.

**Inka...fe**, Choquechaca 131-A, T084-258073, www.inkafe.com.pe. Good coffee and desserts, set breakfasts and good-value lunch menus. Range of sandwiches in French bread. Sit by the window and watch the world go by.

### Cafés, delis, panaderías and heladerías

**Juanito's Sandwich Café**, Carmen Alto 227. Cuzco's answer to a university greasy spoon burger bar. Great grilled veggie and meaty burgers and sandwiches with titles like 'La Cabaña' and the '4 x 4'. Coffee, tea and hot chocolate. Juanito himself is a great character, staff are friendly, and the café stays open late, a classic post club/party retreat.

**Panadería El Buen Pastor**, Cuesta San Blas 579. Very good bread and pastries, the proceeds from which go to a charity for orphans and street children. Serves up *empanadas* and endless hot drinks. Very popular with backpackers. Recommended.

**The Muse**, Tandapata 682, Plazoleta San Blas. Funky little café with a cosy feel and great views over the plaza. Fresh coffee, locally

grown in Quillabamba, good food, including highly recommended vegetarian lasagne, chicken curry and carrot cake. There's often live music in the afternoon/evening with no cover charge. English owner Clair is very helpful. Water bottles refills for a small fee in an attempt to reduce plastic waste in Cuzco.
**Velluto**, Tandapata 700, T084-240966. Great place for crêpes, huge variety of savoury and sweet fillings, good drinks and hot chocolate.

### East and southeast of the Plaza de Armas *p68, map p62*

¥¥¥ **Parrilla Andina**, Maruri. Good-value meat fest. Mixed grill will feed 2 people for around US$15. Features beef, chicken, alpaca and pork. Restaurant is part of the former palace of the Inca, Túpac Yupanqui.
¥¥ **Inkanato**, San Agustín 280, T084-222926, www.perou.net. Good food, staff dressed in Inca outfits and dishes made only with ingredients known in Inca times, calls itself a 'living museum'.
¥¥ **Los Toldos**, Almagro 171 y San Andrés 219. If you're feeling peckish, on a budget and fancy being served by waiters in bow ties you could do worse than try their great chicken *brocheta*. Comes with fries, a trip to the salad bar and is enough for 2 people at just US$2.30. Also *trattoria* with home-made pasta and pizza, delivery T084-229829.
¥ **Chifa Sipan**, Quera 251 (better than their other branch for tourists in Plateros). Owner Carlos may not sound Chinese but he is and joins in the cooking at this excellent place. There is no great ambience but it's busy at lunchtime with locals. Skip to the back of the menu for their better deals and try *chancho* (pork) *con tamarindo* (US$4) or wanton soup and *pollo tipakay* (US$4.20).
¥ **Mao's**, Plaza Túpac Amaru 826, Wanchac, T084-252323 for delivery at no extra cost. Cuzco's answer to KFC/Burger King/ McDonald's, the most popular place in town for wood-oven grilled or roast chicken, crisp French fries, kebabs, huge mixed meat barbecues and salads. It's large, has a games park for kids and electronic and video games. Good value, look out for promotions.

### South and southwest of the Plaza de Armas *p72, map 62*

¥ **Kachivache**, Juan de Dios 260, p 2, T084-255856 (new location). Tasty Spanish cuisine, bruschettas, sandwiches and grilled meats. Vegetarian options are available and prices for all dishes are very reasonable. Relaxed feel, light and airy; a good spot for a leisurely lunch, although service is always much better when the owner is on the scene.
¥ **Puente Rosario**. Between 1200 and 1400 on Puente Rosario, just off Av Sol, pick up a piece of deep-fried potato or deep-fried, battered yucca from one of the street stalls for just US$0.15.
¥ **Santa Ana market** To eat really cheaply, and if your stomach is acclimatized to South American food, make your main meal lunch and escape the Plaza de Armas. Head for the market 5 blocks southwest at Túpac Amaru and eat at one of the many stalls. Food will cost no more than US$0.70 and 3-fruit juices are just US$0.45. Otherwise, look for the set *menús*, usually served between 1200-1500, although they are no good for vegetarians.

#### Cafés, delis, panaderías and heladerías

**Café Manu**, Av Pardo 1046. Good coffee and good food too in a jungle decor. It would be a sin to miss one of their liqueur coffees.
**Moni**, San Agustín 311, T084-231029, www.moni-cusco.com. Peruvian/English-owned, good fresh food and breakfast, British music, magazines, bright, clean and comfy.
**Picarones**, Ruinas y Tullumayo. Good for doughnuts. It is very small, very local and very typical for classic Peruvian sweet stuff.



## Bars and clubs

### Bars

**Plaza de Armas** *p61, map p65*
**Cross Keys Pub**, Portal Confiturías 233 (upstairs). 1100-0130. Run by Barry Walker, a Mancunian ornithologist of **Manu Expeditions**, offering darts, cable sports, pool, great *pisco sours* and bar meals. Happy hours are 1800-1900 and 2130-2200, plus there are daily half-price specials Sun-Wed.

Very popular, loud and raucous, with a great atmosphere.

**Indigo**, inside **Hostal Royal Qosqo**, turn left at the top of Gringo Alley. Shows 3 films a day. Also has a lounge and cocktail bar and serves Asian and local food. A log fire keeps out the night-time cold.

**Norton Rat's Tavern**, Loreto 115, 2nd floor, on the plaza but has a side entrance off a road to the left of La Compañía (same entrance as **Hostal Loreto**), T084-246204, nortonrats@yahoo.com. Pleasant pub with a pool table, dart board, cable TV and lots of pictures of motorbikes! Owner Jeffrey Powers loves the machines and can provide information for bikers. There's a balcony which offers great views of the Plaza de Armas. Juice bar inside the pub serving Amazonian specials – some said to be aphrodisiacs. Happy hour 1900-2100 every night with other daily specials such as Whisky Wednesday.

**Paddy Flaherty's**, C Triunfo 124 on the corner of the plaza, 1300-0100. An Irish theme pub, deservedly popular. Good seating and great food; the jacket potatoes, shepherd's pie and baguettes are all highly recommended.

**Elsewhere** *map p62*

**Amaru Quechua Café Pub**, Plateros 325, 2nd floor, T084-246976. Bar with pizzería, also serves breakfast for US$2.50; games, happy hour 1030-1130, 2000-2200.

**Bar 7**, Tandapata 690, San Blas, T084-506472. Good food and drinks in a trendy bar which specializes in local ingredients.

**Big Blue Martini**, Tecseccocha 148, T084-248839. Sophisticated, split-level sofa bar with funky lighting, very good cocktails, food and a lively music scene. There are jazz sessions on Thu, and on Sat guest DJs stir things up on the decks.

**Km 0 (Arte y Tapas)**, Tandapata 100, San Blas. Owners José Manuel Rabanal (Spanish) and Sara Pereira (Swiss-Italian) have really brought the warmth of Mediterranean Europe with them in this lovely themed bar tucked in behind San Blas. Good snacks and tapas (of course), affordable, and with live music every night (around 2200 – lots of acoustic guitar, etc), this place is a real gem.

**Mandela's Bar**, Palacios 121, 3rd floor, T084-222424. Bar/restaurant with an African theme and adobe-style walls. Good atmosphere and lots of space to spread out and relax. Serves breakfast, lunch and drinks in the evening, also Sun BBQs and special events through the year. Great 360° panorama from the rooftop.

**Los Perros Bar**, Tecseccocha 436, above Gringo Alley (Procuradores). Completely different vibe and a great place to chill out on comfy couches listening to excellent music. The Thai-style wantons are famous in Cuzco, but also give the sauteed chicken salad with avocado a try. In addition, try the thick curried soups and good coffee. The chicken curry is the closest thing to Brick Lane that you'll find in Cuzco, and you even get mango chutney. There's a book exchange, English and other magazines and board games. Opens 1100 for coffee and pastries; kitchen opens at 1300. Occasionally hosts live music and special events.

**Rosie O'Grady's**, at Santa Catalina Ancha 360, T084-247935. It's open 1100 till late (food served till midnight, happy hours 1300-1400, 1800-1900, 2300-2330). Good music, tasty food. English and Russian (!) are both spoken.

## Clubs

Before your evening meal don't turn down flyers being handed out around the Plaza de Armas. Each coupon not only gives you free entry, it's also worth a *cuba libre*. Sadly, the free entry-and-drink system doesn't appear to apply to Peruvians who are invariably asked to pay, even if their tourist companions get in for free. This discrimination should be discouraged. Also note that free drinks are made with the cheapest, least healthy alcohol; always watch your drink being made and never leave it unattended.

If you fancy learning a few Latin dance steps before hitting the dance floor, many of the clubs offer free lessons. Ask at the door for details or look out for flyers.

**Extreme**, on Suecia. An old Cuzco staple. Movies are shown in the late afternoon and early evening, but after midnight this place gets going with an eclectic range of music, from 60s and 70s rock and pop to techno. Offers more free drinks than most, so it's a good option for kicking off a big night out.

**El Garabato Video Music Club**, Espaderos 132, 3rd floor. Daily 1600-0300. Dance area, lounge for chilling, bar with saddles for stools, tastefully decorated in a colonial setting, with live shows 2300-0300 (all sorts of styles) and a large screen showing music videos. Their speciality is *té piteado*, hot tea or *mate de coca* with *pisco* and brown sugar. Recommended.

**Kamikaze**, Plaza Regocijo 274, T084-233865. Peña at 2200, good old traditional rock music, candle-lit cavern atmosphere, entry US$2.50 but usually you don't have to pay.

**Mama Africa**, Portal de Harinas, 2nd floor. Cool music and clubbers' spot. Serves good food from a varied menu, happy hour till 2300, good value.

**Mythology**, Portal de Carnes 298, 2nd floor. Tucked in the corner of the Plaza, this was one of the in spots in 2007, but don't expect cutting-edge tunes. It's more an early 80s and 90s combination of cheese, punk and classic. It also screens movies in the afternoons.

**Siete Angelitos**, Siete Angelitos 638. Tiny hole-in-the-wall club, just a couple of rooms really, but spectacular cocktails, a friendly owner by the name of Walter and an awesome atmosphere when things get going. Often hosts guest DJs, ranging from Latin to trance. Happy hour is often 2 hrs (2000-2200), and as of 2007 there were live reggae nights on Wed and Sat.

**Ukuku's**, Plateros 316. US$1.35 entry or free with a pass. This is somewhat different to the other clubs as every night there is a live band that might play anything from rock to salsa. The DJ then plays a mixture of Peruvian and international music but the emphasis is on local. It has a good mix of Cuzqueños and tourists. Videos are also shown here at 1600 and 1800. Films are free with any purchase.



## Entertainment

There are plenty of places which show videos and DVDs. Some of the restaurants, bars and clubs which show films are listed in the text.

**Centro Qosqo de Arte Nativo**, Av Sol 604, T084-227901. There's a regular nightly folklore show here 1900-2030, entrance by BTG combined entrance ticket (see page 59).

**Teatro Inti Raymi**, Saphi 605. Music nightly at 1845, US$4.50 entry and well worth it.

**Teatro Municipal**, C Mesón de la Estrella 149, T084-227321 for information 0900-1300 and 1500-1900. This is a venue for plays, dancing and shows, mostly Thu-Sun. Ask for their programmes. They also run classes in music and dancing from Jan-Mar which are great value.

## Festivals and events

**20 Jan** Procession of saints in the San Sebastián district of Cuzco.

**Feb/Mar** **Carnival** in Cuzco is a messy affair with flour, water, cacti, bad fruit and animal manure thrown about in the streets. Be prepared.

**Mar/Apr** Easter Mon sees the procession of **El Señor de los Temblores** (Lord of the Earthquakes), starting at 1600 outside the cathedral. A large crucifix is paraded through the streets, returning to the Plaza de Armas around 2000 to bless the tens of thousands of people who have assembled there.

**2-3 May** **Vigil of the Cross**, a boisterous affair, takes place at all mountain tops with crosses on them.

**Jun** **Qoyllur Rit'i** (Snow Star Festival, see box, page 100), held at a 4700-m glacier north of Ausangate, 150 km southeast of Cuzco. It has its final day 58 days after Easter Sun.

**Jun** **Corpus Christi**, on the Thu after Trinity Sun, when all the statues of the Virgin and of saints from Cuzco's churches are paraded through the streets to the cathedral. This is a colourful event. The Plaza de Armas is surrounded by tables with women selling *cuy* (guinea pig), a mixed grill called *chiriuchu* (*cuy*, chicken, tortillas, fish eggs, waterweeds, maize, cheese and sausage) and lots of Cuzqueña beer.

**24 Jun** **Inti Raymi**, the Inca festival of the winter solstice (see page 70), at which locals

## Corpus Christi in Cuzco

Corpus Christi is an annual festival celebrated on the Thursday after Trinity Sunday (generally in early June) by Roman Catholics everywhere. In Cuzco, Corpus is an exuberant and colourful pageant where profound faith and prayer share predominance with abundant eating and copious drinking.

All the Saints and Virgins are paraded through the city to the Plaza de Armas and, after being blessed, they are carried into the great cathedral to be placed in prearranged order, in two rows facing each other. The images are kept in the cathedral until the *octava* (the eighth day after their internment), when they are all escorted in procession back to their respective parishes and churches.

During these days and nights in each other's company, the Saints and Virgins, so the stories go, decide among themselves the future of the people for the forthcoming year. It is also said that they gamble at dice. Five hundred years ago, at the very same time of year and in this precise location, the mummified remains of the Incas were paraded in similar fashion and then laid in state. They consulted the Sun, the Moon, the Lightning and the Rains to learn what fate these elements were to bring in the course of the following year.

The Saints are the first to be paraded. The traditional race between San Jerónimo and San Sebastián is a joyous event. San Cristóbal, carved from a single tree trunk, is a heroic, elaborately painted figure, who leans upon a great staff. His powerful muscles and thick sinews forever shoulder the body of the infant Jesus as they ford a river. It is the heaviest statue of all and popular legend tells that underneath it lies a *huaca*, or sacred rock.

Santiago, the warrior saint and patron of Cuzco, enters astride his white horse, brandishing a sword. Trampled under the hooves of his steed lies a vanquished demon in the likeness of a Moorish soldier. Santiago's name was the battle cry of the Spanish soldiers, but he soon came to represent Illapa, the Andean deity of thunder and lightning.

Next come the Virgins, dressed in pomp, some of them accompanied by archangels and cherubs. They are seen as the equivalent of the Mother Earth, *Pachamama*. The Virgin of Belén is always first, escorted by San José, who then stands to one side of the entrance of the cathedral, waiting for all the Virgins to be carried in. Santa Bárbara, the pregnant virgin, is the last.

Corpus is perhaps the city's greatest event. All the streets and the huge expanse of the Plaza de Armas are thronged with enormous crowds. The revered images, each several hundred years old and from a distinct parish of the city, command a host of fervent followers, including a band of musicians and troupe of dancers. Most important and conspicuous are the bearers, whose strenuous efforts are relieved at resting points, known as *descansos*. The bier carrying the image is placed on top of a scaffold and the bearers and followers are all given a round of *chicha*, and/or beer while the band plays on and *Ave Marias* are prayed one after the other, like a mantra. The respite over, one final toast is made to the statue, also to *Pachamama* and to the surrounding mountain summits, *los apus*. In many cases this is accompanied by fresh coca leaves and lime. Then the parade resumes its journey. As the processions converge upon the centre, they merge together into a larger procession, which becomes engulfed by the multitudes in the Plaza de Armas. The images as they are carried along seem to become swaying vessels navigating a sea of humanity, riding its waves.

## It's no fun at the snow festival

Qoyllur Rit'i is not a festival for the uninitiated or the faint-hearted. It can be very confusing for those who don't understand the significance of this ancient ritual. To get there involves a two-hour walk up from the nearest road at Mawayani, beyond Ocongate, then it's a further exhausting climb up to the glacier. It's a good idea to take a tent, food and plenty of warm clothing. Many trucks leave Cuzco, from Limacpampa, in the days prior to the full moon in mid-June. This is a very rough and dusty overnight journey lasting 14 hours, needing warm clothing and coca leaves to fend off cold and exhaustion. Several agencies offer tours.

Peter Frost writes: "The pilgrimage clearly has its origins in Inca or pre-Inca times, although the historical record dates it only from a miraculous apparition of Christ on the mountain, around 1780. It is a complex and chaotic spectacle, attended by hundreds of dance groups, and dominated by the character of the *ukuku*, the bear dancer, whose night vigil on the surrounding glaciers is the festival's best-known feature. The journey there is lengthy, gruelling and dusty, the altitude (4600 m at the sanctuary) is extremely taxing, the place is brutally cold, unbelievably noisy around the clock (sleep is impossible), and the sanitary conditions are indescribable."



outnumber tourists, is enacted at the fortress of Sacsayhuaman. The spectacle starts at 1000 at the Qoricancha (crowds line the streets and jostle for space to watch), then proceeds to the Plaza de Armas. From there performers and spectators go to Sacsayhuaman for the main event, which starts at 1300. It lasts 2½ hrs and is in Quechua. Locals make a great day of it, watching the ritual from the hillsides and cooking potatoes in pits in the ground. Tickets for the stands can be bought in advance from the **Emufec** office, Santa Catalina Ancha 333, T084-226711, www.emufec.gob.pe, and cost US$80 in June, less March-May. Standing places on the ruins are free but get there at about 1030 as even so-called reserved seats fill up quickly, and defend your space. Travel agents can arrange the whole day for you, with meeting points, transport, reserved seats and packed lunch. Don't believe anyone who tries to persuade you to buy a ticket for the right to film or take photos. On the night before **Inti Raymi**, the Plaza de Armas is crowded with processions and foodstalls. Try to arrive in Cuzco 15 days before Inti Raymi. The atmosphere in the town during the build up is fantastic and something is always going on (festivals, parades, etc).

**Aug** On the last Sun in Aug is the **Huarachicoy Festival** at Sacsayhuaman, a spectacular re-enactment of the Inca manhood rite, performed in dazzling costumes by boys of a local school.

**8 Sep** **Day of the Virgin**, is the occasion for a colourful procession of masked dancers from the church of Almudena, at the southwest edge of Cuzco, near Belén, to the Plaza de San Francisco. There is also a fair at Almudena, and a bullfight on the following day.

**8 Dec** **Cuzco Day**, when churches and museums close at 1200.

**24 Dec** **Santuranticuy**, 'the buying of saints' is a huge celebration of Christmas shopping with a big crafts market in the Plaza de Armas, which is very noisy. It lasts until the early hours of the 25th.

# Shopping

## Arts and crafts

Cuzco has some of the best craft shopping in all Peru. In the Plaza San Blas and the surrounding area, authentic Cuzco crafts still survive and woodworkers can be seen in almost any street. A market is held on Sat.

In its drive to 'clean up' Cuzco, the authorities have moved the colourful artisans' stalls from the pavements of Plaza Regocijo to the main market at the bottom of Av Sol. There are, however, small markets of 10 or so permanent stalls dotted around the city which offer goods made from alpaca as well as modern materials such as fleece.

Cuzco is also the weaving centre of Peru and excellent textiles can be found at good prices; but watch out for sharp practices when buying gold and silver objects and jewellery. Note that much of the wood used for picture frames, etc, is *cedro*, a rare timber not extracted by sustainable means.

### Artisans

**Antonio Olave Palomino**, Plazoleta San Blas 651, makes reproductions of pre-Columbian ceramics and colonial sculptures.
**Edilberta Mérida**, Carmen Alto 133, makes earthenware figures showing the physical and mental anguish of the indigenous peasant.
**Hilario Mendivil**, Plazoleta San Blas 634 and 619, makes biblical figures from plaster, wheat flour and potatoes.
**Maximiliano Palomino de la Sierra**, Triunfo 393, produces festive dolls and traditional woodcarvings.
**Nemesio Villasante**, Av 24 de Junio 415, T084-222915, sells Paucartambo masks.
**Santiago Rojas**, Suytuccato 751, above San Blas, makes statuettes.

### Craft shops

**Agua y Tierra**, Plazoleta Nazarenas 167, and also at Cuesta San Blas 595, T084-226951. Excellent quality crafts from lowland rainforest communities, largely the Shipibo and Ashaninka tribes from the Selva Central whose work is considered to be among the finest in the Amazon Basin.
**Apacheta**, Santa Catalina 313, T084-238210, www.apachetaperu.com. Replicas of Pre-Inca and Inca textiles, ceramics, alpaca goods, contemporary art gallery, and books on Andean culture.
**Coordinadora Sur Andina de Artesanía**, C del Medio 130, off Plaza de Armas, has a good assortment of crafts and is a non-profit organization.
**Inkantations**, Choquechaca 200. Radical baskets made from natural materials in all sorts of weird and wonderful shapes. Also ceramics and Andean weavings. Interesting and original.
**La Mamita**, Portal de Carnes 244, Plaza de Armas. Sells the ceramics of Seminario-Behar, (see page 134), plus cotton, basketry, jewellery, etc. A visit is highly recommended for those who cannot get to their studio in Urubamba.
**La Pérez**, Urb Mateo Pumacahua 598, Wanchac, T084-232186. A big co-operative with a good selection; they will arrange a free pick-up from your hotel.
**Maky Artesanías**, Carmen Alto 101, T084-653643. A great place to buy individually designed ceramics. Ask for discounts if buying several pieces.
**Mercado Artesanal**, Av Sol, block 4. Good for cheap crafts.
**Pedazo de Arte**, Plateros 334B. A tasteful collection of Andean handicrafts, many designed by Japanese owner Miki Suzuki.
**Primitiva**, Hatunrumiyoc 495, T084-260152, San Blas, www.coscio.com. Excellent Peruvian contemporary art gallery, largely featuring the work of Federico Coscio.

### Fabric and clothing

**Alpaca 111**, Plaza Regocijo 202, T084-243233. High-quality alpaca clothing, with shops also in hotels **Monasterio**, **Libertador** and **Machu Picchu Sanctuary Lodge**, the Museo de Arte Precolombino and at the airport.
**Alpaca 3**, Ruinas 472. Quality alpaca items.
**Arte Vivo del Cusco al Mundo**, on the right-hand side in Capilla San Ignacio, Plaza de Armas. Open 1030-1300, 1530-2100. The outlet for 2 cooperatives of weavers.
**Center for Traditional Textiles of Cusco**, Av Sol 603, T084-228117, www.textilescusco.org. A non-profit

organization that seeks to promote, refine and rediscover the weaving traditions of the area. Tours of workshops in Chinchero and beyond can de arranged, also weaving classes. In the Cuzco outlet you can watch weavers at work. The textiles are of excellent quality and the price reflects the fact that over 50% goes direct to the weaver. Recommended.

**Hilo**, Carmen Alto 260, T084-254536. Fashion gear for ladies and gents. Each item in this tiny little shop is designed separately and hand made onsite. Influences seem to range from Inca to Heidi and back to Madonna's finest hour. Run by patrons Eibhlin Cassidy and Avikal Elphee (Evi and Avi), they can adjust and tailor their designs, and they sometimes offer 'The best Chai this side of Mumbai' to their customers.

**Josefina Olivera**, Portal Comercio 173, Plaza de Armas. She sells old ponchos and antique *mantas* (shawls), without the usual haggling. Her prices are high, but it is worth it to save pieces being cut up to make other items, open daily 1100-2100.

**Mundo Alpaca**, T054-202525, www.mundoalpaca.com.pe. Alpaca boutique, art gallery, museum and coffee shop.

**Store of Weavers** (Asociación Central de Artesanos y Artesanas del Sur Andino Inkakunaq Ruwaynin), Av Tullumayo 274, T084-233466, www.cbc.org.pe/tejidosandinos. A store administered by 6 local weaving communities, some of whose residents you can see working on site. All profits go to the weavers themselves. Most of the work utilizes traditional dyes and the fine quality of the *mantas* and other textiles on sale makes this store well worth a visit.

### Jewellery

**Calas**, Siete Angelitos 619-B, San Blas. Handmade silver jewellery in interesting designs and alpaca goods from the community of Pitumarca.

**Carlos Chaquiras**, Triunfo 375, T084-227470, www.carloschaquiras.com. 1000-1930. Very upmarket, with lots of Inca figures, among other designs, enhanced with semi-precious stones and shells.

**Ilaria**, Portal Carrizos 258, T084-246253, in hotels **Monasterio** and **Libertador** and at the airport. The Cuzco branches of a highly regarded Lima silver and jewellery store.

**Joyería H Ormachea**, Plateros 372, T084-237061. Handmade gold and silver items.

**Mullu**, Triunfo 120, T084-229831. Contemporary silver jewellery with semi-precious stones and cotton clothing with interesting designs, Mon-Sat 1000-2100.

**Spondylus**, Cuesta San Blas 505 y Plazoleta San Blas 617, T084-226929, spondyluscusco@mixmail.com. Interesting jewellery in gold and silver, also using semi-precious stones and shells. They will make your own design for you for a reasonable fee. They sell some nice T-shirts with Inca and pre-Inca designs.

### Musical instruments

**Taki Museo de Música de los Andes**, Hatunrumiyoc 487-5. Shop and workshop selling and displaying musical instruments, knowledgeable owner, who is an ethno-musicologist. Recommended for anyone interested in Andean music.

## Bookshops

**Centro de Estudios Regionales Andinos Bartolomé de las Casas**, Av Tullumayo 465, T084-233472, www.cbc.org.pe. Good books on Peruvian history, archaeology, etc, Mon-Sat 1100-1400, 1600-1900.

**Jerusalem**, Heladeros 143, T084-235408. English books, guidebooks, music, postcards, expensive book exchange.

**The Sun**, Plazoleta Limacpampa Chico 471. This café/restaurant has the best book exchange, 1 for 1, maintained by an Australian.

## Camping equipment

There are several places on Plateros which rent out equipment but check it carefully as it is common for parts to be missing. A deposit of US$100 is required, plus credit card, passport or plane ticket. Wherever you hire equipment, check the stoves carefully. White gas (*bencina*) costs US$1.50 per litre and can be bought at hardware stores, but check the purity. Stove spirit (*alcohol para quemar*) is available at pharmacies. Blue gas canisters, costing US$5, can be found at some hardware stores and at shops which rent gear. You can also rent equipment through travel agencies.

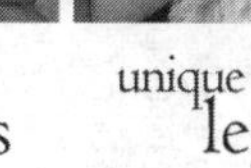
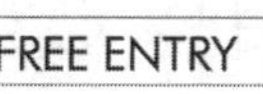
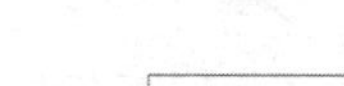

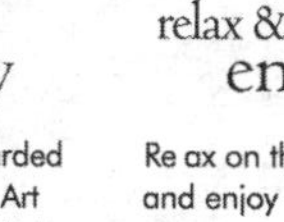
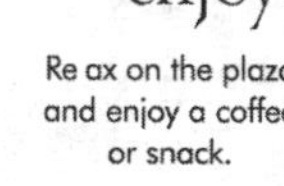

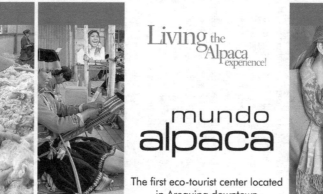

**Edson Zuñiga Huillca**, Mercado Rosaspata, Jr Abel Landeo P-1, T084-802831, T993-7243 (mob). 3 mins from Plaza de Armas, for repair of camping equipment and footwear, also equipment rental, open 24 hrs a day, 7 days a week, English and Italian spoken.
**Soqllaq'asa Camping Service**, Plateros 365 No 2F, T084-252560. Owned by English-speaking Sra Luzmila Bellota Miranda. Good for equipment hire: down sleeping bags; gas stoves; ThermaRest mats. Pots, pans, plates, cups and cutlery are provided free by the friendly staff. Also buys and sells camping gear and makes alpaca jackets. Mon-Sat 0900-1300, 1600-2030, Sun 1800-2030.
**Tatoo**, C del Medio 130, T084-254211, tatoocusco@terandes.com. High-quality hiking, climbing and camping gear, not cheap, European prices in fact, but western brand names: Colombia, Gore-Tex, Polartec, etc. The house brand, Tatoo, produces good trousers, thermals, fleeces and jackets. Imported hiking boots. Another branch in the Larcomar shopping centre in Lima.



## Food

**Casa Ecológica Cusco**, Triunfo 393, www.casaecologicacusco.com. Organic foods, wild honey, coffee, granola. Also natural medicines, indigenous art and weavings. They claim to pay fair prices when dealing with local suppliers.
**La Cholita**, Portal Espinar 142-B and at airport. Extra-special chocolates made with local ingredients.

## Markets

**San Jerónimo**, just out of town (see page 196), is the location of the wholesale Sat morning fruit and vegetable market. Porters struggle past carrying heavy loads and there is a huge array of colourful fruit and vegetables, as well as *campesinos* in for the day to sell their produce and wares. Get there for 0800, but be aware that 'gringos' stick out like a sore thumb so take no valuables.

Food that's just as good, washed and not much more expensive can be bought at the markets in **Wanchac**, Av Garcilaso (not to be confused with C Garcilaso), or **Santa Ana**, opposite Estación San Pedro, which sells a variety of goods. The best prices are at closing time or in the rain. Take care after dark. Sacks to cover rucksacks are available in the market for US$0.75. Both Wanchac and Santa Ana are open every day from 0700.

Just down from **Santiago Church** (unsafe area at night) is a sprawling area of stalls laid out on the pavements. Everything from stolen car jacks to useless junk is for sale – well, would you have use for the arm of a doll or a broken-off piece of computer motherboard? To buy back your stolen camera, visit the Santiago area of Cuzco on Sat morning. It's a fascinating sight – just be sensible and leave the other camera at home.

The second less-legitimate market – but also tolerated by Cuzqueño authorities – is **El Molino**, under the Puente Grau, which sells contraband imported goods brought in without duty or tax being paid. Everything from computers to personal stereos to trekking boots, pirated CDs and DVDs, cheap camera film and wine can be bought here (take a taxi for US$0.60). It is clean and safe (but take the usual precautions about valuables) and is open daily 0600-2030.

On Sat mornings you may see small plazas around the city with furniture markets where beds and wardrobes are sold at a fraction of the store price. **Plaza Túpac Amaru** doubles this up with a flower market, running from around 1000.

## Supermarkets

**La Canasta**, Av La Cultura 2000 block. Very well stocked, takes credit cards, ATM outside.
**D'Dinos Market**, Av La Cultura 2003, T084-252656 for home delivery. Open 24-hrs, well supplied, takes credit cards.
**Gato's Market**, Portal Belén 115.
**Mega Market**, Matará 271 y Av Garcilaso at Plaza Túpac Amaru, US style.

# Activities and tours

There are a million and one tour operators in Cuzco, most of which are packed into the Plaza de Armas. The sheer number and variety of tours on offer is bewildering and prices for the same tour can vary dramatically. Do not deal with guides who claim to be employed by the agencies listed below without verifying their credentials. You should only deal directly with the agencies and seek advice from visitors returning from trips for the latest information. Most agencies offer 4-hr city tours, US$7; to avoid disappointment, check that the tour offers a good selection of sites and that the guide is experienced.

Agencies listed below are included under the field in which they are best known and for which they receive consistent recommendations. Many of these, and the alternatives they offer, can be found in the trip reports in the **South America Explorers'** clubhouse at Choquechaca 188 #4, www.saexplorers.org. You must join first – it's great value and an excellent source of information. Beware also of tours which stop for long lunches at expensive hotels.

Ask questions such as: what is the itinerary? How many meals a day are there? What will the food be? Does the guide speak English (some have no more than a memorized spiel and every ruin is a 'sacred special place')? In general also beware of agencies quoting prices in dollars then converting to soles at an unfavourable rate when it's time to pay (see page 43 on price rises). Check if there are cancellation fees. Students will normally receive a discount on production of an ISIC card.

## Inca Trail and general tours

It is not possible to trek the Inca Trail independently following regulations brought in at the beginning of 2001. Spaces on the Inca Trail are limited to 500 per day (including porters, guides and cooks), and spaces sell out quickly, especially in the high season; this means that booking at least 2 months in advance is essential (see page 160). Alternative Inca Trail routes, such as Santa Teresa and the High Inca Trail treks (see pages 166 and 168) are also being subject to permits and limits on numbers, so it's worth checking with some of the agencies listed below in advance of you're trip. These factors, combined with Machu Picchu winning a place in the 'New 7 Wonders of the World' awards, have meant rapidly rising prices. Prices given below were valid at the time of going to press, but cannot be guaranteed to hold into 2008.

**Amazing Peru**, C Yepez Miranda, C-6, Magisterio, T084-224644 (9 Alma Rd, Manchester M19 2FG, T0808 2346805), www.amazing peru.com. Professional and well organized, "perfect tour", knowledgeable guides.

**Amazon Trails Peru**, C Tandapata 660, San Blas, T084-437499, www.amazontrails peru.com. German speaking guides and family orientated. See also page 112.

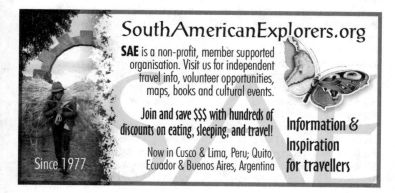

**Andina Travel**, Plazoleta Santa Catalina 219, T084-251892, www.andinatravel.com. Agency specializing in trekking and biking. Prices are dependent on group numbers – latest prices are always available on the website. Among treks offered are Salkantay and the Inca Trail, 7 days, US$750 for 4 people, and the Ausangate Circuit, 6 nights, US$430 for 6-12 people. One of the company's specialities is the Lares Valley programme, which works together with

## Choosing a tour operator for the Inca Trail

To choose a tour group, start first with the price. If the cost is under US$350, then you should be concerned. Bear in mind that the company has to pay for your permit and entry to Machu Picchu, US$120, and the train fare back (US$73 for the full Backpacker fare from Cuzco, US$57 from Ollantaytambo), plus supply food and equipment. If they're cutting costs this means that something has to give and usually this is the salary of the guides and porters (see page 164). However, you won't always get what you pay for. Agencies often pool their clients together to create commercially viable groups and trekkers can find, en route, that they paid hundreds of dollars more than others.

Ask the tour agencies some general questions and, if you're lucky, get them to put their answers in writing. Then, if you have a complaint, you can take it to Indecopi (see pages 50 and 60) on your return and seek compensation. As well as the questions listed below, also ask if there's a toilet and dining tent (if this concerns you); if they carry a first aid kit which must (under the new regulations) include an oxygen bottle; do they carry radios; and, most of all, does the price include the return train ticket? There are ATMs in Aguas Calientes, but the ticket should be included. Check also if the train takes you back all the way. The budget tour companies buy the cheapest ticket back to Ollantaytambo and from there put you on a bus. This does, in fact, shave an hour off the 4½-hr return journey, but many are expected to find a bus seat and stump up the US$2.85 bus fare. This should be part of the deal. Ask to see the equipment if possible (it has been known for tent pegs to be missing!), otherwise ask what tents they supply (some leak – this is the most frequent complaint we hear of). How good is the sleeping mat and sleeping bag (you need a down bag – Paluma), if these are supplied?



some of the valley's traditional weaving communities and provides employment for village residents – many trekking variations are possible in this area; 4 days/3 nights with 3 people, US$405. Recommended.

**Apu Expediciones**, T084-969 8311, www.geocities.com/TheTropics/Cabana/4037/. Operator with many years of experience in adventure and cultural travel. Deals with customers mostly online.

**Big Foot**, Triunfo 392 (oficina 213), T084-991 3851, www.bigfootcusco.com. Specialists in tailor-made hiking trips, especially in the remote corners of the Vilcabamba and Vilcanota mountains. They can arrange Inca Trail, Salkantay and Ausangate hikes. Prices depend on the routes taken and group size; give them a call or check the website.

**Ch'aska**, Plateros 325, 2nd floor, T084-240424, www.chaskatours.com. Dutch-Peruvian company offering cultural, adventure, nature and esoteric tours. They specialize in the Inca Trail, but also llama treks to Lares and 4, 5 and 9 day trips to Choquequirao and beyond.

**Cóndor Travel**, C Saphi 848-A, T084-225961, www.condortravel.com.pe (for flights diviajes@condortravel.com.pe). A high-quality, exclusive agency that will organize trips throughout Peru and the rest of the world. They have a specialized section for adventure travel and are an excellent port of call if looking for international flight tickets. They are representatives for **American Airlines, Servivensa, Avensa, Continental** and most other international airlines. They have many programmes to complement business trips and conferences.

**Destinos Turísticos**, Portal de Panes 123, oficina 101-102, Plaza de Armas, T084-228168, www.destinosturisticos

peru.com. The owner speaks Spanish, English, Dutch and Portuguese and specializes in package tours from economy to 5-star budgets. Individuals are welcome to come in for advice on booking jungle trips to renting mountain bikes. Sacred Valley tours cost US$20 excluding lunch and groups are a maximum of 20 people. Ask in advance if you require guides with specific languages. Very informative and helpful.

**Ecotrek Peru**, T084-247286, T970 4847 (mob), www.ecotrekperu.com. Scot and long-time Cuzco resident Fiona Cameron runs this environmentally friendly tour agency from her home a couple blocks from the Plaza San Blas. Ecotrek offer a wide range of adventures through their excellent website, specializing in little-visited areas such as the Pongo de Mainique and Espíritu Pampa/Vilcabamba Vieja. Fiona's partner, David Ugarte, is a mountain biking specialist, and will tailor 2-wheeled adventures from mellow day-runs to multi-day madness as required. David speaks fluent English, has a degree in tourism, and is great fun to hang out with. Contact him direct on T974 4810 (mob). Both David and Fiona pride themselves on fair treatment of local staff and communities. Tour prices (mid-range) depend on group numbers and type of service. Contact Fiona through her website or by phone and she'll give a prompt response. Fiona also manufactures a range of excellent organic soaps.

**Enigma Adventure**, Jr Clorinda Matto de Turner 100, Urb Magisterial, 1a Etapa, T084-222155, www.enigmaperu.com. Adventure tour agency run by Spaniard Silvia Rico Coll. **Enigma** has rapidly gained an excellent reputation for well-organized and innovative trekking and expeditions throughout the region. In addition to the regular Inca Trail, there are a variety of challenging alternatives; for example, a 7-day programme to the remote and beautiful Laguna Sibinacocha, nestled deep within the wilds of the Vilcanota Mountains, or a 3-night trek into the culturally rich Lares Valley. Set departures and fixed prices are offered on some routes, but on the more remote excursions prices depend on group numbers – costs are clearly explained on the website. Silvia also runs cultural tours, such as visits to traditional weaving communities or Ayahuasca therapy, and can arrange exciting climbing and biking itineraries on demand.

**Explorandes**, Av Garcilaso 316-A (not to be confused with C Garcilaso in the centre), T084-238380, www.explorandes.com. Experienced high-end adventure company. Their main office is in Lima (San Fernando 320, Miraflores, T01-445 0532); however, trips can also be arranged from Cuzco. A 5-day/4-night Inca Trail costs US$625. They arrange a wide variety of mountain treks including some in Cordillera Blanca and Huayhuash further north. Also offered are single and multi-day sea kayaking trips on Lake Titicaca using professional equipment. Vast range of trips available in both Peru and Ecuador, easily booked through their well organized website. They also arrange specialist tours across Peru for lovers of orchids, ceramics or textiles. Award-winning environmental practices.

**Flamenco Travels**, Portal de Confiturias 265, oficina 3, info@ponyexpeditions.com. Associated with **Pony's Expeditions** of Caraz (Cordillera Blanca). They run the Classic Inka

Trail pooled trek at budget end prices, with daily departures (average of 8-10 people). Also the 5-day Salkantay trek.

**Gatur Cusco**, Puluchapata 140 (a small street off Av Sol 3rd block), T084-223496, www.gaturcusco.com. Esoteric, ecotourism, and general tours. Owner Dr José (Pepe) Altamirano is knowledgeable about Andean folk traditions. Excellent conventional tours, bilingual guides and transport. City tour, including visits to sites outside the city proper – Qenqo, Tambomachay, Puca Pacara and Sacsayhuaman US$37.50 (good for visitors with limited time; remember that the BTG entry ticket is not included), Sacred Valley US$24, includes lunch. They also run a 1-day 1st-class train excursion to Machu Picchu with lunch in the **Machu Picchu Sanctuary Lodge Hotel**. Guides speak English, French, Spanish and German. They can also book internal flights.

**Hiking Peru**, Portal de Panes 109, office 6, T084-247942, T965-1414 (mob), www.hikingperu.com. Options include 8-day treks to Espíritu Pampa; 7 days/6 nights around Ausangate; 4-day/3-night Lares Valley Trek.

**Inca Explorers**, Ruinas 427, T084-241070, www.incaexplorers.com. Specialist trekking agency with a good reputation for small group expeditions executed in a socially and environmentally responsible manner. They offer 4-day/ 3-night Inca Trail US$379, while more demanding, adventurous trips include a 2-week hike in the Cordillera Vilcanota (passing Nevado Ausangate), based on a group of 10, and Choquequirao to Espíritu Pampa, again for 2 weeks.

**Liz's Explorer**, Medio 114B, T084-246619, www.lizexplorer.com. Inca Trail 4-day/ 3-night US$385 (minimum group size 10, maximum 16), other lengths of trips available including 1 day for US$110. Liz gives a clearly laid-out list of what is and what is not included. Down and fibre sleeping bags can be hired. If you need a guide who speaks a language other than English let her know in advance. Also city tours (entry fees not included) and Sacred Valley (not including lunch). The majority of reports are good.

**Machete Tours**, Tecseccocha 161, T084-224829, T963-1662 (mob), info@machetetours.com. Founded by born-and-bred jungle hand Ronaldo and his Danish partner Tina, Machete was originally a specialist Manu operator for budget clients (to the cultural zone), but now includes many innovative trekking trips. Especially recommended is a complete 9-day traverse of the Cordillera Vilcabamba from the Apurímac Canyon and Choquequirao across the range to Machu Picchu itself. They also offer expeditions to Espíritu Pampa, Ausangate and, of course, the Inca Trail. They also have a rainforest lodge on the remote Río Blanco, south of the Manu Biosphere Reserve and have set up a series of camps deep in the forest. These jungle trips are focused more on hiking and rustic 'adventure' than those of the classic Manu operators. Not all of the guides speak English so check this before trip details are confirmed. Eric is a recommended guide for Choquequirao.

**Perú Etico**, Matará 437, T084-232069, www.peruetico.com. Part of the Italian/Peruvian family company that includes the **Piccola Locanda** (see Sleeping, above) and the **Osteria della Locanda** restaurant. Good reports, and a clearly stated quota of the tour cost goes towards their children's projects in Huaro and Urubamba, projects that are often visited on the tours.

**Peru Treks and Adventures**, Garcilaso 265 oficina 11 (2nd floor), T084-505863, www.perutreks.com. Set up by Englishman Mike Weston and his wife Koqui González. They pride themselves on good treatment of porters and support staff and have been consistently recommended for their professionalism and standard of customer care. Treks offered include Salkantay, the Lares Valley and Vilcabamba Vieja. Prices depend on group size. Mike also runs the **Andean Travel Web**, www.andeantravelweb.com, with a focus on sustainable tourism in the region.

**Peruvian Andean Treks**, Av Pardo 705, T084-225701, www.andeantreks.com. Mon-Fri 0900-1300, 1500-1800, Sat 0900-1300. Manager Tom Hendrickson has 5-day/4-night Inca Trail using high-quality equipment and satellite phones. His 7-day/ 6-night Vilcanota Llama Trek to Ausangate includes a collapsible pressure chamber for altitude sickness. Tom also organizes interesting extended trekking itineraries, for example an 18-day trip connecting Machu Picchu, Vitcos and Choquequirao.

**Q'ente**, Choquechaca 229, p 2, T084-233722, www.qente.com. Their Inca Trail service is recommended. They will organize private treks to Salkantay, Ausangate, Choquequirao, Vilcabamba and Q'eros. Prices depend on group size. Sacred Valley tours US$20, also day tours to Piquillacta and Tipón, and Moras and Moray, enquire for prices. Horse riding to local ruins costs US$35 for 4-5 hrs. Very good, especially with children.

**SAS Travel**, Portal de Panes 143, T084-237292/249194, www.sastravel peru.com. Discount for SAE members and students. Inca Trail 4-day/3-night US$400 excludes sleeping bags (can rent down bags for US$15), the bus down from Machu Picchu to Aguas Calientes and lunch on the last day. SAS have their own hostel in Aguas Calientes – if clients wish to stay in Aguas after the trail and return the next morning this can be arranged. SAS offer a variety of alternatives to the classic Inca Trail, including a good 5-day/4-night route via Salkantay and Santa Teresa. Group sizes are between 8 and 16 people. To go in a smaller group, costs rise considerably. A personal porter costs US$40 for up to 9 kg carried and US$80 for up to 18 kg. They carry a cooking, dining and toilet tent. Before setting off they ensure you are told everything that is included and give advice on what personal items should be taken. Manu 8-day/7-night US$870, combination of platform camping and lodges. Also mountain biking, horse riding and rafting trips can be organized. All guides speak English (some better than others). They can book internal flights at much cheaper rates than booking from overseas. SAS have a solid reputation for good equipment, guiding and excellent food on the trail, although some recent reports on organization have been mixed.

**Sky Travel**, Santa Catalina Ancha 366, interior 3-C (down alleyway next to Rosie O'Grady's

pub), T084-261818, www.skyperu.com. English spoken. General tours around city (US$8, not including entry tickets) and Sacred Valley (US$18 including buffet lunch). Prides itself on leaving 30 mins before other groups, thus reaching sights and the lunch spot (!) before anyone else. 4-day/3-night Inca Trail uses good-sized double tents and a dinner tent. The group is also asked what it would like on the menu 2 days before departure. Other trips include Vilcabamba and Ausangate (trekking only).
**Tambo Tours**, 4405 Spring Cypress Rd Suite #210, Spring, TX, 77388, USA, T1-888-2-GO-PERU (246-7378), T+1-281 528 9448, www.2GOPERU.com. Long-established adventure and tour specialist with 20 years' experience in Peru, with offices in Peru and the USA. Customized trips for families, individuals and groups to the Amazon and archaeological sites.
**Trekperu**, Ricaldo Palma N-9, Santa Mónica, T084-252899, www.trekperu.com. Experienced trek operator as well as other adventure sports and mountain biking. Offers 'culturally sensitive' tours. 5-day/4-night Cuzco Biking Adventure visits Tipón ruins, Huacarpa Lake, Ninamarca burial towers, Paucartambo, Tres Cruces (superb views over Manu) as well as Pisac and Cuzco. Includes support vehicle and good camping gear. Sleeping bag needed.
**United Mice**, Plateros 351 y Triunfo 392, T084-221139, www.unitedmice.com. A company with 15 years' experience. They offer the Inca Trail, 4 days/3 nights, and Salkantay, Choquequirao, Espíritu Pampa and Ausangate treks. Good English-speaking guides; Salustio speaks Italian and Portuguese. Discount with student card, good food and equipment. They also run rafting and mountain biking tours.
**Wayki Trek**, Procuradores 351, 2nd floor, T084-224092, www.waykitrek.net. Budget travel agency, recommended for their Inca Trail service 4 days/3 nights. Owner Leo grew up in the countryside near Ollantaytambo and knows the area very well. They run treks to several almost unknown Inca sites including Quillarumiyoc, described as a structure for mapping the lunar year. Leo offers many interesting variations on the 'classic' Inca Trail and runs a programme where clients can visit porters' communities before starting treks, hopefully resulting in a deeper cultural understanding for both parties. Wayki also run treks to Ausangate, Salkantay and Choquequirao.

## Adventure tours

### River rafting, mountain biking and trekking

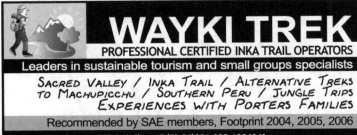

When looking for an operator please consider more than just the tour price. Competition between companies in Cuzco is intense and price wars can lead to compromises on safety as corners are cut or less experienced (and therefore cheaper) guides are hired. Consider the quality of safety equipment (life jackets, etc) and the number and experience of rescue kayakers and support staff. On a large and potentially dangerous river like the Apurímac (where fatalities have occurred), this can make all the difference. Much of the advice given on page 104 also applies here. See also pages 14-21.
**Amazonas Explorer**, Av Collasuyo 910, Miravalle, PO Box 722, T084-252846,

T084-976 5448 (mob), www.amazonas-explorer.com. Experts in rafting, hiking and biking; used by BBC. English owner Paul Cripps has great experience, but takes most bookings from overseas (in UK, T01437-891743). However, he may be able to arrange a trip for travellers in Cuzco. Rafting includes Río Apurímac and Río Tambopata including Lake Titicaca and Cuzco, with all transfers from Lima. Also 5-day/4-night Inca Trail trip of the highest quality, and alternatives to the Inca Trail and Choquequirao to Vitcos. Amazonas offer an excellent variation of the Ausangate Circuit, featuring an extension to the little visited Laguna Singrenacocha and an opportunity for ice-climbers to tackle the remote Campa Peak with experienced guides. Multi-activity and family trips are a speciality, catering for all ages, but juniors in particular. All options are at the higher end of the market and are highly recommended.

**Apumayo**, Av Garcilaso 316, Wanchaq, T084-246018, www.apumayo.com. Mon-Sat 0900-1300, 1600-2000. Urubamba rafting (from 0800-1530 every day) and 3- to 4-day Apurímac trips. Also mountain biking, eg full day trip to Maras and Moray in Sacred Valley, or 5-day epic biking adventure from Cuzco to the jungle town of Quillabamba. They also offer the 4-day/ 3-night standard Inca Trail. This company also offers tours for people with disabilities, including rafting.

**Camp Expeditions**, Av Manco Capac 414, of 403, T084-431468, www.campexpedition.net. All sorts of adventure tours, but specialists in climbing – recommended as the most reliable – and trekking.

**Eric Adventures**, Velasco Astete B-8-B, T084-234764, www.ericadventures.com. Specialize in adventure activities. They clearly explain what equipment is included in their prices and what you will need to bring. Rafting 1-day Río Urubamba, Class III from Jun-Dec, Class IV-V rest of year, US$35; 3-day/2-night Apurímac Canyon Class IV-V in high season (not viable in the low season) US$330; kayak course 3-day/2-night US$190; canyoning, Level 1 initiation course, 1-day, US$75; hydrospeed, 1-day in Río Urubamba Class II-III; mountain biking to Maras and Moray, 1-day, US$55; Inca Trail to Machu Picchu, 4-day/3-night, from US$490. Many other activities available. They also rent motorbikes for US$70-90 (guide is extra) and cars. Prices are more expensive if you book by email, you can get huge discounts if you book in the office. A popular company.

**Land of the Inkas**, Av de la Cultura 1318, Wanchaq, T084-233451, www.landofthe inkas.com. Run by the very experienced Juan and Benjamín Muñiz, this company now largely operates through web-based bookings, arranging both multi-week expeditions and shorter adventures for those already on the ground in the Cuzco area. For many years a rafting specialist, Instinct now offers activities as diverse as surf safaris on Peru's north coast and multi-day horseriding tours in the Sacred Valley.

**Mayuc Expediciones**, Portal Confiturías 211, Plaza de Armas, T084-242824, www.mayuc.com. One of the longest-running river-rafting adventure companies in Cuzco. Rafting 1-day Río Urubamba Class III US$27; 3-day/2-night Río Apurímac Class III-V US$180, 9-day/8-night Tambopata-Cadamo jungle expedition Class III-IV US$1197 (4-6 people), US$997 (7 or more people). Fixed departures are on the 1st and 3rd Sun of every month May-Nov. Mayuc now have a permanent lodge, **Casa Cusi**, on the upper Urubamba, which forms the basis of 2-day, Class III-IV trips in the area. **Casa Cusi** certainly makes a night on the Urubamba fairly comfortable but the real highlight is the on-location sauna to warm you up after a hard day on the river. Other tours include Inca Trail 4-day/3-night premium service US$467 (4-7 people); they also offer an alternative route into Machu Picchu via Salkantay 6-day/5-day and many other adventure trips.

**Medina Brothers**, contact Christian or Alain Medina on T084-225163 or T965-3485 (mob). Friendly family-run rafting company with good equipment and plenty of experience. They usually focus on day rafting trips in the Sacred Valley, but services are tailored to the needs of the client. Reasonable prices dependent on client numbers. Recommended.

**River Explorers & Peru Treks Explorers**, Plateros 328, T084-260926 or T993 9883, T990 9249 (mob), www.riverexplorers.com. A new adventure company in Cuzco, offering mountain biking, trekking and rafting trips (on the Apurímac and Urubamba).

Experienced and qualified guides and, so far, seem to present a good emphasis on safety and environmental awareness. Apurímac Rafting Trips from US$300.

**Swissraft-Peru**, Plateros 361, T084-264124, www.swissraft-peru.com. This company has professionally run tours on the Apurímac and Urubamba rivers, with the focus above all on safety. Equipment is new and of good quality. 4-day expeditions on the Apurímac will cost US$250.

**Terra Explorer Peru**, T084-237352, www.terraexplorerperu.com. Offers a wide range of trips from high-end rafting in the Sacred Valley and expeditions to the Colca and Cotahuasi canyons, trekking the Inca Trail and others, mountain biking, kayaking (including on Lake Titicaca) and jungle trips. All guides are bilingual.



### Paragliding and ballooning

**Cloud Walker Paragliding**, T084-993 7333 (mob), www.cloudwalkerparagliding.com. Richard Pethigal offers a condor's-eye view of the Sacred Valley. From May-Sep he runs half-day tandem paraglider flights from Cuzco. He is a very experienced, licensed pilot and uses high-quality equipment. Be aware that the Sacred Valley offers exciting but challenging paragliding so, if wind conditions are bad, flights may be delayed till the following day. Magnificent scenery, soaring close to snow-capped mountains makes this an awesome experience. The standard cost is US$70 but, if weather conditions are good, he can fly you all the way back to Cuzco, via the ruins of Sacsayhuaman above the city, for US$120.

**Globos de los Andes**, Av de la Cultura 220, suite 36, T084-232352, www.globosperu.com. Hot air ballooning in the Sacred Valley, and expeditions with balloons and 4WD lasting several days.

## Jungle tours

### Manu Biosphere Reserve *p231*

For Manu you're unlikely to go wrong. The pristine reserve area within the park (where hunting is prohibited) is worked by only 9 licensed operators. Those which have received favourable reports are listed below. If any other agency is offering Manu, they will be taking you only to the cultural area within the park, which receives less protection and therefore it's tougher to spot wildlife. If you see Manu promoted in the many agencies along Plateros for US$300-400, it will be a trip to the cultural zone – whatever they tell you. This doesn't mean you are in for a bad trip but the destination and the experience will not be the same.

**Amazon Trails Peru**, C Tandapata 660, San Blas, T084-437499, T974 1735 (mob), www.amazontrailsperu.com. Small agency operated by ornithologist Abraham Huaman, who has many years' experience guiding in the region, and his German wife Ulla Maennig. Mainly offers itineraries in the buffer zones surrounding Manu, including the Amarakaeri Reserved Zone and Blanquillo, but trips to the former reserved zone (now part of the National Park) and Casa Machiguenga are also possible. Abraham offers an adventurous itinerary involving building your own balsa raft and running the Alto Madre de Dios river to the Blanquillo Macaw Collpa. Economical rates: an 8-day/7-night trip into the former reserved zone costs US$825. Guaranteed departure dates with a minimum of 2 people.

**Bonanza Tours**, Suecia 343, T084-507871, www.bonanzatoursperu.com. 3 to 8-day tours to Manu with local guides, plenty of jungle walks, rafting, kayaking and camp-based excursions. Tours go down the Madre del Dios as far as the Blanquillo clay lick, not to the reserve area.

**Expediciones Vilca**, Plateros 359, T084-244751, www.manuvilcaperu.com. Manu jungle tours: in by bus, out by plane, 8 days/7nights US$835 (plus park fees and US$105 for return flight). Plenty of time in the reserved zone with this itinerary. Other lengths of stay are available. Will supply sleeping bags at no extra cost. Minimum 5 people, maximum 10 per guide. This is the only economical tour which stops at the Otorongo camp, which is supposedly quieter than Salvador where many agencies overnight. Clients returning to Cuzco by boat and bus stay at the **Yanayaco Lodge**, situated close to a small parrot clay lick (*collpa*). There are discounts for students and members of SAE.

**InkaNatura Travel**, Plateros 361, T084-255255, www.inkanatura.com (also in Lima at Manuel Bañón 461, San Isidro, T01-440 2022). **InkaNatura** states that it is

a non-profit organization where all proceeds are directed back into projects on sustainable tourism and conservation. It runs a variety of tours to Manu, staying in tented camp and lodges: 5-day/4-night from US$1060 andUS$1090, 7-day/6-night, US$1190, which takes you through the Andes to lowland jungle; **Sandoval Lake Lodge** in Tambopata, 4-day/3-night, US$295-335 (2 people). Trips can get booked up months in advance so contact them early. Having said that, they guarantee departures even if they only have 1 passenger, so don't rule out booking with them once you are in Cuzco. In the office they sell copies of a book called *Peru's Amazonian Eden-Manu* for US$80, whose proceeds are invested in the projects. The same title can be found in other bookshops at a much inflated price. 10% discount on all trips for *Footprint Handbook* readers.

**Manu Ecological Adventures**, Plateros 356, T084-261640, www.manuadventures.com. This company operates one of the most physically active Manu programmes, with options for a mountain biking descent through the cloudforest and 3 hrs of white-water rafting on the way to **Erika Lodge** on the upper Río Madre de Dios. They operate with a minimum of 4 people and a maximum of 10 people per guide. With a minimum of 8 people they will run specialized programmes.

**Manu Expeditions**, C Humberto Vidal Unda G-5, p 2, Urb Magisterial, T084-226671, www.manuexpeditions.com. English spoken, Mon-Fri 0900-1300, 1530-1900; Sat 0900-1300. Owned by ornithologist and British Consul Barry Walker of the **Cross Keys Pub**. Three trips available: US$1810, 9-day/8-night (leaves Sun), visits reserve and Manu Wildlife Centre; US$1410, 6-day/5-night (leaves Sun), takes passengers to the reserve only and US$1110, 4-day/3-night (leaves Fri), goes only to wildlife centre. The first two trips visit a lodge run by Machiguenga people on the first Sun of every month. Also tailor-made birdwatching trips in cloud and rainforest, horse riding and a 9-day /8-night trip to Machu Picchu along a different route from the Inca Trail, rejoining at Sun Gate. Barry runs horse-supported treks to Choquequirao, starting at Huancacalle. Highly recommended.

**Manu Nature Tours**, Av Pardo 1046, T084-252721, www.manuperu.com. Owned by Boris Gómez Luna, with over 20 years experience. English spoken. This company aims more for the luxury end of the market and owns 2 comfortable lodges in the cloud forest and reserved zone. Tours are very much based around these sites, thus entailing less travel between different areas. The standard tours do not include a visit to the Blanquillo Macaw Lick, preferring instead to focus on the macaw colonies close to the **Manu Lodge**. The lodge has an extensive trail system and also offers canopy climbing for an additional US$45 per person. In the cloud forest zone a novel 'Llama Taxi' service is offered, in conjunction with the local community of Jajahuana. An 8-day/7-night tour staying at both lodges costs US$1980 (for 2 or more clients); 4-day/3-night to **Manu Lodge** US$981; 3-day/2-night at **Manu Cloud Forest Lodge** US$498. Extensions to the Blanquillo Macaw Lick cost US$250.

**Oropéndola Tours**, Calle 7 Cuartones, 284 interior 3-D, T084-241428, 968 5990 (mob), www.oropendolaperu.org. English-, Spanish- and Japanese-speaking guides specializing in Manu National Park, birdwatching, nature and cultural experience tours. Guide Walter Mancilla is an expert on flora and fauna. Uses lodges run by indigenous communities. Good reports of attention to detail and to the needs of clients.

**Pantiacolla Tours**, C Saphy 554, T084-238323, www.pantiacolla.com. Manu jungle tours: 5-day, €585 per person; 7-day, €635 per person; 9-day €605 per person. The 5- and 7-day trips include return flights, the 9-day trip is an overland return. Prices do not include US$50 park entrance fee. 9-day trips include a night at **Pantiacolla Lodge**, nestled beneath the mountains of the same name. The lodge boasts an excellent trail system in the transition zone between montane and lowland ecosystems. Guaranteed departure dates regardless of number, maximum 10 people per guide. The trips involve a combination of camping, platform camping and lodges. All clients are given a booklet entitled, *Talking About Manu*, written by the Dutch owner, Marianne van Vlaardingen, a biologist who studied Tamarin monkeys at the Cocha Cashu biological station within Manu. She is

extremely friendly and helpful. Marianne and her Peruvian husband Gustavo Moscoso have recently opened an ecotourism lodge in conjunction with the Yine native community of Diamante. The lodge is a base for cultural tours in the area and will eventually (the project runs for 10 years) be independently owned and managed by the village. Yine guides are used and community members are being trained in the various aspects of running the project.

**Tambopata National Reserve** *p240*
For Tambopata the picture is not so clear because operators do not have to be licensed. However, the market does not appear to be unscrupulous in the manner of the Inca Trail firms. Use one of the firms listed here, ask the right questions and you should be fine.
From the list above, contact **Explorandes**, **Mayuc** and **InkaNatura**. In Lima, see **Peruvian Safaris**.
**Rainforest Expeditions**, Portal de Carnes 236, Plaza de Armas, T084-246243,

www.perunature.com. This company has developed an excellent reputation for their Tambopata services. They own 3 lodges on the Río Tambopata. **Posada Amazonas**, close to Puerto Maldonado, is run in conjunction with local community of Infierno. Several of the guides are community members. Further upriver is the **Refugio Amazonas**, and further still, in an area of pristine primary forest, is the **Tambopata Research Center**, situated next to the area's famed Macaw Lick. Due to its remote location this is superb area for observing rainforest wildlife, including large mammals. They also have an office in Lima, C Aramburu 166-4B, Lima 18, T01-421 8347.



## Conservation

**The Condor Lodge**, Nueva Alta 432-A, T084-221287, www.thecondorlodge.com. Multidisciplinary organization dedicated to the preservation of the condor and other species. Offers 2 and 3-day tours to the Apurímac canyon to look for condors, with riding, trekking, fishing, visits to ruins and hot springs. Recommended.

## Cultural tours

**Milla Tourism**, Av Pardo 689 and Portal Comercio 195 on the plaza, T084-234181, www.millaturismo.com. Mon-Fri 0800-1300, 1500-1900, Sat 0800-1300. Mystical tours to Cuzco's Inca ceremonial sites such as Pumamarca and The Temple of the Moon. Guide speaks only basic English. Prices depend on group numbers; quotes through the website. They also arrange cultural and environmental lectures and courses.
**Mystic Inca Trail**, Unidad Vecinal de Santiago, bloque 9, dpto 301, T084-221358, ivanndp@terra.com.pe. Specialize in tours of sacred Inca sites and study of Andean spirituality. This takes 10 days but it is possible to have shorter 'experiences'.

### Shamans and drug experiences

San Pedro and Ayahuasca have been used since before Inca times, mostly as a sacred healing experience. The plants are prepared with special treatments for curative purposes; they have never been considered a drug. If you choose to experience these incredible healing/teaching plants, only do so under the guidance of a reputable agency or shaman and always have a friend with you who is not partaking. If the medicine is not prepared correctly, it can be highly toxic and, in rare cases, severely dangerous. Never buy from someone who is not recommended, never buy off the streets and never try to prepare the plants yourself. We suggest the following, whom we know to be legitimate:
**Another Planet**, Triunfo 120, T084-229379, www.anotherplanetperu.net. Run by Lesley Myburgh (who also runs **Casa de La Gringa**, Pasñapacana y Tandapata 148, San Blas, T241168, 965 2006 (mob), sleeping in **E** range), who operates all kinds of adventure tours and conventional tours in and around Cuzco, but specializes in jungle trips anywhere in Peru. Lesley is an expert in San Pedro cactus preparation and she arranges San Pedro journeys for healing at physical, emotional and spiritual levels in beautiful remote areas.
**Eleana Molina**, T084-975 1791, misticanativa @yahoo.com. For Ayahuasca ceremonies.

## Private guides

All of those listed are bilingual. Set prices: City tour US$15-20 per day; Urubamba/ Sacred Valley US$25-30, Machu Picchu and other ruins US$40-50 per day. **Leap Local**, www.leaplocal.org, is a good website that recommends good quality local guides.

### Classic standard tours

**Boris Cárdenas**, boriscar@telser.com.pe. Esoteric and cultural tours.
**José Cuba and Alejandra Cuba**, Urb Santa Rosa R Gibaja 182, T084-226179, T968-5187 (mob), ale17ch1@yahoo.com. Both speak English, Alejandra speaks German and French, very good tours.
**Percy Salas Alfaro**, c/o Munditur, T084-2402887, T962-1152 (mob), smunditur@hotmail.com. Serious, friendly.
**Victoria Morales Condori**, San Juan de Dios 229, T084-235204.

### Adventure trips

**Carlos Gutierrez V**, carloshuascaran@ hotmail.com. A qualified (VIAGM) and recommended mountain guide, based in Huaraz (central Peru), but available for climbs in the Southern Cordilleras.

**David Ugarte**, T084-247286, T974-4810 (mob). Specialist in mountain biking and trekking, contact through **Ecotrek Perú** (see above).
**Miguel Angel Jove Mamari**, T084-979 2227 (mob), miguelJ24@hotmail.com. Also rents and sells camping equipment. Best contacted by phone or email or through SAE in Cuzco.
**Roger Valencia Espinoza**, José Gabriel Cosio 307, T084-251278, vroger@qenqo.rcp.net.pe.

# Transport

## Air

See also Getting around, page 23, and Lima transport, page 278.

### Airline offices

**Aero Cóndor**, at the airport, T084-252774. **Lan**, Av Sol 627-B, T084-225552. **Star Perú**, Av Sol 679, of 1, T084-234060. **Taca**, Av Sol 602, T084-249921, good service.

## Bus

### Local

**El Tranvía de Cusco** is actually a motor coach which runs on the route of the original Cuzco tramway system which operated from 1910-1940. The route starts in the Plaza de Armas (except on Sun morning when the weekly flag ceremony takes place) and ends at the Sacsayhuaman Archaeological Park. There is a 10-min stop at the *mirador* by the Cristo Blanco before descending to the Plaza de Armas. Departures 1000, 1150 and 1500, 1 hr 20 mins, with explanations of the city's history, architecture, customs, etc; US$2, US$1.40 for students with ID. For group reservations, T084-740640.

### Long distance

The bus terminal, **Terminal Terrestre**, is on Prolongación Pachacútec. All direct buses to **Lima** go via **Abancay** (Department of Apurímac, 195 km, 5 hrs or longer in the rainy season, US$3.65), and **Nazca** (Department of Ica, US$17-20), on the Panamerican Highway, reaching Lima after about 25 hrs, US$20-31.25 (**Wari** fares) to US$37 (**Cruz del Sur**, *Imperial* class) and US$47-57 (**Cruz del Sur**, *Cruzero* regular and *VIP* classes). **Ormeño**'s *Royal* class costs US$55. This route is paved, however floods in the wet season often damage large sections of the highway. If prone to car sickness, be prepared on the road to Abancay, there are many, many curves, but the scenery is magnificent (it also happens to be a great route for cycling). At Abancay, the road forks, the other branch going to **Andahuaylas**, a further 138 km, 10-11 hrs from Cuzco, US$6, and **Ayacucho** in the Central Highlands, another 261 km, 20 hrs from Cuzco, US$12. On both routes at night, take a blanket or sleeping bag to ward off the cold.

**Molina**, who also has an office at Av Pachacútec, just past the railway station, has buses on both routes. It runs 3 services a day to **Lima** via **Abancay** and **Nazca**, and one, at 1900, to **Abancay** and **Andahuaylas**. **Wari** has 6 departures daily to **Abancay**, **Nazca** and **Lima**. **Cruz del Sur**'s cheaper *Imperial* service leaves once a day to **Lima** via **Abancay**, while their more comfortable *Cruzero* service departs once or twice daily. **San Jerónimo** and **Los Chankas** have buses to **Abancay**, **Andahuaylas** and **Ayacucho**, **San Jerónimo** at 1830. **Turismo Ampay**, **Turismo Abancay**, **Expreso Huamanga** and **Bredde** all have buses daily to Abancay.

**Lake Titicaca and Bolivia** To **Juliaca**, 344 km, 5-6 hrs, US$3-4, the road is fully paved, but after heavy rain buses may not run. To **Puno**, 44 km from Juliaca, US$4.50-6; there is a good service with **Ormeño** at 0900, US$10, 6 hrs. This service continues to **La Paz**, Bolivia. **First Class**, Av Sol 930, have a service at 0800, calling at Andahuaylillas church, Raqchi, La Raya and Pucará, US$25. Travel agencies sell this ticket. Other services are run by **Tour Perú** and **Libertad** (at night), US$8.60, 6½-8 hrs. **Note** We've received many reports of robbery on night buses on the Juliaca–Puno–Cuzco route; travel by day, or by train.

To **Arequipa**, 521 km, Cruz del Sur use the direct paved route via **Juliaca** and have a *Cruzero* service at 2030, 10 hrs, US$23. Other buses join the new Juliaca-Arequipa road at Imata, 10-12 hrs, US$7.75 (eg **Carhuamayo**, 3 a day).

For bus services to other destinations, see the Transport section of the relevant chapter.

## Car

**Avis**, Av El Sol 808 and at the airport, T084-248800, avis-cusco@terra.com.pe. **Touring y Automóvil Club del Perú**, Av Sol 349, T084-224561, www.touringperu.com.pe. A good source of information on motoring, car hire and mechanics (membership is US$45 per year).

## Combi and taxi

### Local

**Combis** run from 0500 to 2200 or 2300, US$0.15. Combis run to all parts of the city, including the bus and train stations and the airport, but are not allowed within 2 blocks of the Plaza de Armas. Stops are signed and the driver's assistant calls out the names of stops. By law all passengers are insured. After 2200 combis may not run their full route; demand to be taken to your stop, or better still, use a taxi late at night.

**Taxis** have fixed prices: in the centre US$0.60 (50% more after 2100 or 2200); and to the suburbs US$0.85-1.55 (touts at the airport and train station will always ask much higher fares). In town it is advisable to take municipality-authorized taxis which have a blue ticket on the windscreen. Safer still are licensed taxis, which have a sticker with a number in the window and a chequerboard pattern on the sides. These taxis are summoned by phone and are more expensive, in the centre US$1-1.25 (**Ocarina** T084-247080, **Aló Cusco** T084-222222, radio taxi T084-222000).

### Long distance

Taxi trips to **Sacsayhuaman** cost US$10; to the ruins of **Tambo Machay** US$15-20 (3-4 people); a whole-day trip costs US$40-70. For US$50 a taxi can be hired for a whole day (ideally Sun) to take you to **Chinchero**, **Maras**, **Urubamba**, **Ollantaytambo**, **Calca**, **Lamay**, **Coya**, **Pisac**, **Tambo Machay**, **Qenqo** and **Sacsayhuaman**.

## Cycle

For tours and mountain biking, see page 110. **Team Bike**, Tullumayo 438, T084-224354. A shop selling good quality parts and boxes for shipping.

## Train

Details of the train services out of Cuzco can be found on www.perurail.com. For details of trains to Aguas Calientes for Machu Picchu, see page 154.

The train to **Juliaca** and **Puno** leaves at 0800, on Mon, Wed and Sat, arriving in Puno at 1730 (sit on the left for the best views). The train makes a stop to view the scenery at La Raya. Trains return from Puno on Mon, Wed and Sat at 0800, arriving in Cuzco at 1730, tourist class US$19, 1st class US$130.

Tickets can be bought up to 5 days in advance. The ticket office at Wanchac station is open Mon-Fri 0800-1700, Sat 0900-1200. Tickets sell out quickly and there are queues from 0400 before holidays in the dry season. In the low season tickets to Puno can be bought on the day of departure. You can buy tickets through a travel agent, but check the date and seat number. You will to show your passport, or a copy, to buy train tickets. Meals are served on the train. Always check whether the train is running, especially in the rainy season, when services might be cancelled.

# Directory

## Banks and money exchange

### Banks

All the banks along Av Sol have ATMs from which you can withdraw dollars or soles at any hour. Whether you use the counter or an ATM, choose your time carefully as there can be long queues at both. Most banks are closed between 1300 and 1600. **BCP**, Av Sol 189. Gives cash advances on Visa and changes TCs to soles and dollars (3% commission). It has an ATM for Visa. It also handles Amex. **Interbank**, Av Sol y Puluchapata. Charges no commission on TCs and has a Visa ATM which gives dollars as well as soles. Accepts Visa, Amex, Maestro, Cirrus, MasterCard and Plus. Next door is **Banco Continental**, also has a Visa ATM but charges up to US$4 commission on TCs. **BSCH**, Av Sol 459. Changes Amex TCs at reasonable rates. Has Red Unicard ATM for Visa/Plus and MasterCard. **Banco Latino**, Almagro 125 y Av Sol 395. Has ATMs for MasterCard. **Scotiabank**, Maruri between Pampa del Castillo and Pomeritos. Gives cash advances on MasterCard, Maestro, Cirrus and Visa in dollars. Emergency number for lost or stolen Visa cards, 0800-1330.

### ATMs

As well as the ATMs in banks (most of which have 24-hr police protection), there are others, accepting a wide range of international cards (the symbols of which are clearly displayed), on the Plaza de Armas at the entrance to Inka Grill, Portal de Panes, Incanto (Santa Catalina Angosta 135, for Citibank), Supermercado Gato's, Portal Belén, and the entrance to Cross Keys and Tunupa, Portal de Confiturías. There are other ATMs on Av la Cultura, beside Supermercado Mega and beside Supermercado La Canasta. Machines are now also appearing in the San Blas area. **Western Union** at Santa Catalina Ancha 165, T084-233727. Money transfers in 10 mins; also at **DHL**, see Post, page 122.

### Casas de cambio

Many travel agencies and *casas de cambio* change dollars. Some of them change traveller's cheques as well, and some charge 4-5% commission. There are many *cambios* on the west side of the Plaza de Armas and on the west side of Av Sol, most change TCs. **LAC Dólar**, Av Sol 150, T084-257762, Mon-Sat 0900-2000, with delivery service to central hotels, cash and TCs, is recommended. The street changers hang around Av Sol, blocks 2-3, every day. Some of them will also change TCs. Whether in banks or on the street, check the notes carefully.

## Embassies and consulates

**Belgium**, Av Sol 954, T084-221098. Mon-Fri 0900-1300, 1500-1700. **France**, Jorge Escobar, C Micaela Bastidas 101, 4th floor, T084-233610. **Germany**, Sra Maria-Sophia Júrgens de Hermoza, San Agustín 307, T084-235459, acupari@terra.com.pe. Mon-Fri, 1000-1200, appointments may be made by phone, it also has a book exchange. **Ireland**, Charlie Donovan, Santa Catalina Ancha 360 (Rosie O'Grady's), T084-243514. **Italy**, Sr Fedos Rubatto, Av Garcilaso 700, T084-224398. Mon-Fri 0900-1200, 1500-1700. **Netherlands**, Sra Marcela Alarco, Av El Sol 954, T084-224322, marcela_alarco@ yahoo.com. Mon-Fri 0900-1500. **UK**, Barry Walker, Av Pardo 895, T084-239974, bwalker@amauta.rcp.net.pe. **US Agent**, Dra Olga Villagarcía, T084-962 1369, consagentcuzco@terra.com.pe, or at the Binational Center (ICPNA), Av Tullumayo 125, T084-224112S.

## Immigration

Av Sol, block 6, close to post office, T084-222741. Mon-Fri 0800-1300. Reported as not very helpful.

## Internet

You can't walk for 5 mins in Cuzco without running into an internet café, and new places are opening all the time. Most have similar rates, around US$0.50 per hr, although if you look hard enough you can find cheaper places. The main difference between cafés is the speed of internet connection and the facilities on offer. The better places have scanners, webcams and

CD burners, among other gadgets, and staff in these establishments can be very knowledgeable. The best cafés are usually those who have most recently updated their equipment, a constantly changing situation, so trial and error is the rule of the day. Many cafés now offer international telephone calls at very reasonable rates.

## Language classes

**Academia Latinoamericana de Español**, Plaza Limacpampa 565, T084-243364, www.latinoschools.com. The same company also has schools in Ecuador (Quito) and in Bolivia (Sucre). They can arrange courses that include any combination of these locations using identical teaching methods and materials. Professionally run with experienced staff. Many activities per week, including dance lessons and excursions to sites of historical and cultural interest. Private classes US$360 for 20 hrs, groups, with a maximum of 4 students US$275, again for 20 hrs.

**Acupari**, San Agustín 307, T084-242970, www.acupari.com. The German-Peruvian Cultural Association. Spanish classes.

**Amauta Spanish School**, Suecia 480, 2nd floor, T084-241442, www.amautaspanishschool.org. Spanish classes, individual or in small groups, also Quechua classes and workshops in Peruvian cuisine, dance and music, US$10.50 per hr individual, but cheaper and possibly better value for group tuition (2-6 people), US$98 for 20 hrs. Pleasant accommodation on site, as well as a free internet café for students, and excursions. They can help find voluntary work, too. School in Urubamba and courses in the Manu rainforest, with **Pantiacolla Tours**.

**Amigos Spanish School**, Zaguán del Cielo B-23, T084-242292, www.spanishcusco.com. Profits from this school support a foundation for disadvantaged children. Private lessons for US$8 per hr, US$141 for 20 hrs of classes in a group. Homestays available.

**Cervantes**, C Camino Real Nuevo 10, Urb Fideranda, Wanchac. Reasonably priced, small school with patient teachers (Rocsana is recommended).

**Cusco Spanish School**, Garcilaso 265, oficina 6 (2nd floor), T084-226928, www.cuscospanishschool.com. US$160 for 20 hrs of private classes, cheaper in groups. School offers homestays, optional activities including dance and music classes, cookery courses, ceramics, Quechua, hiking and volunteer programmes. They also offer courses on a hacienda at Cusipata in the Vilcanota Valley, east of Cuzco.

**Excel Spanish Language Center**, Cruz Verde 336, T084-235298, www.excel-spanishlanguageprograms-peru.org. Very professional, offering private one-to-one lessons, small group courses, or homestays with one-to-one tuition.

**Fairplay Spanish School**, Choquechaca 188, No 5 (same building as **SAE**), T084-978 9252, www.fairplay-peru.org. This relatively new NGO teaches Peruvians who wouldn't normally have the opportunity (Peruvian single mothers, for example) to become Spanish teachers themselves over several months of training. The agency then acts as an agent, allowing these same teachers to find work with visiting students. Classes with these teachers cost US$4.50 or US$6 per hr, of which 33% is reinvested in the NGO, the rest going direct to the teachers. A highly recommended self-sustaining project. The organization can also arrange volunteer work and homestay programmes. **La Casona de la Esquina**, Purgatorio 345, T084-235830, www.spanishlessons.com.pe. US$122 for one-to-one classes for 20 hrs, with additional classes in salsa, cooking, or art. Several private or small group options, homestays and Quechua classes. Recommended.

**Mundo Verde Spanish School**, C Nueva Alta 432-A, T084-221287, www.mundoverdespanish.com. Spanish lessons with the option to study in the rainforest and the possibility of working on environmental and health projects while studying. Some of your money goes towards developing sustainable farming practices in the area. Works with Ecotrek and South American Explorers. US$250 for 20 hrs individual tuition with homestay.

**Peru Language Center**, T084-242562, www.perulanguage.com. Individual part-time, intensive (US$110 for 20 hrs one-to-one) and professional courses, also links classes with salsa, adventure and culture.

**San Blas Spanish School**, Tandapata 688, T084-247898, www.spanishschoolperu.com. Groups, with 4 clients maximum, US$90 for 20 hrs tuition. US$130 for the same thing one-to-one. Also arranges homestay, voluntary work and can arrange lessons in the village of Cai Cay.

**Wiracocha**, Cuesta San Blas 561, T084-242562, 967 0918 (mob), www.wirachochaschool.org. Individual tuition US$7 per hr. The emphasis is on conversation, with volunteer opportunities, accommodation, activities and cooking classes.

## Laundry

There are several cheap laundries on Procuradores, and also on Suecia and Tecseccocha. **Adonai**, C Choquechaca 216-A. Good hole-in-the-wall laundry, US$0.60 per kg for wash and dry, very friendly and usually reliable service. Small book exchange. **Dana's Laundry**, Nueva Baja y Unión. US$2.10 per kg, takes about 6 hrs. **Lavandería**, Saphi 578. Mon-Sat 0800-2000, Sun 0800-1300. Good, fast service, US$1 per kg. String markers will be attached to clothes if they have no label. **Lavandería Louis**, Choquechaca 264, San Blas. US$0.85 per kg, fresh, clean, good value. **Lavandería T'aqsana Wasi**, on Ruinas. Same-day service, they also iron clothes, US$2 per kg, good service, speak English, German, Italian and French, Mon-Fri 0900-2030, Sat 0900-1900. **Splendid Laundry Service**, Carmen Alto 195. Very good, US$1 per kg, laundry sometimes available after only 2 hrs.

## Medical services

### Clinics and doctors

**Clínica Panamericana**, Urb Larapa Grande C-17, T084-270000, T978 5303 (mob), www.cuscohealth.com. 24-hr emergency and medical attention. Good.

**Clínica Pardo**, Av de la Cultura 710, T084-240387, www.clinicapardo.com. 24-hr emergency and hospitalization/ medical attention, international department, trained bilingual personnel, handles complete medical assistance coverage with international insurance companies, free ambulance service, visit to hotel, discount in pharmacy, dental service, X-rays, laboratory, full medical specialization. The most highly recommended clinic in Cuzco.

**Hospital Regional**, Av de la Cultura, T084-227661, emergencies T084- 223691. Very basic. **Dr Ilya Gomon**, Av de la Cultura, Edif Santa Fe, oficina 207, T965 1906 (mob). Good Canadian chiropractor, reasonable prices, hotel or home visits. **Dr Gilbert Espejo** and **Dr Boris Espejo Muñoz**, both in the Centro Comercial Cuzco, oficina 7, T084-228074 and T084-231918 respectively. **Dr Johanna Menke**, T084-971 4558 (mob, 24 hrs). European qualified, Peruvian registered doctor who speaks German, English and some French, swift service.

### Dentists

**Dr Eduardo Franco**, Av de la Cultura, Edif Santa Fe, oficina 310, T084-242207, T965-0179 (mob). 24-hr. **Dr María del Carmen Velásquez and Jesús Velásquez**, Av de la Cultura, Edif Santa Fé, of 310, T084-244557. Husband and wife team. Mon-Fri 0900-1200, 1500-2000. Open Sat mornings also. Recommended.

### Massage and therapies

**Casa de la serenidad**, Pumacurco 636, T084-233670, www.shamanspirit.net. A shamanic therapy centre run by a Swiss-American healer and Reiki Master who uses medicinal 'power' plants. It also has bed and breakfast and has received very good reports.
**Healing Hands**, based at Loki Hostel. Angela is a reiki, shiatsu and craniosacral therapist. Very relaxing and recommended, track Angela down at Loki or drop her line at faeryamanita@hotmail.com.

## Post offices

**Central office**, Av Sol at the bottom end of block 5, T084-225232. Mon-Sat 0730-2000, 0800-1400 Sun and holidays. Poste restante is free and helpful. Sending packages is not cheap. **DHL**, Av Sol 627, T084-244167. For sending packages or money overseas.

## Telephone

There are independent phone offices in the centre. **Telefónica**, Av del Sol 386, T084-241111. For telephone and fax, Mon-Sat 0700-2300, 0700-1200 Sun and holidays.

### Radio messages

**Radio Alex**, Quinta Jardín 288, Villa Militar, T084-238219. For radio use to and from the jungle and other regions, with the potential to connect with phone lines. Alex Galindo charges 1 sol per min (plus phone charges if required); very reliable. You can also try **Radio América**, Túpac Amaru E-6, San Sebastián, T084-271428 and **Radio Tawantinsuyo**, Av Sol 806, T084-228411. Mon-Fri 0730-1900, Sat 0700-1300, messages are sent out between 0500 and 2100 (you can choose the time), in Spanish or Quechua, price per message is US$1. This is sometimes helpful if things are stolen and you want them back.

## Toilets

Conveniences can be found at the top of Plateros, at its junction with Saphi. Cost: US$0.50.

# The Sacred Valley

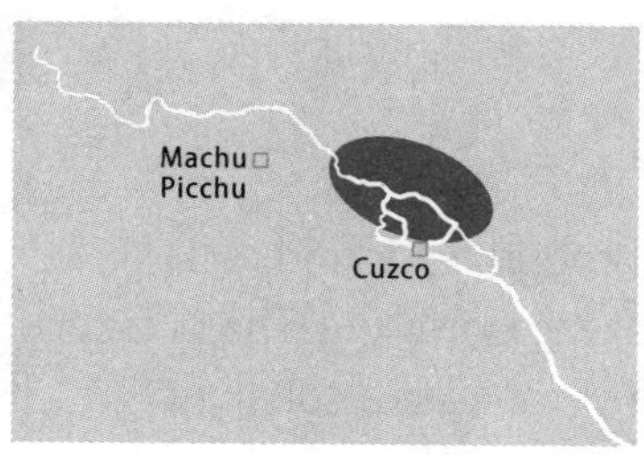




## Footprint features

# Introduction

The Río Urubamba cuts its way through fields and rocky gorges beneath the high peaks of the Cordillera. The presence of giants such as Pitusiray and La Verónica is a constant reminder that to the Incas such mountains were *apus* (beings to be worshipped). The landscape is forever changing as shafts of sunlight fall upon plantations of corn, precipitous Inca terraces, tiled roofs, or the waters of the river itself. Brown hills, covered in wheat fields, separate Cuzco from this beautiful high valley. Major Inca ruins command the heights – Pisac, Huchuy Cuzco and Ollantaytambo are the best examples – and traditional villages guard the bridges or stand on the highlands.



The road from Cuzco climbs up to a pass, then continues over the pampa before descending into the densely populated Urubamba Valley, which stretches from Sicuani (on the railway to Puno) to the gorge of Torontoi, 600m lower, to the northwest of Cuzco. Upstream from Pisac, the river is usually called the Vilcanota, downstream it is the Urubamba.

Beyond Ollantaytambo, the river begins its descent to the Amazonian lowlands, becoming wilder as it leaves the valley behind. That the river was of great significance to the Incas can be seen in the number of strategic sites they built above it. They enhanced the valley's fertility by building vast stretches of terraces on the mountain flanks and the Inca rulers had their royal estates here. It is from the Incas' own name for the river that the section from Pisac to Ollantaytambo is called 'Sacred' today.

## Don't miss ...

1 **Pisac** After a good breakfast at the Residencial Beho, walk up to the ruins at Pisac. As you climb, the views of the Urubamba Valley just get better and better, page 127. Afterwards, stop for a pick-me-up at Ulrike's Café, page 147.

2 **Urubamba** Visit the pottery workshop of Seminario-Behar, where pre-Columbian designs and techniques are used to make very desirable ceramics, page 134.

3 **Salineras** The extraordinary, ancient *salineras* (salt pans) are quite spectacular, page 136.

4 **Moray** In the hills above Urubamba, Moray's three large depressions, converted into terraced crop laboratories, show to perfection the Incas' thorough understanding of their environment, page 136.

5 **Ollantaytambo** Don't only see the Inca ruins here, but also the town, half of which retains its Inca layout (the llaqta). The town's museum is well worth a visit too, page 138.

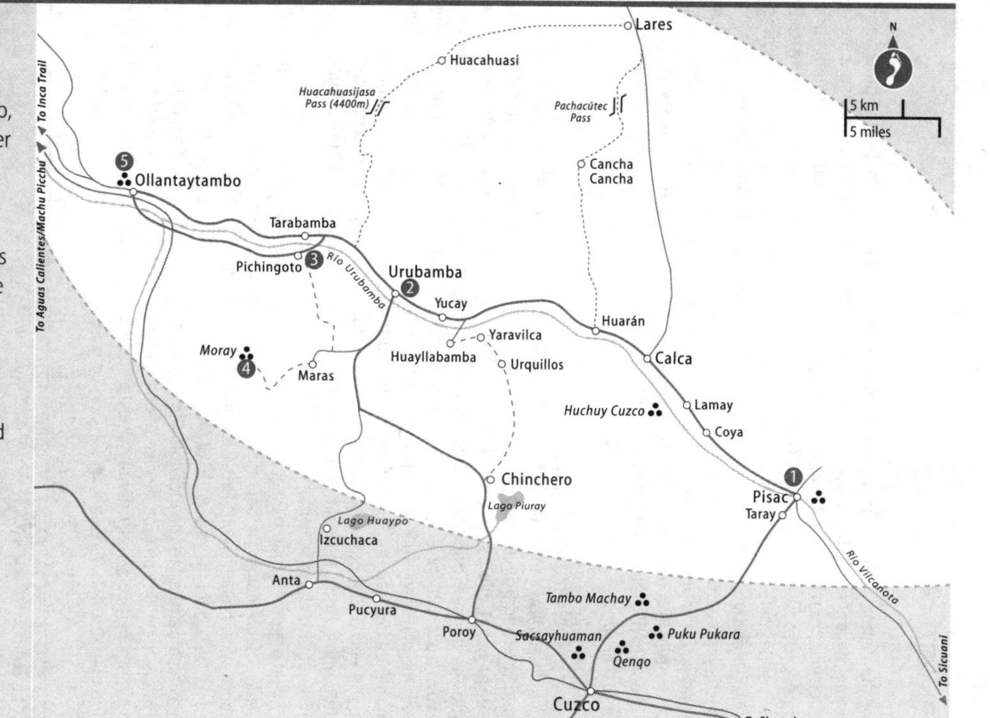

# Ins and outs

For the visitor, paved roads, plentiful transport and a good selection of hotels and eating places make this a straightforward place to explore. You can choose either a quick visit from the city or, better still, linger for a few days, savouring the sights and atmosphere. The valley itself is great for cycling and there are plenty of walking trails for one-day or longer excursions. Horse riding and rafting are also popular in this most visitor-friendly of tourist destinations. Furthermore, if the altitude of Cuzco itself is too much, you can hop on a minibus down to the valley – the 500-m difference can do wonders for your health. The best time to visit this area is April to May or October to November. The high season is from June to September, but the rainy season, from December to March, is cheaper and pleasant enough. » *For Sleeping, Eating and other listings, see pages 144-150.*

## Getting there and around

From Cuzco you can get to the Sacred Valley by bus, car, taxi or as part of an organized tour. The road from Cuzco which runs past Sacsayhuaman and on to Tambo Machay (see page 75), climbs up to a pass, then continues over the pampa before descending into the densely populated Urubamba Valley. As the road drops from the heights above Cuzco, there are two viewpoints, Mirador C'orao and Mirador Taray, looking over the plain around Pisac and, beyond, the Pitusiray and Sawasiray mountains. This road then crosses the Río Urubamba by a bridge at Pisac and follows the north bank to the end of the paved road at Ollantaytambo. It passes through Calca, Yucay and Urubamba. Urubamba can also be reached from Cuzco by the beautiful, direct road through Chinchero (see page 134).

An organized tour to Pisac, Urubamba, Ollantaytambo and Chinchero, as the main places of interest in the Sacred Valley, can be fixed up anytime with a travel agent for about US$20 per person. These tours last only one-day may be too brief. A taxi costs about US$60 for the round trip of the main sites of the valley and back to Cuzco. Taxis may also be hired to the individual towns, eg US$10 to Pisac. For a less hurried visit, explore the valley on foot, by bike or on horseback. Using public transport and staying overnight in Urubamba, Ollantaytambo or Pisac allows much more time to see the ruins and markets. » *For further details, see Tour operators, page 104, and Transport, page 149.*



# Pisac

» *pp144-150. Colour map 2, B3.*

→ *Phone code: 084.*

Only 30 km north of Cuzco is the village of Pisac, which is well worth a visit for its superb Inca ruins, perched precariously on the mountain, above the town. Pisac is usually visited as part of a tour from Cuzco but this often allows only 1½ hours here, not enough time to take in the ruins and splendid scenery.

## Pisac village and market

The ruins are considered to be amongst the very finest in the valley. Strangely, however, most visitors don't come to Pisac for the ruins. Instead, they come in droves for its Sunday morning market, which is described variously as colourful and interesting, or touristy and expensive. This is, in part, explained by the fact that it contains sections for both the tourist and the local community. Traditionally, Sunday is the day when the people of the highlands come down to sell their produce (potatoes, corn, beans, vegetables, weavings, pottery, etc). These are traded for essentials such as salt, sugar, rice, noodles, fruit, medicines, plastic goods and tools. The market comes to life after the arrival of tourist buses around 1000, and is usually

## A market for beads

A major feature of Pisac's popular market is the huge and varied collection of multicoloured beads on sale. Although they are commonly called Inca beads, this is, in fact, something of a misnomer. The Incas were highly talented potters and decorated their ware with detailed geometric motifs, but they are not known to have made ceramic beads.

These attractive items have become popular relatively recently. They used to be rolled individually by hand and were very time-consuming to produce. Now, in a major concession to consumerism, they are machine-made and produced in quantity, then hand-painted and glazed.

Today, the clay beads are produced in countless, often family-run, workshops in Cuzco and Pisac. Some are made into earrings, necklaces and bracelets, but many thousands are sold loose.

over by 1500. However, there is also an important ceremony every Sunday at 1100 sharp, in which the *Varayocs* (village mayors) from the surrounding and highland villages participate in a Quechua Catholic mass in **Pisac church**. It is a good example of the merging of, and respect for, different religious cultures. Pisac has other somewhat less crowded, less expensive markets on Tuesday and Thursday morning; it's best to get there before 0900.

On the plaza, which has several large *pisonay* trees, are the church and a small interesting **Museo Folklórico**. The town, with its narrow streets, is worth strolling around and, while you're doing so, look for the fine facade at Grau 485. There are many souvenir shops on Bolognesi.

## Inca ruins

ⓘ *Daily 0700-1730. If you go early (before 1000) you'll have the ruins to yourself. Entry with BTG (see box, page 59). Guides US$5, but the wardens on site are very helpful and don't charge anything to give out information. Combis US$0.60 per person up to the ruins; taxis US$3 one way from near the bridge; if you want the taxi to take you back down, negotiate a fare. Horses US$3 per person. Overnight parking is allowed in the car park.*

The ruins of Inca Pisac stand on a spur between the Río Urubamba to the south and the smaller Chongo to the east. It is not difficult to imagine why this stunning location was chosen, as it provides an ideal vantage point over the flat plain of the Urubamba, the terraces below and the terraced hillsides across the eastern valley. In *The Conquest of the Incas*, John Hemming describes Pisac as one of the Incas' 'pleasure houses' in the Yucay Valley (another name for this stretch of

### Pisac

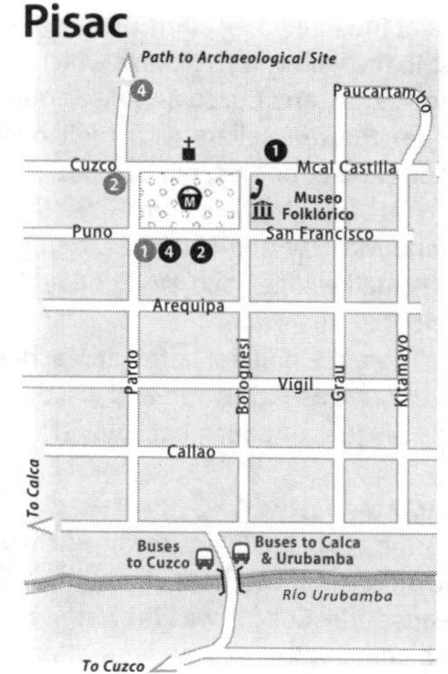

100 metres
100 yards

**Sleeping**
Parador 2
Pisaq 1
Residencial Beho 4
Royal Inca Pisac 5

**Eating**
Bakery 1
Doña Clorinda 2
Ulrike's Café 4

the Urubamba). If it were merely that, it would have been some country estate. There were, however, many other facets to the site – defensive, religious and agricultural – all contributing to one of the largest Inca ruins in the vicinity of Cuzco. The buildings that can be seen today have been dated to the reign of Pachacútec (see page 284), to whom, it is said, the estate belonged.

To appreciate the site fully, allow five or six hours on foot. Walking up, although tiring, is recommended for the views and location. It's at least one hour uphill all the way but the descent takes 30 minutes. Road transport approaches the site from the Kanchiracay end; the drive up from town takes about 20 minutes. Even if you're going by car, do not rush as there is a lot to see and a lot of walking to do at the site.

The walk up to the ruins begins from the town plaza, passing the Centro de Salud and a control post. The path goes through working terraces, giving the ruins a context. The first group of buildings is **Pisaqa**, with a fine curving wall. Climb up to the central part of the ruins, the **Intihuatana** group of temples and rock outcrops in the most magnificent Inca masonry. Here are the **Reloj Solar** (Hitching Post of the Sun) – now closed because thieves stole a piece from it – palaces of the moon and stars, solstice markers, baths and water channels. From Intihuatana, a path leads around the hillside through a tunnel to **Q'Allaqasa** (military area). Across the valley at this point, a large area of Inca tombs in holes in the hillside can be seen. The end of the site is **Kanchiracay**, where the agricultural workers were housed. At dusk you will hear, if not see, the *pisaca* (partridges), after which the place is named, and you may see deer too.



## Pisac to Urubamba » pp144-150. Colour map 2, B2/3.

### Calca and around

The first villages on the road from Pisac towards Urubamba are **Coya** and **Lamay** and the nearby warm springs, which are highly regarded locally for their medicinal properties. **Calca**, 18 km beyond Pisac at 2900 m, was the headquarters of Manco Inca at the beginning of his uprising against the Spaniards in 1536. Today it is a busy hub in the valley, with a plaza which is divided into two parts. Urubamba buses stop on one side, and Cuzco and Pisac buses on the other side of the dividing strip. Look out for the *api* sellers with their bicycles loaded with a steaming kettle and an assortment of bottles, glasses and tubs.

It is a two-day hike from Cuzco to Calca, via Sacsayhuaman, Qenqo, Puka Pukara, Tambo Machay and Huchuy Cuzco with excellent views of the eastern cordilleras, past small villages and along beautifully built Inca paths. There are many places to camp, but take water.

There are mineral baths at **Machacancha**, 8 km east of Calca. These springs are indoors, pleasantly warm and will open at night for groups. They are half an hour by taxi from town. About 3 km beyond Machacancha are the Inca ruins of **Arquasmarca**.

### Huchuy Cuzco

The ruins of a small Inca town, Huchuy Cuzco, are reached across the Río Urubamba and after a stiff two-hour climb. Huchuy Cuzco (also spelt Qosqo), which in Quechua means 'Little Cuzco', was the name given to this impressive Inca site sometime in the 20th century. Its original name was Kakya Qawani, which translates as 'from where the lightning can be seen'. According to the Spanish chronicler Pedro de Cieza de León, the palaces and temples at Huchuy Cuzco were built by the eighth Inca, Viracocha, who conquered the area by defeating the ethnic groups settled there.

Huchuy Cuzco is dramatically located on a flat esplanade almost 600 m above Lamay and Calca in the Sacred Valley. The views from the site are magnificent, with the Río Urubamba far below meandering through fertile fields, and the sombre Pitusiray massif opposite, surrounded by other snowy peaks.

### Rivers of rubbish

Every year on 15-16 September hundreds of students, *campesinos*, gringos, local companies and other volunteers board a bus in Cuzco with rubber gloves and rubbish bags in their hands. What are they doing? Saving the Río Urubamba.

The Urubamba, sacred river of the Incas, is a Peruvian national treasure. This historic waterway, however, is being polluted. El Río Willkamayu (as it is known in Quechua) is a danger to the health of the local people as it is seriously contaminated by plastic, oil, petrol and any number of other non-biodegradable products. During the 2002 clean-up, nappies, clothing and labels that have been out of production for more than 10 years were found.

The Día del Río (Day of the River) is used as a celebration of ecology and education. The idea is to enlighten the young people of Peru through teaching and by example. South American Explorers leads the clean-up effort in partnership with many other companies. Meetings are held roughly once a month at the South American Explorers clubhouse at Choquechaca 188, Cuzco, T084-245484, and have generated lots of ideas concerning cleaning the river in particular and recycling in general.

Cuzco is becoming more progressive on all ecological subjects. A new recycling plant has been opened to deal with the inorganic rubbish. It will take time but it is hoped that, in a few years, all households in Cuzco will be separating their refuse.

What you can do:
→ Bring a water bottle and fill it in designated areas.
→ Always leave plastic bottles in recycling bins.
→ Bring or buy biodegradable soap.
→ Say no to plastic bags in shops.
→ Carry a backpack.
→ Join the next Día del Río.



The ruins themselves consist of extensive agricultural terraces with high retaining walls. There are several buildings made from both the finely wrought stonework the Incas reserved for their most important constructions, and adobe mud bricks.

There are several ways to reach Huchuy Cuzco. The ruins can be accessed most easily by following the steep trail behind the village of Lamay, which is reached by crossing the bridge over the river. There is also a clearly marked trail from the village of Calca. Another longer route leads to Huchuy Cuzco from Tambo Machay near Cuzco, a magnificent one- or two-day trek along the route once taken by the Inca from his capital to his country estate at Huchuy Cuzco; some sections of the original Inca highway remain intact.

## Yucay

A few kilometres east of Urubamba, Yucay has two large grassy plazas divided by the restored colonial church of **Santiago Apóstol**, with its oil paintings and fine altars. On the opposite side from Plaza Manco II is the **adobe palace** built for Sayri Túpac (Manco's son) when he emerged from Vilcabamba in 1558.

Back along the road towards Calca a bridge crosses the river to the village of **Huayllabamba** (see page 135). If you are not dashing along the road at the speed of a local minibus, it is pleasant to cross the river and amble along the quieter bank, through farmland and small communities.

# Valle de Lares » pp144-150.

To the north of Urubamba and Calca, beyond the great peaks that tower above the Sacred Valley, lies the valley of **Lares**, an area famed for its traditional Quechua communities and strong weaving traditions. The mountainous territory that lies between these two valleys offers a great deal to the ambitious trekker, as do the valleys themselves, and, although the area is slowly being 'discovered' by some Cuzco agencies, you are still likely to have it largely to yourself. The entire Cordillera Urubamba is threaded with tracks and the remains of ancient Inca trails and, as you might expect, the variety of trekking routes is almost endless. Many of the locals may offer to sell weavings or *mantas* along the route, at prices a fraction of those in Cuzco. Remember, if you bargain, that many of these items take weeks, perhaps a month or more, to complete, so always give a fair price – at least here all the money goes to the weavers themselves!

Lares is also a perfect example of Peru's fabulous biking opportunities and it has something for everyone, suiting all levels of daring and technical ability. In two days you can freewheel from chilly mountain passes, past llamas and traditional Quechua communities, on unpaved but drivable roads, or follow old Inca trails down technical single tracks and through precipitous canyons alongside rushing mountain torrents.



## Lares trek: Huarán to Yanahuara → *4 days*

The trek from Huarán to Yanahuara via Lares takes you through ancient native forests, past some of the Cordillera Urubamba's greatest snow peaks, their waters feeding jewelled lakes and cascades below, and provides an insight into the communities that inhabit this rugged and challenging land. Enjoy the trek and have a good soak in the hot springs in Lares.

**Day one** The trek begins in the small community of **Huarán**, 6 km to the west of Calca, just off the main highway heading for Urubamba. Public transport along the highway, in the form of combis and buses, is cheap and plentiful. The first day's hike is around four hours of actual walking time up a very steep, exceptionally beautiful and surprisingly wild valley directly to the north of, and above, Huarán. The path stays close to the sparkling water of the **Quebrada Cancha Cancha**, which runs in the valley's centre and is crossed by traditional wood/adobe bridges. It's hard to get lost as you are hemmed in by the steep valley walls: just keep heading north and up.

The lower section of the valley is heavily cultivated, but quite soon enters areas of ancient (highly endangered), red-barked *Polylepis* (*quenoal*) forest, then cloudforest full of bromeliads, cacti and more. The smooth rocks and boulders, rich vegetation and rushing stream conjure up an image of a Japanese garden, but on a vast scale, and all presided over by the turrets and battlements of the valley's sheer rock faces.

The village of **Cancha Cancha** is friendly and very scenic, nestled beneath impressive snow peaks. The small houses are reminiscent of the hobbits' village in *Lord of the Rings*. The mountain up to the left of the pass is **Sirihuani** (5399 m) and you can also see the back of **Chicón/Pico San Juan** to the west. A good campsite for the night is the grassy area just beyond the village.

**Day two** This is a long day's hiking – eight hours of walking plus breaks – but there are hot springs at the end. Cancha Cancha lies at the confluence of two valleys. Your route lies up the right-hand valley and high on its right flank. From Cancha Cancha you can see the Patchacútec pass on a bearing of 40° from your position. You pass through a heavily cultivated area: traditional grass-roofed houses, dry stone walls and potato fields. The following timings until the Pachacútec pass are taken from Cancha Cancha.

After about 50 minutes a beautiful steep peak comes into view on the left. This is Sirihuani, visible earlier from Cancha Cancha up the left hand valley, which becomes increasingly Matterhorn-like as you head towards the pass. 1 hour 20 minutes: it's very important to stay high on the valley's shoulder to get above the vast cliffs dominating the head of the valley. One hour 30 minutes: you're now high above the cliffs. Two clear lakes come into view; a third is just visible higher up the mountain. One hour 40 minutes: the three lakes are in line; Sirihuani, at a bearing of 300° behind the lakes, is now a sheer pyramid. One hour 50 minutes: turn a corner and the great peaks of **Pitusiray** and **Sawasiray** loom into view, their flanks coated with vast glaciers. Sawasiray (sometimes spelt Sahuasiray) has an estimated altitude of around 5770 m, making it possibly the highest peak in the Urubamba range, contested only by Verónica. One local legend recounts how Pitusiray and Sawasiray were once Inca lovers, bound together in death by an icy embrace. If using the IGN 1:100,000 map of the area, Sawasiray lies just to the east of the Urubamba sheet (27-R) on the Calca Map (27-S), and is referred to as Colquecruz.

The pass now lies between two black hills/mountains to the north. Three rocky fingers just to the right of the pass are visible from a great distance, even from Cancha Cancha on a clear day. After two hours 40 minutes you reach a hill just before the pass. This one actually has better 360° views than the pass itself: get your photos here! Dropping into a small dip, climb up the rounded hill and continue north around the base of the small rocky peak of **Cerro Azulorjo** (4958 m). Three hours after leaving Cancha Cancha you reach the summit of the **Pachacútec Pass**. There's a small lake below but it's not visible from the pass itself – have a look just before. Don't forget to build up the *apachetas* (pyramids of standing stones to honour the *apus*, or mountain spirits). Missionary groups have destroyed those on the pass.



## Lares trek

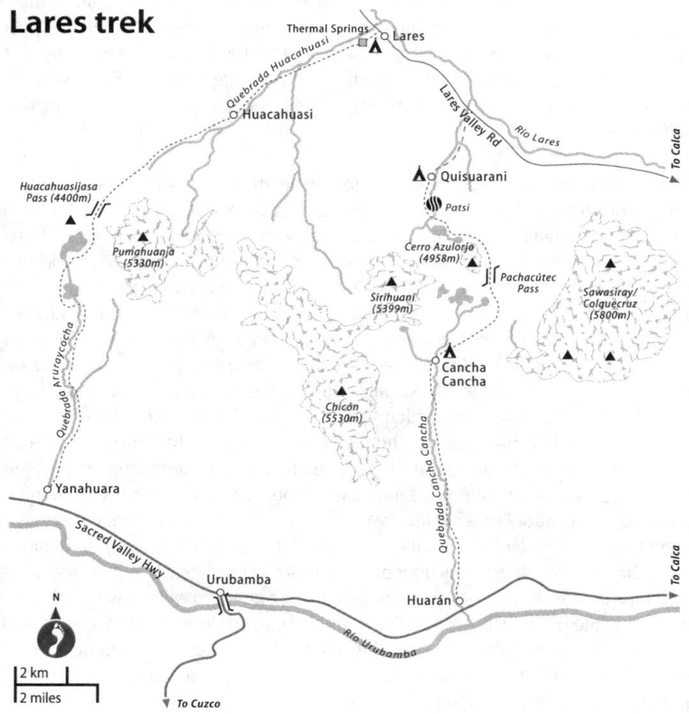

Head north off Pachacútec; 20 minutes beyond the pass a huge valley, flat like a landing strip, opens up to the right, beneath you. Don't descend into the valley, stay high on its left flank. Your route lies left, branching off to the northwest just before the black rocky peak in front of you. Forty minutes beyond the pass you enter a new valley. The mountains in the distance lying at 320° are those of the **Terjuay Massif**, rising to 5330 m. This is considered a separate and distinct range, lying north of and parallel to the Cordillera Urubamba. Heading northwest descend a slippery shale /scree slope towards two lakes. The nearer lake has dried out considerably in the last few years; the further one is the larger. Still heading northwest, transfer in the saddle between the lakes from the left to the right side of the valley. There is a clear trail on the right side of the second, larger lake, and this curves to the left around its circumference. This route leads to the lake's exit stream at its western end. The trail follows the stream away from the lake, turning sharply to the north and descending beside a beautiful waterfall, known locally as the **Patsi** waterfall, whose multiple streams tumble 20 metres or more over the cliff. You're now 1½ hours from the pass. Thirty minutes beyond the falls you reach the settlement of **Quisuarani** on the left side of the river. You've been walking on the right until this point. It's possible to camp here. Five minutes beyond the settlement cross back to the right side. Shortly after the village the path becomes a motorable track, which you can follow or cut off the curves using the many linked walking trails. After another 50 minutes you turn left onto the main Calca to Lares road.

About 1½ hours after joining the road you'll reach the main square of **Lares**, a sleepy town with a couple of basic hostels and shops. Beyond the town centre and up a small river valley are hot springs where you can bathe. To reach them, leave the square from its far corner and take the second left once on the street. An extra 15 minutes walking up the valley to the left of the river brings you to the pools. Ask for directions if unsure. The pools underwent renovations in mid 2005, unfortunately incorporating the typical Peruvian love of concrete, but they are still excellent spots to unwind, especially at night, staring up at the star-studded night sky. Entry to the springs costs US$1.25 and space to pitch a tent a further US$1.50. Some very basic accommodation is also available with negotiation. There's a small shop selling drinks and snacks.



**Day three** A nice easy day, in terms of both navigation and length (just 3½ hours of hiking), with plenty of time to relax at the springs or explore Lares town (not a very daunting task!). Head west up the valley above the springs on the trail/road. After one hour the road crosses the stream to the right hand side. A log bridge aided the crossing at the time of writing. At this point the valley splits in two: take the larger right hand (western) valley. Your trail runs at 300° between ancient stone walls. After around one hour 20 minutes from the springs, original sections of Inca trail begin to appear. The path is on the left of the river, the valley a steep 'V', your course more southwest at this point. You're basically following the road, but it's far more pleasant to use the sections of Inca trail, which sometimes cut off the corners, where possible. As you continue, you gradually ascend higher on the side of the valley; the Inca trails now have marked drainage channels, a feature typical of ancient trails in this region. Two and a half hours after leaving Lares you reach the large community of **Huacahuasi**. **Nevado Pumahuanja** is visible to the southwest. Walk through the village towards the head of the valley. Passing the church bear slightly right and pick up the trail behind the small houses. The route climbs gently out of the village, continuing up the valley on its right side. After some time you will see waterfalls on the far (south) side of the valley. Forty-five minutes beyond Huacahuasi the valley splits and your trail curves to the right following into the near valley and heading away from the waterfalls. About 30 minutes further on are some flat grassy areas good for camping and for the assault on the final pass tomorrow.

**Day four** Six to seven hours' walking time, plus breaks. Head southwest above camp on the track towards the head of the valley. The pass soon becomes visible at 240° between the mountains, the trail clear at this point. It takes just under two hours to reach the top of the pass, the **Abra Huacahuasijasa** at an altitude of approximately 4400 m. Above you and to the left towers the snow peak of **Pumahuanja**, rising to 5330 m. A beautiful lake can now be seen to the southwest. Descending into this valley, leave the lake to your right and continue out of the lake basin into the valley proper, which now runs south towards the Sacred Valley and **Yanahuara**, your final destination. About an hour beyond the Abra Huacahuasijasa you continue past a second lake, this time passing it to your left. Now transfer back to the left side of the Quebrada. The valley takes its name from Aruraycocha, a higher and larger lake, and still boasts extensive stands of ancient *qenoal* trees: however, severe deforestation is taking place and it is feared that these woods may disappear entirely over the next few years. Beyond the second lake the valley drops away steeply, passing huge boulders of the glacial moraine, a remnant of the last ice age, and vast glaciers that once carved the Urubamba range. Now a couple of hours beyond the pass you come to the village of Mantanay. Just keep heading south, through another section of deep forest. Cactuses and bromeliads begin to make an appearance again as you head for the warmer climate of the Sacred Valley. A further two hours, through increasingly settled and cultivated land, brings you to the village of **Yanahuara**.

From Yanahuara infrequent combis and trucks leave for Urubamba: ask around in the village for the latest intelligence. If you find yourself marooned for the night, a further 30 minutes' slog down the rough road will bring you to the highway, with plentiful transport to Urubamba, Ollantaytambo and beyond.

## Cycling route: Valle de Lares → *2 days*

Several agencies in Cuzco can offer biking in this area and it's a good idea to take advantage of their services because, unless you're super fit, or a masochist, you're going to need some transport to get you to the top of the Abra de Lares twice, for the start of each day's ride. By the same token, a professional biking guide will be able to show you interesting sections of single track, provide technical advice and mechanical support. If you want to go it alone, local buses running between Calca and Lares will carry bikes on the roof; just make sure they're well tied on. And don't forget that you can spend the first night soaking away your bumps and bruises in the thermal springs at Lares (see page 132). ▸▸ *For further information, see Cuzco Tour operators, page 104.*

**Day one: Abra de Lares to Lares** The bus ride itself from Calca up to the pass is spectacular and provides an insight into the second day's biking. Reaching the pass at 4400 m you have a spectacular view in both directions: down the valley to Lares, back to Calca and also above to the glaciers of the Urubamba range – not a bad spot to start the day. In clear weather, the northward skyline beyond Lares is dominated by the Nevados of Quilloc and Terijuay, isolated peaks rising to more than 5300 m.

After the first 15 to 20 minutes of downhill on the road, you reach a left-hand turn-off leading you to a faint Inca trail running close to the stream for perhaps 40 minutes. The terrain varies from smooth grassy runs to some serious rocky sections requiring a fair amount of skill, but you can walk them if you're not sure. Just before rejoining the main road you pass the tiny rural community of **Charalpampa**, its small grass-roofed huts backed by the imposing glacier of Sawasiray (5770 m), one of greatest peaks of the Urubamba range. After rejoining the road another hour's biking will take you to a lush meadow beside the river, ideal for lunch. Ambitious bikers can take several short cuts, avoiding the bends, to reach this point. Beyond the meadow the valley drops away steeply, the river carving a deep white-water canyon to the right of the road. It's not long before you reach Lares (see page 132).

**Day two: Abra de Lares to Calca** The second day sees you return to the dizzy heights of the *abra* before hurling yourself downhill once more, this time towards the Sacred Valley. From the heights of the pass a distinct Inca Trail is visible running along the right side of the valley, above the stream which lies at its centre. Like the previous day, a short downhill section on the road leads to a turn-off onto single track. This time the route diverges from the road for several hours. The trail kicks off through rolling farmland and pasture, fields of potatoes and flocks of sheep and alpacas. Despite its great age, the trail is clear, with some small sections of paving still visible, along with many drainage channels cutting across the route. These provide plenty of biking challenges. All the time, the main road to Calca is visible on the far side of the valley, rising high on its left shoulder.

Beyond the gentle valley the route becomes more technically challenging, with some sections providing thrills even for hardened biking addicts. Running close to the river the path enters a sheer canyon and a series of steep rocky descents. There are original sets of Inca stairs to be negotiated and several river crossings on traditional wood and adobe bridges – be as daring as you wish, or walk the tough bits! Emerging from the gorge you ride through the village of Tortora and out onto the main road. From Tortora onwards it's a long but straightforward descent on the road to Calca. There are plenty of short cuts eliminating the curves for those looking for a little excitement, otherwise look out for the traffic and enjoy the views on the way down. Calca itself is a pleasant town (see page 128), with a couple of decent cafés on the main square and good transport links to Cuzco and the rest of the Sacred Valley. Alternatively you can just keep on riding!



## Urubamba and around » pp144-150.

*Colour map 2, B2.*

→ *Phone code: 084. Altitude: 2863 m.*

Like many places along the valley, Urubamba has a fine setting, with views of the Chicón snow-capped peaks and glaciers, and enjoys a mild climate. The main plaza, with a fountain capped by a maize cob, is surrounded by blue-painted buildings. Calle Berriózabal, on the west edge of town, is lined with *pisonay* trees. The large market square is one block west of the main plaza. The main road skirts the town and the bridge for the road to Chinchero is just to the east of town.

### Sights

**Seminario-Behar Ceramic Studio** ⓘ *C Berriózabal 111, a right turning off the main road to Ollantaytambo. T084-201002, www.ceramicaseminario.com, open daily (just ring the bell)*, was founded in 1980 and is located in the beautiful grounds of the former **Hostal Urpihuasi**. Pablo Seminario has investigated the techniques and designs of pre-Columbian Peruvian cultures and has created a style with strong links to the past. Each piece is handmade and painted, using ancient glazes and minerals, and is then fired in reproduction pre-Columbian kilns. The resulting pieces are very attractive. Visitors are welcome to meet the artists (Pablo and Marilú), if they book in advance.

### Chinchero → *Phone code: 084. Colour map 2, B3. Altitude: 3762 m.*

ⓘ *Site open daily 0700-1730. Entry by BTG (see page 59).*

Chinchero is northwest from Cuzco, high on the pampa just off a direct road to Urubamba. The streets of the village wind up from the lower sections, where transport stops, to the **plaza**, which is reached through an archway. The great square appears to be stepped, with a magnificent Inca wall separating the two levels. Let into the wall is a row of trapezoidal niches, each much taller than a man. From the paved lower section another arch leads to an upper terrace, upon which the Spaniards built an attractive **church**. It is open on Sunday for mass and at festivals but ask in the tourist office in Cuzco if it is open at other times, as it is worth spending a quiet moment or two inside to admire the ceiling, beams and walls, which are covered in beautiful floral and religious designs. The altar, too, is fine. From the upper earth- and grass-covered plaza, there are superb views over the mountain ranges. Opposite the church is a small local **museum**. Excavations have revealed many Inca walls, terraces and various other features.

The local produce **market** on Sunday morning is fascinating and very colourful, and best before the tour groups arrive. It's on your left as you come into town. There's also a small handicraft market, also on Sunday, up by the church. Chinchero attracts few tourists, except on Sunday. ›› *For Festivals, see page 148.*

## Chinchero to Huayllabamba → *3-4 hrs*

There is a scenic path from Chinchero to Huayllabamba, the village on the opposite side of the Río Urubamba from the main road, between Yucay and Calca (see page 129). The hike is quite beautiful, with fine views of the peaks of the Urubamba Range. The trail starts on the hill across the valley from the Chichero ruins and leads down to the village of Urquillos. From here it's a short distance to Huayllabamba. The end of the hike is about 10 km before the town of Urubamba. You can either go on to Urubamba or back to Cuzco by looking for transport on the main road. Another trail follows the old Chinchero-Urubamba dirt road, to the left of the new paved road. Ask the locals if you are not sure. It runs over the pampa, with a good view of Chinchero, then drops down to the Urubamba Valley.



## Urubamba

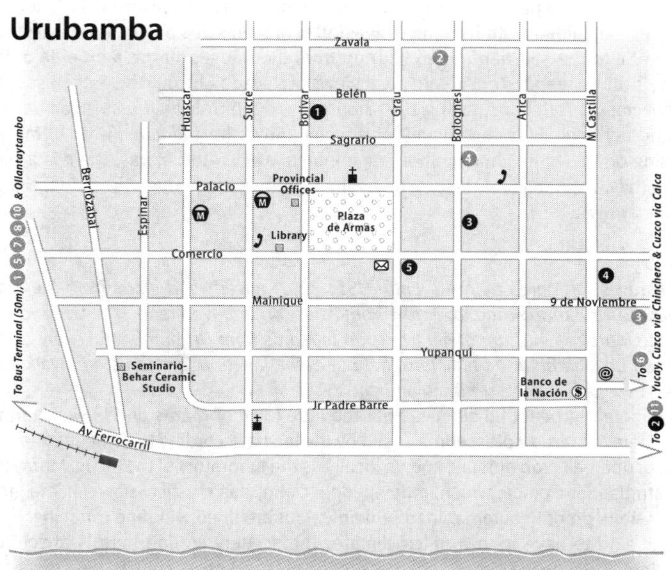


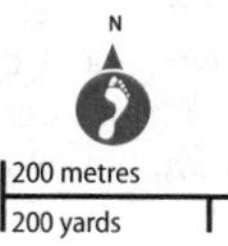


**Sleeping**
Casa Andina Private Collection Sacred Valley **1**
Hospedaje Los Jardines **6**
Hospedaje Perla de Vilcanota **3**
Hostal Urubamba **4**
K'uychi Rumi **8**
Las Chullpas **10**
Las Tres Marías **2**
Libertador Valle Sagrado Lodge **5**
San Agustín Urubamba **11**
Sol y Luna **7**

**Eating**
La Casa de la Abuela **1**
Pintacha **3**
Pizzonay **4**
Quinta los Geranios **2**
The Muse Too **5**

> **“” The cascade of centuries-old rectangular basins is like a giant artwork by a Cubist painter obsessed with the colour white.**

An alternative hike from Chinchero follows the spectacular Maras-Moray-Pichingoto salt mines route (see below). This brings you to the main Urubamba valley road, about 10-12 km beyond the town of Urubamba. You could also take the more direct main road from Chinchero to Urubamba, with occasional short cuts, but this route is a lot less interesting.

## Salineras

Five kilometres west of Urubamba is the village of **Tarabamba**, where a bridge crosses the Río Urubamba. If you turn right after crossing the bridge you'll come to **Pichingoto,** a tumble-down village built under an overhanging cliff. Also, just over the bridge and before the town, to the left of a small walled cemetery, is a salt stream. Follow the footpath beside the stream and you'll come to **Salinas,** a small village below which are over 5000 terraced Inca *salineras* (salt pans) ⓘ *entry US$1.80*, still in production after hundreds of years. The cascade of centuries-old rectangular basins is like a giant artwork by a Cubist painter obsessed with the colour white. These are now a fixture on the tourist circuit and can become congested with buses. It's a 45-minute walk from Urubamba to the salt pans. The climb up from the bridge, on the right side of the valley, is fairly steep but easy, with great views of Nevado Chicón. The path passes by the spectacular salt pans, taking 1½-2 hours to the top. Take water as it can be very hot and dry here. From the summit of the cliff above the *salineras*, walk to **Maras,** focusing on the white church, about 45 minutes' away. After Maras, there is a blue sign with two options for Moray, 9 km by the road, or 5 km through the fields, signed by blue arrows.

## Moray

ⓘ *9 km west of Maras by road. Entry US$1.80. A paved road leads from the main Chinchero-Urubamba road to Maras, from where an unpaved road in good condition leads to Moray. If you cannot get transport to Maras from Urubamba, take any combi between Urubamba and Chinchero, get out at the junction for Maras and walk from there.* ▸▸ *For further details, see Transport, page 150.*

This remote but beautiful site lies near the little town of **Maras** and is well worth a visit. There are three 'colosseums', used by the Incas, according to some theories, as a sort of open-air crop nursery, known locally as the laboratory of the Incas. Moray is a very atmospheric place, which, many people claim, has mystical powers. The great depressions do not contain ruined buildings, but are lined with fine terracing. Each level is said to have its own microclimate. The scenery around here is absolutely stunning. As you leave Maras, look back to the village with its church, tiled roofs and adobe walls framed by snowy mountains. All around are fields of wheat and other crops, such as *kiwicha*, whose tall, thin, violet-coloured flowers produce a protein-rich grain. At harvest-time the whole area turns from rich green to every shade of gold and brown imaginable. To the northwest stands the majestic white peak of La Verónica. The light is wonderful in the late afternoon, but for photography it's best to arrive in the morning. The road eventually arrives at the guardian's hut, but there is little indication of the scale of the colosseums until you reach the rim.

To return from Moray to the main road takes about three hours: 1½ hours to Maras, 45 minutes to the *salineras* and 45 minutes down to the road (much quicker than going up!). Hitching back to Urubamba is quite easy, but take care not to be stranded. One option is to hire a taxi which will take you to Moray, wait an hour, then take you to the Salineras, from where you can walk down to rejoin the main road between Urubamba and Ollantaytambo, US$20.

## Cycling route: Chinchero to Urubamba → *1 day; 40 km*

This day trip is one of the best you can do from Cuzco, taking in fabulous mountain scenery, mysterious archaeology (Moray), and giving an insight into the living culture of the Andes. You pass rich farmlands and finally take on a wild descent past the fascinating *salineras* (salt pans) beneath the picturesque town of Maras. All in all this biking odyssey covers around 40 km on two wheels, ranging from mellow peddles on relatively flat and well-surfaced roads to the truly demanding descent on narrow single track past the *salineras* themselves.

Don't underestimate this trip: you should be in relatively good shape and, remember, if you're not sure of a section, getting off and pushing is better than an impromptu flying lesson! This is a long day, so make sure you bring food and plenty of water. A good biking helmet, sunblock, sunglasses and a warm fleece are also advised. The IGN 1:100,000 topographic sheet covering the Urubamba area (available through the SAE in Cuzco) is of relatively little use here, as information on roads and tracks is seriously outdated. This fact, combined with difficulties of navigating over the relatively featureless agricultural landscape at the start of the ride, means that we recommend using a professional guide or specialist agency for this trip.

*At Tiobamba, near Maras, a fascinating indigenous market festival is held on 15 Aug, where Sacred Valley yellow maize is exchanged for pottery from Lake Titicaca.*

Guides with local knowledge will also find exciting off-road sections for ambitious clients. Many agencies hire private transport to get you and the bikes to Chinchero and back to Cuzco. If you're on a tight budget it's quite possible to use public buses, loading the bikes onto the roof rack; most guides and agencies won't have a problem with this, but watch those bikes carefully. » *For further details, see Activities and tours, page 104.*

The day's adventure usually starts at Chinchero, from where you head west on a good track, across expansive open farming country to the north of Laguna Huaypo. This is mostly easy riding over gently undulating land, with occasional diversions on single track. Views on clear days are spectacular, with the entire Cordillera Urubamba from Chicón/Pico San Juan to the impressive ice pyramid of Verónica laid out before you. Prior to arriving at Moray you join the main surfaced road. Moray is a good lunch spot, with drinks and snacks often available.

*Depending on your biking ability any timings given may vary greatly.*

Heading out of Moray you ride east, taking in some good off-road sections before reaching the historic colonial town of Maras. From here it's all downhill as you race north towards the Sacred Valley. The day's most challenging riding is ahead! Have US$1.80 ready to gain entry to the *salineras* road. The trail is narrow, steep, with precipitous drops to the right, and has some treacherously sharp turns, so be careful; it's exciting, awesome fun though! The terraced salt pans, worked as they have been for centuries, are a great backdrop to a true biking adventure.

Reaching the Sacred Valley, cross the bridge to the north side of the Río Urubamba and on to the highway. Turn right for Urubamba 5 km away, and watch out for crazy drivers.

# Ollantaytambo and around

» pp144-150.

*Colour map 2, A2.*

→ *Phone code: 084. Altitude: 2800 m.*

A trip to Ollantaytambo is a journey into the past, to a world governed by a concept of time very different to the one which holds sway nowadays. Today, the descendants of the people who founded Ollantaytambo continue to live there, watched over still by the sacred mountains of Verónica and Alankoma. They work the land as they have always done, with the same patience and skill that their ancestors employed to shape and then move the huge blocks of stone with which they built both their homes and the temples in which they worshipped. The attractive little town now sits at the foot of some spectacular Inca ruins and terraces, and is built directly on top of the original Inca town.

## Ins and outs

**Getting there** Ollantaytambo can be reached by bus from Cuzco, Urubamba and Chinchero. It is also one of the principal stations for catching the train to Machu Picchu; see page 154 for details. You won't be allowed on to Ollantaytambo station unless you have previously bought a ticket for the train; the gates are locked and only those with tickets can enter. » *For further details, see Transport, page 150.*

## History

The Tambo Valley, as the Spanish chroniclers called it, is a fertile stretch of land sown with fields of maize which hug the banks of the Río Urubamba (Vilcanota) from Ollantaytambo to Machu Picchu. Long before the arrival of the Incas, the valley was inhabited by the Ayarmaca, who had migrated from Lake Titicaca, far to the southeast. On their long journey, this race of farmers followed the course of the Vilcanota, abandoning the harsh *altiplano* in search of a better climate for their agricultural activities. The Ayarmacas, known in the Spanish chronicles as Tampus, came from the same ethnic stock as the Incas of Cuzco, and maintained with them many cultural, linguistic and family ties which would ensure them, at least for a while, a degree of regional autonomy during the period of Inca imperial expansion. When Inca Pachacútec did begin to take control of neighbouring areas (see History, page 284), one of his first conquests was the Tambo Valley. The chronicles tell of two *curacas* (local chieftains), Paucar Ancho and Tokori Tupa, who led the resistance against the Inca, only to be defeated in the mid-15th century. Pachacútec sacked their town, subjugated its people and made their lands his royal estate.

On the death of Pachacútec in 1471, his properties were passed to the members of his *panaca* (royal household), the Hatun Ayllu (Great Clan). This was the Inca's extended family and formed the social, political and religious elite from whose ranks the new Inca would emerge. The Hatun Ayllu set about converting Ollantaytambo into a great agricultural complex by extending its terraces beyond the town. To reclaim still more land for cultivation, they straightened a 3-km stretch of the river, as well as building canals and irrigation channels to bring fresh water from the area's snow-capped peaks and highland lakes. They ordered the construction of *qolqas* (barns) to store the harvest, as well as establishing checkpoints to control access to the centre known today as Ollantaytambo. To link Ollantaytambo to the rest of their empire via the Royal Inca Highway (*Capac Ñan*), the Incas built a tremendous suspension bridge across the river. Still standing after more than five centuries, the single central buttress of that ancient bridge now supports a modern metal structure.

When Manco Inca decided to rebel against the Spaniards in 1536, he fell back to Ollantaytambo from Calca to stage one of the greatest acts of resistance to the *conquistadores*. Hernando Pizarro led his troops to the foot of the Inca's stronghold, which Hernando's brother Pedro later described as "so well fortified that it was a thing of horror". Under fierce fire, Pizarro's men failed to capture Manco and retreated to Cuzco, but Manco could not press home any advantage. The Inca siege of the Spaniards in Cuzco turned into stalemate and Manco was unable to capitalize on the arrival of Diego de Almagro's army from Chile to threaten the Pizarro brothers' hold on Cuzco. In 1537, feeling vulnerable to further attacks, Manco left Ollantaytambo for Vilcabamba (see page 187).

It is easy to see, even today, how daunting an assault on the Inca's defences must have seemed to Pizarro. Great walled terraces of fine masonry climb the hillside, at the top of which is an unassailable sanctuary. The entire construction is superb, including the curving terraces, which follow the contours of the rocks overlooking the Urubamba. It was these terraces which were successfully defended by Manco Inca's warriors. Manco built the defensive wall above the site and another wall closing the Yucay Valley against attack from Cuzco. These are still visible on either side of the valley. Walking up the terraces is taxing enough, but imagine how impossible it must have been for armed *conquistadores* trying to scale the hill under a hail of missiles.

## Entering Ollantaytambo

Entering Ollantaytambo from Urubamba, the road is built along the **Long Wall of 100 Niches**. Note the inclination of the wall towards the road. Since it was the Incas' practice to build walls leaning towards the interiors of buildings, it has been deduced that the road, much narrower then, was built inside a succession of buildings. The road leads into the main plaza, in the middle of which is a fountain on whose top rim stand the statues of two white geese. Public transport congregates in the centre of the square and there is a small church in the southeast corner. The original Inca town is behind the north side of the plaza and you can enter it by taking any of the streets off the plaza, or the street that runs beside the Río Patacancha. The road from the northwest corner of the plaza looks up to the Inca temple, but to get there you have to cross the bridge over the river and go down to the colonial church with its *recinto* (enclosure). Beyond is a grand plaza (and car park) with entrances to the archaeological site.

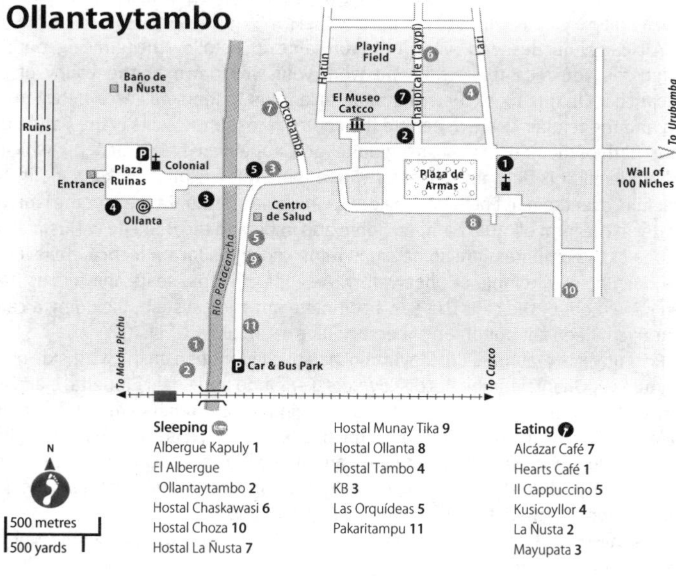


**Sleeping**
Albergue Kapuly **1**
El Albergue Ollantaytambo **2**
Hostal Chaskawasi **6**
Hostal Choza **10**
Hostal La Ñusta **7**
Hostal Munay Tika **9**
Hostal Ollanta **8**
Hostal Tambo **4**
KB **3**
Las Orquídeas **5**
Pakaritampu **11**

**Eating**
Alcázar Café **7**
Hearts Café **1**
Il Cappuccino **5**
Kusicoyllor **4**
La Ñusta **2**
Mayupata **3**

## The Fortress

ⓘ *Daily 0700-1730; if possible, arrive very early, 0700, before the crowds, and avoid Sun afternoons, when tour groups from Pisac descend in their hundreds. Entry US$6.50 or by BTG (see box, page 59), which can be bought at the site; guides at the entrance charge US$2.*

The ruins, known as the 'Fortress', were, in fact, a religious complex, with temples dedicated to the many divinities which comprised the Inca pantheon. The gods the Incas worshipped represented the forces of nature, and were seen, therefore, to control the agricultural life of the community. At the Fortress, we find the Temple of Viracocha, the creator god, as well as those devoted to the sun, water, earth and lightning. The magnificent terraces which lead up to the temple site were almost certainly used by astronomer-priests for the cultivation of corn for ceremonial purposes; the maize they grew there would mark the seasons for planting and harvesting for the rest of the community.

When you visit Ollantaytambo you will be confronted by a series of 16 massive stepped terraces of the very finest stonework, after crossing the great high-walled trapezoidal esplanade known as *Mañariki*. Beyond these imposing terraces lies the so-called Temple of Ten Niches, a funeral chamber once dedicated to the worship of the Pachacútec *panaca* (royal household). Immediately above this is the site popularly known as the Temple of the Sun, although it is not known for certain whether it was ever intended for that purpose. The remains of this temple consist of six monolithic upright blocks of rose-coloured rhyolite, forming a wall which, in common with other Inca temples, runs from east to west. A narrow, vertical course, like stone beading, separates the giant monoliths, on which traces of relief carving can be seen. Typical Andean motifs such as the *chakana* (Andean cross) are just visible, as well as other zoomorphic figures. These designs were defaced by the Spanish shortly after the conquest, as part of a systematic campaign by the victors physically to erase the indigenous religion. They have also suffered from erosion, however; sketches by the American traveller Ephrain George Squier, who visited Ollantaytambo in the 1870s, show that the figures were much more complete then. Below the Temple of the Sun, the dark grey stone is embellished today with bright orange lichen. Note how most of the stones have one or two protrusions at the bottom edge, a feature you will not see in Cuzco or Pisac.

You can either descend by the route you came up, or follow the terracing round to the left (as you face the town) and work your way down to the Valley of the Patacancha. On this route there are more Inca ruins in the small area between the town and the temple fortress, behind the church. Most impressive is the **Baño de la Ñusta** (Bath of the Princess), a grey granite rock, about waist high, beneath which is the bath itself. It is delicately finished with a three-dimensional *chakana* motif. The water falls over the relief arch into the pool, which was probably used for the worship of water in the form of ritual bathing. Some 200 m behind the Baño de la Ñusta along the face of the mountain are some small ruins known as **Inca Misanca**, believed to have been a small temple or observatory. A series of steps, seats and niches have been carved out of the cliff. There is a complete irrigation system, including a canal some 15 cm deep cut out of the sheer rock face at shoulder level.

Recently a two-dimensional **'pyramid'** has been identified on the west side of the main ruins of Ollantaytambo. Its discoverers, Fernando and Edgar Elorietta, claim it is the real Pacaritambo, from where the four original Inca brothers emerged to found their empire (see page 141). Whether or not this is the case, it is still a first-class piece of engineering with great terraced fields and a fine 750-m wall creating the optical illusion of a pyramid. The wall is aligned with the sun's rays at the winter solstice, on 21 June. People gather at midwinter dawn to watch this event.

The mysterious 'pyramid', which covers 50-60 ha, can best be seen from the other side of the river. This is a pleasant, easy one-hour walk west from the Puente

## The Inn of Origin

One of the Incas' three creation stories is the *Inn of Origin*. This legend tells of Pacaritambo (the Inn, or House of Origin), which is also associated with another name, Tambotocco (the Place of the Hole). Like the *Children of the Sun* story, (see page 285), there are variations on the basic theme, which relates that four brothers and four sisters (three of each in some versions) emerged from the central cave of three in a cliff. The names of the brothers and sisters vary, but usually the men were called Ayar Cachi, Ayar Manco, Ayar Uchu and Ayar Sauca, and the women Mama Huaco, Mama Ocllo, Mama Coya and Mama Rahua. The brothers and sisters set out in search of good land on which to settle and on the way fell out with Ayar Cachi, who was much stronger, more violent and more arrogant than the others. They lured him back to the cave and walled him up inside before recommencing their journey. Soon, though, Ayar Cachi miraculously reappeared, telling them to move on to the valley of Cuzco and found the city. He then went to the mountain of Huanacauri where his spirit remained, becoming a place of veneration for the Incas. In return for their worship of him on the mountain, Ayar Cachi would intercede with the gods on their behalf to ensure prosperity and success in war. Ayar Manco then proceeded with his sisters to Cuzco, where, according to some versions, he built Qoricancha as his first house and quickly earned the respect of the local people. A bloody twist to this story recounts how one of the sisters, on the lookout for the ideal land, came to Cuzco and petrified the inhabitants by killing one of them, ripping out his lungs and inflating them as she entered the village.

This myth has several elements in common with the *Children of the Sun*: siblings teaching the unenlightened people and founding Cuzco and the Inca dynasty; the discovery of fertile land on which to base the kingdom; the role of Huanacauri Mountain. Whereas the *Children of the Sun* borrows from the Lake Titicaca creation myth, the *Inn of Origin* borrows from another major American tradition; ancestors, especially brothers, coming out of rocks or the ground.

For the sake of completeness, the third main creation story concerns a shining mantle, the brightness of which as it reflected the sun's rays so dazzled the people that the wearer deceived them into believing that he descended from the Sun. Some versions say that Ayar Manco was the instigator of this trickery after he and his brothers emerged from Pacaritambo. He used sheets of silver strapped to his body to flash in the sun as he strode along a hilltop. An alternative version says that it was Sinchi Roca, Manco's successor, who was dressed in this magnificent robe by his mother. She thus led the people to believe that the boy was a ruler sent by the Sun.

Inca, just outside the town. You'll also be rewarded with great views of the Sacred Valley and the river, with the snowy peaks of the Verónica massif as a backdrop.

### The town

Tucked away below its more famous ruins and rarely visited, the town of Ollantaytambo gives those few travellers who do wander its narrow streets, unchanged for 500 years, a much clearer idea of what life must have been like under Inca rule. Unlike modern cities, *llaqtas* (Inca towns) were not designed to house large populations. Inca society was essentially agrarian and, among the common people, almost everyone worked and lived on the land. The towns and cities that the Incas did build were meant to serve as residential areas for the state's administrative and religious elite.

Throughout the Inca Empire of Tawantinsuyo, the *llaqtas* were divided into two zones, along blood lines, between the two principal *ayllus* (clans), of Hanan and Urin. In Ollantaytambo, the Urin occupied the area which corresponds to the present-day village. Called *Qosqo Ayllu*, it was both an administrative centre and the home of the Pachacútec *panaca*. The streets were laid out in a simple grid pattern, with the whole forming the Inca trapezoid (see page 289). These streets, whose corners are marked with huge stone blocks, surround *canchas* (communal enclosures which house many families). Each *cancha* occupies half a block, with just one entrance on those streets which run parallel to the Río Patacancha. It is clear, from the elaborate double-jamb porticos which form their entrances, that these *canchas* were built for members of the Incas' social and religious elite. The Inca nobility did not work on the land: their *yanaconas* (servants) did it for them, and the remains of the homes of this servant class, built from much simpler materials, have been found in the northern part of the town.

If you are visiting Ollantaytambo, begin your tour at **El Museo Catcco** (**Centro Andino de Tecnología Tradicional y Cultural de las Comunidades de Ollantaytambo**) ⓘ *Casa Horno, Patacalle, 1 block from plaza, T084-204024, www.catcco.org, daily 0900-1900, US$1.50 requested as a donation*. The museum was started with help from the British Embassy and run by Sr Joaquín Randall. It houses a fine ethnographical collection and offers tourist information on day-hikes, things to see and places to eat and stay. Local guides, trained at museum workshops, are available for tours of the town and surrounding areas. Outside the museum, Catcco runs non-profit making cultural programmes, temporary exhibitions, concerts and lectures. Also on site is a ceramics workshop, a textile revitalization programme and an educational theatre project. Ceramics and textiles are sold in the museum shop; proceeds help fund the museum and other Catcco programmes. The museum has internet access. Note the canal down the middle of the street outside the museum.



## Inca quarries at Cachiccata

It takes about a day to walk to the Inca quarries on the opposite side of the river and return to Ollantaytambo. The stone quarries of Cachiccata are located on the lands of the hacienda of the same name, some 9 km from Ollantaytambo. There are three quarries at the site: **Molle Puqro**, which the Incas were gradually abandoning at the time of the conquest; **Sirkusirkuyoc** and the smaller **Cachiccata**, which both seem to have been fully operational. The stone at Cachiccata, rose-coloured rhyolite, is just one of many types of stone used in the construction of Ollantaytambo, and it is still not known where the others came from. It would seem that all the quarries were abandoned when Manco Inca retreated from Ollantaytambo after confronting Hernando Pizarro's cavalry there in 1537.

Standing to the left of the six monolithic blocks which form the so-called Temple of the Sun at Ollantaytambo, you can see, looking west-southwest across the valley, the quarries of Cachiccata, below a mountain called Yana Urco. From here, you can appreciate the Herculean nature of the task that the builders of Ollantaytambo's magnificent temples set themselves.

Several generations of stonemasons and labourers must have worked in their thousands to quarry the huge blocks that the Incas used in the construction of the Temple of the Sun and the Royal House of the Sun. Once extracted, the stones would have been roughly shaped before being transported to the building site. Possibly using rollers, or more probably using the simple brute force of the thousands of men that the Incas' highly organized society would have been able to dedicate to the task, the blocks were then dragged for more than 6 km across open country. 

The Incas would only have been able to cross the Río Urubamba in winter, when its waters are at their lowest ebb, and even then they could probably only have done so by diverting the river's course. It is thought that they dug two channels; the stones would then have been dragged across the dry left-hand channel while the river was being diverted through the right-hand one. This right-hand channel would then be drained in its turn to allow the stones to continue their painstaking progress.

The next task was to raise the rhyolite blocks from the valley floor up to the site known as the Fortress and, to accomplish this, the Incas' engineers built a great ramp. Looking down from the Temple of the Sun, to the left of the six monoliths, the remains of this ramp can still be seen, and they are even more clearly visible when you look up at the ruins from the valley floor. It is difficult to appreciate from today's highly mechanized perspective just how hard the Incas laboured to build Ollantaytambo, employing as they did a patience and skill born of a concept of time very different to our own. The stones were found near the summit of a mountain on the other side of the river valley after a prolonged search. They then had to be quarried, hewn into a rough shape, and hauled across the valley floor and up to the temple. Once there, they were sculpted by the master masons to fit together perfectly, to the design of an architect, or architects, of consummate skill.

Between the ruins and the quarries of Cachiccata, more that 50 enormous stones that never reached their destination lie abandoned. The inhabitants of the area call them **Las Piedras Cansadas** (the tired stones). It is still not known whether work on the temples ceased when the Spanish arrived, or whether it stopped during the civil war between Atahualpa and Huascar. The thousands of workers who were involved in the construction of Ollantaytambo, over a period of generations, almost certainly worked under the *mit'a* system (see page 286). For several months of each year they would have to leave their work to tend their crops and, in times of war, construction would have been abandoned and the workers integrated into the enormous conscripted armies upon which the Inca state depended. Another suggestion is that Colla workers from Lake Titicaca were employed in the construction of the site. This conclusion has been drawn from the similarities between the monoliths facing the central platform and the Tiahuanaco remains. According to this theory, the Colla are believed to have deserted halfway through the work, leaving behind all the unfinished blocks visible today. While most experts agree that the work on Ollantaytambo was begun under Pachacútec, it will probably never be known for certain exactly when Cachiccata's great stones first began to tire.



## Pinkuylluna

Pinkuylluna Hill, on the western edge of Ollantaytambo, is home to the Sacred Valley's most impressive collection of *qolqas* (storehouses), structures which have often (and erroneously) been called prisons by local guides. The reason why these granaries were built so high up on the hillside is given by the 17th-century Spanish chronicler Bernabé Cobo: "[the Incas] built their storehouses outside their towns, in the high places that were fresh and well-ventilated ...". It is impossible to know with any certainty what kinds of produce were stored at Pinkuylluna, but the main harvest was certainly maize, which was probably stored alongside other crops. When viewed from the bridge in front of the ruins, a gigantic image, known locally as the Tunupa, can be seen on the hillside; it is thought by many observers to be a carved likeness of the Inca creator god, Viracocha.

Pinkuylluna can be climbed with no mountaineering experience, although there are some difficult stretches – allow two or three hours going up. The path is difficult to make out, so it's best not to go on your own. Walk up the valley to the left of the mountain, which is very beautiful and impressive, with Inca terraces after 4 km.

## Pumamarca

Hidden away in the hills beyond the historic town, Pumamarca lies about two hours on foot from Ollantaytambo through fertile countryside sculpted long ago into a series of agricultural terraces which to this day are sown with corn and *kiwicha*. Pumamarca is a small, well-preserved Inca citadel 7 km north of, and 800 m above, Ollantaytambo. It lies at the confluence of the Río Patacancha and its tributary, the Yuracmayo (or White River). From there it dominates a strategic point, commanding a privileged view of both valleys, and would once have controlled access to Ollantaytambo from that direction, as well as guarding the canal which bears its name.

The ruins' high surrounding wall with its numerous zigzags suggests that the site was a fortress, although (as at Ollantaytambo) all the *qolqas* (storehouses) were built outside the main complex. Nobody knows for sure exactly when this citadel was built. Some researchers believe that it may have been another checkpoint, designed to limit access to Ollantaytambo from Antisuyo, the eastern *suyo* (quarter) of the Inca Empire. But the impressive nature of Pumamarca, built in classic Inca style, leads many scholars to conclude that it may have been one of the first Inca settlements in the area, and not just a simple outpost of Ollantaytambo.

The path to Pumamarca passes through the village of Munaypata and follows the Río Patacancha. At Pallata, 6 km from Ollantaytambo and 30 minutes before Pumamarca, the Miranda family will look after bicycles and other gear. They live in the first house in the village; the path from the road to the footbridge over the river passes their front door. Up the same valley are the indigenous villages of Marcacocha, Huilloc and Patacancha.

## Cusichaca Valley

A major excavation project has been carried out since 1977 under the direction of Ann Kendall in the Cusichaca Valley, 26 km from Ollantaytambo, at the intersection of the Inca routes ⓘ *see www.cusichaca.org*. Only 9 km of this road are passable by ordinary car. The Inca fort, **Huillca Raccay**, was excavated in 1978-1980, and work is now concentrated on **Llactapata**, a site of domestic buildings. Ann Kendall is now working in the Patacancha Valley northeast of Ollantaytambo. Excavations are being carried out in parallel with the restoration of Inca canals to bring fresh clean water to the settlements in the valley.

## Sleeping

**Pisac** *p126, map p127*

**A Royal Inca Pisac**, Carretera Ruinas Km 1.5, T084-203064, www.royalinkahotel.com/hpisac.html. In the same chain as the **Royal Incas** I and II in Cuzco, this hotel can be reached by the hotels' own bus service. It is a short distance out of town, on the road that goes up to the ruins, a taxi ride after dark. Price includes taxes and breakfast. A guide for the ruins can be provided. The rooms are comfortable, in a number of blocks in the grounds of a converted hacienda; they are pleasantly furnished, with all conveniences. There is a pool, sauna and jacuzzi (US$7), tennis court, horse riding and bicycle rental. The restaurant is good and there is a bar. The hotel is popular with day trippers from Cuzco. Staff are very helpful and accommodating.

**C Paz y Luz**, T084-203204, www.pazyluzperu.com. 10-15 mins' walk from Pisac Plaza, close to the river. American expat Diane Dunn owns this relatively new hotel with a pleasant garden, nicely designed rooms, all with private bath and breakfast included in the price. Good place to chill and admire the rural surroundings and impressive mountain landscapes that rise dramatically above Pisac. Diane also offers healing from many traditions (including Andean), sacred tours, workshops and gatherings. Recommended.

*For an explanation of the sleeping and eating price codes used in this guide, see inside front cover. Other relevant information is found on pages 27-32.*

**D-E Pisaq**, at the corner of Pardo on the Plaza, Casilla Postal 1179, Cuzco, T084-203062, www.hotelpisaq.com. Bright and charming local decor and a pleasant atmosphere at this hotel, with private and shared bathrooms, hot water, sauna and massage. Good breakfast, basic, clean and friendly. The restaurant serves meals using local ingredients, some nights pizza is served, café.

**F Residencial Beho**, Intihuatana 642, 50 m up the hill from the plaza, T/F084-203001. Ask for a room in the main building. They serve a good breakfast for US$1. The *hostal* has a shop selling local handicrafts including masks. The owner's son will act as a guide to the ruins at the weekend.

**G Parador**, on the plaza, T084-203061. Price per person. All rooms share bathrooms, which have hot water. Breakfast is not included, but the restaurant serves other meals.

### Pisac to Urubamba *p128*

**AL Inkaterra Urubamba Villas**, in the hamlet of Higuspurco, between Urubamba and Yukay, www.inkaterra.com. Price is per person in one of two self-contained villas in spacious gardens, fully-equipped, breakfast and dinner included, lunch optional, courtesy bottle of wine, also has a bar, access to excursions and activities with car and driver available.

**AL Sonesta Posadas del Inca**, Plaza Manco II, Yucay 123, T084-201107, www.sonestaperu.com. A converted 300-year-old monastery is now a hotel which is like a little village with plazas, lovely gardens, a chapel and 69 comfortable, heated rooms. The price includes buffet breakfast, but not taxes. The restaurant serves an excellent buffet lunch. Lots of activities can be arranged, canoeing, horse riding, mountain biking, etc. There is a conference centre. Highly recommended.

**A La Casona de Yucay**, Plaza Manco II 104, Yucay, T084-201116, www.cusco.net/casona yucay/index.htm. This colonial house was where Simón Bolívar stayed during his liberation campaign in 1824. The price includes taxes and breakfast. The rooms have heating and, outside, there are 2 patios and gardens. **Don Manuel** restaurant is good, also has bar. Helpful staff.

**C Hostal Y'Llary**, Plaza Manco II, Yucay, T084-201112, www.reservasperu.com/hostalyllary/. The price includes bathroom and breakfast. The *hostal* is in a remodelled building fronting the plaza, with gardens.

### Valle de Lares *p130, map p131*

**L-AL Urubamba Boutique Lodge**, Huarán, Calca, T084-251563, www.urubambaboutiquelodge.com, or www.pebhl.com. Brand new hotel in the same group as the Casa San Blas in the city. All rooms with bath and balconies, **Mayu Cocina Fuzion** restaurant, travel and medical assistance.

### Urubamba and around *p134, map p135*

**L Libertador Valle Sagrado Lodge**, 5° paradero, Yanahuara, T084-961 3316, http://en.vallesagradolodge.com/about/. Affiliated to the Libertador group, a colonial-style hotel with 16 rooms in extensive grounds. Libertador's own **Tambo del Inka** on Av Ferrocarril, www.libertador.com.pe, was being completely rebuilt in 2007 and will reopen as a luxury hotel with 128 rooms.

**AL Casa Andina Private Collection Sacred Valley**, 5° paradero, Yanahuara, between Urubamba and Ollantaytambo, T084-976 5501, www.casa-andina.com. In its own 3-ha estate, with all the facilities associated with this chain, plus a gym, organic garden and restaurant with *novo andino* cuisine. Adventure activities can be arranged here. It also has a spa offering a range of massages and treatments, a gym and a planetarium and observatory, showing the Inca view of the night sky (US$10).

**AL Sol y Luna**, west of town, T084-201620, www.hotelsolyluna.com. Charming round bungalows set off the main road in lovely gardens, pool, excellent buffet in restaurant, French-Swiss owned. Has **Viento Sur** adventure travel agency, www.aventuras vientosur.com, for mountain biking, trekking and paragliding, also has its own riding centre with Paso horses, and provides cultural events and meals, and a spa .

**AL-A K'uychi Rumi**, Km 73.5 on the road to Ollantaytambo, 3 km from town, T084-201169, www.urubamba.com. 6 cottages for rent with 2 bedrooms, fully equipped, fireplace, terrace and balcony, surrounded by gardens. Price is for 1 or 2 people, each house can accommodate 6.

**A San Agustín Monasterio de la Recoleta**, Jr Recoleta s/n, T084-201666, recoleta@hotelessanagustin.com.pe. In a converted monastery (the earliest in the region) on the outskirts, this new hotel has suites and standard rooms with heating, TV and all facilities, plus the **San Isidro** restaurant.
**A San Agustín Urubamba**, Ctra Cuzco–Pisac, Km 69, T084-201444, urubamba@hotelessanagustin.com.pe. An upgraded hotel in a lovely setting just out of Urubamba, also with suites and standard rooms, swimming pool, sauna, massage and jacuzzi, **Naranjachayoc's** restaurant and bar.
**C Las Tres Marías**, Zavala 307, T084-201006. Beautiful gardens and rooms with hot water. Hosts are welcoming. Recommended.
**D-E Hospedaje Los Jardines**, Jr Convención 459, T084-201331, www.machawasi.com. An attractive guesthouse with comfortable rooms, non-smoking, delicious breakfast extra (vegans catered for), safe, lovely garden, laundry. **Sacred Valley Mountain Bike Tours** is also based here.
**E** per person **Las Chullpas**, 3 km west of town in the Pumahuanca Valley, T084-201568, www.uhupi.com/chullpas. Very peaceful, includes excellent breakfast, vegetarian meals, English and German spoken, Spanish classes, natural medicine, treks, horse riding, mountain biking, camping US$3 with hot shower. *Mototaxi* from town US$0.85, taxi US$2 (ask for Querocancha).
**F Hostal Urubamba**, Bolognesi 605, T084-201062. Basic but pleasant, rooms with bath and cold water, cheaper without bath.
**G Hospedaje Perla de Vilcanota**, 9 de Noviembre, T084-809791. Price is per bed, without bath, but shared bathrooms have hot water; some rooms are even cheaper.

### Chinchero *p134*

**C La Casa de Barro**, T084-306031 www.lacasadebarro.net. New modern hotel, price includes American breakfast, with bath, hot water, bar, restaurant, tours arranged.

### Ollantaytambo and around *p138, map p139*

**AL Pakaritampu**, C Ferrocarril s/n, T084-204020, www.pakaritampu.com. The price includes breakfast and taxes. This modern, 3-star hotel has 20 rooms with bath and views. It is owned by a former Peruvian women's volleyball star. There is a TV room, restaurant and bar, internet service for guests, laundry, safe and room service. Adventure sports such as rafting, climbing, trekking, mountain biking and horse riding can be arranged. Meals are extra: buffet US$20, dinner US$17. Excellent quality and service.
**A-B El Albergue Ollantaytambo**, within the railway station gates, T084-204014, www.rumbosperu.com/elalbergue/. Owned by North American Wendy Weeks, the *albergue* has 8 rooms with bath. Price includes breakfast; packed lunch available, full dinner on request. The rooms are full of character and are set in buildings around a courtyard and lovely gardens. There is also a eucalyptus steam sauna. The whole place is charming, very relaxing and homely. See the office-cum-shop-cum-exhibition where interesting handicrafts can be bought. Also for sale is Wendy's digestif, Compuesto Matacuy. It's very convenient for the Machu Picchu train and good place for information. Private transport can be arranged to the salt mines, Moray, Abra Málaga for birdwatching and taxi transfers to the airport. Highly recommended.
**A-B Ñustayoc Mountain Lodge and Resort**, about 5 km west of Ollantaytambo, just before Chillca and the start of the Inca Trail, T01-275 0706, www.nustayoclodge.com. Large and somewhat rambling lodge in a wonderful location with great views of the snowy Verónica massif and other peaks. Lovely flower-filled garden and grounds. Nicely decorated, spacious rooms, all with private bath. Price includes continental breakfast served in the large restaurant area.
**C Hostal Munay Tika**, on the road to the station, T084-204111, www.munaytika.com. Price includes breakfast and bath. Dinner is served by arrangement. To use the sauna costs US$5 with prior notice. Also has a nice garden. New and good.
**C-E KB**, between the main plaza and the ruins, T084-204091, www.kbperu.com. Spacious, comfortable rooms, cheaper without bath, also has budget lodging (**G**), hot water, flower-filled garden, very good restaurant (🍴). Also offers adventure tours.
**D Albergue Kapuly**, at the end of the station road, T084-204017. Prices are lower in the off

season. A quiet place with spacious rooms, with or without bath. The garden is nice and the price includes a good continental breakfast. Recommended.

**E Hostal La Ñusta**, C Ocobamba, T084-204035. Ask about accommodation in the shop/restaurant of the same name on the plaza or in the **Gran Tunupa** restaurant. A decent although uninspiring budget option. Proprietor Rubén Ponce loves to share his knowledge of the ruins with guests. You get a good view of the ruins from the balcony. For details of the restaurant, see Eating.

**E Hostal Tambo**, T084-204003, just walk up the street called Lari that heads north from the plaza. After 20 m or so you'll see an unmarked blue door on the left-hand side; bang on the door. If this doesn't work keep walking, turn left down the first small alley and bang on that blue door instead! Once past this unassuming exterior you emerge into a mini Garden of Eden, full of fruit trees, flowers, dogs, cats and domesticated parrots in the trees. There are only 3 basic rooms with shared bath (some hot water), but the family is very friendly and the *señora* is a real character.

**E Las Orquídeas**, near the start of the road to the station, T084-204032. Good accommodation at this *hostal*, price includes breakfast and meals are available.

**F Hostal Chaskawasi**, Chaupicalle (also called Taypi) north of the plaza, T084-204045, katycusco@yahoo.es. A *hostal* snuggled away in the small alleys behind the plaza. Owner Anna is very friendly.

**F Hostal Ollanta**, south side of the plaza, T084-204116. Basic and clean, with a great location. All rooms with shared bath.

**G Hostal Choza**, just below the main plaza in town, T084-204113. Very clean and friendly with safe motorcycle parking. They have a TV in the front room for guests and one of the rooms features a wonderful view of the ruins with the Nevado de Verónica framed perfectly behind – a great sight to wake up to in the morning. Recommended, but cold water only.

## Eating

**Pisac** *p126, map p127*

**ŸŸ-Ÿ Miski Mijuna Wasi**, on the Plaza de Armas, T084-203266. Serves very tasty local food, typical and *novo andino*, also international dishes. Has a *pastelería* also.

**ŸŸ-Ÿ Mullu**, Mcal Castilla 375, T084-208182. Tue-Sun 0900-1900. Café/restaurant related to the Mullu store in Cuzco, also has a gallery promoting local artists.

**Ÿ Doña Clorinda**, on the plaza opposite the church. A very friendly place; it doesn't look very inviting but cooks tasty food, including vegetarian options.

### Cafés

**Bakery**, Av Mcal Castilla 372. Sells excellent cheese and onion *empanadas* for US$0.25, suitable for vegetarians, and good wholemeal bread. The oven is tremendous – take a look even if you aren't hungry.

**Ulrike's Café**, Plaza de Armas 828, T084-203195, ulrikescafe@terra.com.pe. On the plaza, this comfortable café has possibly the best apple crumble with ice-cream on the planet, to say nothing of great coffee, smoothies and wide range of international cuisine. A good place to chill out after a hard day exploring the markets and ruins.

**Calca and around** *p128*

There are some basic restaurants around the plaza in Calca.

**Urubamba and around** *p134, map p135*

**ŸŸŸ Tunupa**, on left side of the road on the riverbank, in a new, colonial-style hacienda (same ownership as Tunupa in Cuzco), zappa@ terra.com.pe. Excellent food served indoors or out, bar, lounge, library, chapel, gardens, stables and an alpaca/jewellery shop. Outstanding exhibition includes pre-Columbian objects and colonial paintings, and **Seminario** ceramics feature in the decor. People on valley tours (Tue, Thu, Sun) are served a varied buffet including *novo andino* cuisine: buffet lunch, daily 1200-1500, US$15; dinner daily 1800-2030.

**ŸŸ El Fogón**, Parque Pintacha, T084-201534. Traditional Peruvian food, large servings, nice atmosphere. Recommended.

**ŸŸ El Maizal**, on the road before the bridge, T084-201454. Country-style restaurant with a good reputation, buffet service with a variety of typical *novo andino* dishes, plus international choices, beautiful gardens with native flowers and fruit trees. Recommended (they also have a hotel of the same name).

ŸŸ **La Casa de la Abuela**, Bolívar 272, 2 blocks up from the Plaza de Armas, T084-622975. Excellent restaurant with rooms grouped around a small courtyard. The trout is fantastic and food is served with baskets of roasted potatoes and salad. Recommended.

ŸŸ **Quinta los Geranios**, on the main road before the bridge, T084-201043. Regional dishes, excellent lunch with more than enough food, average price US$13.

Ÿ **Pintacha**, Bolognesi 523. Pub/café serving sandwiches, burgers, coffees, teas and drinks. Has games and book exchange, cosy, open till late.

Ÿ **Pizzonay**, Av Mcal Castilla, 2nd block. Pizzas, mulled wine, excellent spinach ravioli and not-so-good lasagne are served in this small restaurant with nice decor. Clean, good value. Recommended.

### Cafés

**The Muse Too**, Comercio 347 y Grau, on the corner of the plaza, T084-980 7970, themusecusco@yahoo.com. Cuzco restaurant-owner Clare's new version of her restaurant/café (Tandapata 684, Cuzco), similar idea with colourful walls, comfortable sofas, good coffee and breakfasts, plus the occasional good curry or chocolate brownie into the bargain.

### Ollantaytambo and around
*p138, map p139*

ŸŸ **Fortaleza**, 2 branches, one on Plaza Ruinas, the other on the north side of the main plaza (although not the same company). Basic but good food, breakfasts, pizza and pasta – all the gringo restaurant favourites are on offer, as well as some more local dishes.

ŸŸ **Il Cappuccino**, just before the bridge on the right-hand side. Offers the best cappuccino in town, great coffee generally, also café latte and expresso. Continental and American breakfasts are good. Slightly more sophisticated ambience and service than many other establishments in town.

ŸŸ **Kusicoyllor**, on the Plaza Ruinas. The same owners as **Il Cappuccino**, serving pizza, pasta and, once again, good coffee.

ŸŸ **Mayupata**, Jr Convención s/n, across the bridge on the way to the ruins, on the left, T084-204083 (Cuzco). Serving international choices and a selection of Peruvian dishes, desserts, sandwiches and coffee. It opens at 0600 for breakfast, and serves lunch and dinner. The bar has a fireplace; river view, relaxing atmosphere.

Ÿ **Alcázar Café**, C del Medio s/n, 50 m from the plaza, T084-204034, alcazar@ollantaytambo.org. A mainly vegetarian restaurant, but also serving fish and meat dishes, with pasta specialities. Offers excursions to some traditional Andean communities.

Ÿ **La Ñusta**, on the plaza, with the same owner as the hostel, see Sleeping. Popular, serves good food; snacks available.

### Cafés

**Heart´s Café**, on Plaza de Armas, T084-204078, www.heartscafe.org. Brand new wholefood restaurant serving western and Asian dishes, including chicken and fish, owned by SAE member Sonia, whose expertise is in vegetarian food. Clean and bright, open from 0700, run by villagers with all proceeds going to local communities. Popular.

## Festivals and events

**Pisac** *p126, map p127*
A local fiesta is held on **15 Jul**.

**Pisac to Urubamba** *p128*
Fiesta de la Virgen Asunta is held in Coya on **15-16 Aug**. Lamay hosts a festival on **15 Aug**.

**Urubamba and around** *p134, map p135*
**May** and **Jun** are the harvest months, with many processions following mysterious ancient schedules. Urubamba's main festival, El Señor de Torrechayoc, takes place during the first week of Jun. Chinchero celebrates the Day of the Virgin on **8 Sep**.

**Ollantaytambo and around**
*p138, map p139*
On **6 Jan** there is the Bajada de Reyes Magos (the Magi), when people from the highland communities bring down to Ollantaytambo the Niño Jesús, dressed in a poncho, etc. There is some traditional dancing, a bull fight, local food and a fair. The Fiesta de Compadres, a moveable feast 10 days before Carnavales and 13 days

before Ash Wednesday, is celebrated in the small, indigenous village of **Marcacocha**, close to Ollantaytambo by local transport or on foot. There is a delightful chapel on an Inca site, the dance of the *huayllata* (Andean goose), a mass and a bullfight in the smallest bullring imaginable, all in beautiful surroundings. As elsewhere, **Semana Santa**, the week before **Easter**, is a lovely time of year. **Pentecost**, 50 days after Easter, is celebrated by the **Fiesta del Señor de Choquekillca**, patron saint of Ollantaytambo. There are several days of dancing, weddings, processions, masses, feasting and drinking (the last opportunity to see traditional Cuzqueño dancing). On **29 Jun**, following Inti Raymi in Cuzco, there is a colourful festival, the **Ollanta-Raymi**, at which the Quechua drama, *Ollantay*, is re-enacted. **29 Oct** is the **Aniversario de Ollantaytambo**, a festival with dancing in traditional costume and many local delicacies for sale.

## Activities and tours

### Urubamba and around *p134, map p135*

**Agrotourism**

**Chichubamba**, Casa de ProPerú, Jr Rejachayoc, Urubamba, T084-201562, www.agrotourismsacredvalley.com. A community tourism project which lets visitors take part in a number of traditional activities (culinary, horticulture, textiles, ceramics, beekeeping, etc, US$3 pp, cheaper for groups), hiking US$10, lodging **E** per person and local meals. It's about 10 mins' walk from Urubamba; follow the signs.

**Horse riding**

**Perol Chico**, 5 km from Urubamba at Km 77, T01-9822 3297 (mob), office T054-284732, www.perolchico.com. Owned and operated by Eduard van Brunschot Vega (Dutch/ Peruvian), 1- to 14-day trips from Urubamba, good horses, riding is Peruvian Paso style; 1-day trip to Moray and the salt pans costs US$110 (minimum 2 people, starting in Cuzco). Recommended.

**Trekking**

**Haku Trek**, contact Javier Saldívar or Yeral Quillahuman, T084-961 3001 (mob). A cooperative tourism project in the Chicón valley (the mountain valley above Urubamba), run by residents of the community. 3 different hiking trips are offered: two 1-day hiking options (US$20 per person including food and accommodation) and a third, 2-day hike up to the Chicón Glacier itself (US$45 all inclusive). Hikes are based at a simple, but beautifully located eco-lodge in the valley and profits are used to fund reforestation of native forest in the area.

## Transport

**Getting there from Cuzco**

Combis and colectivos for **Chinchero** leave from the 300 block of Av Grau in Cuzco, 1 block before crossing the bridge (23 km, 45 mins, US$0.60), continuing to **Urubamba**, a further 25 km, 45 mins, US$0.45. There are also direct buses to **Urubamba**, US$1, or US$1.20 for a seat in a colectivo.

Colectivos, minibuses and buses for **Urubamba** via **Pisac** leave daily 0600-1600, when full, from C Puputi on the outskirts of Cuzco, near the Clorindo Matto de Turner school and Av de la Cultura (32 km, 1 hr, US$0.85).

There is a direct bus service from Av Grau to **Ollantaytambo**, 0745 and 1945 direct. At other times catch a bus to **Urubamba** and change there, US$0.30.

Buses to **Calca** via **Pisac** leave from Av Tullumayo 800 block in Wanchac.

To organize your own Sacred Valley transport, try one of these taxi drivers, recommended by **South America Explorers**: **Manuel Calanche**, T084-227368, T969 5402 (mob); **Carlos Hinojosa**, T084-251160; **Ferdinand Pinares Cuadros**, Yuracpunco 155; Tahuantinsuyo, T084-225914, T968 1519 (mob), speaks English, French and Spanish); **Eduardo**, T084-231809, speaks English. Also recommended are: **Angel Marcavillaca Palomino**, Av Regional 877, T084-251822, amarcavillaca@yahoo.com, helpful, patient, reasonable prices; **Movilidad Inmediata**, Juan Carlos Herrera Johnson, T962 3821 (mob), runs local tours with an English-speaking guide. **Angel Salazar**, Marcavalle I-4 Wanchac, T084-224679 (to leave messages), is English-speaking and arranges good tours, very knowledgeable and enthusiastic; **Milton Velásquez**, T084-222638, T968 0730 (mob), is a tour guide and anthropologist and also speaks English.

**Pisac** *p126, map p127*
From Pisac, buses continue to **Calca** and **Urubamba** (1 hr, US$0.80). Buses returning to **Cuzco** from Pisac are often full; the last one leaves at around 2000.

**Urubamba and around** *p134, map p135*
**Bus**
The bus terminal is just west of Urubamba on the main road. Buses run from here to **Calca**, **Pisac** (1hr, US$0.80) and **Cuzco** (2 hrs, US$1), from 0530 onwards. There are also buses to Cuzco via **Chinchero**, same fare; crowded after 1730. Colectivos to **Cuzco** can be caught from outside the terminal and on the main road, US$1.20. Combis run to **Ollantaytambo** when full, 45 mins, US$0.30. There are also buses to **Quillabamba**.

**Train**
For details of the Sacred Valley Railway to **Aguas Calientes**, see box, page 154.

**Chinchero** *p134*
Buses from Cuzco to Chinchero continue to **Urubamba**, 25 km, 45 mins, US$0.45. The last return bus to **Cuzco** leaves Chinchero at 1900 and is usually very crowded.

**Maras** and **Moray** are visited most easily from Chinchero nowadays. There is public transport to Maras as well as regular pick-up trucks which carry people and produce in and out. Transport stops running after 1700 or 1800 and costs US$0.60-1.

**Ollantaytambo and around**
*p138, map p139*
Those visiting the Sacred Valley by car and intending to continue on to Machu Picchu are advised to leave the car at Ollantaytambo railway station, which costs US$1 a day, or at suitable hotels (see Sleeping, above). For details of the Sacred Valley Railway, see box, page 154.

The station is 10-15 mins' walk from the plaza (turn left at the sign that says 'Centro de Salud' between the Plaza de Armas and the ruins). Colectivos run from the plaza to the station when trains are due. A bus leaves the station at 0900 for **Urubamba** (US$0.30) and **Chinchero** (US$1). Return buses to **Cuzco** leave from the station at 0715 and 1945, US$2.85. Colectivos run all day to **Urubamba** from one block east of the main plaza.

## Directory

**Pisac** *p126, map p127*
**Banks** A shop on M Castilla, heading away from the plaza, near where the road bends, will change TCs. **Internet and telephone** The municipal building, on the same side of the plaza as the museum, has an internet centre (closed Sun morning, US$0.75 per hr) and a public phone booth.

**Pisac to Urubamba** *p128*
**Internet** The municipal library in **Calca** has internet connection.

**Urubamba and around** *p134, map p135*
**Banks** Banks in the town centre on Comercio. ATM on the main road not far from the bridge. **Internet** Connections, corner of Av M Castilla and Av La Convención. **Post** Serpost is on the Plaza de Armas. **Telephone** There are several phone booths around the centre.

**Ollantaytambo and around**
*p138, map p139*
**Banks** ATM at C Ventiderio 248, between the Plaza and Av Ferrocarril.
**Internet** Several places in town, US$0.30 for 30 mins.

# Machu Picchu & the Inca trails

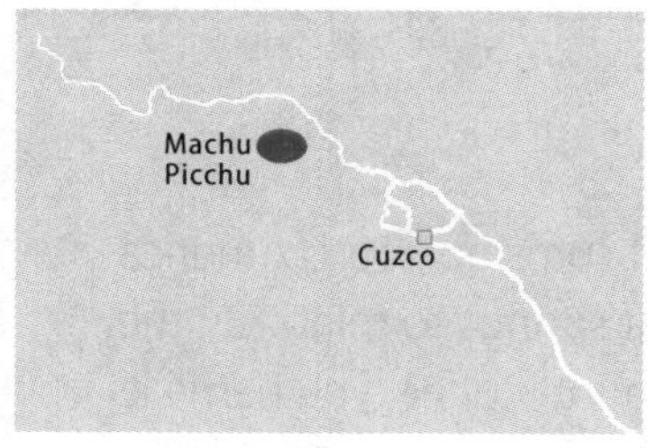




## Footprint features

# Introduction

If you're looking for a picture that sums up South America, Machu Picchu is usually what first springs to mind. On the television, in brochures, on packets of coffee, you name it, Machu Picchu has become a kind of shorthand for lost civilizations, the thrill of discovery, exotic travel and, above all, the mystery that can still be found in an increasingly technological world. At the same time it is accessible; hundreds of thousands of tourists visit it each year. And yet it transcends the many roles that it has acquired – photogenic image, tourist magnet, centre of controversy – through the strength of its stones, the way it is intimately tied to its surroundings, its enigmas and its beauty. The wonder of Machu Picchu has been well documented over the years. Equally impressive is the centuries-old Inca Trail that winds its way from the Sacred Valley near Ollantaytambo and is encompassed by the 325 sq-km Machu Picchu Historical Sanctuary. Machu Picchu itself cannot be understood without the Inca Trail. Its principal sites are ceremonial in character, apparently in ascending hierarchical order. The trail is essentially a work of spiritual art, like a Gothic cathedral, and walking it was formerly an act of devotion. It is unfortunate that the number of tourists who have committed themselves to repeating this Inca devotion, or at least undergoing the necessary penance of four exhausting days, has exceeded the tolerance of the trail itself, leading to severe damage. In addition, the Inca Trail has become, in many tourists' minds, the only Inca trail, when in fact there are many others which lead to Machu Picchu, perhaps without the same ceremonial meaning but with just as much great trekking through fine landscapes. These are now being sold as Inca Trail alternatives, avoiding, it is hoped, the risk of over-exploitation.

## Don't miss ...

1 **Watchman's Hut** This is the ideal place to spend the last few minutes of daylight, page 157.

2 **Intihuatana** This was the key point of Machu Picchu, where the sun's cycle was symbolically tied to the Inca world. Even if you miss the sacred significance, it is a wonderful work of art, page 159.

3 **Huayna Picchu** Make the vertiginous climb to the summit to see Machu Picchu in its glorious context, page 159.

4 **Intipunku** Congratulate yourself on reaching the end of the Inca Trail and be humbled by the view from the Sun Gate, page 164.

5 **Salkantay** This is the highest peak in the Vilcabamba mountains and even when viewed from a distance, it's clear why the Incas saw these heights as the realm of the gods. Various treks pass its glaciers and snowfields, page 165.

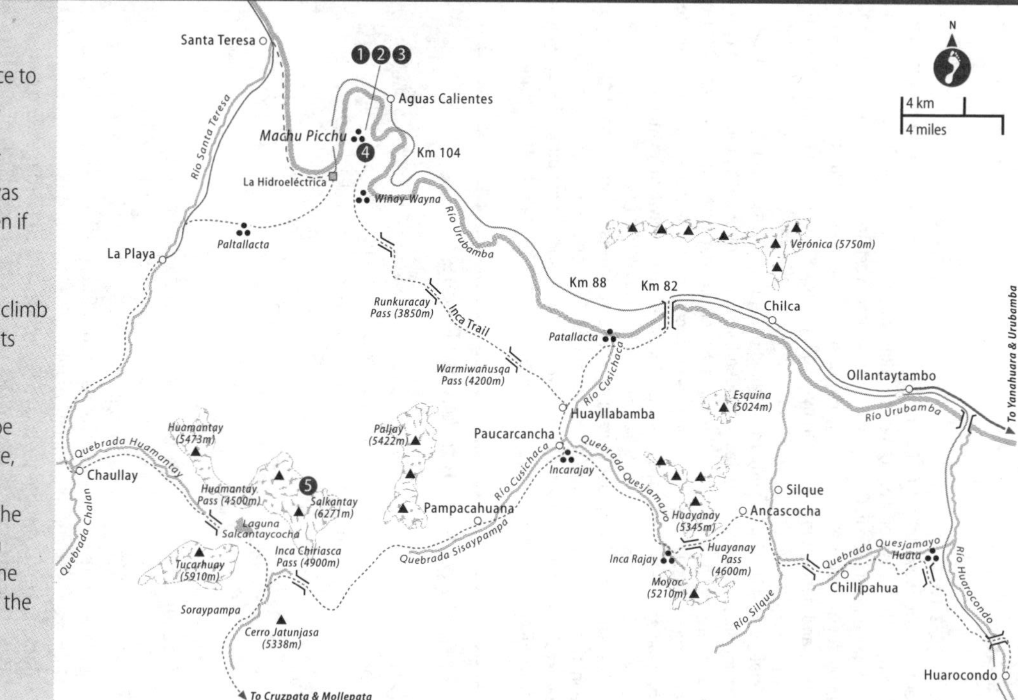

# Ins and outs

## Getting there

There are two ways to get to Machu Picchu. The easy way is by **train** from Cuzco, Ollantaytambo or Urubamba to Aguas Calientes (see box below). **PerúRail** trains run from San Pedro station in Cuzco, following the road west from the city through the Anta canyon for 10 km, before heading north at a sharp angle through the Urubamba canyon, and descending along the river valley, flanked by high cliffs and peaks. The route passes through Poroy and Ollantaytambo, terminating at Aguas Calientes station (officially called Machu Picchu). From Aguas Calientes buses run along a paved road in poor condition to Puente Ruinas, a disused station at the start of the road up to the ruins. There's a final climb to the ruins either on foot (following an Inca path) or continuing by bus. On leaving the site, don't forget that the last bus to Aguas Calientes departs at 1730; walking down to Aguas Calientes takes between 30 minutes and one hour. » *For further details, see box below and Transport, page 177.*

The strenuous but most rewarding way to arrive is on foot. Traditionally, this meant the hike along the Inca Trail, which is described on page 160. The introduction of new regulations for walking the trail have opened up additional options for trekking to Machu Picchu, some shorter, some longer than the popular route (see page 165).



### Travelling by train to Machu Picchu

There are two classes of tourist train: Vistadome and Backpacker. Note that timetables and prices are subject to frequent change. Tickets for all trains should be bought at Wanchac station in Cuzco, Avenida Pachacútec, T084-238722 (extension 318, 319 or 320) or via PerúRail's website, www.perurail.com. Services other than those listed here are run entirely at the discretion of PerúRail.

**From Cuzco**

**Vistadome** (US$66 single, US$113 return) departs San Pedro station daily at 0600 and 0700, arriving Aguas Calientes (Machu Picchu) at 0940 and 1100. It stops at Ollantaytambo en route, some 2 hours after leaving Cuzco. It returns from Machu Picchu at 1530 and 1700, reaching Cuzco at 1920 and 2125, also with a stop in Ollantaytambo.

**Backpacker** (US$46 single, US$73 return) departs San Pedro station daily at 0615, passing Ollantaytambo at 0840 and reaching Aguas Calientes at 1015. It returns at 1555, passing Ollantaytambo at 1740, getting to Cuzco at 2020. If you do not want to arrive in Cuzco in the dark (especially if you have no hotel booked), ask to get off the train at Poroy and take a bus from there. This saves about an hour.

**Hiram Bingham** (US$325 single Poroy-Machu Picchu, US$275 single Machu Picchu-Poroy, US$547 return) is a super-luxury train with dining car and bar. It leaves Poroy (west of Cuzco) at 0900 with brunch on board, reaching Aguas Calientes at 1230. It leaves Aguas at 1800, cocktails, dinner and live entertainment on board, arriving in Poroy at 2125 with a bus service back to Cuzco hotels. The cost includes all meals, buses and entry to the ruins.

Licensed tour operators in Cuzco will be able to show you the alternatives. Whichever route you walk, going on foot is the only true way to get to Machu Picchu and will allow you to see it in its proper context. You are not allowed to walk back along the Inca Trail though you can pay US$4.50 at Intipunku to be allowed to walk back as far as Wiñay-Wayna (see page 164).



## Visitor information

Tickets for Machu Picchu must be purchased in advance from the **Instituto Nacional de Cultura (INC)** ⓘ *Av Pachacútec cuadra 1, Aguas Calientes, www.inc-cusco.gob.pe (for the Cuzco office, see page 59)*. The INC website has information on national heritage sites in the Cuzco area, plus all regulations covering Machu Picchu and the Inca Trail (look under 'Sistema de Reservas RCI'). It also lists the tour operators and guides who are permitted to take tourists on the Inca Trail. The agency officially responsible for the Inca Trail is **Unidad Gestión de Machupicchu** ⓘ *Garcilaso 223, Cuzco, T084-242103*. It is an excellent source of information on Machu Picchu and is the place to which any complaints or observations should be directed. **i perú** ⓘ *in the INC office, as above, Of 4, Aguas Calientes, T084-211104, iperumachupicchu@promperu.gob.pe, 0900-2000 (for the Cuzco office, see Ins and outs, page 58)*, can also provide general information.

▸▸ *For Sleeping, Eating and other listings, see pages 174-178.*



**From Urubamba**

**Sacred Valley Railway Vistadome** (US$46 single, US$77 return) departs Urubamba at 0610, reaching Aguas Calientes at 0820. The return service leaves at 1645, reaching Urubamba at 1915. You must reserve seats 10 days in advance. Several hotels in Urubamba and Yucay offer free transport to and from the station in Urubamba. (Always check in advance that this train is running.)

**From Ollantaytambo** (see also Cuzco services, above)

**Ollantaytambo Vistadome** (US$46 single, US$77 return) leaves Ollantaytambo at 0705, 1030 and 1455, and returning from Aguas Calientes at 0835, 1320 and 1645; journey time 1 hr 20 mins. Tickets include food in the price. These trains have toilets, video, snacks and drinks for sale.

**Ollantaytambo Backpacker Shuttle** (US$57 return, no one-way tickets) only runs 1 Apr to 31 Oct, departing at 0905, arriving at 1100, returning from Aguas Calientes at 1620, reaching Ollantaytambo at 1800. Seats can be reserved even if you're not returning the same day.

There is also a cheap, unscheduled Backpacker train from Ollantaytambo (US$20 single, US$40 return), leaving at 2000, arriving in Aguas Calientes at 2120, returning from Aguas at 0545 the following morning and arriving in Ollantaytambo at 0740. Tickets can be bought in advance at Wanchac station in Cuzco or at Ollantaytambo but check on the train's existence at the time of travel as it is not included on regular timetables. Note that, if you use this service, you will have to spend two nights in Aguas Calientes if you want to see Machu Picchu.

See Train, under Transport, page 178, on an alternative to Peru Rail's services to Machu Picchu.

# Background

For centuries Machu Picchu was buried in jungle, until Hiram Bingham stumbled upon it in July 1911. It was then explored by an archaeological expedition sent by Yale University. Machu Picchu was a stunning find. The only major Inca site to escape 400 years of looting and destruction, it was remarkably well preserved. And it was no ordinary Inca settlement. It sat in an inaccessible location above the Urubamba Gorge, and contained so many fine buildings that people have puzzled over its meaning ever since.

Bingham claimed he had discovered the lost city of Vilcabamba, and for 50 years everyone believed him. But he was proved wrong, and the mystery deepened. Later discoveries revealed that Machu Picchu was the centre of an extensive Inca province. Many finely preserved satellite sites and highways also survive. This is craggy terrain and the value of a province with no mines and little agricultural land – it was not even self-sufficient – is hard to determine. Bingham postulated it was a defensive citadel on the fringes of the Amazon. But the architecture fails to convince us, and in any case, defence against whom?

The Incas were the first to build permanent structures in this region, which was unusual because they arrived at the tail end of 4000 years of Andean civilization. Sixteenth-century land titles discovered in the 1980s revealed that Machu Picchu was built by the Inca Pachacútec, founding father of the Inca Empire. But they do not tell us why he built it. One reasonable speculation is that this area provided access to coca plantations in the lower Urubamba Valley. However, the fine architecture of Machu Picchu cannot be explained away simply as a coca-collecting station.

Recent studies have shown that the Temple of the Sun, or Torreón, was an observatory for the solstice sunrise, and that the Intihuatana stela is the centre point between cardinal alignments of nearby sacred peaks. The Incas worshipped nature: the celestial bodies, mountains, lightning, rainbows, rocks – anything, in fact, that was imbued with spiritual power.

This spiritual component is the key to understanding Machu Picchu. The Bingham expedition identified 75% of the human remains as female, and a common belief is that Machu Picchu was a refuge of the Inca 'Virgins of the Sun'. However, the skeletons were re-examined in the 1980s using modern technology, and the latest conclusion is that the gender split was roughly 50/50.

Machu Picchu was deliberately abandoned by its inhabitants – when, we do not know. This may have happened even before the Spanish conquest, perhaps as a result of the Inca civil wars, or the epidemics of European diseases which ran like brushfires ahead of the Spanish in the New World. One theory proposes that the city ran dry in a period of drought; another suggests a devastating fire. Or the city may have been evacuated during the period of Inca resistance to the Spanish, which lasted nearly 40 years and was concentrated not far west of Machu Picchu.



# Visiting Machu Picchu

» *pp174-178. Colour map 2, A2.*

ⓘ *Daily 0600-1730. Entrance fee is US$40, to be purchased in advance from the INC (see page 155). It is possible to pay in soles or dollars, but only clean, undamaged notes will be accepted. Tickets are valid for 3 days, but once you have entered the site you may not use that ticket for a visit on a second day. At the time of writing, a further increase in the entry fee (even to US$100) was being considered. You cannot take backpacks into the site; leave them at the entrance for about US$1. Guides at the site are often very knowledgeable and worthwhile; they charge US$20 for 2½ hrs, but less per person if you join a group.*

## Making the most of Machu Picchu

- Allow at least a day to appreciate the ruins and their surroundings fully. Although there is still a thriving business in one- or two-day trips, a quick visit hardly gives you time to recover from the initial sense of awe.
- Avoid Monday and Friday when there is usually a crowd of guided tours en route to or from Pisac's Sunday market, all wanting lunch at the same time.
- Visit early or late. The ruins are at their busiest in the morning after 0830. The site is quieter after 1530 although a lot of people do stay on to see the sun setting behind the mountains.
- Try to be there for dawn or dusk to enjoy the changing of the light. A good time to visit is before 0830, when the views are at their best.
- Find time to peer into corners, investigate the angles of stones, the weight of lintels, the outlook of windows. See how rocks and openings align themselves with peaks across the valley.
- Take your own food and plenty of drinking water. The Machu Picchu Sanctuary Lodge (see Sleeping, page 174 ) has a restaurant serving buffet lunch and there's a snack bar beside the entrance but neither place is cheap. Note, too, that food is not officially allowed into the site.
- In the dry season sandflies can be a problem, so take insect repellent and wear trousers and long-sleeved shirts.



There is a tremendous feeling of awe on first witnessing this incredible sight. The ancient citadel of Machu Picchu, 42 km from Ollantaytambo by rail, straddles the saddle of a high mountain at 2380 m, with steep terraced slopes falling away to the fast-flowing Río Urubamba snaking its hairpin course far below in the valley floor. Towering overhead is Huayna Picchu, and green jungle peaks provide the backdrop for the whole majestic scene. In comparison with many archaeological ruins, there are so many standing buildings that it requires no stretch of the imagination to work out what the city looked like. What function some of those buildings had and the meaning of their enigmatic symbols is harder to guess at, but this adds to the allure of the site.

*Numbers in the text correspond to numbered sights on the map, page 158.*

Once you have passed through the ticket gate you follow a path to a small complex of buildings which now acts as the **main entrance (1)** to the ruins. It is set at the eastern end of the extensive **terracing (2)** which must have supplied the crops for the city. Above this point, turning back the way you have come, is the final stretch of the Inca Trail leading down from **Intipunku** (Sun Gate), see page 164. From a promontory here, on which stands the building called the **Watchman's Hut (3)**, you get *the* perfect view of the city (the one you've seen on all the postcards), laid out before you with Huayna Picchu rising above the furthest extremity. Go round the promontory and head south for the **Intipata** (Inca bridge), see page 160.

The main path into the ruins comes to a **dry moat (4)** that cuts right across the site. At the moat you can either climb the long staircase which goes to the upper reaches of the city, or you can enter the city by the baths and Temple of the Sun.

The more strenuous way into the city is by the former route, which takes you past quarries on your left as you look down to the Urubamba on the west flank of the mountain. To your right are roofless buildings where you can see in close-up the general construction methods used in the city. Proceeding along this level, above the main plazas, you reach the **Temple of the Three Windows (5)** and the **Principal**

 **Temple** (6), which has a smaller building called the **Sacristy (7)**. The two main buildings are three-sided and were clearly of great importance, given the fine stonework involved. The wall with the three windows is built onto a single rock, one of the many instances in the city where the architects did not merely put their construction on a convenient piece of land. They used and fashioned its features to suit their concept of how the city should be tied to the mountain and its forces, and the alignment of its stones should relate to the surrounding peaks. In the Principal

## Machu Picchu

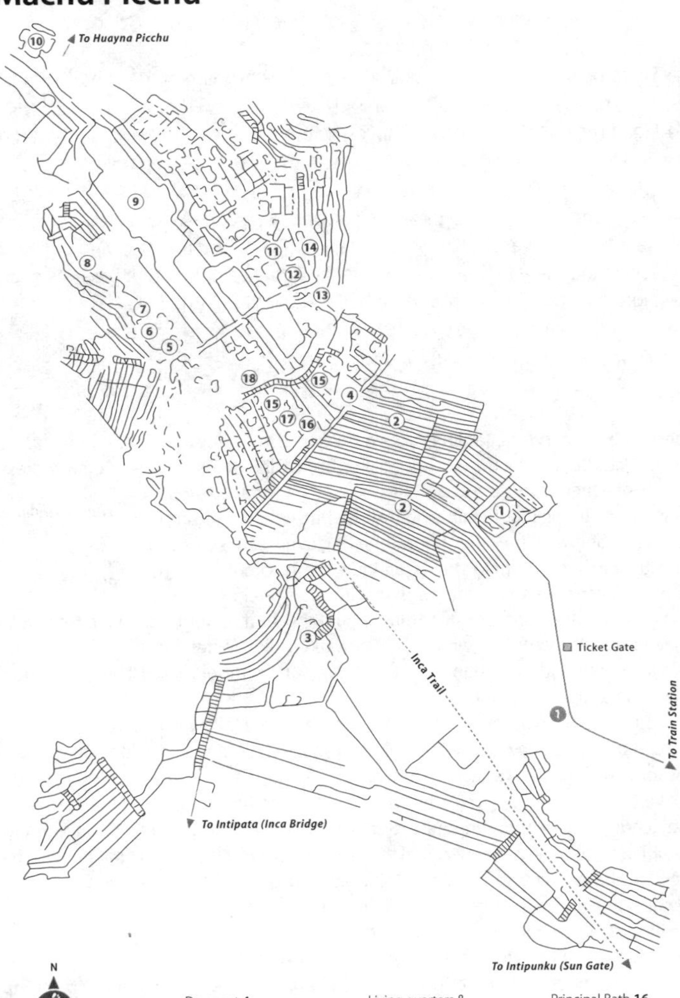


N

50 metres
50 yards

Main entrance **1**
Terracing **2**
Watchman's Hut **3**
Dry moat **4**
Temple of the Three Windows **5**
Principal Temple **6**
Sacristy **7**
Intihuatana **8**
Main Plaza **9**
Sacred Rock **10**
Living quarters & workshops **11**
Mortar buildings **12**
Prison Group & Condor Temple **13**
Intimachay **14**
Ceremonial baths or Fountains **15**
Principal Bath **16**
Temple of the Sun **17**
Royal Sector **18**

**Sleeping**
Machu Picchu Sanctuary Lodge **1**

Temple, a diamond-shaped stone in the floor is said to depict the constellation of the Southern Cross.



Continue on the path behind the Sacristy to reach the **Intihuatana (8)**, the 'hitching-post of the sun'. The name comes from the theory that such carved rocks (*gnomons*), found at all major Inca sites, were the point to which the sun was symbolically 'tied' at the winter solstice, before being freed to rise again on its annual ascent towards the summer solstice. The steps, angles and planes of this sculpted block appear to indicate a purpose beyond simple decoration, and researchers, such as Johan Reinhard in *The Sacred Center*, have sought to explain the trajectory of each alignment. Whatever the motivation behind this magnificent carving, it is undoubtedly one of the highlights of Machu Picchu.

Climb down from the Intihuatana's mound to the **Main Plaza (9)**. Beyond its northern end is a small plaza with open-sided buildings on two sides and on the third, the **Sacred Rock (10)**. The outline of this gigantic, flat stone echoes that of the mountains behind it. From here you can proceed to the start of the trail to Huayna Picchu (see page 159). Returning to the Main Plaza and heading southeast you pass, on your left, several groups of closely packed buildings which are thought to have been **living quarters** and **workshops (11)**, **mortar buildings (12)** – look for the house with two discs let into the floor – and the **Prison Group (13)**, one of whose constructions is known as the **Condor Temple**. Also in this area of the site is a cave called **Intimachay (14)**.

A short distance from the Condor Temple is the lower end of a series of **ceremonial baths (15)** or fountains. They were probably used for ritual bathing and the water still flows down them today. The uppermost, **Principal Bath (16)**, is the most elaborate. Next to it is the **Temple of the Sun (17)**, or Torreón. This singular building has one straight wall from which another wall curves around and back to meet the straight one, but for the doorway. From above, it looks like an incomplete letter P. It is another example of the architecture being at one with its environment as the interior is taken up by the partly worked summit of the outcrop on which the building is constructed. All indications are that this temple was used for astronomical purposes. Underneath the Torreón a cave-like opening has been formed by an oblique gash in the rock. Fine masonry has been added to the opposing wall, making a second side of a triangle, which contrasts with the rough edge of the split rock. The blocks of masonry appear to have been slotted behind another sculpted piece of natural stone, which has been cut into a four-stepped buttress. Immediately behind this is a two-stepped buttress. This strange combination of the natural and the man-made has been called the Tomb or Palace of the Princess. Across the stairway from the complex which includes the Torreón is the group of buildings known as the **Royal Sector (18)**.



## Huayna Picchu

ⓘ *Daily 0700-1300, with the latest return time at 1500. Only 400 people per day are allowed to climb Huayna Picchu.*

Synonymous with the ruins themselves is Huayna Picchu, the verdant mountain overlooking the site. There are also ruins on the mountain itself and steps to the top for a superlative view of the whole magnificent scene, but this is not for vertigo sufferers. The climb takes up to 90 minutes but the steps are dangerous after bad weather and you shouldn't leave the path. You must register at a hut at the beginning of the trail. To reach the **Temple of the Moon** from the path to Huayna Picchu, take the marked trail to the left; it is in good shape but descends further than you think it should, down to near the Urubamba. The Temple of the Moon consists of two caves, one above the other, with Inca niches inside that are sadly blemished by graffiti. Beyond the temple the path to Huayna Picchu is overgrown, slippery when wet and has a crooked ladder on an exposed part about 10 minutes before the top (not for the faint-hearted). It is therefore safer to return to the main trail to Huayna Picchu, adding about 30 minutes to the climb. The round trip takes about four hours.

## Intipata

The famous Inca bridge – Intipata – is about 45 minutes along a well-marked trail south of the Royal Sector. The bridge – which is actually a couple of logs – is spectacularly sited, carved into a vertiginous cliff face. The walk is well worth it for the fine views, but the bridge itself is closed to visitors. Not only is it in a poor state of repair, but the path beyond has collapsed. There have been several accidents.

# The Inca Trail » *pp174-178.*

The classic Inca Trail is a three- to four-day route to Machu Picchu, starting from the Sacred Valley near Ollantaytambo. What makes this hike so special is the stunning combination of Inca ruins, unforgettable views, magnificent mountains, exotic vegetation and extraordinary ecological variety. With your rucksack on your back you will be following in the footsteps of the Incas and making a true pilgrimage. The sweat and struggle is all worth it when you set your eyes on this mystical site at sunrise from the Inca sun gate above the ruins. Afterwards you recover in Aguas Calientes and soothe those aching limbs in the hot springs. » *For alternative Inca routes, see page 165.*

## Ins and outs

**Booking** Unlicensed agencies will sell Inca Trail trips but then pass clients on to a licensed operator. This can cause confusion and problems at busy times. Although there is a quota for agencies and groups to use the trail, modifications to the procedures in 2004 encouraged some agencies to make block bookings way in advance of departure dates. This made it much harder for agencies to guarantee their clients' places on the trail. Current advice is to book your preferred dates as early as possible, up to a year in advance, then confirm nearer the time. You should also verify your operator's cancellation fees. There have been many cases of disappointed trekkers whose bookings did not materialize, so don't wait until the last minute. Check in advance with a reputable tour company in Cuzco (see page 104), with a government agency such as **INC** (www.inc-cusco.gob.pe) or with **South American Explorers** (www.saexplorers.org) in Lima for booking procedures and also for changes in regulations.

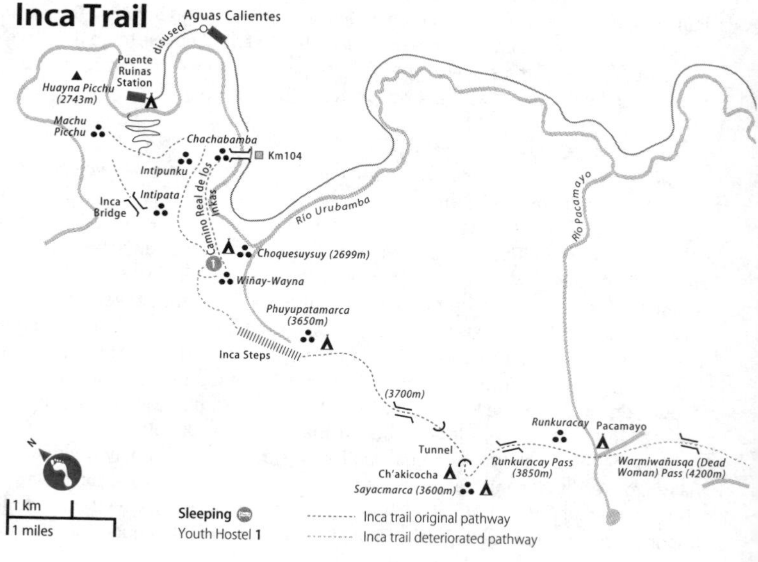

**Entrance tickets and tours** An entrance ticket for the trail or its variations must be bought at the **Instituto Nacional de Cultura (INC)** office in Cuzco; no tickets are sold at the entrance gates. Furthermore, tickets are only sold on presentation of a letter from a licensed tour operator on behalf of the visitor. There is a 50% discount for students, but note that officials are very strict, only an ISIC card will be accepted as proof of status. Tickets are checked at Km 82, Huayllabamba and Wiñay-Wayna.

On all hiking trails (Km 82 or Km 88 to Machu Picchu, Salkantay to Machu Picchu, Km 82 or Km 88 to Machu Picchu via Km 104) adults must pay US$73 (not including entrance to Machu Picchu), students and children under 15 US$36. On the Camino Real de los Inkas from Km 104 to Wiñay-Wayna and Machu Picchu the fee is US$30 per adult, US$15 for students and children. On the trail from Salkantay to Huayllabamba and Km 88 the fee is US$30 per adult, US$17.45 for students and children. The Salkantay trek is also supposed to be subject to a charge of US$36, but a dispute between the INC and the mayor of Mollepata meant that it was not being collected in 2007. It is expected that the charge will be applied in 2008 and that limits on the numbers of hikers will be imposed. It is probably safe to assume that INC will raise charges on trails again in the future.

Tour operators in Cuzco will arrange transport to the start, equipment, food, etc, for an all-in price of US$350-450 per person. Remember that you get what you pay for, but also bear in mind that the cheaper the price the more corners may be cut and the less attention paid to the environment and the porters. Avoiding exploitation is, after all, the goal of the 2001 legislation.

You can save a bit of money by arranging your own transport back to Ollantaytambo in advance, either for the last day of your tour, or by staying an extra night in Aguas Calientes and taking the early morning train, then a bus back to Cuzco. If you take your own tent and sleeping gear, some agencies give a discount. Make sure your return ticket for the tourist train to Cuzco has your name on it, otherwise you have to pay for any changes. » *For advice on tour operators, see box page 106.*

**Advice and information** Although in recent years security has improved, it's still best to leave all your valuables in Cuzco and keep everything inside your tent, even your shoes. Avoid the July and August high season and the rainy season from November to April (note that this can change, so check in advance). In the wet it is cloudy and the paths are very muddy and difficult. Also watch out for coral snakes in this area (black, red, yellow bands). Please remove all your rubbish, including toilet paper, or use the pits provided. Do not light open fires as they can get out of control. The annual **Inca Trail Clean-up** takes place usually in September. Many organizations and agencies are involved and volunteers should contact **South American Explorers** in Cuzco (see page 58) for full details of ways to help.

**Equipment** Note that it is cold at night on the Inca Trail and weather conditions change rapidly, so it is important to take strong footwear, rain gear and warm clothing (this includes long johns if you want to sleep rather than freeze at night):

## Inca Trail regulations

The year 2001 signalled the beginning of strict new rules on the Inca Trail; tourists should be aware of the following regulations:

- All agencies must have a licence to work in the area.
- Groups of up to seven independent travellers who do not wish to use a tour operator are allowed to hike the trail accompanied by an independent, licensed guide, as long as they do not employ any other support staff, such as porters or cooks.
- A maximum of 500 visitors and support staff per day are allowed on the trail.
- Operators pay US$12 for each porter and other trail staff to use the Trail. A porter's wage should be US$50 (165.60 soles). Porters are not permitted to carry more than 20 kg (less scrupulous agencies find ways to circumvent these requirements).
- Littering is banned. Plastic water bottles may not be carried on the trail; only canteens are permitted.
- Pets and pack animals are prohibited, although llamas are allowed as far as the first pass.
- Groups have to use approved campsites; on the routes from Km 82, Km 88 and Salkantay, the campsites may be changed with prior authorization.
- The Inca Trail is closed each February for maintenance.



dress in layers. Also take food, water, water purification tablets, insect repellent, sunscreen, a hat and sunglasses, a supply of plastic bags, a good sleeping bag, a torch and a stove for preparing hot food and drink to ward off the cold at night. It is worth paying extra to hire a down sleeping bag if you haven't brought your own.

A tent is essential: if you're hiring one in Cuzco, check carefully for leaks. Walkers who have not taken adequate equipment have died of exposure. Caves marked on some maps are little better than overhangs and are not sufficient shelter to sleep in. You could also take a first-aid kit; if you don't need it the porters probably will, given their rather basic footwear.

It is forbidden to use trekking poles because the metal tips damage the trail. Instead, buy a carved wooden stick on sale in the main plaza in Ollantaytambo or at the trail head. Many will need this for the steep descents on the path. If you need knee/ankle/thigh supports go to **Ayala**, a shop in Cuzco. (It's in a small arcade to the right of **Taca Peru**, opposite the Palacio de Justicia near the top of Avenida Sol.)

All the necessary equipment can be rented in Cuzco (see page 102). Good maps of the trail and area can be bought from **South American Explorers** in Cuzco or Lima (see pages 58 and 257). If you have any doubts about carrying your own pack, porters/guides are available through Cuzco agencies. Carry a day-pack, water and snacks, in case you walk at a different pace from the porter who is carrying the rest of your supplies.

### The trek → *3½ days*

**Day one** The trek to the sacred site begins either at Km 82, **Piscacucho**, or at Km 88, **Qorihuayrachina**, at 2600 m. In order to reach Km 82, hikers are transported by their tour operator (see above) in a minibus on the road that goes to Quillabamba. From Piri onward the road follows the riverbank and ends at Km 82. Where there used to be an *oroya* (cable crossing), there is now a bridge. You can depart as early as you like and arrive at Km 82 faster than going by train. The Inca Trail equipment, food, fuel and field

**“” The feeling of relief on reaching the top is immense and there's the added, sadistic pleasure of watching your fellow sufferers struggling in your wake ...**

personnel reach Km 82 (depending on the tour operator's logistics) for the Inrena staff to weigh each bundle before the group arrives. When several groups are leaving on the same day, it is more convenient to arrive early.

Km 88 can only be reached by train, subject to schedule and baggage limitations. The train goes slower than a bus but you start your walk nearer to Patallacta (also known as Llaqtapata) and Huayllabamba.

The first ruin is **Patallacta**, near Km 88, the utilitarian centre of a large settlement of farming terraces which probably supplied the other Inca Trail sites. From here, it is a relatively easy three-hour walk to the village of **Huayllabamba**. Note that the route from Km 82 goes via **Cusichaca**, the valley in which Ann Kendall worked (see page 144), rather than Patallacta.

A series of gentle climbs and descents leads along the Río Cusichaca, the ideal introduction to the trail. Huayllabamba is a popular camping spot for tour groups, so it's a better idea to continue for about an hour up to the next site, **Llulluchayoc** (Three white stones), which is a patch of green beside a fast-flowing stream. It's a steep climb but you're pretty much guaranteed a decent pitch for the night. If you're feeling really energetic, you can go on to the next camping spot, a perfectly flat meadow, called **Llulluchapampa**. This means a punishing ascent for one hour 30 minutes through cloudforest, but it does leave you with a much easier second day. There's also the advantage of relative isolation and a magnificent view back down the valley.

**Day two** For most people the second day is by far the toughest. It's a steep climb to the meadow, followed by an exhausting 2½-hour haul up to the first pass – aptly named **Warmiwañusqa** (Dead Woman's Pass) – at 4200 m. The feeling of relief on reaching the top is immense and there's the added, sadistic pleasure of watching your fellow sufferers struggling in your wake. After a well-earned break it's a sharp descent on a treacherous path down to the Pacamayo Valley, where there are a few flat camping spots near a stream if you're too weary to continue.

**Day two/three** If you're feeling energetic, you can proceed to the second pass. Halfway up comes the ruin of **Runkuracay**, which was probably an Inca *tambo* (post-house). Camping is no longer permitted here. A steep climb up an Inca staircase leads to the next pass, at 3850 m, with spectacular views of Pumasillo (6246 m) and the Vilcabamba range. The trail descends to **Sayacmarca** (Inaccessible town), a spectacular site over the Aobamba Valley, where it's possible to camp. Just below Sayacmarca lies **Conchamarca** (Shell town), a small group of buildings standing on rounded terraces.

**Day three** A blissfully gentle two-hour climb on a stone highway, leads through an Inca tunnel and along the enchanted fringes of the cloudforest, to the third pass. This is the most rewarding part of the trail, with spectacular views of the entire Vilcabamba range, and it's worth taking the time to dwell on the wonders of nature. Then it's down to the extensive ruins of **Phuyupatamarca** (Cloud-level town), at 3650 m, where Inca observation platforms offer awesome views of nearby Salkantay and surrounding

## A porter's lot is not a happy one

When you're slogging up Dead Woman's Pass, sweating away and feeling sorry for yourself, spare a thought for the guy who just ran past you with your pack and half a kitchen on his back.

Being a porter on the Inca Trail, or anywhere else in the Andes for that matter, is a tough business. Four days of literally back-breaking work and you'd be a lucky porter indeed to come away with US$60. Add to that the unscrupulous tour operators who insist porters carry far in excess of the official 20-kg weight limit and fail to provide adequate shelter (most porters sleep under a plastic sheet rather than in a waterproof tent) and you have a line of work that no sane Westerner would contemplate.

Competition between tour agents in Cuzco is fierce and, in the battle to maximize profits and minimize costs (and prices), it's often the porters who lose out. If you find this situation as frustrating as we at Footprint do, don't despair, there's a lot that you, the client, can do to help improve working conditions.

Hire a porter! Providing paid employment is the most direct form of aid and you'll save yourself some pain on the trail as well!

→ Ask your agent how much porters are paid. 165.60 soles (plus tips, travel expenses and food) for four days is the official wage, but in many casas 120 soles is the norm. Cheap trips often entail badly paid porters.

→ Let your agent know that porters' welfare is of concern to you.

→ Don't start out carrying your own pack, realize after a short while that it's too heavy and load it onto a porter already laden to the maximum.

→ Spend time with your porters – they are amazing people, and many have fascinating tales to tell.

→ Tip your porter. Get together with your group on the last night and arrange a tip. Thirty soles per porter (US$8.50) is fair. Give your tips directly to the porters themselves.

→ Make sure your guide takes care of sick porters on the trail.

→ If you feel that your porters have been neglected or abused tell your tour agency, inform the South American Explorers and drop us a line at www.footprintbooks.com or at our Bath address in the UK. We read all your letters, and agencies who repeatedly mistreat porters will be removed from our publications.



peaks. There is a 'tourist bathroom' here, where water can be collected, but purify it before drinking.

From here an Inca stairway of white granite plunges more than 1000 m to the spectacularly sited and impressive ruins of **Wiñay-Wayna** (Forever young) ⓘ *entry US$5.75*, offering views of recently uncovered agricultural terraces at **Intipata** (Sun place). A trail, not easily visible, goes from Wiñay-Wayna to the terracing. There is a youth hostel at Wiñay-Wayna (see Sleeping, page 174) and there are spaces for a few tents, but they get snapped up quickly. After Wiñay-Wayna there is no water, and no place to camp, until Machu Picchu. A gate by Wiñay-Wayna is locked between 1530 and 0500, preventing access to the path to Machu Picchu at night.

**Day four** From Wiñay-Wayna it is a gentle hour's walk through a forest of trees and giant ferns to a steep Inca staircase, which leads up to **Intipunku** (Sun gate), where you look down, at last, upon Machu Picchu, basking in all her glory. Your aching muscles will be quickly forgotten and even the presence of the functional hotel building cannot detract from one of the most magical sights in all the Americas.

# Alternative Inca routes » pp 174-178.

To the environmental benefits of choosing an alternative to the classic Inca Trail, trekkers used to be able to add the advantage of fewer regulations. Not any longer; those alternatives that meet up with the classic trail are subject to the same entrance fees. An additional charge is almost certainly to be levied on the Salkantay/Santa Teresa trek (see Ins and outs, page 160). As of 2008 expect trekker numbers and the licensing of guides to come under tighter scrutiny on alternative routes as well.

## Camino Real de los Inkas → *4-5 hrs*

This short Inca trail is used by those who don't want to endure the full hike. It starts at Km 104, where a footbridge gives access to the ruins of **Chachabamba**. The trail ascends to the main trail at Wiñay-Wayna. Half way up is a good view of the ruins of **Choquesuysuy**. This first part is a steady three-hour ascent (take water) and the trail is narrow and exposed in parts. About 15 minutes before Wiñay-Wayna is a waterfall where fresh water can be obtained (best to purify it before drinking).

## Salkantay treks

Four hours' drive west of Cuzco is **Mollepata**, starting point for two major alternatives to the 'classic' Inca Trail. Both treks pass beneath the magnificent glacial bulk of **Salkantay**, at 6271 m the loftiest peak of the Vilcabamba range. The first trek (see page 166) takes the northwestern pass under Salkantay, leading into the high jungles of the Santa Teresa valley and eventually down to the town of Santa Teresa itself at the confluence with the Río Urubamba, from where Aguas Calientes and Machu Picchu are accessible.

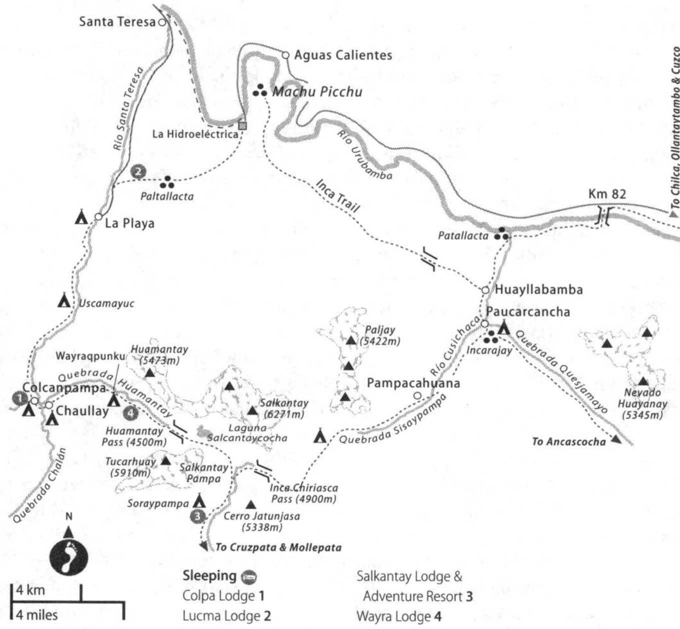

The second trek (see page 168) often referred to as the **High Inca Trail**, follows the same route up to the base of Salkantay before turning east across the Inca Chiriasca Pass at approximately 4900 m. This route then descends via Sisaypampa, from where you trek to Pampacahuana, an outstanding Inca ruin. The remains of an Inca road then go down to the singular Inca ruins of Paucarcancha, also known as Incarajay. Paucarcancha is also an important camping site on the Ancascocha trek (see page 169).

On the third day you join the classic Inca Trail at Huayllabamba, before continuing to Machu Picchu. Because the route follows the Km 88 trail in its second half, fees are payable, permits are required and thus booking at least two months in advance is highly recommended. Due to regulations it is not possible to trek this route without a registered Peruvian guide. There is an obligatory change from animals to porters before you reach Huayllabamba.

The initial road journey to Mollepata is in itself quite spectacular, passing through lush agricultural land and winding through and above steep-sided river canyons. The rivers here run from the peaks of the Vilcabamba mountains and into the mighty Río Apurímac gorge just to the south of the road. Keep your eyes peeled to the right and, weather permitting, you can catch glimpses of La Verónica (5750 m) at the western end of the Urubamba range, and Salkantay itself, protruding like a bleached shark's tooth above the lower ridges of the Cordillera Vilcabamba. The road is good-quality tarmac until the turn-off just beyond Limatambo, in the Río Colorado valley floor. A dirt road then winds steeply up to Mollepata, a relaxed and picturesque rural community. For independent trekkers this is an excellent spot to find guides and mules for the Santa Teresa route; they can sometimes be encountered later in the trek but don't rely on this, especially in the high season. Note that as of 2008 independent trekking and unlicensed guides may not be permitted on this route. Improvements in the road now mean most supported treks begin at **Cruzpata**, a little further up the track to the north of Mollepata. This cuts out a few hours' walk and makes the first day's trek to Soraypampa more relaxed.



## Santa Teresa trek: Cruzpata to Santa Teresa → *4 days*

**Day one** Start the trek from Cruzpata at 3100 m, or walk up to this point following the road from Mollepata. Trek north-northwest on the left side of valley, following the clear trail/road on a very gentle climb into the mountains. Your route takes you inexorably closer to the great peak of **Tucarhuay** (5910 m) which stands above Soraypampa, your destination for today's hike. You'll pass small mountain settlements and areas of montane forest rich in Andean flowers. Look out for mountain caracaras and hummingbirds. After four to five hours' hiking, streams begin to cross the trail with increasing regularity. The vegetation begins to thin out and about 30 minutes before reaching Soraypampa the awesome silhouette of Salkantay starts to reveal itself to your right.

**Soraypampa**, the grassy plain cradled beneath the peaks, is divided by a large stream running through its centre. Make sure you camp on the better-drained land above the stream. The air is wonderfully clear, with luminous stars at night. If you're feeling energetic, or want to cut down walking time over the pass tomorrow, it's possible to camp further up the valley towards Salkantay (see next paragraph).

**Day two** One hour's walking on the left side of the valley heading northeast brings you to **Salkantay Pampa**, below the mountain's glacial moraines. There's a nice rest spot just after a wall and before a stream. Over the next 1½ hours you will climb steeply up the left side of the valley on switchbacks above the pampa. The trail now begins to swing to the left, taking you northwest to west-northwest between the bulk of Tucarhuay and Salkantay. The latter's glaciers tower almost two vertical kilometres above you, a sight that draws your gaze again and again. You now pass a small lake filled with green algae on your right. This is referred to as **Salcantaycocha** on the IGN sheet. 

Thirty minutes above the lake you reach the pass at approximately 4500 m. (There is some confusion over the name of this pass; we call it the Huamantay Pass for ease of reference.) Views are stunning with Salkantay to the north and east, Tucarhuay to the south and, running to the northwest, **Huamantay**, Salkantay's smaller extension, nonetheless impressive with two jagged, glaciated peaks rising to over 5400 m. Visible far away down the valley to the northwest lies the vast bulk of the **Pumasillo/Sacsarayoc** massif, another of Vilcabamba's little-known giants. Standing stones cover the highest points of the pass, built and balanced to honour Pachamama and the *apus* of the mountains.

On the far side of the pass the path descends steeply, twisting down into the valley of the **Quebrada Huamantay** (according to the IGN sheet once again – local names may vary). After an hour or so the trail crosses a stream and the valley begins to flatten out into an area of rugged *puna* grasses and pastures. The route generally follows the left-hand side of the valley and, after a further two hours, reaches a wide pampa, **Wayraqpunku**, to the left of the Quebrada. If you're tired, or want to add an extra day to the trek, many areas along this section of the valley would make fine camping spots with magnificent sunrise views of the mountains behind. Another 25 minutes and the pampa drops away suddenly into a steep-sided canyon. Your route still on the left side of the valley, you leave the *puna* behind and enter the realm of the forest. The vegetation is stunted at first, known as dwarf or elfin forest, the trees gradually gaining height as you descend and finally becoming true cloudforest a few hundred metres above **Chaullay**. Bamboo also becomes more prevalent as you descend and the trail sometimes steeper with sharp drops on the right. Half an hour before arriving at Chaullay, the destination for the day's hike, there are two small, earthen cliffs on the far side of the valley. These are clay licks, or *collpas*, used by parakeets to supplement their diets with minerals and to help them cleanse their systems of toxins sometimes found in unripe fruit. Chaullay is a small community with plenty of space for camping and a few stores from which basic supplies are sometimes available. Keep all valuables, including hiking boots, inside your tent at night.



**Day three** On leaving Chaullay you cross a bridge over the **Quebrada Chalán** almost immediately. From this point on, the route takes a roughly north or north-northeast direction (always downstream) in the Santa Teresa valley until its confluence with the Urubamba tomorrow. Thirty minutes later you reach a second village, **Colcanpampa**, and its surrounding fields, which is a possible alternative campsite. Ten minutes after the field the track branches: take the right, more heavily used track. After a further five minutes go straight on at the junction. This entire area is dense high-altitude rainforest clinging to steep slopes, utterly wild apart from the occasional clearing in the valley bottoms. The trail itself is not for those with vertigo problems, as it is often narrow, steep and has sheer drops on one side. A second river crossing is reached after 10 minutes. You're crossing the **Río Totora** where it merges with the Quebrada Chalán, the result of which is **Río Santa Teresa**. On the far side of the bridge is a grassy area ideal for a quick break, and just a few metres up the Totora, on the far side, is a hot sulphur spring, although it's far from easy and possibly dangerous to reach.

Thirty minutes more and you pass a small farm, but you're still enveloped in the forest. Butterflies abound, the sound of cicadas fills the air, along with the roar of water rushing towards the vastness of the Amazon. Everywhere you look is thick with living forms, and the contrast to the sterile glacial world above is quite mind-blowing. Ten minutes more and you cross a big stream flowing down from the left. Climb 20 m up the streambed and you'll see the trail continuing on the far side. Twelve minutes beyond, you reach a lovely three-tiered waterfall, great for a refreshing dip, but be careful of sharp stones and other refuse in the churning pool below. Forty-five minutes beyond this the trail emerges briefly onto a stony beach, possibly flooded in times of very high water. Another stream is crossed, and after a further 45 minutes you reach **Uscamayuc,** a clearing with huts and running water, a good lunch stop and possible campsite. Sometimes fruits from the local *chakras* (smallholdings) are available.

From this point onwards the trail begins to flatten out and the land is increasingly utilized for agriculture. Over the next one to two hours you cross three small bridges until reaching a sandy beach. This is a good place for a wash and rest, and if you want to camp a little away from civilization this could be a good option, as **La Playa** lies only 10 minutes or so down the track. Compared with other settlements on the route so far, this is a sprawling metropolis, with lots of houses, a large school and a drivable road connecting it to the outside world across the bridge. The football field just before the bridge makes a decent campsite for those who prefer company and easy access to beer and other luxuries. Make sure all valuables are locked away safely in your tent.

**Day four** If you don't fancy walking down the valley to Santa Teresa town, it may be possible to hitch a ride on one of the trucks that work this road. If you want to walk, keep reading the description below. Cross the bridge to the right or eastern side of the Santa Teresa. The road runs high above the river, passing through coffee and banana plantations. Thirty minutes' walk from the bridge you have the option to hike on a restored Inca trail, up the steep mountain to the right (east), towards the recently discovered ruins of **Patallacta,** and on to the hydroelectric station just below Aguas Calientes. For a full description of this route see Day 7 of the Vilcabamba Traverse Trek (see page 224).

The second option, not as spectacular but easier on weary muscles, is to continue down the road to Santa Teresa. A couple of hours after leaving La Playa you once again cross the river back to the left-hand bank. After just over three hours' walking in total you reach another bridge crossing the **Río Sacsara,** just above its confluence with the Santa Teresa. You're now in the ghost town of Santa Teresa Vieja with its pretty church, abandoned after a devastating flood several years ago. Hundreds of people died as flood waters rushed off the heavily deforested and eroded mountains above. The new village is located on a hill just above the old town. Thirty minutes more and you cross another bridge, this one just below the Santa Teresa's confluence with the Sacsara. A few minutes more and you arrive at **La Oroya,** a fun basket-and-wire crossing above the raging Río Urubamba. *Camiones* costing US$1.25 leave on the rough road to **La Hidroeléctrica,** from where you can catch the local train US$8 for tourists to Aguas Calientes at 1520. Alternatively, walk along the railway tracks into town, a further 2-3 hours through subtropical forest, before emerging into the concrete jungle of Aguas. Take yourself to the hot springs and soothe those aches away!



## High Inca Trail: Cruzpata to Huayllabamba → *3 days*

**Day one** This trail uses the same route as the Santa Teresa Trek (see page 166) until reaching Salkantay Pampa, just underneath the glacial moraines. It's a good idea to camp as far up the valley as possible, due to the demanding nature of the pass on the following day.

**Day two** Today's trek takes you over the **Inca Chiriasca** pass. Not to be underestimated, the pass lies at 4900 m (some estimates state over 5000 m) making proper acclimatization to altitude essential. You should also be prepared for severe weather conditions, including the possibility of snow, at any time of year. At the foot of the glacial moraines turn right, crossing the stream and beginning your climb steeply up the valley's flank. The pass lies to the west of your position, just underneath and to the south of Salkantay's southernmost glaciers and snowfields. Following the fairly clear path you've got three or four hours' tough slog ahead of you, battling up steep trails and loose scree slopes. All the time the vast bulk of **Salkantay** looms above you, drawing increasingly close and entirely dominating the vista to the north. The pass itself lies just underneath a steep rocky spire, and there's precious little room to manoeuvre once up there. The rocky peak of **Cerro Jatunjasa** further hems you in to the south. Salkantay's glaciers seem close enough to touch. Beyond Inca Chiriasca you descend roughly to the southeast, zigzagging down a steep scree slope: be careful, as it's easy to loose your footing, especially if there's some snow cover. You're heading into the valley of the **Quebrada Sisaypampa**, which quickly shifts its course 90 degrees and continues its descent to the northeast. About 2½ hours beyond the pass you reach some areas flat enough for camping. Take a break, you deserve it after a long day (eight hours in all).



**Day three** A short day today, 3½ hours following the stream down into the valley. You pass the friendly village of **Pampacahuana** and the village school on the left of the stream. The local teacher enjoys visitors and can always use extra materials (pens, books, etc) if you have them spare. Beyond the community, the trail shifts to the right-hand side of the Quebrada and you arrive at your destination, the village of **Paucarcancha** and its ruins, also known as **Incarajay**. You can camp below the ruins or near the small shop on the far side of the bridge.

From this point onwards you have three options, the first being to descend to **Huayllabamba** on the left side of the river and from there to join the Inca Trail (see page 163 for details). The second option is to continue beyond Huayllabamba and exit the trail at Km 82 near Ollantaytambo, where you can obtain transport back to Cuzco. The third option is to head up the valley of the **Quebrada Quesjamayo** to the southeast, a reverse of the multi-day Ancascocha trek. The second and third options are detailed in the description of the Ancascocha route, see below.

*Permits and a guide are required if you want to continue onto the Inca Trail from Huayllabamba.*



## Ancascocha trek: Huarocondo to Km 82 → *4 days*

Named after a diminutive but beautifully situated community in the Cordillera Vilcabamba's remote eastern fringe, this is a little-known, but worthy addition to the growing list of alternative Inca trails. Crossing three fairly steep passes, it offers fabulous views of some of the region's best-known snow peaks, Salkantay and La Verónica foremost among them. Unsung attractions such as the impressive Nevado Huayanay, which towers above a landscape laced with icy lakes and cascades, are an added bonus. Along with the natural attractions you'll pass interesting ruins, fragmented sections of Inca trail and friendly pastoral communities. Ancascocha can easily be combined with the classic Inca Trail (given the timely reservation of permits), or longer routes into the heart of the Vilcabamba range. For those with more limited time, transport direct to either Aguas Calientes or Cuzco can be obtained from the trail's end.

**Day one** **Huarocondo**, a pretty, untouristy town is the launching point for the trek. The main plaza is worth a look, with its elegant colonial church framed by rugged mountains behind. The town's famed roast pig, *lechón*, is a greasy but tasty treat. Unsurprisingly, the best place to experience this is the **Casa de Lechón** on the north side of the plaza. The start of the trail itself lies to the northwest, about 4 km down the fertile river valley of the **Río Huarocondo**. With wheeled transport it will take you 10 minutes to reach, otherwise bet on an hour's walk to the trailhead, a small footbridge to the left of the road. A yellow sign beneath the bridge states the completion date of 1998, during the service of Alcalde Prof Daniel Vargas. The bridge's location more or less corresponds to **Paropiso** marked on the IGN Urubamba map.

Cross the bridge and the railway tracks immediately after (this is the Cuzco to Aguas Calientes line) and continue straight on, on a bearing of 300°. The trail gently climbs above the tracks, heading through dry, scrubby country, and is now easily followed. After 30 minutes you pass a rustic shelter with fine views, built for trekkers and local mule drivers. On a bearing of 320° you can see your immediate objective, the **Abra Watuq'asa** in a saddle at 3800 m. Above it lies the Inca ruin of **Huata**. An Inca wall running down the ridge, just to the right of the pass, is visible from a great distance. Two hours from the bridge you should reach the pass; there's very little water on this section of trail in the dry season. The ruins of Huata are impressive, with tall lower walls and square bastions resembling a medieval European castle. A short hike up to a second set of walls and fortifications that wrap themselves around the hill's summit rewards you with views of Chicón, Halancoma and La Verónica.

Your route now lies down the impressive valley to the west. From the pass it's a 30- to 40-minute decent to a small glade above the village of **Pomatales**. This might be a good lunch spot. The lower section of the valley boasts significant stands of native Andean woodland. Passing the glade, the trail leads to the far side of the valley and turns back on itself, climbing and heading north for a short distance, initially passing through a quarried defile. Keeping to the main trail, the route follows the contours of the hill, after 15 minutes turning west out of the Pomatales valley and into that of **Chillipahua**. Strange parallel rock formations on the far side of the valley, possibly limestone, lance vertically down towards the river below. Thirty minutes from the glade the trail flattens out, running high on the valley's left shoulder. A further 10 minutes and the way splits: take the lower trail. The valley now turns southwest and tonight's campsite comes into view, the small community of **Chillipahua**. Beyond the school is a football field close to a stream running through the valley's centre, and this is as good a place to pitch your tent as any. Four to five hours in total at a steady pace.



**Day two** Head up the valley from camp. After five minutes cross to the right side of the river just before reaching a wall on the waterway's left bank. Follow the river on its right bank and after about 25 minutes on the trail you'll reach a T-junction: take the left-hand fork, staying close to the river. After a further 20 minutes, turn into the right- hand valley, following the small *quebrada* (stream). You're heading west now, through high *puna*, thick with tough *ichu* grass. If you hike in June or July you might find locals harvesting and drying their annual potato crop. One and a half hours from leaving camp, still climbing up the left-hand side of the valley, a stream crosses the route; don't forget to look behind you for good views of Chicón. The pass, locally known as the **Abra Chillipahua** or **Chochoccasa**, lies slightly to the left of a jagged rocky mountain, the 4500-m **Cerro Chachicata**. Heavy use from both man and beast has led to significant erosion, making the pass easy to identify. Two hours from camp brings you to the pass's summit at 4525 m. A precipitous view greets you on the far side, the vista dropping sharply down below you to the valley of the **Río Silque**, and northwest across the valley to the rugged and magnificent 5345-m **Nevado Huayanay**.

Descend on the steep western path straight over the pass and into the valley. After 20 minutes of descent into the *quebrada* you pass the tiny house of local herders. Ten minutes more and you come to the Río Silque valley floor. Cross the river and follow the trail right/north/downstream on the far (left) side. After a few minutes you pass a house with a walled *chakra* where a stream enters from the left-hand valley with a steep cliff rising above. Don't follow this *quebrada*; keep following the Río Silque. Views of Verónica become increasingly impressive, perfectly framed by the valley's dark walls.

One and a quarter hours after leaving the *abra* you cross a significant landslide, and a further 25 minutes beyond this, a wide *quebrada* enters from the west. The small, fairly traditional community spread out across the valley floor is **Ancascocha**, with the rectangular schoolhouse visible from the trail. Head down into the

Ancascocha valley. You'll find the locals welcoming and it's possible to camp on the school football pitch or further up the valley with the residents' permission. The river running through the valley is marked as the **Quebrada Huayanay** on the IGN Urubamba sheet. It'll take four or five hours at a steady pace.

With its spectacular location at the foot of snow-capped Huayanay, it would easily be possible to spend a second day exploring the valley and its surroundings. A nice walk takes you up to a waterfall at the right-hand side of the valley's head, above a marshy area rich in birdlife (Andean geese, caracaras, etc); this takes an hour return. With a spare day you can hike high above the village to the little-visited source of this cascade, an isolated glacial lake. Ask the villagers for directions.

**Day three** Continue up the valley above Ancascocha and then take the southwest/left-hand branch under the bulk of Huayanay, keeping to the left-hand side of this *quebrada* as you steadily ascend. You're heading towards to the black triangular rock peak, the non-glaciated face of **Nevado Moyoc** that comes into view a short distance up the trail. Maintain a heading following trails of around 240°, and after just over an hour a beautiful emerald lagoon comes into view beneath you and to the right. A waterfall feeds the lake from its far end. The Huayanay pass, the highest on the trek at 4600 m, lies at 240° between the peak of Moyoc and vast mass of Huayanay's glaciers above you. The easiest route to the pass starts from the left-hand corner of the lake, and rises on a clear diagonal, running high above both lagoon and falls. A second, very steep route leads up a trail to the right of the falls – this one looks impossible for pack animals.

Two hours after leaving camp you pass some interesting sections of ancient Inca wall on the way to the high *abra* and soon after this the trail flattens into a high-altitude grassy valley, only slowly gaining height. You pass a chain of jewel-like lakes framed by the snows behind. The lakes are surprisingly rich in water plants and

## Ancascocha trek

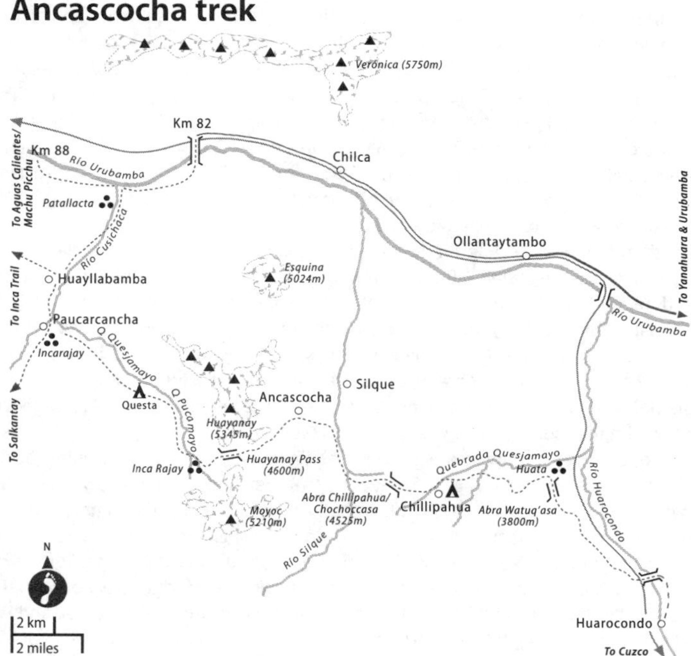

aquatic insects. The surrounding area is rich pasture, used by locals to graze sheep, horses and alpacas. A final steep push leads you to the pass, marked by an *apucheta* (a group of standing stones built to honour the spirits of the mountains), almost three hours after leaving Ancascocha. Spectacular views surround and you get a peek at the almost-vanished Moyoc glacier.

After the pass the trail turns to the west/right. On a clear day the razor peak of Salkantay is an awe-inspiring reference point in front of you. Maintaining a roughly westward heading, you descend into the northward-running valley below the pass. This should take about 20 minutes. Cross the stream to the left-hand side of the *quebrada*, referred to as **Pucamayo** on the IGN sheet. Just above the stream lies the ancient Inca ruin of **Inca Rajay**, its low walls studded with flowers and mosses. At this point you turn northwest heading down the Pucamayo valley. To the right lie the vast ramparts of **Huayantay**, this time its rear or western aspect. As you continue down the valley, the stream quickly drops away below you, running deep in a ravine to your right. Twenty minutes from Inca Rajay you cross a stream entering from the left, and 10 minutes after this you pass a steep cliff to your right, braided by two elegant waterfalls. After a further 20 minutes you cross a stream and enter the now-much-flatter valley floor, shortly afterwards passing the small settlement of **Muya Muya**. Beyond the village the valley drops steeply, turning to the left, now running more to the west. For the first time bushes and trees appear en masse. The trail crosses and re-crosses a dried out streambed before arriving at **Questa** (pronounced Keska), a settlement lying at 3700 m, some two hours after passing Inca Rajay. It's usually possible to camp next to the school.

**Day four** On leaving the village, the valley once again heading northwest, cross a wood and adobe bridge to the left-hand side of river. Below Questa the pastoral landscape seems timeless and tranquil, untouched by the modern world. Stick to the high left-hand side of the valley to avoid a small canyon 25 minutes' walk beyond your camp. The trail continues a further 45 minutes before skirting above the extensive ruins of **Paucarcancha** (also referred to as Incarajay), the site dominating a village of the same name. At this point the **Río Quesjamayo** flows into the **Río Cusichaca**. Cross a bridge to the far (west) bank of the Cusichaca. A small house here doubles as a shop, with basic supplies – rice, pasta, tomato sauce and, of course, Coca Cola. The terraces are a good place to camp if you fancy walking beyond Questa on Day 3.

You can extend this trek into the Vilcabamba range, for example either to on the traverse trek to Choquequirao (see page 220) or the valley of Santa Teresa (see page 166) by turning south up the Cusichaca valley towards Salkantay and the Inca Chiriasca pass, a substantial undertaking at 4900 m.

Otherwise, after leaving the shop, head downriver, following the path through increasingly lush vegetation. Bamboo and bromeliads make an appearance for the first time, perhaps the remnants of a section of cloudforest before cultivation. You reach a junction after 15 minutes: take the right, more heavily used trail. Another five minutes and you arrive at **Huayllabamba**, one of the camps on the classic Inca Trail to Machu Picchu. If you have obtained Inca Trail permits (booking months in advance essential) and have a licensed guide, a left turn on the far side of Huayllabamba will start you on the route to Dead Woman's Pass (see page 163).

If concluding the trek at either Km 88 (for train transport to Aguas Calientes) or Km 82 (for bus transport to the Sacred Valley or Cuzco) keep heading north down the valley on what would normally be the first day of the Inca Trail. If you're hiking later in the day you will encounter a great number of porters and tourists heading for Huayllabamba. After about 1½ hours you reach a junction above the ruins of Patallacta. Turn right, initially up a hill, for Km 82, or left, then left again for Km 88, which lies just beyond the ruins. It takes another 2½ hours to reach the bridge crossing the Río Urubamba and Km 82. Early in the morning buses dropping tourists onto the 'Trail' will take hikers back to

Cuzco for a small fee. Make sure you get to Km 82 before midday to maximize chances of finding transport. If catching the train from Km 88, make sure you've pre-booked tickets and confirmed times in Cuzco, and that the train has clear instructions to stop at the station.

## Other routes

There are other routes which approach the Inca Trails to Machu Picchu, such as the access through the Millpo Valley in the Salkantay area. A three-night trek goes from Km 82 to Km 88, then along the Río Urubamba to Pacaymayo Bajo and Km 104, from where you take the Camino Real described on page 165 to Wiñay-Wayna and Machu Picchu. Good day hiking trails have also been opened along the left bank of the Urubamba river, starting from Aguas Calientes and crossing the bridge of the hydroelectric plant to Choquesuysuy. You can use the trail along the Urubamba river as an alternative route when leaving Machu Picchu: it is 27 km from Aguas Calientes to Km 82, from where you can catch a bus to Ollantaytambo or Cuzco. Allow at least 5½ hours to get to Km 82 on the rough track. Food and drinks are sold at Km 88, but there is nowhere to stay en route.

**Inca Jungle Trail** This is offered by several tour operators in Cuzco: on the first day you cycle downhill from Abra Málaga to Santa María, 4-5 hours of beautiful, easy riding. The second day is a hard seven-hour trek from Santa María to Santa Teresa. It involves crossing three adventurous bridges and bathing in the hot springs at Santa Teresa (US$1.65 entry). The third day is a six-hour trek from Santa Teresa to Aguas Calientes and the final day is a guided tour of Machu Picchu.

# Aguas Calientes

» *pp174-178. Colour map 2, A2.*
*See also map, page 175.*

→ *Phone code: 084.*

The last stop on the train route to Machu Picchu, Aguas Calientes (or just Aguas) is also a popular resting place for those recovering from the rigours of the Inca Trail. It is named after the hot springs above the town. It is also known, officially, as Machu Picchu Pueblo. Most activity is centred around the old railway station, on the plaza, or on Avenida Pachacútec, which leads from the plaza to the **thermal baths** ⓘ *10 mins' walk from town, daily 0500-2030, US$3.15*. These consist of a rather smelly communal pool, with basic toilets, changing facilities and showers. You can rent towels and bathing costumes for US$0.65 at several places on the road to the baths. Take soap and shampoo and keep an eye on your valuables. There is a new museum in the town, **Museo Manuel Chávez Ballon** ⓘ *Carretera Hiram Bingham, Wed-Sun 0900-1600, US$6*, displaying objects found at Machu Picchu.

## Putucusi

An interesting day hike out of Aguas Calientes ascends Putucusi Mountain. Local people consider Putucusi to be a protector mountain for the area and it gives stupendous views of Machu Picchu and its surroundings. Follow the railway line out of town towards Machu Picchu and look for some stone stairs and a trail on your right (there is a blue sign). The climb to the top takes up to two hours, is very steep and involves several ladder sections, so it's not for the faint-hearted.

## Sleeping

**Machu Picchu** *p156, map p158*
LL **Machu Picchu Sanctuary Lodge**, under the same management as the **Hotel Monasterio** in Cuzco, T01-610 8303, http://machupicchu.orient-express.com. This hotel bills itself as an eco lodge with biodegradable products and recycling. The rooms are comfortable, the service is good and the staff helpful. Electricity and water are available 24 hrs a day. Food in the restaurant is well cooked and presented; the restaurant is for residents only in the evening, but the buffet lunch is open to all. Prices start at US$795 per room, per night, all-inclusive. Packages with guided tours of Machu Picchu are available.

### Camping

Camping is not allowed at Intipunku, nor anywhere else at the site; guards may confiscate your tent. There is a free campsite beside the rail tracks at Puente Ruinas station.

**The Inca Trail** *p160, map p160*
G **Youth Hostel**, Wiñay-Wayna. Price per person, with bunk beds, showers and a small restaurant. It is often fully booked. You can sleep on the floor of the restaurant more cheaply, but it is open for diners until 2300. There are also spaces for a few tents, but they get snapped up quickly too. The hostel's door is closed at 1730.

### Camping

The approved campsites are currently at **Huayllabamba**, **Llulluchayoc**, **Llulluchapampa**, **Pacaymayo Valley**, **Runkuracay** and **Phuyupatamarca**.

**Salkantay treks** *p165, map p165*
**Machu Picchu Lodge to Lodge**, T084-243636(in Lima T01-421 6952, in North America T1-949-679 1872, in Europe T43-664-434 3340), www.mountainlodgesofperu.com. **Mountain Lodges of Peru** have set up a series of lodges on the Santa Teresa trek to Machu Picchu. Fully guided tours take 7 days, going from lodge to lodge, which are at Soraypampa (**Salkantay Lodge and Adventure Resort**), Huayraccmachay (**Wayra Lodge**), Collpapampa (**Colpa Lodge**) and Lucmabamba (**Lucma Lodge**). Contact **Mountain Lodges of Peru** for rates, departure dates as well as all other details.
G **Hospedaje Mollepata**, Mollepata, just above the plaza, behind the solid, elegant church, T084-832103, or in Cuzco 084-245449. Price per person. Hot water electric shower, nice courtyard with café and **Ñan Tika** restaurant attached. Swings in the courtyard are a real bonus!

**Aguas Calientes** *p173, map p175*
Some hotels in Aguas Calientes have increased their prices in response to the rising costs of train services and excursions on the Inca Trail. Bargain hard for good value accommodation and always book in advance from Cuzco.
LL **Inkaterra Machu Picchu**, Km 110, T084-211122. Reservations: Jr Andalucía 174, Miraflores, Lima, T01-610 0404; in Cuzco at Plaza las Nazarenas 167, p 2, T084-245314, www.inkaterra.com. Beautiful colonial-style bungalows have been built in a village compound surrounded by cloudforest 5 mins' walk along the railway from the town. The hotel has lovely gardens in which there are many species of birds, butterflies and orchids. There is a pool, an expensive restaurant, but also a **campsite** with hot showers at good rates. It offers tours to Machu Picchu, several guided walks on the property and to local beauty spots. The buffet breakfasts, included in price, are great. It also has the **Café Inkaterra** by the railway line. The hotel is involved in a project to rehabilitate spectacled bears and release them back into the wild. Recommended, but there are a lot of steps between the public areas and rooms.
LL-L **Hatuchay Tower**, Ctra Puente Ruinas block 4, T084-211201, www.hatuchaytower.com. This smart, modern hotel is below the old station. Buffet breakfast and all taxes are included. There

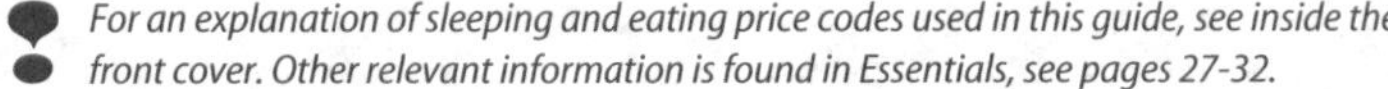
*For an explanation of sleeping and eating price codes used in this guide, see inside the front cover. Other relevant information is found in Essentials, see pages 27-32.*

are standard rooms and luxury suites with hot water.

**AL Machu Picchu Inn**, Av Pachacútec 101, T084-211057, mapiinn@peruhotel.com.pe. The price includes bathroom and breakfast. A modern hotel, functional atmosphere.

**AL-A Gringo Bill's**, Colla Raymi 104, T084-211046, www.gringobills.com. Price includes bathroom, breakfast and lunch or dinner. **Gringo Bill's** is an Aguas Calientes institution, it's friendly and relaxed, with lots of coming and going, hot water, good beds, luggage store, laundry and money exchange. Good meals are served in the restaurant; breakfast starts at 0530 and they offer a packed lunch to take up to the ruins.

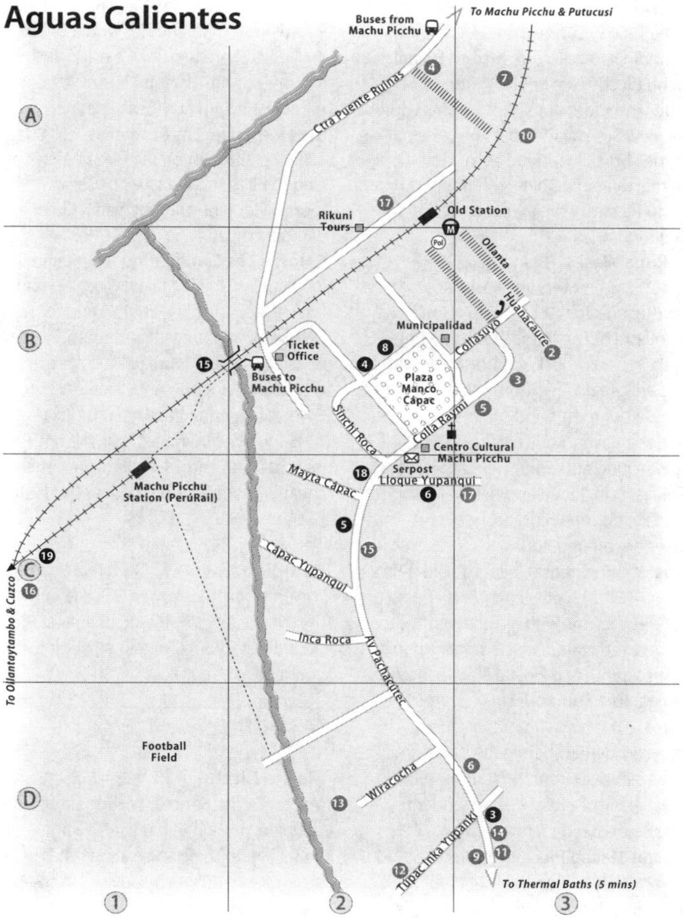

## Aguas Calientes

Not to scale

**Sleeping**
Gringo Bill's **3** *B3*
Hatuchay Tower **4** *A2*
Hospedaje Las Bromelias **5** *B3*
Hospedaje Quilla **6** *D3*
Hostal Continental **7** *A3*
Hostal Ima Sumac **9** *D3*
Hostal Los Caminantes **10** *A3*
Hostal Machu Picchu **17** *A2*
Hostal Pachakúteq **11** *D3*
Hostal Samana Wasi **12** *D2*
Hostal Wiracocha Inn **13** *D2*
Inkaterra Machu Picchu **16** *C1*
La Cabaña **14** *D3*
Machu Picchu Inn **15** *C2*
Presidente **17** *A2*
Rupa Wasi **2** *B3*

**Eating**
Café Inkaterra **19** *C1*
Govinda **3** *D3*
Illary **4** *B2*
Inca Wasi **5** *C2*
Indio Feliz **6** *C2*
Inka's Pizza Pub **8** *B2*
Pueblo Viejo **18** *C2*
Toto's House **15** *B1*

**Bars & clubs**
Waisicha Pub **17** *C3*

**A La Cabaña**, Av Pachacútec M20-3, T084-211048. Price includes bathroom and continental breakfast. Rooms have hot water. There is a café, laundry service and a DVD player and TV (with a good selection of movies) for clients in the lounge. The staff are helpful and can provide information on interesting local walks. The hotel is popular with groups.

**A Presidente**, at the old station, T084-211065 (Cuzco T084-244598), sierrandina@gmail.com. Next to **Hostal Machu Picchu**, see below, in the same group, and more upmarket. Rooms without river view are cheaper, but the price includes breakfast. There seems to be only minimal difference between this and **Hostal Machu Picchu**, which represents better value for money.

**A-B Rupa Wasi**, C Huanacaure 180, T084-211101, www.rupawasi.net. Rustic 'eco-lodge', located up a small alley off Collasuyo. The lodge and its owners have a very laid-back, comfortable style, there are great views from the balconies of the 1st-floor rooms and purified water (so you don't have to buy more plastic). Birdwatching and other treks available. Breakfast is included and half board is available: gourmet cuisine. Cookery classes are offered, too.

**C Hostal Continental**, near the old train station, T084-211065, sierrandina@gmail.com. Very clean rooms with good beds, hot showers, renovated, in the same group as the **Presidente** and **Hostal Machu Picchu**.

**C Hostal Ima Sumac**, Av Pachacútec 173, T084-232111, hostalimasumac@perucuzco.com. 5 mins before the baths, so quite a climb up from the station. Rooms are generally of a reasonable standard; they also exchange money.

**C Hostal Machu Picchu**, at the old station, T084-211065 (Cuzco T084-244598), sierrandina@gmail.com. Price includes breakfast and taxes. A clean, functional establishment, which is quiet and friendly (especially Wilber, the owner's son). There is hot water, a nice balcony overlooking the Urubamba, a grocery store and travel information is available. Recommended.

**C Hostal Pachakúteq**, up the hill beyond **Hostal La Cabaña**, T084-211168. Rooms with bathroom and 24-hr hot water. Good breakfast is included, quiet, family run. Recommended.

**D Hospedaje Quilla**, Av Pachacútec, T084-211009, between Wiracocha and Túpac Inka Yupanki. Price includes breakfast, bath and hot water. They rent bathing gear for the hot springs if you arrive without your costume and towel.

**D Hostal Wiracocha Inn**, C Wiracocha, T084-211088, www.wiracochainn.com. Rooms with bath and hot water. Breakfast included. There is a small garden at this very friendly and helpful *hostal*. It's popular particularly with European groups.

**D-E Hospedaje Las Bromelias**, Colla Raymi, T084-211145. Just off the plaza before **Gringo Bill's**, this is a small place which has rooms with bath and hot water. Cheaper without bath.

**E Hostal Los Caminantes**, Av Imperio de los Incas 140, by the railway just beyond the old station, T084-211007. Price is per person for a room with bathroom. Hot water available but breakfast costs extra. It's basic but friendly and clean.

**E Hostal Samana Wasi**, C Túpac Inka Yupanki, T084-211170, quillavane@hotmail.com. Price includes bath and 24-hr hot water. There are cheaper rooms without bath at this friendly, pleasant place.

### Camping

The only official campsite is in a field by the river, just below Puente Ruinas station. Do not leave your tent and belongings unattended at any time.

## Eating

**Machu Picchu** *p156, map p158*

Machu Picchu Sanctuary Lodge (see Sleeping, page 174) has a restaurant serving buffet lunch. There's also a snack bar beside the entrance but you're advised to take your own food and drink.

**Aguas Calientes** *p173, map p175*

Pizza seems to be the most common dish in town, but many *pizzerías* serve other types of food as well. Many restaurants add 10% service to the bill; protest if you do not wish to pay it. The old station and Av Pachacútec are lined with eating places.

**Café Inkaterra**, on the railway, just below the **Inkaterra Machu Picchu**. US$15 for a great lunch buffet with scenic views of the river.

**Inca Wasi**, Av Pachacútec. A very good place to eat.

**Indio Feliz**, C Lloque Yupanqui, T084-211090. Great French cuisine, excellent value and service, set 3-course meal for US$10, good *pisco sours*. Highly recommended.

**Inka's Pizza Pub**, on the plaza. Good pizzas, changes money and accepts traveller's cheques. Next door is **Illary**, which is popular.

**Pueblo Viejo**, Av Pachacútec, near the plaza. Good food in a warm and spacious environment. Price includes salad bar.

**Toto's House**, Av Imperio de los Incas, on the railway line. Same owners as **Pueblo Viejo**. Good value and quality *menú*.

**Govinda**, Av Pachacútec y Túpac Inka Yupanki. Vegetarian restaurant with a cheap set lunch. Recommended.

## Bars and clubs

**Aguas Calientes** *p173, map p175*

**Waisicha Pub**, C Lloque Yupanqui. For good music and atmosphere.

## Activities and tours

For details of specialist operators in Cuzco, see Activities and tours, page 104.

**Tambo Tours**, 4405 Spring Cypress Rd Suite #210, Spring, TX, 77388, USA, T1-888-2-GOPERU (246-7378), T+1-281 528 9448, www.2GOPERU.com. Long-established adventure and tour specialist with 20 years' experience in Peru, with offices in Peru and the USA. Customized trips for families, individuals and groups to the Amazon and archaeological sites.

## Transport

For details of travelling by rail to Machu Picchu, see box, page 154.

**Aguas Calientes** *p173, map p175*

**Bus**

Buses leave Aguas Calientes for **Machu Picchu** (via the disused station at Puente Ruinas) every 30 mins 0630-1300, US$12 return, US$6 single, valid for 48 hrs. The bus stop in Aguas Calientes is 50 m from the railway station, with the ticket office opposite. Tickets can also be bought in advance at **Consetur**, Sta Catalina Ancha, Cuzco, which saves queuing when you arrive in Aguas Calientes. Buses return from the ruins to Aguas 0700-0900 and 1200-1730.

**Train**

The station for the tourist trains at Aguas Calientes is on the outskirts of town, 200 m from the **Inkaterra Machu Picchu Hotel**. The ticket office is open 0630-1730; there is a guard on the gate.

**Getting to Machu Picchu on the cheap**

Tourists are not permitted to travel on the local train from Cuzco to Machu Picchu, but you can board the local train from the station at Hidroeléctrica. This can be combined with local buses and walking for a cheap route to Machu Picchu as follows: take a bus from Cuzco towards Quillabamba at 1900, US$6. Get out at Santa María where minibuses wait to go to Santa Teresa, 2 hrs, US$2.10. You reach Santa Teresa by sunrise in time to buy breakfast. Cross the new bridge and walk 6 km to the Central Hidroeléctrica on a nice, flat road or hitch a ride on a workers' truck, US$0.60. From the Hidroeléctrica train station it's 40 mins on the local train to Aguas Calientes at 1520 (US$8 for tourists), or you can walk along the railway in 2-3 hrs. (At Km 114.5 along the track is **G** pp **Hospedaje Mandor**, with garden, about 2 km from the bridge to Machu Picchu.) To return, leave Aguas Calientes at 0600 to walk to Santa Teresa, where you catch the 1000 bus to Santa María, arriving at 1200. At 1300 take a bus to Cuzco, arriving around 1900-2000. Or take the local train from Aguas Calientes to Santa Teresa at 1210, stay in a hostal, then take the 1000 bus to Santa María. This route can also be combined with a one-way ticket Ollantaytambo-Machu Picchu. If using this route, don't forget to get your ticket for Machu Picchu in Cuzco, unless you want to buy it in Aguas Calientes.

## Directory

**Aguas Calientes** *p173, map p175*

**Banks** There are several ATMs in town.

**Internet** Many internet shops, average price US$1 per hr; slow connection.

**Medical services** Urgent Medical Center, Av de Los Incas 119, T084-211005, 084-976 1314 (mob). Good care at affordable prices.

**Post** Serpost (post office), just off the plaza, between the Centro Cultural Machu Picchu and Galería de Arte Tunupa.

**Telephone** Oficina on C Collasuyo, and plenty of phone booths around town.

# Beyond Machu Picchu

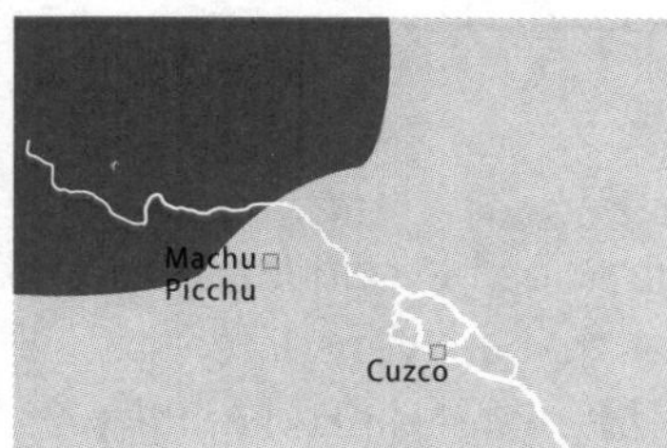




## Footprint features

# Introduction

The lower reaches of the Río Urubamba beyond Machu Picchu are the gateway to regions that are very different from the highlands of Cuzco, yet intimately linked to it by history. Peru's rugged and largely unexplored Vilcabamba Mountains lie to the north and east of the main Andean chain, situated between the canyons of the mighty Apurímac and Urubamba rivers. Extending a mountainous limb into the Amazon Basin, they rise from tropical rainforest to the freezing glaciers of Nevado Salkantay at 6271 m, an area of around 30,000 sq km.



The most important town in this area is Quillabamba, where, they say, it is summer all year round. From here you head north to the end of the Andes and the beginning of the vast jungle. The limit between the two is marked by the waterfalls and canyon of the Pongo de Mainique, frequently described as one of the most beautiful places on earth. East of Quillabamba is Vilcabamba Vieja, the mysterious last stronghold of the Incas, where Manco Inca and his followers maintained Inca traditions, religion and government outside the reach of the Spanish authorities. Long sought by *conquistadores* and archaeologists, Vilcabamba Vieja is now the destination of one of Peru's hardest treks.

## Don't miss ...

1 **Quillabamba** After some hard travelling or long-distance trekking, relax in the City of Eternal Summer, page 182.

2 **Pongo de Mainique** Witness the Río Urubamba's glorious finale as it tumbles into the Amazon Basin, page 184.

3 **Yurac Rumi** Take a moment to investigate and honour the White Rock, the most sacred site of the Incas, page 185.

4 **Hiking to Espíritu Pampa** This trek allows you to follow in the footsteps of the last Incas and the *conquistadores* who so ruthlessly pursued them to their hideaway in the Vilcabamba mountains. Imagine the heavily armoured and mounted Spaniards and the brutal struggles that must have taken place, page 186.

5 **Birdwatching** The wide range of altitudes and habitats in the Vilcabamba region, including areas of relatively pristine forest, make it ideal for birdlife, pages 183 and 189.

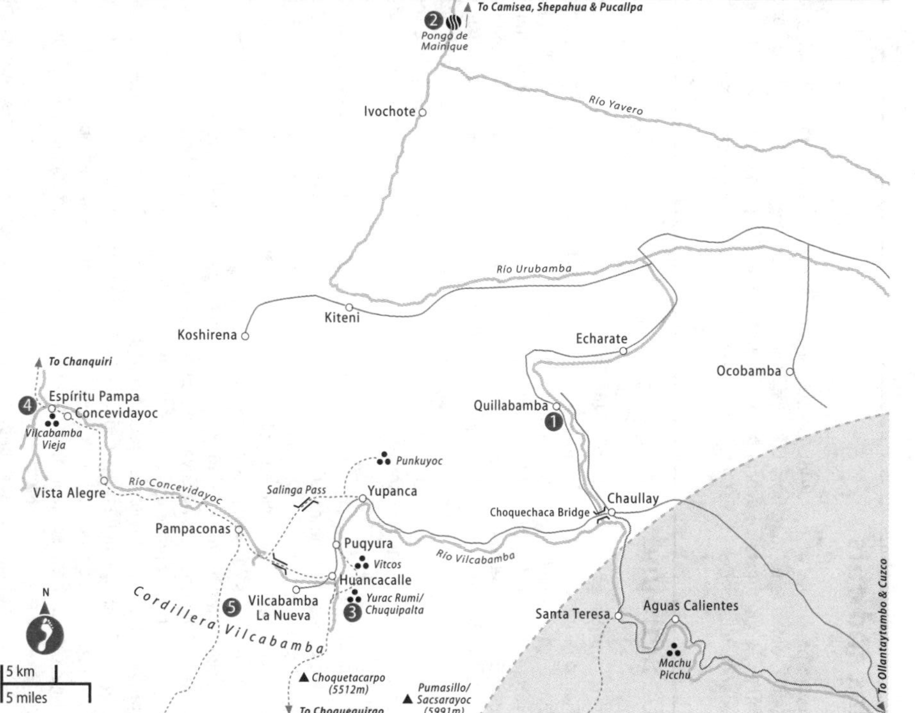

## Ins and outs

As no passenger trains for tourists run beyond Aguas Calientes, the only route to Quillabamba is by road from Cuzco via Ollantaytambo. Beyond Quillabamba, road transport continues to Ivochote, for boats to the Pongo de Mainique, and to Huancacalle for treks to Espíritu Pampa. » *For further details see Transport, page 191.*

## Background

In 1536, three years after the fall of the Inca Empire to the Spanish *conquistadores*, Manco Inca led a rebellion against the conquerors (see box, page 187). Retiring from Cuzco when Spanish reinforcements arrived, Manco and his followers fell back to the remote triangle of Vilcabamba and established a centre at Espíritu Pampa. Centuries after the eventual Spanish crushing of Inca resistance, the location of the neo-Inca capital of Vilcabamba was forgotten; the search for it provoked Hiram Bingham's expeditions and his discovery of Machu Picchu. Bingham also discovered Vilcabamba Vieja, without realizing it, but its true location at Espíritu Pampa was only pinpointed by Gene Savoy in the 1960s, and was not confirmed irrefutably until the work of Vincent Lee in the 1980s.

Vilcabamba lies in a region of immense biological diversity known as the Tropical Andes Eco-region, the meeting of the Andes and the Amazon, which supports the greatest range of animal and plant life on the planet. This diversity is the result of massive variations in altitude, climate and habitat within a relatively small area. Vilcabamba's isolation has also meant that many high-altitude species have been cut off from other populations for thousands, perhaps millions of years, developing separate characteristics and eventually becoming new species, endemic to the region.

In the face of growing threats from oil and gas companies and settlement from the more densely populated mountain regions of Peru, Conservation International and the Smithsonian Institute conducted a 'rapid assessment programme' finding, among others, 12 previously unknown species of amphibian and reptile, plus a very large rodent. These studies aided the recent creation of the Otishi National Park in some of the range's most remote recesses.

In the foothills and surrounding river valleys live four indigenous groups: the Nahua, Nanti, Kirineri and Machiguenga. Some of these people live in voluntary isolation from the outside world. Sadly, both the people and wilderness are under threat; it's an all-too-familiar story. Shell explored the area in the early 1980s and its encounters with uncontacted tribes led to the deaths of at least 42% of the Nahua population, largely through introduced diseases to which these people had little or no immunity. Despite improving its social and environmental practices, Shell pulled out of the region in the late 1990s, but the gas field it discovered, Camisea, is still under development.

## Quillabamba and around » *pp190-191.*

*Colour map 2, A2.*

→ *Phone code: 084.*

*La Ciudad de Eterno Verano* (The City of Eternal Summer), as it is known, was once a prosperous town from the sale of coffee. It has now become the overnighting spot for people going to Vilcabamba, Espíritu Pampa and the magnificent Pongo de Mainique, the region's gateway to the Amazon. This delightful market town now survives on the export of fruit, coffee, honey and other produce to Cuzco. There is a

### Camisea Natural Gas Project

Construction of a pipeline taking gas from the Camisea field to Lima cut a swathe of destruction across the Vilcabamba range. The pipe heads for the coast, an export terminal and liquefaction plant in the buffer zone of the Paracas National Reserve, which has some of the most significant bird and marine mammal populations on the entire Pacific coast of South America. Serious environmental and social risks scared off a number of investors, but in September 2003 the Camisea Consortium received funding worth US$135 million from the Interamerican Development Bank. The bank has refused to disburse final instalments until social and environmental conditions are met. Meanwhile, in a quietly issued Peruvian Supreme Decree, the Nahua Kugakapori Reserve (for uncontacted or little-contacted tribal groups) was opened to oil and gas development. There have been reports of forced relocation of tribes within the reserve.

By 2005 pressure was being exerted to begin development of 'block 56', 56,680 ha within Nahua territory. This project is now known as Camisea 2. A major liquid-gas spill from a ruptured pipe occurred in December 2004, and this, together with diesel spills totalling several thousand gallons, has increased indigenous opposition to the current project, not to mention Camisea 2. Local tribal groups state that both fish and wildlife populations have decreased significantly since the initiation of the project.

Deforestation of the Vilcabamba range's western slope began in Inca times, but the east has remained unaffected by population pressure and cultivation. Conservationists and, increasingly, ecotourism interests are fighting to preserve its treasures. Can they succeed? Only time will tell.

See also Robert Goodland's Peru: Camisea Natural Gas Project. Independent Assessment of the Environmental and Social Priorities. Other sources are www.shinai.org.pe and www.amazonwatch.org.

Dominican mission here. The tourist season is from June to July, when Peruvian holidaymakers descend on the town to absorb its wonderful warm and sunny climate and relaxed atmosphere. Although Quillabamba has plenty to offer, it's normally overlooked by foreign tourists because of the incredibly bumpy but beautiful ride to get there.

## The road to Quillabamba

After leaving Ollantaytambo, the road passes through **Peña**, a place of great beauty. Once out of Peña, the paved road climbs on endless zigzags, offering breathtaking views, to reach the **Abra Málaga Pass**, just below the beautiful glaciated peak of Verónica. Here, where the paving ends, at 4000 to 4300 m, are some patches of *polylepis* woodland, which contain a number of endangered birds. These include the white-browed tit spinetail, the ash-breast tit tyrant and the royal cinclodes. Since it is so accessible, this has become a prime site for birdwatchers, and conservationists are working hard to protect the area. At Chaullay the road meets the old Machu Picchu to Quillabamba railway and continues parallel to the Río Urubamba to Quillabamba.

## Around Quillabamba

For the weary traveller one of the biggest attractions, about 1.5 km from Quillabamba, is **Sambaray** ⓘ *US$0.20; combi US$0.20, taxi US$0.60*, a recreation area with an outdoor swimming pool, restaurant, volleyball and football field. As Sambaray is situated on the Río Alto Urubamba, you can also swim in the river, or, if you're feeling brave, tube down it. Ask locals for the best place to start, as the river can be quite rapid. **Siete Tinajas** (Seven Small Baths) is a beautiful waterfall some 45 minutes by combi from town (take the bus from Paradero El Grifo, US$1). It is well worth the trip for the photos alone, although be careful when climbing to the top, as it can be very slippery.

## Pongo de Mainique and the Amazon Basin

Before the Río Urubamba enters the vast plain of the Amazon Basin it carves its way through one last wall of foothills and the result is spectacular. The Pongo de Mainique is a sheer rainforest canyon, hundreds of metres deep with the Urubamba surging through its centre and many small waterfalls tumbling in on either side. The Machiguenga people who live in the area believe this to be a portal to the afterlife and it's easy to see why. It is an awe-inspiring journey. The Machiguengas, however, are very private people and do not take kindly to uninvited strangers; if you wish to visit them on their reserve take someone who has contact with them. The jungle surrounding the canyon is home to much wildlife, including many species of macaw.

**Ecotrek Peru** ⓘ *in Cuzco, T084-247286, T970 4847 (mob), www.ecotrekperu.com*, runs tours in the region. To make the journey independently, take a bus from Quillabamba's northern bus 'terminal' (a dusty outdoor affair with many foodstalls and the occasional ticket booth) to **Ivochote**, via a new road into the jungle (see Transport, page 191). The road can be in terrible condition in places. En route you'll pass **Kiteni**, a rapidly expanding jungle town. Ivochote is the end of the road, literally, but it develops a party atmosphere on Saturdays, market day in the jungle. Due to the Camisea Natural Gas Project (see page 183), downriver boat traffic is fairly intense. *Lanchas* (boats) head downstream early in the morning on most days during the dry season. In the wet season (roughly December to April) the river may be too dangerous to navigate, especially the rapids in the Pongo itself. When the river is high you rocket through in about five minutes; in the dry season, it's a more leisurely drift through the Pongo. Depending on your bargaining ability, passage downriver to the Pongo or to the **Casa de los Ugarte** (see Sleeping, page 190) will set you back between US$6 and US$8.50, providing the captain has trading business downstream. Hiring a boat independently will cost a lot more. To return upstream prices are roughly one-third higher, owing to the increased amount of fuel required to motor against the current. Round trips are sold for about US$17 per person. Two to three hours downstream from the Casa de los Ugarte, on the right-hand bank of the river, you pass the Machiguenga community of **Timpía**. Here is the community-run **Sabeti Lodge** (see Sleeping, below), which has a number of activities and excursions in the region, including trips to the Pongo and visits to two of the best *colpas*, clay-licks, in Peru.

Beyond the Pongo a day's boat travel will bring you to **Malvinas**, centre of the hugely controversial Camisea Natural Gas Project, and on to **Camisea** itself. If you wish to stay here, you must ask the *presidente* of the community first. From the Pongo downstream to Camisea will cost US$6 by boat. Another day downriver and you'll reach **Sepahua**, a largely indigenous village on the edge of the Alto Purús region. It has a few *hostales* and you can buy pretty much anything. Those with time and an adventurous spirit can continue downriver to **Pucallpa** via Atalaya (several *hostales*, market and a tourist office on the plaza which will help with day trips). To go all the way to **Iquitos** in the north means, overall, a journey of 2500 km by boat, an incredible opportunity to see the Peruvian jungle.

## Huancacalle and around » pp190-191.

At **Chaullay**, the historic **Choquechaca Bridge**, built on Inca foundations, permits drivers to cross the river to the village of Huancacalle, a two-street village (a few shops, one with a *comedor* – book a meal an hour in advance, vegetarians not catered for) between four and seven hours from Quillabamba. Huancacalle is the best base for exploring the nearby Inca ruins of Vitcos and the starting point for the trek to Espíritu Pampa. You can also hike up to **Vilcabamba La Nueva** from Huancacalle. It's a three-hour walk through beautiful countryside with Inca ruins dotted around. There is a mission run by Italians, with electricity and running water, where you may be able to spend the night.

### Walking tour of Vitcos and Yurac Rumi → *3-4 hrs*

The Inca sites of Vitcos and Yurac Rumi lie behind the hill that rises immediately on the far side of the river from Huancacalle. Both sites are easily accessible and well worth the effort of a visit. Allow plenty of time for hiking to and visiting the ruins, although three hours is sufficient for a whirlwind tour. Guides can be hired in Huancacalle for a small fee (US$2-3 for a guided walk to both sites).

Just past the **Hospedaje Sixpac Manco**, cross the bridge on your left. On the far side of the river the trail splits – take the left-hand fork. The right-hand trail leads to the Choquetacarpo pass and, eventually, to **Choquequirao**, a magnificent Inca citadel (see page 218). The left-hand track leads up an impressive restored Inca stairway to a small field. It's a steep climb. Follow the incline of the field and another small restored section of Inca Trail. From this point you will see the beautifully sculpted **Yurac Rumi**, the **White Rock** of the Incas (also referred to as **Chuquipalta**), once the most sacred site in South America. The rock is very large (8 m high and 20 m wide), with intricate and elaborate carvings, now covered in lichen. The rock has an intricate system of water channels surrounding it and these run into a finely carved Inca bath, in excellent condition. Underneath the White Rock on the right-hand side lies a series of 'seats'; local guides claim these were used by the Inca's chosen virgins during ceremonies held at the site. Shadows and light play strangely on the rock's finely carved features; take the time if you can to return later in the day and have another look.

From the White Rock continue downhill, following the contour of the hill to the left. As you walk down the valley, **Ñustahispanan** comes into view – agricultural terraces, another sacred rock and a stone mimicking the shape of the mountains down the valley.

Following the trail on the left-hand side of the valley takes you to **Vitcos**. The path climbs higher on the left-hand side and very soon Vitcos comes into view, with mountains silhouetted behind. At Vitcos you will find **Manco Inca's Palace**, a beautiful multi-doored building with excellent stonework. It was the palace of the last four Inca rulers from 1536 to 1572 and was discovered by Hiram Bingham in 1911, the same year he discovered Machu Picchu. Unlike that more famous site, Vitcos has documented historical associations which make a visit particularly interesting and rewarding. Above the palace is a flat area, perhaps originally used for ceremonial purposes, with fantastic 360° views, from the snowy peaks of the Vilcabamba range to the verdant valleys below. The entire site is highly defensible, surrounded on three sides by steep drops and accessed by a thin bridge of land on the fourth. To return to Huancacalle, retrace your steps or descend to the road on the far side of the river.

# Huancacalle to Espíritu Pampa trek » pp190-191.

The trek to Espíritu Pampa from Huancacalle takes three days, but would be a more comfortable undertaking in four. Vilcabamba Vieja itself is quite a large site, and further groups of buildings may still be awaiting discovery in the densely forested mountains surrounding the valley. Give yourself at least a day at the site to soak up the atmosphere before continuing a further six hours to Chanquiri, the starting point for transport to Kiteni and Quillabamba.

## Ins and outs

The **Instituto Nacional de Cultura** is considering introducing charges for this trek and entering Espíritu Pampa in 2008.

**Guides and supplies** An excellent guide is Jesús Castillo Alveres who can be contacted through the **Hospedaje Sixpac Manco** in Huancacalle (see page 191). Many members of the Cobos family (see page 189) are guides; Juvenal Cobos has guided for BBC documentary teams among others. A good rate of pay for guides/mule drivers is US$8 per day, plus expenses, and US$6 per mule or horse used (in some seasons, the trail is unsuitable for horses). A professional guide will charge US$50-60 per day, plus all expenses. Before you leave be very clear about your exact itinerary and expectations; some guides have been known to leave clients in Espíritu Pampa, half a day's hike from the roadhead in Chanquiri. Always ask if you have to provide sufficient food and a waterproof tent by way of accommodation for your guide on the trail. If you enjoy your trip give your guide a tip; it will be appreciated. Remember, *arrieros* (mule drivers) based in Huancacalle have to walk all the way back along the route, a journey of at least two and a half days, and for this they don't charge. Always take all plastic and non-biodegradable rubbish back to Cuzco for more efficient disposal. All supplies must be brought from Huancacalle as even basic items are scarce on the trail.

**Best time to visit** The best time of year is from May to November, possibly December. Outside this period it is very dangerous as the trails are extremely narrow and can be thick with mud and very slippery. Insect repellent is essential; there are millions of mosquitoes. Also take along painkillers and other basic medicines, which will be much appreciated by the local people should you need to take advantage of their hospitality.

## Day one: Huancacalle to Río Chalcha → *6-7 hrs' walking.*

From **Hospedaje Sixpac Manco** follow the course of the Río Vilcabamba upstream, staying on the right side. Your compass bearing is roughly west and you'll maintain this direction for most of the first day and, indeed, the trek to Espíritu Pampa itself. You're heading towards the Abra Colpapasa (Colpapasa Pass), which lies to the right of the jagged peaks in front of you. Climb up the right bank until you reach the road heading for Vilcabamba La Nueva. Near a slightly Swiss-looking house with a diamond-shaped image of Christ, turn right up the hill. After 70 m or so, turn left off the road up the dirt track. The trail starts edging towards the peaks, beginning to leave the river's course behind. This whole area is a picturesque mix of cloudforest remnants and farmland. Just before another crucifix and where the stream crosses the trail (you're back on the road again!) turn right and traverse the small concrete bridge. On the far side head up this valley, keeping on the left of the stream. After a short time you rejoin the road once more. Turn right and keep ascending the valley. From here to Vilcabamba La Nueva you can essentially follow the road, electricity cables and river up the valley. Look out for short cuts to avoid the bends. As you

## The last Incas of Vilcabamba

After Pizarro killed Atahualpa in 1532 the Inca Empire disintegrated rapidly, and it is often thought that native resistance ended there. But in fact it continued for 40 more years, beginning with Manco, a teenage half-brother of Atahualpa.

In 1536, Manco escaped from the Spanish and returned to lead a massive army against them. He besieged Cuzco and Lima simultaneously, and came close to dislodging the Spaniards from Peru. Spanish reinforcements arrived and Manco fled to Vilcabamba, a mountainous forest region west of Cuzco that was remote, but still fairly close to the Inca capital, which he always dreamed of recapturing.

The Spanish chased Manco deep into Vilcabamba but he managed to elude them and continued his guerrilla war, raiding Spanish commerce on the Lima highway, and keeping alive the Inca flame. Then, in 1544, Spanish outlaws to whom he had given refuge murdered him, ending the most active period of Inca resistance.

The Inca line passed to his sons. The first, a child too young to rule named Sayri Túpac, eventually yielded to Spanish enticements and emerged from Vilcabamba, taking up residence in Yucay, near Urubamba in 1558. He died mysteriously – possibly poisoned – three years later.

His brother Titu Cusi, who was still in Vilcabamba, now took up the Inca mantle. Astute and determined, he resumed raiding and fomenting rebellion against the Spanish. But in 1570, Titu Cusi fell ill and died suddenly. A Spanish priest was accused of murdering him. Anti-Spanish resentment erupted, and the priest and a Spanish viceregal envoy were killed. The Spanish Viceroy reacted immediately, and the Spanish invaded Vilcabamba for the third and last time in 1572.

A third brother, Túpac Amaru was now in charge. He lacked his brother's experience and acuity, and his destiny was to be the sacrificial last Inca. The Spanish overran the Inca's jungle capital, and dragged him back to Cuzco in chains. There, Túpac Amaru, the last Inca, was publicly executed in Cuzco's main plaza.

approach Vilcabamba La Nueva the valley floor begins to flatten out into agricultural and grazing land. An Italian-sponsored programme is supporting a carpentry project here, hence the impressive buildings in parts of the village.

When you enter Vilcabamba take the first right at the junction. You want to head up the large valley to the right, not the smaller valley rising above the town to your left. You're heading roughly north-northwest at this point. Cross the stream at the bottom of the smaller valley, following the road along the left-hand side of the larger westerly valley. Holding your course up the river, you reach the **Abra Colpapasa** at over 4000 m. Here there's a sign announcing government plans to improve the route to Espíritu Pampa. From the pass, given clear weather (which the author didn't have!) you can see many of the great snow peaks in the Vilcabamba range, including Salkantay and Pumasillo (also marked as Sacsarayoc on many Peruvian maps). Once through, follow the left side of the pass, descending gently. There's a 'road' – possibly work in progress – that follows a high line in early sections of the valley, and several short-cut paths cutting off the bends beneath. You're still heading west. After one hour there's a magnificent set of Inca steps dropping steeply towards the river and the valley floor. The trail turns to the left slightly, crossing another stream entering the main flow from the left by a nicely constructed wooden bridge, the **Puente Malcachaca**. Before crossing the bridge two trails come into view on the far side. The higher one leads to the village of Pampaconas and on to Espíritu Pampa. The lower trail (described below) circumvents the village, following the river directly to Espíritu Pampa. This route also leads to several beautiful potential campsites by the river, the best of which are another 15 to 20 minutes' walk from the bridge. If you still feel energetic, you could continue to the Pampas just below the tiny settlement of Ututu (see Day two, below). The river here carries the local name of the **Río Chalcha**. It is generally marked on maps as the **Río Concevidayoc**, but carries local names in several sections.

## Day two: Río Chalcha to Vista Alegre → *A total of 6½-7 hrs' walking.*

From the campsites near the Chalcha, carry on descending further into the valley – and the Amazon Basin. As you advance the vegetation becomes wilder and less disturbed. The hills on the far side of the river are dominated by stands of virgin cloudforest. With the continuing loss in elevation the trees become studded with epiphytes, plants that make their home on the branches of large trees. They lack root systems so obtain all nutrients and moisture directly from the humid atmosphere and thus are indicators of cloudforest and rainforest environments. The path follows the river closely, passing through a patchwork of fields and natural vegetation. You can feel the air become stickier and more humid as you descend. The tiny and idyllic settlement of **Ututu** is reached 1½ hours after the camp. Perhaps only 10 or 20 people call Ututu home and their lifestyle seems little influenced by the modern world. Just beyond, through picturesque *pampa*, you cross an orange suspension bridge across the Chalcha to its right bank. The path now enters a spectacular stretch of ancient cloudforest, choked with mosses and vines. In many sections the route follows wonderful sections of Inca trail, stairs, etc. All the time the river roars on your left, gathering strength from the many small creeks that join it. This section lasts between one and 1½ hours, but serious birdwatchers with a day to spare would be well rewarded. The area abounds in birdlife, with many colourful species of tanager, among others. Throughout this section of the trail you're heading more or less northeast.

You now come to a second orange suspension bridge, crossing back to the left-hand side of the valley. A brief climb offers splendid views of the densely forested peaks in the Vilcabamba range, especially on the right side of the river. Sadly, much of the forest on the trail side in this section has been cut or burned to create small farming plots or *chacras*. Walking close to the ridgeline, the river far below, you pass lush secondary forest and scrub before descending to **Vista Alegre** through a more heavily populated area. The Concevidayoc now carries the local name of Río Vista Alegre. Before you reach camp, located in a convenient football field, you cross three bridges. The first is a fragile construction of dubious safety, made with rough-hewn logs balanced against each other in the centre. In the dry season it's possible to wade across the river and this could be a better option. The second bridge, Cedrochaka, is a simple log affair, but secure. The third, Puente Vista Alegre, just before the field, is adequate for most walkers.

## Day three: Vista Alegre to Espíritu Pampa → *About 7 hrs' walking.*

Carry on downstream. After a couple of minutes you'll cross a stony riverbed – a stream entering the Río Vista Alegre. A few logs form a rough bridge which may be impassable in heavy rain. The path continues on the far side towards a junction – take the right-hand path. The trail follows the river's left bank, largely surrounded by forest, heading roughly north-northeast. After an initial alternation between forest and stony beaches the track enters the largest stretch of primary forest on the route. For the next four or five hours, it is broken only by the tiny dwellings of five or six families who live in the area. The route ascends and descends many times between feeder streams entering the main river. You've now returned to your northwesterly course. There are great views of the jungle from various viewpoints on the route.

Again, this is a great area for birding, this time in the transition zone between the cloudforest and the lowland tropical forest. The area seems especially rich in examples of the trogon family, with quetzals very much in evidence. As the trail continues the river drops further and further beneath you. You're walking high on the left slope of the valley. After two hours you reach the tiny settlement of **Urpipata**, set on a hilltop. The **Río Tunqimayo**, 15 minutes further on, is crossed by a spectacular wooden bridge. There are crystal-clear pools in the river, ideal for a refreshing dip. This could be a good campsite if you have time, though space for tents is very limited. A second bridge, 1½ hours further on, crosses the **Río Yuquemayo**.

The dispersed settlement of **Concevidayoc** comes into view 5½ hours from the start of the day's trek. The river below now carries the same name. After another hour you come to the **Puente Pumachaca**, crossing another of the Concevidayoc's tributaries. Around Concevidayoc there are many small side trails leading to houses and fields, but the main trail is obvious. You pass the small ruin of the house of Don Cobos on the left-hand side. If you don't want to proceed further this would be a good camping spot. The Cobos family has been instrumental in the most significant explorations of the Espíritu Pampa area and still guide today, based at the **Hospedaje Sixpac Manco** in Huancacalle.

Shortly after the Cobos' house the trail splits, but a blue arrow indicates the higher trail and route to Espíritu Pampa. Finally you reach the **Abra Tucuiricco** and the foundations of a small but well-constructed Inca house, perhaps built as a lookout to warn of approaching enemies. From here you can look down on Espíritu Pampa and Manco's Vilcabamba Vieja. A flight of restored Inca stairs leads downhill and 20 minutes later you come to the small settlement of **Espíritu Pampa**. A large sign announces the restoration of Espíritu Pampa and Vilcabamba. There's a modest shop in the village run by the wife of Américo, Vilcabamba's caretaker. The shop has a pretty limited selection of goods, but sells biscuits, rice, eggs and, of course, Coca Cola. In front of the houses themselves is a small field which is perfect for camping.

## Day four: Vilcabamba Vieja

A trail leads up behind the houses to the ruins of Vilcabamba Vieja, a mere 10 minutes' walk away. Some of the lower ruins are being restored but the ruins on higher ground are still romantically consumed by the jungle, with vines and the huge root systems of forest giants wrapped around the remains of finely built houses. What is also apparent is how different this city is, compared with others in the Inca Empire, set as it is in a low valley on the edge of the Amazon Basin. This is a city and a civilization out of its element, the Incas far from their beloved mountains, forced to the very edge of their empire by the European invaders. For birdwatchers there are several leks (display grounds) of the Andean cock-of-the-rock, Peru's national bird. Its strange calls echo throughout the ruins.

## Day five: Espíritu Pampa to Chanquiri → *About 5 hrs' walking.*

To leave Espíritu Pampa, follow the path that crosses directly in front of the houses, leaving from the north side of the field. The path then crosses the **Río Santa Isabel** after 10 to 15 minutes on a suspension bridge carrying the same name. You are now heading east-northeast, swinging more to the north as you continue. You're on the left bank of the Santa Isabel, following the river downstream towards its confluence with the Río Concevidayoc. The valley is quite densely populated here, with much slash and burn agriculture and consequent forest clearance. After an hour or so you pass **Chuntabamba**, a small settlement with a school, small shop, etc. There are many little side trails leading to fields and houses in this area, but the main trail is always obvious. You're still heading north at this point. The Santa Isabel merges with the Río Concevidayoc after about 2½ hours and enters a steep forested canyon. You follow the trail to the left in a picturesque valley of a tributary entering from the west, crossing the **Puente Santa Victoria,** before returning to the course of the main river. You now descend steeply to the river and cross the **Azulmayo** (or Asolmayo) suspension bridge.

The route begins to climb steeply on the far side. At a split in the trail turn left (north) – if you've taken the correct turn you'll come to a small concrete bridge over a stream five minutes later. It's a very tough, steep climb for up to 1½ hours. **Chanquiri** comes into view in the valley below from the highest point of the climb, high on the side of the hill (but below the summit). This small town lies on the right-hand side of the valley that joins the Santa Isabel, just below the confluence of the two. The valley is that of the **Río San Miguel.** Following the hill into the San Miguel Valley, cross the sturdy **Puente La Resistencia.** Head up the opposite bank until it meets with a road. The road is impassable for vehicles in the higher section, because of many landslides. Some 30 minutes later you arrive in Chanquiri.

## Sleeping

**Quillabamba** *p182*
**E Hostal Quillabamba**, Prolongación y M Grau, just behind the main market, T084-281369, hostalquillabamba@latinmail.com. The highly kitsch design will remind you of some 1960s Californian motel, marooned on the edge of the Amazon Basin. This is one of the largest *hostales* in Quillabamba, all rooms have private bath, TV (local channels only) and telephone. There's a swimming pool, which occasionally has water in it, a restaurant and parking facilities. Less appealing is the small zoo with several inadequately housed species of macaw and toucan. They also have a cockfighting school for the championship, held every year in late Jul.
**F** per person **Hostal Alto Urubamba**, Jr 2 de Mayo 333, T084-281131, altourub@ec-red.com. Rooms bath, hot water and TV; those with shared cold shower are **G** per person. Spotlessly clean, pleasant hotel,, can be noisy from TV in courtyard. One block from the Plaza de Armas, near internet place and laundry. Staff are very friendly and knowledgeable. Small local restaurant attached and there are great views over the town from the roof. Highly recommended.
**F Hostal Don Carlos**, Jr Libertad 566, T084-281371. Clean and simple, all rooms have private shower with occasional hot water, TV and sofa. Bar and restaurant.

There are other places to stay (**G**) around the main market.

**Pongo de Mainique and the Amazon Basin** *p184*
**G Hostales**, Kiteni. There are several cheap *hostales* along the main street, but they are almost exclusively occupied by workers from the Camisea Gas Project.
**G Hostal La Casa de los Ugarte**, just beyond the Pongo, on the left bank of the river (if heading downstream). The small hacienda of Ida and Abel Ugarte, who are very helpful and will let you camp on their land for a small fee. They have a modest general store and basic supplies; fruit and very fresh eggs are available. The forest behind the hacienda is rich in wildlife and the family may be able to arrange expeditions in the jungle, if given time.
**G Hostal Pongo de Mainique**, Ivochote, just behind the **Señor de Huanca** (**G**), which is on the right once over the footbridge. Both are basic. The former has tiny, insecure rooms, while the latter is more spacious and safer, but older. Both have basic restaurants. There is also **Hostal Marvin**, price unknown.
**G Hostal Vanessa**, Sepahua. On the main street close to the port, very pleasant.
**Sabeti Lodge**, Timpía, www.sabetilodge.com, or contact CEDIA, T01-420 4340. The lodge founded by the Machiguenga community, the Centro para el Desarrollo del Indígena

*For an explanation of sleeping and eating price codes used in this guide, see inside the front cover. Other relevant information is found in Essentials, see pages 27-32.*

Amazónico (CEDIA) and Perú Verde (see page 60). Offers 4- and 5-night packages for eco and eco-mystical tourism with guided tours. Restaurant, bar.

**Huancacalle** *p185*
**F Sixpac Manco** This hostel, managed by the Cobos family, is fairly comfortable and has good beds.
**G** Villagers will accept travellers in their very basic homes (take a sleeping bag).

**Huancacalle to Espíritu Pampa** *p186*
**Chanquiri** has no hostel, but you can sleep on someone's floor, perhaps at the small restaurant/shop on the west side of the plaza. If they like you and you buy a meal and a couple of drinks they may not charge for accommodation. The main plaza isn't ideal for camping.

## Eating

**Quillabamba** *p182*
ꝩ **El Gordito**, Jr Espinar. A good place for chicken.
ꝩ **Pizzería Venecia**, Jr Libertad 461, on the Plaza de Armas, T084-281582. Decent pizza, delivery available.
ꝩ **Pub Don Sebas**, Jr Espinar 235 on Plaza de Armas. Good, great sandwiches, run by Karen Molero who is very friendly and always ready for a chat.

There are many *heladerías* (ice cream shops), the best of which are on the west side of the Plaza de Armas. Quillabamba's a great place for freshly squeezed fruit juices – head for the 2nd floor in the main market. **Gabbi's Juice Stall**, on the far right-hand side, is especially recommended.

## Transport

**Quillabamba** *p182*
**Bus** Most buses leave **Cuzco** for Quillabamba from the Terminal Terrestre de Santiago between 1800 and 2000. Journey time is approximately 8 hrs, although expect 14 hrs or more in the rainy season, because of landslides. 4 bus companies on this route are: **Valle de los Incas**, T084-244787, **Ben Hur**, T084-229193, **Ampay**, T084-245734, and **Selva Sur**, T084-247975. **Ampay** has good modern buses, while **Selva Sur** has 2 buses on the route, one of which is quite comfortable, with good reclining seats. Buy tickets in advance, US$6.

The bus station in Quillabamba is on Av 28 de Julio and buses depart for **Cuzco** daily, at all hours of the day and night. There are extra services at weekends. There are also buses to **Ivochote** from the northern bus terminal (for boats to the Pongo de Mainique), 8-10 hrs, US$4 (all companies sell tickets on C Ricardo Palma, opposite the main market). Ask locals for their opinions on the best bus companies for this route. Some companies drop passengers off outside **Hotel Quillabamba** on the return. Combis leave Quillabamba for **Huancacalle** daily at 0900 and 1200, US$3.30. The journey takes 4-7 hrs. On Fri they go all the way to **Vilcabamba La Nueva**.

**Pongo de Mainique and the Amazon Basin** *p184*
In **Ivochote**, you may have to wait a few days for a boat downstream, but try to get as far as **Bajo Pongo** or **Timpía**, 4 hrs, US$10. It's a further 4 hrs, US$10 to **Camisea**. After **Sepahua**, boats are larger and more frequent and distances are greater. To **Atalaya** you can take an express, 10 hrs, US$15, or a delivery boat, up to 2 days. From there you can take a boat (36 hrs, US$16) or a plane (several per week, according to demand) to **Pucallpa**.

**Huancacalle to Espíritu Pampa** *p186*
**Bus** From **Chanquiri**, at the end of the Espíritu Pampa trail, trucks and buses leave for **Kiteni** and **Quillabamba** on Wed and Sun. It's an 8- to 12-hr ride, US$3.30. Finding transport at other times of the week can be problematic.

## Directory

**Quillabamba** *p182*
**Banks** BCP, Jr Libertad, is good for TCs. **Banco Continental**, Av F Bolognesi, accepts Visa and Cirrus. **Internet** Ciber Master, Jr Espinar, on the plaza.

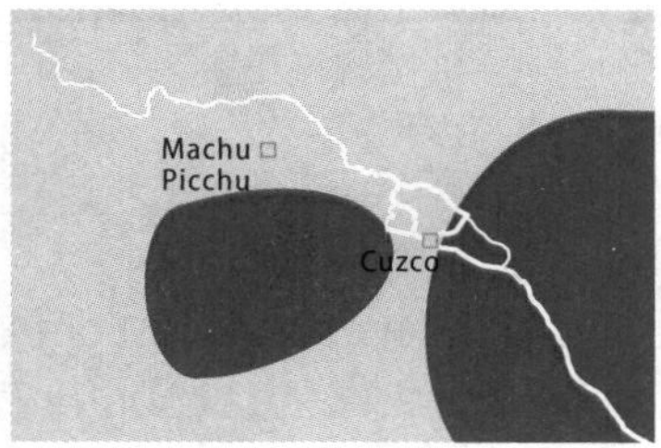


# East & West of Cuzco



## Footprint features

# Introduction

Most visitors to Cuzco, after seeing the city, head for the Sacred Valley and Machu Picchu, but to the east and west are many equally tempting propositions. This part of the country is singularly off the beaten track in relation to the rest of the region. It's an area of myths, reputed to be where the founders of the Inca dynasty emerged into the world.

Along or near the main road from Cuzco to Lake Titicaca are a number of archaeological sites, the most prominent of which are Tipón and Raqchi, while the colonial churches at Andahuaylillas and Huaro are among the most fascinating in the whole region. There are beautiful lakes, too; four of them are near the village of Acomayo, while Huacarpay is an excellent place for walking and birdwatching. Also accessible from this road is the majestic Ausangate massif, where you can do some serious high-altitude trekking.

And not to be outdone, the western part of the region also boasts its own 'lost city', at Choquequirao. As impressive as Machu Picchu but, in comparison, much less visited, this is a tremendous site, and getting there requires an expedition of four days or more.

## Don't miss ...

1 **Paucartambo** In mid-July the unmissable festival of the Virgen del Carmen is one of the highlights of the Cuzco departmental calendar, page 201.

2 **Andahuaylillas** Visit the Sistine Chapel of the Andes and, nearby, the equally remarkable church at Huaro. For the best view, take a strong torch as they are not lit, page 205.

3 **Ausangate** Trek for six days around the glaciers and lakes on the flanks of one of the Incas' most sacred mountains, page 206.

4 **Acomayo** Tired of ruins, churches, roads and people? Then take a trip to the four lakes near this peaceful waterside village, page 211.

5 **Raqchi** This highly spirited place contains the remnants of one of the tallest Inca buildings ever constructed, the temple to the creator god Viracocha. It is now a centre for the local ceramics industry, page 212.

6 **Choquequirao** The latest addition to the 'lost cities' trail, only reached by adventurous trekking, page 218.

# East of Cuzco

*A paved road runs southeast from Cuzco to Sicuani, at the southeastern edge of the Department of Cuzco. It follows the valley of the Río Vilcanota (the upper stretch of the Urubamba) as it cuts through the altiplano. Ruins dot the hillsides, demonstrating the spread of the Incas' influence towards their spiritual home at Lake Titicaca, which is also the road's destination at Puno. A smattering of distinctive colonial churches can be found along the route. Northeast of the Vilcanota is the mountain range of the same name, crowned by the snowy summit of Ausangate, one of the Incas' great apus. Its glaciers and lakes are the backdrop to one of the region's finest treks. At the other extreme, the deep canyons of the Río Apurímac are a side trip away.* » *For Sleeping, Eating and other listings, see pages 214-216.*

### Ins and outs

Combis run every 15-20 minutes between Cuzco and Sicuani, and more frequently to the villages and towns in between. To visit the beautiful mountain lakes and Inca bridge west of the main road, it would be worthwhile renting a 4WD for two days. Giving locals a lift is both fun and helpful – they will make sure you take the right road. » *For further details, see Transport, page 215.*



## South to Pacarijtambo

Pacarijtambo is a good starting point for the three to four hours' walk to the ruins of **Maukallaqta**, which contain good examples of Inca stonework. From there, you can walk to **Pumaorca**, a high rock carved with steps, seats and a small puma in relief on top. Below this are more Inca ruins.

From Cuzco there are buses and trucks to Pacarijtambo, US$2. You can find lodging for the night at the house of the Villacorta family and leave for Cuzco by truck the next morning. On the way back, you'll pass the caves of **Tambo Toco**, where a legend says that the four original Inca brothers emerged into the world, thus contradicting the story that the brothers emerged at Ollantaytambo (see page 141).

## San Jerónimo to Huanca trek » *pp214-216.*

Leaving Cuzco, you will soon pass the condor monument (see box, page 73) of San Sebastián then enter the old colonial town of **San Jerónimo**, which has become almost a suburb of the sprawling city and is now home to Cuzco's wholesale Saturday morning food market (see page 104). San Jerónimo is the starting point for an excellent trek to Huanca.

### San Jerónimo to Huaccoto → *4-5 hrs*

From San Jerónimo, head north along Calle Clorinda Matto de Turner (past the main produce market on the left and the **Andenes de Andrea** restaurant). Further along is the cemetery. The street becomes an unpaved road, swings to the right (east) for 500 m and then left (north) again on its definite course up the mountain. There is a 4WD road which connects San Jerónimo with Huaccoto, laboriously winding its way for 15 km from 3200 m up to 4000 m. Much more interesting and worthwhile, is to follow the old Inca and Spanish colonial track, which ascends the *quebrada* (ravine) of the Huaccotomayu and is only about half as long and more direct, but also steep in places. This road is wide, very clearly marked and widely travelled. Heading north by northwest, the pedestrian road leaves the narrow streets of the town. On the way out, the road winds past the remains of once great colonial *estancias*.

The most striking feature of the landscape is the thousands of eucalyptus trees covering the slopes of all the surrounding hillsides. Few truly old trees remain (the eucalyptus was first introduced to this region in the 1870s and 1880s). There are large groves of 20- to 40-year-old trees growing out of older and thicker stumps, harvested in the mid-20th century, interspersed with extensive patches of much younger trees. The air is dense with that most invigorating and promising aroma of menthol.

Below you can see the red-tiled roofs of San Jerónimo and the broader expanse of the valley of the Río Huatanay, gradually making its way southeast towards its confluence with the Río Urubamba – only 20 km away – whose waters will eventually flow into the Amazon region and on to the Atlantic Ocean.

The broad trail climbs the mountainside, intersecting the many turns and twists of the little-used track. The walking trail pretty much follows the course of a fast-flowing *acequia* (irrigation channel), no doubt originally constructed by the Incas or their predecessors, the Huari-Tiahuanacos, who built Piquillacta (see page 202). There are other canals and aqueducts, which distribute the water from the numerous *puquios* (natural springs) that sprout from the slopes and gullies of **Cerro Pachatusan** (the pillar, or pivot of the world), which, although its main peak and summit are not yet visible, we have been ascending since San Jerónimo.

As the eucalyptus groves begin to thin out, the ridge line and highlands finally become visible. Due north is the prominent, pyramidal summit of **Pikol**, a minor *apu* (mountain) but an important landmark. Its name is clearly carved on its slopes. To the right of it, at roughly two o'clock, a short segment of jagged dark grey boulders and rocks can clearly be seen. This is the first hint of the **Huaccoto** quarries and the principal reference point to head for. In Inca times and throughout the colonial and republican periods, Huaccoto was the site of an important stone quarry and a principal source of building materials for the Inca temples and Spanish colonial mansions of Cuzco. To the immediate right is the gully formed by the **Río Huaccotomayu**, which will somehow vanish into the mountain slope a few hundred metres beyond and above.

The treeline is at about 3700 or 3800 m. You emerge from it into an altogether different world. The panorama is wide and very luminous (assuming, of course, that the weather is fine). The landscape is composed of rolling hills, dotted with tarns that can swell into flooding lakes during the rainy season. Although the ever-growing African *kikuyo* grass (introduced to the area in the early 20th century) has already made



## San Jerónimo to Huanca trek

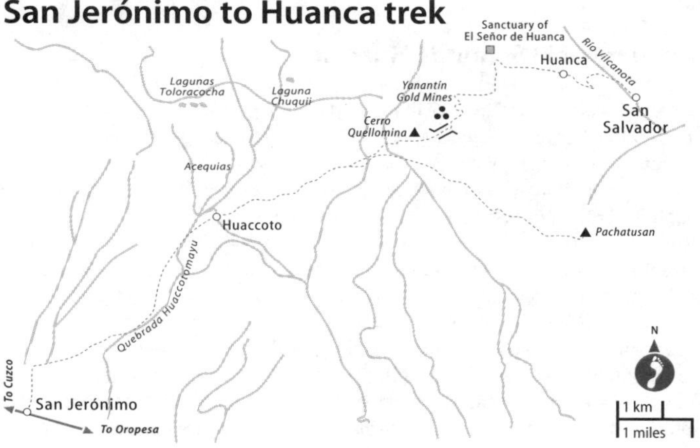

headway into this last pocket of native highland flora, it is the native grasses – the *ichu* and its nearest relatives – which predominate, but only briefly. Soon you reach a landscape devoid of trees, with cushion plants growing low to preserve heat and moisture. The most common is the *yareta*, a bright green bubble-like growth, reminiscent of coral and often, incorrectly, referred to as tundra. Beyond the foreground of rolling hills of *yareta*, scattered with tarns, are several chains of great mountain peaks.

## Huaccoto to Huanca

From Huaccoto it is possible for experienced climbers to make a detour to the summit of **Pachatusan**, heading for the first of its many false summits (east, then south along the slope of the mountain). Alternatively, continue on the same well-worn path that brought you to this point. A gentle climb of a few more metres over the next 1 km, veering slightly east by northeast, sets course towards an obvious breach between Pachatusan and its northwestern extension, known as **Cerro Quellomina**. This pass and a winding trail descend through a maze of impregnable crags, all the way down to the green valley of the Urubamba, which makes its way from southeast to northwest, splaying out into various branches and channels, creating islets and sandbanks which disappear in the rainy season.

Along the crest, close to the pass, are numerous wooden crosses draped in long, flowing, veil-like cloths, many of them well over 3 m tall. These have been erected by pilgrims and devotees and each year they are clad in fresh garments. A few hundred metres along the pass, on the left, is the entrance to what were once the famous **Yanantín** gold mines, belonging to the Marqués de Valleumbroso, which now yield only copper. The entire area was once known as the Marquesado de Oropeza. The trail, very wide and easily recognizable, twists down through the rock spires. Another 200 m beyond is a small Inca fortress perched on one of the buttresses. Closer inspection reveals the remains of other observation points and Inca constructions among the rock towers. Just below this point, another major trail branches off to the left (northwest), climbing up to a well-marked pass. This is an original Inca road, leading back up to Ccoricocha and eventually Huchuy Cuzco and on to Chinchero.

Soon, although still far below your present position, a large, relatively flat area comes into view, with many buildings, cereal cultivation and groves of very tall, old eucalyptus trees. This green belt of fertility amid the seemingly relentless precipices of Pachatusan's northeastern face is **Huanca**, site of the famous sanctuary, one of the great religious shrines of the Andes. Its fame spreads far beyond its immediate vicinity. Devotees, belonging to branches and brotherhoods, come from as far as Ecuador and Bolivia.



## Sanctuary of El Señor de Huanca

The Sanctuary of El Señor de Huanca stands above the clouds, surrounded by flower-filled gardens and trees of many kinds. It is a great gathering place of so many hopes and wishes for goodness, protected by the great misty crag, Pachatusan. From Huaccoto, three hours' hiking, not counting the unavoidable stops to appreciate the scenery, should bring you to the grounds of the sanctuary. The Mercedarian fathers, though fewer than in the past, are still there to greet visitors. The father in charge, whose title is Comendador Capellán, requests that all hikers descending from Huaccoto past the springs pick up all the garbage they can, as a contribution to the conservation of the sanctuary grounds. Lodging and meals are available for pilgrims and hikers (see Sleeping, page 214). There is also a public telephone. Note that there is always a ride available from the sanctuary, as the priests are more than willing to help the faithful who need transport; ring the bell of the private quarters and the resident priest will assist. Of course, a contribution to the sanctuary will be appreciated. » *For details of how to reach the sanctuary by road, see Transport, page 215.*

**History of the sanctuary** We know from Spanish chroniclers of the mid-16th century, such as Pedro de Cieza de León and Juan Polo de Ondegardo, that the Apu Pachatusan was a major *huaca* (shrine) long before the conquest. It was the origin of the ashlars and stone used for building Imperial Cuzco of Pachacútec. It had numerous springs on both its western and eastern slopes. Last but not least, as the later exploitation of the rich mines of the Marqués de Valleumbroso confirmed, it was a source of gold, silver and copper, all of great importance in pre-Columbian Peru, but of much greater value to the piratical economy of 16th-century Europe. (The gold was weighed in the aptly named town of Oropesa, some 10 km beyond San Jerónimo and close to Piquillacta, which was founded by the Spaniards in the boom years of the late 16th century.) Even before the Incas and Spaniards (as well as the Huari-Tiahuanacos of Piquillacta), two fundamental elements characterized the mountain: the abundance of fresh water springs and a large population of puma. Today the puma have disappeared, but the deer that must have constituted their prey can still be seen in groups in more isolated parts of the mountain.

Instead of succumbing to the zeal of the early crusading *conquistadores*, Pachatusan's sacredness was absorbed and adapted in the more enlightened approach of religious syncretism that prevailed in the mid-17th to late 18th century. How else was the Marqués de Valleumbroso going to get the locals to work the mines? At Huanca, the necessary Christian miracle took place in 1675, 25 years after the great earthquake of 1650. It was a time when miracles, no matter their provenance, were universally required.

In May that year, one Diego Quispe, a native of Chincheros working in the Yanantín mines, committed some grave disciplinary error for which he was to be dealt severe punishment the next day. He fled into the crags and gullies of Apu Pachatusan, trusting more in the justice of the earth than that of his overlords. He crept into the furthest depths of an overhang and began to pray. As night fell and Quispe prepared to resume his flight to freedom, the miracle took place. Jesus appeared to him, wearing the crown of thorns and bleeding from the lashes on his back. He spoke the words: "Diego, I have chosen this site to be a volcano of love and a pure spring of regeneration and forgiveness. Go to your home and let the local priest and all your people know. I shall await you here." Diego took a silver chain from his neck and laid it at the base of the rock where the apparition occurred (the first of many centuries of gifts and tributes to El Señor de Huanca).

Diego's life was spared, and more miracles followed. In the course of the next two generations, the boulder acquired a painting of Christ being whipped by a stylized, Moorish-looking ruffian (an ironic echo of the treatment inflicted upon the mineworkers by the Marqués de Valleumbroso). In time, ownership of the land passed to the religious order of La Merced of Cuzco (Mercedarios). A large sanctuary was built over the original boulder and among the devotees whose generosity contributed to its construction are various South American presidents, the elder Alessandri of Chile prominent among them.

Today, the boulder and traces of the painting are partially visible through glass. Nearly 400 years' accumulation of plaques, icons and messages are everywhere. People come on foot, on horseback and by car to fill empty coke bottles and glass jars with the magic water that flows out of Apu Pachatusan just above the sanctuary.

## Towards Paucartambo » *pp214-216.*

### Saylla to Oropesa

Southeast from San Jerónimo the valley begins to narrow as you reach **Saylla**, famous for its *chicharrones* – deep-fried pieces of pork. Between here and Oropesa are the extensive ruins of **Tipón** ⓘ *entry US$1.80, or BTG ticket, 1 hr on foot from Tipón village* *(taxis available)*. They include baths, terraces, irrigation systems and a temple complex, accessible by a path leading from just above the last terrace, all in a fine setting. If you head to the left at the back of the site, there is a small pathway. Follow the trail round to where you will see more small ruins. From there you will find an amazing Inca road with a deep irrigation channel, which can be followed to reach **Cerro Pachatusan** in two to three days (see also San Jerónimo to Huanca trek, page 196).

Further on is **Oropesa**, which has been known as Cuzco's breadbasket since colonial times and is the national capital of this staple foodstuff. Try the delicious large, circular loaves. The church has a fine ornately carved pulpit. Next comes the village of **Huacarpay**, near the shores of Laguna de Huacarpay, in the **Piquillacta Archaeological Park**. For details of Inca ruins and walks around this area, see page 202.

## Huambutío to Pisac

About 3 km beyond Oropesa, just past Huacarpay, is a turning left to **Huambutío**. Here the road divides. The higher road, called Carretera Carmen Bonita, goes north to Paucartambo, on the eastern slope of the Andes (see below), and on to Manu. The other road heads northwest, following the river bank past Huambutío, Vilcabamba and San Salvador (for access to the sanctuary at Huanca, see page 198) and on to Pisac (see page 126). At Pisac the road connects with the road to the Sacred Valley of the Urubamba, as well as the road back to Cuzco via Sacsayhuaman.

The 20 km stretch from Huambutío to Pisac is fully paved and is an access road for the first river-rafting section on the Río Urubamba, which also connects with another rafting route from Piñipampa. In the rainy season, and for less experienced rafters, the Huambutío (Piñipampa) to Pisac river section is safer to run. The rapids are Class II to III. The rafting trip is 30-35 km long with spectacular views of the Urubamba valley that are not seen on a conventional valley tour. This part of the river offers views of the Sanctuary of El Señor de Huanca. » *For Cuzco operators offering rafting trips, see Activities and tours, page 110. See also Rafting, page 18.*



## Paucartambo and around

This once remote town, 80 km east of Cuzco, is on the road to Pilcopata, Atalaya and Shintuya and is now the overland route used by tour companies from Cuzco into Manu National Park (see page 235). Consequently, it has become a popular tourist destination. On 15-17 July, the **Fiesta of the Virgen del Carmen** is a major attraction and well worth seeing. Masked dancers enact rituals and folk tales in the streets (see page 201).

Since colonial times Paucartambo was on the route for produce brought from the jungle to the sierra and thence to the coast. King Carlos III of Spain had a stone bridge built across the river here in the 18th century to replace the previous rope bridge. The locals claimed that the reason the king lost such a large proportion of the *diezmos reales* (tithes, or one-tenth tax on annual produce) due to him from the area was that the mule loads were too heavy for the original bridge. The stone bridge may have solved his tax problem, but it also furthered his aim of promoting the development of Paucartambo and encouraging scientific and exploratory expeditions in the region.

You can walk from Paucartambo to the *chullpas* of **Machu Cruz** in about an hour, or to the *chullpas* of **Pijchu** (take a guide). You can also visit the Inca fortress of **Huatojto**, which has fine doorways and stonework. A car will take you as far as Ayre, from where the fortress is a two-hour walk. From Paucartambo, in the dry season, you can go 44 km to **Tres Cruces**, along the Pilcopata road, turning left after 25 km. Señor Cáceres in Paucartambo will arrange this trip for you. Tres Cruces gives a wonderful view of the sunrise in June and July: peculiar climatic conditions make it appear as if three suns are rising. Tour operators in Cuzco (see page 104) can arrange transport and lodging.

## The fiesta of the Virgen del Carmen

In the village of Paucartambo, 80 km east of Cuzco, a pagan-Christian festival celebrates the Virgen del Carmen annually on 15-17 July. Her feast days are in the Quechua month of Earthly Purification. There are two popular myths surrounding the history of the Virgen del Carmen.

The first tells how the Virgin appeared in Paucartambo. The story goes that a rich Ccolla woman called Felipa Begolla came to Paucartambo to trade goods. One day she was unloading her wares, when, in one of her earthenware pots, the head of a beautiful woman appeared and a sweet voice spoke to her: "Do not be afraid, my dear, my name is Carmen". The head shone like the rays of the sun. Felipa contracted a great cabinetmaker in the town to carve a body made of fine wood on which to place the beautiful head. She brought the statue of the Virgin into the town's church and all the Ccolla people celebrated because the Virgin had arrived in a pot from Ccollao, an area beginning 150 km southeast of Cuzco, beyond the Ausangate massif, covering the enormous highland plateau that includes Titicaca and stretching as far as northern Argentina. The Ccolla swore to come to Paucartambo every year on 16 July so that the Virgin would not feel sad at being away from her own land. The Virgen del Carmen festival became popular and so, each year, dancing groups dressed in colourful costumes with decorated masks came to re-enact the old folk tales. (Sra Betty Yabar, *Testimonio de Cheqec*, 1971)

In the other popular myth, the Chontakirus, a tribe from the jungle, tell that the Ch'unchos, who in history and fables embody profanity and contempt for sacred things, stole the statue of the Virgin from the Ccollas of Puno who were taking it to Paucartambo for the Corpus Christi celebrations. During the confrontation the Ch'unchos killed the Ccollas and threw the statue into the Río Amaru (river of the serpent). From that day, the river was renamed the Madre de Dios, after the Mother of God. The statue was rescued from the waters and taken to the church in Paucartambo, where she remains. Scars from the arrows in her chest can still be seen (Sra Alfonsina Barrionuevo, *Cuzco Mágico*, 1968).

For the festival, the church is decorated, with the Mamacha Carmen dressed in fine clothes, and she is visited by the dancing Comparsas. Some travel from far away, such as the Negritos who, in colonial times, came to dance for the Virgin, praying for their freedom. The Ch'unchos, her captors, are her main dancers and they guard her along the route of the procession. The party continues for the next two days with lots of dancing and music. Each dancing group has its own station in town and every year important people are named as Carguyocs, who are in charge of a particular dancing group at every ceremony. The Carguyocs cover all the costs of the festivity for the dancers and for all the people who visit. They provide lodging, food and drink.

The Mamacha Carmen is taken out on her final procession to the colonial stone bridge (built by King Carlos III of Spain in the 18th century). She then blesses the four Suyos, or cardinal points. The Saqras (demons) scurry over the rooftops trying to tempt her, but the Virgin with her kindness makes them repent. In the afternoon, a re-enactment of the battle between the Ccollas and the Ch'unchos, called the Guerrilla, takes place. The whole town gets involved and the music, dancing and drinking continue.

# Piquillacta Archaeological Park » pp214-216.

The Piquillacta Archaeological Park is 30 km southeast of Cuzco, off the main road to Sicuani. It has an area of 3421 ha and its nucleus is the remains of a lake, the Laguna de Huacarpay, around which are many pre-Columbian archaeological sites. The principal ones are Piquillacta, Choquepuquio, Kañarakay, Urpicancha and Rumicolca.

## Piquillacta

ⓘ *Daily 0700-1730. Entry US$1.80 or with BTG (see box, page 59). Buses to Urcos from Av Huáscar in Cuzco will drop you at the entrance on the north side of the complex, though this is not the official entry.*

Piquillacta, which translates as the City of Fleas, is a large site, with some reconstruction in progress. It was an administrative centre at the southern end of the Huari Empire. The Huari, contemporaneous with the Tiahuanaco culture (AD 600-1000), were based near present-day Ayacucho in the Central Highlands, almost 600 km north of Cuzco by road. However, Huari influence covered most of what we now know as Peru, from Cajamarca and the Pacific coast in the north to the borders of the Tiahuanaco in the south. The Huari system of regional storehouses, irrigation, roads and government was similar to that of the Incas, who adopted it from them.

Archaeological evidence from Piquillacta is confusing, but mostly suggests that this was not a place for permanent residents but rather a base for storing supplies, housing itinerant groups of workers, gathering and distributing tributes, and conducting ceremonies. The whole site is surrounded by a wall, there are many enclosed compounds with buildings of over one storey and it appears that the walls were plastered and finished with a layer of lime.

## Rumicolca

On the main road to Sicuani and Puno, shortly after the turn-off to Piquillacta, you will see, on the right, the huge gateway of Rumicolca. You can walk around it for free. This was a Huari aqueduct, built across a narrow stretch of the valley, which the Incas clad in fine stonework to create this gateway. If you look at the top you can see the original walls, four tiers high. It is now being 'restored', which in Cuzco means rebuilt – a highly controversial topic.

Rumicolca itself (the name means depository or storage site for rocks) was a control point and parallel set of gateways through which in Inca times all traffic between Cuzco and Collasuyo (the southeastern quarter of the Inca dominions) had to pass. It is very imposing. The wall through which the gates pass is of common enough composition, rough-hewn rock bound by a hardened clay mortar. There is evidence that this was covered in stucco and painted in ochres and reds. The gateways, though, are some of the finest Inca masonry. Large, perfectly cut, polished andesite ashlars fit together exactly, without mortar, demonstrating a quality of workmanship equal to anything in Cuzco, Ollantaytambo or Pisac. The finely dressed gateways probably date from the 14th century, contemporary with the monumental phase of Inca architecture in the era of Pachacútec or his successor Túpac Yupanqui. The wall which the gateway crosses is 600 to 800 years older and supported a Huari aqueduct which brought water to Piquillacta.

## Laguna de Huacarpay

The lake, also known as **Laguna de Lucre**, is smaller now than it was in ancient times, when it was called Muyna. The basin of the lake lies at an altitude of 3200 m and is surrounded by several hills no higher than 3350-3400 m. Its shape is roughly circular and its circumference is presently about 8 km. Sections of the lake are overgrown with thick beds of *totora* reeds and other Andean lakeside vegetation. As the lake is gradually drying up, the reeds are spreading and fragmenting the open water, but several large sections of water remain. Water levels fluctuate between the dry and rainy seasons and as a result of other climatic events, such as El Niño. The village of Huacarpay, on its northern shore, can be subjected to damaging floods.

The Laguna de Huacarpay is the habitat of a variety of birdlife. In the open water, flocks of puna teals, pochards and pintails can be seen, as well as more scattered individual Andean ruddy ducks, with their conspicuous blue beaks. The *totora* reed banks are home to several varieties of gallinules and coots, the giant and the red-fronted being most noticeable. Along the shores of the lake and the neighbouring marshlands live puna ibis (though not in large numbers) and sometimes white-faced ibis; also some herons and occasional egrets. There are also lapwings, terns and Andean gulls. Most of these are present year-round. Huacarpay is the area most readily accessible from Cuzco in which to observe a typical Andean highland lake environment.

## Around Laguna de Huarcarpay

A good way to see both the ruins and some varied wildlife is to hike or cycle around the lake, on 8 km of level, paved minor road, which few motor vehicles use. The main focus of this basic circuit is birdwatching and only two or three secondary archaeological sites, but the hike can be lengthened to include the majority of the sites built on the surrounding hills. Some can be visited independently, but on an anticlockwise circuit of the lake basin they can easily be taken in.

From the main Cuzco–Urcos highway, take the turning south towards Lucre. At the southern end of the lake the road begins to swing slightly to the left (east) and soon splits: right to the town of Lucre and left around the lake. **Lucre** has been associated with textiles since Inca times. In the 1850s and 1860s, the area was owned by the Garmendia family who pioneered the first industrial production of textiles (worsteds, tweeds, alpaca and vicuña finished cloth) in this area, maybe in all Peru. To do this they imported a complete textile mill from England, the whole works, including the engineers and mechanics. It was shipped to Mollendo, thence to Arequipa and on over the Andes by mule. For many years it played a significant part in the local economy, but today there is no sign of it.

The left-hand fork continues east and shortly begins to climb a little and heads northeast. Here a really nice hike starts. On some maps this is marked Morada de Huascar, but its true name is **Kañarakay**. From this point, angling away and above the modern road, following the gently rising crest and the various converging trails and footpaths, you begin to glimpse the layers of history of this area. Looking north, some 5 km across the lake, as if moulded onto its hill, lies the rectilinear grid of Piquillacta. West of it and slightly lower are the less regular, but taller walls of Choqepuquio, while slightly lower but close by are the remains of a colonial hacienda, also named Choqepuquio. Much further away, 20-30 km north, is the unusual, stark profile of Cerro Pachatusan. Meanwhile, looking to the east of Piquillacta, the gates of Rumicolca are visible, the irrigation canals contouring the mountains from distant, forgotten

 sources. Also visible is the unmistakable architectural harmony between structure and environment that characterizes Inca building, in this case, the terraces of Urpicancha. That's the entire hike which lies ahead.

From Kañarakay start hiking northeastward. What at first sight appears to be arid, rocky country interspersed with crumbling ridges and strewn with loose rocks and scree, is in fact the remnants of a vast network of roads, passageways, buildings, retaining walls and stairways. Several cities lie scattered here, successively inhabited, abandoned and repopulated. This is also the realm of the cacti: *opuntia* predominate, but also thin, elongated prickly pears, enormously tall flat *nopales*, small barrel cacti, some with huge bright scarlet and yellow flowers. There are seven-pointed San Pedro cacti, with lily-white flowers which bud at dawn, blossom at noon and wither by sunset. *Epyphitic bromeliads*, most of them *tsillandsias* with bushy crowns of long thin leaves armed with sharp thorns, cling to ancient walls and grow in empty windows. There are also aloes and agave, and almost everywhere are blankets of Spanish moss. The fauna is limited to lizards and rodents, which keep the insect population under control. Most common are black widow spiders, which live under stones (it is best to leave rocks where they are and watch carefully where you sit down for a break!). Kestrels and hawks streak overhead, but the most typical of local birds are the Andean flicker, a large bright yellow-greenish speckled ground woodpecker, fond of lizards, and the giant hummingbirds – Patagonia gigas – with their nests strategically placed among the thick branches of a thorny cactus.

After 1 km of this jumble of stone, you come to the ruins of **Urpicancha** (*urpi* meaning dove, and *cancha* an enclosed field). Some legends say this was the birthplace of the Inca Huáscar, who waged war with his half-brother Atahualpa. Urpicancha is like a small oasis in the middle of the dusty environment surrounding the lake. It consists of a succession of a terraces on the hillside, descending almost to the lakeshore. At its base are two partial enclosures, made of well-fitted rocks which have acquired a striking orange hue from the lichen. A freshwater spring descends the hillside, partially piped, and there's an old colonial house, closed for some years now. It's a shady spot, with eucalyptus, willows and some mature elderberry trees (*sauco*).

From here, the hike climbs up to **Rumicolca** (see page 202). Several paths meander along the western slope of the large hill called Cerro Combayoc. All these trails will lead to Rumicolca but the routes closest to Urpicancha are the most scenic. The entire Muyna basin can be seen, and the eastern side of Combayoc, including 40 km of the Vilcanota river valley, Andahuaylillas and sections of the Rumicolca quarries. Rumicolca is a few metres from the modern Cuzco to Puno road. On the other side of the road, less than 50 m away, lies the entrance to the Huari adobe wall ruins of **Piquillacta** (see page 202).

From Piquillacta, head west into a valley through which runs the paved road from Cuzco to Paucartambo. Cross it and continue for about 50 m until you come to the remains of the old dirt road which runs parallel to the modern one for a short stretch and then veers left, crossing an old bridge. Over the bridge head west by southwest, past the site of a lime crusher (some houses, a small adobe factory); on the right is a marshy extension of Huacarpay lake. Here is some of the best birdwatching on the entire trek. Follow the main (or any secondary) path up the side of the valley, gaining the first ridge about 100 m beyond.

Look south and see the dark walls of **Choquepuquio**, perhaps the most mysterious of the archaeological sites on the trek. The walls suggest two-storeyed houses but also a redoubt, built to withstand siege and attack. Choquepuquio was erected as a stronghold in insecure times. Its drama derives from the fact that it is not being restored (unlike most other sites in the park). It is unkempt, there are thistles and brambles and, when seen up close, its walls appear even taller and more enigmatic than at first glance. From Choqepuquio follow any of the paths leading to the road which goes to Cuzco. You will emerge directly opposite the Lucre turn-off where the hike began.

# Southeast towards Urcos » pp214-216.

## Andahuaylillas

Continuing southeast towards Urcos you reach Andahuaylillas and the first of three fascinating 17th-century churches. This is a simple structure, but it has been referred to as the Andean Sistine Chapel because of its beautiful frescoes and internal architecture. Go in, wait for your eyes to adjust to the darkness, then turn to look at the two pictures either side of the splendid door. On the right is the path to heaven, which is narrow and thorny; on the left the way to hell, which is wide and littered with flowers. They are attributed to the artist Luis de Riaño. Above is the high choir, built in local wood, where there are two organs. Craning your neck further you will see the remarkable painted and carved ceiling. The main altar is gilded in 24-carat gold leaf and has symbols from both the Quechua and Christian religions, such as the sun and the lamb, respectively. Many of the canvases depict the lives of the church's patron saints, St Peter and St Paul. Ask for Sr Eulogio; he is a good guide, but speaks Spanish only. Outside, around the peaceful plaza, are massive pisonay trees dripping with red seeds and hanging moss.

*The church is likely to be locked. For the giant key, look for Sr Pablo Ticuña at 2 de Mayo 367, a block away. He will show you around for US$0.85 per person (he only speaks Spanish).*

## Huaro

Before the next major town of Urcos is the quiet village of Huaro; turn left off the main road to reach the appalling main plaza, dominated by a concrete lookout tower. The church on this plaza is stunning inside. Walking in takes your breath away. The walls are plastered with frescoes used to evangelize the illiterate. Grinning skeletons compete with dragons and devils ushering the living into the afterlife and punishing them thereafter. Completed in 1802 by Tadeo Escalante, they are now mostly in a sad state of repair. Tour groups come here, but there is precious little money being spent on preservation. The first fresco on the right as you enter shows the torment of sinners in hell. A liar has his tongue torn out with pliers, a drunk has boiling alcohol poured down his throat through a funnel and others are impaled on a wheel. The torture is not confined to the masses. In a boiling cauldron, among the tortured, writhing, naked bodies are a priest, a cardinal and a bishop, identified by their hats.

Looking left of the door there is a priest giving absolution at the death of a girl in a poor house while below, a rich house plays host to a sumptuous banquet (with roasted guinea pig on the menu, of course). A woman here is choking and being led away by the skeleton of Death. The moral is clear. Right of the entrance, below another portrait of rich people having a feast, is the Tree of Life with good versus evil as Death wields an axe and Jesus sounds a bell.

To the right of this, on the left wall, is Judgement Day at its grimmest. Centre stage is a graveyard, the coffins of which are being yanked open by skeletons to drag the dead to either the underworld on the right (entered via the mouth of a dragon) or heaven (complete with Pearly Gates and musicians playing trumpets).

On the left are people being pulled from flames by angels. This is Purgatory and its inhabitants are those who have committed minor sins. Having paid their dues they will now be allowed into heaven. The democracy of the Catholic vision again allows these sinners to include cardinals and bishops.

To the right of this painting we see that Death is never far away. A huge skeleton containing the body of a woman (for we are all born of woman) has at its feet the paraphernalia of the rich, which cannot be taken into the next life. More skeletons stand behind people ignorant of their destiny. An angel sounds a trumpet from the top of a pillar at the moment of death. Meanwhile, the devil can be seen lurking under the bed of a person being given absolution. Again, look up at the wonderful ceiling.

## Urcos

Beyond Huaro is Urcos. There are lodgings here, but they are basic to say the least. A spectacular road runs from Urcos across the Eastern Cordillera to Puerto Maldonado in the jungle (see below and page 239).

# Cordillera Vilcanota

» *pp214-216. Colour map 2, B4.*

East of Cuzco lies the **Cordillera Vilcanota**, the greatest concentration of mountains and glaciers in southern Peru. With at least four great peaks towering above 6000 m (depending on which map you're looking at!) in densely packed icy masses, this area is reminiscent of the Cordillera Huayhuash further to the north. Viewed from the ruins of Sacsayhuaman above Cuzco, **Ausangate**, at 6384 m the range's loftiest peak, is impressive even from a distance of nearly 100 km, but in the Vilcanota mountains Ausangate is just the beginning. Unlike both the Cordilleras of Vilcabamba and Urubamba, which plunge precipitously from sheer glaciers into lush subtropical valleys, the Vilcanota rises from the northern Altiplano, and treks into the region rarely, if ever, drop below 4000 m.

Life is harsh for the communities who live in the shadow of these great peaks. Knowledge of Spanish is often limited or non-existent and the people's respect of ancient ways and the power of the *apus* (mountain spirits), runs strong. Survival is eked from a meagre diet of potatoes, *cuy* (guinea pig) and the meat and wool of the large herds of domesticated llamas and alpacas that roam the valleys. In this land of wild and austere beauty the relatively sparse human population has allowed the continued survival of rare Andean wildlife. Vicuña are sometimes seen grazing on isolated mountain slopes, and viscacha, a relative of the chinchilla, are often seen in rocky areas. Sacred beasts to the Incas, the puma and the condor, though rarely seen, still inhabit this desolate kingdom.



## The road to Puerto Maldonado

The small town of **Tinqui**, east of Urcos is the traditional starting point for treks into the region and is a good place to find local guides and *arrieros* (muledrivers). Some 82 km from Urcos, at the base of Ausangate, is the town of **Ocongate**, which has two hotels. Some 47 km after passing the snowline Hualla-Hualla pass, at 4820 m, the super-hot thermal baths of **Marcapata** ⓘ *173 km from Urcos, entry US$0.10*, provide a relaxing break.

## Ausangate circuit → *6 days*

This is the most popular trekking route and involves fairly tough hiking around the peak itself, featuring icy mountain vistas, high passes (including two over 5000 m) and some beautiful turquoise lakes. As an added bonus, there are two geothermal springs to thaw out in at the beginning and end! In addition to the 'circuit', there is a great variety of other options, including treks around the range's northern peaks and routes to the magnificent **Laguna Sibinacocha**, a stunning 15-km long lake set at 4800 m in remote territory to the east of Ausangate. Described below is the classic Ausangate Circuit, with an additional two-day extension to the isolated northern lake, **Laguna Singrenacocha**.

**Preparations** A standard fee for locals hired independently is US$7 per day for an *arriero* and US$6 per horse per day. You are also expected to provide sufficient food and a tent for the *arriero*. Tiofilo is a recommended guide/*arriero* who can be contacted through Tinqui's radio station, located just of the town's main plaza. The IGN 1:100,000 Ocongate map (available at **South American Explorers** in Cuzco) covers all trekking areas described below and is fairly accurate. Note that as you leave

Tinqui you will be charged a community fee for using the Ausangate trail; at the time of writing this was S/.10 per person (US$4).



**Day one** Four hours' walking in total. From Tinqui head southeast towards the radio and TV aerials on the hill overlooking town. This is **Concacancha**. A couple of families rent camping space up here, if you don't want to stay in one of Tinqui's cheap *hostales*. To get to Concacancha you must cross a bridge to the south side of the Río Pinchimuro Mayo and climb the trail up the far bank. Ausangate's northern face dominates the landscape to the south on clear days. Just to the left of the small hill and radio masts a clear dirt road heads south towards the mountains. The road twists sharply in a small dip, then establishes itself on a heading of 150°, contained neatly between adobe walls. The landscape here is high-altitude *puna* with the occasional small dwelling. Don't be surprised, either here or further into the trek, if friendly, industrious locals, dressed in beautiful traditional clothing, track you down looking to sell alpaca goods and drinks. Please treat them with respect, they're just trying to make a living. After 1½ hours heading more or less south you cross a stream running across the trail, next to a Km 7 marker. A couple of minutes after the stream, turn right at the Y junction on a bearing of 220°. it's a good path, slightly less used than the previous one. After a further 10 minutes the trail fades a little, heading 150° again. You

## Ausangate trek

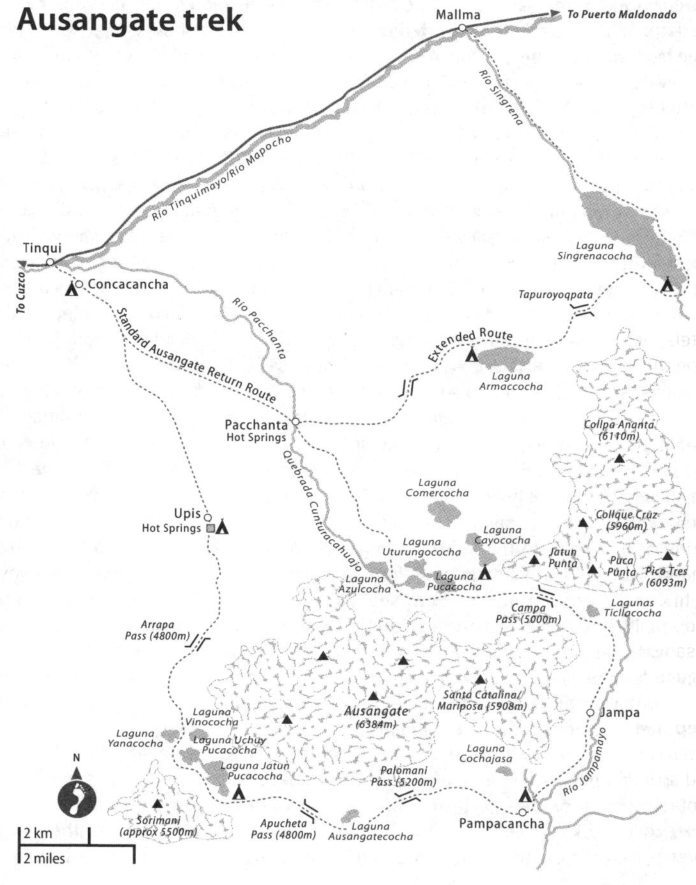

 cross a second stream and keep your southeast course, crossing a small adobe bridge over an irrigation channel 2¼ hours after leaving Concacancha. Fifteen minutes more and you arrive at the crest of the hill, with spectacular views of Ausangate and a glacier tumbling into a narrow valley to the southeast. This valley and its hot springs are the destination for the day's hike.

Using trails contouring around the hills on the left side of the swampy **Upismayo** valley, head to the valley's eastern end and a small collection of buildings. This is **Upis**, reached after about three hours from Concacancha. The valley often contains interesting bird-life in addition to horses, llamas and alpacas. Bird species often spotted include Andean geese and puna ibis. From the settlement the glacial valley lies at 140°. Continue around the swamp and up the valley to the left of the stream that runs through its centre. About 30 minutes beyond the houses you pass the Upis hot springs. A further 20 minutes takes you to some decent camping areas with plenty of space. There seem to be several areas of hot pools, the cleanest being on the right hand side of the valley: soak in the pools and admire the snow.

**Day two** Five to six hours walking. Cross the stream to the far (right hand) side of the valley and hike towards the imposing north face of Ausangate. After 25 minutes the pass area comes into view, just to the right of a rocky triangular peak on a bearing of around 200°. The trail continues to ascend gradually to the right side of the valley, still holding roughly the same course, crossing areas of cushion moss after another 20 minutes or so, and all the time offering a stunning close-up of the craggy peaks and vast ice formations before you. After 1¼ hours take a sharp right, about 240°, up a grassy valley about 300 m before the black peak. Walking on the left side of this valley the route curves back to the left slightly, and, about 1¾ hours after leaving camp you reach the 4800 m **Arrapa** pass. Fabulous desolate views surround you, with a deep valley to your right, and rugged, often snow-dusted hills beyond that.

From this point and for the next few days always keep Ausangate on your left. After the pass continue at 240° under a low line of hills. A little further and a huge, seemingly uninhabited valley opens out before you. This is the **Jalacocha** valley, a place that, to this author at least, seems to possess a primeval, 'lost world' quality... let your imagination run wild! Turn hard left (140°) and descend gently across the top of the valley heading upstream; don't go down into the bottom of the valley. To the south, across the valley, rise the jagged spires of **Nevado Sorimani**. An hour from the *abra* you pass a small lake on your right. This is possibly **Yanacocha** on the IGN sheet, or perhaps a smaller unmarked lake. Just beyond this another much larger emerald lake comes into view, **Laguna Uchuy Pucacocha**, and this is your immediate destination. Steep winding paths take you south, down towards the lake. After 10 minutes you cross a flat pampa criss-crossed with clear streams, a decent snack or lunch stop. From here head south towards the stream and waterfall that flow from the lake's western end; 15 minutes should see you arrive at the crossing above the falls. Cross at this point to the right/southern side of the valley and climb up through interesting boulder-like rock formations before arcing around and emerging above Uchuy Pucacocha. You can now see yet another lake, the largest yet, **Jatun Pucacocha**, just beyond (to the east of) Uchuy and connected to it by another stream and waterfall. To the right of these connecting waterfalls lies a large rocky hill. Tonight's camp lies at the far end of Jatun Pucacocha and the easiest way of reaching it lies with the trails running to the right of the hill and down the valley, definitely the best option for those with pack animals.

An alternative route passes some *campesino* houses beneath the hill, and contours around its left side, offering better views of the lake and the giant seracs and crevasses of the glacier tumbling down from Ausangate's southern flank towards the lakes. Keeping to the lake's southern side, once around the corner close to the falls, climb high to avoid some scrambling later and follow the lake to its eastern end. There's good flat ground for camping just to the north of the stream and the boggy ground. This campsite can be very exposed in windy weather. 

**Day three** A long day, seven to eight hours with breaks. Walk east up the valley, crossing to the right side of the stream. After 10 minutes the trail turns to the right above some *campesinos*' houses, circumventing a steep rise in the valley floor. There are constant views of the great southern glaciers and, after about 50 minutes, views down to two small lakes on the left, one clear, the other milky turquoise. Forty minutes' more gentle climbing and you reach the first pass of the day, the 4800-m **Apucheta** pass, named after the standing stones that crown the summit in honour of the surrounding *apus*. As you'd expect by now, there are great views of Ausangate and her snowfields, and from a little further down, **Ausangatecocha**, a beautiful, luminous lake (120° from the pass) nestled in the valley below. Head down into the valley below the lake, still heading east. This is a good place for a break, as the next couple of hours will see you climb to the highest pass on the route, the formidable 5200-m **Abra Palomani**.

From the valley floor the pass lies up a valley at about 70°, just to the right of Ausangate's huge glaciers threaded with crevasses and jutting seracs, and a black rocky outcrop just below the snow line. Twenty minutes' climb from the bottom the valley splits in two: take the left-hand route heading towards Ausangate. Another 10 minutes and the trail swings back to the right, climbing a ridge, crossing a small valley and resuming its initial 70°-80° course. Looking back, you're treated to spectacular views of **Nevado Sorimani**, **Nevado del Inca** and, far to the southeast, **Nevado Cóndor Tuco**. One and a half hours from the valley floor you reach the pass, exposed and crowded with *apuchetas*. There are fabulous views in both directions, as you'd expect, and now another peak reveals itself, **Santa Catalina** (5908 m), or Mariposa, as it is locally known, lying just to the east of the main Ausangate peak.

On the far side of the pass a clear trail descends over a desolate landscape into the valley below. At first the trail keeps to its east-northeast course, and then turns to the east in the second half of its descent, reaching the floor of this next valley just over an hour from the pass. Skirt the valley floor on its left side heading down for a further 45 minutes to its confluence with the larger **Jampamayo** valley. Here lies Pampaconcha, a small indigenous community, and a couple minutes beyond this, northeast and to the left of the stream, is a sheltered camping spot.

**Day four** Five to six hours in total. Start the day hiking more or less northeast up the valley, always keeping to its left side. After about 30 minutes a huge snow peak comes into view at the head of the valley. This is **Señal Nevado Pico Tres** (6093 m), and it's this mountain's triple summit that dominates much of the day's walk. Jagged coal-black mountains on the right contrast sharply with the glaciers ahead. An hour from camp the trail begins to turn to the north and by the time you're 45 minutes further up the valley you're heading towards the left-hand edge of Pico Tres, passing a large community marked as **Jampa** on the IGN map. Above Jampa more great peaks edge into view to the west of Pico Tres. According to the map these are **Jatun Punta** (the Matterhorn style peak to the left), **Puca Punta** just to the right and the massive **Collque Cruz** (5960 m) behind. Having said that, local names vary considerably and some refer to the entire massif that stretches to Laguna Armaccocha as **Ccallangate**. Continuing north you begin to climb higher on the left slope of the valley towards your immediate destination, the 5000-m **Campa** pass. Just under 3 hours from last night's camp the trail swings sharply to the west, and it's this bearing that you'll more or less maintain for the rest of the day.

A chain of small lakes comes into view at the foot of the mountains across the valley to the north, the **Lagunas Ticllacocha**. Look out for wild vicuñas in this section of the valley, their delicate forms blending easily into the super-sized landscape. Keep to trails high on the left to avoid steeper terrain lower in the valley. Very soon the pass area begins to flatten out and a group of *apuchetas* are reached; slightly deceptive as the pass lies about 10 minutes further, with a second set of *apuchetas* about 3½ hours' walking time from the start of the day's hike. The pass rivals Palomani in terms of its beauty, with a vast wall of razor peaks, ridges and glaciers always to your right. Descending from the pass, many lakes come into view far below and to the west. The valley below is empty and lifeless with huge piles of boulders deposited close to the lakes, demonstrative of massive and continuing glacial retreat. Tonight's campsite, about an hour from the pass, lies on the far side of a small ridge, sheltered and directly south of the closest lake, **Laguna Cayococha**. The site boasts great views of Ausangate, the trekking peak of **Campa** (marked as María Huamantilla) and **Nevado Yanajaja**. Viscachas are easily observed by patient trekkers amongst the boulders near camp.

**Day five** Three to four hours in total. Leave camp heading west. After 10-15 minutes a large chain of lakes, each a different colour, comes into view: **Lagunas Pucacocha, Uturungococha** and **Minaparayoc**. On a clear day you can see the entire Urubamba range stretching across the horizon from La Verónica beyond Cuzco to its end in the east above the Manu National Park. Skirting the left side of the lakes, you cross an area of swampy ground (much favoured by the local alpacas) with the help of strategically placed local bridges. An unhindered view of Ausanagate's north face is visible above you. The path passes a tiny crystalline lake, **Cocha Otorongo** or Jaguar Lake, very clear even by Vilcanota standards. Locals say the lake is used in the ceremonies of traditional medicine men. Passing two smaller lakes on the right, the path turns north after just over an hour. Yet another large shallow lake reveals itself to the left, **Laguna Azulcocha**. Leaving the lakes behind you continue north over rough hilly country, dropping into a small valley after a further 40 minutes. Head northwest to the community marked on the IGN map as **Cullpaca**. At Cullpaca the valley joins the larger **Quebrada Cunturacahuajo**; follow this Quebrada north or north-northeast for 30 minutes until reaching the village of **Pacchanta**. This is positively a city by local standards, with a school, two-storey buildings, some super basic hostels if you're fed up with camping, and hot springs into the bargain!



**Day six** If you now want to head back to Tinqui on the 'standard' route leave Pacchanta following clear trails to the northwest. Cross the small range of hills above the town, then gently descend, crossing open *puna* towards Tinqui. In three hours you should be back in town.

Alternatively, to continue to the northern lakes, on leaving Pacchanta turn right/east. You're aiming for a pass lying just to the left/north of a large black hill (4800 m **Cerro Quimsa Puca Orjo**) which quickly comes into view ahead of you as you hike out above the village. The pass is reached after an hour's hiking from the village. If you feel inclined to climb to the hill's summit, you'll be rewarded with fabulous 360° views of Ausangate to the south, the Collque Cruz/Ccallangate massif to the east and, far to the north, the range of mountains (also part of the Vilcanota range) that play host to the Qoyllur Rit'i festival each summer (see page 98). You'll also find a rustic altar for sacrifices in honour of the great peaks.

From the pass, descend into the **Quillhuahuayjo** valley below you to the east. You can see two *quebradas* (streams) entering the Quillhuahuayjo from the west. Don't take the valley immediately to the east of the pass; rather, on reaching the valley floor, head north past a small community, then, after 15-20 minutes, turn right up the **Quimsacocha** valley. Heading roughly east, hike on the right side of the valley for 20 minutes before crossing a bridge to the left and continuing in the same direction. The valley is reminiscent of the Scottish highlands until the immense snow peaks poke over the horizon a few minutes later! Carry on following the main stream east, taking a slight left at the end of the valley. Fifteen minutes later pass just to the left of a *campesino*'s house, at which point the dark waters of **Laguna Armaccocha** come into view below you to the right, cradled beneath the icy peaks. Five minutes further and there's a good campsite in a flat 'step' high above the lake, with great views of both lake and mountains. If you want somewhere less windy there are also some good sites lower down, closer to the shore. Three or four hours in total.

**Day seven** About three hours relaxed hiking. Start the day hiking eastwards and upwards on a diagonal above the ash-grey Armaccocha lake. The sound of a small river entering the lake on its far side echoes up through the valley and seems disproportional to its size. After about 40 minutes the trail begins to swing more northeast and flattens out towards the top of the pass. Five more minutes and you reach the summit, known locally as **Tapuroyoqpata** for its location close to some ancient looted tombs. From this vantage point the Qoyllur Rit'i range becomes visible to the north once more. Continuing northeast over rocky country for a further 45 minutes brings you to a viewpoint over the fabulous turquoise **Laguna Singrenacocha**, 3.5 km long and perhaps the most impressive of all the lakes on the trek. Head down to the shore and make your way to the lake's southern end where there's a flat area ideal for camping. A powerful river enters here, with tumbling waterfalls flowing down from higher up the valley. Camp on the southern side or, if crossing, wade across where the river meets the lake and loses its power – be careful.

**Day eight** Follow trails north-northwest along the right-hand shore of the lake. Once at the far end after about 1½ hours, follow the Río Singrena and paths, then drivable roads, down to the small town of **Mallma**. Bank on a walk of around four hours. Mallma is on the Ocongate–Puerto Maldonado road, along which unscheduled trucks and, very occasionally, buses head towards Cuzco and the Sacred Valley. More reliable buses usually leave Tinqui and Ocongate for Cuzco in the afternoon or evening. Combis leave when they have enough passengers to cover the petrol and make a profit. Neither bus, truck nor combi makes for a particularly pleasant journey, so take a sleeping bag to fend off the frostbite at midnight!

## Southeast from Urcos » pp214-216.

Southeast from Urcos, the main road passes through **Cusipata**, with an Inca gate and wall. Here the ornate bands for the decoration of ponchos are woven. Close by is the Huari hilltop ruin of **Llallanmarca**. Beyond Cusipata on the main road is **Checacupe** which has a fine church with good paintings and a handsome carved altar rail. Before you get there, however, it's worth heading west off the main road to visit the pretty village of Acomayo, the Inca bridge at Qeswachaka and four beautiful mountain lakes. You are advised to hire a 4WD or a vehicle with a driver for this side-trip but it is also feasible by combi, if you have more time. » *For further details, see Transport, page 216.*

### Acomayo and around

To get to Acomayo, take the road that branches off the main road between Cusipata and Checacupe, turning into a dirt track soon afterwards. At the first fork, just before **Lago Pomacanchi**, turn right to travel past a small community and on to Acomayo. The chapel here is decorated with mural paintings of the 14 Incas.

From Acomayo, you can walk to **Huáscar**, which takes one hour, and from there to **Pajlia**; a climb which leads through very impressive scenery. The canyons of the upper Río Apurímac are vast beyond imagination. Great cliffs drop thousands of metres into dizzying chasms and huge rocks balance menacingly overhead. This river, whose source is accepted as being the source also of the Amazon, rises in the mountains near Arequipa. The ruins of **Huajra Pucará** lie near Pajlia. They are small, but in an astonishing position.

Near Acomayo are four lakes. To reach them drive back along the dirt track from the village, as if you were going towards the main road. When you reach the first lake, Lago Pomacanchi, instead of continuing east, take a sharp right along the eastern shores of the lake. You will travel past three more beautiful lakes: Lago Acopia, Lago Asnacocha and Lago Pampamarca. Stop awhile beside **Lago Pampamarca**. It is absolutely quiet here and a great place to recharge your soul. Set against the pale green grass banks, serene waters reflect the red soil of the hills behind. The only sound is the occasional splash and hoot of a white-beaked Andean coot. The air is thin, clear and crisp.

## Towards the Inca bridge

Beyond Pampamarca, the road continues to **Yanaoca**, where you'll find basic accommodation and restaurants. From here it is possible to head southeast to Sicuani but continuing to **Qeswachaka** and the grass Inca bridge 30 km away is well worth the effort. Just before you leave Yanaoca, turn right to join a road which, at times, is very rough. The way is marked with kilometre signs: turn right just after Km 22 where another road begins, marked with a Km 0. You will find steps down to the bridge shortly before Km 31, two bends from the bright orange road bridge.

The footbridge has been rebuilt every year for the past 400 years during a three-day festival, which starts on 10 June and is celebrated by the three communities who use the bridge. It is built entirely of *pajabrava* grass, woven and spliced to make six sturdy cables which are strung across the 15-m chasm. Look in the water at the far side and you will probably see the remains of the previous year's effort; the work lasts five months, after which the fibres deteriorate and you should not attempt to cross.

About two hours before you reach Qeswachaka is the **Carañawi Cave** (at 4100 m). From Yanaoca find transport towards Livitaca and ask locals where to get off for Carañawi. There is also a large sign. You may only enter the cave between June and October as there is too much water at other times of the year. Camping is possible, but be prepared for extreme cold; there is no water available. It is certainly also possible to drive here in a rented car, but the road is terrible so taking a 4WD is a good idea.



## Raqchi → *Colour map 2, B4.*

ⓘ *San Pedro de Cacha, 120 km southeast of Cuzco. Entry US$1.65. There is a basic shop at the site. The school next door greatly appreciates donations of books and materials.*

In the province of Canchis, in a fertile tributary valley of the Vilcanota, lies the colonial village of **San Pedro de Cacha**. Although unremarkable in itself, the village stands within Raqchi, one of the most important archaeological sites in Peru.

A few hundred metres beyond the village are the principal remains, the once great **Temple of Viracocha**, the pan-Andean god, creator of all living creatures. This is one of the only remaining examples of a two-storey Inca building. It was 90 m long and 15 m high and was probably the largest roofed building ever constructed by the Incas. Above walls of finely dressed masonry 3-4 m high – stonework equal to that found in Cuzco or Machu Picchu – rise the remains of another 5-6 m high wall of adobe brickwork of which only isolated sections remain. Similarly, of the 22 outer columns, which supported great sloping roofs, just one or two remain complete, the others being in various states of preservation. There are numerous other buildings, including *acllahuasi* (houses of chosen women, spinners and weavers of ceremonial cloth), barracks, granaries, reservoirs, baths and fountains. The burial site includes round *chullpa* tombs of the sort found around Lake Titicaca. Much of it was damaged and demolished by looters in search of treasure during or after the Spanish conquest. According to some accounts, the temple was built by Inca Viracocha in the late 14th century, but some chronicles attribute it to Pachacútec.

*If you get lost ask for Tungasuca (a settlement to the south) via the 'circuito de las cuatro lagunas'.*

Archaeological research has shown that Raqchi was always a place associated with religious and ceremonial activity. This predates not only the Incas, but also the Canches (an ethnic group which flourished in the middle horizon of Tiahuanaco), who were conquered and incorporated into the Inca Empire. Since Raqchi was the principal religious site of the Canches, it was natural that the Incas should dedicate their own temple on their allies' hallowed ground. Perhaps the most significant reason behind the choice of this as a sacred site is that Raqchi stands on the slopes of the only dormant volcano in the Cuzco region, Kimsachata. The name in Quechua means 'three-cornered' or 'triplets'. Various myths of Viracocha's travels in the area tell of a hostile reception by local inhabitants, resulting in their destruction by fire and brimstone invoked by Viracocha; others show him taming and overcoming a devastating eruption of Kimsachata.

On the volcano's slopes are pure water springs and sulphurous thermal springs, salt and rich clay deposits. The clay provides the region's principal industry, pottery and ceramics (whence its other name, Raqchi, which in Quechua is a large vessel or pot used in the preparation of *chicha*), as well as building materials such as tiles and particularly strong bricks. » *For information on local festivals, see page 215.*

## South to Sicuani

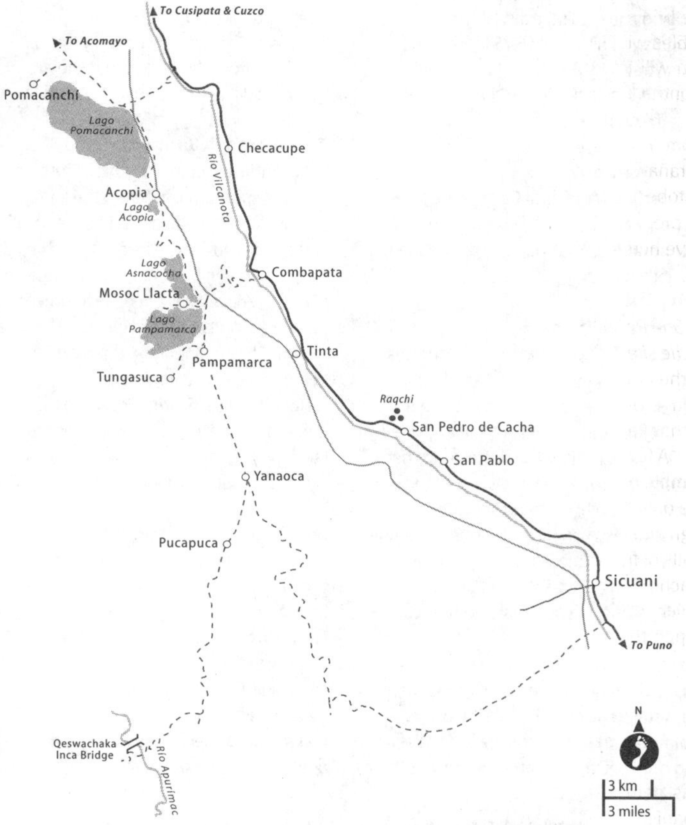

## Sicuani → *Phone code: 084. Colour map 2, B4. Altitude: 3690 m.*

Sicuani is an important agricultural centre and an excellent place for items of llama and alpaca wool and skins. They are sold at the railway station and at the excellent Sunday morning market. The plaza is not as bad as the aberrations found in villages in the nearby mountains, but it is flanked along one entire side by a mirror-glass-fronted, purple-painted concrete monstrosity. On the other side are examples of what might have been much more appropriate colonial-style, balconied buildings. Around the plaza are several shops selling local hats. The bus terminal is in the newer part of town, which is separated from the older part and the Plaza de Armas by a pedestrian walkway and bridge. At the new end of the bridge, but also close to the centre of town, are several *hostales* advertising hot water and private bathrooms.

*23 km before Sicuani on the main road is Tinta, whose church has a brilliant gilded interior and an interesting choir vault.*

Beyond Sicuani the road continues 250 km to Puno. **La Raya** pass (4321 m), the highest on this route, is 38 km beyond the town and marks the divide between Cuzco Department and the altiplano which stretches to Lake Titicaca.

## Sleeping

**San Jerónimo to Huanca** *p196*

G **Sanctuary of El Señor de Huanca**. Lodging and meals are available for pilgrims and hikers: US$5.75 for bed and board, free for somewhere to sleep only (but you can cook). Both include full use of bath and toilet.

**Paucartambo** *p200*

G **Albergue Municipal Carmen de la Virgen**. Fairly basic.

G **Quinta Rosa Marina**, near the bridge. Similarly basic.

**Andahuaylillas** *p205*

F **La Casa del Sol**, close to the central plaza on Garcilaso. Relaxing, clean and bright hostel. Well-decorated rooms set around a courtyard, this is excellent value. Owned by Dr Gladys Oblitas, the hostel funds her project to provide medical services to poor *campesinos*. While staying you can take a course or take part in workshops on natural and alternative medicine. She also has a practice in Cuzco, Procuradores 42, T084-227264, medintegral@hotmail.com.

**Urcos** *p206*

G **Hostal Luvic**, on the plaza. Cheap, basic.

G **Hostal Señor de Qoillurrit'i**, on the main road on the central plaza. Best of a bad bunch. Dormitory rooms are very basic but clean; also a private double of similar quality. Showers are cold in a separate block outside.

Hotel LaTerraza in Urcos may look upmarket from the outside but should be avoided if at all possible.

**Cordillera Vilcanota** *p206*

G **Ausangate**, Tinqui. Very basic but warm, friendly atmosphere. Sr Crispin (or Cayetano), the owner, is knowledgeable and can arrange guides, mules, etc. He and his brothers can be contacted in Cuzco on F084-227768. All have been recommended as reliable sources of trekking and climbing information, for arranging trips and for being very safety conscious.

G **Hostal Tinqui Guide**, Tinqui, on the right-hand side as you enter the village. Friendly, with meals available, the owner can arrange guides and horses.

**Southeast from Urcos** *p211*

G **Casa Comunal**, Tinta. Clean dormitory accommodation and good food.

**Camping**

There are many places to camp wild by the lakes near **Acomayo**. Take warm clothing for night-time and plenty of water. At **Qeswachaca** there's good camping downstream, but take water.

*For an explanation of sleeping and eating price codes used in this guide, see inside the front cover. Other relevant information is found in Essentials, see pages 27-32.*

**Sicuani** *p214*

**F Obada**, Jr Tacna 104, T084-351214. Has seen better days. There are large, clean rooms with hot showers.

**F Royal Inti**, Av Centenario 116, T084-352730, on the west side of the old pedestrian bridge across the river. Modern, clean and friendly.

**F Samariy**, Av Centenario 138 (next to Royal Inti), T084-352518. Offers good-value rooms with bathrooms.

**G José's Hostal**, Av Arequipa 143, T084-351254. Good, clean rooms with bath. Prices per person.

## Eating

**Urcos** *p206*

**Restaurante Pollería**, on the main plaza. Acceptable and cheap.

**Sicuani** *p214*

There are several cafés on 2 de Mayo, running northeast from the plaza, which are good for snacks and breakfasts.

**El Fogón**, Zevallos, the main drag down from the plaza, smart, painted pink, on the left heading down. Serves up good chicken and chips for US$1.70.

**Mijuna Wasi**, Jr Tacna 146. Closed Sun. One of several *picanterías*, which prepares typical dishes such as *adobo* served with huge glasses of *chicha* in a dilapidated but atmospheric courtyard. Recommended.

**Pizzería Bon Vino**, 2 de Mayo 129, 2nd floor, off the east side of the plaza. Good for an Italian meal.

## Bars and clubs

**Sicuani** *p214*

**Piano Bar**, just off the first block of 2 de Mayo, is the best nightspot in town.

## Festivals and events

**Sanctuary of El Señor de Huanca** *p198*

**14-21 Sep** Señor de Huanca celebrations. The pilgrimage continues throughout Oct.

**Paucartambo** *p200*

**15-17 Jul** Fiesta of the Virgen del Carmen (see page 201).

**Towards the Inca bridge** *p212*

**10 Jun** A 3-day festival is celebrated for the rebuilding of the grass Inca footbridge at Qeswachaka.

**Raqchi** *p212*

Raqchi is still a venue for ceremonial events.

**24-29 Jun** Wiracocha festivities in San Pedro and neighbouring San Pablo start on 24 Jun. This date marks the dual Andean celebration of the ancient Inca festival of the sun, **Inti Raymi**, and the Christian feast day of **San Juan Bautista**, closely associated with water, streams and bathing, as well as being the patron saint of cattle and cattle breeders. It is the time of branding. On the eve of the fiesta, bonfires are lit across the Andes and fortunes are divined. Dancers come to Raqchi from all over Peru and through music and dance they illustrate everything from the ploughing of fields to bull fights. This leads into the feast of San Pedro and San Pablo on **29 Jun**.

## Transport

**San Jerónimo to Huanca trek** *p196*

**Bus**

The most convenient place in central Cuzco to board a bus to San Jerónimo is Av Sol 3rd block. Three services stop here: **ET León de San Jerónimo** (from Puquín District, on the road to Chinchero); **Santiago Express** (from plaza of Santiago district, a few blocks from La Virgen de Belén and the Antonio Lorena Hospital) and **Chaska** (from Villa El Sol-Independencia in the Santiago district). All services run 0530-2200 and go through the downtown area, Wanchac district and along Av de la Cultura all the way to San Jerónimo, US$0.15.

Alight in front of San Jerónimo police station; C Clorinda Matto de Turner is 1½ blocks away, for the start of the trek. This street is also where the San Jerónimo main market is located and has the cemetery at its very end. .

**Sanctuary of El Señor de Huanca** *p198*

**Bus**

Transport from Cuzco leaves from the Coliseo Cerrado and the back of the Social Security Hospital compound, 2 blocks beyond the Hospital Regional main bus stop, to the right on Av de la Cultura going southeast. Buses run 0700-1200 on weekends and daily during the Señor de Huanca celebrations and pilgrimage in Sep and Oct (see Festivals and events, above). Buses make the return trip 1200-1600.

The priests have their own private transport, which can be rented for a ride from the sanctuary to connect with transport to Cuzco or Pisac.

**Taxis**

Taxis from Cuzco to the sanctuary cost about US$10 one way or US$20-25 return with waiting time.

### Humbutio to Pisac *p200*

**Bus**

**Empresa de Transportes Paucartambo y Pitusiray**, Av Tullumayo 202 (lower part), run from Cuzco to **San Salvador**, 0640 and 1300 Mon-Sat, 1½ hrs, US$0.75, returning to Cuzco at 0800 and 1330. There's also a bus from San Salvador to **Pisac** at 1400, 45 mins-1 hr, US$0.60.

### Paucartambo *p200*

Private car hire for a round trip from Cuzco to **Paucartambo** on 15-17 Jul costs US$30 and can be arranged by tour operators in Cuzco. A minibus leaves for Paucartambo from Av Huáscar in Cuzco, every other day, 3-4 hrs, US$4.50; alternate days Paucartambo-Cuzco. Trucks and a private bus leave from the Coliseo, behind Hospital Segura in Cuzco; 5 hrs, US$2.50.

### Piquillacta Archaeological Park *p200, map p203*

Buses to **Lucre** leave from the bus station on Av Huáscar in Wanchac district, on a side street ½ block from the market, 1 hr, US$0.45. Small cars wait at the start of the 8-km circuit around the Huacarpay lake charging US$1.50 (Ruperto Valencia and Ernesto Arredondo are recommended drivers). To go directly to **Piquillacta** and **Rumicola**, catch the Urcos bus from Av de la Cultura, see below.

### Southeast to Urcos *p205*

**Transportes Vilcanota** depart daily 0500-2100 from the terminal on Av de la Cultura, Cuzco, at the Paradero Hospital Regional (on a side street) and run to **Urcos** (US$0.72) via **San Jerónimo**, **Saylla**, **Huasao**, **Tipón**, **Oropesa**, **Piquillacta/ Huacarpay** and **Andahuaylillas**.

To **Andahuaylillas** you can also take a taxi, or the **Oropesa** bus from Av Huáscar in Cuzco, via Tipón, Piquillacta and Rumicolca.

### Cordillera Vilcanota *p206*

Buses for **Tinqui** leave from C Tomasatito Condemayta, near the Coliseo Cerrado in Cuzco, 1000 Mon-Sat, 6-7 hrs, US$3.50.

### Southeast from Urcos *p211*

Combis run every 15-20 mins between Cuzco and **Sicuani** (137 km, US$1.25) via Tinta and **Raqchi**. Note that it is impossible to buy unleaded petrol in Sicuani. From Sicuani there are buses and trucks to **Acomayo** (3 hrs, US$1); alternatively, get off at Checacupe and take a truck from there. To get to the **Inca bridge** catch a *combi* or *colectivo* from the plaza in Combapata to **Yanaoca** (30 km, US$0.50); they leave when full. Then hitchhike to **Quehue** (no accommodation), a 1½-hr walk from Qeswachaka, or to **Qeswachaka** itself, on the road to Livitaca. Be prepared for long waits on this road. On Wed and Sat there are direct buses to **Livitaca** from Cuzco with the **Warari** and **Olivares** companies which pass Qeswachaka, returning on Mon and Thu.

## Directory

### Sanctuary of El Señor de Huanca *p198*

**Telephone** A public telephone is at the Sanctuary.

### Sicuani *p214*

**Banks** Banco de la Nación has a branch on the plaza, as does BCP, but the one cash machine takes only local cards.

# West of Cuzco

*From Cuzco a road heads west to the city of Ayacucho in the central highlands. At the town of Abancay in the Department of Apurímac the road divides, with one branch forming the principal overland route to Lima, via Nazca – of the famous lines – and the coastal city of Pisco (destroyed in the earthquake of 2007). There are enough Inca sites on or near this road in the Department of Cuzco to remind us that the empire's influence spread to all four cardinal points. Add to this some magnificent scenery, especially in the canyon of the Río Apurímac, and you have the makings of some fascinating excursions away from the centre. One, to the ruins of Choquequirao, is a tough but rewarding trip.* ▸▸ *For Sleeping, Eating and other listings, see page 225-226.*

## Ins and outs

All direct buses from Cuzco to Lima go via Abancay, 195 km, five hours (longer in the rainy season). There are also local buses between Cuzco and Abancay, which stop at places en route. The road is paved, but floods in the wet season may damage large sections of the highway. If prone to car sickness, be prepared, as there are many, many curves, but the scenery is magnificent (it also happens to be a great route for cycling). ▸▸ *For further details, see Transport, pages 117 and 226 .*

## Anta to Abancay ▸▸ *p225-226.*

### Anta to Limatambo

The road heads west (alongside the Machu Picchu railway) to **Anta**, where felt trilby hats are on sale. Beyond Anta, heading towards Abancay, are the ruins of **Tarahuasi** ⓘ *76 km west of Cuzco, 2 km before Limatambo, US$1.65*. A few hundred metres from the road is a very well-preserved Inca temple platform, with 28 tall niches, and a long stretch of fine polygonal masonry. The ruins are impressive, enhanced by the orange lichen which gives the walls a beautiful honey colour. Near here the Spanish *conquistadores* on their push towards the Inca capital of Cuzco suffered what could have been a major setback. Having crossed the Río Apurímac, the expeditionary force under the command of Hernando de Soto encountered an Inca army at Vilcaconga. On the first day of the battle, de Soto's men were almost routed, although only five were killed, but in the night reinforcements led by Almagro arrived. The following morning the Incas were demoralized to see a larger force than the one they had defeated the day before and, after renewed fighting, left the field to the Spaniards.

### Apurímac canyon

One hundred kilometres from Cuzco along the Abancay road is the exciting descent into the **Apurímac canyon**. Nearby is the former Inca suspension bridge that inspired Thornton Wilder's *The Bridge of San Luis Rey* (see Books, page 315), which won the 1928 Pulitzer prize. The bridge itself was made of rope and was where the royal Inca road crossed the river. When the *conquistadores* reached this point on the march to Cuzco, they found the bridge destroyed. But luck was on their side since, it being the dry season, the normally fierce Río Apurímac was low enough for the men and horses to ford. In colonial times the bridge was rebuilt several times but it no longer exists.

Thornton Wilder (1897-1975) uses an imagined episode in the bridge's history to meditate upon individual destiny. His novel describes how, on 20 July 1714, five travellers are on the bridge when its ropes snap and it plummets into the river. A

**“” Roughly translated from Quechua, Apurímac means ‘the river that speaks’. The roaring rapids along its course give ample justification for this title.**

monk, Brother Juniper, witnesses their death and investigates the lives of each, trying to understand the role of divine providence in their demise. Three of the characters are fictional but the other two are the son and teacher of La Perricholi, the most famous actress in Peru at the time and one-time mistress of the Viceroy Amat. For his efforts, and for his questioning of God's purpose, Juniper is declared heretical by the Inquisition and burned at the stake.

Not far from the new road bridge over the Apurímac are the thermal baths of **Cconoc** ⓘ *US$1.80*. An unmade road twists down to the river's edge where several pools and spouts are fed by warm water coming out of the cliffs. They are fairly clean, but watch out for the biting midges.

## Curahuasi and around

The road continues to **Curahuasi**, which has several roadside restaurants and *hospedajes*. From here it's a good two-hour walk up Cerro San Cristóbal to **Capitán Rumi**, a huge rock overlooking the Apurímac canyon. The views are staggering, particularly if Salkantay and its snowy neighbours are free of cloud. Ask for directions, especially at the start.

About 20 minutes from Curahuasi at an altitude of 3500 m is the **Saywite Stone** ⓘ *3 km from main road at Km 49, well-signposted, entry US$3*, a large carved rock that is said to represent the three regions of jungle, sierra and coast, with the associated animals and Inca sacred sites of each. It is now the centrepiece of a UNESCO World Heritage Site, consisting of six main areas falling away from the stone and its neighbouring group of buildings. There is a staircase beside an elegant watercourse of channels and pools, a group around a stone (split by lightning), called the Casa de Piedra or Rumi Huasi, an Usnu platform and another monolith, called the Intihuatana. The holes around the perimeter of the Saywite Stone suggest that it was once covered in gold. It is said to have been defaced by ‘people from Lima’ when they took a cast of it, breaking off many of the animals' heads. It is fenced in and clean; ask the guardian for a closer look.

## Cachora

This village is the starting point for the trek to Choquequirao (see page 221). It lies in a magnificent location on the south side of the Apurímac, reached by a side road from the Cuzco–Abancay highway, shortly after Saywite. It is four hours by bus from Cuzco to the turn-off, then a two-hour descent from the road at 3695 m to Cachora at 2875 m. Accommodation, guides (Celestino Peña is the official guide) and mules for the trek are available here.

## Choquequirao → *Colour map 2, B2.*

ⓘ *Entry US$3.35 (this may be increased in 2008).*

Choquequirao is another ‘lost city of the Incas’, built on a ridge spur almost 1600 m above the Apurímac. Its Inca name is unknown, but research by US archaeologist Gary Ziegler suggests that it was built during the reign of Topa Inca. Although only 30% has been uncovered, it is believed to be a larger site than Machu Picchu, but with fewer buildings. The stonework is different from the classic Inca construction and masonry, simply because the preferred granite and andesite are not found in this region. A number of high-profile explorers and archaeologists, including Hiram Bingham, researched the site, but its importance has only recently been recognized. And now tourists are venturing in there, too. With new regulations being applied to cut congestion on the Inca Trail, Choquequirao is destined to replace the traditional hike as the serious trekker's alternative.

**Ins and outs** The shortest route to Choquequirao is from **Cachora** (see above). The two-day hike from Cachora can be undertaken as part of the Vilcabamba traverse trek detailed on page 220. It is also possible to reach Choquequirao from either Huancacalle or Aguas Calientes by doing the trek in reverse, although this will take a minimum of eight days and require thorough preparation.

**Exploring the site** The main features of Choquequirao include the **Lower Plaza**, considered by most experts to be the focal point of the city. Double-jammed doorways and high-quality stonework suggest that the buildings were used by high-ranking members of Inca society. Three of the main buildings were two-storey structures. The **Upper Plaza**, reached by a huge set of steps or terraces, has what are possibly ritual baths. Some have speculated that this area was occupied by the priesthood of Choquequirao. The lesser quality of the stonework and the absence of double-jammed doorways suggest slightly lower status than the Lower Plaza. A beautiful set of slightly curved agricultural terraces runs for over 300 m east-northeast of the Lower Plaza.

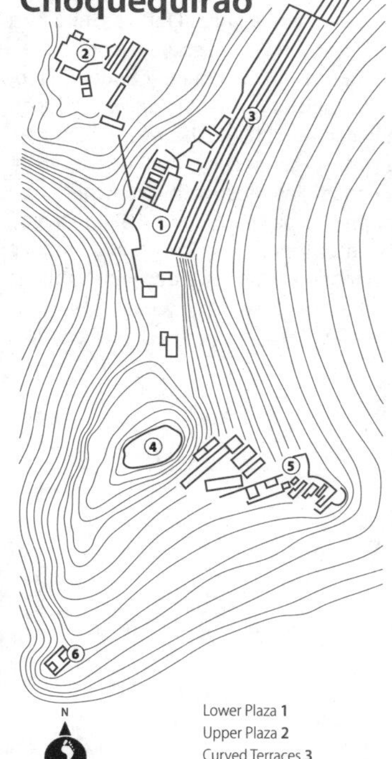


The **Usnu** is a levelled hilltop platform, ringed with stones and giving awesome 360-degree views. Perhaps it was a ceremonial site, or was used for astronomical and solar observations. The **Ridge Group**, still shrouded in vegetation, is a large collection of buildings some 50-100 m below the Usnu. Unrestored, with some significant hall-like structures, this whole area makes for great exploring. Perhaps this extensive and complex set of buildings formed the living quarters for the site's residents.

The **Outlier Building**, isolated and surrounded on three sides by sheer drops of over 1500 m into the Apurímac Canyon, possesses some of the finest stonework within the Choquequirao site. The Outlier's separation from the other structures must also be significant in some way, but exactly how, like so many other questions regarding the Incas and their society, remains a mystery.

**Capuliyoc** (viewpoint), nearly 500 m below the Lower Plaza, is a great set of agricultural terraces, visible on the approach from the far side of the valley. These terraces enabled the Incas to cultivate plants from a significantly warmer climate in close geographical proximity to their ridge-top home. Further terraces decorated with llamas in white stone have been uncovered; ask if they are open to the public.

## Abancay → *Phone code: 083. Colour map 2, B1.*

Nestled between mountains in the upper reaches of a glacial valley at 2378 m, this friendly town is a functional, commercial centre, growing in importance now that the paved Lima–Nazca–Cuzco road passes through it. It also hopes to benefit from the tourist trade to Choquequirao and much investment is taking place in hotels and generally improving the town. It celebrates the **Yawar Fiesta** in July. **Tourist office** ⓘ *Lima 206, T083-321664, open 0800-1430*, or **Dircetur** ⓘ *Av Arenas 121, p 1, T083-321664, apurimac@mincetur.gob.pe.*

Half-day tours are run to nearby sites such as the former haciendas of **Yaca** and **Illanya**. Near the former is a place where silkworms are bred. Also included is the colonial bridge at **Pachachaca**, the Mirador at **Taraccasa**, for good views over the city, and the thermal baths of **Santo Tomás**. The **Santuario Nacional de Ampay**, north of town, has lagoons called Angasccocha (3200 m) and Uspaccocha (3820 m), a glacier on Ampay moutain at 5235 m and flora and fauna typical of these altitudes. By public transport, take a colectivo to Tamburco and ask the driver where to get off. To reach the glacier requires two days of trekking, with overnight camping.

# Vilcabamba traverse trek → *Colour map 2, B2.*



The Vilcabamba range was the last refuge of the Inca Empire and, under Manco Inca and his sons, resistance endured for decades after the initial conquest (see page 187). Hemmed in between two great rivers, the mountains form a natural fortress, and Inca ruins, many little known and unrestored, lie scattered across the entire region.

Described below is a trek across the mountains from Cachora to Choquequirao, continuing from there to the Yanama river valley and on to Santa Teresa or Machu Picchu itself. The full route crosses the entire Vilcabamba range, between the mighty canyons of the Apurímac and Urubamba rivers, connecting two of the most impressive archaeological sites in South America. For those with time this is an excellent alternative to the classic Inca Trail and in places follows well-preserved examples of Inca road. It passes the mines of La Victoria and involves an incredible number of strenuous ascents and descents. En route you are rewarded with fabulous views of the Sacsarayoc massif (also called Pumasillo), Salkantay, other snow peaks and the deep canyons of the Río Blanco and the Apurímac. You will also see condors

and meet very friendly people, but the highlight is Choquequirao itself. Those with less time to spare can follow the first part of the route only, from Cachora to Choquequirao, and return via the same trail.

A third alternative splits from the main route in the Yanama Valley and goes to Huancacalle (see page 185), via the pass of Choquetacarpo, 4600 m high. From Huancacalle it's possible to continue on to Espíritu Pampa on the edge of the rainforest. Both routes can be undertaken in reverse.

## Ins and outs

It is recommended that you hire a guide, either locally in Cachora (see page 218) or in Cuzco. Not only will you obtain local knowledge of the area and route, but also you will be helping to bring employment to an extremely isolated region of Peru and at the same time give an incentive to preserve the region's cultural and environmental resources. The 1:100,000 IGN sheet Machu Picchu completely covers the route, although in some places accuracy is not great. Maps are available at the **Instituto Geográfico Nacional** in Lima or at **South American Explorers** in Cuzco. Some agencies in Cuzco are beginning to offer organized treks on these routes.

## Cachora to Choquequirao → *2 days*

**Day one** From Cachora take the road heading down, out of the village, through lush cultivated countryside and meadows. On a clear day you should have good views of the snow peak of **Padrayoc**, roughly to the north, on the far side of the Apurímac canyon. There are many trails close to the village; if uncertain of the trail, ask; the locals are very friendly. After 15 minutes of descent, a sign for Choquequirao points to a left-hand path, initially following the course of a small stream. Follow the trail and cross a footbridge to the other side of a large stream. From here the track becomes more obvious, with few paths diverging from the main route. The trail follows the left side of the valley, more or less flat, passing an old hacienda on the right-hand side. To your right is the Apurímac Canyon, the river flowing far beneath (although difficult to see at this point), and the Vilcabamba range.

After 9 km, two or 2½ hours from the start of the trek, is the wonderful *mirador* (viewpoint) of **Capuliyoc**, at 2800 m, with fantastic vistas of the Apurímac Canyon and the snowy Vilcabamba range across the river. (Many organized treks start here.) With a pair of binoculars it's just possible to recognize Choquequirao, etched into the forested hills to the west. Condors are sometimes seen in this area. Beyond Capuliyoc the trail begins to descend towards the river. Here, away from the village, there exist some excellent examples of dry forest, largely devoid of leaves in the dry season. Further down the valley lies **Cocamasana**, a rest spot with a rough covered roof. From this point the river is clearly visible, running emerald green when the water level is low, a rushing white torrent during the rains. At Km 16 is **Chiquisca** (1930 m), a lovely wooded spot and home to a local family. Chiquisca has a fairly clean water supply, so it's an opportunity to fill bottles. If you don't want to continue any further on the first day, this is a good campsite, with flush toilets, a shower and drinks on sale. Another one-hour descent leads you to the suspension bridge crossing the Río Apurímac (1500 m). Currents are strong on the river, but a few sheltered spots are good for a refreshing dip. By the bridge, camping is possible at Playa Rosalina.

Crossing the bridge the path ascends very steeply for one and a half hours. **Santa Rosa**, a good area for camping, again near the property of a local family, is just after the Km 21 sign. Clean water is available and there is a small store in the village. If this area is occupied, another larger site is available 10 minutes further up the hill. Ask residents for directions.

**Day two** From Santa Rosa continue uphill on a steep zigzag for two hours to the *mirador* of **Marampata**. The **Huanpaca** waterfall can be seen on the far side of the valley. From Marampata the trail flattens out, following the right side of the canyon, downstream, towards Choquequirao. In the valley below the guard post and underneath the main site, you can see some excavated agricultural terraces. Far below, in a different warmer microclimate, these terraces enabled the inhabitants to cultivate lower-altitude fruits and vegetables in close proximity to their highland staples. After 1½ hours on this flatter trail you enter some beautiful stretches of cloudforest, before a final short climb and arrival at **Choquequirao** itself.

Most groups camp on the great set of terraces reached upon arrival at the site. The warden will show you where to camp. At an altitude of 3000 m the nights can be cold. If coming from Santa Rosa you should have the afternoon free to explore the complex. There is much more to Choquequirao than at first appears, so, given time, you could easily allow an extra day here. Many people find the unrestored buildings below the main plaza particularly enchanting, with the remains of terraces and living quarters still smothered in dense forest. They also give an impression of what the site must have looked like when first discovered, a great contrast to the restored Lower and Upper Plaza areas. To return to Cachora at this point, simply retrace the route, possibly camping at Chiquisca to give a nice break to the two-day return trek.

## Choquequirao to Yanama → *2 days*

**Day three** The third day, if completed in one day as described below, is almost certainly the toughest on the trek. It will keep you walking pretty much all day, and there's a steep ascent to the campsite, just to add to your pleasure!

Climb to the Upper Plaza complex roughly to the northwest of the Main Plaza and terraces. There are spectacular vistas of the canyon, the surrounding peaks, including Ampay to the west, and also over the central areas of Choquequirao itself. A rough and sometimes overgrown trail climbs steeply up the hill behind, following sections of old Inca trail and drainage channels, and passing some small ruins. The route traverses cloudforest, festooned with mosses, around the left side of the mountain for one hour, with some precipitous drops on the left. Beyond Choquequirao many sections of trail will prove a challenge to those with severe vertigo! The path then emerges into an area of alpine grassland and starts to descend steeply, zigzagging into the valley of the **Quebrada Victoria**. Towards the lower section of the grassland is a green glade, used to graze pack animals. It's possible to camp here, but water could be a problem in the dry season.

After the glade the path continues its descent, once again entering scrub and then dry forest. Note the contrast between the dry vegetation on this side of the valley, which receives sun for most of the day, and the damp and green forest on the far side, which is often in shadow. This is a vivid illustration of how mountain ranges such as the Vilcabamba create a vast range of microclimates and, therefore, biodiversity, in an extremely limited geographical area. After 30 minutes the trail passes close to the unrestored houses and terraces of **Pinchiunuyoc**. It's possible to obtain water here as the original Inca water channels are still flowing. After another 1½ or two hours of steep descent you reach the Quebrada Victoria at around 2000 m. The climate here is subtropical and, except for the large numbers of sandflies, this is a great spot for lunch and a bracing dip in the river. In the wet season or during flash floods the Quebrada Victoria could be impossible to cross; seek local information.

Continue downstream along the right-hand bank of the *quebrada* (ravine) for perhaps 200 m and you'll come to the beginning of the trail leading up the other side, running almost entirely through thick forest. This is a brutal ascent, climbing for three or four hours until reaching the campsite at roughly 3500 m. The campsite, which has a limited water supply, is, once again, on the land of a local family who live perched on the edge of the abyss, with the forest and towering glacial peak of Corihuaynachina as a backdrop. Several trails branch off the main route near the family's land and potentially this could be confusing. Perhaps the surest way to locate your home for the night is to listen for the sounds of domestic animals, the barking of dogs and crowing of cockerels coming from the family's home. It's a magnificent campsite, but cold at night. Enjoy the view from your tent!



**Day four** Carry on up the trail from camp, following the left side of the valley, roughly in the direction of Corihuaynachina. The **Abra San Juan** (San Juan Pass) is to the left of this peak. Continue through cloudforest for 2½ hours. The trail can be very muddy in places. There are some beautiful examples of mountain cedar in the area and the valley supports much wildlife, including spectacled bears. Birdlife is prolific and diverse, with many species of mountain tanager, solitary eagles in the valley's lower reaches, mountain caracaras, and sometimes condors soaring above the peaks. The route passes several abandoned mine shafts, which can be explored (at your own risk) with flashlights.

After the initial 2½ or three hours' hiking from camp, the forest fades, replaced by high Andean *puna* (grassland) studded with flowers and, in places, a strange blood-red lichen covering the rocks. The path follows a section of original Inca trail, arriving at the Abra San Juan (4200 m) roughly four hours after leaving camp. On a clear day there are magnificent views of the *nevados* (snowy peaks) of Choquetacarpo and Sacsarayoc (also known as Pumasillo). Below them is the valley of the Río Yanama. The alternative route to Huancacalle can be seen to the north on the far side of the Yanama. Follow the path roughly east-northeast, descending for 2½ or three hours, and this will bring you to the small traditional village of **Yanama,** at around 3500 m. On the way down to Yanama some of the drop-offs are very steep. The valley is full of wild flowers. In the village it's usually possible to camp in front of the school buildings and to buy basic food. It may also be possible to hire mules and guides. Yanama has no roads to the outside world and traditional cultures are still strong. Please respect these people's ways and don't offer children sweets, etc. Note the excellent quality of the stonework in many of the traditional dwellings, and also the fine grass roofing.

## Yanama to La Playa → *2 days*

**Day five** Ascend the Yanama Valley for 1½ hours, following the course of the Río Yanama, which runs on your left. Waterfalls can be seen on either side, snowmelt from glaciers high above. Towards the head of the valley the trail starts to veer away from the river to the right, beginning the ascent to the 4800-m **Abra Apacheta** (Apacheta Pass). It's a hard climb of around three hours and the altitude can take its toll. To the right of Apacheta is **Padrayoc**, the mountain visible from Cachora, towering above the Apurímac. From the pass, in clear weather, it's possible to see **Salkantay,** at 6271 m the highest peak in the Vilcabamba range. The descent from the pass is long and some trails lead away from the main route to houses and farms – be careful, especially in foggy conditions. The path tends to veer to the right and leads into the valley of the **Quebrada Tortora**. This area is badly marked on the IGN 1:100,000 sheet, and a stream that you keep on your left, and that runs into the Quebrada Tortora, appears not to be marked. Once in the valley, you follow the Río Tortora for about an hour before crossing to the other side via a small bridge just before a metal-roofed house. Continue with the river on your right until you reach a flat grassy area with several houses. This is **Hornopampa**. From here you can see Tortora village, 1 km or so down the valley. Tortora appears to be marked too far up the valley on the IGN 1:100,000 sheet, which could cause confusion. In Tortora you can camp near the medical post. The biting insects here can be awful but, to make up for the bugs, there are lovely views of many tall peaks, including **Huamantay**, visible down the valley.

**Day six** Walk downhill through forest for two hours, staying on the right side of the river. Just before you come to a big wedge-shaped hill at the bottom of the valley cross to the other side. Tortora bridge lies just below a series of grassy meadows in this region. The trails in this area are often affected by landslides, so seek local information. On crossing the bridge follow the gently sloping trail through fairly undisturbed sections of forest for four or five hours until reaching the small community of **La Playa** where it is possible to camp. About halfway between the bridge and La Playa the trail crosses a rocky stream bed; the path doesn't continue directly on the other side. Climb about 50 m up the rocky stream bed and you'll see the trail continuing on the right. A short distance after this, a beautiful waterfall tumbles across the trail, perhaps 100 m high. Next to the trail, under the fall, is a pool that is perfect for bathing and a (very!) refreshing shower.

**La Playa** has a run-down feel and doesn't give the most welcoming impression to the passing hiker, so you may want to camp slightly before the village, for greater privacy. The town centre and the road (see below) are both located across the bridge on the right side of Río Santa Teresa. You can obtain basic supplies at a couple of small stores in the town centre.

## La Playa to Aguas Calientes → *1 day*

**Day seven** La Playa marks the beginning of a rough road that runs to Santa Teresa. To finish the hike, you can simply follow the road downhill to Santa Teresa, or catch the early morning *camión* if you're feeling lazy; *camiones* (trucks) leave for Santa Teresa at 0600 on most days, although the road may be closed in the wet season.

Alternatively, to continue the hike from La Playa, the more interesting route is to follow the Santa Teresa road for 30 minutes to the tiny settlement of **Lucmabamba**. On the right-hand side a restored section of Inca trail leads into the hills. Follow this trail uphill, towards the ruins of **Paltallacta**, which lie over the ridge in the next valley. From the road it's 2½ or three hours' climb through scrubby bush and sections of cloudforest until reaching the pass. The restored section of Inca road runs out after about 1 km and a narrow but clear trail takes its place. In one or two places it's possible to see small sections of the original Inca trail. At the summit of the hill is a magnificent area of virgin cloudforest, worth the climb in itself. Once you begin to descend on the other side it's possible, weather conditions allowing, to view Machu Picchu from a very interesting perspective, encircled by hills, and behind, the snow-covered peaks of the Urubamba range. The large waterfall you can see, spilling out from the mountain in front of Machu Picchu is La Hidroeléctrica, designed to generate power for the surrounding area. Half an hour below the summit you reach the dispersed ruins of **Paltallacta**, unrestored walls and terraces that must have once represented a substantial settlement. Recent expeditions in the area have uncovered many new finds, including one originally described by Hiram Bingham and subsequently lost for almost a century. Who knows what remains to be discovered? Just below the ruins, to the left of the trail, are some grassy areas which give a wonderful perspective on the whole scene.

From Paltallacta, a steep descent of at least one hour leads to **Ahobamba Valley** and a cable bridge crossing the Río Ahobamba. Take care crossing the bridge as the wooden planks have been known to break. Once on the other side follow the path along the river, past the waterfall (La Hidroeléctrica), keeping to the right, past some fenced facilities, presumably associated with the hydroelectric project. You're now in the valley of the **Río Urubamba**, having crossed the entire Vilcabamba range. From here there should be plenty of people to ask directions.

There are two levels of railway track in the area. To get the local train to Aguas Calientes you need to climb up the bank to reach the main, higher track. Here there is a small railway station from which trains normally leave in the afternoon for Aguas Calientes. Alternatively you can walk to Aguas Calientes, 9 km, 2-3 hours' walk, simply by following the railway tracks (see also box, page 154). At several points there are good views of Machu and Huayna Picchu, towering above the Urubamba. Be careful of speeding trains! Near the Hidroeléctrica train station are the well-preserved ruins of an Inca temple (ask the locals for directions). This site features an intricately carved sacred rock, similar to that at Machu Picchu, which almost perfectly mirrors the contour of the mountain on the other side of the valley. If you still have energy this is certainly worth a look before getting to Aguas Calientes. ▸▸ *For details of Sleeping, Eating and other facilities in Aguas Calientes, see pages 174-178.*

## Sleeping

**Anta to Limatambo** *p217*

**G Hostal Central**, Jr Jaquijahuanca 714, Anta. A basic, friendly place with motorbike parking; beware of water shortages.

**G Hostal Rivera**, near the river, Limatambo. An old stone house built round a courtyard, clean, quiet and full of character.

**Curahuasi and around** *p218*

**G Hostal San Cristóbal**, Curahuasi. Clean, nice decor, pleasant courtyard, shared bath, cold shower. A new bathroom block is currently being built.

**Camping** in Curahuasi is possible on the football pitch, but ask the police for permission first.

**Cachora** *p218*

**D Casa de Salcantay**, Prolongación Salcantay s/n, www.salcantay.com. Price is per person and includes breakfast, dinner available if booked in advance. New Dutch-run hostel with links to community projects, comfortable, small, Dutch, English and German spoken, can help with arranging independent treks, or organize treks with tour operator.

**E-F Los Tres Balcones**, Jr Abancay s/n, Cachora, www.choquequirau.com. New hostel designed as start and end point for the trek to Choquequirao. Price is per person, breakfast included, more expensive rooms have Roman bath. Comfortable rooms with hot showers, camping available and there's a restaurant and pizza oven. Shares information with the town's only internet café. It runs a trek to Choquequirao, US$400, including transport from Cuzco, camping gear, mules and porters, all the meals, snacks, fruit, water, entrance ticket to the ruins, horses for riding, bilingual tour guide and lunch at the hostel afterwards.

**G La Casona de Ocampo**, San Martín 122, T084-237514, lacasonadeocampo@yahoo.es. Price per person. Rooms with hot shower all day, free camping, owner Carlos Robles is knowledgeable and friendly.

**Abancay** *p220*

**C-D Turistas**, Av Díaz Bárcenas 500, T083-321017, hotursa@terra.com.pe. With bathroom, breakfast included. The original building is in colonial style, but there is a new block and the whole hotel has been refurbished, with new bedrooms, a bigger restaurant, gardens and a travel agency, **Apu-Rimac Tours y Travel**. Rooms are large and, in the old block, the better and more expensive ones are on the top floor. Quiet, clean, good restaurant, internet (US$0.60 per hr), parking space.

**E Imperial**, Díaz Bárcenas 517, T083-321538. Rooms are around the central parking space in this hospitable, efficient and spotless hotel. Great beds, TV and hot water (also in the shared bathrooms). The price of rooms without bath does not include breakfast. Helpful and good value.

**E Kavaxio Palace**, Díaz Bárcenas 1112, at El Olivo, T083-803050. New, rooms with bath have hot water, TV; hot water also in the shared bathrooms. Breakfast extra. Good service, welcoming.

**F Arenas**, Av Arenas 192, T083-322107. A brand-new hotel is constructed beside the old one, with plain but well-appointed rooms, good beds, big showers, hot water, internet, restaurant, TV, parking and a lift to the top floor, which has good views. Hospitable.

**G Apurímac Tours**, Jr Cuzco 421, T083-321446. Another new building; rooms upstairs with bath and hot water. The *comedor* in the courtyard serves breakfast and lunch, pay extra for either.

## Eating

**Anta to Limatambo** *p217*

**Tres de Mayo**, Anta. Very good and popular, with top service.

There is also a good cheap restaurant in **Limatambo**, hidden from the road by trees.

### Curahuasi and around *p218*

¥ **La Amistad**, Curahuasi. The best restaurant in town, popular, with good food and moderate prices, but has poor service.

### Abancay *p220*

¥¥-¥ **La Valera**, Arenas 150. An Argentinian-style steak house.

¥ **Chifa Shanghai**, Arenas 129. Large helpings, popular with locals.

¥ **Focarela Pizzería**, Díaz Bárcenas 521, T083-322036. Simple but pleasant decor, pizza from a wood-burning oven, fresh, generous toppings, popular. Ask for *vino de la casa*!

¥ **Pizzería Napolitana**, Díaz Bárcenas 208. With a wood-fired clay oven and wide choice of toppings.

### Cafés

**Café Mundial**, Arequipa 301. Open early for breakfast and also for evening snacks.

**Dulce & Salad**, Arequipa y 2 de Mayo. A pleasant café and *heladería*, 4 types of breakfast, daily salad specials, sandwiches, hot and cold drinks, cakes and a bar.

**La Delicia**, Díaz Bárcenas 210. A small vegetarian place serving breakfast, lunch buffet, juices, yoghurts and other products.

**Natur Center**, Díaz Bárcenas 211. An equally small vegetarian café with breakfast, lunch *menú*, juices and treatments.

**Panadería Buen Gusto**, Núñez 209. Good bread and cakes baked on the premises, also has a café.

**Panadería Cynthia**, Huancavelica 311. With café serving enormous croissants.

## Activities and tours

### Abancay *p220*

Local tour prices US$32-28 per person, depending on numbers.

**Apurimak Tours**, at **Hotel Turistas**, see Sleeping. Runs local tours and 1- and 2-day trips to Santuario Nacional de Ampay: 1-day, 7 hrs, US$40 per person for 1-2 people (cheaper for more people). Also a 3-day trip to Choquequirao including transport, guide, horses, tents and food, just bring your sleeping bag, US$60 per person.

**Carlos Valer**, guide in Abancay. Ask for him at **Hotel Turistas**, very knowledgeable and kind.

## Transport

### Anta to Limbatambo *p217*

The bus fare to **Anta** from **Cuzco** is US$0.30.

### Cachora *p218*

There are buses from Cachora to **Abancay** at 0630 and 1100, 2 hrs, US$1.50; also colectivo taxis.

### Abancay *p220*

The following bus companies (office addresses are given in brackets) all depart from the Terminal Terrestre, on Av Pachacútec, on the west side of Abancay: **Bredde** (Gamarra 423, T083-321643; Av Arenas 210), 5 daily to **Cuzco**, including 0600, 1300. **Cruz del Sur** (Díaz Bárcenas 1151, T083-323028), serves the whole country. **Los Chankas** (Díaz Bárcenas 1011, El Olivo, T083-321485), to **Cuzco**. **Molina** (Gamarra 422, T083-322646), 3 daily to **Cuzco**. **San Jerónimo** to **Cuzco** at 2130.

The terminal has a restaurant, internet and phones, a *cambio*, toilets and shops. Taxi to centre US$0.60, otherwise it's a steep 5 blocks up Av Juan Pablo Castro to Jr Lima, another block to Jr Arequipa and cheap hotels, and one more to hotels **Turistas** and **Imperial**. Several bus companies have offices on or near the El Olivo roundabout at Av Díaz Bárcenas y Gamarra.

Buses to **Cachora** (for the Choquequirao trek) depart from Jr Prado Alto, between Huancavelica and Núñez (5 blocks uphill from Díaz Bárcenas; it's not the first Jr Prado you come to), 0500 and 1400, 2 hrs, US$1.50. Alternatively, hire a car with driver from the Curahuasi terminal on Av Arenas, next to the Wari office, charge US$10.

## Directory

### Abancay *p220*

**Banks** BCP, Jr Arequipa 218, has ATM outside, Visa and Amex. There are several *cambios* on Jr Arequipa, opposite the *mercado central*, including **Machi**, No 202 (also at Díaz Bárcenas 105) and **Oro Verde**.

**Internet** The town is full of internet places. Some have phone cabins.

# Southern jungle

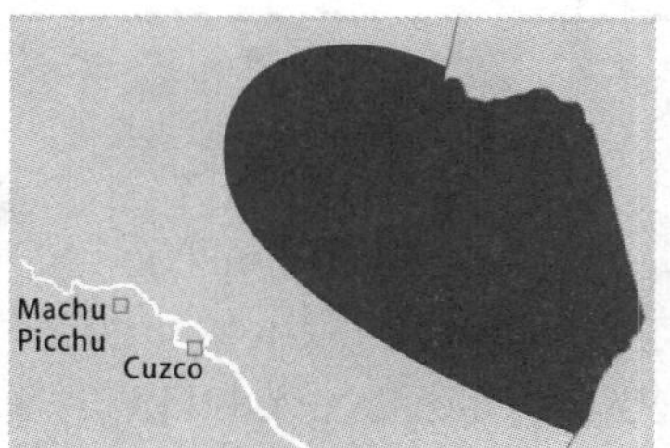




**Footprint features**

# Introduction

The immense Amazon Basin covers a staggering 4 million sq km, an area roughly three quarters the size of the United States. But despite the fact that 60% of Peru is covered by this green carpet of jungle, less than 6% of its population lives there. This lack of integration with the rest of the country makes transportation difficult but does mean that much of Peru's rainforest is still intact.

The Peruvian jungles are home to a diversity of life unequalled anywhere on earth, and it is this great diversity which makes the Amazon Basin a paradise for nature lovers, be they scientists or simply curious amateurs. Overall, Peru's jungle lowlands contain some 10 million living species, including 2000 species of fish and 300 mammals. They also contain over 10% of the world's 8600 bird species and, together with the adjacent Andean foothills, 4000 butterfly species.

The southern part of Peru's Amazon jungle contains the Manu National Biosphere Reserve (1.9 million ha), the Tambopata National Reserve (254,358 ha) and the Bahuaja-Sonene National Park (1.1 million ha). These three great protected areas are in the department of Madre de Dios, adjoining the eastern edge of the department of Cuzco and extending to the borders of Brazil and Bolivia.

## Don't miss ...

1 **Ox-bow lakes** You may catch a glimpse of giant otters if you take a trip on one of the many *cochas* (ox-bow lakes), page 230.

2 **Cock-of-the-rock lek** Watch these dazzling birds dance for the favours of their mate in the clearings in the cloudforest, page 234.

3 **Rainforest canopy** Climb to the highest possible level of the tower at Manu Wildlife Centre to listen to the birdsong and the chatter of the monkeys going about their business, page 234.

4 **Collpa Colorado** See the multitude of macaws and parrots getting their essential minerals from this famous macaw lick in Tambopata, page 241.

5 **The night sky** After your cold shower and dinner by the light of an oil lamp, go outside and marvel at the night sky, with its shooting stars and fireflies in the bushes; but be careful – it's a jungle out there.

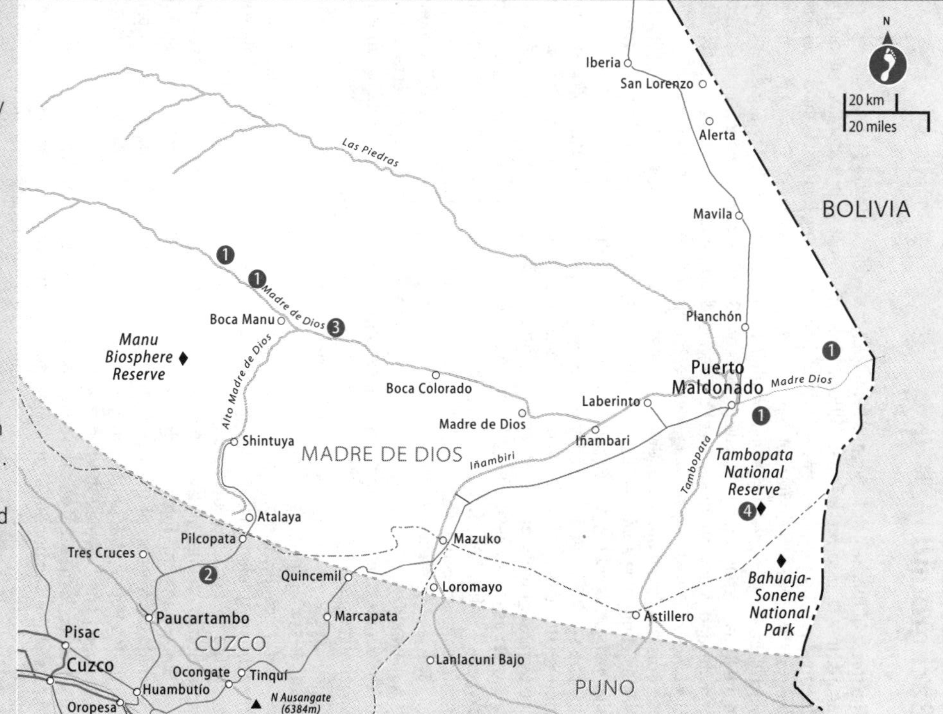

# Background

The forest of this lowland region is technically called Subtropical Moist Forest, which means that it receives less rainfall than tropical forest and is dominated by the floodplains of its meandering rivers. One of the most striking features is the former river channels that have become isolated as *cochas* (ox-bow lakes). These are home to black caiman, giant otter and a host of other living organisms. Other rare species living in the forest are jaguar, puma, ocelot and tapir. There are also capybara, 13 species of primate and many hundreds of bird species. If you include the cloudforests and highlands of the Manu Biosphere Reserve, the bird count almost totals 1000.

This incredible biological diversity brings with it an acute ecological fragility. As well as containing some of the most important flora and fauna on earth, the region also harbours gold-diggers, loggers and hunters. For years, logging, gold prospecting and the search for oil and gas have endangered the unique rainforest. Fortunately, though, the destructive effect of such groups has been limited by the various conservation organizations working to protect it. Ecologists consider the Amazon rainforest as the lungs of the earth – the Amazon Basin produces 20% of the earth's oxygen – and any fundamental change in its constitution, or indeed its disappearance, could have disastrous implications for our future on this planet.

The relative proximity to Cuzco of Manu in particular has made it one of the prime nature-watching destinations in South America. Manu is heavily protected, with visitor numbers limited and a large percentage of the park inaccessible to tourists. Nevertheless, there is no need to worry that this level of management is going to diminish your pleasure. There is more than enough in the way of birds, animals and plants to satisfy the most ardent wildlife enthusiast.

Until recently, the area around Puerto Maldonado and Tambopata was under threat from exploitation and settlement. However, the suspension of oil exploration in 2000 led to a change of status for a large tract of this area, giving immediate protection to another of Peru's zones of record-breaking diversity.

Since 2003 the forests of Madre de Dios have been under threat from the planned construction of the *Transoceánica*, a road linking the Atlantic and Pacific oceans via Puerto Maldonado and Brazil. The paving of this road system, creating a high-speed link between the two countries, will certainly bring more uncontrolled colonization in the area, as seen so many times in the Brazilian Amazon, placing the forests of the Tambopata region under further pressure. Uncontrolled colonization along Bahuaja-Sonene's southern border, in the Tambopata headwaters area, is another cause of growing concern, which, at the time of writing, had failed to be addressed by either the government or local conservation groups.

## Climate

The climate is warm and humid, with a rainy season from November to March and a dry season from April to October. Cold fronts from the South Atlantic, called *friajes*, are characteristic of the dry season, when temperatures drop to 15-16°C during the day, and 13°C at night. The best time to visit is in the dry season, when there are fewer mosquitoes and the rivers are low, exposing the beaches. Trips, especially lodge-based, can also be planned during the rainy season. The dry season is a good time to see birds nesting and to view the animals at close range, as they stay near to the rivers and are easily seen.

# Manu Biosphere Reserve

→ Colour map 2, A3/4.

*The Manu Biosphere Reserve covers an area of 1.9 million ha (almost half the size of Switzerland) and is one of the largest conservation units on earth, encompassing the complete drainage of the Manu River, with an altitudinal range from 200 m to 4100 m above sea level. No other rainforest can compare with Manu for the diversity of life forms. The reserve is one of the great birdwatching spots of the world; a magical animal kingdom which offers the best chance of seeing giant otters, jaguars, ocelots and several of the 13 species of primates which abound in this pristine tropical wilderness. The more remote areas of the reserve are home to indigenous groups with little or no knowledge of the outside world.* ▸▸ For Sleeping, Eating and other listings see pages 237-239.

## Tours to Manu

There are about 15 authorized agencies in Cuzco (see page 112) offering tours to Manu. Prices vary considerably, from as little as US$600 per person for a six-day tour up to US$1000-1500 per person with the more expensive, usually lodge-based, tours. Note that tourists are only allowed to visit authorized areas of the former Manu Reserved Zone and the Cultural Zone (see Park areas, page 233). From 2008 tax will be applied to all tours to the southern jungle (formerly it was a tax free zone). Prices will therefore rise by at least 15%. Also, the instability of the US dollar in 2007 was forcing operators to reconsider their pricing policy, some choosing to price in soles or euros.

The cheaper tours usually travel overland there and back, which takes at least three full days (in the dry season), meaning you'll spend much of your time on a bus or truck and will end up exhausted. Going overland does, however, allow you to see Manu's full range of ecosystems and increases your chance of seeing some rare wildlife species (for example, cock-of-the-rock). Another important factor to consider is whether or not your boat has a canopy, as it can be very uncomfortable sitting in direct sunlight or rain for hours on end.

The quality of guides varies a lot, but all are now supposed to have official qualification. You might want to meet your guide before deciding on a trip if you are in Cuzco. You can only enter the former Reserved Zone of Manu with a recognized guide who is affiliated to an authorized tour company. Beware of pirate operators on the streets of Cuzco who offer trips to the former Reserved Zone and end up halfway through the trip changing the route 'due to emergencies', which, in reality, means they have no permits to operate in the area. For a full list of all companies who are allowed access to the former Reserved Zone, contact the Manu National Park office (see Ins and outs, below).

Take finely woven, long-sleeved and long-legged clothing and effective insect repellent. Lodge reservations should be made at the relevant offices in Cuzco as they are often not set up to receive visitors without prior notice.

**Eco-tour Manu** is a non-profit-making organization made up of tour operators, which assures quality of service and actively supports conservation projects in the area. When you travel with an Eco-tour member you are ensuring that you support tropical rainforest conservation projects. Eco-tour Manu comprises Manu Expeditions, Manu Nature Tours, Pantiacolla Tours, InkaNatura Travel, Aventuras Ecológicas Manu , Expediciones Vilca and Tapir Tours. Contact any member company for further information.

## Ins and outs

**Getting there** Cuzco is the starting point for trips to Manu. Almost all visitors go with a specialist tour operator (see box above), with accommodation and transport – either a flight to the airstrip at Boca Manu or overland in a private vehicle – included in the tour price. For independent travellers, the road trip over the Andes to Itahuania takes a whole day by local truck (16 to 18 hours in the dry season, 20 to 40 hours in the wet). It is an uncomfortable journey, but you will see some spectacular scenery. Only basic supplies are available after leaving Cuzco, so take all your camping and food essentials, including insect repellent. Transport can be disrupted in the wet season because the road is in poor condition (tour operators have latest details). Alternatively, flights from Cuzco to Boca Manu can be arranged the day before, usually by Manu tour operators, if there are enough passengers. »For further information see Transport, page 238. 

**Visitor information** **Manu National Park Office** ⓘ *Av Micaela Bastidas 310 (Casilla Postal 591), Cuzco, T084-240898, pqnmanu@terra.com.pe, daily 0800-1400*, issues permits for the National Park for S/.150 per person (about US$46), plus US$10 per person for entry to the Reserved Zone (see below). Information on conservation issues in the park can be obtained from **Asociación Peruana para la Conservación de la Naturaleza (Apeco)** ⓘ *Parque José Acosta 187, p 2, Magdalena del Mar, Lima 17, T01-264 0094, www.apeco.org.pe*, and from **Pronaturaleza** ⓘ *Alfredo León 211, Miraflores Lima 18, T01-447 9032; also Jr Cajamarca, cuadra 1 s/n, Puerto Maldonado, T082-571585, www.pronaturaleza.org*. **Perú Verde** ⓘ *Ricaldo Palma J-1, Santa Mónica, Cuzco, T084-226392, www.peruverde.org*, is a local NGO that can help with information and has free video shows about Manu National Park and Tambopata National Reserve. Staff are friendly and helpful and also have information on programmes and research in the jungle area of Río Madre de Dios.

## Park areas

The Biosphere Reserve comprises the **Manu National Park** (1,692,137 ha), which only government-sponsored biologists and anthropologists were allowed to visit with permits from the Ministry of Agriculture in Lima; the **Manu Reserved Zone** (257,000 ha), set aside for applied scientific research and ecotourism; and the **Cultural Zone** (92,000 ha), containing acculturated native groups and colonists, where the locals still employ their traditional way of life.

In 2003 the former Manu Reserved Zone was absorbed into the Manu National Park, increasing its protected status. Ecotourism activities have been allowed to continue in specially designated tourism and recreational zones along the course of the Lower Manu River. These tourism and recreational areas are accessible by permit only. Entry is strictly controlled and visitors must go under the auspices of an authorized operator with an accredited guide. Permits are limited and reservations should be made well in advance, though it is possible to book a place on a trip at the last minute in Cuzco. In the former Reserved Zone there are tented safari camps around Cocha Salvador and two lodges, the rustic **Casa Machiguenga** run by the Machiguenga communities of Tayakome and Yomibato with the help of a German NGO, and the upmarket **Manu Lodge**.

The Cultural and Multiple Use Zones are accessible to anyone and several lodges exist in the area. It is possible to visit these lodges under your own steam. The Multiple Use Zones are a system of buffer areas surrounding the core of Manu. Among the ethnic groups in these areas are the Harakmbut, Machiguenga and Yine in the **Amarakaeri Reserved Zone**, on the east bank of the Río Alto Madre de Dios, who have set up their own ecotourism activities, entirely managed by local indigenous people. Associated with Manu are other areas protected by conservation groups, or local people, for example the **Blanquillo Reserved Zone** (around Tambo Blanquillo), a conservation concession in the adjacent Los Amigos river system, and some cloudforest parcels along the road; see also page 236. The **Nuhua-Kugapakori Reserved Zone** (443,887 ha), set aside for these two nomadic native groups, is the area between the headwaters of the Río Manu and headwaters of the Río Urubamba, to the north of the Río Alto Madre de Dios. » *For details of lodges and other accommodation, see Sleeping, page 237.*

## Birdwatching in Manu

Much of the Manu National Park is totally unexplored and the variety of birds is astounding: about 1000 species, significantly more than in the whole of Costa Rica and over a tenth of all the birds on earth. Although there are other places in the Manu area where you can see birdlife and an astonishing variety of other wildlife, an excellent place for the visiting birder with limited time is the **Manu Wildlife Centre**.

A typical trip starts in Cuzco and takes in the wetlands of Lake Huacarpay (to the south of the city – see page 202) where a variety of Andean waterfowl and marsh birds can be seen. Here, the beautiful and endemic mountaineer hummingbird can be seen feeding on tree tobacco. Then the route proceeds to the cloudforest of the eastern slopes of the Andes. Driving slowly down the road through the cloudforest, every 500 m loss in elevation produces new birds. This is the home of the Andean cock-of-the-rock, and a visit to one of their leks (courtship areas) is one of the world's top ornithological experiences. These humid montane forests are home to a mind-boggling variety of multicoloured birds, and a mixed flock of tanagers, honeycreepers and conebills turns any tree into a Christmas tree! There are two species of quetzal here, too.

Levelling out onto the forested foothills of the Andes, the upper tropical zone is then reached. This is a forest habitat that in many parts of South America has disappeared and been replaced by tea, coffee and coca plantations. In Manu, the forest is intact, and rare species such as the Amazonian umbrellabird and blue-headed and military macaws can be found.

Good places to base yourself for upper-tropical birding and an introduction to lowland Amazon species are **Amazonia**, **Erika** and **Pantiacolla** lodges, all on the Río Alto Madre de Dios. From here on, transport is by river and the beaches are packed with nesting birds in the dry season. Large-billed terns scream at passing boats and Orinoco geese watch warily from the shore. Colonies of hundreds of sand-coloured nighthawks roost and nest on the hot sand.

As you leave the foothills behind and head into the untouched forests of the western Amazon, you are entering forest with the highest density of birdlife per square kilometre on earth. Sometimes it seems as if there are fewer birds than in an English woodland; only strange calls betray their presence. Then a mixed flock comes through, containing maybe 70-plus species, or a brightly coloured group of, say, rock parakeets dashes out of a fruiting tree.

This forest has produced the highest day-list ever recorded anywhere in the world and holds such little-seen gems as black-faced cotinga and rufous-fronted ant-thrush. Antbirds and ovenbirds creep in the foliage and give tantalizing glimpses until they reveal themselves in a shaft of sunlight. Woodcreepers and woodpeckers climb tree-trunks and multicoloured tanagers move through the rainforest canopy. To get to this forest is difficult and not cheap, but the experience is well worth it.

Some good places for lowland birding are the **Manu Wildlife Centre** and **Tambo Blanquillo,** both of which are located close to a large *collpa* (macaw lick) and to *cochas* (ox-bow lakes) crammed with birds. There's an excellent walk-up canopy tower at the Manu Wildlife Centre where rainforest canopy species can be seen with ease. There are many excellent areas; the entire **Lower Manu River** is superb, and **Cocha Salvador**, deep inside the pristine forests of the national park, is hard to beat.

A trip to Manu is one of the ultimate birding experiences and topping it off with a *collpa* is a great way to finish; hundreds of brightly coloured macaws and other parrots congregate to eat the clay essential to their digestion, in one of the world's great wildlife spectacles.

## The road to Manu

The arduous trip over the Andes from Cuzco to the end of the road at Itahuania is a long and uncomfortable journey, but, throughout the route, you will see some spectacular scenery.

From Cuzco you climb up to the **Huancarani Pass** (3½ hours) and then drop down to the picturesque mountain village of **Paucartambo** in the Mapacho Valley (see page 214). You can make a detour to **Tres Cruces**, 44 km from Paucartambo, for a great view of the sunrise over the Amazon. The road then ascends to the **Acjanacu Pass** (cold at night), after which it goes down to the cloudforest and then the rainforest. On the way, you pass **Manu Cloudforest Lodge**, **Cock-of-the-Rock Lodge** and the **San Pedro Biological Station**. This last is owned by **Tapir Tours** and is usually visited as part of a larger Manu tour programme. After 12 hours you reach **Pilcopata** at 650 m. One hour more – the route is hair-raising and breathtaking – and you are in Atalaya, which is the jump-off point for river trips further into the Manu.

**Atalaya**, the first village on the Río Alto Madre de Dios, consists of a few houses and some basic accommodation. Even in the dry season this part of the road is appalling and trucks often get stuck. In Atalaya, boats are available to take you across the river to **Amazonia Lodge**. The route continues to **Salvación**, where a Manu park office is situated and there are a few basic hostels and restaurants. ⏩ *For details of lodges and other accommodation, see Sleeping, page 237.*

## Shintuya and Itahuania

The road now bypasses Shintuya, a commercial and social centre, from where wood from the jungle is transported to Cuzco. There are two Shintuyas: one is the port and mission and the other is the native village. There are a few basic restaurants, but supplies here tend to be expensive.

*You can't arrange trips to the tourist zones of the national park from Shintuya; arrangements must be made in Cuzco.*

The end of the road is **Itahuania**, the starting point for river transport. Rain often disrupts wheeled transport, though. The road is scheduled to continue to Nuevo Edén, 11 km away, and Diamante, so the location of the port will be determined by progress on the road. Eventually, the road will go to Boca Colorado. **Note** It is not possible to arrange trips to the Manu Reserved Zone in Itahuania, owing to park regulations. All arrangements must be made in Cuzco.

## Boca Manu to Boca Colorado → *Colour map 2, A4/A5.*

From Itahuania you can catch one of the infrequent cargo boats that sail downriver to the gold-mining centre of Boca Colorado on the Río Madre de Dios, via Boca Manu, and pass several ecotourism lodges en route including **Pantiacolla Lodge** and **Manu Wildlife Centre**. Boca Manu is the connecting point between the Alto Madre de Dios, Manu and Madre de Dios rivers. It has a few houses, an airstrip and some well-stocked shops. It is also the entrance to the Manu Reserve and to go further north you must be part of an organized group (see page 232).

Between Boca Manu and Boca Colorado is **Blanquillo**, a private reserve of 10,000 ha. Bring a good tent and all your food if you want to do it yourself, or, alternatively, accommodation is available at **Tambo Blanquillo**. Wildlife is abundant, especially macaws and other parrots at the macaw lick near **Manu Wildlife Centre**. There are occasional boats to Blanquillo from Shintuya (six to eight hours).

From Boca Colorado a road now runs to **Puerto Maldonado** (see page 239), three hours by *colectivo*. Boca Colorado has some very basic accommodation but it is not recommended for single women travellers. ⏩ *For details of lodges and other places to stay around Boca Manu see Sleeping, page 237.*

## Reserved Zone

The entrance fee to the Reserved Zone is S/.150 per person (about US$40) and is included in package-tour prices. The park ranger station is located in **Limonal**, 20 minutes by boat from Boca Manu. You need to show your permit here and, provided you have one, camping is allowed.

Upstream on the Río Manu you pass **Manu Lodge**, on the Cocha Juárez, after three or four hours by boat. You can continue to Cocha Otorongo (2½ hours) and Cocha Salvador (30 minutes), the biggest lake with plenty of wildlife, where **Casa Machiguenga Lodge** is located and several companies have safari camp concessions. From here it is two hours to **Pakitza**, the entrance to the National Park Zone. This is only for biologists with a special permit. ⏩ *For details of lodges and other accommodation around the Reserved Zone, see Sleeping, page 238.*

## Sleeping

Lodges in the Southern jungle are usually included as part of a package run by tour operators from Cuzco, see page 112.

### The road to Manu *p235, map p231*

**Proyecto Selva Inca/Hacienda Villa Carmen**, Av Sumar Pacha s/n, Pilcopata, T084-231625 or 084-975 6207 (mob), www.selvainka.com. Run by Evelyne Oblitas, this is a safe, friendly and inexpensive lodge in Pilcopata. Due to its village position this is more a social project than an opportunity to see rare wildlife, but we've received several positive reports regarding their sustainable development programmes and work with local communities. A 3-day/2-night programme costs US$230; other options available. Book first by phone or online.

F **Sra Rubella** runs an unnamed place in Pilcopata, very basic but friendly.

### Lodges

**Amazonia Lodge**, Cuzco office at Matará 334, T084-231370, www.amazonialodge.com. On the Río Alto Madre de Dios just across the river from Atalaya, an old tea hacienda run by the Yábar family, famous for its bird diversity and fine hospitality, a great place to relax, contact in advance to arrange transport. Price is US$60 per person per night, full board.

**Cock-of-the-Rock Lodge**, San Pedro, on the road from Paucartambo to Atalaya, at 1500 m. This is next to a cock-of-the-rock lek and the San Pedro Biological Station. It is run by the **Perú Verde** group (see Visitor information, page 233). Double rooms with shared bath and 7 private cabins with en suite bath.

**Erika Lodge**, contact **Aventuras Ecológicas Manu**, Plateros 356, Cuzco, T084-261640, www.manuadventures.com/erika.html. On the Alto Madre de Dios, 25 mins from Atalaya. Like **Amazonia Lodge**, this is a good place for birds. It offers basic facilities and is cheaper than the other and more luxurious lodges.

**Manu Cloud Forest Lodge**, owned by **Manu Nature Tours** (page 114). Located at Unión at 1800 m on the road from Paucartambo to Atalaya, before San Pedro. 6 rooms with 16-20 beds in total.

**Posada San Pedro Cloud Forest Lodge**, San Pedro, on the road from Paucartambo to Atalaya, before Pilcopata. 14 rooms. Included as an overnight stop in many tour operators' Manu programmes.

### Shintuya and Itahuania *p235, map p231*

The priest will let you stay in the dormitory rooms at Shintuya mission (**G**) and you can camp, but beware of thieves.

### Lodges

**Pantiacolla Lodge**, 30 mins downstream from Shintuya. Book through **Pantiacolla Tours** (see page 114). Owned by the Moscoso family. This lodge is located underneath the Pantiacolla Mountains, which, due to the large altitudinal range in a small area, boasts great biological diversity, particularly with birds. Good trail system.

**Yanayaco Lodge**, in Cuzco, Procuradores 330, T084-248122, www.yanayacolodge.com. Approximately 1 hr by boat above Diamante village on the southern bank of the Madre de Dios, close to a small parrot *collpa* (mineral lick); claims to offer frequent sightings of large mammals. The lodge also offers several different itineraries including all transport to the Manu Cultural and the Manu Reserved Zones, prices depend on length of stay and number of passengers.

### Boca Manu to Boca Colorado *p236, map p231*

C **Boca Manu Lodge**, opposite Boca Manu airstrip, book through **Emperadores Tours**, Procuradores 190, Cuzco, T084-239987. This reasonably priced place is run by Juan de Dios Carpio, who owns a general store in Boca. If stranded here, ask at the store about the lodge.

### Lodges

**Manu Wildlife Centre**, book through **Manu Expeditions, InkaNatura** (see page 112), or **Perú Verde**. 2 hrs down the Río Madre de Dios from Boca Manu, near the Blanquillo macaw

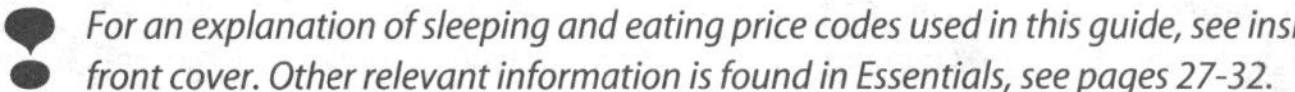
*For an explanation of sleeping and eating price codes used in this guide, see inside the front cover. Other relevant information is found in Essentials, see pages 27-32.*

lick. There's also a tapir lick and walk-up canopy tower. 22 double cabins with private bathroom and hot water. Also canopy towers for birdwatching (see page 234).

**Turismo Indígena Wanamei**, Clorinda Matto I-1, Urb Magisterio, 1ra Etapa, Cuzco, T084-254033, T965 2520 (mob), or Av 26 de Diciembre 276, Puerto Maldonado, T082-572539, www.ecoturismowanamei.com. New initiative by the people of the Amarakaeri Communal Reserve, located between Manu and Tambopata. They offer 4-9 day trips starting and ending in Cuzco. Accommodation includes lodges, communities and camping. The trips aim to offer excellent wildlife viewing opportunities and an insight into the daily life of indigenous peoples. It's advised that you speak Spanish. The 5 day/4 nights trip costs US$200 and includes all transport, meals, lodging and a guide.

**Yine Lodge**, next to Boca Manu airport. Book through **Pantiacolla Tours** (page 114). A smart cooperative project, managed with the native Yine community of Diamante.

**Reserved Zone** *p236, map p231*

In the Cocha Salvador area, several companies have tented safari camp infrastructures, some with shower and dining facilities, but all visitors sleep in tents. Some companies have installed walk-in tents with cots and bedding.

**Casa Machiguenga**, contact **Manu Expeditions** (page 114) or the **Apeco NGO** (page 233), T084-225595. Near Cocha Salvador, upriver from Manu Lodge, Machiguenga-style cabins run by the local community of Tayakome with NGO help.

**Manu Lodge**, run by **Manu Nature Tours** (page 114) and only bookable as part of a full package deal with transport, is situated on the Manu River, 3 hrs upriver from Boca Manu towards Cocha Salvador. It's in a fine location overlooking Cocha Juárez, an ox-bow lake which often has a family of giant otters. The lodge has an extensive trail system, and stands of mauritia palms near the lake provide nesting sites for colonies of blue and yellow macaws.

## Eating

**The road to Manu** *p235, map p231*

**Rosa and Klaus**, Atalaya. Very friendly people; meals are at their home; camping.

## Activities and tours

For Cuzco-based tour operators who specialize in trips to Manu and Tambopata, see Activities and tours, page 112. For international operators, see page 47.

**Amazon Trails Peru**, C Tandapata 660, San Blas, Cuzco, T084-437499, T974 1735 (mob), www.amazontrailsperu.com. Tours to Manu and Blanquillo. See also page 112.

**Pantiacolla Tours**, C Saphy 554, Cuzco, T084-238323, www.pantiacolla.com. Manu jungle tours, see page 114. Some trips include a night at **Pantiacolla Lodge**, see page 237.

## Transport

**Manu Biosphere Reserve** *p231, map p231*

**Air**

A private flight will set you back around US$750 one-way (this cost can be divided between the number of passengers). Contact **Transandes**, T084-224638, or **Aerocóndor**, T084-252774. Both airlines have offices in the Cuzco airport terminal. Flights, which use small propeller-engined aircraft, can sometimes be delayed by bad weather.

**Bus and truck**

From the Coliseo Cerrado in Cuzco 3 bus companies run to **Pilcopata** Mon, Wed, Fri, returning same night, US$10. They are fully booked even in low season. Trucks to Pilcopata run on same days, returning Tue, Thu, Sat, 10 hrs in wet season, less in the dry. Transport can be disrupted in the wet season because the road is in poor condition; paving is under way as part of the Carretera Interoceánica (tour companies have latest details). *Camioneta* service runs between Pilcopata and **Salvación** to connect with the buses, Mon, Wed, Fri. The same *camionetas* run **Itahuania-Shintuya-Salvacion** regularly, when sufficient passengers, once a day, and 2 trucks a day. On Sun, there is no traffic. To **Boca Manu** you can hire a boat in Atalaya, US$212 for a *peke peke*, or US$400 for a motor boat. It's cheaper to wait or hope for a boat going empty up to Boca Manu to pick up passengers, when the fare will be US$12.50 per passenger. Itahuania-Boca Manu in a shared boat with other passengers is US$6.25. A private, chartered boat would be US$105. From Itahuania, cargo boats leave for **Boca Colorado**, via Boca Manu, but only when the boat is fully laden; about 6-8 a week, 9 hrs, US$15. From Boca Colorado colectivos leave from near football field for Puerto Carlos, 1 hr, US$5, ferry across river 10 mins, US$1.65; colectivo Puerto Carlos–Puerto Maldonado, 3 hrs, US$10, rough road, lots of stops (in Puerto Maldonado **Turismo Boca Colorado**, Tacna 342, T082-573435, leave when full). Tour companies usually use their own vehicles for the overland trip from Cuzco to Manu.

# Puerto Maldonado and around

➔ *Phone code: 082. Colour map 2, A6.*

***Puerto Maldonado is a key hub for visiting the rainforest, or for departing to Brazil or Bolivia. Most visitors are whisked through town on their way to a lodge on the Río Madre de Dios or the Río Tambopata, but the city dwellers would prefer tourists to spend some time in town, which is an important timber, gold mining and tourism centre. It's a safe place, with chicha music blaring out from most street corners.*** ▸▸ *For Sleeping, Eating and other listings, see pages 245-250.*

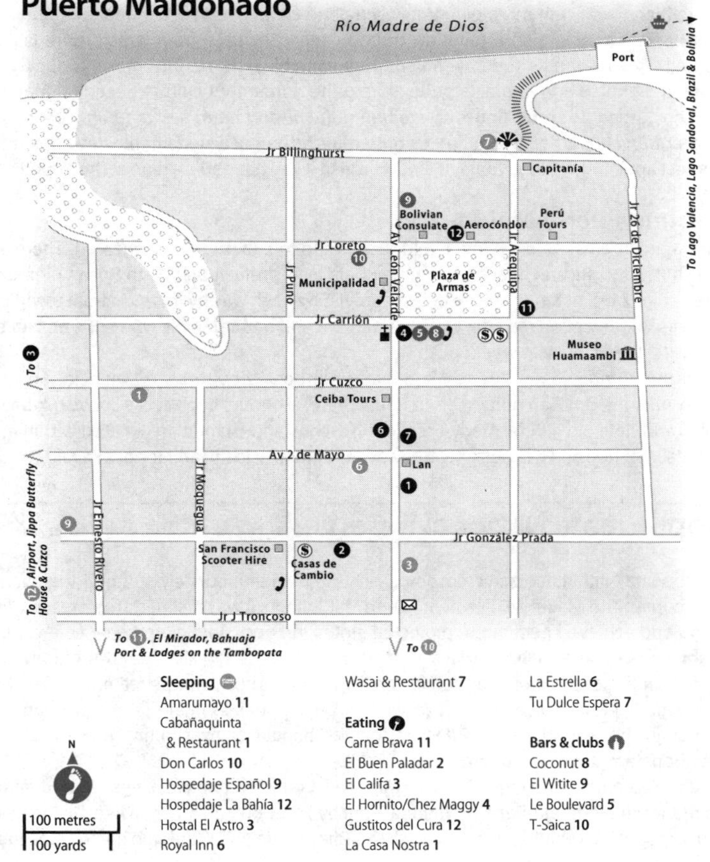


**Sleeping**
Amarumayo 11
Cabañaquinta & Restaurant 1
Don Carlos 10
Hospedaje Español 9
Hospedaje La Bahía 12
Hostal El Astro 3
Royal Inn 6
Wasai & Restaurant 7

**Eating**
Carne Brava 11
El Buen Paladar 2
El Califa 3
El Hornito/Chez Maggy 4
Gustitos del Cura 12
La Casa Nostra 1
La Estrella 6
Tu Dulce Espera 7

**Bars & clubs**
Coconut 8
El Witite 9
Le Boulevard 5
T-Saica 10

## Ins and outs

**Getting there** Most people visiting the jungle around Puerto Maldonado fly in from Lima or Cuzco (30 minutes). A yellow fever vaccination is offered free at the airport on arrival but check that a new needle is used. Combis to the airport run along Avenida 2 de Mayo every 10 to 15 minutes, US$0.60; a *mototaxi* from town to the airport is US$2. As an alternative to flying, there are buses from both Cuzco and Urcos. The road from the cold of the high Andes to the steamy heat of the Amazon jungle can only be described as a challenge (see box, page 249). You should take a mosquito net, insect repellent, sunglasses, sunscreen, a plastic sheet, a blanket, food and water. » *For further details, see Transport, page 248.*

**Tourist office** At the airport.

## Sights

Overlooking the confluence of the Ríos Tambopata and Madre de Dios, Puerto Maldonado is a major logging and brazil nut processing centre. From the park at the end of Jirón Arequipa, across from the Capitanía, you get a good view of the two rivers, the ferries across the Madre de Dios and the lumber at the dockside. The brazil nut harvest is from December to February and the crop tends to be good on alternate years. Nuts are sold on the street, plain or coated in sugar or chocolate. **El Mirador** ⓘ *Av Fitzcarrald and Av Madre de Dios, Mon-Sat 0900-1700, Sun 1200-1700, US$0.60*, is a 47-m-high tower with three platforms giving fine views over the city and surrounding rainforest. There is also a toilet at the top – no curtains – from which there is an equally fine view over the city! **Museo Huamaambi** ⓘ *26 de Diciembre 360, US$1*, contains photos and artefacts pertaining to the Harakmbut culture of central Madre de Dios. **Jippa Butterfly House** ⓘ *adjoining the airport entrance (a 5-min walk from the terminal building), US$3*, breeds butterflies as part of a sustainable development project and offers guided tours. It's worth a visit if you have spare time at the airport.

## Around Puerto Maldonado

If you are interested in seeing a gold rush, a trip to **Laberinto** is suggested. There is one hotel and several poor restaurants. Boats leave from Laberinto to Boca Colorado (see page 236). At Km 13 on the Cuzco road (US$2 each way by *mototaxi* from town) is a pleasant recreational centre with a restaurant and natural pools where it's possible to swim. It gets busy at weekends.

Tour companies in Puerto Maldonado run boat trips to **Lago Valencia**, 60 km away near the Bolivian border – four hours there, six hours back. It is a *cocha* (ox-bow lake) with lots of wildlife. Many excellent beaches and islands are located within an hour's boat ride and it is possible to stay overnight with local families or at a refuge.



# Tambopata National Reserve

» *pp245-250. Colour map 2, A6.*

Tambopata National Reserve encompasses the area immediately south of the rivers Tambopata and Madre de Dios near Puerto Maldonado. It was first declared a reserve in 1990 and achieved permanent protected status in 2000. Adjoining the reserve is the **Bahuaja-Sonene National Park**, which extends from the Río Heath and the Bolivian border in the east, across to the Río Tambopata, 50 to 80 km upstream from Puerto Maldonado. Tambopata is open to visitors but Bahuaja-Sonene is out of bounds, although those visiting the *collpa* on the Tambopata or river rafting down the Río Tambopata will travel through it.

In September 2007, the Peruvian Ministers Council proposed a legal amendment to reduce the Bahuaja-Sonene National Park by 209,000 ha and open it to oil and gas exploration. This would put at huge risk the Tambopata and Candamo basins. See the websites www.amazonwatch.org and www.thepetitionsite.com/1/save-candamo-heart-of-the-bahuaja-sonene-national-park-peru.

Tambopata is a very reasonable alternative for those who do not have the time to visit Manu. It is a close rival in terms of seeing wildlife (notably giant otters) and boasts some superb *cochas* (ox-bow lakes). Perhaps the most famous feature are the **collpas**, Chuncho and Colorado, where macaws and parrots, in particular, congregate to extract minerals from the clay river bank. The latter, in the southwest of the reserve, is in an area surrounded by pristine primary rainforest with excellent wildlife viewing. Primates are abundant and other large mammals, such as tapir and jaguar, are often seen, especially in the dry season.

## Ins and outs

**Getting there** From Puerto Maldonado access to the reserve is either by travelling west along the Río Tambopata or east along the Río Madre de Dios. Although Lago Sandoval can be visited on day trips from Puerto Maldonado (see page 242), overnight stays in the reserve can only be arranged as part of a tour and lodge package. You could turn up at Puerto Maldonado and try to get on a tour but this takes time and patience so you're better off booking in advance from Cuzco or from your home country. Lodges on the Tambopata are reached by road to Bahuaja port, 15 km upriver from Puerto Maldonado close to the community of Infierno, then continuing by boat.

**Visitor information** The fee for a day visit in the reserve between Lago Salvador and the Collpa de Chuncho is US$9 per person, or US$20 per person for 2 visits in up to 5 days (plus US$7.55 per day); between the Collpa de Chuncho and the Collpa Colorado

**Sleeping**
Casa de Hospedaje Mejía **5**
Casa de Hospedaje Picaflor **6**
Eco Amazonia Lodge **2**
El Corto Maltés **3**
Explorers' Inn **4**
Inkaterra Reserva Amazónica **8**
Libertador Tambopata Lodge **11**
Posada Amazonas Lodge **7**
Refugio Amazonas **1**
Sandoval Lake Lodge **10**
Tambopata Research Centre **12**
Wasai Lodge **13**

costs US$30-45 per person depending on length of stay. If staying at a lodge, they will organize the payment of the fee, otherwise, you need to visit **INRENA** ⓘ *Av 28 de Julio s/n, block 8, Puerto Maldonado, T082-573278, Mon-Fri 0830-1300, 1430-1800, Sat 0900-1200*. Long-term visitors should be aware that leishmaniasis exists in this area.

## Lodges

Most lodges are clustered along the Río Madre de Dios and on Lago Sandoval on the northern edge of the Tambopata Reserve. Other lodges are along the Río Tambopata, on the west side of the Tambopata Reserve. A number are excellent for lowland rainforest birding. **Explorer's Inn,** 58 km from Puerto Maldonado on the Río Tambopata, is perhaps the most famous: more than 580 bird species have been recorded here, as well as 1230 species of butterflies, and giant river otters. The **Posada Amazonas/Tambopata Research Centre** and **Libertador Tambopata Lodge** are also good. » *For details of lodges and other accommodation, see Sleeping, page 245.*

## Lago Sandoval

ⓘ *US$9 entry for independent travellers accompanied by a guide; this can be arranged by the boatman in Puerto Maldonado. Boat hire US$25 per day plus petrol.* This beautiful and tranquil lake is a one-hour boat ride along the Río Madre de Dios, and then a 5-km walk into the jungle. There are two jungle lodges at the lake (see page 246) and it is regularly included on tour packages. At weekends, especially on Sundays, the lake gets quite busy. It is sometimes possible to see giant river otters early in the morning and several species of monkey, macaw (especially the smaller red-bellied macaws, which maintain a large breeding population near the lake) and hoatzin.

Upstream from Lago Sandoval is the wreck of a steamer that resembles the *Fitzcarrald*. This lies a few metres from the Río Madre de Dios in the bed of a small stream.

### The giant otters of Río Madre de Dios

Giant otters (*Pteronura brasiliensis*) are the largest and most spectacular of the world's 13 otter species, sometimes reaching 1.8 m (6 ft) in length. The otters live and hunt in family groups and local people call them *lobos del río* (wolves of the river), as a mark of respect for their supreme hunting abilities.

The giant otters in the Peruvian Amazon are endangered. The species as a whole has been pushed to the very edge of extinction by the skin trade, and now perhaps less than 2000 remain in South America, the only continent in which they occur. Despite legal protection the otters now face a new threat, this time from uncontrolled tourism, as guides anxious to earn tips or under pressure from tourists, approach the otters too closely.

Giant otters are highly territorial and sensitive animals that require large areas of pristine lake and river habitat to survive. This habitat is shrinking fast owing to human encroachment, and areas such as Tambopata and Manu offer the best chance of the species' survival. According to studies carried out by the Frankfurt Zoological Society you should always maintain a distance of at least 70 m from giant otters. Keep quiet and move slowly. Approaching or chasing giant otters causes stress, which eventually can lead to the death of pups or to otters leaving their lake habitat entirely.

As a tourist visiting the protected areas of Madre del Dios or *cochas* (ox-bow lakes) in the forest beyond, you MUST share the responsibility for preserving these magnificent predators. If your guide or other tourists in the group wish to approach the otters, please insist that they adhere to the above conditions and keep your distance; if you explain why, most tourists will be happy with your decision. By keeping to these simple rules you will be making a small but very significant contribution to the survival of giant otters in the wild.

The story of the rubber baron Fitzcarrald's attempt in 1894 to haul a boat across the watershed from the Ucuyali to the Madre de Dios drainage basin inspired the German director, Werner Herzog, to make his famous film, *Fitzcarraldo* (1982).

## Río Las Piedras

The little-visited **Las Piedras** river, running roughly parallel to the Río Manu, flows for some 700 km from remote rainforest headwaters in the Alto Purús region. **Alto Purús**, recently upgraded to national park status, encompasses vast expanses of scarcely explored rainforest, home to indigenous people with little or no contact with the outside world, not to mention priceless wildlife resources, little studied, but already under considerable threat (see box, page 244). Las Piedras is navigable for about 500 km northwest of Puerto Maldonado, a journey that takes three weeks. Despite the impact of loggers, there are still reports of excellent wildlife sightings all along its length.

The lower, more easily accessible section of the river, closer to Puerto Maldonado and currently outside state protection, runs through rich tropical forests, very similar to those in the Manu and Tambopata areas. Overshadowed by these justly famous reserves, the Piedras area receives only a handful of western visitors each year, a fact which many would consider an attraction in itself. Lured by the region's untapped ecotourism potential and a desire to protect the river's rich wildlife, a couple of

## Logging, corruption and the death of mahogany

Despite being a protected area, recently upgraded to full national park status, Alto Purús is currently an illegal logging frontier. Huge demand for mahogany and cedar driven by increasing scarcity, and mahogany's recent appearance on the IUCN (World Conservation Union) endangered species list, have driven prices sky high. Vast numbers of largely poor loggers and their families are pushing further and further upriver looking to profit from southern Peru's last unlogged region, outside of the more strongly enforced park zones of Manu and Tambopata/Bahuaja-Sonene. Widespread corruption has ensured that officials and police at all levels have 'looked the other way' in return for handsome pay-offs, and wood is licensed as if originating from legal concessions, when in reality it is coming from areas in which logging is prohibited.

The loggers in turn are coming into conflict with the real owners of this land, the indigenous people, causing some tribes to migrate away from their traditional territories and bringing them into contact with diseases to which they have little resistance – often with fatal results. Extensive subsistence hunting by the loggers is also affecting local wildlife populations, which again has a knock-on effect for the tribes of the area. Where the loggers and their families will go after the last of the commercial timber is gone is anyone's guess, but thoughts of the future are of little importance when tomorrow's dinner is far from certain. To the corrupt government officials and businessmen making huge profits from the trade, the suffering of both the forest and its people is a minor concern compared to their rapidly fattening bank accounts.

On a slightly more positive note the lower Río Las Piedras is the site of a burgeoning ecotourism industry with several excellent lodges already open and offering perhaps a more sustainable future for the river, its people, and the surrounding wilderness.

How can you help?

→ Never buy products made from or containing tropical hardwoods.
→ Check for FSC (Forest Stewardship Council) label of sustainability on wood products in general. Look at www.fsc.org for more information.
→ Support a local or international conservation organization.



environmentally sound tourism and research projects have opened several hours upriver from Puerto Maldonado. Due to its lack of protected status it's also fairly straightforward to tailor your own itinerary in this part of the forest. By visiting the Río Las Piedras to view wildlife, you are encouraging the sustainable use of another precious section of the Peruvian wilderness.

### Wildlife

So what exactly does the Piedras offer in terms of wildlife? Close to 600 species of birds, a least eight primate species and the possibility of spotting some of the Amazon's larger mammals: jaguar, puma, tapir and giant anteater are all present. Healthy populations of giant otters exist in the rivers and ox-bow lakes, and, last but not least, there are several collpas or clay licks that attract parrots, macaws and, in some cases, larger mammals as well. The only real downside is that recent or continued hunting pressure has resulted in wildlife being somewhat shier and more secretive than in Manu or Tambopata. Nevertheless this remains an excellent wildlife destination.

## Sleeping

Accommodation in jungle lodges is usually included as part of a package run by tour operators from Cuzco, see page 112.

**Puerto Maldonado** *p239, map p239*

B **Wasai Lodge & Expeditions**, Billinghurst opposite the Capitanía, T082-572290, reservations: Las Higueras 257, Residencial Monterrico, La Molina, Lima 12, www.wasai.com. Price includes breakfast, a/c, TV, shower. In a beautiful location overlooking the Río Madre de Dios, with forest surrounding cabin-style rooms which are built on a slope down to the river. Small pool with waterfall, good restaurant (local fish a speciality). Recommended. They can organize local tours and also have a lodge on the Río Tambopata (see below).

C **Cabañaquinta**, Cuzco 535, T571045, www.hotelcabanquinta.com. With breakfast, a/c (cheaper rooms without a/c and hot water), free drinking water, internet, good restaurant, lovely garden, very comfortable, airport transfer. Recommended.

C **Don Carlos**, Av León Velarde 1271, T082-571029. Good place with a nice view over the Río Tambopata. Rooms have a/c, TV and phone, and there's a restaurant.

E **Amarumayo**, Libertad 433, 10 mins from the centre, T082-573860, residencial amarumayo@hotmail.com. Comfortable lodging, with pool and garden. Good restaurant. Recommended.

E **Hospedaje Español**, González Prada 670, T082-572381. Very clean, comfortable rooms in a nice building, garden setting, friendly.

E **Hospedaje La Bahía**, Av 2 de Mayo 710, T082-572127. Large clean rooms. Cheaper without bath or TV. This is one of the best budget options.

E **Royal Inn**, Av 2 de Mayo 333, T082-571048. Modern and clean, one of the best of the cheaper hotels, rooms at the back are less noisy.

F **Hostal El Astro**, Av León Velarde 617, T082-572128. Clean, safe, family-run.

**Tambopata National Reserve** *p240, map p241.*

Apart from the **Tambopata Research Centre** the lodges in the Tambopata area all lie on the edge of the reserve or across the water from it. Most of the lodges use the term 'ecotourism', or something similar, in their publicity material but this is applied pretty loosely. Fortunately no lodge offers trips where guests hunt for their meals but Posada Amazonas' collaboration with the local community is unique in this area. See box, page 13, for points to note when choosing a lodge. Some of the lodges offer guiding and research placements to biology and environmental science graduates. For further details send a SAE to **TReeS**, c/o J Forrest, PO Box 33153, London NW3 4DR.

**Río Madre de Dios**

**El Corto Maltés**, Billinghurst 229, Puerto Maldonado, T082-573831, cortomaltes@terra.com.pe. On the south side of the Río Madre de Dios, halfway to Sandoval, the focus of most visits. Hot water, huge dining room, well run. Attracts a lot of French groups. 3 days/2 nights cost US$180.

**Eco Amazonia Lodge**, book through their office in Lima: Av Larco 1083, of 408, Miraflores, T01-242 2708, in Cuzco T084-225068, www.ecoamazonia.com.pe. On the Río Madre de Dios, 1 hr downriver from Puerto Maldonado. Room for up to 80 in basic bungalows and dormitories, good for birdwatching with viewing platforms and tree canopy access, has its own Monkey Island. US$150 for 3 days/2 nights.

**Estancia Bello Horizonte**, 20 km northwest of Puerto Maldonado, Loreto 258, Puerto Maldonado, T082-572748 (in **Heladería Gustitos del Cura**), www.estanciabello horizonte.com. In a nice stretch of forest overlooking the Madre de Dios, a small lodge with bungalows for 25 people, with private bath, hammock and pool. 3 days/2 nights US$95-140, depending on the package. It is part of the scheme to train and employ young people. Suitable for those wanting to avoid a river trip.

**Inkaterra Reserva Amazónica**, book through **Inkaterra**, Andalucía 174, Lima 18, T01-610 0404; Cuzco, T084-245314; Puerto Maldonado T082-572283, www.inkaterra.com. 45 mins by boat down the Río Madre de Dios. Tastefully decorated, a hotel in the jungle with 6 suites and 38 rustic bungalows with private bathrooms, solar power, friendly staff, very good food in a huge dining room supported by a big tree. Caters mainly for large groups. The lodge is surrounded by its own 10,000-ha reserve, which boasts the largest number of ant species recorded in a single location: 342. It also has a new canopy walk and a Monkey Island (Isla Rolín) for the recovery of primates, which are introduced back in to their natural environment. Jungle tours available with multilingual guides; most are to Lago Sandoval. US$345 per person for 3 days/2 nights package, up to US$1381 for 5 days/4 nights.

### Lago Sandoval

**C Casa de Hospedaje Mejía**, to book T082-571428, visit **Ceiba Tours**, L Velarde 420, T082-573567, turismomejia@hotmail.com. An attractive rustic lodge close to Lago Sandoval, full board can be arranged, canoes are available. 3 days/2 nights cost US$70.

**Sandoval Lake Lodge**, book through **InkaNatura**, Manuel Bañón 461, San Isidro, Lima, T01-440 2022, www.inkanatura.com (page 112). 1 km beyond **Mejía** on Lago Sandoval, usually accessed by canoe across the lake after a 3-km walk or rickshaw ride along the trail, can accommodate 50 people in 25 rooms, bar and dining area, electricity, hot water. A short system of trails is nearby. Guides are available in several languages. US$215 per person for 3 days/ 2 nights.

### Río Tambopata

**Casas de Hospedaje Baltimore**, several families in the community of Baltimore on the banks of the Río Tambopata, 60 km upriver, www.baltimoreperu.com. They are developing accommodation for visitors (with EU funding), 4-12 tourists per home. They offer the opportunity to experience the forest close-up and an insight into daily life in the forest at a more economical price. Prices vary depending on method of access: about US$120, 3 days/2 nights. Guiding in Spanish, English speaking guide can be arranged. Researchers and volunteers also welcomed by arrangement.

**Casa de Hospedaje Picaflor**, Casilla 105, Puerto Maldonado, picaflor_rc@yahoo.com. A small, 4-room, family run guesthouse with solar lighting, a good library, great cakes and fresh bread baked daily. It's located just downriver from **Libertador Tambopata Lodge**. Guiding in English/Spanish, good trail system, visits are made to Lago Condenado. Suited to backpackers and birders wanting a more intimate rainforest experience. US$20 per person per night plus TNR fee and transport. Special arrangements also for researchers and volunteers wanting to stay 4 weeks or more .

**Explorer's Inn**, book through **Peruvian Safaris**, Alcanfores 459, Miraflores, Lima, T01-447 8888, or Plateros 365, Cuzco, T084-235342, or Fonavi H15, Puerto Maldonado, T/F082-572078, www.peruviansafaris.com. Just before the La Torre control post, adjoining the TNR, in the part where most research work has been done, 58 km from Puerto Maldonado. 2½-hr ride up the Río Tambopata (1½ hrs return, in the early morning, so take warm clothes and rain gear). One of the best places in Peru for seeing jungle birds. Also tours through the adjoining community of La Torre to meet local people and find out about their farms (*chacras*) and handicrafts. The guides are biologists and naturalists from around the world who undertake research in the reserve in return for acting as guides. They provide interesting wildlife treks, including one to the macaw lick. US$450 for 5 days/4 nights.

**Libertador Tambopata Lodge**, on the Río Tambopata, to make reservations Suecia 343, Cuzco, T084-245695, www.tambopatalodge.com. Affiliated to the **Libertador** hotel chain, the lodge has rooms with solar-heated water, sleeps 60. Good guides, excellent food. Trips go to Lake Condenado, some to Lake Sachavacayoc and to the Collpa de Chuncho, guiding mainly in English and Spanish, usual package US$200 per person for 3 days/2 nights, naturalists' programme provided.

**Posada Amazonas Lodge**, on the Tambopata river, 1½ hrs by vehicle and boat upriver from Puerto Maldonado. Book

*For an explanation of sleeping and eating price codes used in this guide, see inside the front cover. Other relevant information is found in Essentials, see pages 27-32.*

through **Rainforest Expeditions**, Aramburú 166, of 4B, Miraflores, Lima 18, T01-421 8347, or Portal de Carnes 236, Cuzco, T084-246243, in Puerto Maldonadao T082-572575, www.perunature.com. A collaboration between the tour agency and the local native community of Infierno. Attractive rooms with cold showers, visits to Lake Tres Chimbadas, with good birdwatching including the Collpa. Offers trips to a nearby indigenous primary health care project where a native healer gives guided tours of the medicinal plant garden. Service and guiding is very good. Recommended. Prices start at US$225 for a 3 day/2 night package, or US$745 for 5 days/4 nights including the **Tambopata Research Centre**, the company's more intimate, but comfortable lodge, about 6 hrs further upriver. Rooms are smaller than Posada Amazonas, shared showers, cold water. The lodge is next to the Colorado macaw clay lick. 2 hrs from Posada Amazonas, Rainforest Expeditions also has the **Refugio Amazonas**, close to Lago Condenados. It is the usual stopover for those visiting the collpa. 3 bungalows accommodate 70 people in en suite rooms, large, kerosene lit, open bedrooms with mosquito nets, well designed and run, atmospheric. Prices are as for Posada Amazonas.

**Wasai Lodge**, run by **Hotel Wasai** in Puerto Maldonado (see above). On the Río Tambopata, 120 km (4½ hrs) upriver from Puerto Maldonado, small lodge with 3 bungalows for 30 people, 15 km of trails around the lodge, guides in English and Spanish. The Collpa de Chuncho is only 1 hr upriver; 3-day/2-night trips US$300, 5-day/4-night US$400, including 1 night in Puerto Maldonado.

### Río Las Piedras *p243*

**Amazon Rainforest Conservation Centre**, contact Pepe Moscoso, Jr Los Cedros B-17, Los Castaños, Puerto Maldonado, T082-573655, www.laspiedrasamazon.com. A well set-up jungle lodge roughly 8 hrs up Río Las Piedras, in a magnificent location overlooking a beautiful 4-km long ox-bow lake, Lago Soledad. The lake has a family of giant otters and the surrounding 7000-ha private reserve is home to 8 monkey species, peccaries, tapir and large cats, among others. Eight comfortable bungalows, with bath, hot water, small balcony, some have lake views. Activities include night-time caiman spotting, a viewing platform 35 m up an ironwood tree, a hide overlooking a macaw lick, and walks on the extensive trail network. Most trips break the long river journey roughly half way at the simple but pleasant Tipishca Camp, overlooking a second ox-bow lake with its own family of otters. Prices depend on group numbers: a 6-day/5-night programme with 5-7 people costs US$985.

**Las Piedras Biodiversity Station**, contact Emma Hume and Juan Julio, T082-573922, T960 0109 (mob), www.rainforestresearch.netfirms.com. About 6 hrs upriver from Puerto Maldonado, this lodge offers good opportunities for scientific research and long-term volunteer projects, in addition to more conventional rainforest tours. It's close to both macaw and mammal clay licks and has an extensive trail system, hides and a canopy platform. Accommodation for 20 people in double rooms with shared showers. Volunteer/research rates start at US$15/US$18 per day and include transport to and from the lodge if you're staying more than a month. A 4-day/3-night tour for 4-5 people costs US$315. Tours up the Río Tambopata are also offered. Excellent value for no frills expeditions into a rich area of the Piedras forest.

## Eating

### Puerto Maldonado *p239, map p239*

**TT-T Carne Brava**, on the Plaza de Armas. One of the smart new joints for a steak and chips. Similar, also on the Plaza, is **Vaka Loca**.

**TT-T El Califa**, Piura 266. Often has bushmeat, mashed banana and palm hearts on the menu. Recommended.

**TT-T El Hornito/Chez Maggy**, on the plaza. Good pizzas served in a cosy atmosphere, pasta dishes are not such good value.

**T El Buen Paladar**, González Prada 365. Good-value lunch menu.

**T La Casa Nostra**, Av León Velarde 515. The best place for snacks and cakes.

**T La Estrella**, Av León Velarde 474. The smartest and the best of the *pollos a la brasa* places.

**Cafés**

**Gustitos del Cura**, Loreto 258, Plaza de Armas. An ice-cream parlour run by a project for homeless teenagers, offering delicious and unusual flavours such as lúcuma and brazil nut, only US$0.30 for a large cone!

**Tu Dulce Espera**, Av L.Velarde 475. Good for evening juices and snacks.

## Bars and clubs

**Puerto Maldonado** *p239, map p239*

There is a **billiard hall** at Puno 520.

**Coconut**, east side of the plaza. Disco.

**El Witite**, Av León Velarde 153. A popular, good disco, latin music, open Fri and Sat.

**Le Boulevard**, behind **El Hornito**. Live music, popular.

**T-Saica**, Loreto 335. An atmospheric bar with live music at weekends.

## Activities and tours

For Cuzco-based tour operators who specialize in trips to Tambopata, see Activities and tours, page 115. For international agencies, such as **Tambo Tours**, see Tour operators, page 47.

**Puerto Maldonado** *p239, map p239*

The usual price of trips to **Lago Sandoval** is US$25 per person per day (minimum 2 people) and US$35 per person per day for longer trips lasting 2-4 days (minimum of 4-6 people). All guides should have a *carnet* issued by the Ministry of Tourism (DIRCETUR), which authorizes them as suitable guides and confirms their identity. Check that the *carnet* has not expired. Reputable guides are: **Hernán Llave Cortez**, **Romel Nacimiento** and the **Mejía** brothers, all of whom can be contacted on arrival at the airport, if available. Also recommended is **Víctor Yohamona**, T968 6279 (mob), victorguideperu@hotmail.com, who speaks English, French and German. **Perú Tours**, Loreto 176, T082-573244, perutoursytravel@hotmail. com. Organizes local trips. See also **Ceiba Tours**, under Casa de Hospedaje Mejía, above.

## Transport

**Puerto Maldonado** *p239, map p239*

**Air**

To **Lima** via Cuzco, daily with **Aerocóndor** and **Lan**.

**Bus**

Daily combis and trucks to **Laberinto**, 1½ hrs, US$2.50; they return in the afternoon. There are daily buses from the Terminal Terrestre in **Cuzco** with **Transportes Iguazú** and **Mendivil**. Both on Av Tambopata, blocks 3 and 5 in Puerto Maldonado. 19 hrs (potentially much longer in the wet), US$15, depart 1400 from Puerto Maldonado. Another option is to go from Cuzco to **Urcos**, 1 hr, US$2.25, then look for the **Transportes Juan Carlos** bus in Urcos' main plaza. This is a Volvo truck modified with seats and windows. In the dry season this takes 26 hrs to Puerto Maldonado, US$13; it leaves about 1500 daily. There are also daily buses from **Mazuko** to Puerto Maldonado with **Transportes Bolpebra** and **Transportes Señor de la Cumbre**, 4 hrs, US$3.

For **Boca Manu** and **Itahuania** take a colectivo to **Boca Colorado** (see above) and then take a cargo boat (no fixed schedule). From Itahuania there is transport to Pilcopata and Cuzco.

**Mopeds and mototaxis**

Scooters and mopeds can be hired from **San Francisco**, on the corner of Puno and González Prada for US$1.15 per hr or US$10 per day. No deposit is required but your passport and driving licence need to be shown. Mototaxis around town charge US$0.60; riding pillion on a motorbike is US$0.30.

**River**

Transport to the river lodges is always organized as part of a tour package; it is not possible to travel independently to the lodges. Boats to **Lago Sandoval** or **Lago Valencia** can be arranged through the **Capitanía del Puerto** (Río Madre de Dios), T082-573003.

## Truckin' the hard way!

If you are still feeling adventurous when you emerge at Puerto Maldonado from the depths of the jungle, try getting back to Cuzco by truck. You'll need plenty of time and patience: the trip takes between two days and a week depending on the weather and the number of breakdowns along the way. And you'll have to be confident of your ability to withstand high levels of discomfort for the duration of the trip. It is said that least comfortable of all are the petrol trucks, as passenger space is very limited. Our author, however, had the good fortune to miss the petrol truck and ride for two days atop empty (alas) beer bottles, which wasn't exactly luxurious either!

Trucks leave daily from PetroPerú on the outskirts of Puerto Maldonado and charge about S/.30 (US$9) for the whole trip. Make sure you are well-equipped with warm clothes and blankets as, however cleverly you try to time your departure, you can guarantee that fate, the weather and the famous law of sod will combine to ensure that you will reach the top of the 4000-m-plus pass at some ungodly hour when temperatures are well below freezing even without factoring in wind chill. The journey begins, however, in heavily cultivated lowland rainforest, rolling along a dirt track that was once described by Peruvian engineers as the country's worst road. Muddy ruts more than a metre deep threaten first to send passengers flying from the top of the truck and then to swallow the entire vehicle. Freeing a loaded truck from such a rut requires the involvement of all aboard and a good hour or so. Anyone lacking a sense of humour is advised to take the aeroplane.

After a few hours you start climbing into the cloudforest on a narrow, rocky, winding road with beautiful scenery all around, and precipitous cliffs plunging down beside you. Potential hazards are best left unanalysed, but if you suffer from vertigo, you'll be happiest asleep on this stretch. Before reaching the highest point of the journey, you pass through Quincemil where there are some very basic hostels for those who really need a break. During the day the views of Nevado Ausangate are magnificent as you go over the pass. During the night, however, which is when most trucks somehow cross, all you can be aware of is the cold. Should your driver decide that this would be an ideal place to snooze in his nice warm cabin, the words "vamos maestro" shouted with sufficient volume and frequency, combined with some energetic window-tapping, may prove effective in persuading him to move on a little. In Ocongate the townsfolk keep a night-time vigil and offer something vaguely coffee-like to those truck passengers brave or foolish enough to emerge from their blankets. From here it is just five hours or so along an abominably dusty road to Urcos, the resting place for the trucks.

Frequent buses leave Urcos for Cuzco, just an hour along the valley floor, where hot showers, good food and all those glorious Inca walls await. One thing's for sure, if you make this trip, you won't forget it in a hurry.

## ❻ Directory

**Puerto Maldonado** *p239, map p239*
**Airline offices** Aerocóndor, Loreto 222, T082-571733. **Lan**, Av León Velarde y 2 de Mayo, T082-573677.
**Banks and money exchange** BCP, cash advances with Visa, no commission on TCs. **Banco de la Nación**, cash on Mastercard, reasonable rates for TCs. Both are on the south side of the Plaza. The best rates for cash are at the *casas de cambio*/gold shops on Puno 6th block, eg *Cárdenas Hnos*, Puno 605.
**Embassies and consulates** Bolivian Consulate, on the north side of the plaza.
**Immigration** Peruvian immigration, Jr Ica 727, p 2, T082-571069. Get your exit stamp here if you're heading to Brazil or Bolivia.
**Internet** All over town, including along Av León Velarde and most main streets.
**Post** Serpost, Av León Velarde, cuadra 6.
**Telephone** **Telefónica**, on west side of plaza, adjoining the Municipalidad. A phone office on the plaza, next to **El Hornito**, sells cards for national and international calls.

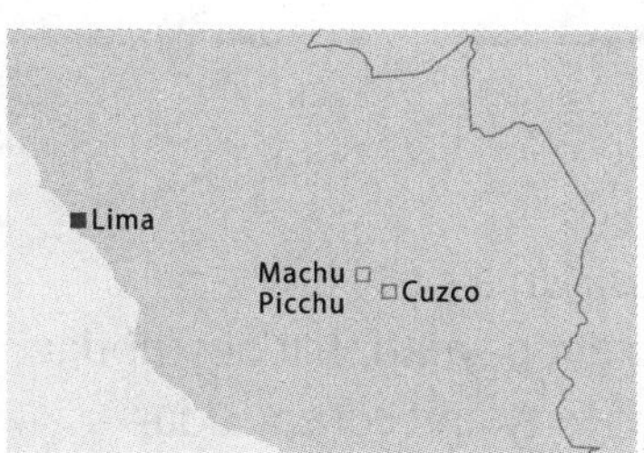

# Lima



## Footprint features

# Introduction

It is a well-established cliché to call Lima a city of contradictions, but it's difficult to get beyond that description. Here you'll encounter grinding poverty and conspicuous wealth in abundance. The hardships of the poor in this sprawling metropolis of 8,000,000 inhabitants are all too evident in the lives of those struggling to get by in the crowded streets and frantic bus lanes. The rubbish-strewn districts between airport and city and, even more so, the shantytowns on the outskirts emphasize the vast divisions within society. Most visitors head for Miraflores, San Isidro or Barranco, whose chic shops, bars and cafés would grace any major European city. Here, smart restaurants and elegant hotels rub shoulders with pre-Inca pyramids; neat parks and the cliff-top Larcomar shopping centre overlook the ocean and parapenters fly on the Pacific winds. Lima's image as a place to pass through quickly is enhanced by the thick grey blanket of cloud that descends in May and hangs around for the next seven months. Wait until the blanket is pulled aside in November to reveal bright blue skies and suddenly all Limeños descend on the city's popular beach resorts. While Lima has the ability to incite frustration and despair, it can also, given the chance, entertain, excite and inform. It has some of the finest historical monuments and museums in the country. The colonial centre, with its grand Plaza de Armas, fine churches and beautiful wooden balconies, is one of Peru's 10 UNESCO World Heritage sites and strenuous efforts are being made to refurbish the historical districts. The city's cuisine has earned it the title 'Gastronomic Capital of the Americas' and the bars, discos and *peñas* of Barranco and Miraflores ring to the sounds of techno and traditional music, and everything in between. Scratch beneath that coating of grime and decay and you'll find one of the most vibrant and hospitable cities in the world.

## Don't miss ...

1 **Plaza de Armas** Enclosed wooden balconies and a great cathedral. Seek out a colonial mansion, such as the Palacio Torre Tagle, to see the opulence of Spanish secular architecture, page 258.

2 **Museo de la Nación** Housed in a spectacular modern building, it has the most complete overview of precolonial Peruvian culture, page 262.

3 **Museo Larco** Some excellent exhibitions and lovely gardens, page 263.

4 **Circuito de Playas** If the sea and sky aren't merging into one on a cloudy day, late afternoon would be a good time to do this drive or taxi ride along the foot of the cliffs beside the Pacific, page 265.

5 **Barranco** Spend all evening in this suburb, where restaurants, bars, *peñas* and discos are all within walking distance, especially on Bolognesi, page 265.

6 **Eating out** For top-quality dining with a difference (setting and menu) try Huaca Pucllana at the foot of the pyramid, in Miraflores, page 272. Cheaper and more relaxed is Dalmacia, on Calle San Fernando, which has a Spanish feel, page 273.

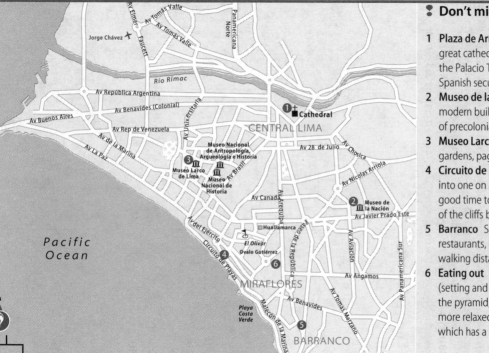

# Ins and outs → *Phone code: 01. Population: 8,000,000.*

## Getting there

### From the airport

All international flights land at **Jorge Chávez Airport** ⓘ *16 km west of the centre of the city, deep in the district of Callao, arrivals and departures information T511 6055, www.lap.com.pe*. Passengers arriving from international flights will find the *aduana* (customs) process to be relatively painless and efficient (a push-button, red light/green light system for customs baggage checks).

Transport into town is easy if a bit expensive. Tickets for official taxis are bought inside the airport building; the cheaper option is the taxis waiting outside the airport building, but within the airport perimeter fence. **Remise taxis** have representatives at desks outside both international and domestic arrivals. **Taxi Green** ⓘ *T01-484 4001, www.taxigreen.com*, has been recommended: US$8 to San Miguel, US$13 to the city centre, US$11.50 to San Isidro, US$15 to Miraflores and Barranco. **CMV** ⓘ *T01-422 4838, cmv@exalmar.com.pe*, charges US$17 to San Miguel, US$22 to the centre, US$26 to San Isidro and Miraflores and US$31 to Barranco; **Mitsui** ⓘ *T01-349 7722, remisse@mitsuiautomotriz.com*, charges US$22, US$27, US$31 and US$36 respectively

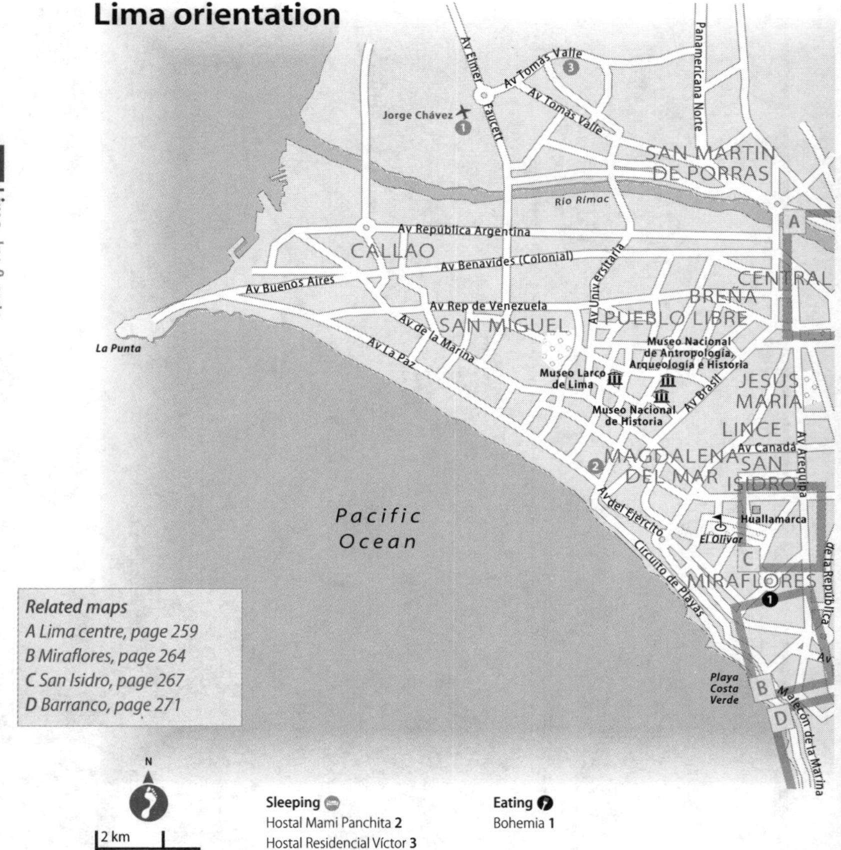

(prices for 3 people sharing).There are many taxi drivers offering their services outside arrivals with similar or higher prices (more at night). No taxis use meters, so make sure you fix the price before getting in and insist on being taken to the hotel of your choice, not the driver's. It's always best to have exact change in soles to avoid having to break a large banknote along the way. If you are feeling confident and not too jetlagged, go to the car park exit and find a taxi outside the perimeter, by the roundabout. They charge US$4-7 to the city centre. The security guards may help you find a taxi.

**Note** All vehicles can enter the airport for 10 minutes at no charge. After that, a fee is charged and taxis that have been waiting for more than the allotted free time will try to make the passenger pay the toll upon leaving the airport. Always establish who will pay before getting in.

The **Bus Super Shuttle** ⓘ *T01-517 2556, www.supershuttleairport.com*, runs from the airport to the San Miguel, US$15, and the centre, San Isidro, Miraflores and Barranco for US$19 (prices for 6 people sharing). To get to Miraflores by combi, take the one that says "Callao-Ate" with a big red "S". Known as "La S", the only direct connection between the airport and Miraflores. Catch it outside of the airport, on Av Faucett, US$0.45. From downtown Lima go to the junction of Alfonso Ugarte and Av Venezuela where many combis take the route "Todo aeropuerto – Avenida Faucett": US$0.35-0.45. At busy times (which is anytime other than very late at night or early in the morning) luggage may not be allowed on buses.

**Note** If arriving on a flight which lands late at night and you have a connection to Cuzco early next morning, you can stay the night at the airport.

**Airport facilities** All car hire firms have offices at the airport. The larger international car hire chains, such as **Budget, Dollar** and **Hertz,** are usually cheaper and have better-maintained vehicles than local firms. The larger, more expensive hotels in Miraflores and San Isidro have their own buses at the airport, and charge for transfer. For details of hotels near the airport, see page 265. **Global Net** ATM (accepting American Express, Visa, Mastercard and the Plus, Cirrus and Maestro systems), a *casa de cambio* (money changing desk) and a bank can be found at the same end as the stairs up to national departures. There are also exchange facilities in international arrivals, but rates are poorer than outside. There are public telephones around the airport and a **Teléfonica** *locutorio*, open 0700-2300 daily. Internet facilities are more expensive than in the city. The airport has an office of **i perú** ⓘ *T01-574 8000, daily 24 hrs*. Information desks can be found in the national foyer and in the international foyer. There is also a helpful desk in the international arrivals hall. It can make hotel and transport reservations. The **Perú Perú** shops sell gifts and books, including a selection of English-language guidebooks.

**Note** It is very important to reconfirm your flights when flying internally in Peru or leaving the country. This is generally done 48 to 72 hours in advance by phoning or visiting the airline office directly or, sometimes, by going to a travel agent for which you may have to pay a service charge. If you do not reconfirm your internal or international flight, you may not get on the plane. See also Customs, page 35. Airlines recommend that you arrive at the airport three hours before international flights and two hours before domestic flights. Check in for international flights closes one hour before departure, 30 minutes for domestic flights, after which you may not be permitted to board. Drivers of cars entering the car park are subject to a document check.

### From the bus terminal

If you arrive in Lima by bus, it is likely you'll pull into the main terminal at Jirón Carlos Zavala, just south of the historical centre of Lima. It is essential that you take a taxi to your hotel even if it's close, as this area is not safe day or night. Most of the hotels are to the west. Some of the high-class bus companies have terminals in safer areas.

## Getting around

Downtown Lima can be explored on foot in the daytime, but take all the usual precautions. At night, taxis are a safer option. The central hotels are fairly close to many of the tourist sites. Miraflores is 15 km south of the centre. Many of the better hotels and restaurants are located here or in neighbouring San Isidro.

The Lima public transport system, at first glance very intimidating, is actually quite good. There are three different types of vehicles that will stop whenever flagged down: buses, combis and colectivos. They can be distinguished by size; big and long, mid-size and mini-vans, respectively. The flat-rate fare for the first two types of vehicle is US$0.35; a little more for the third. Note that on public holidays, Sundays and from 2400 to 0500 every night, a small charge is added to the fare. Always try to pay with change to avoid delays and dirty looks from the *cobrador* (driver's assistant). » *For further details, see Getting around, page 23, and Transport, page 278.*

## Best time to visit

Only 12° south of the equator, you would expect a tropical climate, but Lima has two distinct seasons. Winter is from May to November, when a damp *garúa* (sea mist) hangs over the city, making everything look greyer than it is already. It is damp and cold, 8° to 15°C. The sun breaks through around November, revealing bright blue skies, and temperatures rise as high as 30°C. This is beach weather for all Limeños, when weekends become a very crowded raucous mix of sun, sea, salsa and *ceviche*. Note that the temperature in the coastal suburbs is lower than in the centre because of the sea's influence. You should protect yourself against the sun's rays when visiting the beaches around Lima, and elsewhere in Peru.

## Tourist information

Official tourist information is provided by offices of **i perú** ⓘ *Jorge Chávez International Airport, T01-574 8000, daily 24 hrs; Casa Basadre, Av Jorge Basadre 610, San Isidro, T01-421 1627, iperulima@promperu.gob.pe, Mon-Fri 0830-1830; Larcomar shopping centre, Módulo 14, Plaza Gourmet, Miraflores, T01-445 9400, Mon-Fri 1100-1300, 1400-2000.* Ask for the free *Peru Guide* published in English by Lima Editora, T01-444 0815, available at travel agencies.

As much an agency as a tourist office, but highly recommended nonetheless, is Siduith Ferrer de Vecchio of **Fertur Peru** ⓘ *Jr Junín 211, Plaza de Armas, T01-427 1958;*

*Schell 485, Miraflores, T01-242 1900, www.fertur-travel.com, Mon-Sat 0900-1900. In USA/Canada T(1)-877-247-0055 and in UK T020-3002 3811.* Her agency offers not only up-to-date, correct tourist information on a national level, but also great prices on national and international flights, discounts for those with ISIC and youth cards and for **South American Explorers** members (of which she is one). Other services include flight reconfirmations, hotel reservations, transfers to and from the airport or bus stations and tours.

**Info Perú** ⓘ *Jr de la Unión (Belén) 1066, of 102, T01-431 0117, www.infoperu.com.pe, Mon-Fri 0930-1800, Sat 0930-1400*, is a helpful private travel agency with lots of good advice; English and French spoken.

**South American Explorers** ⓘ *Piura 135, Miraflores (Casilla 3714, Lima 100), T01-445 3306, limaclub@saexplorers.org, Mon-Fri 0930-1700 (Wed 0930-2000) and Sat 0930-1300 (see also page 46)*, has a well-stocked map room for reference, an extensive library in English, a book exchange and provides access to member-written trip reports. Members are welcome to use the SAE's PO Box for receiving post and can also store luggage and valuables in their very secure deposit space. SAE sells official maps from the Instituto Geográfico Nacional, SAE-produced trekking maps, used equipment and a large variety of Peruvian crafts. Note that all imported merchandise sold at SAE is reserved for members only, no exceptions. They host regular presentations on various topics ranging from jungle trips to freedom of the press. SAE, apart from the services mentioned above, is simply a great place to step out of the hustle and bustle of Lima and delight in the serenity of a cup of tea, a magazine and a good conversation with a fellow traveller. » *For further sources of information, see Tourist information, page 46.*

## Background

Lima, originally named *La Ciudad de Los Reyes*, The City of Kings, in honour of the Magi, was founded on Epiphany in 1535 by Francisco Pizarro. From then until the independence of the South American republics in the early 19th century, it was the chief city of Spanish South America. The name Lima, a corruption of the Quechua name *Rimac* (speaker), was not adopted until the end of the 16th century.

At the time of the Conquest, Lima was already an important commercial centre. It continued to grow throughout the colonial years and by 1610, the population was 26,000, of whom 10,000 were Spaniards. This was the time of greatest prosperity. The commercial centre of the city was just off the Plaza de Armas in the Calle de Mercaderes (first block of Jirón de la Unión) and was full of merchandise imported from Spain, Mexico and China. All the goods from the mother country arrived at the port of Callao, from where they were distributed all over Peru and as far away as Argentina.

There were few cities in the Old World that could rival Lima's wealth and luxury, until the terrible earthquake of 1746. The city's notable elegance was instantly reduced to dust. Only 20 of the 3000 houses were left standing and an estimated 4000 people were killed. Despite the efforts of the Viceroy, José Manso de Velasco, to rebuild the city, Lima never recovered her former glory.

During the 19th century, the population dropped from 87,000 in 1810 to 53,000 in 1842, after the Wars of Independence, and the city suffered considerable material damage during the Chilean occupation which followed the War of the Pacific.

By the beginning of the 20th century the population had risen to 140,000 and the movement of people to the coastal areas meant that unskilled cheap labour was available to man the increasing numbers of factories. Around this time, major improvements were made to the city's infrastructure in the shape of modern sanitation, paved streets, new markets and plazas. For the entertainment of the burgeoning middle classes, a modern race track was opened in what is now the

Campo de Marte, as well as the municipal theatre, the Teatro Segura. Large-scale municipal improvements continued under the dictatorship of Augusto Leguía and the presidency of Oscar Benavides, who focused on education for the masses, housing facilities for workers and cheap restaurants in the slum areas which were growing up around Lima.

Lima, a city of over 8,000,000 people, continues to struggle to live up to its former reputation as the City of Kings. It is seriously affected by smog for much of the year and is surrounded by *pueblos jóvenes*, or shanty settlements of squatters who have migrated from all parts of Peru in search of work and higher education. Villa El Salvador, a few miles southeast of Lima, may be the world's biggest squatters' camp, with 350,000 people building up an award-winning self-governing community since 1971.

The city has changed drastically in the last few years. The commercial heart of Lima has begun to move away from the centre of town and has taken root in more upmarket districts such as Miraflores and San Isidro. Amid the traditional buildings which still survive soar many skyscrapers that have changed the old skyline.

# Sights

## Central Lima » *pages 265-281.*

### Plaza de Armas

One block south of the Río Rímac lies the Plaza de Armas, which has been declared a World Heritage site by UNESCO. The plaza used to be the city's most popular meeting point and main market. In the centre of the plaza is a bronze fountain dating from 1650.The **Palacio de Gobierno** (Government Palace) on the north side of the plaza stands on the site of the original palace built by Pizarro. When the Viceroyalty was founded it became the official residence of the representative of the crown. Despite the opulent furnishings inside, the exterior remained a poor sight throughout colonial times, with shops lining the front facing the plaza. The facade was remodelled in the second half of the 19th century, then transformed in 1921, following a terrible fire. In 1937, the palace was totally rebuilt. The changing of the guard is at 1200. **Tours** are available in Spanish and English Monday-Friday 1400-1730, or 1100 for groups, 45 minutes, free; book 2 days in advance at the Oficina de Turismo, of 201 (ask guard for directions); foreigners must take passport. Shorts may not be worn.

Lima **cathedral** ⓘ *T01-427 9647, Mon-Sat 0900-1630, all-inclusive entrance ticket US$1.50*, stands on the site of two previous buildings. The first, finished in 1555, was partly paid for by Francisca Pizarro on the condition that her father, the *conquistador*, was buried there. A larger church, however, was soon required to complement the city's status as an Archbishopric. In 1625, the three naves of the main building were completed while work continued on the towers and main door. The new building was reduced to rubble in the earthquake of 1746 and the existing church, completed in 1755, is a reconstruction on the lines of the original.

The interior is immediately impressive, with its massive columns and high nave. Also of note are the splendidly carved stalls (mid-17th century), the silver-covered altars surrounded by fine woodwork, the mosaic-covered walls bearing the coats of arms of Lima and Pizarro and an allegory of Pizarro's commanders, the 'Thirteen Men of Isla del Gallo'. The assumed remains of Francisco Pizarro lie in a glass coffin in a small chapel on the right of the entrance, though more recent research has indicated that they actually reside in the crypt.

There is a **Museo de Arte Religioso** in the cathedral, with free guided tours (English available, give tip); ask to see the picture restoration room.

Next to the cathedral is the **Archbishop's Palace**, rebuilt in 1924, with a superb wooden balcony. On the opposite side of the plaza is the **Municipalidad de Lima**, just

## Lima centre

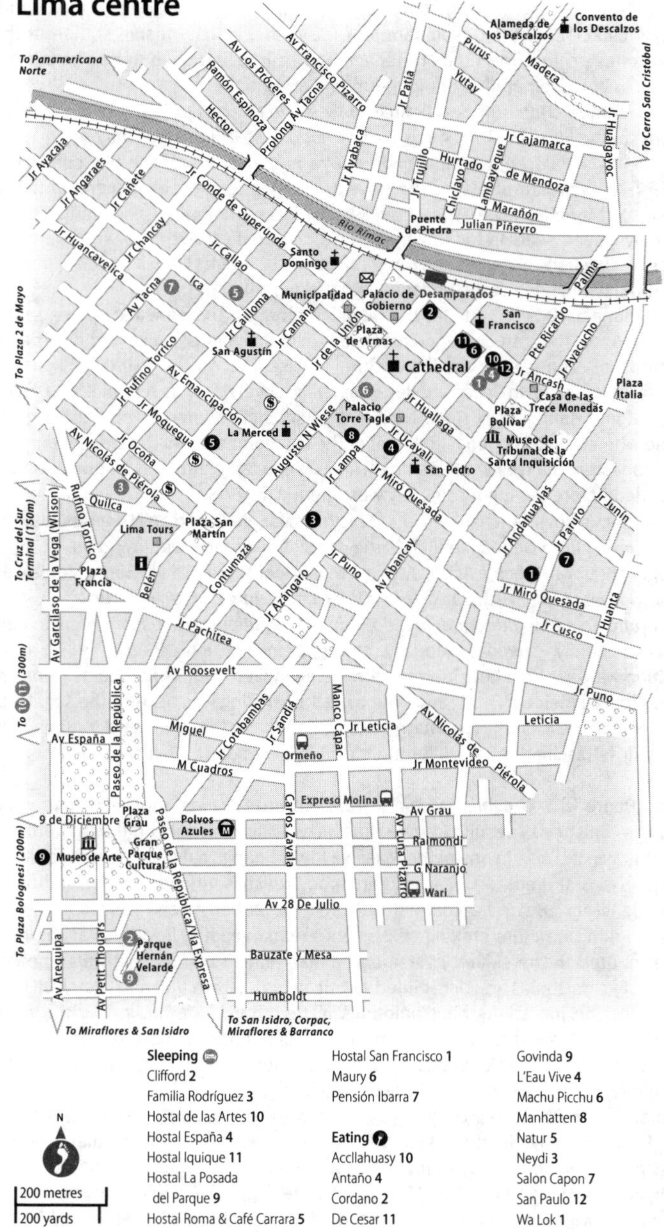

 behind which is **Pasaje Ribera el Viejo**, a pleasant place to hang out with several good cafés with outdoor seating.

## Around the Plaza de Armas → *Clockwise from north to northwest*

The **Puente de Piedra**, behind the Palacio de Gobierno, is a Roman-style stone bridge built in 1610. Until about 1870 it was the only bridge strong enough to take carriages across the Río Rímac to the district of the same name. East of the bridge is the Central Railway's **Estación de los Desamparados**. The name, which means 'station of the helpless ones', comes from the orphanage and church that used to be nearby. The station now holds temporary, but long-running exhibitions.

The baroque church of **San Francisco** ⓘ *Jr Lampa, corner of Ancash, 1st block northeast of the Plaza de Armas, T01-427 1381, daily by guided tour only 0930-1730, US$2, US$0.50 children*, was finished in 1674 and was one of the few edifices to withstand the 1746 earthquake. The nave and aisles are lavishly decorated in the Moorish, or Mudéjar, style. The choir, which dates from 1673, is notable for its beautifully carved seats in Nicaraguan hardwood and its Mudéjar ceiling. There is a valuable collection of paintings by the Spanish artist, Francisco de Zubarán (1598-1664), which depict the apostles and various saints.

The **monastery** is famous for the Sevillian tilework and panelled ceiling in the cloisters (1620). The 17th-century *retablos* in the main cloister are carved from cedar and represent scenes from the life of San Francisco, as do the paintings. A broad staircase leading down to a smaller cloister is covered by a remarkable carved wooden dome dating from 1625. Next to this smaller cloister is the Capilla de la Soledad where a café is open to the public. The catacombs under the church and part of the monastery are well worth seeing. This is where an estimated 25,000 Limeños were buried before the main cemetery was opened in 1808.

Two blocks down Ancash, at No 536, is the **Casa de las Trece Monedas**, built in 1787 by counts from Genoa. It still has the original doors and window grills.

Turn right down Avenida Abancay to the **Museo del Tribunal de la Santa Inquisición** ⓘ *Plaza Bolívar, C Junín 548, near the corner of Av Abancay, daily 0900-1700, free, students offer to show you round for a tip; good explanations in English.* The main hall, with a splendidly carved mahogany ceiling, remains untouched. The Court of Inquisition was first held here in 1584, after being moved from its first home opposite the church of La Merced. From 1829 until 1938 the building was used by the senate. In the basement there is an accurate recreation in situ of the gruesome tortures. The whole tour is fascinating, if a little morbid. A description in English is available at the desk.

**San Pedro** ⓘ *Jr Ucayali, 3rd block from Plaza de Armas, Mon-Sat 0930-1145, 1700-1800*, finished by Jesuits in 1638, has an unadorned facade, different from any other church in the city. In one of the massive towers hangs a five-tonne bell called *La Abuelita* (the Grandmother), first rung in 1590, which sounded the Declaration of Independence in 1821. The contrast between the sober exterior and sumptuous interior couldn't be more striking. The altars are marvellous, in particular the high altar, attributed to the skilled craftsman, Matías Maestro. The church also boasts Moorish-style balconies and rich, gilded woodcarvings in the choir and vestry, all tiled throughout. The most important paintings in the church are hung near the main entrance. In the monastery, the sacristy is a beautiful example of 17th-century architecture. Also of note are La Capilla de Nuestra Señora de la O and the penitentiary. Several viceroys are buried below.

**Palacio Torre Tagle** ⓘ *Jr Ucayali 363, Mon-Fri during working hours, visitors may enter the patio only*, is the city's best surviving specimen of secular colonial architecture. It was built in 1735 for Don José Bernardo de Tagle y Bracho, to whom King Philip V gave the title of First Marquis of Torre Tagle. The house remained in the family until it was acquired by the government in 1918. Today, it is still used by the foreign ministry but visitors are allowed to enter courtyards to inspect the fine Moorish-influenced woodcarving in the balconies, the wrought-iron work, and a 16th-century coach complete with commode. From the palace, turn right then left to return to the Plaza de Armas.

**Santo Domingo** ⓘ *Jr Camaná, 1 block northwest from the Plaza de Armas past the post office, T01-427 6793, Mon-Sat 0900-1230, 1500-1800, Sun and holidays, mornings only, US$0.75*. The church and monastery were built in 1549. The church is still as originally planned, with a nave and two aisles covered by a vaulted ceiling, though the present ceiling dates from the 17th century. The cloister is one of the most attractive in the city and dates from 1603. There is a second, much less elaborate cloister. A chapel, dedicated to San Martín de Porres, one of Peru's most revered saints, leads off from a side corridor. Between the two cloisters is the Chapter House (1730), which was once the premises of the Universidad de San Marcos. Beneath the sacristy are the tombs of San Martín de Porres and Santa Rosa de Lima (first saint of the Americas and patron saint of Lima). In 1669, Pope Clement presented the alabaster statue of Santa Rosa in front of the altar.

Behind Santo Domingo is the **Alameda Chabuca Granda**, named after one of Peru's most famous singers and composers. Every afternoon musicians and artists give free shows and you can sample Peruvian dishes and sweets.

## Southwest of the Plaza de Armas

**Jirón de La Unión**, the main shopping street, runs southwest from the Plaza de Armas. It has been converted into a pedestrian precinct which teems with life in the evening. In the two blocks south of Jirón Unión, known as Calle Belén, several shops sell souvenirs and curios.

The first mass in Lima was said on the site of the first church to be built at **La Merced** ⓘ *Plazuela de la Merced, Unión y Miró Quesada, T01-427 8199, church open Mon-Sat 0800-1245, 1600-2000, Sun 0700-1300, 1600-2000; monastery open daily 0800-1200, 1500-1730*. At Independence the Virgin of La Merced was made a marshal of the Peruvian army. The restored colonial facade is a fine example of baroque architecture. Inside are some magnificent altars and the tilework on some of the walls is noteworthy. A door from the right of the nave leads into the monastery where you can see some 18th-century religious paintings in the sacristy. The cloister dates from 1546.

South of Jirón de la Unión, the **Plaza San Martín** has a statue of San Martín in the centre. The plaza has been restored and is now a nice place to sit and relax.

The **Gran Parque Cultural de Lima** ⓘ *daily 0800-2030*, was inaugurated in January 2000 by both the mayor of Lima, Alberto Andrade, and the then-president Alberto Fujimori. It has a medium-sized outdoor amphitheatre, Japanese garden, food court and children's activities. Relaxing strolls through this green, peaceful and safe oasis in the centre of Lima are recommended. Within the park is the **Museo de Arte** ⓘ *9 de Diciembre (Paseo Colón) 125, T01-423 4732, http://museoarte.perucultural.org.pe/, Thu-Tue 1000-1700, US$3.65, free guide, signs in English*, which was built in 1868 as the Palacio de la Exposición. The building was designed by Alexandre Gustave Eiffel. There are more than 7000 exhibits, giving a chronological history of Peruvian cultures and art from the Paracas civilization up to today. They include excellent examples of 17th- and 18th-century Cuzco paintings, a beautiful display of carved furniture, heavy silver and jewelled stirrups and also pre-Columbian pottery. A *filmoteca* (cinema club) is on the premises and shows films almost every night; consult the local paper for details, or look in the museum itself.

## North of the centre

Though this part of the city enjoyed considerable popularity in colonial times, it could no longer be considered fashionable. North of the Río Rímac, the **Alameda de los Descalzos** was designed in the early 17th century as a restful place to stroll and it soon became one of the city's most popular meeting places. On the Alameda is the **Convento de los Descalzos** ⓘ *T01-481 0441, 1000-1300, 1500-1800, closed Tue, US$1, by guided tour only, 45 mins in Spanish.* Founded in 1592, it contains over 300 paintings of the Cuzco, Quito and Lima schools, which line the four main cloisters and two ornate chapels. The chapel of El Carmen was constructed in 1730 and is notable for its baroque gold leaf altar. A small chapel dedicated to Nuestra Señora de la Rosa Mística has some fine Cuzqueño paintings. The museum shows the life of the Franciscan friars during colonial and early republican periods. The cellar, infirmary, pharmacy and a typical cell have been restored.

## San Borja

The district of San Borja lies southeast of the centre. From Avenida Garcilaso de la Vega in downtown Lima take a combi with a window sticker that says 'Javier Prado/ Aviación'. Get off at the 21st block of Javier Prado at Avenida Aviación. From Miraflores take a bus down Avenida Arequipa to Avenida Javier Prado (27th block), then take a bus with a window sticker saying 'Todo Javier Prado' or 'Aviación'. A taxi from downtown Lima or from the centre of Miraflores costs US$2.

### Museo de la Nación

ⓘ *Av Javier Prado Este 2465, T01-476 9876, Tue-Sun 0900-1700, closed on major public holidays, US$2.50, 50% discount with ISIC card, guided tours last about 4 hrs.* This is the anthropological and archaeological museum for the exhibition and study of the art and history of the aboriginal races of Peru. There are good explanations in Spanish and English on Peruvian history, and ceramics, textiles and displays of many ruins in Peru. The museum is arranged so that you can follow the development of Peruvian pre-colonial history through to the time of the Incas. A visit is recommended before you go to see the archaeological sites themselves. There are displays on the tomb of El Señor de Sipán, artefacts from Batán Grande near Chiclayo (Sicán culture), reconstructions of the friezes found at Huaca La Luna and Huaca El Brujo, near Trujillo, and of Sechín and other sites. Temporary exhibitions are held in the basement, where there is also an Instituto de Cultura bookshop. The museum has a cafeteria.



## Pueblo Libre

Pueblo Libre is west of the centre and is the location of three museums. To get there take any public transport on Avenida Brasil with a window sticker saying 'Todo Brasil'. For the Museo Arqueológico Rafael Larco Herrera, get off at the 15th block and take a bus down Avenida Bolívar. For the Museo Nacional de Antropología, Arqueología e Historia, get off at the 21st block called Avenida Vivanco; walk about five blocks down Vivanco and the museum will be on your left. A taxi from downtown Lima costs US$1.50-2.50.

From Miraflores, you need to take bus SM 18 Carabayllo-Chorrillos, marked 'Bolívar, Arequipa, Larcomar'. For the Museo Arqueológico Rafael Larco Herrera get off at block 15 of Bolívar. For the Museo Nacional de Antropología, Arqueología e Historia get out at block 8 of Bolívar, by the Hospital Santa Rosa, and walk down San Martín 5 blocks till you see the 'blue line'; turn left. A taxi from Miraflores costs US$2-2.50.

### Museo Nacional de Antropología, Arqueología e Historia

ⓘ *Plaza Bolívar (not to be confused with Plaza Bolívar in the centre), T01-463 5070, http://museonacional.perucultural.org.pe, Tue-Sun 0930-1700 (closed 25 Dec and 1 Jan), US$3.35, students US$1, guides available for groups.*

On display are ceramics of the Chimú, Nazca, Mochica and Pachacámac cultures, various Inca curiosities and works of art, and interesting textiles. The museum houses the Raimondi Stela and the Tello obelisk from Chavín, and a reconstruction of one of the galleries at Chavín. It also has a model of Machu Picchu.

## Museo Nacional de Historia

ⓘ *Plaza Bolívar, next to the Museo de Antropología y Arqueología, T01-463 2009, Tue-Sat 0900-1700, Sun and holidays 0900-1600, US$3.*

This museum is housed in a mansion built by Viceroy Pezuela and occupied by San Martín (1821-22) and Bolívar (1823-26). The exhibits comprise colonial and early republican paintings, manuscripts, portraits, etc. The paintings are mainly of historical episodes.

## Museo Larco de Lima

ⓘ *Av Bolívar 1515, T01-461 1312, www.museolarco.org, daily 0900-1800 including holidays, US$10 (half price for students), disabled access, guides, texts in English, Spanish and French. Photography not allowed.*

Located in an 18th-century mansion, itself built on a seventh-century pre-Columbian pyramid, this museum has a collection which gives an excellent overview of the development of Peruvian cultures through their pottery. It has the world's largest collection of Moche, Sicán and Chimú pieces. There is a Gold and Silver of Ancient Peru exhibition, a magnificent textile collection and a fascinating erotica section. It is surrounded by beautiful gardens and has the highly regarded *Café del Museo* (www.cafedelmuseo.com).

> *A 'blue line' marked on the pavement (very faded in places), links the Museo Nacional de Antropología, Arqueología e Historia to the Museo Larco de Lima, 10 mins' walk away.*

## San Isidro » pages 265-281. See also map, page 267.

The district of San Isidro combines some upscale residential areas, important commercial zones, many of Lima's fanciest hotels, numerous good restaurants and a huge golf course, smack in the middle. Along Avenida La República is **El Olivar**, an old olive grove planted by the first Spaniards. It's now a beautiful park and definitely worth a stroll by day or night.

At Avenida Rosario and Avenida Rivera are the ruins of **Huallamarca**, or **Pan de Azúcar** ⓘ *US$1.75*, a restored adobe pyramid of the Maranga culture, dating from about AD 100-500. There is a small site museum on the premises.

## Miraflores » pages 265-281.

Miraflores, apart from being an attractive residential part of Lima, is also full of fashionable shops, cafés, discotheques, fine restaurants and good hotels and guesthouses. In the centre of all this is the beautiful Parque Central de Miraflores – **Parque Kennedy** – between Avenida Larco and Avenida Oscar Benavides (locally known as Avenida Diagonal). This well-kept park has a small open-air theatre with performances from Thursday to Sunday, ranging from Afro-Peruvian music to rock'n'roll. Towards the bottom of the park is a nightly crafts market open from 1700 to 2300.

At the end of Avenida Larco and running along the Malecón de la Reserva is the renovated **Parque Salazar** and the very modern shopping centre called **Centro Comercial Larcomar**. Here the shopping centre's terraces, which have been carved out of the cliff, contain expensive shops, hip cafés and restaurants, an open-air internet café and discos. The balustrades have a beautiful view of the ocean and sunset. The 12-screen cinema is one of the best in Lima and even has a cine-bar in the twelfth theatre. Don't forget to check out the Cosmic Bowling Alley with its black lights and fluorescent balls. A few hundred metres to the north is the renovated Parque Champagnat and then, across the bridge over the gorge, the famous **Parque del Amor**

## Miraflores

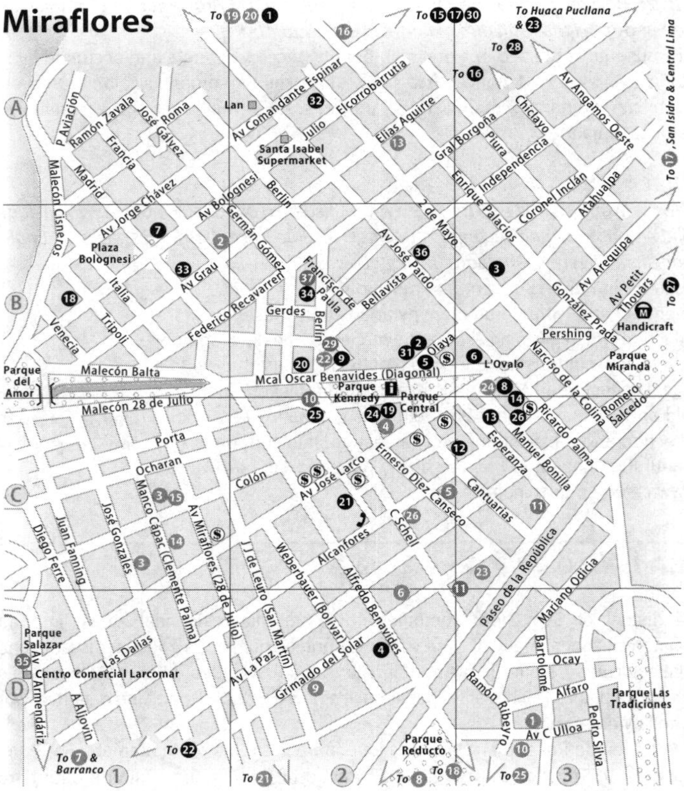

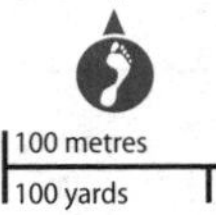


**Sleeping**
Adventures House **20** *A2*
Albergue Turístico Juvenil Internacional **1** *D3*
Albergue Verde **9** *D2*
Antigua Miraflores **2** *B1*
Casa Andina **21** *D2*
Esperanza **11** *C3*
Eurobackpackers **14** *C1*
Explorer's House **19** *A1*
Flying Dog Backpackers **4** *C2*
Friend's House **3** *C1*
Home Perú **17** *A3*
Hostal El Patio **5** *C2*
Hostal José Luis **18** *D3*
Hostal La Castellana **6** *D2*
Inka Lodge **13** *A2*
José Antonio **15** *C1*
Lion Backpackers **23** *C3*
Loki Backpackers **24** *B3*
Mansión San Antonio **25** *D3*
Miraflores Park **7** *D1*
San Antonio Abad **10** *D3*
Sipán **8** *D2*
Sonesta Posadas del Inca **26** *C2*
Stop & Drop **22** *B2*
Wayruro's Backpackers **16** *A2*

**Eating**
Astrid y Gaston **12** *C3*
Bohemia **30** *A3*
Café Beirut **31** *B2*
Café Café **2** *B2*
Café de la Paz **19** *C2*
Café Tarata **21** *C2*
Café Voltaire **3** *B3*
Café Z **20** *B2*
C'est Si Bon **15** *A2*
Chez Philippe **32** *A2*
Coco de Mer **33** *B1*
Dalmacia **22** *D1*
Dino's Pizza **17** *A2*
Dove Vai **5** *B2*
El Kapallaq **27** *B3*
El Parquetito **24** *C2*
El Señorío de Sulco **1** *A1*
Fluid **34** *B2*
Haiti **6** *B3*
Huaca Pucllana **23** *A3*
Las Brujas de Cachiche **7** *B1*
La Tiendecita Blanca **8** *B3*
La Trattoria **13** *C3*
Madre Natura **16** *A3*
Pardo's Chicken **4** *D2*
Pizza Street **9** *B2*
Ricota **21** *C2*
Sandwich.com **5** *B2*
Shehadi **5** *B2*
Sí Señor **18** *B1*
Super Rueda **25** *C2*
Tapas Bar **26** *C3*
Vivaldi **14** *C3*
Wa Lok **28** *A3*

**Bars & clubs**
Bartinis **35** *D1*
Dubliner's Irish Pub **37** *B2*
Media Naranja **10** *C2*
Murphys **11** *C3*
The Old Pub **29** *B2*
Voluntarios Pub **36** *B2*

where on just about any night of the week you'll see at least one wedding party taking photos of the happy couple. Peruvians are nothing if not romantic.



**Huaca Pucllana** ⓘ *at the intersection of C Borgoña y Tarapacá, near the 45th block of Av Arequipa, T01-445 8695, http://pucllana.perucultural.org.pe, Wed-Mon 0900-1600, closed holidays, US$2, includes compulsory guide in Spanish*, is a fifth- to eighth-century ceremonial and administrative centre of the pre-Inca Lima culture. The small adobe-brick pyramid is 23 m high. It has a museum and handicrafts shop.

## Barranco and the seaside

» *pages 265-281.*

*See also map, page 271.*

South of Miraflores is Barranco, which was already a seaside resort by the late 17th century. During Spanish rule, it was a getaway for the rich who lived in or near the centre. It's now an intellectual haven with artists' workshops and chic galleries.

The attractive public library, formerly the town hall, stands on the delightful plaza. Nearby is the interesting *Bajada*, a steep path leading down to the beach, where many of Lima's artists live. The **Puente de los Suspiros** (Bridge of Sighs) leads towards the Malecón, with fine views of the bay.

*The beach, although not safe to walk at night, has a great view of the whole Lima coastline from Chorrillos to La Punta.*

Barranco is a quiet, sleepy suburb in the day but comes alive on weekend nights when the city's young flock here to party. Squeezed into a few streets are dozens of good bars and restaurants. No visit to Lima would be complete without a tour of Barranco's 'sights'.

### Lima's beaches

Lima sits next to an open bay, with its two points at **La Punta** (Callao) and **Punta La Chira** (Chorrillos). During the summer (December-March), beaches get very crowded all week, even though all beaches lining Lima's coast have been declared unsuitable for swimming. A stroll on the beach is pleasant during daylight but, when the sun goes down, the thieves come out and it is very dangerous. Camping is a very bad idea.

The **Circuito de Playas**, beginning with **Playa Arica** (30 km from Lima) and ending with **San Bartolo** (45 km from Lima), has many great beaches for all tastes. For a beach that is always packed with people, there's **El Silencio** or **Punta Rocas**. Quieter options are **Señoritas** or **Los Pulpos**. **Punta Hermosa** has volleyball tournaments and surfing.

## Sleeping

All hotels and restaurants in the upper price brackets charge 19% state tax (IVA) and 10% service on top of prices. In hotels foreigners pay no IVA and the amount of service charged is up to the hotel. Neither is included in the prices below, unless indicated otherwise. The more expensive hotels charge in dollars according to the parallel rate of exchange at midnight. The central colonial heart of Lima is not as safe at night as the more upmarket areas of San Isidro, Miraflores and Barranco. If you are only staying a short time and want to see the main sights, the centre is convenient, but do take care. San Isidro is the poshest district, while Miraflores has a good mix of places to stay, great ocean views, bookshops, restaurants and cinemas. From here you can commute to the centre by bus (30 to 45 mins) or by taxi (20 to 30 mins). Barranco, which is more bohemian, is further out.

**Near the airport** *map p254*

There are lots of places to stay on **Av Tomás Valle**, the road from the airport to the Panamericana Norte, but they are almost without exception short stay and unsafe.

**L Ramada Costa del Sol**, Av Elmer Faucett s/n, T01-711 2000, www.ramada.com. New hotel within the airport perimeter. Offers day rates as well as overnights if you can't get into the city.

B-D **Hostal Residencial Victor**, Manuel Mattos 325, Urb San Amadeo de Garagay, Lima 31, T01-569 4662, hostalvictor@terra.com.pe. 5 mins from the airport by taxi, or phone or email in advance for free pick-up, large comfortable rooms, with bath, hot water, cable TV, free luggage store, free internet and 10% discount for Footprint book owners, American breakfast, evening meals can be ordered locally, mall with restaurants, fast food and gym nearby, very helpful, owner Víctor Melgar has a free reservation service for Peru and Bolivia.

**Central Lima** *p258, map p259*

B **Maury**, Jr Ucayali 201, T01-428 8188, http://ekeko2.rcp.net.pe/hotelmaury/. Fancy, secure, breakfast included, most luxurious hotel in the historical centre.

B **The Clifford Hotel**, Parque Hernán Velarde 27, near 2nd block of Av Petit Thouars, Sta Beatriz, T01-433 4249, www.thecliffordhotel.com.pe. Nicely converted, republican town house with 20 rooms in a quiet and leafy park. Also has suites (**A**), price includes breakfast, a welcome drink and an airport transfer (either there or back), good value. Bar and conference room.

C **Hostal La Posada del Parque**, Parque Hernán Velarde 60, near 2nd block of Av Petit Thouars, Santa Beatriz, T01-433 2412, www.incacountry.com. Run by Sra Mónica Moreno and her husband Leo Rovayo who both speak good English, a charmingly refurbished old house in a safe area, excellent bathrooms, cable TV, breakfast US$3 extra, airport transfer (24 hrs) US$14 for up to 3 passengers. Highly recommended as excellent value.

D **Hostal Roma**, Jr Ica 326, T/F01-427 7576, www.hostalroma.8m.com. With bath, **E** without bath, hot water all day, safe to leave luggage, basic but clean, often full, internet extra but good, motorcycle parking (**Roma Tours**, helpful for trips, reservations, flight confirmations, Errol Branca speaks English). Highly recommended.

E **Hostal Iquique**, Jr Iquique 758, Breña, T01-433 4724, http://barrioperu.terra.com.pe/hiquique. With bathroom. Discount for SAE members. Clean but noisy and draughty, friendly, use of kitchen, warm water, storage facilities, safe, internet, rooms on the top floor at the back are best. Repeated recommendations.

E-F **Hostal de las Artes**, Jr Chota 1460, Breña, T01-433 0031, http://arteswelcome.tripod.com. **F** without bath (no singles with bath), **G** pp in dormitory, Dutch owned, English spoken, safes in rooms and safe luggage store, nice colonial building, solar hot water system, book exchange, airport transfer US$12. Recommended.

F **Hostal España**, Jr Azángaro 105, T01-427 9196, www.hotelespanaperu.com. **E** with private bath (3 rooms), **G** per person in dormitory, fine old building, shared bathroom, hot showers, friendly, French and English spoken, internet service, motorcycle parking, luggage store (free), laundry service, don't leave valuables in rooms, roof garden, good café, can be very busy.

F **Hostal San Francisco**, Jr Azángaro 125-127, T01-426 2735, hostalsf@lanpro.com.pe. Dormitories with and without bathrooms, safe, Italian/Peruvian owners, good service, internet and *cafetería*.

G per person **Familia Rodríguez**, Av Nicolás de Piérola 730, 2nd floor, T01-423 6465, jotajot@terra.com.pe. With breakfast, clean, friendly, popular, some rooms noisy, stores luggage, also has dormitory accommodation with only 1 bathroom (same price), transport to airport US$10 per person for 2 people, US$4 per person for 3 or more, offers good information, secure. Recommended.

G **Pensión Ibarra**, Av Tacna 359, 14th-16th floor (no sign), T01-427 8603, pensionibarra@ekno.com. Breakfast US$2, discount for longer stay. Use of kitchen, balcony with views of the city, clean, friendly, very helpful owner, hot water, full board available (good small café next door).

**San Isidro** *p263, map p267*

LL **Country Club**, Los Eucaliptos 590, T01-611 9000, www.hotelcountry.com.

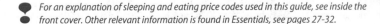

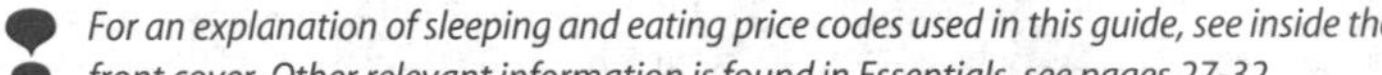
*For an explanation of sleeping and eating price codes used in this guide, see inside the front cover. Other relevant information is found in Essentials, see pages 27-32.*

Excellent service and luxurious rooms in this National Monument, safes in rooms, cable TV, free internet for guests, good bar and restaurant. It also has all the fitness options you'd expect, plus privileges at the San Isidro golf club. Classically stylish.

**LL Sonesta Hotel El Olivar**, Pancho Fierro 194, T01-712 6000, www.sonesta.com/peru_lima/. One of the top 5-star hotels in Lima, luxurious, modern, with many eating options, bar, garden, swimming pool, quiet, popular and very good.

**L Libertador**, Los Eucaliptos 550, T01-421 6666, www.libertador.com.pe (reservations: Las Begonias 441, office 240, T01-442 1995/444 3720). **Golden Tulip** hotel, overlooking the golf course, full facilities for business travellers, comfortable rooms, fine service, good restaurant. A rich collection of true hospitality and Peruvian culture with hotels in Arequipa, Cuzco, Huaraz, Máncora, Puno, Tambopata, Trujillo, Valle del Colca, Urubamba and Valle Sagrado.

**AL Garden Hotel**, Rivera Navarrete 450, T01-442 1771, reservas@gardenhotel.com.pe. Price includes tax, breakfast and internet. Good, large beds, shower, small restaurant, ideal for business visitors. Recommended.

**C Hostal Mami Panchita**, Av Federico Gallessi 198, T01-263 7203, www.mami panchita.com. Dutch and Peruvian owned, English, French, Dutch, Spanish and German

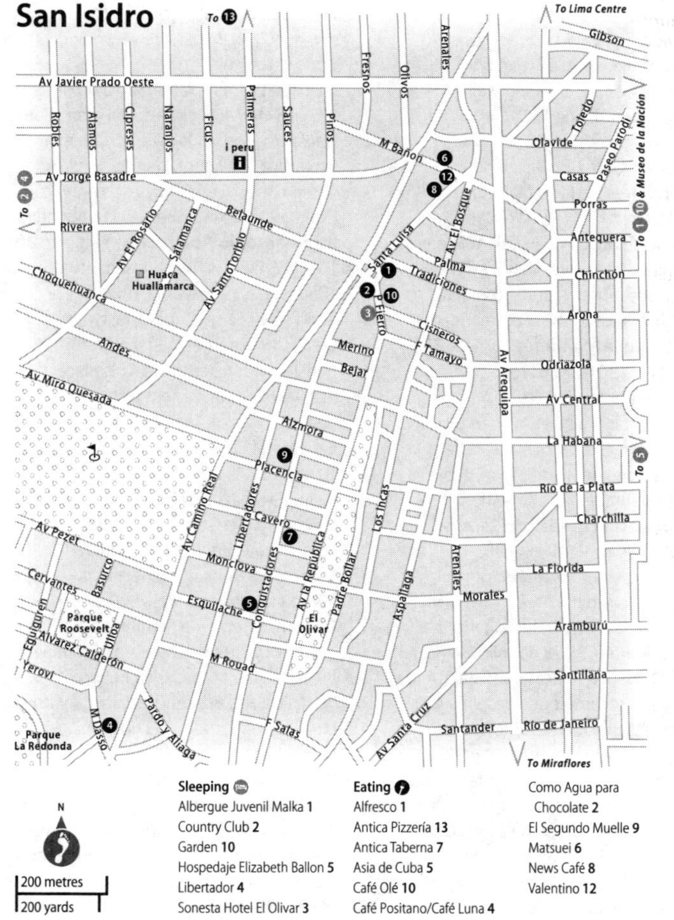

spoken, includes breakfast and welcome drink, comfortable rooms with bath, hot water, living room and bar, patio, email service, book exchange, **Raymi Travel** agency (good service), 15 mins from airport, 15 mins from Miraflores, 20 mins from historical centre.

**D-E Hospedaje Elizabeth Ballon**, Av del Parque Norte 265, San Isidro, T01-980 07557, http://chezelizabeth.typepad.fr. Family house in residential area 7 mins' walk from Cruz del Sur bus station. Shared or private bathrooms, TV room, laundry, luggage storage, breakfast extra, airport transfers US$12.

**F Albergue Juvenil Malka**, Los Lirios 165 (near 4th block of Av Javier Prado Este), T01-442 0162, hostelmalka@terra.com.pe. Youth hostel, 20% discount with ISIC card, dormitory style, 4-8 beds per room, English spoken, cable TV, laundry, kitchen, nice café, climbing wall. Highly recommended.

**Miraflores** *p263, map p264*

**LL Miraflores Park**, Av Malecón de la Reserva 1035, T01-242 3000, www.mira-park.com. An **Orient Express** hotel, beautiful ocean views, excellent service and facilities, at the top of the range in Lima. Highly recommended.

**AL-A Antigua Miraflores**, Av Grau 350 at C Francia, T01-241 6116, www.peru-hotels-inns.com. A small, elegant hotel in a quiet but central location, very friendly service, tastefully furnished and decorated, gym, cable TV, good restaurant. Recommended.

**AL-A Sonesta Posadas del Inca**, Alcanfores 490, T01-241 7688, www.sonestaperu.com. Part of renowned chain of hotels, convenient location, cable TV, a/c, restaurant.

**A Casa Andina**, Av 28 de Julio 1088, T01-241 4050, www.casa-andina.com.pe. One of this recommended chain, with similar facilities and decor to those in the Cuzco area. Very neat, with many useful touches, comfortable beds, internet access and Wi-Fi, a/c, fridge, safe, laundry service, buffet breakfast, other meals available.

**A José Antonio**, 28 de Julio 398, T01-445 7743, www.hotelesjoseantonio.com. This clean, friendly hotel is good in all respects, including the restaurant, huge rooms with jacuzzi baths, helpful, some English spoken, internet, swimming pool. Recommended.

**A Mansión San Antonio**, Av Tejada 531, T01-445 9665, www.mansionsanantonio.com. Bed and breakfast, 7 suites of varying standards on 3 floors in a quiet residential area, safe, bar, coffee shop, Wi-Fi in public areas, swimming pool, stylish and gay friendly.

**B Esperanza**, Esperanza 350, T01-444 2411, http://barrioperu.terra.com.pe/htlesperanza. A clean, modern hotel with 40 en suite rooms. The rooms can't boast a lot of character, but the location, only a few mins' walk from Parque Central in Miraflores, is excellent. Good hot water and the staff, including the manager Max Vargas, are very friendly. Good value.

**B Hostal La Castellana**, Grimaldo del Solar 222, T01-444 4662, lacastellan@terra.com.pe. Pleasant, good value, nice garden, safe, expensive restaurant, laundry, English spoken, special price for South American Explorers (SAE) members. Recommended.

**B San Antonio Abad**, Ramón Ribeyro 301, T01-447 6766, www.hotelsanantonio abad.com. Clean, secure, quiet, good service, welcoming, tasty breakfasts, internet, 1 free airport transfer with reservation. This place is justifiably popular and it is frequently recommended.

**B-C Hostal El Patio**, Diez Canseco 341, T01-444 2107, www.hostalelpatio.net. Includes breakfast, reductions for long stays, very nice suites and rooms, comfortable, English and French spoken, convenient, *comedor*, gay friendly. Recommended.

**C Sipán**, Paseo de la República 6171, T01-447 0884, www.hotelsipan.com.pe. Breakfast and tax included in price. Very pleasant, in a residential area, with bath, cable TV, fridge, security box, internet access.

**D-E Home Perú**, Av Arequipa 4501 (no sign), T01-241 9898, www.homeperu.com. In a 1920s mansion with huge rooms, with breakfast, **E-F** pp with shared bath, group discounts, very welcoming and helpful, use of kitchen, luggage store, English spoken, laundry service, internet, safe, near Plaza Vea hypermarket. Can help with bus and plane tickets, connected to other *hostales* in the country. Recommended.

**D-E Lion Backpackers**, Grimaldo del Solar 139, T01-447 1827, www.lionbackpackers.com. Double rooms and dormitories, 3 blocks from Parque Kennedy, nice atmosphere, safe, breakfast, very helpful.

**E** per person **Inka Lodge**, Elias Aguirre 278, T01-242 6989, www.inkalodge.com. Also with dormitories (**F** per person), convenient, fresh breakfast included, internet, laundry, very welcoming.

**E** per person **Hostal José Luis**, Francisco de Paula Ugarriza 727, San Antonio, T01-444 1015, www.hoteljoseluis.com. Price includes breakfast. Rooms with bath, hot water, safe, quiet, clean, internet, kitchen facilities, friendly, popular, English spoken.

**E-F** per person **Eurobackpackers**, Manco Cápac 471 (no sign, look for the cat with the world on his stick), T01-791 2945, www.eurobackpackers.com. Dormitory, also doubles, breakfast included, family atmosphere, comfortable, safe, internet. Good reputation although rooms downstairs are not as airy as those on first floor.

**F** pp **Adventures House**, Jr Cesareo Chacaltana 162, T01-241 5693, www.adventureshouse.com. Rooms for up to 4 people, with bath and hot water, free internet access, national calls, pleasant, quiet, a short walk from all main facilities, airport transfer, use of kitchen, bike rental US$15/day. Associated with **Fly Adventures**, see Paragliding, below.

**F Albergue Turístico Juvenil Internacional**, Av Casimiro Ulloa 328, San Antonio between San Isidro and Miraflores, T01-446 5488, www.limahostell.com.pe. Youth hostel, dormitory accommodation. Price per person, **D** in a double private room. Basic cafeteria for breakfasts, travel information, lounge with cable TV, laundry facilities, swimming pool often empty, extra charge for use of the minimal kitchen facilities, clean and safe, situated in a nice villa. Recommended.

**F** per person **Albergue Verde**, Grimaldo del Solar 459, T01-445 3816, www.albergue verde.com. Nice small *hostal*, comfortable beds, **C** pp in double, friendly owner, Arturo Palmer, breakfast included, airport transfers US$15.

**F** per person **Explorer's House**, Av Alfredo León 158, by 10th block of Av José Pardo, T01-241 5002, explorers_house@yahoo.es. No sign, but plenty of indications of the house number, with breakfast, dormitory with shared bath, or double rooms with bath, hot water, use of kitchen, laundry service, Spanish classes, English spoken, very welcoming.

**F** per person **Flying Dog Backpackers**, Diez Canseco 117, T01-445 6745, www.flyingdog.esmartweb.com. Price includes breakfast in *El Parquetito* café, small dormitories or private rooms, comfortable, shared bath (**D-E** in en suite room), hot water, secure, free internet and local calls, book exchange, kitchen facilities. Central and very popular so book through the web. Transport information and tickets can be arranged.

**F Friend's House**, Jr Manco Cápac 368, T01-446 6248, friendshouse_peru@ yahoo.com.mx. Dormitory accommodation with hot water, cable TV, use of kitchen, includes breakfast, very popular with backpackers, near Larcomar shopping centre, plenty of good information and help. Highly recommended. They have another branch at José Gonzales 427, T446 3521. **E** per person with bath, same facilities, except private rooms only and more like a family home. Neither branch is signposted.

**F** per person **Loki Backpackers** (formerly Incahaus), Av Larco 189, T01-242 4350, www.lokihostel.com. Restored house built in the 1920s, keeping period details but with modern facilities. The capital's sister to the party hostel of the same name in Cuzco, **D** in double room, good showers, with breakfast (cooked breakfast extra), Fri barbecues, use of kitchen, free internet, lockers, airport transfer extra.

**F Stop & Drop Backpacker Hotel & Guesthouse**, Berlin 168, 2nd floor, T01-243 3101, www.stopandrop.com. Price per person. **D** double rooms with private bath. Backpacker hotel and guest house, also Spanish school. Bar, kitchen facilities, luggage store, laundry, TV, movies, internet, games, comfortable beds, safe, hot showers 24 hours, adventure sports and volunteer jobs. Airport pick up US$17.

**F** per person **Wayruro's Backpackers**, Enrique Palacios 900, T01-444 1564, www.wayruros.com. Comfortable dormitories, hot water, kitchen facilities, internet, breakfast and laundry service, cable TV and DVD, luggage store, airport pick-up.

**Barranco and the seaside** *p265, map p271*

C **Domeyer**, Domeyer 296, T01-247 1413, www.domeyerhostel.net. Hot water 24 hrs, laundry service, secure, gay friendly.

E per person **Barranco's Backpackers Inn**, Malecón Castilla 260, T01-247 3709, www.trekinnperu.com. Ocean View, colourful rooms, all en suite, shared and private rooms (with cable TV), free internet with Wi-Fi, kitchen facilities. Breakfast included. Discount for SAE members.

E **Casa Barranco**, Av Grau 982, T01-477 0984, www.lacasabarranco.8m.com. No sign on the street, just ring. Friendly owner Felipe offers clean rooms all with shared bathroom. Bed in dormitory for **F**, also monthly rentals available (US$150). Kitchen, DVD room, cable TV and PS1. Discount for SAE members.

E **Safe in Lima**, Alfredo Silva 150, T01-252 7330, www.safeinlima.com. Quiet, Belgian-run *hostal* with family atmosphere in new premises, with breakfast, very helpful, airport pick-up US$14, good value, reserve in advance, lots of information for travellers.

F per person **The Point**, Malecón Junín 300, T01-247 7997, www.thepointhostels.com. Rooms range from doubles to large dormitories, all with shared bath, very popular with backpackers (book in advance at weekends), breakfast included, internet, cable TV, laundry, kitchen facilities, gay friendly, party atmosphere most of the time, **The Pointless Pub** open 2000 till whenever, weekly barbecues, therapeutic massage next door, can arrange bungee jumping, flight tickets and volunteering. Also has hostels in Arequipa and Cuzco.

## Eating

**Central Lima** *p258, map p259*

ƒƒ **Antaño**, Ucayali 332, opposite the Torre Tagle palace, T01-426 2372. Good, typical Peruvian food, nice patio. Recommended.

ƒƒ **L'Eau Vive**, Ucayali 370, opposite Torre Tagle palace, T01-427 5612. Mon-Sat 1230-1500 and 1930-2130. Run by nuns, fixed-price lunch menu, Peruvian-style in interior dining room, or à la carte in either of the dining rooms that open onto the patio, excellent, profits go to the poor. Ave Maria is sung nightly at 2100.

ƒƒ **Manhatten**, Jr Miró Quesada 259. Mon-Fri 0700-1900, low-end executive-type restaurant, local and international food, good.

ƒƒ **Wa Lok**, Jr Paruro 864, Barrio Chino, T01-427 2656. Good dim sum, cakes and fortune cookies (when you pay the bill). Owner Liliana Com speaks fluent English, very friendly.

ƒƒ-ƒ **De Cesar**, Ancash 300, T01-428 8740. 0700-2300. Seafood, including *ceviche* and *chirrones de marisco*. Meat dishes include *lomo saltado*. Good food.

ƒƒ-ƒ **San Paolo**, Ancash 454, T01-427 4600. 0600 till midnight. Peruvian food, also has a good *menú diario* for US$3-4.

ƒ **Cordano**, Jr Ancash 202. Typical old Lima restaurant and watering hole, slow service and a bit grimy but full of character. Definitely worth the time it takes to drink a few beers.

ƒ **Govinda**, Av Garcilaso de la Vega 1670, opposite Gran Parque de Lima. Vegetarian food and natural products, good.

ƒ **Kin Ten**, Ucayali y Paruro, Barrio Chino. Excellent vegetarian options at this *chifa*.

ƒ **Machu Picchu**, Jr Ancash 312. Huge portions, grimy bathrooms (to say the least), yet very popular, closed for breakfast.

ƒ **Natur**, Moquegua 132, 1 block from Jr de la Unión, T01-427 8281. The owner, Humberto Valdivia, is also president of the South American Explorers' board of directors; the casual conversation, as well as his vegetarian restaurant, is certainly recommended.

ƒ **Neydi**, Puno 367. Daily 1100-2000. Good, cheap seafood, popular.

ƒ **Salon Capon**, Jr Paruro 819. Good dim sum at this recommended *chifa*. Also has a branch at Larcomar shopping centre, which is ƒƒƒ, elegant and equally recommended.

**Cafés**

**Accllahuasy**, Jr Ancash 400. Around the corner from **Hostal España**, open daily 0700-2300, good Peruvian dishes.

**Café Carrara**, Jr Ica 330, attached to **Hostal Roma**. Daily until 2300, multiple

# Barranco

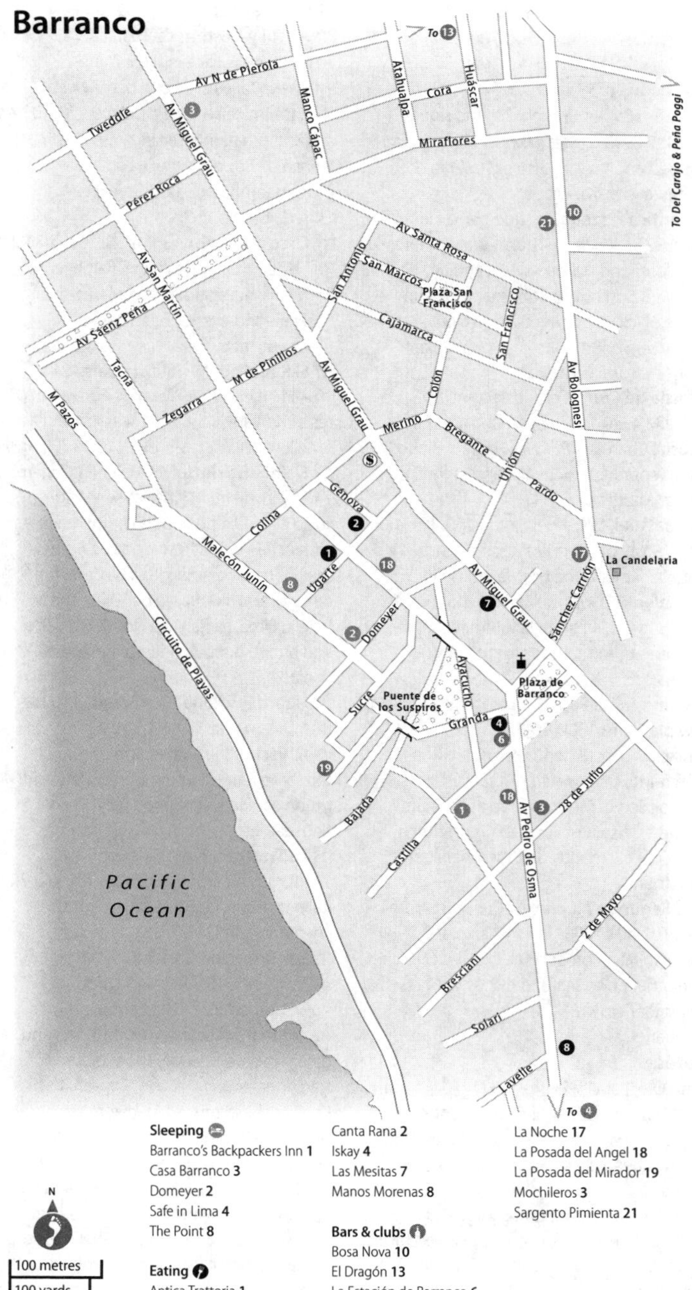


**Sleeping**
Barranco's Backpackers Inn **1**
Casa Barranco **3**
Domeyer **2**
Safe in Lima **4**
The Point **8**

**Eating**
Antica Trattoria **1**
Canta Rana **2**
Iskay **4**
Las Mesitas **7**
Manos Morenas **8**

**Bars & clubs**
Bosa Nova **10**
El Dragón **13**
La Estación de Barranco **6**
La Noche **17**
La Posada del Angel **18**
La Posada del Mirador **19**
Mochileros **3**
Sargento Pimienta **21**

N

100 metres
100 yards

breakfast combinations, pancakes, sandwiches, nice ambience, good.

**San Isidro** *p263, map p267*

TTT **Alfresco**, Santa Lucía 295 (no sign), T01-422 8915. Best known for its tempting seafood and *ceviche*, also pastas and rice dishes, expensive wines.

TTT **Antica Pizzería**, Av 2 de Mayo 728, T01-222 8437. Very popular, great ambience, excellent food, Italian owner, and an excellent bar, **Antica Taberna**, with a limited range of food at Conquistadores 605, San Isidro, very good value, fashionable, get there early for a seat.

TTT **Asia de Cuba**, Conquistadores 780, T01-222 4940. Popular, serving a mix of Asian, Cuban and Peruvian dishes. It also has a reputation for its bar and nightclub; try the Martinis.

TTT **Matsuei**, C Manuel Bañon 260, T01-422 4323. Sushi bar and Japanese dishes, very popular, among the best Japanese in Lima.

TTT **Valentino**, Manuel Bañon 215, T01-441 6174. One of Lima's best international restaurants, formal, look for the tiny brass sign.

TT **Como Agua Para Chocolate**, Pancho Fierro 108, T01-222 0297, aguapachocolat@terra.com.pe. Dutch-Mexican owned restaurant, specializing in Mexican food as the name suggests, also has a very amusing Dutch night once a month. SAE members get a discount.

TT **El Segundo Muelle**, Av Conquistadores 490, T01-421 1206, and Av Canaval y Moreyra (aka Corpac) 605. Excellent *ceviche* and other good seafood dishes. Attracts a younger crowd.

**Cafés**

**Café Olé**, Pancho Fierro 115 (1 block from Hotel Olivar). Huge selection of entrées and desserts, also serves breakfast and sandwiches, very smart with prices to match.

**Café Positano/Café Luna**, Miguel Dasso 147. Popular with politicians, café and bistro.

**News Café**, Av Santa Luisa 110. Another elegant café serving great salads and desserts, popular and expensive.

**Miraflores** *p263, map p264*

TTT **Astrid y Gaston**, Cantuarias 175, T01-444 1496. Excellent local and international cuisine, one of the best.

TTT **Café Voltaire**, Av 2 de Mayo 220, T01-447 4807. International cuisine with emphasis on French dishes, beautifully cooked food, pleasant ambience, good service. Closed Sun.

TTT **Coco de Mer**, Av Grau 400, T01-243 0278. Run by Englishwoman Lucy Ralph, popular for Mediterranean and Peruvian dishes, cocktails and events, open daily 1200 till whenever.

TTT **El Kapallaq**, Av Petit Thouars 4844, T01-444 4149. Prize-winning Peruvian restaurant specializing in seafood and fish, excellent *ceviches*. Mon-Fri 1200-1700 only.

TTT **El Señorío de Sulco**, Malecón Cisneros 1470, T01-441 0183, http://senoriodesulco.com. Overlooking a clifftop park, with ocean views from upstairs. Forget the Footprint grading, this is a 'five-fork' restaurant which some believe is the best in Lima, all Peruvian food, à la carte and buffet, piscos, wines, piano music at night.

TTT **Huaca Pucllana**, Gral Borgoña cuadra 8 s/n, alt cuadra 45 Av Arequipa, T01-445 4042. Facing the archaeological site of the same name, contemporary Peruvian fusion cooking, very good food in an unusual setting, popular with groups.

TTT **La Trattoria**, C Manuel Bonilla 106, 1 block from Parque Kennedy, T01-446 7002. Italian cuisine, popular, serving the best cheesecake in Lima.

TTT **Las Brujas de Cachiche**, Av Bolognesi 460, T01-447 1883, www.brujasdecachiche.com.pe. An old mansion converted into bars and dining rooms, beautifully decorated, traditional food (menu in Spanish and English), best *lomo saltado* in town, buffets 1230-1430 daily except Sat, live *criollo* music. Highly recommended.

TTT **Rosa Náutica**, Espigón No 4, Lima Bay, T01-445 0149, www.larosanautica.com. Built on an old British-style pier. Delightful opulence, finest fish cuisine, experience the atmosphere by buying an expensive beer in the bar at sunset, 1230-0200 daily.

**Sí Señor**, Bolognesi 706, T01-445 3789, www.sisenor.org. Mexican food, cheerful, lots of low-slung lights over the table, huge portions.

**Wa Lok**, Av Angamos Oeste 703, T01-447 1280. A branch of the famous Barrio Chino *chifa*, also serving good food in a tasteful, modern setting.

**Bohemia**, Av Santa Cruz 805, on the Ovalo Gutiérrez, T01-445 0889. Large menu of international food, great salads and sandwiches. Highly recommended. Also at Av El Polo 706, 2nd floor, Surco, T01-435 9924, and at Pasaje Nicolás de Rivera 142, opposite the main post office near Plaza de Armas, Lima centre, T01-427 5537.

**Café Tarata**, Pasaje Tarata 260. Good atmosphere, family run, good varied menu.

**Chez Philippe**, Av 2 de Mayo 748, T01-222 4953. Pizza, pasta and crêpes, with a wood oven and rustic decor.

**Dalmacia**, San Fernando 401, T01-445 7917. Spanish-owned, casual gourmet restaurant, excellent, seating on the terrace.

**Fluid**, Berlín 333, T01-242 9885, www.fluidperu.com. Restaurant and couch bar serving Thai and oriental food, plenty of vegetable dishes, good cocktails, mellow atmosphere, good contemporary music from rock to dance and trance, often has live bands later in the evenings. Professional-size pool table, British/Peruvian owned. Closed Sunday. Discount for SAE members.

**Ricota**, Pasaje Tarata 248, T01-445 2947. Charming café on a pedestrian walkway, with a huge menu, big portions and very friendly staff.

**Café Beirut**, Mártir Olaya 204, T01-243 3605. Excellent mid-range Middle-Eastern restaurant, close to the centre of Miraflores, a strange pink colour, but enthusiastic waiters, superb falafel and Arabic favourites, both sweet and savoury.

**Shehadi**, Av Diagonal 220, T01-444 0630. Facing Parque Kennedy, US-owned, brightly-lit restaurant specializing in pizza but also serving typical Peruvian fare. Good value daytime menus. Popular with locals and foreigners alike.

**El Parquetito**, Diez Canseco 150. Good cheap menu, serves breakfast, eat inside or out.

**Dino's Pizza**, Av Comandante Espinar 374 (and many other branches), T01-219 0909, www.pizza.com.pe. Great pizza at a good price, delivery service.

**Madre Natura**, Chiclayo 815. Natural foods shop and eating place, very good, closes 2100.

**Pardo's Chicken**, Av Benavides 730. Chicken and chips, very good and popular (branches throughout Lima).

**Sandwich.com**, Av Diagonal 234. Good, cheap sandwiches with interesting combinations of fillings.

**Super Rueda**, Porta 133, also Av Pardo 1224. Mexican food à la Peru, fast-food style.

**Pizza St**, the unofficial name for C San Ramón (across from Parque Kennedy), is a pedestrian walkway lined with bars, restaurants and discotheques open until the small hours of the morning. Very popular, with good-natured touts trying to entice diners and drinkers with free offers.

### Cafés

**Café Café**, Martín Olaya 250, near the Parque Kennedy roundabout. Very popular, good atmosphere, over 100 different blends of coffee, good salads and sandwiches, very popular with well-to-do Limeños. Also at Larcomar (good sea views).

**Café de la Paz**, Lima 351, middle of Parque Kennedy. Good café right on the park, a nice place for an outdoor drink, good cocktails, meals on the expensive side.

**Café Z**, Mcal Oscar R Benavides 598 y José Gálvez, past Parque Kennedy. American-owned, excellent Peruvian coffee, teas, hot chocolate, and the best home-made cakes away from home, cheap too.

**C'est si bon**, Av Comandante Espinar 663, T01-446 9310. Excellent cakes by the slice or whole, among the best in Lima.

**Dove Vai**, Diagonal 228. A bright *heladería* in this block of eating places; try the *encanto* with lumps of chocolate brownie.

**Haiti**, Av Diagonal 160, Parque Kennedy. Open almost 24 hrs daily, large terrace, decent food and coffee, great for spotting politicians, journalists and artists.

**La Tiendecita Blanca**, Av Larco 111 on Parque Kennedy. One of Miraflores' oldest; expensive, with good people-watching and very good cakes, European-style food and delicatessen.

**Tapas Bar**, Manuel Bonilla 103, T01-242 7922. Expensive but very good tapas bar behind huge wooden doors, the tapas are a meal in themselves, extensive wine list, reserve a table at weekends.

**Vivaldi**, Av Ricardo Palma 258, 1 block from Parque Kennedy. Good, expensive, reminiscent of a gentlemen's club. Also **Vivaldi Gourmet**, Conquistadores 212, San Isidro, an international restaurant.

### Barranco and the seaside *p265, map p271*

**TTT Antica Trattoria**, Alfonso Ugarte 242. Barranco branch of the popular San Isidro *pizzería* (see above).

**TTT Canta Rana**, Génova 101, T01-477 8934. Sun-Mon 1200-1800, Tue-Sat 1200-2300, good *ceviche* but expensive, small portions.

**TTT La Costa Verde**, on Barranquito beach, T01-441 3086. Excellent fish and wine, expensive but recommended as the best by Limeños, daily 1200-2400, Sun buffet.

**TTT Manos Morenas**, Av Pedro de Osma 409, T01-467 0421. Open 1230-1630, 1900-2300, creole cuisine with shows some evenings (cover charge for shows).

**TT Las Mesitas**, Av Grau 341, T01-477 4199. Traditional tea-room-cum-restaurant, serving creole food and old sweet dishes which you won't find anywhere else.

**TT-T Iskay**, Pedro de Osma N 106, T01-247 2102, iskay@iskayperu.com. Mon-Sat 0900-2300. Cultural café, art gallery and handicrafts, excellent service, well-decorated, daily *menú* is great value at US$2.50. Recommended.

## Bars and clubs

Lima has excellent nightlife, with a lot of variety. Often there is a cover charge ranging from US$3-10 per person. For details of *peñas*, see Entertainment, below.

### Central Lima *p258, map p259*

The centre of town, specifically Jr de la Unión, has many discos. It's best to avoid the nightspots around the intersection of Av Tacna, Av Piérola and Av de la Vega. These places are rough and foreigners will receive much unwanted attention.

For latest recommendations for gay and lesbian places, see www.deambiente.com, www.gayperu.com and http://lima.queercity.info/index.html.

**El Rincón Cervecero**, Jr de la Unión (Belén) 1045. German pub without the beer, fun.

**Estadio Futbol Sports Bar**, Av Nicolás de Piérola 926 on the Plaza San Martín, T01-428 8866. Beautiful bar with a disco on the bottom floor, international football theme, good international and creole food.

**Piano Bar Munich**, Jr de la Unión 1044 (basement). Small and fun.

**Yacama Arte & Rock Bar**, Jr de la Unión 892, T01-427 7897. Unpretentious rock bar on 2nd floor; serving cheap beer.

### Miraflores *p263, map p264*

**Bartinis**, in Larcomar, T01-445 4823. Good cocktails, trendy crowd; expensive.

**Dubliner's Irish Pub**, Berlín 327, T01-242 3588, dubliners-peru@hotmail.com. One in an ever-expanding list of Irish bars in Peru. Easygoing atmosphere, friendly, there's usually some rugby or football on the TV. Attracts a wide range of punters, local and foreign.

**La Tasca**, Av Diez Canseco, very near Parque Kennedy, part of the **Flying Dog** group and underneath one of the hostels (see Sleeping, above). Spanish-style bar with cheap beer (for Miraflores). Attracts an eclectic crowd including ex-pats, travellers and locals. Gay-friendly. Small and crowded.

**Media Naranja**, Schell 130, at the bottom of Parque Kennedy. Brazilian bar with typical drinks and food.

**Murphys**, C Schell 627. Best known for live music on Thu, Fri and Sat night, often rock covers. Occasional Guinness in cans. Discount for SAE members on draught beer.

**The Old Pub**, San Ramón 295 (Pizza Street). Cosy, with live music most days.

**Voluntarios Pub**, Independencia 131, T01-445 3939, www.voluntariospub.org. All staff are volunteers from non-profit organizations which benefit by receiving 90% of the profits made by the pub. Good atmosphere, music and drinks, nice to know that while you are partying other people are benefiting.

**Barranco and the seaside** *p265, map p271*

Barranco is the capital of Lima nightlife. The following is a short list of some of the better bars and clubs. Pasaje Sánchez Carrión, commonly called El Bulevar, right off the main plaza, used to be the heart of it all. Watering holes and discos line both sides of this pedestrian walkway, but crowds and noise are driving people elsewhere. Some places have been closed for safety reasons. Av Grau, just across the street from the plaza, is also lined with bars, eg **El Ekeko**, Av Grau 266, and **Las Terrazas,** Av Grau 290. Many of the bars in this area turn into discos later on.

**Bosa Nova**, Bolognesi 660. Chilled student-style bar with good music.

**El Dragón**, N de Piérola 168, T01-797 1033, dragoncultural@hotmail.com. Popular bar and venue for music, theatre and painting.

**El Grill de Costa Verde**, part of the **Costa Verde** restaurant on Barranco beach. Young crowd, packed at weekends.

**Juanitos**, Av Grau, opposite the park. Barranco's oldest bar, and perfect to start the evening.

**La Noche**, Bolognesi 307, at Pasaje Sánchez Carrión. A Lima institution with a high standard of live music. Mon is jazz night, kicks off around 2200.

**La Posada del Angel**, 3 branches, 2 in the first block of Pedro de Osma and the third at Av Prol San Martín 157, T01-247 5544. These are popular bars serving snacks and meals.

**La Posada del Mirador**, near the Puente de los Suspiros (Bridge of Sighs). Beautiful view of the ocean if you pay for the privilege.

**Mochileros**, Av Pedro de Osma 135. Good pub in a beautiful house, holds events at weekends.

**Sargento Pimienta**, Bolognesi 755. Live music, always a favourite with Limeños. Opposite is the relaxed **Trinidad**.

## Entertainment

### Cinemas

The newspaper *El Comercio* lists cinema information in the section called *Luces*. Tue is reduced price at most cinemas. Most films are in English with subtitles and cost US$2 in the centre and around US$4-5 in Miraflores. The best cinema chains in the city are **Cinemark, Cineplanet** and **UVK Multicines**.

### Peñas

**Central Lima** *p258, map p259*

**Las Brisas de Titicaca**, Pasaje Walkuski 168, at 1st block of Av Brasil near Plaza Bolognesi, T01-332 1881. A Lima institution.

**Miraflores** *p263, map p264*

**De Cajón**, Merino 2nd block, near 6th block of Av del Ejército. Good *música negra*.

**Sachun**, Av del Ejército 657, T01-441 0123/4465. Great shows on weekdays as well.

**Barranco** *p265, map p271*

**De Rompe y Raja**, Manuel Segura 127, T01-247 3271, www.derompeyraja.net. Popular, Thu, Fri, Sat, music, dancing and criolla food.

**Del Carajo**, Catalino Miranda 158, www.del-carajo.com. All types of traditional music, open Fri-Sat from 2130.

**La Candelaria**, Av Bolognesi 292, T01-247 1314, www.lacandelariaperu.com. A good *peña*, Fri-Sat 2130 onwards.

**La Estación de Barranco**, Pedro de Osma 112, T01-477 5030. Good, family atmosphere, varied shows.

## Festivals and events

**18 Jan** is the anniversary of the founding of Lima, with a Peruvian music festival on the previous night (17 Jan), culminating in the Plaza de Armas.

**Semana Santa**, or Holy Week, is a colourful spectacle with processions.

**28-29 Jul**, Independence, has music and fireworks in the Plaza de Armas.

Oct is the month of **Our Lord of the Miracles** with impressive processions starting at Las Nazarenas church on the 4th block of Av Tacna.

## Shopping

Supermarket chains include **E Wong**, **Metro**, **Plaza Vea**, **Santa Isabel** and the upmarket **Vivanda**. They are all well stocked and carry a decent supply of imported goods.

**Central Lima** *p258, map p259*

On C García Naranjo, La Victoria, just off Av Grau in the centre of town is **Polvos**

**Azules**, the official black market of Lima. The normal connotations of a 'black market' do not apply here as this is an accepted part of Lima society, condoned by the government and used by people of all backgrounds. It's good for cameras, hiking boots and music equipment. Be careful, this is not a safe area, so be alert and put your money in your front pockets.

**Miraflores** *p263, map p264*
**Parque Kennedy**, the main park of Miraflores, has a daily crafts market open 1700-2300. Av Petit Thouars runs parallel to Av Arequipa. Its 54 blocks end at Av Ricardo Palma, a few blocks from Parque Kennedy. At the 51st block there's a crafts market area with a large courtyard and small flags. This is the largest crafts arcade in Miraflores. From here to C Ricardo Palma the street is lined with craft stalls. All are open daily until late(ish).

## Activities and tours

Do not conduct business anywhere other than in the agency's office and insist on a written contract. Bus offices or the airport are not the places to arrange and pay for tours. You may be dealing with representatives of companies that either do not exist or which fall far short of what is paid for.

Most of those in Lima specialize in selling air tickets, or in setting up a connection in the place where you want to start a tour. Shop around and compare prices; also check all information carefully. It's best to use a travel agent in the town closest to the place you wish visit; it's cheaper and they're more reliable.

**Near the airport** *map p254*
**Escorted Economic Overland Peru**, T/F01-567 5107, victormelgar777 @yahoo.com. Run by experienced tour guide Víctor Melgar (of **Hostal Víctor** – see Sleeping), who escorts individuals, families and groups throughout Peru and Bolivia, safely and economically.

**Central Lima** *p258, map p259*
**Lima Tours**, Jr Belén 1040, T01-619 6900, www.limatours.com.pe. Recommended both for tours in the capital and around the country.
**Roma Tours**, Jr Ica 330, next to Hostal Roma, T/F01-427 7572, dantereyes@hotmail.com. Good and reliable. Administrator Dante Reyes is very friendly and speaks English.
**Victor Travel Service**, Jr de la Unión (Belén) 1068, T01-433 5547, T9335 0095 (24 hrs), victortravelservice@terra.com.pe. Hotel reservations (no commission, free pick-up), free maps of Lima and Peru, Mon-Sat 0900-1800, very helpful.

**San Isidro** *p263, map p267*
**AQP**, Los Castaños 347, T01-222 3312, www.saaqp.com.pe. Comprehensive service, tours offered throughout the country.
**InkaNatura Travel**, Manuel Bañón 461, T01-440 2022, www.inkanatura.com. Also in Cuzco, offers good tours with knowledgeable guides, special emphasis on sustainable tourism and conservation.

**Miraflores** *p263, map p264*
**Amazing Peru**, C Ramon Ribeyro 264, Urb San Antonio, T0808-234 6805 (UK). Professional and well organized. Knowledgeable guides.

**Andean Tours**, Schell 319, of 304-305, T01-444 8665, www.andean-tours.com. Bespoke tours all over Peru.
**Aracari Travel Consulting**, Av Pardo 610, No 802, T01-242 6673, www.aracari.com. Regional tours, also offers themed and activity tours, has a very good reputation.
**Class Adventure Travel** (**CAT**), San Martin 800, T01-444 2220 (Centro Comercial Sol Plaza, Av El Sol 948 Office 311, Cuzco, T02-535 5263), www.classadventure.travel. Dutch owned and run. One of the best, with offices in several Latin American countries. Tailor-made travel. Highly recommended.
**Coltur**, Av Reducto 1255, T01-615 5555, www.coltur.com.pe. Very helpful, experienced and well-organized for tours throughout the country.
**Dasatariq**, Jr Francisco Bolognesi 510, T01-447 7772, www.dasatariq.com. Also in Cuzco. A well-organized company with a good reputation and helpful staff.
**Domiruth Travel Service SAC**, Jr Rio de Janeiro 216-218, Lima 18, T01-610 6022, www.domiruth.com.pe. Tours throughout Peru, from the mystical to adventure travel.
**Explorandes**, C San Fernando 320, T01-445 0532, www.explorandes.com.pe. Award-winning company. Offers a wide range of adventure and cultural tours throughout the country. Also has an office in Cuzco.
**Fertur Peru**, Schell 485, T01-445 1760, USA/Canada T+1-877-247 0055 toll free, UK T+44-(0)20-3002 3811, www.fertur-travel.com. Up-to-date tourist information. Good prices for domestic and international flights. Discounts for ISIC and youth card holders.
**Fly Adventure**, Cesareo Chacaltana 162, T01-241 5693, T9754 2011 (mob – Luis Munárriz, instructor), T9752 0598 (Julie Peton, manager), www.adventureshouse.com/servicesing.htm. Paragliding, US$40 for 15-min tandem flight over the cliffs, 1-day course US$80, 7-day course US$450. Recommended.
**Masi Travel Sudamérica**, Porta 350, T01-446 9094, www.masitravel.com. Tours throughout Peru, plenty of information

on the website. Contact Verónika Reategui for an efficient service.

**Peru for Less**, Jorge Leguia 142, T01-272 0542, US office: T+1-877-269 0309; UK office: T+44-(0)20-3002 0571; www.peruforless.com. Claims to meet or beat any published rates on the internet from outside Peru.

**Peruvian Safaris**, Alcanfores 459, T01-447 8888, www.peruviansafaris.com. For tours throughout Peru, including to Tambopata. Reservations for the **Explorer's Inn**, 3-day/2-night US$180, excluding park entrance fees and flights.

**Rutas del Peru SAC**, Av Enrique Palacios 1110, T01-444 5405, www.rutasdelperu.com. Tailor-made trips and overland trips in trucks.

**Viajes Pacífico (Gray Line)**, Av La Mar 163, T01-610 1900, www.graylineperu.com. Expanded service with tours throughout Peru and within South America.

**Viracocha**, Av Vasco Núñez de Balboa 191, T01-445 3986, peruviantours@viracocha .com.pe. Very helpful for flights, adventure, birdwatching, cultural and mystical tours.

## Transport

### Air

For information on international flights, see Getting there, page 21. For airport facilities, see page 255. For information on domestic flights, see Getting around, page 23. For transport to and from Lima airport, see Ins and outs page 254. To enquire about arrivals or departures, T01-511 6055, www.lap.com.pe.

### Airlines

**Domestic** Aero Cóndor, Juan de Arona 781, San Isidro, T01-614 6000. **Lan**, Av José Pardo 513, Miraflores, T01-213 8200. **LC Busre**, Los Tulipanes 218, Lince, T01-619 1313. **Star Perú**, Av José Pardo 485, Miraflores, T01-705 9000. **Taca Perú**, Av Pardo 811, Miraflores, T01-511 8222. **International** Air France-KLM, Av Alvarez Calderón 185, p 6, San Isidro, T01-213 0200, Reservations.Peru@klm.com. **American Airlines**, Av Canaval y Moreyra 390, San Isidro, and in Hotel Las Américas, Av Benavides y Av Larco, Miraflores, T01-211 7000. **Continental**, 147 Via Principal 110 of 101, Edificio Real 5, San Isidro, and in the Hotel Marriott, Av Larco 1325, Miraflores, T01-712 9230, or 0800-70030. **Delta**, Víctor Belaúnde 147, San Isidro, T01-211 9211. **Iberia**, Av Camino Real 390, p 9, San Isidro, T01-411 7800. **Lloyd Aéreo Boliviano**, Av José Pardo 231, Miraflores, T01-241 5210. **Lufthansa**, Av Jorge Basadre 1330, San Isidro, T01-442 4455, lhlim@terra.com.pe. **Tame**, Av La Paz 1631, Miraflores, T01-422 6600.

### Bus

#### Local

**Lima centre–Miraflores**: Av Arequipa runs 52 blocks between downtown Lima and Parque Kennedy in Miraflores. There is no shortage of public transport on this avenue; they have 'Todo Arequipa' on the windscreen. When heading towards downtown from Miraflores the window sticker should say 'Wilson/Tacna'. To get to Parque Kennedy from downtown look on the windshield for 'Larco/Schell/ Miraflores', 'Chorrillos/Huaylas' or 'Barranco/Ayacucho'.

**Lima centre–Barranco**: Lima's only urban freeway, Vía Express, runs from Plaza Grau in the centre of town, to the northern tip of Barranco. This 6-lane thoroughfare, locally known as *El Zanjón* (the Ditch), with a separate bus lane in the middle, is the fastest way to cross the city. In order from Plaza Grau the 8 stops are: 1) **Av México**; 2) **Av Canadá**; 3) **Av Javier Prado**; 4) **Corpac**; 5) **Av Aramburu**; 6) **Av Angamos**; 7) **Av Ricardo Palma**, for Parque Kennedy; 8) **Av Benavides**. Buses downtown for the Vía Expresa can be caught on Av Tacna, Av Wilson (also called Garcilaso de la Vega), Av Bolivia and Av Alfonso Ugarte. These buses, when full, are of great interest to highly skilled pickpockets who sometimes work in groups. If you're standing in the aisle be extra careful.

#### Long distance

Although Lima is home to a seemingly neverending list of bus companies, only a small percentage are actually recommended. Confirm that the bus leaves from the place where the ticket was purchased.

One company that is recommended for service to all parts of Peru is **Cruz del Sur**, www.cruzdelsur.com.pe. The website accepts Visa bookings without surcharge. Its main terminal is at Av Javier Prado Este

1109, San Isidro, T01-225 5748. This terminal offers the *Cruzero* service (luxury buses), more expensive and direct, with no chance of passengers in the aisle, and *VIP* service (super luxury buses). They go to **Cuzco** (US$47-57), to other parts of the country and to **La Paz**. It also has a terminal at Jr Quilca 531, in the centre, T01-431 5125, which has routes to many destinations in Peru with *Imperial* service (Cuzco US$37), meaning quite comfortable buses and periodic stops for food and bathroom breaks, a cheap option with a quality company. Other companies that offer a service between Cuzco and Lima include **Expreso Molina** and **Wari**, Av Luna Pizarro 343, La Victoria, T01-330-3543, www.expresowari.com.pe (US$20-31.25 to Cuzco).

### Taxi colectivos

Regular private cars acting as taxis charge US$0.50. They are a faster, more comfortable option than municipal public transportation, but they are no safer. There are 3 routes: 1) between Av Arequipa and Av Tacna which runs from Miraflores to the centre of Lima; 2) between Plaza San Martín and Callao; 3) between the Vía Expresa and Chorrillos. Look for the coloured sticker posted on the windscreen. These cars will stop at any time to pick people up. When full (usually 5 or 6 passengers) they only stop for someone getting off, then the process begins again to fill the empty space.

### Taxis

Meters are not used, so the fare should be agreed upon before you get in. Drivers don't expect tips; give them small change from the fare. The following are taxi fares for some of the more common routes, give or take a sol. From downtown Lima to: Parque Kennedy (Miraflores), US$3. Museo de la Nación, US$3. South American Explorers, US$3. Archaeology Museum, US$3. Immigration, US$2.15. From Miraflores (Parque Kennedy) to: Museo de la Nación, US$3. Archaeology Museum, US$4. Immigration, US$3, Barranco, US$4. From outside airport terminal to centre US$4-7, San Isidro/Miraflores US$7-9. Whatever the size or make, yellow taxis are usually the safest since they have a number, the driver's name and radio contact. A large number of taxis are white, but as driving a taxi in Lima (or for that matter, anywhere in Peru) simply requires a windshield sticker saying 'Taxi', they come in all colours and sizes. Licensed and phone taxis are safest and, by law, all taxis must have the vehicle's registration number painted on the side.

### Telephone taxis

There are several reliable phone taxi companies, which can be called for immediate service, or booked in advance; prices are 2-3 times more than ordinary taxis; eg to the airport US$11-15, to suburbs US$8-9. Some are **América Taxi**, T01-265 2588; **Moli Taxi**, T01-479 0030; **Taxi Real**, T01-470 6205; **Taxi Seguro**, T01-415 2525; **Taxi Tata**, T01-274 5151; **TCAM**, run by Carlos Astacio, T01-9983 9305, safe, reliable. If hiring a taxi for over 1 hr agree on price per hr beforehand. Recommended, knowledgeable drivers: **César A Canales N**, T01-436 6184, T01-9687 3310 (mob) or through *Home Perú*, only speaks Spanish, reliable. **Hugo Casanova Morella**, T01-485 7708 (he lives in La Victoria), for city tours, travel to airport, etc. **Mónica Velásquez Carlich**, T01-425 5087, T9943 0796 (mob), vc_monica@hotmail.com. For airport pick-ups, tours, speaks English, very helpful.

## Directory

### Banks and money exchange

### Banks

**BCP**, Jr Lampa 499, Central Lima (main branch), Av Pardo 425 and Av Larco at Pasaje Tarata, Miraflores, Av Pardo y Aliaga at Av Camino Real, San Isidro. Mon-Fri 0900-1800, Sat 0930-1230. Accepts and sells American Express TCs only, accepts Visa card and branches have Visa/Plus ATM. **Banco de Comercio**, Av Pardo 272 and Av Larco 265, Miraflores, Jr Lampa 560, Central Lima (main branch). Mon-Fri 0900-1800, Sat 0930-1200. Changes and sells American Express TCs only, ATM accepts Visa/Plus. **BBVA Continental**, corner of Av Larco and Av Benavides and corner of Av Larco and Pasaje Tarata, Miraflores, Jr Cuzco 286, Lima centre near Plaza San Martín. Mon-Fri 0900-1800, Sat 0930-1230. TCs (American Express). Visa/Plus ATM. **Banco Financiero**, Av Ricardo

Palma 278, near Parque Kennedy (main branch). Mon-Fri 0900-1800, Sat 0930-1230. TCs (American Express), ATM for Visa/Plus. **Banco Santander Central Hispano (BSCH)**, Av Pardo 482 and Av Larco 479, Miraflores, Av Augusto Tamayo 120, San Isidro (main branch). Mon-Fri 0900-1800, Sat 0930-1230. TCs (Visa and Citicorp). ATM for Visa/Plus and Mastercard. **HSBC**, Amador Merino Reyna 307, p 10, San Isidro, T01-512 3000. **Scotiabank**, Av Diagonal 176 on Parque Kennedy, Av José Pardo 697, Miraflores, Av Alfonso Ugarte 1292, Breña, Miguel Dasso 286, San Isidro. Mon-Fri 0915-1800, Sat 0930-1230. TCs (American Express only), ATM for Visa, Mastercard, Maestro and Cirrus. **Citibank**, in all Blockbuster stores, and at Av 28 de Julio 886, Av Benavides 23rd block and Av Emilio Cavenecia 175, Miraflores, Av Las Flores 205 and branch in Centro Comercial Camino Real, Av Camino Real 348, San Isidro. Blockbuster branches open Sat and Sun 1000-1900. Changes and sells Citicorp cheques. **Interbank**, Jr de la Unión 600, Central Lima (main branch). Mon-Fri 0900-1800. Also Av Pardo 413, Av Larco 690 and in Larcomar, Miraflores, Av Grau 300, Barranco, Av Pezet 1405 and Av Pardo y Aliaga 634, San Isidro, and supermarkets Wong and Metro. Accepts and sells American Express TCs, ATM for Visa/Plus, Mastercard, Maestro, Cirrus and Amex.

### Cambistas

On the corner of Ocoña and Jr Camaná you'll no doubt see the large concentration of *cambistas* (street changers) with huge wads of dollars and soles in one hand and a calculator on the other. They should be avoided. Changing money on the street should only be done with official street changers wearing an identity card with a photo. Keep in mind that this card doesn't automatically mean that they are legitimate but most likely you won't have a problem. Around Parque Kennedy and down Av Larco in Miraflores are dozens of official *cambistas* with ID photo cards attached to their usually blue, sometimes green vest. There are also those who are independent and are dressed in street clothes, but it's safer to do business with an official money changer.

### Casas de cambio

There are many *casas de cambio* on and around Jr Ocoña off the Plaza San Martín. Repeatedly recommended is **LAC Dolar**, Jr Camaná 779, 1 block from Plaza San Martín, 2nd floor, T01-428 8127. Also at Av La Paz 211, Miraflores, T01-242 4069. Mon-Sat 0900-1900, Sun and holidays 0900-1400, good rates, very helpful, safe, fast, reliable, 2% commission on cash and TCs (Amex, Citicorp, Thomas Cook, Visa), will come to your hotel if you're in a group. Also recommended is **Virgen P Socorro**, Jr Ocoña 184, T01-428 7748. Daily 0830-2000, safe, reliable and friendly.

### Currency and card services

**American Express Office**, *Travex SA*, Av Santa Cruz 621, Miraflores, T01-710 3900, info @travex.com.pe. Mon-Fri 0830-1730, Sat 0900-1300. Replaces lost or stolen Amex cheques of any currency in the world. Purchase Amex cheques with Amex card only. Or branches of *Viajes Falabella*, eg Jr Belén 630, T01-428 9779, or Av Larco 747-753, Miraflores, T01-444 4239, lgutierrez @ viajesfalabella.com.pe. **Mastercard**, Porta 111, 6th floor, Miraflores, T01-242 2700.

### Embassies and consulates

**Australia**, Av Víctor Andrés Belaúnde 147, Vía Principal 155, Ed Real 3, of 1301, San Isidro, Lima 27, T01-222 8281, info.peru@austrade .gov.au. **Austria**, Av República de Colombia 643, p 5, San Isidro, T01-442 0503. **Belgian Consulate**, Angamos Oeste 392, Miraflores, T01-241 7566. **Bolivian Consulate**, Los Castaños 235, San Isidro, T01-422 8231, open 0900-1330 or 24 hrs for visas (except those requiring clearance from La Paz). **Canada**, Libertad 130, Casilla 18-1126, Lima, T01-444 4015, lima@dfait-maeci.gc.ca. **France**, Arequipa 3415, San Isidro, T01-215 8400, www.ambafrance-pe.org. **Germany**, Av Arequipa 4210, Miraflores, T01-212 5016, kanzlei@embajada-alemana.org.pe. **Israel**, Natalio Sánchez 125, p 6, Santa Beatriz, T01-418 0500. **Italy**, Av G Escobedo 298, Jesús María, T01-463 2727, www.italemb peru.org.pe. **Japan**, Av San Felipe 356, Jesús María, T01-218 1130. **Netherlands Consulate**, Torre Parque Mar, Av José Larco 1301, p 13, Miraflores, T01-213 9800, info@nlgovlim.com, open Mon-Fri 0900-1200. **New Zealand Consulate**, Av Camino Real 390, Torre Central, p 17 (Casilla 3553), San Isidro, T01-221 2833, reya@ nzlatam.com, Mon-Fri 0830-1300, 1400-1700. **Spain**, Jorge Basadre 498, San Isidro, T01-212 5155, open 0900-1300. **Sweden**, C La Santa María 130, San Isidro, T01-442 8905, konslima@ terra.com.pe. **Switzerland**, Av Salaverry 3240, Magdalena, Lima 17, T01-264 0305, vertretung@ lim.rep.admin.ch. **UK**, Torre Parque Mar, p 22, T01-617 3000, www.britishembassy.gov.uk/ peru, 1300-2130 (Dec-Apr to 1830 Mon and Fri, and Apr-Nov to 1830 Fri), good for security information and newspapers. **USA**, Av Encalada block 17, Surco, T01-434 3000, http://lima.usembassy.gov, the consulate is in the same building.

### Internet and email

Lima is completely inundated with internet cafés, so you will have no problem finding one regardless of where you are. An hour will cost you around US$0.60-0.90.

### Police and immigration

### Immigration

Av España 700 y Jr Huaraz, Breña, 0900-1330. See page 51 for procedures on visa extensions. Provides new entry stamps if passport is lost or stolen.

### Police

PNP, Policía Nacional del Perú, T01-475 2995, Lima. They have stations in every town.

### Tourist police

Jr Moore 268, Magdalena at the 38th block of Av Brasil, T01-460 1060, open daily 24 hrs. For public enquiries, Jr Pachitea at the corner of Tambo de Belén (10th block of Jr de la Unión), Lima, T01-424 2053, and Calle Colón 246, Miraflores, T01-243 2190. They are friendly and very helpful, English spoken. It is recommended to visit if you have had property stolen.

### Post offices

**Central Post Office**, Jr Camaná 195, near the Plaza de Armas. Mon-Fri 0730-1900, Sat 0730-1600. **Poste Restante** is in the same building but is considered unreliable. **Miraflores Post Office** is on Av Petit Thouars 5201. There are many other small branches around Lima but these are usually less reliable.

### Telephone

Easiest to use are the many independent phone offices, *locutorios*, all over the city. They take phone cards, which can be bought in *locutorios*, or in the street nearby. There are payphones all over the city. Some accept coins, some only phone cards and some both. For full details on phone operation, see Essentials, page 45.

# Background

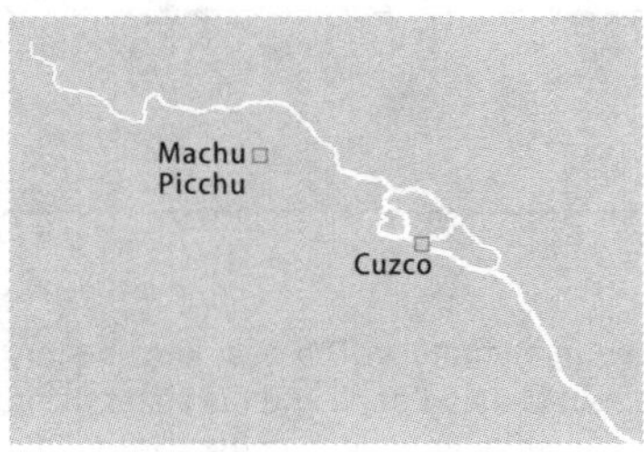




## Footprint features

# History

## Inca Dynasty

The origins of the Inca Dynasty are shrouded in mythology. The best-known story reported by the Spanish chroniclers talks about Manco Cápac and his sister rising out of Lake Titicaca, created by the Sun as divine founders of a chosen race. This was in approximately AD 1200. Over the next 300 years the small tribe grew to supremacy as leaders of the largest empire ever known in the Americas, the four territories of Tawantinsuyo, united by Cuzco as the umbilicus of the universe. The four quarters of Tawantinsuyo, all radiating out from Cuzco, were: 1 Chinchaysuyo, north and northwest; 2 Cuntisuyo, south and west; 3 Collasuyo, south and east; 4 Antisuyo, east.

At its peak, just before the Spanish Conquest, the Inca Empire stretched from the Río Maule in central Chile, north to the present Ecuador-Colombia border, containing most of Ecuador, Peru, western Bolivia, northern Chile and northwest Argentina. The area was roughly equivalent to France, Belgium, Holland, Luxembourg, Italy and Switzerland combined (980,000 sq km).

The Incas, under their first ruler, Manco Cápac, migrated north to the fertile Cuzco region, settling between the rivers Saphi and Tullumayo (marked today by the two Cuzco streets which still bear their names). Here, they established Cuzco as their capital. They were initially a small group of *ayllus*, or family-based clans, devoted to agriculture. They began their expansion gradually, by forging links over a long period of time with other ethnic groups in the area in order to acquire more land for cultivation. Successive generations of rulers were fully occupied with overcoming local rivals, such as the Colla and Lupaca to the south, and the Chanca to the northwest. The Incas had had a long-running dispute with the Chanca, a powerful people based around Ayacucho, whose lands adjoined theirs. The Inca oral histories recorded by the Spanish recount that, towards the end of the reign of Viracocha, the Chanca finally felt strong enough to launch an all-out attack on Cuzco itself and that the people of Cuzco emerged victorious under the command of a young general called Cusi Yupanqui, who would later take the name Inca Pachacútec (Earth changer). The hero was subsequently crowned as the new ruler.

From the start of Pachacútec's own reign in 1438, barely 100 years before the arrival of the Spanish, imperial expansion grew in earnest, the defeat of the Chanca being the trigger. With the help of his son and heir, Túpac, territory was conquered from the Titicaca Basin south into Chile, and all the north and central coast down to the Lurin Valley. The Incas also subjugated the Chimú, the highly sophisticated rival empire who had re-occupied the abandoned Moche capital at Chan Chán, in the north, near present-day Trujillo. Typical of the Inca method of government, some of the Chimú skills were assimilated into their own political and administrative system, and some Chimú nobles were even given positions in Cuzco.

Perhaps the pivotal event in Inca history came in 1527 with the death of the ruler, Huayna Cápac. Civil war broke out in the confusion over his rightful successor. One of his legitimate sons, Huáscar, ruled the southern part of the empire from Cuzco. Atahualpa, Huáscar's half-brother, governed Quito, the capital of Chinchaysuyo. In 1532, soon after Atahualpa had won the civil war, **Francisco Pizarro** arrived in Tumbes with 179 *conquistadores*, many on horseback. Atahualpa's army was marching south, probably for the first time, when he clashed with Pizarro at Cajamarca, in the northeastern Peruvian Andes.

## Children of the Sun

Like any agrarian society, the Incas were avid sky watchers, but their knowledge of astronomy was naturally limited to what could be of practical use to them with regard to their farming activities. In common with other cultures throughout the world, they realized that the seasons on which their subsistence depended were governed by the apparent movement of the sun, who they called Inti, and placed at the head of their pantheon of gods. As the Inca Garcilaso de la Vega explains in his Royal Commentaries (1609), the Incas gave the name *huata* to the sun's annual motion, which in Quechua can mean either 'year', or 'to attach'. They believed that the sun had been created by the supreme creator god Viracocha, who caused it to rise from an island on Lake Titicaca now known as Isla del Sol, and that the moon goddess, the sun's sister, called Mama Killa, rose from the nearby island of Coatí (known today as the Island of the Moon). Lake Titicaca is central to the creation legends of the Incas, having also been the birthplace of the first two Incas (also brother and sister) and the scene of a great flood sent, it is said, by Viracocha, to punish mankind for having disobeyed his teachings. Colourful as they may seem, such myths were also central to the political structure of the Inca State, in that they established the Inca's divine right to rule, as a direct descendant of the sun god Inti and, therefore, his representative on earth.

Any agrarian society learns over time when to sow and harvest its crops by observing the cycle of nature around it. But in a planned, centralized economy governed by a self- proclaimed elite, the seasons of the year must be anticipated and, if it is to remain in power, that elite must be seen to monopolize the knowledge required for such predictions. The Incas, therefore, recruited the high priests, or tarpuntaes, who made astronomical observations from the empire's many temples dedicated to the sun, from the ranks of their own nobility, who were essentially the Inca's extended family. These priests observed solar and lunar eclipses, which were variously interpreted as the sexual union of the two astral bodies or, more calamitously, manifestations of their anger with their chosen people, a warning of the imminent death of a public figure, or indications that they themselves were under attack.

These astronomer-priests divided the year into twelve lunar months, which they themselves realized fell short of the solar year. They corrected this discrepancy by carefully following the course of the sun using cylindrical stone columns erected on the hills around the city of Cuzco and measuring their shadows to calculate the solstices, placing their new year at the time of the summer solstice and their greatest celebration, Inti Raymi, during the winter solstice (June in the modern calendar). The equinoxes were calculated using a single stone pillar placed in the centre of each temple dedicated to the sun. At noon, when the stone barely cast a shadow, Inti was said to be sitting 'with all his light on the column'. As the Incas extended their empire towards present-day Ecuador, they realized that at the new temples they established, the further north they went, the more the shadow cast by the stones they erected was reduced. Quito's temple, therefore, just 22 km south of the equator, where the sun casts no shadow at midday, was held to be the favourite resting place of Inti, thereby rivalling the importance of the oldest and most venerated shrine in the empire at Qoricancha, in Cuzco.

This was one of the biggest cities in the Inca Empire and was where the Incas and Spanish had their first showdown. Here Pizarro ambushed and captured Atahualpa and slaughtered his guards. Despite their huge numerical inferiority, the heavily armed Spaniards took advantage of an already divided Inca Empire to launch their audacious attack. The Incas attempted to save their leader by collecting the outrageous ransom demanded by Pizarro for Atahualpa's release. This proved futile as the Spanish, fearing a mobilization of Inca troops, executed the Inca leader once the treasure had been collected. There was no army coming to Atahualpa's rescue. Pizarro and his fellow *conquistador*, Diego de Almagro, had reacted hastily to a false rumour and their fatal decision was criticized at the time, including by Emperor Charles V. Pushing on to Cuzco, Pizarro was at first hailed as the executioner of a traitor: Atahualpa had ordered the death of Huáscar in 1533, while himself a captive of Pizarro, and his victorious generals were bringing the defeated Huáscar to see his half-brother. Panic followed when the *conquistadores* set about sacking the Inca capital and they fought off with difficulty an attempt by Manco Inca to recapture Cuzco in 1536.

## Inca society

The people we call the Incas were a small aristocracy numbering only a few thousand, centred in the highland city of Cuzco. They rose gradually as a small regional dynasty, similar to others in the Andes of that period, starting around AD 1200. Then, suddenly, in the mid-1400s, they began to expand explosively under Pachacútec, a sort of Andean Alexander the Great, and later his son, Túpac. Less than 100 years later, they fell before the rapacious warriors of Spain. The Incas were not the first dynasty in Andean history to dominate their neighbours, but they did it more thoroughly and went further than anyone before them.

## Empire building

Enough remains today of their astounding highways, cities and agricultural terracing for people to marvel and wonder how they accomplished so much in so short a time. They seem to have been amazingly energetic, industrious and efficient – and the reports of their Spanish conquerors confirm this hypothesis.

They must also have had the willing cooperation of most of their subject peoples, most of the time. In fact, the Incas were master diplomats and alliance-builders first, and military conquerors only second, if the first method of expansion failed. The Inca skill at generating wealth by means of highly efficient agriculture and distribution brought them enormous prestige and enabled them to 'out-gift' neighbouring chiefs in huge royal feasts involving ritual outpourings of generosity, often in the form of vast gifts of textiles, exotic products from distant regions, and perhaps wives to add blood ties to the alliance. The 'out-gifted' chief was required by the Andean laws of reciprocity to provide something in return, and this would usually be his loyalty, as well as a levy of manpower from his own chiefdom.

Thus, with each new alliance the Incas wielded greater labour forces and their mighty public works programmes surged ahead. These were administered through an institution known as *mit'a*, a form of taxation through labour. The state provided the materials, such as wool and cotton for making textiles, and the communities provided skills and labour.

*Mit'a* contingents worked royal mines, royal plantations for producing coca leaves, royal quarries and so on. The system strove to be equitable, and workers in such hardship posts as high altitude mines and lowland coca plantations were given correspondingly shorter terms of service.

## Organization

Huge administrative centres were built in different parts of the empire, where people and supplies were gathered. Articles such as textiles and pottery were produced there

## All roads lead to Cuzco

There was a time when roads of colossal dimensions and magnificent construction crossed the difficult Andean terrain, thousands and thousands of kilometres in the most amazing network ever seen in antiquity. Through the building and management of this complex system, the Inca empire achieved both its expansion and its consolidation.

Cuzco, navel of the world and capital of the powerful Tawantinsuyo, was where these roads began and ended. From the city's civic arena, Huacaypata (today's Plaza de Armas), the four trunk roads set out to each of the four (*tahua*) quarters (*suyus*) into which the empire was divided: **Chinchaysuyo** to the northwest as far as Quito and the Colombian border; **Collasuyu** to the south, incorporating the altiplano as far as Argentina and Chile; **Cuntisuyu** to the west, bound by the Pacific Ocean; and **Antisuyu** to the east and the Amazon lowlands.

The limits presented by sea and jungle made the roads to north and south into a great axis which came to be known as **Capaq Ñan** (Royal, or Principal Road). They became the Incas' symbol of power over men and over the sacred forces of nature. So marvellous were these roads that the Spaniards who saw them at the height of their glory said there was nothing comparable in all Christendom and that, for example, a young girl from court could run their length barefoot as they were even swept clean. Amazement was not the sole preserve of the Europeans, as an early chronicle reveals. A settler who lived a long way from the capital reached the road in his district and said, "At last, I have seen Cuzco."

Imperial life revolved around these roads. Via them the produce of the coastal valleys and Amazonia were collected in tribute, to be exchanged prudently with those of the sierra, or to be stored for times of shortage. Whole communities were moved along these roads, to keep rebellion in check or to take the skills they possessed to another corner of the empire. These people had been conquered by armies thousands strong who advanced, unstoppable, along the roads, their supplies guaranteed at the *tambos* (storehouses) that were placed at regular intervals. News and royal decrees travelled with all haste, delivered by the famous *chasquis*, a race of men dedicated exclusively to running in relay along the roads.

While the roadbuilding did not happen all at once, the speed with which Pachacútec and his successors transformed the Andean world was incredible. In scarcely a century the most important civilization of the southern hemisphere had been created, only to be destroyed as the Spaniards capitalized on the fratricidal war between Huáscar and Atahualpa. What happened to the roads after that parallels what happened to the civilization itself. For a while the Spaniards used the very same roads which had been used to feed this immense body, only to leave it weakened and lifeless. Then, the large populations which the roads connected were exiled to live in reductions in the valleys where they could be controlled more easily and the roads, now running from one ghost town to the next, faded into oblivion.

The Incas, however, built for eternity. Many sections of the great network can be found today, not only in good condition but still in use, like the Inca Trail to Machu Picchu. Many other sections are lost under vegetation. But today Inca roads are considered of national importance and there is a hope that work will begin on their conservation, especially the singularly important Capaq Ñan.

in large workshops. Work in these places was carried out in a festive manner, with plentiful food, drink and music. Here was Andean reciprocity at work: the subject supplied his labour, and the ruler was expected to provide generously while he did so.

Aside from *mit'a* contributions there were also royal lands claimed by the Inca as his portion in every conquered province, and worked for his benefit by the local population. Thus, the contribution of each citizen to the state was quite large, but apparently, the imperial economy was productive enough to sustain this.

Another institution was the practice of moving populations around wholesale, inserting loyal groups into restive areas, and removing recalcitrant populations to loyal areas. These movements of *mitmakuna*, as they were called, were also used to introduce skilled farmers and engineers into areas where productivity had to be raised.

## Communications

The huge empire was held together by an extensive and highly efficient highway system. There were an estimated 30,000 km of major highway, most of it neatly paved and drained, stringing together the major Inca sites. Two parallel highways ran north to south, along the coastal desert strip and the mountains, and dozens of east-west roads crossing from the coast to the Amazon fringes. These roadways took the most direct routes, with wide stone stairways zigzagging up the steepest mountain slopes and rope suspension bridges crossing the many narrow gorges of the Andes.

Every 12 km or so there was a *tambo*, or way station, where goods could be stored and travellers lodged. The *tambos* were also control points, where the Inca state's accountants tallied movements of goods and people. Even more numerous than *tambos*, were the huts of the *chasquis*, or relay runners, who continually sped royal and military messages along these highways.

The Inca state kept records and transmitted information in various ways. Accounting and statistical records were kept on skeins of knotted strings known as *quipus* (see box, page 290). Numbers employed the decimal system, and colours indicated the categories being recorded. An entire class of people, known as *quipucamayocs*, existed whose job was to create and interpret these. Neither the Incas nor their Andean predecessors had a system of writing as we understand it, but there may have been a system of encoding language into *quipus*.

Archaeologists are studying this problem today. History and other forms of knowledge were transmitted via songs and poetry. Music and dancing, full of encoded information which could be read by the educated elite, were part of every major ceremony and public event information was also carried in textiles, which had for millennia been the most vital expression of Andean culture.



## Textiles

Clothing carried insignia of status, ethnic origin, age and so on. Special garments were made and worn for various rites of passage. It has been calculated that, after agriculture, no activity was more important to Inca civilization than weaving. Vast stores of textiles were maintained to sustain the Inca system of ritual giving. Armies and *mit'a* workers were partly paid in textiles. The finest materials were reserved for the nobility, and the Inca emperor himself displayed his status by changing into new clothes every day and having the previous day's burned.

Most weaving was done by women and the Incas kept large numbers of 'chosen women' in female-only houses all over the empire. Among their duties was to supply textiles to the elite and the many deities, to whom the weavings were frequently given as burned offerings. These women had other duties, such as making *chicha* – the Inca corn beer which was consumed and sacrificed in vast quantities on ceremonial occasions. They also became wives and concubines to the Inca elite and loyal nobles. And some may have served as priestesses of the moon, in parallel to the male priesthood of the sun.

## Religious worship

The Incas have always been portrayed as sun-worshippers, but it now seems that they were just as much mountain-worshippers. Recent research has shown that Machu Picchu was at least partly dedicated to the worship of the surrounding mountains, and Inca sacrificial victims have been excavated on frozen Andean peaks at 6700 m. In fact, until technical climbing was invented, the Incas held the world altitude record for humans.

Human sacrifice was not common, but every other kind was, and ritual attended every event in the Inca calendar. The main temple of Cuzco was dedicated to the numerous deities: the Sun, the Moon, Venus, the Pleiades, the Rainbow, Thunder and Lightning, and the countless religious icons of subject peoples which had been brought to Cuzco, partly in homage, partly as hostage. Here, worship was continuous and the fabulous opulence included gold cladding on the walls, and a famous garden filled with life-size objects of gold and silver. Despite this pantheism, the Incas acknowledged an overall Creator God, whom they called Viracocha. A special temple was dedicated to him, at Raqchi, about 100 km southeast of Cuzco. Part of it still stands today.

## Military forces

The conquering Spaniards noted with admiration the Inca storehouse system, still well-stocked when they found it, despite several years of civil war among the Incas. Besides textiles, military equipment, and ritual objects, they found huge quantities of food. Like most Inca endeavours, the food stores served a multiple purpose: to supply feasts, to provide during lean times, to feed travelling work parties, and to supply armies on the march.

Inca armies were able to travel light and move fast because of this system. Every major Inca settlement also incorporated great halls where large numbers of people could be accommodated, or feasts and gatherings held, and large squares or esplanades for public assemblies.

Inca technology is usually deemed inferior to that of contemporary Europe. Their military technology certainly was. They had not invented iron-smelting and basically fought with clubs, palmwood spears, slings, wooden shields, cotton armour and straw-stuffed helmets. They did not even make much use of the bow and arrow, a weapon they were well aware of. Military tactics, too, were primitive. The disciplined formations of the Inca armies quickly dissolved into melees of unbridled individualism once battle was joined.

This, presumably, was because warfare constituted a theatre of manly prowess, but was not the main priority of Inca life. Its form was ritualistic. Battles were suspended by both sides for religious observance. Negotiation, combined with displays of superior Inca strength, usually achieved victory, and total annihilation of the enemy was not on the agenda.

## Architecture

Other technologies, however, were superior in every way to their 16th-century counterparts: textiles, settlement planning and agriculture in particular with its sophisticated irrigation and soil conservation systems, ecological sensitivity, specialized crop strains and high productivity under the harshest conditions.

Unlike modern cities, Inca towns, or *llaqtas*, were not designed to house large, economically active populations. Inca society was essentially agrarian and, among the common people, almost everyone worked and lived on the land. The towns and cities that the Incas did build were meant to serve as residential areas for the state's administrative and religious elite. Throughout Tawantinsuyo, the *llaqtas* were divided into two zones, along blood lines, between the two principal *ayllus*, of Hanan and Urin. The streets were laid out in a simple grid pattern, with the whole forming a trapezoid. The trapezoid was the fundamental basis of Inca architecture,

## Quipus: holding the strings of empire

Despite their extraordinary advances in the fields of government, agriculture, architecture, astronomy and engineering, it is generally agreed that the Incas never developed a written language. But given the phenomenal degree to which the Inca State was centrally planned and governed, it should come as no surprise to learn that they did employ a complex mnemonic device for the keeping of state records.

The *quipu*, an invention which predates the Incas, consisted of a series of strings with knots tied in them. Those *quipus* found so far by archaeologists vary in length from just a few centimetres to more than a metre. By varying the colour of the strings, and the position and type of knot, the Incas were able to record vast amounts of information related to the affairs of the empire in a series of censuses of its entire population of more than 10 million.

The *quipucamayocs*, an hereditary group trained in the art of compiling and deciphering the *quipus*, were charged with keeping a complete demographic record from births and deaths to age groups, the number of men-under-arms, marriages, and the material wealth of the empire, which comprised great storehouses like those discovered by the Spanish when they reached Cuzco in 1533. These huge rectangular sheds contained everything that was grown or manufactured in an empire where private ownership was almost unknown, including grain, cloth, military equipment, coca, metal, shoes and items of clothing. All of this vast treasure, which the gold-hungry Spanish completely ignored, would have been precisely documented using *quipus*.

The Inca social system of *ayllus*, or clans, was based on groups of multiples of 10, and its arithmetical system was therefore also decimal. Apparently the concept of zero was understood but had no symbol; on those *quipus* deciphered by researchers it is represented by the absence of a knot. The data recorded on a *quipu* was calculated using an abacus, or *yupana*, which was fashioned from a rectangular tablet divided into smaller rectangular blocks, upon which grains of quinoa and corn of different colours were used to add, subtract, multiply and divide complex sums. The Spanish chronicler José de Acosta (1590) was astonished by the dexterity and exactitude of the Incas' *yupanacamayocs*, who he claimed never made a mistake and were much faster and more accurate than the Spanish accountants who used pen and paper.

While most scholars maintain that *quipus* were only used to record numbers, some others assert that they were also utilized to record other kinds of information, and that they were therefore effectively written records, or books. Recent research has suggested that the Incas employed a decimal alphabet in which consonants were represented by numbers and vowels were omitted, enabling them to communicate, and conserve, abstract concepts like poetry and storytelling on both their *quipus* and in the geometric designs of their weavings.

If such theories can be proved, they would make the Incas the inventors of written language in South America, and the *quipucamayocs* their court historians and Peru's first chroniclers. See http://agutie.homestead.com/files/Quipu_B.htm for a selection of articles.

from niches and doorways to buildings and entire towns, and has been called the Inca version of the arch. 

The Incas fell short of their Andean predecessors in the better-known arts of ancient America – ceramics, textiles and metalwork – but it could be argued that their supreme efforts were made in architecture, stoneworking, landscaping, road building, and the harmonious combination of these elements. These are the outstanding survivals of Inca civilization, which still remain to fascinate the visitor: the huge, exotically close-fit blocks of stone, cut in graceful, almost sensual curves; the astoundingly craggy and inaccessible sites encircled by great sweeps of Andean scenery; the rhythmic layers of farm terracing that provided land and food to this still-enigmatic people. The finest examples of Inca architecture can be seen in the city of Cuzco and throughout the Sacred Valley.

### Ruling elite

The ruling elite lived privileged lives in their capital at Cuzco. They reserved for themselves and privileged insiders certain luxuries such as the chewing of coca, the wearing of fine vicuña wool, and the practice of polygamy. But they were an austere people, too. Everyone had work to do, and the nobility were constantly being posted to state business throughout the empire. Young nobles were expected to learn martial skills, besides being able to read the *quipus*, speak both Quechua and the southern language of Aymara, and know the epic poems.

The Inca elite belonged to royal clans known as *panacas*, which each had the unusual feature of being united around veneration of the mummy of their founding ancestor – a previous Inca emperor, unless they happened to belong to the *panaca* founded by the Inca emperor who was alive at the time. Each new emperor built his own palace in Cuzco and amassed his own wealth rather than inheriting it from his forebears, which perhaps helps to account for the urge to unlimited expansion.

This urge ultimately led the Incas to overreach themselves. Techniques of diplomacy and incorporation no longer worked as they journeyed farther from the homeland and met ever-increasing resistance from people less familiar with their ways. During the reign of Huayna Cápac, the last emperor before the Spanish invasion, the Incas had to establish a northern capital at Quito in order to cope with permanent war on their northern frontier. Following Huayna Cápac's death came a devastating civil war between Cuzco and Quito, and immediately thereafter came the Spanish invasion. Tawantisuyo, the empire of the four quarters, collapsed with dizzying suddenness.



## Conquest and after

Peruvian history after the arrival of the Spaniards was not just a matter of *conquistadores* versus Incas. The vast majority of the huge empire remained unaware of the conquest for many years. The Chimú and the Chachapoyas cultures of northern Peru were powerful enemies of the Incas. The Chimú developed a highly sophisticated culture and a powerful empire stretching for 560 km along the coast from Paramonga south to Casma. Their history was well recorded by the Spanish chroniclers and continued through the conquest possibly up to about 1600. The Kuélap/Chachapoyas people were not so much an empire as a loose-knit 'confederation of ethnic groups with no recognized capital' (Morgan Davis *Chachapoyas: The Cloud People*, Ontario, 1988). But the culture did develop into an advanced society with great skill in roads and monument building. Their fortress at Kuélap, in the northeast, where the Andes meet the Amazon, was known as the most impregnable in Tawantinsuyo. It remained intact against Inca attack and Manco Inca even tried, unsuccessfully, to gain refuge here against the Spaniards.

## Exploration of the Vilcabamba

The Peruvian Vilcabamba remained virtually unexplored until the 20th century, both because of its geographical isolation and a lack of interest. The few travellers who went there, like the **Comte de Sartiges** in 1833, concentrated on the southwestern fringes and the site of Choquequirao.

Then in 1910 **Sir Clements Markham**, the President of the Royal Geographical Society, published *The Incas of Peru*, which focused attention on the late 'neo-Inca' period when they fled from Cuzco deep into the Vilcabamba heartland after the Spanish invasion. This whetted the interest of a young American academic from Yale called **Hiram Bingham**.

Bingham's subsequent reporting of Machu Picchu in 1911 is so famous that it has at times obscured the other discoveries he made in the area: Vitcos, which the last Incas used as their capital in exile for 35 years after the Spanish had conquered the rest of their empire; and another mysterious site down below in the jungle, whose significance evaded Bingham at the time, in an area called Espíritu Pampa which he evocatively translated as 'the Plain of Ghosts'.

Over the course of two subsequent expeditions, in 1912 and 1914-1915, he went on to report many other sites and cover an awe-inspiring amount of ground. It is fair to say that almost a century later, many explorers and archaeologists are still just adding footnotes and elucidations to Bingham's pioneering work.

Another less heralded but important contribution came from the mining prospector **Christian Bües**, who roamed the area in the 1920s and left a meticulously detailed map which is still used by today's explorers. He was the first to visit the remote and well-preserved ruin of Inca Wasi in the Puncuyoc hills.

Significant discoveries were made in 1941 by an American expedition led by the film-maker and anthropologist **Paul Fejos**, which investigated the Inca Trail. They found the dramatic site of Wiñay Wayna ('forever young'), which was named after an orchid found locally, and the nearby Inti Pata. The expedition was accompanied by a young scholar called **John H Rowe**, who went on over a long career to become the most influential Andeanist of his generation.

**Gene Savoy** made a swashbuckling entrance into the exploring world in 1964 with his discovery that the Espíritu Pampa site Bingham had partially found down in the jungle 50 years before was actually far larger than had been suspected. It could now be properly identified as the site of Old Vilcabamba, the city the Incas escaped to right at the end of their 'kingdom in exile' when they were driven out of Vitcos. The Spanish burnt and looted it in 1572 before capturing Túpac Amaru.

Savoy's methods were often unorthodox and his work at Espíritu Pampa was cut short when a *denuncia* was issued against him by the local community. A search party was sent down from Lima to apprehend him, led by an American archaeologist called **Gary Ziegler**. Savoy escaped and has since concentrated very successfully on exploring Chachapoyas in the north.

In the 1980s, architect and ex-Marine called **Vince Lee** retraced much of Savoy's route and made positive identifications of many Inca fortresses along the way. Lee brought draughtsmanship and much-needed humour to the study of Inca ruins in the area, as the title of his entertaining book *Sixpac Manco* exemplifies.

My own introduction to exploration in the area came at roughly the same time, when I joined some of the reconnaissance groups organized by the Cusichaca Project, run by the British archaeologist Ann Kendall, who reported on the area around the Aobamba and Santa Teresa valleys.

The Vilcabamba became difficult to travel in during the height of the Sendero Luminoso years and it was not until 2002 that interest in the area was reawakened with the discovery of a hill-top Inca site on Cerro Victoria by a National Geographic team led by Peter Frost and Gary Ziegler – the same Ziegler who had chased after Gene Savoy several decades before.

This was followed in the same year by the discovery of another site by Ziegler and myself called Cota Coca, which lies in the lower Yanama Valley and has been concealed for many years because the sides of that valley have collapsed.

In 2003, another Thomson – of the Ziegler Research Expedition, this time supported by the Royal Geographical Society – used thermal imaging cameras to fly over the cloudforest and find the outlines of stone buildings beneath the vegetation. The main Inca site under investigation was called Llactapata – appropriately one of the very sites Bingham had first reported partially on, in 1912. As with Espíritu Pampa, Llactapata was found to be considerably larger than Bingham had initially realized.

The above is a short summary only of the many expeditions that have been made into the Vilcabamba. Unlike mountaineering and the climbing of summits, therei s no 'registered log' for the discovery of Inca sites and, while I have tried to attribute each successive discovery in the area to the correct team, there may be some unpublished explorers of whom I am unaware. I apologize to anyone who may have been inadvertently omitted as a result. In the words of Vince Lee: "I don't know who you are. I wish I did."

Why are discoveries still being made here when the rest of the world is so well mapped? It is partly because the Vilcabamba is such a dense quadrant of twisting river canyons and thick cloudforest, making it easy to pass within 3 m of a ruin and miss it.

Both for aesthetic and strategic reasons, the Incas chose to build on remote, isolated sites, as even the most casual visitor to Machu Picchu can observe. They also often built settlements in sectors scattered at different levels on a hillside, so that while one sector may have been found, others remain hidden.

All these factors mean that it is highly likely more ruins will be found in the years to come. The Vilcabamba has by no means given up all its secrets.

For more information see Hugh Thomson's book *The White Rock: An Exploration of the Inca Heartland*, Phoenix (UK)/Overlook Penguin (USA) and the website www.thewhiterock.co.uk, which has up-to-date links with the most recent discoveries.

In 1535, wishing to secure his communications with Spain, Pizarro founded Lima, near the ocean, as his capital. The same year Diego de Almagro set out to conquer Chile. Unsuccessful, he returned to Peru, quarrelled with Pizarro, and in 1538 fought a pitched battle with Pizarro's men at the salt pits, near Cuzco. He was defeated and put to death. Pizarro, who had not been at the battle, was assassinated in his palace in Lima by Almagro's son three years later.

For the next 27 years each succeeding representative of the Kingdom of Spain sought to subdue the Inca successor state of Vilcabamba, north of Cuzco, and to unify the fierce Spanish factions. Francisco de Toledo (appointed 1568) solved both problems during his 14 years in office: Vilcabamba was crushed in 1572 and the last reigning Inca, Túpac Amaru, put to death.

For the next 200 years the Viceroys closely followed Toledo's system, if not his methods. The Major Government – the Viceroy, the *Audiencia* (High Court), and *corregidores* (administrators) – ruled through the Minor Government – Indian chiefs in charge of large groups of natives – an approximation to the original Inca system.

### Towards Independence

The Indians rose in 1780, under the leadership of an Inca noble who called himself Túpac Amaru II. He and many of his lieutenants were captured and put to death under torture at Cuzco. Another Indian leader in revolt suffered the same fate in 1814, but this last flare-up had the sympathy of many of the locally born Spanish, who resented their status, inferior to the Spaniards born in Spain, the refusal to give them anything but the lowest offices, the high taxation imposed by the home government, and the severe restrictions upon trade with any country but Spain.

Help came to them from the outside world. José de San Martín's Argentine troops, convoyed from Chile under the protection of Lord Cochrane's squadron, landed in southern Peru on 7 September 1820. San Martín proclaimed Peruvian Independence at Lima on 28 July 1821, though most of the country was still in the hands of the Viceroy, José de La Serna. Bolívar, who had already freed Venezuela and Colombia, sent Antonio José de Sucre to Ecuador where, on 24 May 1822, he gained a victory over La Serna at Pichincha.

San Martín, after a meeting with Bolívar at Guayaquil, left for Argentina and a self-imposed exile in France, while Bolívar and Sucre completed the conquest of Peru by defeating La Serna at the battle of Junín (6 August 1824) and the decisive battle of Ayacucho (9 December 1824). For over a year there was a last stand in the Real Felipe fortress at Callao by the Spanish troops under General Rodil before they capitulated on 22 January 1826. Bolívar was invited to stay in Peru, but left for Colombia in 1826.



# Modern Peru

## Political developments

### 19th century

Independence from Spanish rule meant that power passed into the hands of the Creole elite with no immediate alternation of the colonial social system. The *contribución de indígenas*, the colonial tribute collected from the native peoples was not abolished until 1854, the same year as the ending of slavery. For much of the period since Independence Peruvian political life has been dominated by these traditional elites. Political parties have been slow to develop and the roots of much of the political conflict and instability which have marked the country's history lie in personal ambitions and in regional and other rivalries within the elite.

The early years after Independence were particularly chaotic as rival *caudillos* (political bosses) who had fought in the Independence wars vied with each other for power. The increased wealth brought about by the guano boom (the manure of seabirds had become an important fertilizer in Europe) led to greater stability, though political corruption became a serious problem under the presidency of **José Rufino Echenique** (1851-54) who paid out large sums of the guano revenues as compensation to upper-class families for their (alleged) losses in the Wars of Independence. Defeat by Chile in the War of the Pacific discredited civilian politicians even further and led to a period of military rule in the 1880s.

## Early 20th century

Even though the voting system was changed in 1898, this did little to change the dominance of the elite. Voting was not secret so landowners herded their workers to the polls and watched to make sure they voted correctly. Yet voters were also lured by promises as well as threats. One of the more unusual presidents was **Guillermo Billinghurst** (1912-14) who campaigned on the promise of a larger loaf of bread for five cents, thus gaining the nickname of 'Big Bread Billinghurst'. As president he proposed a publically funded housing programme, supported the introduction of an eight hour day and was eventually overthrown by the military who, along with the elite, were alarmed at his growing popularity among the urban population.

The 1920s was dominated by **Augusto Leguía**. After winning the 1919 elections Leguía claimed that Congress was plotting to prevent him from becoming president and induced the military to help him close Congress. Backed by the armed forces, Leguía introduced a new constitution which gave him greater powers and enabled him to be re-elected in 1924 and 1929. Claiming his goal was to prevent the rise of communism, he proposed to build a partnership between business and labour. A large programme of public works, particularly involving building roads, bridges and railways, was begun, the work being carried out by poor rural men who were forced into unpaid building work. The Leguía regime dealt harshly with critics: opposition newspapers were closed and opposition leaders arrested and deported. His overthrow in 1930 ended what Peruvians call the *Oncenio* (11-year period).

The 1920s also saw the emergence of a political thinker who would have great influence in the future, not only in Peru but elsewhere in Latin America. **Juan Carlos Mariátegui**, a socialist writer and journalist, argued that the solution to Peru's problems lay in the reintegration of the Indians through land reform and the breaking up of the great landed estates.

Another influential thinker of this period was **Víctor Raúl Haya de la Torre**, a student exiled by Leguía in 1924. He returned after the latter's downfall to create the **Alianza Popular Revolucionaria Americana** (APRA), a political party calling for state control of the economy, nationalization of key industries and protection of the middle classes, which, Haya de la Torre argued, were threatened by foreign economic interests.

In 1932 APRA seized control of Trujillo; when the army arrived to deal with the rising, the rebels murdered about 50 hostages, including 10 army officers. In reprisal the army murdered about 1000 local residents suspected of sympathizing with APRA. APRA eventually became the largest and easily the best-organized political party in Peru, but the distrust of the military and the upper class for Haya de la Torre ensured that he never became president.

A turning point in Peruvian history occurred in 1948 with the seizure of power by **General Manuel Odría**, backed by the coastal elite. Odría outlawed APRA and went on to win the 1950 election in which he was the only candidate. He pursued policies of encouraging export earnings and also tried to build up working-class support by public works projects in Lima. Faced with a decline in export earnings and the fall in world market prices after 1953, plus increasing unemployment, Odría was forced to stand down in 1956.

In 1962 Haya de la Torre was at last permitted to run for the presidency. However, although he won the largest percentage of votes he was prevented from taking office by the armed forces who seized power and organized fresh elections for 1963. In these the military obtained the desired result: Haya de la Torre came second to **Fernando Belaúnde Terry**. Belaúnde attempted to introduce reforms, particularly in the landholding structure of the sierra; when these reforms were weakened by landowner opposition in Congress, peasant groups began invading landholdings in protest.

At the same time, under the influence of the Cuban revolution, guerrilla groups began operating in the sierra. Military action to deal with this led to the deaths of an estimated 8000 people. Meanwhile Belaúnde's attempts to solve a long-running dispute with the International Petroleum Company (a subsidiary of Standard Oil) resulted in him being attacked for selling out to the unpopular oil company and contributed to the armed forces' decision to seize power in 1968.

## The 1968 coup and its legacy

This was a major landmark in Peruvian history. Led by **General Juan Velasco Alvarado**, the Junta had no intention of handing power back to the civilians. A manifesto issued on the day of the coup attacked the 'unjust social and economic order' and argued for its replacement by a new economic system 'neither capitalist nor communist'. Partly as a result of their experiences in dealing with the guerrilla movement, the coup leaders concluded that agrarian reform was a priority.

Wide-ranging land reform was launched in 1969, during which large estates were taken over and reorganized into cooperatives. By the mid-1970s, 75% of productive land was under cooperative management. The government also attempted to improve the lives of shanty-town dwellers around Lima, as well as attempting to increase the influence of workers in industrial companies. At the same time attempts were made to reduce the influence of foreign companies with the nationalization of several transnationals.

Understandably, opposition to the Velasco government came from the business and landholding elite. The government's crack-down on expressions of dissent, the seizure of newspapers and taking over of TV and radio stations all offended sections of the urban middle class. Trade unions and peasant movements found that, although they agreed with many of the regime's policies, it refused to listen and expected their passive and unqualified support. As world sugar and copper prices dropped, inflation rose and strikes increased. Velasco's problems were further increased by opposition within the armed forces and by his own ill health. In August 1975 he was replaced by **General Francisco Morales Bermúdez**, a more conservative officer, who dismantled some of Velasco's policies and led the way to a restoration of civilian rule.

Belaúnde returned to power in 1980 by winning the first elections after military rule. His government was badly affected by the 1982 debt crisis and the 1981-83 world recession, and inflation reached over 100% a year in 1983-84. His term was also marked by the growth of the Maoist guerrilla movement **Sendero Luminoso** (**Shining Path**) and the smaller **Túpac Amaru** (MRTA).

Initially conceived in the University of Ayacucho, Shining Path gained most support for its goal of overthrowing the whole system of Lima-based government from highland Indians and migrants to urban shanty towns. The activities of Sendero Luminoso and Túpac Amaru (MRTA) frequently disrupted transport and electricity supplies, although their strategies had to be reconsidered after the arrest of both their leaders in 1992. Víctor Polay of MRTA was arrested in June and Abimael Guzmán of Sendero Luminoso was captured in September and sentenced to life imprisonment. Although Sendero did not capitulate, many of its members took advantage of the Law of Repentance, which guaranteed lighter sentences in return for surrender, and freedom in exchange for valuable information. Meanwhile, Túpac Amaru was thought to have ceased operations (see below).

In 1985 APRA, in opposition for over 50 years, finally came to power. With Haya de la Torre dead, the APRA candidate **Alan García Pérez** won the elections and was allowed to take office by the armed forces. García attempted to implement an ambitious economic programme intended to solve many of Peru's deep-seated economic and social problems. He cut taxes, reduced interest rates, froze prices and devalued the currency. However, the economic boom which this produced in 1986-87 stored up problems as increased incomes were spent on imports. Moreover, the government's refusal to pay more than 10% of its foreign debt meant that it was unable to borrow. In 1988 inflation hit 3000% and unemployment soared. By the time his term of office ended in 1990 Peru was bankrupt and García and APRA were discredited.

## The Fujimori years

In presidential elections held over two rounds in 1990, **Alberto Fujimori** of the Cambio 90 movement defeated the novelist **Mario Vargas Llosa**, who belonged to the Fredemo (Democratic Front) coalition. Fujimori, without an established political network behind him, failed to win a majority in either the senate or the lower house. Lack of congressional support was one of the reasons behind the dissolution of congress and the suspension of the constitution on 5 April 1992.

President Fujimori declared that he needed a freer hand to introduce market reforms and combat terrorism and drug trafficking, at the same time as rooting out corruption. Initial massive popular support, although not matched internationally, did not evaporate. In elections to a new, 80-member Democratic Constituent Congress (CCD) in November 1992, Fujimori's Cambio 90/Nueva Mayoría coalition won a majority of seats. A new constitution drawn up by the CCD was approved by a narrow majority of the electorate in October 1993. Among the new articles were the immediate re-election of the president (previously prohibited for one presidential term), the death penalty for terrorist leaders, the establishment of a single-chamber congress, the reduction of the role of the state, the designation of Peru as a market economy and the favouring of foreign investment. As expected, Fujimori stood for re-election on 9 April 1995 and the opposition chose as an independent to stand against him former UN General Secretary, Javier Pérez de Cuéllar. Fujimori was re-elected by a resounding margin, winning about 65% of the votes cast. The coalition that supported him also won a majority in Congress.

The government's success in most economic areas did not appear to accelerate the distribution of foreign funds for social projects. Rising unemployment and the austerity imposed by economic policy continued to cause hardship for many, despite the government's stated aim of alleviating poverty.

Dramatic events on 17 December 1996 thrust several of these issues into sharper focus: 14 Túpac Amaru terrorists infiltrated a reception at the Japanese Embassy in Lima, taking 490 hostages. Among the rebels' demands were the release of their imprisoned colleagues, better treatment for prisoners and new measures to raise living standards. Most of the hostages were released and negotiations were pursued during a stalemate that lasted until 22 April 1997. The president took sole responsibility for the successful, but risky assault which freed all the hostages (one died of heart failure) and killed all the terrorists.

The popularity that Fujimori garnered from not yielding to Túpac Amaru deflected attention from his plans to stand for a third term following his unpopular manipulation of the law to persuade Congress that the new constitution did not apply to his first period in office. By 1998, opposition to Fujimori standing again had gained a substantial following, but not enough to dissuade the president or his supporters. Until the last month of campaigning for the 2000 presidential elections, Fujimori had a clear lead over his two main rivals, ex-mayor of Lima Alberto Andrade and former social security chief Luis Castaneda. Meanwhile, the popularity of a fourth candidate,

 Alejandro Toledo, a former World bank official of humble origins, surged to such an extent that he and Fujimori were neck and neck in the first poll. Toledo, a pro-marketeer given to left-wing rhetoric, and his supporters claimed that Fujimori's slim majority was the result of fraud, a view echoed in the pressure put on the president, by the US government among others, to allow a second ballot.

The run-off election, on 28 May 2000, was also contentious since foreign observers, including the Organization of American States, said the electoral system was unprepared and flawed, proposing a postponement. The authorities refused to delay. Toledo boycotted the election and Fujimori was returned unopposed, but with scant approval. Having won, he proposed "to strengthen democracy".

This pledge proved to be utterly worthless following the airing of a secretly shot video on 14 September 2000 of Fujimori's close aide and head of the National Intelligence Service (SIN), Vladimiro Montesinos, handing over US$15,000 to a congressman, Alberto Kouri, to persuade him to switch allegiances to Fujimori's coalition. Fujimori's demise was swift. His initial reaction was to close down SIN and announce new elections, eventually set for 8 April 2001, at which he would not stand.

Montesinos was declared a wanted man and fled to Panama, where he was denied asylum. He returned to Peru in October, prompting First Vice-president Francisco Tudela to resign in protest over Montesinos' continuing influence. Fujimori personally led the search parties to find his former ally and Peruvians watched in amazement as this game of cat-and-mouse was played out on their TV screens.

While Montesinos himself successfully evaded capture, investigators began to uncover the extent of his empire, which held hundreds of senior figures in its web. His activities encompassed extortion, money laundering, bribery, intimidation, probably arms and drugs dealing and possibly links with the CIA and death squads. Swiss bank accounts in his name were found to contain about US$70 million, while other millions were discovered in accounts in the Cayman Islands and elsewhere.

Meanwhile, Fujimori, apparently in pursuit of his presidential duties, made various overseas trips, including to Japan. Here, on 20 November, he sent Congress an email announcing his resignation. Congress rejected this, firing him instead on charges of being 'morally unfit' to govern. An interim president, Valentín Paniagua, was sworn in, with ex-UN Secretary General Javier Pérez de Cuéllar as Prime Minister, and the government set about uncovering the depth of corruption associated with Montesinos and Fujimori.



## After Fujimori

In the run-up to the 2001 ballot, the front-runner was Alejandro Toledo, but with far from a clear majority. Ex-President Alan García emerged as Toledo's main opponent, forcing a run-off on 3 June. This was won by Toledo with 52% of the vote. He pledged to heal the wounds that had opened in Peru since his first electoral battle with the disgraced Fujimori, but his presidency was marked by slow progress on both the political and economic fronts. With the poverty levels still high, few jobs created and a variety of scandals, Toledo's popularity plummeted. A series of major confrontations and damaging strikes forced the president to declare a state of emergency in May 2003 to restore order. Nor could Toledo escape charges of corruption being laid at his own door; accusations that he and his sister orchestrated voter fraud in 2000 were upheld by a congressional commission in May 2005 (Toledo was formally charged in December 2006).

The April 2006 elections were contested by Alán García, the conservative Lourdes Flores and Ollanta Humala, a former military officer and unsuccessful coup leader who claimed support from Venezuela's Hugo Chávez and Evo Morales of Bolivia. García and Humala won through to the second round, which García won, in part because many were suspicious, even critical of the 'Chávez factor' and the latter's interference in Peruvian affairs. García was anxious to overcome his past record as president and he pledged to hold back public spending despite consistent economic growth from 2005 to 2007. Labour unions complained that Peru's poor were not benefiting from the strong economy, leading to mass demonstrations against García in mid-2007. The Peruvian Congress, meanwhile, approved a trade pact with the United States in 2006, García's support for this being an indication of his willingness to court orthodoxy, rather than the left-leaning model proposed by his Andean neighbours Hugo Chávez and Evo Morales. The US Congress approved the pact in November 2007.

All the while, the past continued to dog the present. Since 2002, Montesinos has been convicted of a number of crimes in a series trials and yet more prosecutions are in process. In 2004, prosecutors also sought to charge exiled Fujimori with ordering the deaths of 25 people in 1991 and 1992. This followed the Truth and Reconciliation Committee's report (2003) into the civil war of the 1980s-1990s, which stated that over 69,000 Peruvians had been killed. With attempts to extradite Fujimori from Japan coming to nothing, prosecution could not proceed. Meanwhile Fujimori himself declared that he would be exonerated and stand again for the presidency in 2006. To this end he flew to Chile in November 2005 with a view to entering Peru, but the Chilean authorities jailed him for seven months and then denied him exit from Chile pending the outcome of an extradition request by Peru. In September 2007 the Chilean Supreme Court determined that Fujimori should be sent to Peru to stand trial.

## Society

The most remarkable thing about Peru, population 28.7 million in 2007, is its people. For most Peruvians life is a daily struggle to survive in the face of seemingly insurmountable problems. But most people do get by, through a combination of ingenuity, determination and sheer hard work.

Peru may not be the poorest country in South America, and official estimates show the number of poor declining from over 50% of the population to about 44% in 2007, but almost a fifth of people still live in extreme poverty. Over a third of homes have no electricity or running water and a third of children suffer from chronic malnutrition.

### Health

There have been major improvements in health care in recent years, but almost a third of the population have no access to public health services. The infant mortality rate is high – 30 deaths per 1000 births – and the figure rises steeply in some rural areas where one in ten infants die within a year of birth.

As only a small percentage of the population contributes to social security schemes, medical consultations are not necessarily free. People also have to pay for prescribed medicines, which are very expensive, and so rarely finish a course of treatment. Lack of health education and limited primary health care also means that many women die in childbirth. Abortion is illegal in Peru, but those with cash can always find a private doctor. Those without the means to pay for a doctor run the risk of death or infection from botched abortions.

### Education

Education is free and compulsory for both sexes between six and 14. There are public and private secondary schools and private elementary schools. There are 32 state and private universities, and two Catholic universities. But resources are extremely limited and teachers earn a pittance. Poorer schoolchildren don't have money to buy pencils and notebooks and textbooks are few and far between in state schools. Furthermore, many children have to work instead of attending school; a quarter of those who start primary school don't finish. This is also due to the fact that classes are taught in Spanish and those whose native tongue is Quechua, Aymara or one of the Amazonian languages find it difficult and give up.

### Migration

The structure of Peruvian society, especially in the coastal cities, has been radically altered by internal migration. This movement began most significantly in the 1950s and 1960s as people from all provinces of Peru sought urban jobs in place of work on the land. It was a time of great upheaval as the old system of labour on large estates was threatened by the peasant majority's growing awareness of the imbalances between the wealthy cities and impoverished sierra. The process culminated in the agrarian reforms of the government of General Juan Velasco (1968-75). Highland-to-city migration was given renewed impetus during the war between the state and Sendero Luminoso in the 1980s. Many communities which were depopulated in that decade are now beginning to come alive again.

# Culture

## People

Peru has a substantial indigenous population, only smaller as a percentage of the total than Bolivia and Guatemala of the Latin American republics. The literacy rate of the indigenous population is the lowest of any comparable group in South America and their diet is 50% below acceptable levels. The highland Indians bore the brunt of the conflict between Sendero Luminoso terrorists and the security forces, which caused thousands of deaths and mass migration from the countryside to provincial cities or to Lima. Many indigenous groups are also under threat from colonization, development and road-building projects. Long after the end of Spanish rule, discrimination, dispossession and exploitation is still a fact of life for many native Peruvians.

### Quechua

According to Inca legend, the dynasty's forebears were a small group who originally lived near Lake Titicaca. They later moved to Cuzco, from where they expanded to create the Inca Empire. Their culture soon covered an area from the southernmost edge of present-day Colombia, through Quito and Ecuador, Peru and Bolivia to northern Chile and Argentina. Out of this rapid expansion grew the myth that the Quechua language originated with the Incas and spread along with their influence. But linguistic evidence points to Quechua being spoken in northern and central Peru long before the Incas arrived on the scene, even though the precise starting point of the language cannot be pinpointed. So the common idea that Quechua equals Inca is misleading (for more information on this issue, visit www.quechua.org.uk).

Quechua is spoken widely throughout the Andes by people of a predominantly agricultural society, growing potatoes and corn as their basic diet, largely outside the money economy. This society ranges from Bolivia to Ecuador (where the language is known as Quichua). According to some estimates, about two million Quechua-speakers cannot converse in Spanish, but there are many more Indians who now speak only Spanish. Though recognized as an official language, little effort is made to promote Quechua nationally. It is only the remoteness of many Quechua speakers which has preserved it in rural areas. This isolation has also helped preserve many ancient traditions and beliefs. See also Festivals, on page 308.

## The ancient leaf

Coca flourishes in the subtropical valleys of the eastern Andes, as well as in the Sierra Nevada de Santa Marta in Colombia, and for millennia it has been central to the daily life and religious rituals of many of the indigenous cultures of South America. The coca plant (*Erythroxylum coca*) is an evergreen shrub found in warm, fertile valleys. Its leaves are oval, 3-5 cm long and resemble laurel or bay leaves. Chewed with lime, which acts as a catalyst, the leaf releases a mild dose of cocaine alkaloid, numbing the senses, dulling both hunger and pain and even providing some vitamins otherwise absent in the starch-heavy diet of the highland people.

Under the Incas, the use of coca was restricted to ceremonies involving the nobility and priesthood. After the conquest the Spanish promoted it among the half-starved slaves of the mines of Huancavelica and Potosí. It wasn't until 1862 that an Austrian chemist refined the leaf to produce pure cocaine, which was subsequently marketed as a cure for opium addiction, a local anaesthetic, a tonic and (as Coca Cola) a headache remedy. In the 1970s, with the drug's growth in popularity in the US and Europe, cocaine became big business, funding entire guerrilla movements and creating multi-billion dollar fortunes for men like Colombia's Pablo Escobar.

Some ethnobiologists estimate that coca has been cultivated in the Andes for at least 4000 years. Archaeological discoveries in Ecuador from the Valdivia Period (1500 BC) seem to provide early evidence of the use of coca: ceramic figurines have been found showing men with the bulges in the cheeks characteristic of the coca chewer. The traditional consumption of coca remains an important symbol of ethnic identity for the indigenous peoples of the highlands.

Under the Incas, coca was revered as a gift from the gods and was strictly controlled by the state. It was used in religious rites and burials and for divination. After the conquest, the role of coca in indigenous religious practices and divination provoked the Catholic extirpators of idolatry to ban its use. Diego de Robles began the Western-led demonization of coca which continues to this day when he declared that it was "a plant that the devil invented for the total destruction of the natives", and it was condemned outright at the first ecclesiastical council of Lima in 1551.

However, it did not take the Spanish long to recognize the enormous business potential. As the Uruguayan historian Eduardo Galeano writes: "In the mines of Potosí in the 16th century as much was spent on European clothing for the oppressors as on coca for the oppressed. In Cuzco, 400 Spanish merchants made their living from trafficking coca, one hundred thousand baskets, containing a million kilos of coca leaves, entered the silver mines of Potosí annually. The Church extracted taxes from the traffic. Inca Garcilaso de la Vega tells us, in his *Royal Commentaries*, that "the greater part of the income of the bishop, canons and other church ministers came from the tithe on coca. ... With the few coins that they received for their work, the Indians bought coca leaves ... chewing the leaves they could stand better ... the inhuman tasks imposed upon them".

Today coca continues to play an important role in the lives of Peru's indigenous highlanders. The act of chewing coca is a form of social bonding; it can stave off hunger and fatigue, relieve the effects of altitude, help divine the future, or appease Mother Earth in ceremonies as old as the cultures that have guarded them so jealously through the centuries.

## Aymara

High up in the Andes, in the southern part of Peru, lies a wide, barren and hostile plateau, the altiplano. Prior to Inca rule Tiahuanaco on Lake Titicaca was a highly organized centre for one the greatest cultures South America has ever witnessed: the Aymara people. Today, the shores of this lake and the plains that surround it remain the homeland of the Aymara. The majority live in Bolivia, the rest are scattered on the southwestern side of Peru and northern Chile. The climate is so harsh on the altiplano that, though they are extremely hardworking, their lives are very poor. They speak their own language, Aymara. More so than the scattered group of different peoples that speak Quechua, the Altiplano Aymara people form a compact group with a clear sense of their own distinct identity and in many respects have been able to preserve more of their indigenous traditions and belief system.

## Amazonian peoples

Before the arrival of the Europeans, an estimated six million people inhabited the Amazon Basin, comprising more than 2000 tribes or ethnic-linguistic groups who managed to adapt to their surroundings through the domestication of a great variety of animals and plants, and to benefit from the numerous nutritional, curative, narcotic and hallucinogenic properties of thousands of wild plants.

It's not easy to determine the precise origin of these aboriginal people. What is known, however, is that since the start of colonial times this population slowly but constantly decreased, mainly because of western diseases such as influenza and measles. This demographic decline reached dramatic levels during the rubber boom of the late 19th and early 20th centuries as a result of forced labour and slavery.

Today, at the basin level, the population is calculated at no more than two million inhabitants making up 400 ethnic groups, of which approximately 200,000 to 250,000 live in the Peruvian jungle. Within the basin it is possible to distinguish at least three large conglomerates of aboriginal societies: the inhabitants of the *varzea*, or seasonally flooded lands alongside the large rivers (such as the Omagua, Cocama and Shipibo people); the people in the interfluvial zones or firm lands (such as the Amahuaca, Cashibo and Yaminahua) and those living in the Andean foothills (such as the Amuesha, Asháninka and Machiguenga).

The Amazonian natives began to be decimated in the 16th century, and so were the first endangered species of the jungle. These communities still face threats to their traditional lifestyles, notably from timber companies, gold miners and multinational oil companies. There appears to be little effective control of deforestation and the intrusion of colonists who have taken over native lands to establish small farms. And though oil companies have reached compensation agreements with local communities, previous oil exploration has contaminated many jungle rivers, as well as exposing natives to risk from diseases against which they have no immunity.

## Criollos and mestizos

The first immigrants were the Spaniards who followed Pizarro's expeditionary force. Their effect, demographically, politically and culturally, has been enormous. They intermarried with the indigenous population and the children of mixed parentage were called mestizos. The Peruvian-born children of Spanish parents were known as *criollos*, though this word is now used to describe people who live on the coast, regardless of their ancestry, and coastal culture in general.

## Afro-Peruvians

Peru's black community is based on the coast, mainly in Chincha, south of Lima, and also in some working-class districts of the capital. Their ancestors were originally imported into Peru in the 16th century as slaves to work on the sugar and cotton plantations on the coast. Though small – between 2% and 5% of the total population –

the black community has had a major influence on Peruvian culture, particularly in music and dancing and cuisine.

### Asian immigrants

There are two main Asian communities in Peru, the Japanese and Chinese. Large numbers of poor Chinese labourers were brought to Peru in the mid-19th century to work in virtual slavery on the guano reserves on the Pacific Coast and to build the railroads in the central Andes. The culinary influence of the Chinese can be seen in the many *chifas* found throughout the country.

The Japanese community, now numbering some 100,000, established itself in the first half of the 20th century. The normally reclusive community gained prominence when Alberto Fujimori, one of its members, became the first president of Japanese descent outside Japan anywhere in the world. During Fujimori's presidency, many other Japanese Peruvians took prominent positions in business, central and local government. The nickname 'chino' is applied to anyone of Oriental origin.

### Europeans

Like most of Latin America, Peru received many emigrés from Europe seeking land and opportunities in the late 19th century. The country's wealth and political power remains concentrated in the hands of this small and exclusive class of whites, which also consists of the descendants of the first Spanish families. There still exists a deep divide between people of European descent and the old colonial snobbery persists.

## Religion

The Inca religion (described on page 289) was displaced by Roman Catholicism from the 16th century onwards, the conversion of the inhabitants of the 'New World' to Christianity being one of the stated aims of the Spanish *conquistadores*. Today, statistics vary between 81 and 89% of the population declaring itself Catholic.

One of the first exponents of Liberation Theology, under which the Conference of Latin American Bishops in 1968 committed themselves to the 'option for the poor', was Gustavo Gutiérrez, from Huánuco. This doctrine caused much consternation to orthodox Catholics, particularly those members of the Latin American church who had traditionally aligned themselves with the oligarchy. Gutiérrez, however, traced the church's duty to the voiceless and the marginalized back to Fray Bartolomé de las Casas.

The Catholic Church faced a further challenge to its authority when President Fujimori won the battle over family planning and the need to slow down the rate of population growth. Its greatest threat, however, comes from the proliferation of evangelical Protestant groups throughout the country. Some 6% of the population now declare themselves Protestant and one million or more people belong to some 27 different non-Catholic denominations.

Although the vast majority of the population ostensibly belongs to the Roman Catholic religion, in reality religious life for many Peruvians is a mix of Catholic beliefs imported from Europe and indigenous traditions based on animism, the worship of deities from the natural world such as mountains, animals and plants. Some of these ancient indigenous traditions and beliefs are described throughout this section.

## Arts and crafts

Peru is exceptionally rich in handicrafts. Its geographic division into four distinct regions – coast, mountains, valleys and Amazon Basin – coupled with cultural

## The family that weaves together ...

Nowadays, and presumably for at least the last 200 to 300 years, the women weave most of the men's garments and the men weave the women's, or at least a very important part of them: the men weave the women's skirts. It works like this: the women weave the fine warp-faced pieces like *lliclIas* (*mantas*), ponchos, *chumpis* (belts), *ch'uspas*, and similar items. But the plainer elements, men's pantaloons, women's skirts, the colourful wide *golones* (the decorative edging attached to them) are woven by men on large treadle looms, imported from Europe soon after the conquest. The men also weave the thick blankets, but on heavier versions of the traditional backstrap loom (or waist loom). The men are also the knitters and crochet makers. There are a few elements of Andean garb that are not woven at all, the most important being the *chullo* (the classic wool cap with the earl flaps), but there are also *chullos* for children of either sex and, in some areas like Pitumarca, for young girls until puberty. All of these are knitted, the preferred alternative to the standard knitting needles being the spokes of bicycle wheels.

differences, has resulted in numerous variations in technique and design. Each province, even each community, has developed its own style of weaving or carving.

The Incas inherited 3000 years of skills and traditions: gold, metal and precious stonework from the Chimú; feather textiles from the Nazca; and the elaborate textiles of the Paracas. All of these played important roles in political, social and religious ceremonies. Though much of this artistic heritage was destroyed by the Spanish conquest, the traditions adapted and evolved in numerous ways, absorbing new methods, concepts and materials from Europe while maintaining ancient techniques and symbols.

## Textiles and costumes

Woven cloth was the most highly prized possession and sought after trading commodity in the Andes in pre-Columbian times. It is, therefore, not surprising that ancient weaving traditions have survived. **The Incas** inherited this rich weaving tradition. They forced the Aymaras to work in *mit'as* or textile workshops. The ruins of some enormous *mit'as* can be seen at the temple of Raqchi, south of Cuzco (see page 212). Inca textiles are of high quality and very different from coastal textiles, being warp-faced, closely woven and without embroidery. The largest quantities of the finest textiles were made specifically to be burned as ritual offerings – a tradition which still survives. The Spanish, too, exploited this wealth and skill by using the *mit'as* and exporting the cloth to Europe.

**Prior to Inca rule** Aymara men wore a tunic (*llahua*) and a mantle (*llacata*) and carried a bag for coca leaves (*huallquepo*). The women wore a wrapped dress (*urku*) and mantle (*iscayo*) and a belt (*huaka*); their coca bag was called an *istalla*. The *urku* was fastened at shoulder level with a pair of metal *tupu*, the traditional Andean dress pins.

**The Inca men** had tunics (*unkus*) and a bag for coca leaves called a *ch'uspa*. The women wore a blouse (*huguna*), skirts (*aksu*) and belts (*chumpis*), and carried foodstuffs in large, rectangular cloths called *lliclIas*, which were fastened at the chest with a single pin or a smaller clasp called a *ttipqui*. Women of the Sacred Valley now wear a layered, gathered skirt called a *pollera* and a *montera*, a large, round, red Spanish type of hat. Textiles continue to play an important part in society. They are still used specifically for ritual ceremonies and some even held to possess magical powers.

## Textile materials and techniques

The Andean people used mainly alpaca or llama wool. The former can be spun into fine, shining yarn when woven and has a lustre similar to that of silk, though sheep's wool came to be widely used following the Spanish conquest.

A commonly used technique is the drop spindle. A stick is weighted with a wooden wheel and the raw material is fed through one hand. A sudden twist and drop in the spindle spins the yarn. This very sensitive art can be seen practised by women while herding animals in the fields. Spinning wheels were introduced by Europeans and are now prevalent owing to increased demand. Pre-Columbian looms were often portable and those in use today are generally similar. A woman will herd her animals while making a piece of costume, perhaps on a backstrap loom, or waist loom, so-called because the weaver controls the tension on one side with her waist with the other side tied to an upright or tree. The pre-Columbian looms are usually used for personal costume while the treadle loom is used by men for more commercial pieces.

The skills of **dyeing** were still practised virtually unchanged even after the arrival of the Spanish. Nowadays, the word *makhnu* refers to any natural dye, but originally was the name for cochineal, an insect which lives on the leaves of the nopal cactus. These dyes were used widely by pre-Columbian weavers. Today, the biggest centre of production in South America is the valleys around Ayacucho. Vegetable dyes are also used, made from the leaves, fruit and seeds of shrubs and flowers and from lichen, tree bark and roots.

## Pottery

Inca ceramic decoration consists mainly of small-scale geometric and usually symmetrical designs. One distinctive form of vessel which continues to be made and used is the *arybola*. This pot is designed to carry liquid, especially *chicha*, and is secured with a rope on the bearer's back. It is believed that *arybolas* were used mainly by the governing Inca elite and became important status symbols. Today, Inca-style is very popular in Cuzco and Pisac.

With the Spanish invasion many indigenous communities lost their artistic traditions, others remained relatively untouched, while others still combined Hispanic and indigenous traditions and techniques. The Spanish brought three innovations: the potter's wheel, which gave greater speed and uniformity; knowledge of the enclosed kiln; and the technique of lead glazes. The enclosed kiln made temperature regulation easier and allowed higher temperatures to be maintained, producing stronger pieces. Today, many communities continue to apply prehispanic techniques, while others use more modern processes.

## Jewellery and metalwork

Some of the earliest goldwork originates from the Chavín culture – eg the *Tumi* knife found in Lambayeque. These first appeared in the Moche culture, when they were associated with human sacrifice. Five centuries later, the Incas used *tumis* for surgical operations such as trepanning skulls. Today, they are a common motif.

The Incas associated gold with the sun. However, very few examples remain as the Spanish melted down their amassed gold and silver objects. They then went on to send millions of Indians to their deaths in gold and silver mines.

During the colonial period gold and silver pieces were made to decorate the altars of churches and houses of the elite. Metalworkers came from Spain and Italy to develop the industry. The Spanish preferred silver and strongly influenced the evolution of silverwork during the colonial period. A style known as Andean baroque developed around Cuzco embracing both indigenous and European elements. Silver bowls in this style – *cochas* – are still used in Andean ceremonies.

## Woodcarving

Wood is one of the most commonly used materials. Carved ceremonial objects include drums, carved sticks with healing properties, masks and the Incas' *keros* – wooden vessels for drinking *chicha*. *Keros* come in all shapes and sizes and were traditionally decorated with scenes of war, local dances, or harvesting coca leaves. The Chancay, who lived along the coast between 100 BC and AD 1200, used *keros* carved with sea birds and fish. Today, they are used in some Andean ceremonies, especially during **Fiesta del Cruz**, the Andean May festival.

**Glass mirrors** were introduced by the Spanish, although the Chimú and Lambayeque cultures used obsidian and silver plates, and Inca *chasquis* (messengers) used reflective stones to communicate between hilltop forts. Transporting mirrors was costly, therefore they were produced in Lima and Quito. Cuzco and Cajamarca then became centres of production. In Cuzco the frames were carved, covered in gold leaf and decorated with tiny pieces of cut mirror. Cajamarca artisans, meanwhile, incorporated painted glass into the frames.

## Gourd-carving

Gourd-carving, or *mate burilado*, as it is known, is one of Peru's most popular and traditional handicrafts. It is thought even to predate pottery – engraved gourds found on the coast have been dated to some 3500 years ago. During the Inca empire gourd-carving became a valued art form and workshops were set up and supported by the state. Gourds were used in rituals and ceremonies and to make *poporos* – containers for the lime used while chewing coca leaves.

# Music and dance

The music of Peru can be described as the very heartbeat of the country. Peruvians see music as something in which to participate, and not as a spectacle. Just about everyone, it seems, can play a musical instrument or sing. Just as music is the heartbeat of the country, so dance conveys the rich and ancient heritage that typifies much of the national spirit. Peruvians are tireless dancers and dancing is the most popular form of entertainment. Unsuspecting travellers should note that once they make that first wavering step there will be no respite until they collapse from exhaustion.

Each region has its own distinctive music and dance that reflects its particular lifestyle, its mood and its physical surroundings. The music of the sierra, for example, is played in a minor key and tends to be sad and mournful, while the music of the lowlands is more up-tempo and generally happier. Peruvian music divides at a very basic level into that of the highlands (*Andina*) and that of the coast (*Criolla*).

**Highlands** When people talk of Peruvian music they are almost certainly referring to the music of the Quechua- and Aymara-speaking Indians of the highlands which provides the most distinctive Peruvian sound. The highlands themselves can be very roughly subdivided into some half dozen major musical regions, of which perhaps the most characteristic are Ancash and the north, the Mantaro Valley, Cuzco, Puno and the Altiplano, Ayacucho and Parinacochas.

**Urban and other styles** Owing to the overwhelming migration of peasants into the barrios of Lima, most types of Andean music and dance can be seen in the capital, notably on Sundays at the so-called *Coliseos*, which exist for that purpose. This flood of migration to the cities has also meant that the distinct styles of regional and ethnic groups have become blurred. One example is **Chicha music,** which comes from the *pueblos jóvenes*, and was once the favourite dance music of Peru's urban working class. *Chicha* is a hybrid of Huayno music and the Colombian cumbia rhythm – a meeting of the highlands and the tropical coast.

Another recent phenomenon is **tecno-cumbia**, which originated in the jungle region with groups such as **Rossy War**, from Puerto Maldonado, and **Euforia**, from Iquitos. It is a vibrant dance music which has gained much greater popularity across Peruvian society than *chicha* music ever managed. There are now also many exponents on the coast such as **Agua Marina** and **Armonía 10**. Many of the songs comment on political issues and Fujimori used to join **Rossy War** on stage. Tecno-cumbia has evolved into a more sophisticated form with wider appeal across Peruvian society, with **Grupo 5**, from Chiclayo, one of the most popular exponents.

**Música criolla**, the music from the coast, could not be more different from that of the sierra. Here the roots are Spanish and African. The immensely popular **Valsesito** is a syncopated waltz that would certainly be looked at askance in Vienna and the **Polca** has also undergone an attractive sea change.

Reigning over all, though, is the **Marinera**, Peru's national dance, a splendidly rhythmic and graceful courting encounter and a close cousin of Chile's and Bolivia's *Cueca* and the Argentine *Zamba*, all of them descended from the *zamacueca*. The Marinera has its *Limeña* and *Norteña* versions and a more syncopated relative, the *Tondero*, found in the northern coastal regions, is said to have been influenced by slaves brought from Madagascar.

All these dances are accompanied by guitars and frequently the *cajón*, a resonant wooden box on which the player sits, pounding it with his hands. Great names of *música criolla* include the singer/composers **Chabuca Granda** and **Alicia Maguiña**, the singer **Jesús Vásquez** and the groups **Los Morochucos** and **Hermanos Zañartu**.

**Afro-Peruvian** Also on the coast is the music of the small but influential black community, the *Música Negroide* or *Afro-Peruano*, which had virtually died out when it was resuscitated in the 1950s, but has since gone from strength to strength, thanks to **Nicomedes and Victoria Santa Cruz** who have been largely responsible for popularizing this black music and making it an essential ingredient in contemporary Peruvian popular music. It has all the qualities to be found in black music from the Caribbean – a powerful, charismatic beat, rhythmic and lively dancing, and strong percussion provided by the *cajón* and the *quijada de burro*, a donkey's jaw with the teeth loosened. Its greatest star is the Afro-Peruvian diva **Susana Baca**. Her incredible, passionate voice inspired Talking Head's David Byrne to explore this genre further and release a compilation album in 1995, thus bringing Afro-Peruvian music to the attention of the world. Other notable exponents are the excellent **Perú Negro**, one of the best music and dance groups in Latin America, and the singer Eva Ayllón. **Novalima**, a group of internationally based Peruvian musicians, has produced new arrangements of many classic Afro-Peruvian tracks (see www.novalima.net).

**Musical instruments** Before the arrival of the Spanish in Latin America, the only instruments were wind and percussion. Although it is a popular misconception that Andean music is based on the panpipes, guitar and *charango*, anyone who travels through the Andes will realize that these instruments only represent a small aspect of Andean music. The highland instrumentation varies from region to region, although the harp and violin are ubiquitous. In the Mantaro area the harp is backed by brass and wind instruments, notably the clarinet. In Cuzco it is the *charango* and *quena* and on the altiplano the *sicu* panpipes.

The *quena* is a flute, usually made of reed, characterized by not having a mouthpiece to blow through. As with all Andean instruments, there is a family of *quenas* varying in length from around 15 cm to 50 cm. The *sicu* is the Aymara name for the *zampoña*, or panpipes. It is the most important prehispanic Andean instrument, formed by several reed tubes of different sizes held together by knotted string. Virtually the only instrument of European origin is the *charango*. When stringed instruments were first introduced by the Spanish, the indigenous people liked them but wanted something that was their own and so the *charango* was born. Originally, they were made of clay, condor skeletons and armadillo or tortoise shells.

## Dances

The highlands are immensely rich in terms of music and dance, with over 200 dances recorded. Every village has its fiestas and every fiesta has its communal and religious dances. *Comparsas* are organized groups of dancers who perform for spectators dances following a set pattern of movements to a particular musical accompaniment, wearing a specific costume. These dances have a long tradition, having mostly originated from certain contexts and circumstances and some of them still parody the ex-Spanish colonial masters.

Many dances for couples and/or groups are danced spontaneously at fiestas throughout Peru. These include indigenous dances which have originated in a specific region and ballroom dances that reflect the Spanish influence. One of the most popular of the indigenous dances is the **Huayno**, which originated on the altiplano but is now danced throughout the country. It involves numerous couples, who whirl around or advance down the street, arm-in-arm, in a *pandilla*. During fiestas, and especially after a few drinks, this can develop into a kind of uncontrolled frenzy.

# Festivals

Fiestas (festivals) are a fundamental part of life for most Peruvians, taking place up and down the length and breadth of the country and with such frequency that it would be hard to miss one, even during the briefest of stays. This is fortunate, because arriving in any town or village during these inevitably frenetic celebrations is one of the great Peruvian experiences.

While Peru's festivals can't rival those of Brazil for fame or colour, the quantity of alcohol consumed and the partying run them pretty close. What this means is that, at some point, you will fall over, through inebriation or exhaustion, or both. After several days of this, you will awake with a hangover the size of the Amazon rainforest and probably have no recollection of what you did with your backpack.

The object of the fiesta is a practical one, such as the success of the coming harvest or the fertility of animals. Thus the constant eating, drinking and dancing serves the purpose of giving thanks for the Sun and Rain that makes things grow and for the fertility of the soil and livestock, gifts from *Pachamama* (Mother Earth), the most sacred of all gods. So, when you see a Peruvian spill a little *chicha* (maize beer) every time they refill, it's not because they're sloppy but because they're offering a *ch'alla* (sacrifice) to Pachamama.



# Literature

The fact that the Incas had no written texts in the conventional European sense and that the Spaniards were keen to suppress their conquest's culture means that there is little evidence today of what poetry and theatre was performed in pre-conquest times. It is known that the Incas had two types of poet, the *amautas* – historians, poets and teachers who composed works that celebrated the ruling class' gods, heroes and events – and *haravecs* – who expressed popular sentiments. Written Quechua today is less common than works in the oral tradition. Although Spanish culture has had some influence on Quechua, the native stories, lyrics and fables retain their own identity. Not until the 19th century did Peruvian writers begin seriously to incorporate indigenous ideas into their art, but their audience was limited. Nevertheless, the influence of Quechua on Peruvian literature in Spanish continues to grow.

## Colonial period



In 16th-century Lima, headquarters of the Viceroyalty of Peru, the Spanish officials concentrated their efforts on the religious education of the new territories and literary output was limited to mainly histories and letters.

Chroniclers such as **Pedro Cieza de León** (*Crónica del Perú*, published from 1553) and **Agustín de Zárate** (*Historia del descubrimiento y conquista del Perú*, 1555) were written from the point of view that Spanish domination was right. Their most renowned successors, though, took a different stance. **Inca Garcilaso de la Vega** was a mestizo, whose *Comentarios reales que tratan del origen de los Incas* (1609) were at pains to justify the achievements, religion and culture of the Inca Empire. He also commented on Spanish society in the colony. A later work, *Historia general del Perú* (1617), went further in condemning Viceroy Toledo's suppression of Inca culture. Through his work, written in Spain, many aspects of Inca society, plus poems and prayers have survived.

Writing at about the same time as Inca Garcilaso was **Felipe Guaman Poma de Ayala**, whose *El primer nueva corónica y buen gobierno* (1613-1615) is possibly one of the most reproduced of Latin American texts (eg on T-shirts, CDs, posters and carrier bags). Guaman Poma was a minor provincial Inca chief whose writings and illustrations, addressed to King Felipe III of Spain, offer a view of a stable pre-conquest Andean society (not uniquely Inca), in contrast with the unsympathetic colonial society that usurped it.

In the years up to Independence, the growth of an intellectual elite in Lima spawned more poetry than anything else. As *criollo* discontent grew, satire increased both in poetry and in the sketches which accompanied dramas imported from Spain. The poet **Mariano Melgar** (1791-1815), who wrote in a variety of styles, died in an uprising against the Spanish but played an important part in the Peruvian struggle from freedom from the colonial imagination.

## After Independence

After Independence, Peruvian writers imitated Spanish *costumbrismo*, sketches of characters and lifestyles from the new Republic. The first author to transcend this fashion was **Ricardo Palma** (1833-1919), whose inspiration, the *tradición*, fused *costumbrismo* and Peru's rich oral traditions. Palma's hugely popular *Tradiciones peruanas* is a collection of pieces which celebrate the people, history and customs of Peru through sayings, small incidents in mainly colonial history and gentle irony.

Much soul-searching was to follow Peru's defeat in the War of the Pacific. **Manuel González Prada** (1844-1918), for instance, wrote essays fiercely critical of the state of the nation: *Páginas libres* (1894), *Horas de lucha* (1908). **José Carlos Mariátegui**, the foremost Peruvian political thinker of the early 20th century, said that González Prada represented the first lucid instant of Peruvian consciousness.

## 20th century

Mariátegui himself (1895-1930), after a visit to Europe in 1919, considered deeply the question of Peruvian identity, writing about politics, economics, literature and the Indian question from a Marxist perspective (see *Siete ensayos de interpretación de la realidad peruana*, 1928). Other writers had continued this theme. **Clorinda Matto de Turner** (1854-1909), with *Aves sin nido* (1889), was the forerunner by several years of the 'indigenist' genre in Peru and the most popular of those who took up González Prada's cause. Other prose writers continued in this vein at the beginning of the 20th century, but it was **Ciro Alegría** (1909-67) who gave major, fictional impetus to the racial question. Of his first three novels, *La serpiente de oro* (1935), *Los perros hambrientos* (1938) and *El mundo es ancho y ajeno* (1941), the latter is his most famous.

Contemporary with Alegría was **José María Arguedas** (1911-69), whose novels, stories and politics were also deeply rooted in the ethnic question. Arguedas, though not Indian, had a largely Quechua upbringing and tried to reconcile this with the hispanic world in which he worked. This inner conflict was one of the main causes of his suicide. His books include *Agua* (short stories, 1935), *Yawar fiesta* (1941), *Los ríos profundos* (1958) and *Todas las sangres* (1964).

In the 1950s and 1960s, there was a move away from the predominantly rural and indigenist to an urban setting. At the forefront were, among others, **Mario Vargas Llosa**, **Julio Ramón Ribeyro**, **Enrique Congrains Martín**, **Oswaldo Reynoso**, **Luis Loayza**, **Sebastián Salazar Bondy** and **Carlos E Zavaleta**. They explored all aspects of the city, including the influx of people from the sierra. These writers incorporated new narrative techniques in the urban novel, which presented a world where popular culture and speech were rich sources of literary material, despite the difficulty in transcribing them.

**Alfredo Bryce Echenique** (born 1939) has enjoyed much popularity following the success of *Un mundo para Julius* (1970), a brilliant satire on the upper and middle classes of Lima. Other contemporary writers of note are **Rodolfo Hinostrozo** (born 1941), novelist, playwright and poet, **Mario Bellatín** (born 1960 – see *Salón de belleza* and *Damas chinas*), and **Jaime Bayly**, who is also a journalist and TV presenter. His novels include *Fue ayer y no me acuerdo, Los últimos días de la prensa, La noche es virgen* and *Ya de repente, un angel*. Most recently, writers are confronting the violence and the after-effects of the Sendero Luminoso/MRTA and Fujimori/Montesinos period, with powerful, neorrealist novels and stories. Among the best examples are **Alonso Cueto** (born 1954): *Grandes miradas* (2003), *La hora azul* (2005); **Santiago Roncagliolo** (born 1975): *Abril rojo* (2006); and **Daniel Alarcón** (born Lima 1977), who lives in the USA and writes in English: *War by Candlelight* (2005) and *Lost City Radio* (2007).

Without doubt, the most important poet in Peru, if not Latin America, in the first half of the 20th century, was **César Vallejo**, born in 1892 in Santiago de Chuco (Libertad). In 1928 he was a founder of the Peruvian Socialist Party, then he joined the Communist Party in 1931 in Madrid. From 1936 to his death in Paris in 1938 he opposed the fascist takeover in Spain. His first volume was *Los heraldos negros* in which the dominating theme of all his work, a sense of confusion and inadequacy in the face of the unpredictability of life, first surfaces. *Trilce* (1922), his second work, is unlike anything before it in the Spanish language. *Poemas humanos* and *España, aparta de mí este cáliz* (written as a result of Vallejo's experiences in the Spanish Civil War) were both published posthumously, in 1939.



## Painting

The Catholic Church was the main patron of the arts during the colonial period. The innumerable churches and monasteries that sprang up in the newly conquered territories created a demand for paintings and sculptures, met initially by imports from Europe of both works of art and of skilled craftsmen, and later by home-grown products. An essential requirement for the inauguration of any new church was an image for the altar and many churches in Lima preserve fine examples of sculptures imported from Seville during the 16th and 17th centuries. But sculptures were expensive and difficult to import, and as part of their policy of relative frugality the Franciscan monks tended to favour paintings. The Jesuits, too, tended to commission paintings and several major works by Sevillian artists can be seen in Lima's churches.

Painters and sculptors soon made their way to Peru in search of lucrative commissions including several Italians who arrived during the later 16th century. The Jesuit **Bernardo Bitti** (1548-1610), for example, trained in Rome before working in

Lima, Cuzco, Juli and Arequipa. European imports, however, could not keep up with demand and local workshops of creole, mestizo and Indian craftsmen flourished from the latter part of the 16th century. As the Viceregal capital and the point of arrival into Peru, the art of Lima was always strongly influenced by European, especially Spanish models, but the old Inca capital of Cuzco became the centre of a regional school of painting which developed its own characteristics. A series of paintings of the 1660s, now hanging in the Museo de Arte Religioso in Cuzco, commemorate the colourful Corpus Christi procession of statues of the local patron saints through the streets of Cuzco. These paintings document the appearance of the city and local populace, including Spanish and Inca nobility, priests and laity, rich and poor, Spaniard, Indian, African and mestizo. Many of the statues represented in this series are still venerated in the local parish churches. They are periodically painted and dressed in new robes, but underneath are the original sculptures, executed by native craftsmen. Some are of carved wood while others use the pre-conquest technique of maguey cactus covered in sized cloth.



One of the most successful native painters was **Diego Quispe Tito** (1611-81) who claimed descent from the Inca nobility and whose large canvases, often based on Flemish engravings, demonstrate the wide range of European sources that were available to Andean artists in the 17th century. But the **Cuzco School** is best known for the anonymous devotional works where the painted contours of the figures are overlaid with flat patterns in gold, creating highly decorative images with an underlying tension between the two- and three-dimensional aspects of the work. The taste for richly decorated surfaces can also be seen in the 17th- and 18th-century frescoed interiors of many Andean churches, as in Chinchero, Andahuaylillas and Huaro, and in the ornate carving on altarpieces and pulpits throughout Peru.

# Land and environment



## Geography

Peru is the third largest South American country, the size of France, Spain and the United Kingdom combined, and presents formidable difficulties to human habitation. Virtually all of the 2250 km of its Pacific Coast is desert. From the narrow coastal shelf the Andes rise steeply to a high plateau dominated by massive ranges of snow-capped peaks and gouged with deep canyons. The heavily forested and deeply ravined Andean slopes are more gradual to the east. Further east, towards Brazil and Colombia, begin the vast jungles of the Amazon Basin.

### Highlands

The highlands, or sierra, extend inland from the coastal strip some 250 km in the north, increasing to 400 km in the south. The average altitude is about 3000 m and 50% of Peruvians live there. Essentially, it is a plateau dissected by dramatic canyons and dominated by some of the most spectacular mountain ranges in the world.

In spite of these ups and downs which cause great communications difficulties, the presence of water and a more temperate climate on the plateau has attracted people throughout the ages. Present day important population centres in the Highlands include Cajamarca in the north, Huancayo in central Peru and Cuzco in the south, all at around 3000 m. Above this, at around 4000 m, is the 'high steppe' or *puna*, with constant winds and wide day/night temperature fluctuations. Nevertheless, fruit and potatoes (which originally came from the *puna* of Peru and Bolivia) are grown at this altitude and the meagre grasslands are home to the ubiquitous llama.

## Eastern Andes and Amazon Basin

Almost half of Peru is on the eastern side of the Andes and about 90% of the country's drainage is into the Amazon system. It is an area of heavy rainfall with cloudforest above 3500 m and tropical rainforest lower down. There is little savanna, or natural grasslands, characteristic of other parts of the Amazon Basin.

There is some dispute on the Amazon's source. Officially, the mighty river begins as the Marañón, whose longest tributary rises just east of the Cordillera Huayhuash. However, the longest journey for the proverbial raindrop, some 6400 km, probably starts in southern Peru, where the headwaters of the Apurímac (Ucayali) flow from the snows on the northern side of the Nevado Mismi, near Cailloma.

With much more rainfall on the eastern side of the Andes, rivers are turbulent and erosion dramatic. Although vertical drops are not as great – there is a whole continent to cross to the Atlantic – valleys are deep, ridges narrow and jagged and there is forest below 3000 m. At 1500 m the Amazon jungle begins and water is the only means of surface transport available, apart from three roads which reach Borja (on the Marañón), Yurimaguas (on the Huallaga) and Pucallpa (on the Ucayali), all at about 300 m above the Atlantic which is still 4000 km or so downstream. The vastness of the Amazon lowlands becomes apparent and it is here that Peru bulges 650 km northeast past Iquitos to the point where it meets Colombia and Brazil at Leticia. Oil and gas have recently been found in the Amazon, and new finds are made every year, which means that new pipelines and roads will eventually link more places to the Pacific Coast.

## Climate

In the highlands, April to October is the dry season. It is hot and dry during the day, around 20° to 25°C, and cold and dry at night, often below freezing. From November to April is the wet season, when it is dry and clear most mornings, with some rainfall in the afternoon. There is a small temperature drop (18°C) and not much difference at night (15°C). In the Amazonian lowlands April to October is the dry season, with temperatures up to 35°C. In the jungle areas of the south a cold front can pass through at night. November to April is the wet season. It is humid and hot, with heavy rainfall at any time.

# Wildlife and vegetation

Peru is a country of great biological diversity. It contains 84 of the 117 recognized life zones and is one of the eight 'mega-diverse countries' on earth. The fauna and flora are to a large extent determined by the influence of the Andes, the longest uninterrupted mountain chain in the world, and the mighty Amazon river, which has by far the largest volume of any river in the world.

## Andes

From the desert rise the steep Andean slopes. In the deeply incised valleys Andean fox and deer may occasionally be spotted. Herds of llamas and alpacas graze the steep hillsides. Mountain caracara and Andean lapwing are frequently observed soaring, and there is always the possibility of spotting flocks of mitred parrots or even the biggest species of hummingbird in the world (*Patagonia gigas*).

The Andean zone has many lakes and rivers and countless swamps. Exclusive to this area short-winged grebe and the torrent duck which feeds in the fast flowing rivers, and giant and horned coots. Chilean flamingo frequent the shallow soda lakes.

The *puna*, a habitat characterized by tussock grass and pockets of stunted alpine flowers, gives way to relict elfin forest and tangled bamboo thicket in this inhospitable windswept and frost-prone region. Occasionally the dissected remains of a *Puya* plant can be found; the result of the nocturnal foraging of the rare spectacled bear. There are quite a number of endemic species of rodent including the viscacha, and it is the last stronghold of the chinchilla. Here also pumas roam preying on the herbivores which frequent these areas, mountain-pudu, Andean deer or guemal and the mountain tapir. 

## Tropical Andes

The elfin forest grades into mist enshrouded cloudforest at about 3500 m. In the tropical zones of the Andes, the humidity in the cloudforests stimulates the growth of a vast variety of plants particularly mosses and lichens. The cloudforests are found in a narrow strip that runs along the eastern slopes of the spine of the Andes. It is these dense, often impenetrable, forests clothing the steep slopes that are important in protecting the headwaters of all the streams and rivers that cascade from the Andes to form the mighty Amazon as it begins its long journey to the sea.

This is a verdant world of dripping epiphytic mosses, lichens, ferns and orchids which grow in profusion despite the plummeting overnight temperatures. The high humidity resulting from the 2 m of rain that can fall in a year is responsible for the maintenance of the forest and it accumulates in puddles and leaks from the ground in a constant trickle that combines to form myriad icy, crystal-clear tumbling streams that cascade over precipitous waterfalls.

In secluded areas the flame-red Andean cock-of-the-rock give their spectacular display to females in the early morning mists. Woolly monkeys are also occasionally sighted as they descend the wooded slopes. Mixed flocks of colourful tanagers are commonly encountered, and the golden-headed quetzal and Amazon umbrella bird are occasionally seen.

## Amazon Basin

At about 1500 m there is a gradual transition to the vast lowland forests of the Amazon Basin, which are warmer and more equable than the cloudforests clothing the mountains above. The daily temperature varies little during the year with a high of 23° to 32°C falling slightly to 20° to 26°C overnight. This lowland region receives some 2 m of rainfall per year most of it falling from November to April. The rest of the year is sufficiently dry, at least in the lowland areas to inhibit the growth of epiphytes and orchids which are so characteristic of the highland areas. For a week or two in the rainy season the rivers flood the forest. The zone immediately surrounding this seasonally flooded forest is referred to as *terre firme* forest.

The vast river basin of the Amazon is home to an immense variety of species. The environment has largely dictated the lifestyle. Life in or around rivers, lakes, swamps and forest depend on the ability to swim and climb and amphibious and tree-dwelling animals are common. Once the entire Amazon Basin was a great inland sea and the river still contains mammals more typical of the coast, eg manatees and dolphins.

Here, in the relatively constant climatic conditions, animal and plant life has evolved to an amazing diversity over the millennia. It has been estimated that 3.9 sq km of forest can harbour some 1200 vascular plants, 600 species of tree, and 120 woody plants. In these relatively flat lands, a soaring canopy some 50 m overhead is the power-house of the forest. It is a habitat choked with strangling vines and philodendrons among which mixed troupes of squirrel monkeys and brown capuchins forage. In the high canopy small groups of spider monkeys perform their lazy aerial acrobatics, whilst lower down, clinging to epiphyte-clad trunks and branches, groups of saddle-backed and emperor tamarins forage for blossom, fruit and the occasional insect prey.

The most accessible part of the jungle is on or near the many great meandering rivers. At each bend of the river the forest is undermined by the currents during the seasonal floods at the rate of some 10 m or 20 m per year leaving a sheer mud and clay bank, whilst on the opposite bend new land is laid down in the form of broad beaches of fine sand and silt.

A succession of vegetation can be seen. The fast growing willow-like *tessaria* first stabilizes the ground enabling the tall stands of *caña brava gynerium* to become established. Within these dense almost impenetrable stands the seeds of rainforest trees germinate and over a few years thrust their way towards the light. The fastest growing is a species of *cercropia* which forms a canopy 15 m to 18 m over the *caña* but even this is relatively short-lived. The gap in the canopy is quickly filled by other species. Two types of mahogany outgrow the other trees forming a closed canopy at 40 m with a lush understory of shade-tolerant *heliconia* and ginger. Eventually even the long-lived trees die off to be replaced by others providing a forest of great diversity.

## Jungle wildlife

The meandering course of the river provides many excellent opportunities to see herds of russet-brown capybara – a sheep-sized rodent – peccaries and brocket deer. Of considerable ecological interest are the presence of ox-bow lakes, or *cochas*, since these provide an abundance of wildlife which can be seen around the lake margins. The best way to see the wildlife is to get above the canopy. Ridges provide elevated viewpoints for excellent views over the forest. From here, it is possible to look across the lowland flood plain to the very foothills of the Andes, possibly some 200 km away. Flocks of parrots and macaws can be seen flying between fruiting trees and noisy troupes of squirrel monkeys and brown capuchins come very close.

The lowland rainforest of Peru is particularly famous for its primates and giant otters. Giant otters were once widespread in Amazonia but came close to extinction in the 1960s owing to persecution by the fur trade. The giant otter population in Peru has since recovered and is now estimated to be at least several hundred. Jaguar and other predators are also much in evidence. Although rarely seen their paw marks are commonly found along the forest trails. Rare bird species are also much in evidence, including fasciated tiger-heron and primitive hoatzins.

The (very) early morning is the best time to see peccaries, brocket deer and tapir at mineral licks (*collpa*). Macaw and parrot licks are found along the banks of the river. Here at dawn a dazzling display arrives and clambers around in the branches overhanging the clay lick. At its peak there may be 600 birds of up to six species (including red and green macaws, and blue-headed parrots) clamouring to begin their descent to the riverbank where they jostle for the mineral rich clay, a necessary addition to their diet which may also neutralize the toxins in their leaf and seed diet. Rare game birds such as razor-billed curassows and piping guans may also be seen.

A list of over 600 bird species has been compiled. Particularly noteworthy species are the black-faced cotinga, crested eagle, and the spectacular Harpy eagle, perhaps the world's most impressive raptor, easily capable of taking an adult monkey from the canopy. Mixed species flocks are commonly observed containing from 25 to over 100 birds of perhaps more than 30 species including blue dacnis, blue-tailed emerald, bananaquit, thick-billed euphoria and the paradise tanager. Each species occupies a slightly different niche, and since there are few individuals of each species in the flock, competition is avoided. Mixed flocks foraging in the canopy are often led by a white-winged shrike, whereas flocks foraging in the understorey are often led by the bluish-slate ant shrike. (For more information on the birds of Peru, see page 15.)

# Books

## History and culture

**Alden Mason, J**, *The Ancient Civilizations of Peru* (1991).
**Cáceres Macedo, Justo**, *The Prehispanic Cultures of Peru* (1988).
**Hemming, John**, *The Conquest of the Incas* (1970). Essential reading.
**Keatinge, Richard W** (editor), *Peruvian Prehistory. An Overview of Pre-Inca and Inca Society* (1988).
**Kendall, Ann**, *Everyday Life of the Incas* (1978).
**Mosely, Michael E**, *The Incas and their Ancestors: The Archaeology of Peru.*
**Portal Cabellos, Manuel**, *Oro y tragedia de los Incas*. Excellent on the division of the empire, civil war and *huaqueros*.
**Thomson, Hugh** *Cochineal Red: Travels through Ancient Peru* (2006). Exploration of Peru's pre-Inca cultures, drawing on the latest archaeological discoveries.

## Cuzco and Machu Picchu

**Bingham, Hiram**, *Lost City of the Incas* (2002), Weidenfeld & Nicolson. New illustrated edition, with an introduction by Hugh Thomson.
**Frost, Peter**, *Exploring Cusco*. On Cuzco, the Sacred Valley, Inca Trail, Machu Picchu and other ruins.
**Frost, Peter** et al (Edited by Jim Bartle), *Machu Picchu Historical Sanctuary*, Nuevas Imagenes. With superb text and photos on all aspects of the Inca Trail and the endangered ecosystem of the sanctuary.
**Milligan, Max**, *In the Realm of the Incas* (2001) Harper Collins. A beautiful book with photographs and text.
**Morrison, Tony**, *Qosqo. The Navel of the World* (1997), Condor Books. Describes Cuzco's past and present with an extensive section of photographs of the city and its surroundings.
**Reinhard, Johan**, *The Sacred Center*. Explains Machu Picchu in archaeological terms.
**Thomson, Hugh**, *The White Rock* (2002), Phoenix. Highly acclaimed account of Thomson's travels in the Inca heartland, as well as the journeys of earlier explorers and the history of the region.

## The Royal Inca Road

**Espinosa, Ricardo**, *La Gran Ruta Inca, The Great Inca Route* (2002), Petróleos del Perú. A photographic and textual record of Espinosa's walk the length of the Camino Real de los Incas, fro Quito to La Paz.
**Muller, Karin**, *Along the Inca Road. A Woman's Journey into an Ancient Empire* (2000), National Geographic.
**Portway, Christopher**, *Journey Along the Andes* (1993), Impact Books.

## Wildlife and environment

**Clements, James F and Shany, Noam**, *A Field Guide to the Birds of Peru* (2001), Ibis.
**Krabbe, Nils and Fjeldsa, Jon**, *Birds of the High Andes* (1990), University of Copenhagen. Covers all Peruvian birds that occur above 3000 m – a large proportion of the birds likely to be seen in the Andes.
**Hilty, Steve, and Brown, William**, *A guide to the Birds of Colombia* (1986). Covers the vast majority of the Amazonian species likely to be seen.
**Parker, Ted, Parker, Susan, and Plenge, Manuel**, *An Annotated checklist of Peruvian Birds* (1982). Slightly outdated but still useful, it lists all Peruvian birds by habitat type.
**Person, David L and Beletsky, Les**, *Ecotraveller's Wildlife Guide: Peru* (2001), Academic Press. Recommended.
**Ridgely, Robert, and Tudor, Guy**, *Birds of South America Volumes 1 & 2* (1989 and 1994).
**Valqui, Thomas**, *Where to Watch Birds in Peru* (2004), www.granperu.com/bird watching book/. Describes 151 sites, how to get there and what to expect to see once there.
**Walker, Barry, and Fjeldsa, Jon**, *Birds of Machu Picchu.*

# Notes

# Notes

# Notes

# Notes

# Notes

# Notes

# Notes

# Notes

# Notes

# Notes

# Notes

# Notes

# Notes

# Footnotes

# Spanish words and phrases

Volumes of dictionaries, phrase books or word lists will not provide the same enjoyment as being able to communicate directly with the people of the country you are visiting. Learning Spanish is a useful part of the preparation for a trip to Peru and you are encouraged to make an effort to grasp the basics before you go. As you travel you will pick up more of the language and the more you know, the more you will benefit from your stay. The following section is designed to be a simple point of departure.

Whether you have been taught the 'Castilian' pronounciation (z, and c followed by i or e are pronounced as the th in think) or the 'American' pronounciation (they are pronounced as s), you will encounter little difficulty in understanding either. Regional accents and usages vary, but the basic language is essentially the same everywhere. For a basic guide to pronunciation, see page 335.

## Greetings, courtesies

| | |
|---|---|
| good afternoon/evening/night | *buenas tardes/noches* |
| good morning | *buenos días* |
| goodbye | *adiós/chao* |
| hello | *hola* |
| How are you? | *¿cómo está?¿cómo estás?* |
| I do not understand | *no entiendo* |
| leave me alone | *déjeme en paz/no me moleste* |
| no | *no* |
| please | *por favor* |
| pleased to meet you | *mucho gusto/encantado/encantada* |
| see you later | *hasta luego* |
| thank you (very much) | *(muchas) gracias* |
| What is your name? | *¿cómo se llama? ¿cómo te llamas?* |
| yes | *sí* |
| I speak... | *Hablo...* |
| I speak Spanish | *Hablo español* |
| I don't speak Spanish | *No hablo español* |
| Do you speak English? | *¿habla inglés?* |
| Please speak slowly | *hable despacio por favor* |
| I am very sorry | *lo siento mucho/disculpe* |
| I'm fine, thanks | *estoy muy bien gracias* |
| I'm called... | *me llamo...* |
| What do you want? | *¿qué quiere?* |
| I want | *quiero* |
| I don't want it | *No lo quiero* |
| long-distance phone call | *una llamada de larga distancia* |
| good/bad | *bueno/malo* |

## Nationalities and languages

American *americano/a*
Australian *australiano/a*
Austrian *austriaco/a*
British *británico/a*
Canadian *canadiense*
Danish *danés/danesa*
Dutch *holandés/holandesa*
English *inglés/inglesa*
French *francés/francesa*
German *alemán/alemana*
Irish *irlandés/irlandesa*
Italian *italiano/a*
New Zealand *neozelandés/neozelandesa*
Norwegian *noruego/a*
Portuguese *portugués/portuguesa*
Scottish *escocés/escocesa*

Swedish *sueco/a*
Swiss *suizo/a*
Welsh *galés/galesa*

## Basic questions

Have you got a room for two people? *¿Tiene una habitación para dos personas?*
How do I get to_? *¿cómo llego a_?*
How much does it cost? *¿cuánto cuesta?*
How much is it? *¿cuánto es?*
When does the bus leave (arrive)? *¿a qué hora sale (llega) el autobús?*
When? *¿Cuándo?*
Where is_? *¿Dónde está?*
Where is the nearest petrol station? *¿dónde está el grifo más cerca?*
Why? *¿por qué?*

## Basics

bank *el banco*
bathroom/toilet *el baño*
bill *la factura/la cuenta*
cash *el efectivo*
cheap *barato*
church/cathedral *La iglesia/catedral*
exchange house *la casa de cambio*
exchange rate *el tipo de cambio*
expensive *caro*
internet café *cibercafé*
market *el mercado*
notes/coins *los billetes/las monedas*
police (policeman) *la policía (el policía)*
post office *el correo*
supermarket *el supermercado*
telephone office *el centro de llamadas*
ticket office *la boletería/la taquilla*
travellers' cheques *los travelers/los cheques de viajero*

## Getting around

aeroplane/airplane *el avión*
airport *el aeropuerto*
bus station *la terminal de autobús*
bus *el bus/el autobús*
minibus *la combi*
motorcycle taxi *el mototaxi*
bus route *el corredor*
first/second class *primera/segunda clase*
on the left/right *a la izquierda/derecha*
second street on the left *la segunda calle a la izquierda*
ticket *el boleto*
to walk *caminar*
Where can I buy tickets? *¿dónde se puede comprar boletos?*
Where can I park? *¿dónde se puede parquear?*

## Orientation and motoring

arrival *la llegada*
avenue *la avenida*
block *la cuadra*
border *la frontera*
fixed route taxi *el colectivo*
corner *la esquina*
customs *la aduana*
departure *la salida*
east *el este, el oriente*
empty *vacío*
full *lleno*
highway, main road *la carretera*
immigration *la inmigración*
insurance *el seguro*
the insured *el asegurado/la asegurada*
to insure yourself against *asegurarse contra*
luggage *el equipaje*
motorway, freeway *el autopista/la carretera*
north *el norte*
oil *el aceite*
passport *el pasaporte*
petrol/gasoline *la gasolina*
puncture *el pinchazo*
south *el sur*
street *la calle*
that way *por allí/por allá*
this way *por aquí/por acá*
tourist card *la tarjeta de turista*
tyre *la llanta*
unleaded *sin plomo*
visa *el visado*
west *el oeste/el poniente*

## Accommodation

air conditioning *el aire acondicionado*
all-inclusive *todo incluido*
blankets *las mantas*
clean/dirty towels *las toallas limpias/sucias*
dining room *el comedor*
double bed *la cama matrimonial*
guesthouse *la casa de huéspedes*
hot/cold water *el agua caliente/fría*
hotel *el hotel*
Is service included? *¿está incluido el servicio?*
Is tax included? *¿están incluidos los impuestos?*
noisy *ruidoso*
pillows *las almohadas*
power cut *el apagón/corte*
restaurant *el restaurante*
room *el cuarto/la habitación*
sheets *las sábanas*
shower *la ducha*
single/double *sencillo/doble*
soap *el jabón*
to clean *limpiar*
toilet *el sanitario*
toilet paper *el papel higiénico*
with private bathroom *con baño privado*
with two beds *con dos camas*

## Health

aspirin *la aspirina*
blood *la sangre*
chemist *la farmacia*
condoms *los preservativos, los condones*
contact lenses *los lentes de contacto*
contraceptive *anticonceptivo*
(pill) *(la píldora anticonceptiva)*
diarrhoea *la diarrea*
doctor *el médico*
fever/sweat *la fiebre/el sudor*
(for) pain *(para) dolor*
head *la cabeza*
period/towels *la regla/las toallas*
stomach *el estómago*
altitude sickness *el soroche*

## Time

at one o'clock *a la una*
at half past two *a las dos y media*
at a quarter to three *a cuarto para las* tres or *a las tres menos quince*
it's one o'clock *es la una*
it's seven o'clock *son las siete*
it's six twenty *son las seis y veinte*
it's five to nine *son cinco para las nueve/son las nueve menos cinco*
in ten minutes *en diez minutos*
five hours *cinco horas*
does it take long? *¿tarda mucho?*

Monday *lunes*
Tuesday *martes*
Wednesday *miércoles*
Thursday *jueves*
Friday *viernes*
Saturday *sábado*
Sunday *domingo*

January *enero*
February *febrero*
March *marzo*
April *abril*
May *mayo*
June *junio*
July *julio*
August *agosto*
September *septiembre*
October *octubre*
November *noviembre*
December *diciembre*

## Numbers

one *uno/una*
two *dos*
three *tres*
four *cuatro*
five *cinco*
six *seis*
seven *siete*
eight *ocho*
nine *nueve*
ten *diez*
eleven *once*
twelve *doce*
thirteen *trece*
fourteen *catorce*

fifteen *quince*
sixteen *dieciséis*
seventeen *diecisiete*
eighteen *dieciocho*
nineteen *diecinueve*
twenty *veinte*
twenty-one *veintiuno*
thirty *treinta*
forty *cuarenta*
fifty *cincuenta*
sixty *sesenta*
seventy *setenta*
eighty *ochenta*
ninety *noventa*
hundred *cien/ciento*
thousand *mil*

## Family

aunt *la tía*
brother *el hermano*
cousin *el/la primo/a*
daughter *la hija*
family *la familia*
father *el padre*
fiancé/fiancée *el novio/la novia*
friend *el amigo/la amiga*
grandfather *el abuelo*
grandmother *la abuela*
husband *el esposo/marido*
married *casado/a*
single/unmarried *soltero/a*
sister *la hermana*
son *el hijo*
uncle *el tío*
wife *la esposa*

## Food

Avocado *la palta*
baked *al horno*
bakery *la panadería*
beans *los frijoles/las habichuelas*
beef *la carne de res*
beef steak or pork fillet *el bistec*
boiled rice *el arroz blanco*
bread *el pan*
breakfast *el desayuno*
butter *la mantequilla*
cassava, yucca *la yuca*
casserole *la cazuela*
chewing gum *el chicle*
chicken *el pollo*
chilli pepper or green pepper *el ají*
clear soup, stock *el caldo*
cooked *cocido*
dining room *el comedor*
egg *el huevo*
fish *el pescado*
fork *el tenedor*
fried *frito*
fritters *las frituras*
garlic *el ajo*
goat *el chivo*
grapefruit *el pomelo*
grill *la parrilla*
grilled/griddled *a la plancha*
guava *la guayaba*
ham *el jamón*
hamburger *la hamburguesa*
hot, spicy *picante*
ice cream *el helado*
jam *la mermelada*
knife *el cuchillo*
lime *el limón*
lobster *la langosta*
lunch *el almuerzo*
margarine, fat *la manteca*
meal, supper, dinner *la comida*
meat *la carne*
minced meat *el picadillo*
mixed salad *la ensalada mixta*
onion *la cebolla*
orange *la naranja*
pepper *el pimiento*
plantain, green banana *el plátano*
pasty, turnover *la empanada/el pastelito*
pork *el cerdo*
potato *la papa*
prawns *los camarones*
raw *crudo*
restaurant *el restaurante*
roast *el asado*
salad *la ensalada*
salt *la sal*
sandwich *el bocadillo*
sauce *la salsa*
sausage *la longaniza*
scrambled eggs *los huevos revueltos*
seafood *los mariscos*
small sandwich, filled roll *el bocadito*
soup *la sopa*
spoon *la cuchara*

squash *la calabaza*
squid *los calamares*
supper *la cena*
sweet *dulce*
sweet potato *la batata*
to eat *comer*
toasted *tostado*
turkey *el pavo*
vegetables *los legumbres/vegetales*
without meat *sin carne*
yam *el camote*

## Drink

beer *la cerveza*
boiled *hervido*
bottled *en botella*
camomile tea *la manzanilla*
canned *en lata*
cocktail *el coctel*
coconut milk *la leche de coco*
coffee *el café*
coffee, small, strong *el cafecito*
coffee, white *el café con leche*
cold *frío*
condensed milk *la leche condensada*
cup *la taza*
drink *la bebida*
drunk *borracho*
firewater *el aguardiente*
fruit milkshake *el batido*
glass *el vaso*
glass of liquer *la copa de licor*
hot *caliente*
ice *el hielo*
juice *el jugo*
lemonade *la limonada*
milk *la leche*
mint *la menta*
orange juice *el jugo de naranja*
pineapple milkshake *el batido de piña con leche*
rum *el ron*
soft drink *el refresco*
soft fizzy drink *la gaseosa/cola*
sugar *el azúcar*
tea *el té*
to drink *beber/tomar*
water *el agua*
water, carbonated *el agua mineral con gas*
water, still mineral *el agua mineral sin gas*
wine, red *el vino tinto*
wine, white *el vino blanco*

## Key verbs

**To go** *ir*
I go *voy*
you go (familiar ) *vas*
he, she, it goes, you (formal) go *va*
we go *vamos*
they, you (plural) go *van*
**To have** (possess) *tener*
I have *tengo*
You (familiar) have *tienes*
He, she, it, you (formal) have *tiene*
We have *tenemos*
They, you (plural) have *tienen*
(Also used in 'I am hungry' *tengo hambre*)
There is/are *hay*
There isn't/aren't *no hay*
**To be** (in a permanent state) **ser**
*soy; eres; es; somos; son*
**To be** (positional or temporary state) **estar**
*estoy; estás; está ; estamos; están.*

This section has been assembled on the basis of glossaries compiled by André de Mendonça and David Gilmour of South American Experience, London, and the Latin American Travel Advisor, No 9, March 1996

# Spanish pronunciation

The stress in a Spanish word conforms to one of three rules: 1) if the word ends in a vowel, or in n or **s**, the accent falls on the penultimate syllable (*ventana*, *ventanas*); 2) if the word ends in a consonant other than **n** or **s**, the accent falls on the last syllable (*hablar*); 3) if the word is to be stressed on a syllable contrary to either of the above rules, the acute accent on the relevant vowel indicates where the stress is to be placed (*pantalón*, *metáfora*). Note that adverbs such as *cuando*, 'when', take an accent when used interrogatively: *¿cuándo?*, 'when?'

**Vowels**: **a** not quite as short as in English 'cat'; **e** as in English 'pay', but shorter in a syllable ending in a consonant; **i** as in English 'seek'; **o** as in English 'cot' (North American 'caught'), but more like 'pope' when the vowel ends a syllable; **u** as in English 'food'; after 'q' and in 'gue', 'gui', u is unpronounced; in 'güe' and 'güi' it is pronounced; **y** when a vowel, pronounced like 'i'; when a semiconsonant or consonant, it is pronounced like English 'yes'; **ai, ay** as in English 'write'; **ei, ey** as in English 'eight'; **oi, oy** as in English 'voice'

Unless listed below **consonants** can be pronounced in Spanish as they are in English. **b, v** have an interchangeable sound and both are a cross between the English 'b' and 'v', except at the beginning of a word or after 'm' or 'n' when it is like English 'b'; **c** like English 'k', except before 'e' or 'i' when it is as the 's' in English 'sip'; **g** before 'e' and 'i' it is the same as j; **h** when on its own, never pronounced; **j** as the 'ch' in the Scottish 'loch'; **ll** as the 'g' in English 'beige'; sometimes as the 'lli' in 'million'; **ñ** as the 'ni' in English 'onion'; **rr** trilled much more strongly than in English; **x** depending on its location, pronounced as in English 'fox', or 'sip', or like 'gs'; **z** as the 's' in English 'sip'.

# Food glossary

Food has always played an important role in Peruvian culture. The country's range of climates has also made it internationally famed for its cuisine.

## Savoury dishes

**Ají (hot pepper)**
Ají is found in many varieties and is used to add 'spice' to everything from soup to fish to vegetable dishes. It is a staple in Peruvian kitchens from the coast to the most remote jungle villages. These peppers can be extremely spicy, so the inexperienced palate should proceed with caution!

**Papa (potato)**
The potato is as Peruvian as the Inca himself. There are more than 2,000 varieties of tuber although only a fraction are edible. *The International Potato Institute* is located on the outskirts of metropolitan Lima so those with a potato fetish might wish to visit. The *papa amarilla* (yellow potato) is by far the best-tasting of the lot.

**Causa**
A casserole served cold with a base of yellow potato and mixed with hot peppers, onion, avocado, with either chicken, crab or meat. A fantastic starter.

**Estofado**
A mild chicken stew, with lots of potatoes and other vegetables, served with rice.

**Lomo saltado**
Strips of sirloin sautéed with tomato, onion, *ají amarillo* (a spicy orange pepper) and french fried potatoes served with rice.

**Papa Ocopa**
A typical dish from the Arequipa region. A spicy peanut sauce served over cold potatoes with a slice of hard boiled egg.

**Papa a la Huancaína**
A dish which originated in the central department of Huancayo. This creamy cheese sauce served over cold potatoes is a common starter for set menus everywhere.

**Papa rellena (stuffed potato)**
First baked then fried, the potato is stuffed with meat, onions, olives, boiled egg and raisins. *Camote* (yams) can be substituted for potatoes.

**Choclo (corn)**
Another staple in the Peruvian diet. The large kernels are great with the fresh cheese produced all over the country.

**Maíz morado (purple corn)**
This type of corn is not edible for humans. It's boiled and the liquid is used to make *chicha*, a sweet and very traditional Peruvian refreshment.

**Chicha de Jora**
A strong fermented beverage mostly found in mountain communities. The people who make it use their saliva to aid in the fermenting process.

**Granos (grains)**
*Kiwicha* and *quinoa* are very high sources of protein and staples of the Inca diet. *Quinoa* is wonderful in soups and *kiwicha* is a common breakfast food for children throughout the country.

**Arroz (rice)**
Another major staple in Peruvian cooking.

**Anticuchos (beef heart kebabs)**
Beef heart barbecued and served with cold potato and a wonderful assortment of spicy sauces.

**Cuy (guinea pig)**
Prepared in a variety of ways from stewed to fried.

**Cau cau**
Tripe and potatoes.

**Rocoto relleno (stuffed hot peppers)**
Stuffed with meat and potatoes, then baked.

**Pachamanca**
Typical mountain cuisine, so popular it's now prepared everywhere. Beef, pork and chicken mixed with a variety of vegetables, and cooked together over heated stones in a hole in the ground.

**Seco de cabrito**
A favorite dish from the north coast. Roasted goat marinated with fermented *chicha*, served with beans and rice.

**Ají de gallina**
A rich mix of creamed, spicy chicken over rice and boiled potatoes.

**Ceviche**
The national dish of Peru. Raw fish or seafood marinaded in a mixture of lime juice, red onions and hot peppers, usually served with a thick slice of boiled yam (*camote*) and corn. With a coastline of more than 1800 km, the fruits of the sea are almost limitless. Sea bass, flounder, salmon,.red snapper, sole and many varieties of shellfish are all in abundance. Keep in mind that *ceviche* is a dish served for lunch. Most *cevicherías* close around 1600.

## Postres (desserts)

**Arroz con leche**
Rice pudding.

**Manjar blanco**
A caramel sweet made from boiled milk and sugar.

**Picarones**
Deep-fried donut batter bathed in a honey sauce.

**Suspiro a la limeña**
*Manjar blanco* with baked egg white.

**Turrón**
This popular sweet, shortbread covered in molasses or honey, is sold everywhere during the October celebrations of *Señor de los Milagros* (Lord of Miracles) in Lima.

## Fruta (fruit)

There's a great selection of fruit in Peru. Apart from common fruits such as mandarins, oranges, peaches and bananas, there are exotic tropical fruits to choose from.

**Chirimoya**
Custard apple. In Quechua means 'the sweet of the gods'.

**Lúcuma**
Eggfruit.

**Maracuyá**
Passionfruit, often served as a juice.

**Tuna**
Prickly pear.

## Bebidas (drinks)

The national beers include *Cristal, Cusqueña, Barena* and *Pilsen*. There are also some dark beers.

Although not known as a great wine producing country, there are a couple of good quality wines to choose from. *Blanco en Blanco* is a surprisingly pleasant white wine from the Tacama winery which also makes a great red wine called *Reserva Especial*.

*Pisco*, a strong brandy made from white grapes, is produced in the departments of Ica, Moquegua and Tacna. *Pisco sour*, the national drink, is made with lime juice, egg white, sugar and a dash of cinnamon.

# Complete title listing

**Footprint publishes travel guides to over 150 destinations worldwide. Each guide is packed with practical, concise and colourful information for anyone from first-time travellers to travel aficionados. The list is growing fast and current titles are noted below. Available from all good bookshops and online www.footprintbooks.com.**

**(P) denotes pocket guide**

## Latin America & Caribbean

Antigua & Leeward Islands (P)
Argentina
Barbados (P)
Belize, Guatemala & Southern Mexico
Bolivia
Brazil
Caribbean Islands
Chile
Colombia
Costa Rica
Cuba
Cuzco & the Inca Heartland
Dominican Republic (P)
Ecuador & Galápagos
Mexico & Central America
Nicaragua
Patagonia
Peru
Peru, Bolivia & Ecuador
South American Handbook

## North America

Vancouver (P)
Western Canada

## Australasia

Australia
East Coast Australia
New Zealand
Sydney (P)
West Coast Australia

## Africa

Cape Town (P)
Egypt
Kenya
Namibia
South Africa
Tanzania

## Europe

Andalucía
Antwerp & Ghent (P)
Barcelona (P)
Bilbao (P)
Cardiff (P)
Copenhagen (P)
Costa de la Luz (P)
Croatia
Dublin (P)
Lisbon (P)
London
London (P)
Madrid (P)
Naples (P)
Northern Spain
Reykjavik (P)
Scotland Highlands & Islands
Seville (P)
Siena (P)
Tallinn (P)
Turin (P)
Valencia (P)
Verona (P)

## Middle East

Dubai (P)

## Asia

Borneo
Cambodia
India
Laos
Malaysia & Singapore
Northeast India
Rajasthan
South India
Sri Lanka
Thailand
Vietnam
Vietnam, Cambodia & Laos

## Activity guides

Diving the World
Snowboarding the World
Surfing Britain
Surfing Europe
Surfing the World

## Lifestyle guides

Body & Soul Escapes
European City Breaks
Travel with Kids
Travellers Handbook
Wine Travel Guide to the World

# Index

→ *Entries in bold refer to maps*



Footnotes Index

# Advertisers' index

# Acknowledgements

This fourth edition would not have been possible without the help of many people. Steve would like to thank Avikal Elphee and Eibhlin Cassidy of Hilo for their tasty chai and comical lunchtime conversations. Thanks to Fiona Cameron and David Ugarte of Ecotrek Peru for vast amounts of practical advice and always being there for your buddies!

Ben and Steve would like to thank Heather MacBrayne, Manager of South American Explorers in Cuzco and the staff of the Lima clubhouse. Heather has done a fantastic job running the Cuzco Clubhouse and has provided Steve and Ben with great information over the years. Ben and Steve would also like to thank Miles Buesst (former Manager of South American Explorers, Lima) who updated the Lima city section, doing a fine job at short notice. Miles has made plenty of great contributions both in and around the city centre – thanks mate! As we write this Miles is preparing to become a proud father, so good luck with this, the greatest of adventures! As always Marianne Van Vlaardingen of Pantiacolla Tours was a great friend, soulmate and fountain of rainforest wisdom! Another session of trotos' cake n'coffee anyone?!

Steve would like to thank Jane and Gary for always having the doors of Jack's Cafe and Paddy O'Flaherty's open when a break was seriously required. Thanks also to friends Ross Knutson and Simon Leishman for help with previous editions.

Steve's family and friends in Plymouth deserve a place here, specifically Kay Isbell, for teaching him how to write in the first place, Ben Isbell for being basically just 'awesome', and having the force surging through him (?!). Bex King and Mark Isbell have helped when it was most needed and been all over top class.

Lastly, thanks and love to Christine Frankham for being a fabulous mum, and to Jim, Robert Frankham and Jane Deacon, Steve's two brothers and sister, for being the best family he could hope for, providing him with many stunning travel stories of strange and exotic lands as a young man growing up in Southwest England, looking out to sea and a world of adventure.

Finally, this piece wouldn't be complete without mentioning the hard work of all in the Footprint team, particularly Steve's fabulous and inspirational partner in crime Ben Box, the ever reasonable and phenomenally patient Alan Murphy, always juggling 10 different projects at a bare minimum. My thanks also to Jo Williams and all in the mapping, printing and editorial divisions of Footprint in Bath – all your hard work makes the books look stunning on the shelves, and this is greatly appreciated!

Thanks also to the following travellers: Luigi Andretto (Italy); Laralyn Bergstedt (USA); Christian Bieri (Spain); Anne-Leen and Fred De Backer; Alexander de Bont (The Netherlands); Johan de Brui (The Netherlands); Francine Buschel-Gomez (USA); Jonathan and Karen Canaani (Israel); Dr G Reid Dusenberry (USA); Becky Ellis; Herbert Geiges (Switzerland); Reut Gelblum (Israel); Robert Griffiths (USA); Thibault and Olivia Guillemet (Belgium); Will Haig (UK); Céline Hanson (Peru); Sharon Herkes (UK); Alex Higgins (Canada); Golan Hod (USA); Elena Ibello (Switzerland); Robbert Jobse (Peru); Alexandra Jones (Australia); Dalia Karmon and Shai Haim; Kathryn (UK); Lucy Kenward (Canada); Ursula Kirchner (Austria); Susan Landau; Jack Last (Australia); Bert Leffers (The Netherlands); Rachel Loong (Australia); Nick MacLeod; James Michie (Australia); Jill Neff (USA); Robert Ossevoort (The Netherlands); Christian Peters (Germany); Daniel Pfeufer (Germany); Joachim Pietsch (Germany); Bart Van Pottelberge (Belgium); Nicolas Pozzo di Boego (UK); Cecilia Ravnoey López (Norway); Liz and Tom Robins (UK); Yvonne Ward and Penny Russell (Australia); Priska Rutishauser (Switzerland); Marisa Sauder (Switzerland); Klaus Schwab (Austria); Ramon Stevens (USA); Terri Tucker (Chile); Beat Wuersch (Switzerland).

Footprint would also like to thank Professor Larry Goodyer, Head of the Leicester School of Pharmacy and director of Nomad Medical, for providing the health section.

# Map symbols

## Administration

- Capital city
- Other city, town
- International border
- Regional border

## Roads and travel

- National highway
- Paved road
- Unpaved or *ripio* (gravel) road
- Track
- Footpath
- Railway
- Railway with station
- Airport
- Bus station
- Metro station
- Cable car
- Funicular
- Ferry

## Water features

- River, canal
- Lake, ocean
- Seasonal marshland
- Beach, sandbank
- Waterfall
- Reef

## Topographical features

- Contours (approx)
- Mountain, volcano
- Mountain pass
- Escarpment
- Gorge
- Glacier
- Salt flat
- Rocks

## Cities and towns

- Main through route
- Main street
- Minor street
- Pedestrianized street
- Tunnel
- Track
- Footpath
- One way-street
- Steps
- Bridge
- Fortified wall
- Park, garden, stadium
- Sleeping
- Eating
- Bars & clubs
- Building
- Sight
- Cathedral, church
- Chinese temple
- Hindu temple
- Meru
- Mosque
- Stupa
- Synagogue
- Tourist office
- Museum
- Post office
- Police
- Bank
- Internet
- Telephone
- Market
- Medical services
- Parking
- Petrol
- Golf
- Detail map
- Related map

## Other symbols

- Archaeological site
- National park, wildlife reserve
- Viewing point
- Campsite
- Refuge, lodge
- Castle, fort
- Diving
- Deciduous, coniferous, palm trees
- Hide
- Vineyard, winery
- Distillery
- Shipwreck
- Historic battlefield

# Map 1 Urubamba Valley

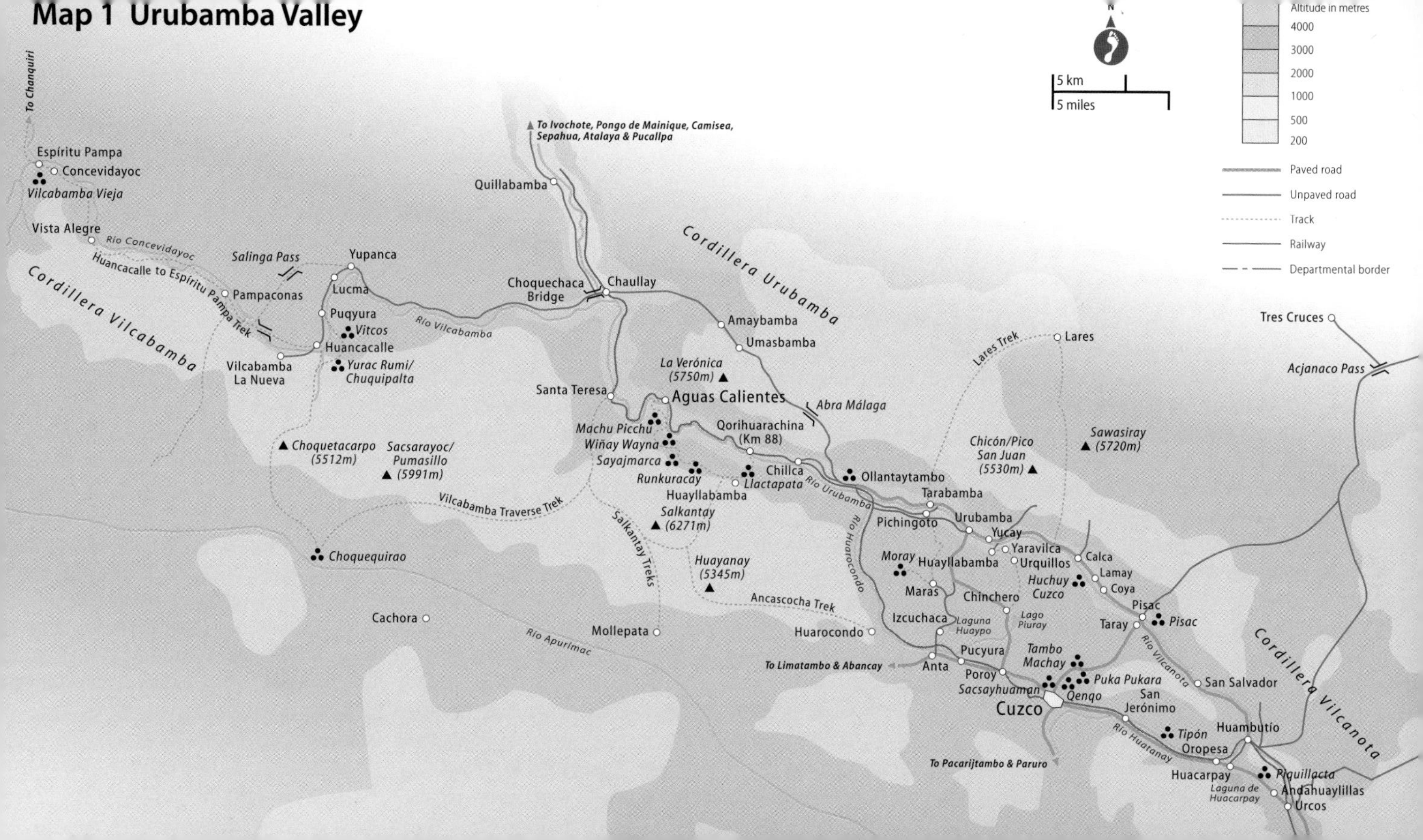

5 km
5 miles

Altitude in metres
4000
3000
2000
1000
500
200

Paved road
Unpaved road
Track
Railway
Departmental border

To Chanquiri
Espíritu Pampa
Concevidayoc
Vilcabamba Vieja
Vista Alegre
Río Concevidayoc
Huancacalle to Espíritu Pampa Trek
Cordillera Vilcabamba
Salinga Pass
Yupanca
Pampaconas
Lucma
Puqyura
Vitcos
Río Vilcabamba
Huancacalle
Vilcabamba La Nueva
Yurac Rumi/ Chuquipalta
To Ivochote, Pongo de Mainique, Camisea, Sepahua, Atalaya & Pucallpa
Quillabamba
Choquechaca Bridge
Chaullay
Cordillera Urubamba
Amaybamba
Umasbamba
La Verónica (5750m)
Santa Teresa
Aguas Calientes
Abra Málaga
Machu Picchu
Wiñay Wayna
Sayajmarca
Runkuracay
Qorihuarachina (Km 88)
Chillca
Llactapata
Huayllabamba
Salkantay (6271m)
Choquetacarpo (5512m)
Sacsarayoc/ Pumasillo (5991m)
Vilcabamba Traverse Trek
Choquequirao
Salkantay Treks
Huayanay (5345m)
Ancascocha Trek
Cachora
Mollepata
Río Apurímac
Huarocondo
Río Urubamba
Río Huarocondo
Ollantaytambo
Tarabamba
Pichingoto
Urubamba
Lares Trek
Lares
Chicón/Pico San Juan (5530m)
Sawasiray (5720m)
Yucay
Yaravilca
Urquillos
Moray
Huayllabamba
Maras
Chinchero
Izcuchaca
Laguna Huaypo
Lago Piuray
Calca
Lamay
Coya
Huchuy Cuzco
Pisac
Taray
Tres Cruces
Acjanaco Pass
To Limatambo & Abancay
Anta
Pucyura
Poroy
Sacsayhuaman
Tambo Machay
Puka Pukara
Qenqo
Cuzco
Río Vilcanota
San Salvador
Cordillera Vilcanota
San Jerónimo
Río Huatanay
Tipón
Huambutío
Oropesa
To Pacarijtambo & Paruro
Huacarpay
Laguna de Huacarpay
Piquillacta
Andahuaylillas
Urcos

# Map 2 Cuzco region

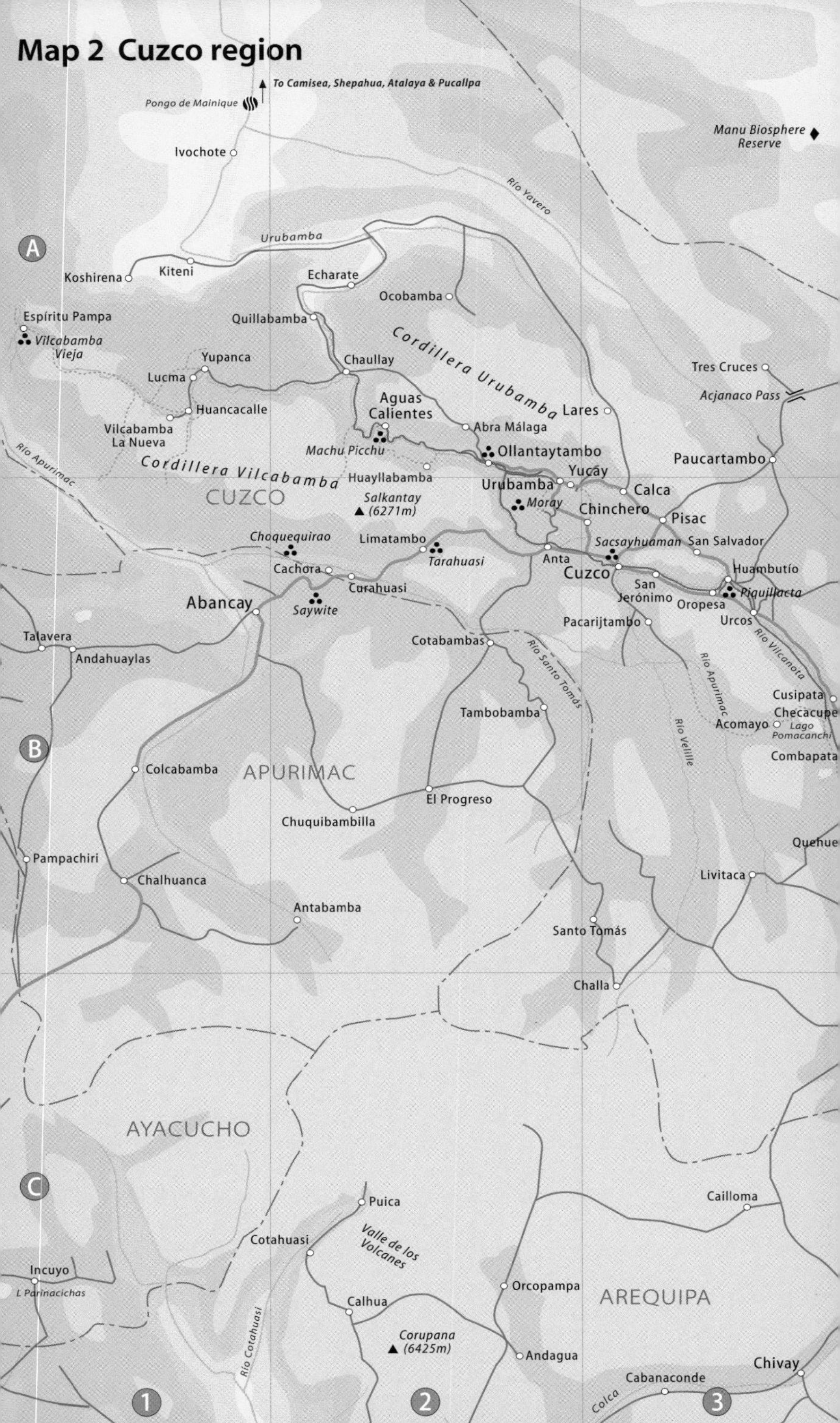

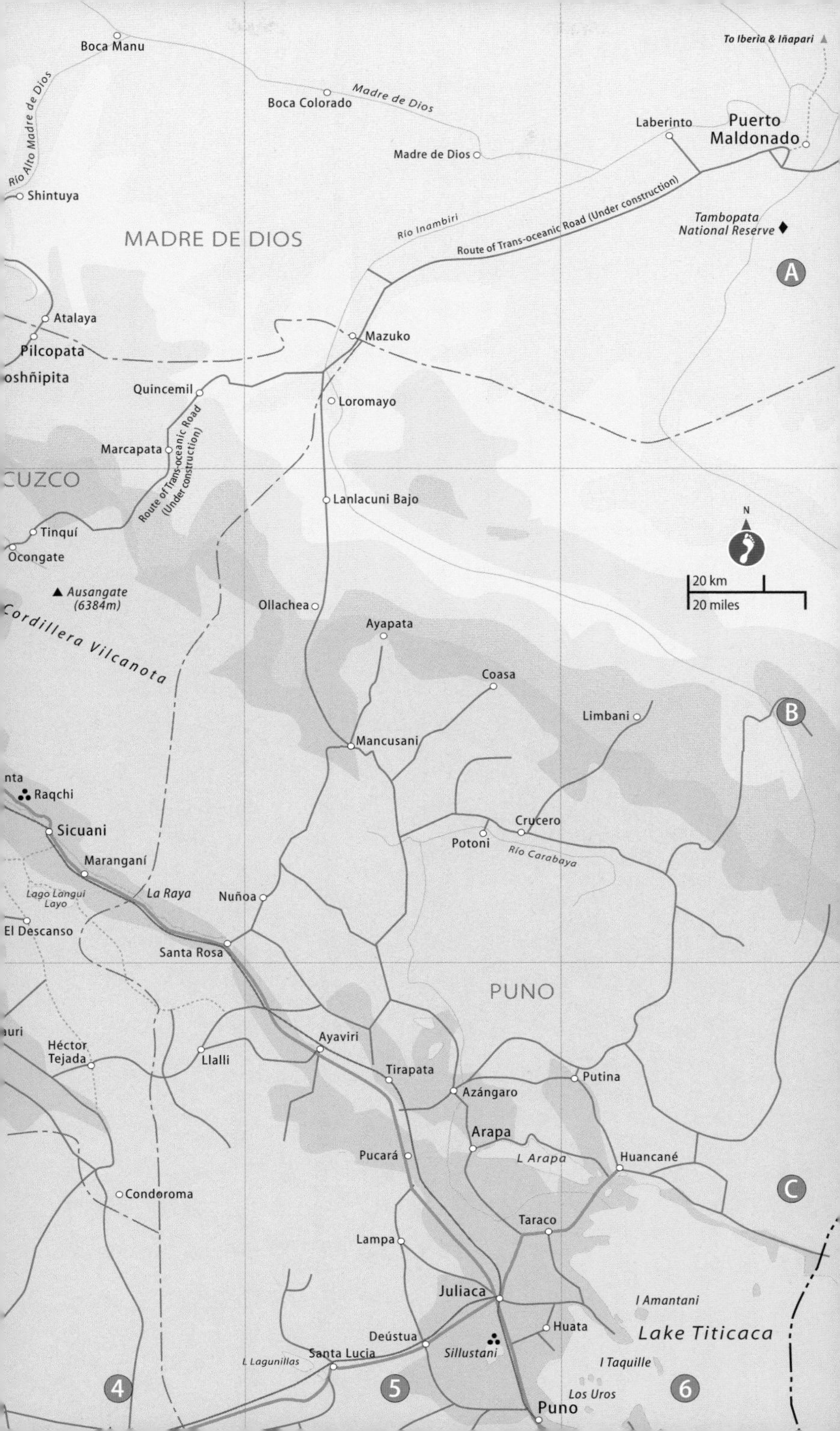

Boca Manu
Río Alto Madre de Dios
Shintuya
Boca Colorado
Madre de Dios
Madre de Dios
Laberinto
Puerto Maldonado
To Iberia & Iñapari
Río Inambiri
Route of Trans-oceanic Road (Under construction)
Tambopata National Reserve
MADRE DE DIOS
A
Atalaya
Pilcopata
oshñipita
Mazuko
Quincemil
Loromayo
Route of Trans-oceanic Road (Under construction)
Marcapata
CUZCO
Lanlacuni Bajo
Tinquí
Ocongate
N
20 km
20 miles
Ausangate (6384m)
Cordillera Vilcanota
Ollachea
Ayapata
Coasa
Limbani
B
Mancusani
nta
Raqchi
Sicuani
Crucero
Potoni
Río Carabaya
Maranganí
Lago Langui Layo
La Raya
Nuñoa
El Descanso
Santa Rosa
PUNO
auri
Héctor Tejada
Llalli
Ayaviri
Tirapata
Putina
Azángaro
Arapa
Pucará
L Arapa
Huancané
Condoroma
C
Taraco
Lampa
Juliaca
I Amantani
Lake Titicaca
Huata
Deústua
Sillustani
Santa Lucia
L Lagunillas
I Taquille
Los Uros
Puno
4
5
6

Map 3 Peru
COLOMBIA
ECUADOR
A
Iquitos
Rio Amazonas
LORETO
Rio Marañón
N
AMAZONAS
100 km
100 miles
Rio Huallaga
Rio Ucuyali
Moyobamba
Chachapoyas
Tarapoto
CAJAMARCA
BRAZIL
SAN MARTIN
Cajamarca
LA LIBERTAD
Pucallpa
Cordillera Blanca
Chimbote
B
ANCASH
HUANUCO
Huaraz
UCAYALI
Huánuco
PASCO
Cerro De Pasco
JUNIN
MADRE DE DIOS
La Oroya
HUANCAYO
Puerto Maldonado
LIMA
CUZCO
LIMA
Huancavelica
Machu Picchu
Ayacucho
HUANCAVELICA
Cuzco
Abancay
Pisco
APURIMAC
Ica
PUNO
BOLIVIA
ICA
Nasca
AYACUCHO
C
AREQUIPA
Juliaca
Lake Titicaca
Puno
Arequipa
MOQUEGUA
Pacific Ocean
Moquegua
TACNA
Ilo
Tacna
1
2
3
CHILE

# Credits


## Footprint credits
**Editor**: Ben Box
**Map editor**: Sarah Sorensen
**Picture editor**: Kevin Feeney

## Credits
**Managing Director**: Andy Riddle
**Publisher**: Patrick Dawson
**Editorial**: Alan Murphy, Sophie Blacksell, Nicola Gibbs, Felicity Laughton, Sara Chare, Jo Williams
**Cartography**: Robert Lunn, Kevin Feeney
**Cover design**: Robert Lunn
**Design**: Mytton Williams
**Sales and marketing**: Zoë Jackson, Hannah Bonnell
**Advertising sales manager**: Renu Sibal
**Finance and administration**: Elizabeth Taylor

## Photography credits
**Front cover**: Textiles, Melvyn Longhurst, Alamy
**Back cover**: Jarno Gonzalez Zarraonandia, Shutterstock
**Inside colour section**: Alex Robinson; Ricardo Beleil/BrazilPhotos, Danita Delimont, David Noton Photography, Joseph Rothe, Mireille Vautier/Alamy; Joseph Calev, Maria Veras, Jarno Gonzalez Zarraonandia/ Shutterstock; age fotostock/Superstock; South American Pictures

## Print
Manufactured in Italy by LegoPrint
Pulp from sustainable forests


## Footprint feedback
We try as hard as we can to make each Footprint guide as up to date as possible but, of course, things always change. If you want to let us know about your experiences – good, bad or ugly – then don't delay, go to www.footprintbooks.com and send in your comments.


## Publishing information
Footprint Cuzco & the Inca heartland
4th edition




ISBN 978 1 906098 20 9
CIP DATA: A catalogue record for this book is available from the British Library





Published by Footprint
6 Riverside Court
Lower Bristol Road
Bath BA2 3DZ, UK
T +44 (0)1225 469141
F +44 (0)1225 469461
discover@footprintbooks.com
www.footprintbooks.com

Distributed in the USA by Globe Pequot Press, Guilford, Connecticut




Neither the black and white nor colour maps are intended to have any political significance.

Every effort has been made to ensure that the facts in this guidebook are accurate. However, travellers should still obtain advice from consulates, airlines etc about travel and visa requirements before travelling. The authors and publishers cannot accept responsibility for any loss, injury or inconvenience however caused.